中国世界遗产影像志

WORLD HERITAGE IN CHINA

赵迎新　主编

中国摄影出版社
China Photographic Publishing House

前　言

葛剑雄　历史地理学家

世界文化遗产和自然遗产是自然和人类共同的杰作，有幸保留到今天并被人类发现和认识的更是可遇不可求的奇迹。

成为世界自然遗产的地质、自然地理或生物结构无不经过漫长的演变，少则以万年计，多则以亿年计。尽管它们的同类曾大量存在，甚至广被全球，但绝大多数已变化消失，或者没有能够形成独特的景观或群落。在地球约50亿年的生命中，能够孕育出像世界自然遗产这样的概率微乎其微。

自从产生人类社会，人类对自然环境的影响不可避免。尽管世界自然遗产基本都是自然本身演化的结果，但其最终的形成往往离不开人类的影响。正面的影响是，由于人类的及时发现和保护，使它们不至于向着发育或消亡的方向继续演化，至少放慢了演化的速度。消极方面的影响，则是某些濒危的自然景观或生物群落正是人类活动的产物。

人类对它们的发现、认识、研究、确定和珍惜，也经历了一个漫长的时期。从早期的恐惧或对抗到逐渐的敬畏、规避、亲近，人类从无意识的反应进化到了自觉的观念。但只有当人类拥有观察、探测、记录、接近和居留在地球上任何地点的手段和能力时，全部业已存在的自然遗产才有可能被发现并列入《世界自然遗产名录》。

世界文化遗产更是人类借助自然环境创造的杰作，其中大部分还是在生产力和科学技术水平低下的情况下，或者是仅仅依靠手工和简单的工具创造出来的。尽管大多数遗产的创造者当初就希望他们的产物能长久存在下去，但他们的主要目的还是为了满足当时特殊人群的物质或精神的需要，而不是为了今天能成为遗产。沧海桑田，天灾人祸，有意无意（包括以往破坏性的保护、修缮和重建），最重要、最辉煌、最宏大、最繁华、最富贵、最有吸引力的往往最先受到破坏，或者被破坏的次数最多，破坏得最彻底。因此，文化遗产只是无数同类中硕果仅存的幸运者。

而且，与自然遗产相比，它们更面临着来自自然和人类两方面的威胁。现有的世界文化遗产绝大多数产生于工业化以前，无论是文物、建筑群还是遗址，构成它们的物质主要是石料、木材、砖瓦、陶瓷、金属、矿物、纸张、纺织品、动植物制品等，很难在自然条件下长期保存。

文化遗产属于不同的人群、民族、国家、文化，出于不同的审美情趣、政治理念、意识形态、价值观念、特殊崇拜、宗教信仰，最易在人类的群体冲突中成为破坏目标和牺牲品。即使因对其他群体有利用价值而得以幸存，其最富特色的部分往往也会被改变或消除。文化遗产一般可以部分或全部被移动、拆除、毁坏，增加了在战争、冲突和动乱中被盗窃、劫掠、破坏的可能性。就是在平时，也往往是盗匪的目标。

正因为如此，世界文化遗产、自然遗产和文化自然双重遗产是地球和我们的祖先对我们最有价值的恩赐，是全人类的财富，也是我们对子孙后代最有意义的馈赠。

中国疆域辽阔，地形复杂，山河壮丽，景观丰富，历史悠久，人口众多，文化发达，大自然和祖先给我们留下了类型和数量都居世界前列的自然遗产和文化遗产。

但毋庸讳言，由于近代的科学技术和经济文化的落后，特别是“文化大革命”的破坏，中国没有及时参与申报和保护世界遗产的行动。1972 年联合国教科文组织通过《保护世界文化与自然遗产公约》时，中国的“文化大革命”还没有结束。在改革开放后，一批专家学者走出国门，其中就有不久前刚去世、享年 102 岁的中科院院士侯仁之先生。侯先生告诉我，在美国参观一所大学时，校长向他展示该校收藏的文物，他看到玻璃盒子里装的是从北京城墙上拆下来的城砖。作为北京城的研究者他完全明白，彻底拆除北京城墙正是“文化大革命”的“成果”。正是侯仁之先生从国外带回了世界文化与自然遗产的信息，并以全国政协委员的身份与其他几位委员一起提案，建议中国加入《公约》，促成中国在 1985 年成为该《公约》的缔约国，并且在 1987 年第 11 届世界遗产大会上将故宫等 6 项列入《世界遗产名录》，到 2013 年中国已经拥有 45 项世界遗产。

设立《世界遗产名录》最根本的目的是为了保护，正如《公约》所明确的，是“注意到文化遗产和自然遗产越来越受到破坏的威胁，一方面因年久腐变所致，同时变化中的社会和经济条件使情况恶化，造成更加难以应付的损害或破坏现象”；“考虑到任何文化或自然遗产的坏变或丢失都有使全世界遗产枯竭的有害影响”；“考虑到国家一级保护这类遗产的工作往往不很完善，原因在于这项工作需要大量手段而列为保护对象的财产的所在国却不具备充足的经济、科学和技术力量”。因此，《公约》要求缔约国“应通过一切适当手段，特别是教育和宣传计划，努力增强本国人民对本公约第一和第二条中确定的文化和自然遗产的赞赏和尊重”；“应使公众广泛了解对这类遗产造成威胁的危险和根据本公约进行的活动”。

旅游、考察和探险无疑是直接了解世界遗产的有效途径，能激发人们对它们的热爱、赞赏和尊重，提高人们保护世界遗产的自觉性。中国的世界遗产不仅是中国人民最主要的旅游目的地，也是世界人民向往的旅游胜地。改革开放以来，越来越多的中国人成为各国世界遗产的游客，今天世界上任何一个文化或自然遗产都已不乏中国人的足迹。

但过度的旅游开发、过多的游客对世界遗产造成的破坏日益严重，一些遗产项目不得不实行严格的人数限制和参观时间、进入范围的限制。这就意味着，世界总人口中能够进入这些世界遗产的人是极少数，而且会越来越少。由于经济能力、身体条件、社会环境等方面的限制，多数人不可能参观大多数世界遗产。另一方面，如果缺乏必要的历史、文化、艺术、科学等方面的知识和欣赏能力，即使身临其境，也未必能认识世界遗产的价值，达到赞赏和尊重的目的。而自然遗产的观赏无不有最佳的季节、气候、时间、位置、角度、距离、光线、气温、环境等苛刻的条件，能够获得最佳效果的人微乎其微。不少自然遗产地域范围广阔，即使多次进入也难以穷尽。

现代科学技术和专业人士已经能为我们提供古人梦想中的“卧游”，即足不出户就能通过视觉和听觉器官全方位获得旅游目的地的信息。专业摄影不仅可以从数百数万公里外俯瞰地球的每个角落，还能捕捉到稍纵即逝的影像，精细展示美妙的微观世界，或者聚焦、定格在一个最佳的瞬间——百年一遇、千年一遇，甚至是绝无仅有的景观。前人留下的照片尽管拍摄的质量未必尽如人意，有的已影像模糊，却为我们留住了历史——显示了已经变化的自然景观和已经消失的人文景观。

这部《中国世界遗产影像志》精选了800多张优秀摄影家拍摄的照片，涵括历史照片、美术作品、地图和图表。这些图像全方位显示了中国47处世界遗产的最佳景观。专家的说明介绍了相关的历史和文化背景、相应的科学知识和研究成果，扩展了读者的视野，更便于从时间、空间和人类历史的广度认识世界遗产。

如果你已经到过某项世界遗产，你肯定能发现比你记忆中更好的视觉效果，或许你会开始新的追求。

如果你还没有到过某项世界遗产，你一定会感受到它惊人的魅力和巨大的吸引力，你的追寻会有更具体的目标。

如果你暂时没有去某项世界遗产的条件，那么就慢慢观赏这些影像吧。如果你再读读相关的文字，也许你能获得身临其境的人也无法享受到的乐趣，因为你的想象和赞赏不受时间和空间的限制。

Foreword

Ge Jianxiong, historical geographer

World cultural heritage and natural heritage are masterpieces of the joint labor of man and nature; those which have survived to be recognized today are wonders hard to find.

The geological, geographical or biological formations in world natural heritage have all undergone long-term evolution over tens of thousands or even hundreds of millions of years. Though fellow formations may once have existed in large quantity or even covered the whole globe, most of them have changed or vanished or failed to form singular landscape or community. In the 5-billion-year life span of the earth few places can generate world natural heritage.

Since the advent of human society, mankind inevitably exerted influence on nature. Though world natural heritage sites are basically results of the evolution of nature, the final formation of them cannot be separated from human interference. A positive influence of mankind may be that their timely identification and protection prevents the further growth or vanishing of those sites or at least slows down the speed of evolution. A negative influence may be that human activity leads to the endangerment of some natural landscape or floras.

Mankind's discovery, recognition, research, identification and valuing of the heritage also have undergone a long process. Man's response to natural heritage has changed from early fear or opposition to gradual reverence, evasion and intimacy. Man's unconscious responses finally have given way to self-awareness. But only when mankind has the means and capacity to observe, explore, record and approach any location on earth can all surviving natural heritage possibly be discovered and entered on the *World Natural Heritage List*.

World cultural heritages are products of man's efforts, aided by the natural environment, and most of them are produced through manual labor or with simple implements. Though most creators of heritage hoped that their products might last forever, their main purpose was to gratify the material or spiritual needs of a particular group instead of leaving relics for today. Transmutation of nature by natural or man-made disasters may damage cultural heritage, with damage caused either deliberately or unintentionally (including protection, repairs or rebuilding that may have had destructive effects). The most important, splendid, prosperous and attractive artefacts are often the first to be destroyed or damaged. As a result cultural heritage sites are only the lucky survivors.

Cultural heritage usually faces threats from both man and nature. Most of the world cultural heritage usually came into being prior to industrialization, no matter whether they are artefacts, architectural complexes or ruins. They are mainly made of stone, wood, brick and tiles, porcelain, metal, mineral, paper, textile, and animal or plant products, and so under natural circumstances they can hardly be conserved indefinitely.

Cultural heritage belongs to different ethnic groups, nationalities, nations, and cultures, and reflects different aesthetics, political views, ideology, values, and particular cultural and religious beliefs, so they are liable to be destroyed and sacrificed in ethnic conflicts. Even though some cultural relics survive due to their value to the new owner, their most distinctive parts often suffer changes or loss. Cultural heritage usually can be partly or totally removed, demolished or destroyed and so has a higher possibility of being stolen or robbed, looted or destroyed in wars, clashes or disturbances. Even in peacetime it is often the target of theft.

It is for this very reason that world cultural heritage, natural heritage and double-identity heritage are most valuable gifts from the earth and from our ancestors; they are the common wealth of all mankind and the most meaningful legacy that we may pass down to our offspring.

In the vast land of China, the complex typology, magnificent nature, long history and advanced culture have generated natural and cultural heritage which excel both in variety and quantity.

Yet, due to slow development in science and technology as well as in the economy and culture of China in modern times, plus the destruction wrought by the Cultural Revolution, China failed to declare and protect its world heritage in a timely way. When *Convention Concerning the Protection of the World Cultural and Natural Heritage* was passed by UNESCO in 1972, the Cultural Revolution was still going on in China. It is only after China carried on the reforms and open-door policy that groups of experts and scholars began to visit foreign countries. Among them there was one academician of the Chinese Academy of Sciences named Hou Renzhi, who just passed away recently at the age of 102. Mr. Hou told me that during his American tour the president of an American university showed him a piece of brick taken from the city wall of Beijing encased in a glass case. Being a researcher of Beijing, Mr. Hou was fully aware that the demolition of the Beijing city wall was deemed one "achievement" of Cultural Revolution. Mr. Hou's visit to the United States brought back information regarding the world cultural and natural heritage. He allied with several other members of China's People's Political Consultative Conference in moving that China should join the *Convention Concerning the Protection of the World Cultural and Natural Heritage* and consequently China became a party to the convention. In the 11th World Heritage Convention of 1987, six sites including the Imperial Palace in Beijing entered *the World Heritage List*; by 2013, the list of sites had expanded to 45.

The primary purpose of drawing up *the World Heritage List* is to protect the heritage, as is stated in the Convention, "Noting that the cultural heritage and the natural heritage are increasingly threatened with destruction not only by the traditional causes of decay, but also by changing social and economic conditions which aggravate the situation with even more formidable phenomena of damage or destruction"; "considering that deterioration or disappearance of any item of the cultural or natural heritage constitutes a harmful impoverishment of all the nations of the world"; "considering that the protection of this heritage at the national level often remains incomplete because of the scale of the resources which it requires and of the insufficient economic, and technological resources of the country where the property to be protected is situated." Therefore the Convention demands that all states and parties "shall endeavor by all appropriate means, and in particular by educational and information programmes, to strengthen appreciation and respect by their peoples for the cultural and natural heritage defined in Articles 1 and 2 of the Convention"; and "shall undertake to keep the public broadly informed of the dangers threatening this heritage and of the activities carried on in pursuance of this Convention."

Tourism, investigation and exploration are undoubtedly effective means to know more about the world heritage directly and so inspire people to love, appreciate and respect the heritage and enhance people's awareness in protecting it. The world heritage in China not only attracts Chinese to visit, but also draws people from everywhere in the world. Since the implementing of reforms, more and more Chinese have gone abroad to visit world heritage in other countries and have left their footprints in every cultural or natural heritage site.

Yet excessive tourism and excessive numbers of tourists have caused more and more serious damages to world heritage. Some heritage sites have to take measures to restrict the number of visitors, visiting hours and visiting places. That means, only a small proportion of the world population have access to these world heritages and the number may drop even lower. Financial position, health and social milieu may also thwart efforts at travel, and so the majority of people will have no chance to visit world heritage. On the other hand, visitors may fail to recognize the value of the world heritage and so fail to appreciate and respect it for lack of essential historical, cultural, artistic and scientific knowledge and sensitivity to heritage appreciation, even if they have access to the heritage. Meanwhile, the appreciation of natural heritage requires appropriate season, climate, time, position, angle, distance, sunshine, temperature and setting, and very few visitors can view the best scenery. Besides, natural heritage site usually covers a wide range and cannot be exhausted even if visitors come more than once.

These limitations may be alleviated with the help of professionals working with modern science and technology, who may provide us with a mental tour of the world heritage without leaving our homes. Professional photographers can not only take aerial pictures of every corner of the world from hundreds to thousands of kilometers away, but also capture unique images at a particular instant. Such pictures can display the wonderful micro-world or focus on a particular moment—the best moment in a hundred years, a thousand years or even the most unique moment ever. As for historical photos, though the quality of them may not be so satisfactory, and some may even become indistinct over time, they record history—reproducing the old landscape and vanished cultural views.

World Heritage in China contains over 800 photos by excellent photographers in addition to historical photos, drawings of fine arts, atlases and charts. These pictures show the best view of the 47 world heritage sites in China in an all-round way, while the explanations by experts introducing the relevant historical and cultural context and corresponding scientific knowledge and research findings may broaden the reader's range of knowledge and facilitate their appreciation of the world heritage from the dimension of time, space and human history.

If you happen to have visited a certain site before, the photos will refresh and jog your memory, and you will be inspired to revisit the place.

If you have not visited a certain site, you will be charmed by it and your search will have more specific goals.

If you have no chance to visit the world heritage for the time being, you may appreciate these beautiful pictures at your leisure. If you further your appreciation by reading the relevant text, you may derive more pleasure than those who are on the spot—your imagination and appreciation will not be bound by time and space.

序：世界的印迹

周梅生　世界遗产影像专家

人与自然，各具其态。万千变化，异彩纷呈。

在地球46亿年和人类50万年的生命历程中，人为创建和自然形成了许多伟大的奇迹。这些奇迹构建了地球生命与人类历史的脉络渊源，确认了思想与物质的普世价值，证明了人与自然的复杂关系。联合国教科文组织世界遗产委员会组织世界各国权威专家，对其进行全面的梳理与考证，逐步确认了世界文化遗产、自然遗产、文化与自然双重遗产及非物质与口头流传遗产四种类型。对于人类思想的肯定、对于居息星球的认知，任何史书无法比拟，它是严谨的考据，它是精准的表述，它是客观的证明，它是恢宏的颂歌。

中国自加入《保护世界文化与自然遗产公约》后，累年申报，以数量计，已居于世界第二的位置。多年来国际国内各种领域对于中国的世界遗产的叙述，多以联合国教科文组织世界遗产委员会的确认时间为序排列先后，《中国世界遗产影像志》汲取诸多专家学者意见，按照中国人的思维方式，以文化属性和物质特征重新梳理这些在中国的世界遗产，在历史时间和地理空间形成的座标系上，凸显中国的世界遗产在整体体系上的鲜明形象。至此，本书将其重新归纳，以摄影、图像、文字诸多语言方式进行表述，在诗意的气氛和科学的论证之中表述中国人的世界遗产观点。

中国世界遗产的类别归纳

第一部分：皇家文化遗产[注]

中国皇家建筑是皇权至上的象征，源于流传有序的礼仪规制，是人类文明从事宏大的政治、经济、军事、文化活动的重要遗存。跨越时间三千多年，纵横地域数万公里，规模巨大，制作精良，是以建筑形式保存下来的中国古人最重要的思想传述，亦是中国列入《世界遗产名录》最重要的项目。

中国皇家建筑依功能分为五种，即：

1. 皇家宫殿。中国古代帝王治理国家、主持朝政、生活起居的地方，以北京故宫为代表。

[注] 本书中列入皇家文化遗产的高句丽是中国古代边疆的少数民族政权。

2. 皇家陵寝。中国古代帝王的墓葬群落，以先古王陵、封建王朝帝陵、历代诸侯贵族墓葬为序，以秦始皇陵和明清皇家陵寝为代表。

3. 皇家园林。古代帝王进行休息、狩猎、文化交流和外交活动的场所，以北京颐和园、承德避暑山庄为代表。

4. 皇家坛庙。中国古代帝王进行祭祀、祈祷的象征性建筑，用以协调人与自然的关系，佑护家国之命运，以北京天坛为代表。

5. 皇家军事、经济设施。以帝王威权，用举国之力，兴废接替，历久不衰，成为国家形象象征的军事、经济设施，以长城、大运河为代表。

第二部分：民间文化遗产

中国民间建筑，地域辽阔，形制各异，功能复杂，材料多样，工艺丰富，是人类建筑文化的实证。其中传承有序、保存完好，具有代表性的建筑群，成为世界文化遗产的重要资源。

中国民间建筑依形制分为三种，即：

1. 古代城池。其功能为基层行政区划的确认，可以进行经济贸易、文化教育、军事防御、养息居住等人类生存活动，以平遥古城、丽江古城为代表。

2. 园邸馆舍。城镇村墟，民之所居，以基本生活功能保障为生，兼及宗族祭祀、文化教育诸方面，集园林、府邸、宗祠、墓地各种形式为一体的中国古代民间建筑群，以苏州园林，曲阜孔庙、孔府、孔林为代表。

3. 家族村落。以家族为中心的聚居村落，体现居住、劳作、自我保护的功能，材质工艺体现地域物产与文化的特点，是农耕文明在中国大地上的重要体现，以皖南古民居、福建土楼为代表。

第三部分：宗教文化遗产

宗教是人类文化的重要表现形式，中国大地上数千年遗留下来的宗教建筑成为典型的文化符号和精神象征。中国本土宗教道教和外来宗教佛教具有代表性，其建筑形式源出本土传统，融合外来精华，殿宇、塔刹、洞窑、石刻雕塑诸般具备。由于大批艺术家的参与，历代沿革，锲而不舍，使得中国古代宗教建筑达到顶端的艺术成就，成为世界建筑艺术史上的东方文化代表。

中国宗教建筑依宗教体系和建筑形制分为三种，即：

1. 道教建筑。以中国古代太极无极、乾坤阴阳的宇宙观规划道教建筑与大自然的关系，宫观殿宇皆应对道法自然、天人合一的哲学思想，是人与自然精神契合、功能协调的物象表现，以武当山古建筑群为代表。

2. 佛教建筑。佛教是中国古代影响力最大的宗教，其寺庙遍布全国。多以中国古代殿宇式建筑为主，吸收佛教原生地建筑精华，融合中国少数民族建筑特点，成为有中国特色的多元文化的建筑类型，以五台山佛教古建筑群、西藏布达拉宫等佛教建筑为代表。

3. 洞窟石刻。石窟形制源于古印度、东南亚地区的佛教建筑，开山凿窟，雕刻佛像，供僧人信士顶礼膜拜、修行居住之用。多因地制宜，依山就势，规模宏大，历时久远，形象众多，成为古代文化生活史的物象实证，以敦煌石窟为代表。

第四部分：自然遗产

人类生养居息的地球在46亿年的成长演化史中，留下许多突出例证，成为地球生命的证明，这些特殊的地质、地貌、地理现象，成为“世界自然遗产”，包括以下四种，即：

1. 代表地球演化史中重要阶段的突出例证，如：宙、代、纪、世、期、时等不同等级地质时代的物质遗存。

2. 代表的重要地质过程、生物演化过程及人类与自然相互关系的突出例证，如：冰川作用、火山作用、生物进化、动植物群系等。

3. 独特、稀有或绝妙的自然现象，地貌及地质结构，如江河湖海、山岳洞穴等。

4. 尚存的珍稀或濒危动植物的栖息地，从科学研究和生产保护的角度具有特殊价值的动植物群落。

综上所述，张家界、九寨沟、大熊猫生存保护区等具有代表性。

另有具备“自然与文化”双重身份的世界遗产，有以下特征：

1. 由地壳运动自然形成的绝妙地貌，符合人类共同的审美趋势。

2. 与地貌相辅相成的以建筑为典型物象的人类文化活动遗址，两相映照，鬼斧神工，浑然天成。

3. 由动物、植物和天文气象共同形成的独特景观，具有象征性和代表性，应和了人类在自然力影响下而产生的心理活动。

中国的双重身份世界遗产，以泰山、黄山为重要代表。

非物质和口头流传世界遗产不在本书表述之列。

本书体例以志为主。

志书是中国典籍特有体例，以自然地域、行政区划为单位，以客观存在为依据，记述历史与现状，用以存史，资政，传播人类思想与文明，了解自然生存与延续。《中国世界遗产影像志》创立了志书类典籍新的形式，以摄影为主要叙述语言，明确精准，解决了旧著志书中单纯以文字描述物象的形状、色彩、质感等实质概念的困难之处，以一图而知天下，具有信息保存与传播的时代气息。

志书结构分明，以编、章、节、目的体系层次顺序而为，主次得当，全而不杂，阅读顺畅，查勘方便。

本书以志为主，传、记、图、表、录、述诸体并用，以“横分门类，纵述始末”为原则，经纬分明，各逞所长，在时间与空间上交待明确，避免概念混淆、内容重复。相互关联的项目，跨篇参见，各有侧重。

照片编排选取当代中国有影响力的摄影家关于世界遗产的重要作品，参以历史老照片，以应“纵述始末”的原则，全面展现中国世界遗产的历史与现状。照片编选以“文献性、学术性，艺术性”为指导原则，以影写志，以志传史，从宏观观照到常识铺陈，追寻世界的印迹，珍重遗产的价值。希望本书能够成为研究中国世界遗产的学术典籍。

Introduction-Footprints of the World

Zhou Meisheng, expert on world heritage images

Humanity and Nature each have their own distinctive guise, displaying their brilliance through countless transformations.

During the life process of the earth and humanity (the former is 4.6 billion years old, while the latter is 0.5 million), each has worked great miracles. These wonders form the veins of the earth's existence and human history, confirming the universal values of thoughts and matter, and demonstrating the complicated relationship between man and nature. The UNESCO World Heritage Committee summoned authorities and experts all over the world to sort through and verify the various forms of heritage, finally recognizing four types of heritage, namely, world cultural heritage, world natural heritage, cultural and natural heritage, and intangible and oral tradition heritage. This kind of affirmation of human thoughts and knowledge of our planet cannot be matched by any historical study. It is rooted in rigorous research, precise formulations, and objective evidence; it is precise formulation; it is objective evidence; it is also a magnificent tribute to the beauty we have inherited.

Ever since China entered *the Convention Concerning the Protection of the World Cultural and Natural Heritage*, she has been bidding year after year and has become the second country in the world in terms of the number of heritage sites. For many years all statements about China World Heritage from any discipline (whether in China or abroad) have tended to arrange the heritage sites according to the date in which they entered *the world heritage list*. Though this arrangement is objective, it ignores the essential attributes of the heritage and may easily lead to misunderstandings. Therefore, in this volume of World Heritage in China, we have absorbed the ideas of many experts and scholars and present the world heritage in China according to the cultural attributes and material characteristics of the heritage sites. This principle of organization accords with the Chinese mode of thinking, which highlights the distinctive images of China world heritage in a coordinated system that takes into account both historical time and geographical space. That is why we reclassify the world heritage sites and narrate them in the form of photography, graphics and text. We aim to state the viewpoint of the Chinese on China world heritage by combining poetic atmosphere with scientific argumentation.

The Classification of China's World Heritage

Part 1 Imperial Cultural Heritage*

Chinese royal architecture symbolizes the imperial power. It comes from the time-honored etiquette rules and is important remains of human civilization engaged in grandiose political, economical, military and cultural activities. The royal architecture covers a span of over three thousand years and is widely distributed over thousand miles. The large-scale, well-made architecture is the most important thought tradition of ancient Chinese passed down in the form of architecture, and also China's most important item in the list of world heritage.

* Note: Koguryo listed as imperial cuttural heritage in this book, was an ethnic regime on the ancient Chinese frontier.

Imperial Palaces. The places where the emperors of China ruled the country, administered national affairs and resided, typified by the Imperial Palace in Beijing.

Imperial Mausoleums. The burial grounds of Chinese imperial families, including tombs of ancient kings, mausoleums of feudal dynastic emperors, and the tombs of princes and peerage. The Mausoleum of Emperor Qin Shi Huang and the Imperial Mausoleums of the Ming and Qing dynasties are representative examples.

Imperial Gardens. The places where the emperors relaxed, went hunting, and carried on cultural exchange and negotiations. Beijing Summer Palace and Chengde Mountain Resort are representatives of this type.

Imperial Temples. The symbolic architecture where the emperors of China offered sacrifices and prayed to Heaven to coordinate the relationship between man and nature, and to plead for heaven's blessing to the country. Typical is the Temple of Heaven in Beijing.

Imperial Defensive or Economic Construction. The emperors summoned the resources of the whole country to build defensive or Economic works which lasted for a long period of time and became a kind of image of the empire. The Great Wall, the Grand Cannal are the representatives of such works.

Part 2 Folk Cultural Heritage

The folk architecture of China, scattered over China's vast territory, has diverse shapes and structures and serves complicated functions. Structures of this kind are made of different materials and built with a range of technologies, exemplifying humanity's architectural culture. Among them, those representative clusters of buildings passed down to later generations in a good state of preservation are important resources of world cultural heritage.

The folk architecture of China can be divided into three categories according to their shape and structure:

Ancient cities. They serve as marks of basic level administrative divisions. Sites for commerce, education, military defense and residence, they are typified by the two ancient cities of Ping Yao and Lijiang.

Gardens and Residences. In cities and villages where people lived, gardens and premises served to guarantee basic life functions and provide a venue for offering sacrifices to ancestors as well as cultural activities and education. In this category are ancient folk architectural complexes unifying garden, residence, ancestral hall and cemetery. Typical representatives are the classical gardens of Suzhou and the Temple of Confucius, Kong Family Mansion, and Cemetery of Confucius, all in Qufu.

Lineage Villages. Village settlements centered on particular lineages served the functions of residence, work and self-protection. The building materials and techniques reveal characteristics of regional produce and culture, making them an important emblem of agricultural civilization in the vast land of China. Representative are the ancient villages in South Anhui Province and the Fujian Tulou.

Part 3 Religious Cultural Heritage

Religion is an important aspect of culture, and the religious architecture left in China over a period of several thousand years has become a quintessential cultural sign and spiritual emblem. Most representative are China's native religion of Taoism and an import from abroad, Buddhism. The architectural forms of both come from local tradition in the main, along with some blending from foreign cultures. There are halls and temples, pagodas, grottoes and stone sculptures. Due to the participation of large numbers of artists and continuous efforts despite historical change, the religious architecture of ancient China reached a peak in craftsmanship and has become a representative of oriental culture in the history of world architecture.

The religious architecture of China may be divided into three types according to the religions they represent and architectural shape and structure:

Taoist Buildings. The great harmony infinite and the cosmos of heaven and earth and yin and yang are used to regulate the relationship between Taoist buildings and nature. The halls and convents are all reflections of the philosophical concepts of Tao, modeling after nature and fusing into one both Nature and Man. These structures embody the spiritual harmony between man and nature and the healthy functioning of both. Representative is the ancient architectural complex on Mount Wudang.

Buddhist Buildings. Buddhism is the most influential religion in ancient China and its temples are scattered everywhere. Most of the temples follow the example of ancient Chinese halls in their main structure, but also incorporate the architectural high points of Buddhist architecture elsewhere and some architectural features of minority nationalities of China. So Buddhist architecture developed into a form of construction reflecting many cultures but having Chinese particularities. Representative are the ancient Buddhist architectural complex of Mount Wutai and the Potala Palace of Tibet.

Grotto Carvings and Stone Sculptures. Grotto carvings originated in ancient India and Southeast Asia, where people dug grottos into cliff-faces and carved statues for monks and believers to worship and practice Buddhism. The grottoes are usually adapted to the shape of the mountain and massive in scale, with many Buddha statues. Such works usually take quite a long period of time and become material objects reflecting ancient cultural life. Representative are Dunhuang Grottoes.

Part 4 Natural Heritage

In the long process of 4.6 billion years the earth on which we live has left prominent evidence to show how it has grown. The specific geological, typographic and geographical phenomena have become world natural heritage. They cover the following categories:

Prominent examples representing important stages in the process of the earth's evolution, such as the material remains of different geologic periods from eon and era to age and period.

Prominent examples showing important geological action in process, the evolution process of species and those revealing the interrelationship between nature and mankind.

Singular, rare or unique natural phenomena, landforms and geological structures, such as rivers, lakes and seas, mountains and caves.

The habitats of rare or endangered species, particular fauna and flora having special value to scientific research or protection.

Of the above mentioned items, representative are Zhangjiajie, Jiuzhaigou, and the habitat of the Giant Panda.

There are also heritage sites enjoying the double identity of both nature and culture. They have the following characteristics:

A unique landform resulting from natural crust movement and according with the aesthetic principles of mankind.

Sites of human cultural activities complementary to the landscape, with architecture as the typical objects. Nature and architecture set each other off and form a unified identity.

Singular landscapes formed by animals, plants, astronomy and weather. They are symbolic and representative, echoing the psychological activities of man under the influence of natural forces.

Typical double-identity world heritage sites in China are Mount Taishan and Mount Huangshan.

Nonmaterial and oral tradition world heritage are not covered in this book.

The book adopts the style of a gazetteer.

Gazetteers are a special genre among Chinese works. They narrate the history and circumstances of a particular natural region or administrative region based on objective existence, in order to record history, provide reference, transmit ideas and culture, and grasp the principle of natural existence and continuity.

World Heritage in China establishes a new form of gazetter. It uses photography as the main narrative language to illustrate the sites clearly and precisely and thereby solve the difficulty of using words to describe notions regarding the shapes, colors and texture of objects. This narrative style is very much in keeping with the present era, which features images in preserving and spreading information.

The gazetteer of China World Heritage is clearly divided into parts, chapters, sections, and items. It is complete without being confusing. We hope you will find the book is easy to follow and consult.

While the gazetteer is the book's primary model, it also adopts other forms such as survey, graphics, charts and historical records. Following the principle of broad coverage and thorough narrative, this book aims to make a well-organized presentation that gives credit to each form. All the sites are clearly introduced temporally and spatially to avoid mixing concepts or creating repetition. Items which are cross-referenced are discussed in each section with a different emphasis.

Regarding the photographs adopted, we have selected important pictures of the world heritage from influential photographers, with old photos as reference to implement the principle of "narrating the whole picture vertically" to present a comprehensive picture of China World Heritage both past and present. The photographs we selected all have the characteristics of being documentary, academic and artistic. We use photographs to present accounts of the world heritage sites and record them in history. We search for footprints of the world, whether in broad observation or factual narration, so as to cherish the value of our heritage. We hope that this book will become a milestone in the research of China's World Heritage.

目　录
CONTENTS

● 前　言 2
Foreword

● 序：世界的印迹 8
Introduction-Footprints of the World

皇家文化遗产 20
Imperial Cultural Heritage

● 明清故宫（北京故宫、沈阳故宫） 28
Imperial Palaces of the Ming and Qing Dynasties in Beijing and Shenyang

● 长　城 56
The Great Wall

● 秦始皇陵及兵马俑坑 80
Mausoleum of the First Qin Emperor

● 北京皇家祭坛——天坛 100
Temple of Heaven:an Imperial Sacrificial Altar in Beijing

● 北京皇家园林——颐和园 112
Summer Palace, an Imperial Garden in Beijing

● 承德避暑山庄及其周围寺庙 130
Summer Mountain Resort and Its Outlying Temples, Chengde

● 明清皇家陵寝 150
The Imperial Tombs of the Ming and Qing Dynasties

● 大运河 168
The Grand Canal

● 殷　墟 188
Yin Xu

● 元上都遗址 196
The Site of Xanadu

● 高句丽王城、王陵及贵族墓葬 206
Capital Cities and Tombs of the Ancient Koguryo Kingdom

民间文化遗产 214
Folk Cultural Heritage

- 曲阜孔庙、孔林和孔府 222
  Temple and Cemetery of Confucius and the Kong Family Mansion in Qufu
- 苏州古典园林 234
  Classical Gardens of Suzhou
- 杭州西湖文化景观 244
  West Lake Cultural Landscape of Hangzhou
- 澳门历史城区 256
  The Historic Centre of Macao
- 福建土楼 268
  Fujian Tulou
- 丽江古城 280
  The Old Town of Lijiang
- 平遥古城 292
  Ancient City of Ping Yao
- 皖南古村落——西递、宏村 300
  Ancient Villages in Southern Anhui—Xidi and Hongcun
- 开平碉楼与村落 308
  Kaiping Diaolou and Ancient Village Cluster
- 青城山—都江堰 318
  Mount Qingcheng and the Dujiangyan Irrigation System
- 红河哈尼梯田 326
  Cultural Landscape of Honghe Hani Rice Terraces
- 周口店“北京人”遗址 334
  Peking Man Site at Zhoukoudian
- 丝绸之路：长安—天山廊道的路网 342
  Silk Roads: the Routes Network of Chang’an-Tianshan Corridor

宗教文化遗产 Religious Cultural Heritage 366

- 拉萨布达拉宫历史建筑群 Historic Ensemble of the Potala Palace, Lhasa 374
- 莫高窟 Mogao Caves 398
- 云冈石窟 Yungang Grottoes 422
- 龙门石窟 Longmen Grottoes 432
- 大足石刻 Dazu Rock Carvings 442
- 峨眉山—乐山大佛 Mount Emei Scenic Area, including Leshan Giant Buddha Scenic Area 450
- 登封“天地之中”历史建筑群 Historic Monuments of Dengfeng in “The Centre of Heaven and Earth” 462
- 武当山古建筑群 Ancient Building Complex in the Wudang Mountains 472
- 五台山 Mount Wutai 482

自然遗产 Natural Heritage 492

- 泰　山 Mount Taishan 500
- 黄　山 Mount Huangshan 510

- 庐山国家公园 518
  Mount Lushan National Park
- 新疆天山 530
  Xinjiang Tianshan
- 武夷山 540
  Mount Wuyi
- 三清山国家公园 550
  Mount Sanqingshan National Park
- 武陵源风景名胜区 558
  Wulingyuan Scenic and Historic Interest Area
- 九寨沟风景名胜区 566
  Jiuzhaigou Valley Scenic and Historic Interest Area
- 黄龙风景名胜区 576
  Huanglong Scenic and Historic Interest Area
- 云南三江并流保护区 584
  Three Parallel Rivers of Yunnan Protected Areas
- 中国南方喀斯特 594
  South China Karst
- 中国丹霞 602
  China Danxia
- 澄江化石遗址 614
  Chengjiang's fossils in Yunnan Province
- 四川大熊猫栖息地 622
  Site of Sichuan Giant Panda Sanctuaries-Wolong, Mt Siguniang and Jiajin Mountains

附录 1：图版 **630**
Appendix 2: Illustration

附录 2：遗产地概述 **656**
Appendix 2: Brief Introduction

中国世界遗产影像志
WORLD HERITAGE IN CHINA

皇家文化遗产
Imperial Cultural Heritage

明清故宫（北京故宫、沈阳故宫） 28
长城 56
秦始皇陵及兵马俑坑 80
北京皇家祭坛——天坛 100
北京皇家园林——颐和园 112
承德避暑山庄及其周围寺庙 130
明清皇家陵寝 150
大运河 168
殷墟 188
元上都遗址 196
高句丽王城、王陵及贵族墓葬 206

北京故宫太和殿广场。（图/李少白）
The square of Hall of Supreme Harmony of the Imperial Palace, Beijing. (Photo by Li Shaobai)

皇家文化遗产

王贵祥　清华大学古建筑研究所所长

建筑作为一种人类文化与文明的物质性遗产，负载历史上不同时代经济的、政治的、宗教的与文化的信息。

如果说西亚、北非、欧洲、印度，以及伊斯兰世界的古代建筑文化遗产的最重要代表，多数是宗教建筑，包括古代神庙、法老陵墓、基督教堂、印度教神庙、伊斯兰清真寺的话，那么中国古代建筑文化遗产的最重要代表，则主要是皇家建筑。这其中包括历代帝王的宫殿、苑囿、陵寝，以及皇家祭祀建筑。每一种类型的皇家建筑遗产，都是当时历史的一部百科全书。透过这些遗产，我们看到的是那个时代的经济、政治、文化、艺术，甚至那个时代的社会组织形式、建筑生产方式、建筑材料来源、材料加工方式，以及由此而透露出来的那个时代的科学技术水平。

中国皇家建筑的建造史，几乎贯穿了中国古代建筑发展的数千年历史。从见于文献的最早的上古黄帝合宫，到见于考古发掘的河南偃师二里头早商宫殿遗址，以及周代宫殿遗址，都属于皇家建筑的范畴。

中国古代皇家建筑，首先包括了象征皇家统治权威，并为皇家统治集团提供日常起居生活空间的宫殿建筑。中国古代宫殿建筑的起源，至少可以追溯到上古商周时代。如果说春秋战国时代周天子的宫殿还不那么宏伟，诸侯国王的宫殿也没有达到后世帝王宫殿的规模，则自秦始皇开始，宫殿建筑的建造，就几乎成为一个帝国最重要的建造活动。秦代都城咸阳，几乎就是一座宫殿之城。其中的阿房宫，仅仅其前殿，就号称："南北五百步，南北五十丈，上可以坐万人，下可以建五丈旗。周驰为阁道，自殿下直抵南山。表南山之巅以为阙。为复道，自阿房渡渭，属之咸阳，以象天极阁道绝汉抵营室也。"由此可见其宫殿规模宏伟之一斑。

汉代的宫殿同样十分宏伟壮观，令当时的皇帝汉高祖都十分震动，所谓："高祖还，见宫阙壮甚，怒，谓萧何曰：'天下苦战匈匈数岁，成败未可知，是何治宫室过度也？'萧何曰：'天下方未定，故可因遂就宫室。且夫天子四海为家，非壮丽无以重威，且无令后世有以加也。'高祖乃说。"

自此之后的东汉刘秀、三国曹魏，以及南北朝各代王朝，直至隋、唐、五代十国、两宋、辽、金，还有后来的元统治者、明清统治者，都建造了宏大的宫殿。如果说隋唐两朝的宫殿规模宏大，宋金时代的宫殿华丽繁缛，则元大都宫殿，集中亚与中土文化为一体，将宫殿与苑囿结合为一个有机的建筑与园林空间整体。有明一代建造了三座宫殿，包括明中都临濠宫殿、明初南京宫殿、永乐朝开始建造的北京宫殿，都是在总结前代宫殿的基础上所建造的空间完整、建筑宏伟的大型宫殿建筑群。清代建造了两个宫殿建筑群，一个是盛京宫殿，另外一个就是在明代紫禁城的基础上修葺完善的北京宫殿。正是这座明清两代建造完成的北京紫禁城，为中国古代宫殿建筑史画上了一个圆满的句号。

皇家祭祀建筑的建造，开始于上古三代，包括夏世室、殷重屋、周明堂。自西汉开始，祭祀最高神灵的明堂的建造，一直是历代帝王最重要的建筑事件。唐代武则天在洛阳建造的明堂，达到了长宽各 300 尺、高 294 尺的巨大规模。明代嘉靖皇帝亲自设计了明堂，就是今日北京天坛祈年殿的前身。

除了明堂之外，历代帝王还要建造祭天的圜丘坛、祭地的方泽坛，以及祭日的日坛、祭月的月坛，还有先农坛、先蚕坛、山川坛，以及祭祀祖先之神的太庙，祭祀社稷之神的社稷坛等等。明初洪武年间，太祖皇帝将南京郊外祭祀天地的地方综合为天地坛。永乐初的北京，也沿袭了天地合祀的做法。后来，又改为天地分祀，才出现了北京的天坛与地坛之分。此外，历代帝王还有尊孔祭孔的习惯。自宋代始，就有了国家祭孔的庙宇。元、明、清三代，除了在京城建立具有国家祭祀功能的国子监与孔庙之外，孔子故乡曲阜的孔庙也具有了国家祭祀庙宇的功能，例如，清代帝王就曾不止一次地远赴曲阜祭孔。

皇家苑囿，或皇家园林，是另外一类重要的皇家建筑遗产。中国园林包括自然山水、树木、花草，也包括建筑，是一个完整的艺术整体，其最高的境界是“虽由人作，宛自天开”。而皇家园林，更以其“移天缩地在君怀”的大气派，成为极其辉煌的建筑艺术作品。秦汉时代的大苑囿，往往有数百平方公里的规模，如秦汉关中上林苑。隋唐时代的园林依然很宏伟，如隋唐长安的禁苑、洛阳的西苑，以及后来的神都苑，都是规模宏伟的大园林。

自宋金时代开始，皇家园林的规模与尺度变得适中，园林景观也变得更加优雅与丰富。宋汴梁城四周都有园林，如金明池、琼林苑等，北宋末年还在汴梁城内建造了著名的艮岳，南宋在临安城凤凰山下的宫殿附近建造了风景优雅的御苑。金元两代的北京城，也是园林滋茂的城市，而金代离宫万安宫，以及元大都城内的西苑海子，都是著名的皇家园林的例子。清代北京城西郊的三山五园，以及后来的承德避暑山庄，更是集历代园林艺术之精华而创造的园林艺术珍品。如自清乾隆帝始创的清漪园，以及后来的颐和园，都是浓缩了中国古代园林艺术之最高水平的园林艺术杰作。

中国皇家建筑遗产中，还包括历代的皇家陵寝。中国是一个重厚葬的国家。安阳殷墟是目前发现的最早的皇家陵寝遗址之一。其中出土的甲骨文与青铜器，都是最重要的古代文化遗产之一。秦始皇陵附近发现的秦兵马俑，是 20 世纪最重要的考古发掘之一。其后的历朝历代，都留下了一些重要的帝王陵寝，如汉代的茂陵，唐代的昭陵、乾陵等。除了陵寝本身及其周围的山水环境之外，陵寝前的神道，以及神道上的石雕艺术，都是皇家陵寝建筑遗产的重要内容。此后的宋代陵寝、明代陵寝、清代陵寝，都保存得相当完好。而明清两代的陵寝，除了完整的陵寝山原空间，陵寝前的牌楼、石桥、神道石雕人兽之外，还有精美的陵寝建筑。正是这些陵寝建筑，最完整准确地保存了不同时代的建筑结构、造型与装饰细部，成为中国古代建筑遗产中的重要组成部分。

当然，中国皇家建筑遗产还不仅包括这些。从更为深入的层面上讲，还包括皇家档案馆皇史宬、皇家钦天监所管理的观象台、皇家宫殿内的图书馆文渊阁等。现存皇家建筑遗产中，以北京明清紫禁城宫殿最为引人瞩目。这是一座沿用了将近 600 年的宫殿建筑群，其中又蕴涵了中国古代宫殿建筑自西周至明清一直延续的“前朝后寝”制度。北京明清紫禁城宫殿，仿中国人信仰中的天界紫薇宫而建，是现存世界上最为宏大的宫殿建筑群，也是中国现存最大的古代建筑群。其中包括了清代、明代，甚至元代的古代建筑，或古代建筑遗迹。

北京颐和园也是一座重要的皇家建筑遗产。中国古代园林的发展历史，可以追溯到三千年前的西周时期。周文王所建造的“灵沼”、“灵台”、“灵囿”是中国历史上最早的皇家园林雏形。历代帝王都有建造园林、苑囿的传统。故而，西方人认为中国古典园林是“世界园林之母”。而北京颐和园的前身，是清代乾隆皇帝所建清漪园。后遭英法联军焚毁，又经慈禧太后时期的重建，才形成了现在这样的园林景观。颐和园保持了中国古典园林“一池三山”象征的传统，并揉和进了江南私家园林的许多优秀设计手法。颐和园所达到的园林艺术水平，无论是其真山真水的自然景观，还是步移景异的园林艺术效果、小中见大的园景处理方法，都可以说是臻于完善之作，因此，可以说颐和园是中国古典园林中之集大成的代表作。

另外一个令世界瞩目的中国皇家建筑遗产是北京天坛。古代中国是一个以儒家文化为代表的社会。自然神崇拜与祖先崇拜是贯穿中国社会数千年的文化传统。而在所有自然崇拜中，历代中国天子最为崇信的是天。对天的祭祀，是历代帝王最重要的祭祀活动之一。所以，历代帝王都在其都城之南建立祭天的圜丘坛，同时，还要建造祭祀万神的明堂。北京天坛是将历史上的圜丘坛与明堂合二为一。所谓祈年殿，最初就是明代嘉靖皇帝所建的明堂。而与祈年殿在一条轴线上的天坛，其原型就是历代帝王的圜丘坛。将圜丘坛与明堂合二为一，则造就了高贵、典雅、清远，且深负文化内涵的天坛景观。

建筑遗产是一部大书，中国皇家建筑遗产更是这部大书中最重要的一个章节。这些遗产并不仅仅属于我们，它首先属于创造它们的那个时代，同时属于我们的子子孙孙。悉心保护好这些珍贵的历史遗产，把它们真实、完好地传送给我们的后代，是每一位遗产保护工作者的责任，也是全社会的责任。

Imperial Cultural Heritage

Wang Guixiang, director of Ancient Architecture Research
Institute of Tsinghua University

As a material heritage of human culture and civilization, architecture carries the economic, political, religious and cultural information of different historical periods. If the most important representatives of the ancient architectural cultural heritage of West Asia, North Africa, India and the Islamic world are mostly religious buildings, including ancient temples, the tombs of Pharaohs, Christian churches, Hindu temples, and Islamic mosques, then the major representatives of China's ancient architectural cultural heritage are mainly imperial buildings, including the palaces, gardens and parks, mausoleums, and ritual sites of successive dynasties. Each type of imperial architectural heritage is an encyclopedia of the history of its time. These heritage sites reveal the economy, politics, culture and art of their era, and also the forms of social organization, the mode of architectural production, the source of architectural materials, the methods of craftmanship, and the technological level of their era.

The history of China's imperial architecture parallels practically the entire development of architecture in ancient China. From the He Palace of the Yellow Emperor in remote times, the earliest palace recorded in literature, to the palace site of the early Shang Dynasty in Erlitou of Yanshi in Henan Province that has been excavated by archaeologists, and the site of the Zhou Dynasty palace, all belong to the category of imperial architecture. Such buildings first of all include the palace structures that symbolized the ruling authority of the imperial family and provided daily living space for the imperial house.

The origin of ancient Chinese palace architecture can be traced back to at least the time of the ancient Shang and Zhou dynasties. If the palace of the Zhou Sons of Heaven (i.e. kings) in the Spring and Autumn and the Warring States periods were not that magnificent, and the scale of the palaces of the various feudal lords could not match those of later emperors, then begining with Emperor Qin Shi Huang, the construction of palace buildings became practically the most important construction activity of an empire. Xianyang, the capital of the Qin Dynasty, was practically a city of palaces. Of simply the front hall of Epang Palace it was said, "It was 500 paces from east to west and 500 feet from north to south. Above it could accommodate ten thousand people, and below one could install a 50 foot flagpole. A covered walkway was built around it that led all the way to the Southern Mountains. An entrance gate was built on the summit of the Southern Mountains. Another double-layer corridor connecting Epang Palace with Xianyang across the Wei River emulated the celestial pathway that the Polaris and the Cassiopeia cross the Milky Way to the Pegasus." This description gives us a glimpse of the grand scale of the palace.

The palaces of the Han Dynasty were just as grand and magnificent, and even the then emperor Han Gaozu found them a little excessive. According to the historian Sima Qian, "Upon Gaozu's return, he was angered upon seeing the imperial palace and said to Xiao He, 'The whole country has been racked by war these several years and the outcome is still not certain, so why build such an extravagant palace?' Xiao He answered, 'Just because it is uncertain, we can take the time to build the palace. For the Son of Heaven, the whole world is his home, and if the palace is not grand and splendid, then it cannot display your awesome power, besides, it should be so perfect that later generations cannot surpass it.' Gaozu then was pleased." From then on, Liu Xiu of the Eastern Han, Cao Wei of the Three Kingdoms period and the Southern and Northern dynasties, all the way down to the Sui, Tang, the Five dynasties and Ten Kingdoms, Northern Song, Southern Song, Liao, Jin, and the later rulers of Ming and Qing dynasties, all built magnificent palaces. If the palaces of the Sui and Tang dynasties were grand in scale, and the palaces of the Song and Jin periods were gorgeous and overelaborate, then the palace in Xanadu combined the cultures of Central Asia and the Chinese heartland, and formed an organic whole of architecture and garden space by combining palace buildings with garden and park. The Ming Dynasty had three palaces, including the palace in Linhao, the Middle Capital, the palace in Nanjing built in the early Ming Dynasty, and the palace in Beijing whose construction started during the Yongle period. All the three palaces were great palace complexes that had abundant space and magnificent buildings and drew on the knowledge acquired from earlier building projects of this kind.

The Qing Dynasty built two palace complexes, one in Shenyang and the other in Beijing, repaired and perfected on the foundation of the Ming Forbidden City. It is the Beijing Forbidden City, built and completed during the Ming and Qing dynasties, that marked the culmination of China's history of palace architecture.

The construction of imperial sacrificial architecture began in high antiquity, including the Shishi (generational edifices) of the Xia, Chongwu (double rooms) of the Yin and Mingtang (bright halls) of the Zhou. Beginning in the Western Han, the construction of Mingtang for worshipping the highest god(s) has always been the most important architectural event for China's rulers. The Mingtang in Luoyang built by Empress Wu Zetian of the Tang Dynasty was vast in size, being 300 feet both in length and width, and 294 feet in height. The site is preserved to this day. Emperor Jiajing of the Ming Dynasty personally designed a Mingtang, the predecessor of the present-day Hall of Prayer for Good Harvest at the Temple of Heaven in Beijing.

In addition to Mingtang, emperors of every generation also built circular mound altars for worshipping heaven, fangze altars for worshipping earth, altars of the sun for worshipping the sun, and altars of the moon for worshipping the moon. They also built altars of agriculture, altars of goddess of silkworms, altars of mountains and rivers, taimiao (imperial ancestral temple) for worshipping ancestors, and altars of land and grain for worshipping the gods of land and grain. In the Hongwu period of the early Ming, Emperor Taizu synthesized the places for worshipping heaven and earth to form the Altar of Heaven and Earth. Beijing in the early Yongle period followed the practice of worshipping heaven and earth at the same time. Later, the worship of heaven and earth was separated and resulted in the division of the Altar of Heaven and the Altar of Earth in Beijing. In addition, successive emperors had the custom of respecting and worshipping Confucius. From the Song Dynasty, the state established a Confucius Temple. During the three dynasties of Yuan, Ming and Qing, the Imperial Academy and Confucius Temple were established and had state sacrifical functions, while at the same time, the Confucius Temple in Qufu, the hometown of Confucius, was also used as the state sacrifical temple. The Emperors of the Qing Dynasty, for example, went to Qufu more than once to worship Confucius.

The imperial park, or imperial garden, is another important type of imperial architectural heritage. The Chinese garden includes natural landscape, trees and flowers, and buildings, which make a complete artistic whole whose highest state is "made by man, yet appearing to be of nature." Imperial gardens, with their air of "moving heaven and shrinking earth to bring them into one's arms", have created very splendid works of imperial garden art. The vast gardens of the Qin and Han dynasties, such as Shanglin Park in Guanzhong , often covered an extensive area. The parks of the Sui and Tang dynasties, such as Forbidden Garden in Changan, Western Garden in Luoyang, and the later Shendu Garden, were also of very imposing scale.

From the time of the Song and Jin dynasties, the size and scale of imperial gardens moderated, and gardening landscape became more elegant and richer. In the Song Dynasty, there were gardens at all four sides of Bianliang, such as Jinming Pool and Qionglin Garden. At the end of Northern Song, the famous Genyue Imperial Garden was also constructed in Bianliang. The Southern Song built a beautiful imperial garden close to the palace under Mt. Fenghuang in Hangzhou. Beijing in the Jin and Yuan dynasties was rich in gardens, and Wanan Palace, the detached palace of the Jin Dynasty, and Xinyuan Haizi inside Xanadu of the Yuan Dynasty, were famous examples of the imperial garden. The Three mountains and Five gardens in the western suburb of Beijing in the Qing Dynasty, and the later Chengde Summer Mountain Resort, were treasures of gardening art created by combining the artistic essence of earlier gardens. Qingyi Park, first created by Emperor Qianlong of the Qing Dynasty, and the later Summer Palace were both outstanding works of gardening art that captured the the highest level of ancient Chinese gardening design.

Imperial mausoleums are also part of China's imperial architectural heritage. In China, elaborate burials were emphasized. The Yin Xu in Anyang are one of the earliest royal tomb sites discovered so far. The oracle bones and bronze vessels excavated there are among the most important ancient cultural heritages. The Terracotta warriors and horses discovered in the vicinity of the mausoleum of Emperor Qin Shi Huang are one of the most important archaeological finds of the 20th century. Later dynasties have all left some important imperial tombs, such as Maoling of the Han Dynasty, Zhaoling and Qianling of the Tang Dynasty, etc. In addition to the tombs themselves and the surrounding landscape environment, the sacred ways in front of the tombs and and the stone carving art along the sacred ways, are also important elements in this architectural heritage. The mausoleums of the Song, Ming and Qing dynasties are quite well preserved. In the case of the tombs of the Ming and Qing dynasties, in addition to the intact burial mounds, ornamental archways, stone bridges, and stone carved human figures and beasts along the sacred ways, there are also exquisite mausoleum buildings. It is these mausoleum builings that most completely and precisely preserve the architectural structures, modeling, and decoration details of various periods, and have become an important part of the ancient Chinese architectural heritage.

Of course, there is still more to China's imperial architectural heritage. On a deeper level, one should also include Huangshicheng, the imperial archives; the observatory managed by Qintianjian, the imperial bureau of astronomy; and Wenyuan Pavilion, the library inside the imperial palace. Among all existing imperial building complexes, the palaces in the Forbidden City of the Ming and Qing dynasties in Beijing are the most remarkable. This palace complex was used for nearly 600 years, and it contains the "audience halls in the front, living quarters in the rear" system that ancient Chinese palace architecture followed all the way from the Western Zhou to the Ming and Qing dynasties.

The palaces in the Forbidden City of the Ming and Qing dynasties in Beijing, whose construction imitated the Ziwei Palace in heaven that existed in Chinese belief, are the most magnificent existing palace complex in the world, and also the biggest existing ancient architectural complex in China. Here are found ancient buildings or ancient architectural sites from the Ming, Qing, and even Yuan.

The Summer Palace in Beijing is also an important imperial architectural heritage. The developmental history of ancient Chinese gardens may date back to the Western Zhou period 3,000 years ago. "Lingzhao", "Lingtai" and "Lingyou", constructed by Emperor Wenwang of the Zhou Dynasty, were the earliest prototypes of imperial garden in Chinese history. Successive generations of emperors had the tradition of constructing gardens and parks, and that is why westerners regard the classical Chinese garden as "the mother of world gardening". The predecessor of the Summer Palace in Beijing is Qingyi Garden, constructed by Emperor Qianlong of the Qing Dynasty. It was burnt down by the Anglo-French allied forces and rebuilt during the period of the Empress Dowager Cixi, forming the gardening landscape that we know now. The Summer Palace maintained the tradition of the symbol of "one pool, three mountains" of the classic Chinese garden, and adopted many excellent design techniques of Jiangnan private gardens. The level that the Summer Palace reached, be it the natural landscape of its mountain and lake, or the artistic effects of varying landscape at different spots and presenting the large within the small, may all be said to be nearly perfect work. The Summer Palace may therefore be regarded as the culmination of classical Chinese gardens.

Another Chinese imperial architectural heritage that catches world attention is the Jemple of Heaven in Beijing. Ancient Chinese society was typified by Confucian culture, and the tradition of worshipping nature and ancestors ran through Chinese society for thousands of years. In terms of reverence for nature, Chinese emperors set greatest store by Heaven, and the worship of heaven was one of the most important sacrificial activities of all emperors. Therefore, all emperors built a circular mound altar to the south of their capital as well as a Mingtang for worshipping all gods. The Temple of Heaven in Beijing combined the two. The so-called Hall of Prayer for Good Harvest originally was the Mingtang built by Jiajing Emperor of the Ming Dynasty. The Temple of Heaven, built on the same axis as the Hall of Prayer for Good Harvest, had as its prototype the circular mound altar of the emperors. The combination of the circular mound altar with the Mingtang creates the spectacle of the Temple of Heaven that is noble, elegant, quietly remote, and rich in cultural meaning.

Architectural heritage is a thick book, and China's imperial architecture is the most important chapter in this thick book. These legacies do not only belong to us, they belong first of all to the age in which they were created, and at the same time they belong to our posterity. It is the responsibility of all engaged in heritage protection, and the responsibility of society as a whole, to carefully preserve these heritage sites and hand them down intact to our children.

中国世界遗产影像志

WORLD HERITAGE IN CHINA

Imperial Palaces of the Ming and Qing Dynasties in Beijing and Shenyang

明清故宫（北京故宫、沈阳故宫）

北京故宫。（图 / 周梅生）

The Imperial Palace, Beijing. (Photo by Zhou Meisheng)

Imperial Palaces of the Ming and Qing Dynasties in Beijing and Shenyang

明清故宫（北京故宫、沈阳故宫）

紫禁城是 5 个多世纪（1416-1911 年）最高权力的中心，它以园林景观和容纳了家具和工艺品的 10000 间房间的庞大建筑群，成为明清时代中国文明无价的历史见证。沈阳清朝故宫建于 1625-1626 年至 1783 年间，共有 114 座建筑，其中包括一个极为珍贵的藏书馆。沈阳故宫是统治中国的最后一个朝代在将权力扩大到全国中心、迁都北京之前，朝代建立的见证，后来成为北京故宫的附属皇宫建筑。这座雄伟的建筑为清朝历史以及满族和中国北方其他部族的文化传统提供了重要的历史见证。

——世界遗产委员会评价

Seat of supreme power for over five centuries (1416-1911), the Forbidden City in Beijing, with its landscaped gardens and many buildings (whose nearly 10,000 rooms contain furniture and works of art), constitutes a priceless testimony to Chinese civilization during the Ming and Qing dynasties. The Imperial Palace of the Qing Dynasty in Shenyang consists of 114 buildings constructed between 1625 - 1626 and 1783. It contains an important library and testifies to the foundation of the last Dynasty that ruled China, before it expanded its power to the centre of the country and moved the capital to Beijing. This palace then became auxiliary to the Imperial Palace in Beijing. This remarkable architectural edifice offers important historical testimony to the history of the Qing Dynasty and to the cultural traditions of the Manchu and other tribes in northern China.

——World Heritage Committee Evaluation

鸟瞰北京故宫三大殿。（图 / 马文晓）

An aerial view of three Halls of the Imperial Palace, Beijing. (Photo by Ma Wenxiao)

北京故宫太和殿内景。（图 / 胡锤）
The interior view of Hall of Supreme Harmony of the Imperial Palace, Beijing. (Photo by Hu Chui)

北京故宫交泰殿内景。（图 / 胡锤）
The interior view of Hall of Union of the Imperial Palace, Beijing. (Photo by Hu Chui)

正大光明
弘敷五典無輕民事惟難
表正萬邦慎厥身脩思永
惟精惟一道積于厥
克寬克仁皇建其有

左图　北京故宫乾清宫内景。（图 / 胡锤）

The left　The interior view of the Palace of Heavenly Purity of the Imperial Palace, Beijing. (Photo by Hu Chui)

右上　北京故宫长春宫宝座间。（图 / 胡锤）

Upper right　The throne room in the Palace of Eternal Spring of the Imperial Palace, Beijing. (Photo by Hu Chui)

右下　北京故宫长春宫东梢间内景。（图 / 胡锤）

Lower right　The interior view of Dong Shao Chamber in the Palace of Eternal Spring of the Imperial Palace, Beijing. (Photo by Hu Chui)

左图　北京故宫漱芳斋戏台天花。建于明永乐十八年（1420 年），后作为清重华宫宴集演戏之所。（图 / 胡锤）

The left　The ceiling of Shufang Hall Stage of the Imperial Palace, Beijing. Built in the 18th Year of Yongle Reign Period (1420 A.D.), later used as the venue for holding banquets and viewing performances. (Photo by Hu Chui)

右上　北京故宫九龙壁。位于紫禁城宁寿宫区皇极门外，建于乾隆三十七年 (1772 年)。（图 / 胡锤）

Upper right　The Nine Dragon Screen of the Imperial Palace, Beijing. It is outside Huangji Gate of Tranquility and Longivity Hall section in Forbidden City and constructed in the 37th year of Qianlong reign period (1772 A.D.). (Photo by Hu Chui)

右下　北京故宫宁寿宫花园禊赏亭。建于清乾隆三十七年（1772 年）。（图 / 胡锤）

Lower right　Xishang Pavilion of Tranquility and Longivity Hall Garden of the Imperial Palace, Beijing. Constructed in the 37th year of Qianlong reign period of the Qing Dynasty (1772 A.D.). (Photo by Hu Chui)

北京故宫的描金斗拱。（图 / 胡锤）
Dougong brackets outlined in gold of the Imperial Palace, Beijing. (Photo by Hu Chui)

上图　北京故宫太和殿藻井。（图 / 胡锤）

The upper　Caisson ceiling of Hall of Supreme Harmony of the Imperial Palace, Beijing. (Photo by Hu Chui)

下图　北京故宫养心殿藻井。（图 / 胡锤）

The lower　Caisson ceiling of Hall of Mental Cultivation of the Imperial Palace, Beijing. (Photo by Hu Chui)

北京故宫藏品：清 · 玉石水仙盆景。（图 / 胡锤）
Qing Dynasty Potted Landscape of Jade Daffodils. (Photo by Hu Chui)

组图：北京故宫藏品。

1. 清 · 金佛塔。（图 / 胡锤）/ 2. 嵌珍珠金佛像。（图 / 胡锤）/ 3. 清 · 金天球仪。（图 / 胡锤）/ 4. 清 · 雍正粉彩天球瓶。（图 / 胡锤）/ 5. 清 · 碧玉觥。（图 / 胡锤）/ 6. 清 · 牙雕群仙祝寿龙船。（图 / 胡锤）/ 7. 清 · 玉雕童子洗象。（图 / 胡锤）/ 8. 清 · 德化窑达摩。（图 / 胡锤）/ 9. 清 · 朱碧山银槎杯。（图 / 胡锤）

1.Qing Gold Pagoda. (Photo by Hu Chui) / 2.Statue of Gold Buddha with Inlaid Pearls. (Photo by Hu Chui) /3.Qing Gold Celestial Globe. (Photo by Hu Chui) / 4.Qing Globe-shaped rose vase of Yongzheng reign period. (Photo by Hu Chui) / 5.Qing Jade Gong. (Photo by Hu Chui) / 6.Qing Ivory Dragon Boat with Eight Immortal Beings Celebrating the Birthday of Xiwangmu. (Photo by Hu Chui) / 7.Qing Jade Sculpture of two Boys Washing an Elephant. (Photo by Hu Chui) / 8.Monk Damo produced by Dehua Kiln. (Photo by Hu Chui) / 9.Boat-shaped Silver Cup. (Photo by Hu Chui)

北京故宫藏品：北宋画家张择端的作品《清明上河图》局部。作品以长卷形式，生动记录了中国 12 世纪北宋汴京的城市面貌和当时汉族社会各阶层人民的生活状况。（图 / 胡锤）

Part of *Riverside Scene at Qingming Festival*, Zhang Zeduan 's masterpiece of the Northern Song Dynasty preserved in the Imperial Palace.The long scroll adopts cavalier perspective and presents a vivid picture of Bianjing in the twelveth century, the capital of the Northern Song Dynasty. (Photo by Hu Chui)

鸟瞰沈阳故宫。（图 / 线云强）
An aerial view of the Imperial Palace of Shenyang. (Photo by Xian Yunqiang)

上图　大政殿外景。（图 / 王瑞琛）

The Upper　External view of Dazheng Hall. (Photo by Wang Ruichen)

下图　崇政殿雪景。（图 / 王瑞琛）

The Lower　Chongzheng Hall in snow. (Photo by Wang Ruichen)

上图　太庙正殿。（图 / 王瑞琛）

The Upper　The main hall of Tai Miao, the Imperial Ancestral Temple. (Photo by Wang Ruichen)

下图　凤凰楼。（图 / 王瑞琛）

The Lower　Fenghuang Lou (the Phoenix House). (Photo by Wang Ruichen)

沈阳故宫崇政殿宝座。（图 / 田立）
The throne at Chongzheng Hall of Shenyang Palace Museum. (Photo by Tian Li)

大政殿内宝座与屏风。(图 / 王瑞琛)

Throne and screen at Dazheng Hall. (Photo by Wang Ruichen)

左上　清宁宫内景。（图 / 王瑞琛）

Upper left　Interior view of Qingning Palace, or Palace of Pure Tranquility. (Photo by Wang Ruichen)

左下　迪光殿内景。（图 / 王瑞琛）

Lower left　Interior view of Diguang Hall. (Photo by Wang Ruichen)

右上　继思斋内景。（图 / 王瑞琛）

Upper right　Interior of Jisi Zhai. (Photo by Wang Ruichen)

右下　颐和殿内景。（图 / 王瑞琛）

Lower right　Interior of Yihe Hall. (Photo by Wang Ruichen)

(Photo by Wang Ruichen)

左上　大政殿藻井。（图 / 王瑞琛）

Upper left　Cassion ceiling of Dazheng Hall. (Photo by Wang Ruichen)

右上　凤凰楼彩画。（图 / 王瑞琛）

Upper right　Color painting at Fenghuang Lou. (Photo by Wang Ruichen)

下图　崇政殿堂陛梵文天花。（图 / 王瑞琛）

The Lower　Sanskrit ceiling of the Tangbi in Chongzheng Hall. (Photo by Wang Ruichen)

左图　清太祖努尔哈赤像。（图 / 王瑞琛）

The Left　Portrait of Nurhachi, Emperor Taizhu of the Qing Dynasty. (Photo by Wang Ruichen)

右上　努尔哈赤玉宝。（图 / 王瑞琛）

Upper right　Jade seal of Nurhachi. (Photo by Wang Ruichen)

右中　努尔哈赤玉宝。（图 / 王瑞琛）

Middle right　Jade seal of Nurhachi. (Photo by Wang Ruichen)

右下　努尔哈赤宝剑。（图 / 王瑞琛）

Lower right　Sword of Nurhachi. (Photo by Wang Ruichen)

右图　清太宗皇太极像。（图 / 王瑞琛）

The Right　Portrait of Huang Taiji, Emperor Taizong of the Qing Dynasty. (Photo by Wang Ruichen)

左上　皇太极玉宝。（图 / 王瑞琛）

Upper left　Jade seal of Huang Taiji. (Photo by Wang Ruichen)

左中　皇太极玉宝。（图 / 王瑞琛）

Middle left　Jade seal of Huang Taiji. (Photo by Wang Ruichen)

左下　皇太极腰刀。（图 / 王瑞琛）

Lower left　Broadsword of Huang Taiji. (Photo by Wang Ruichen)

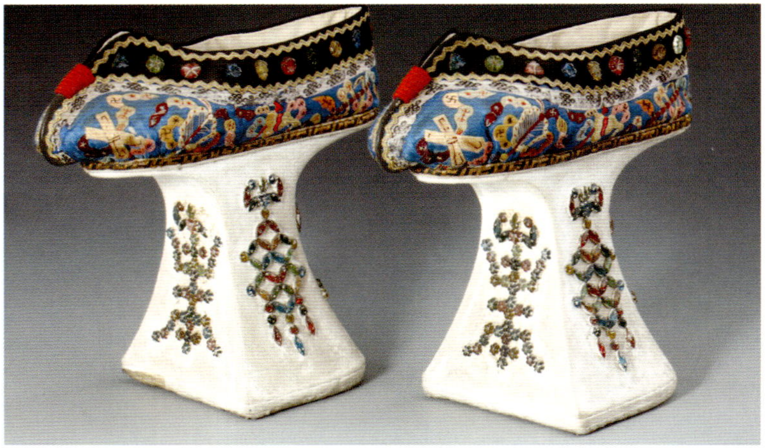

左上　男式便帽。（图 / 王瑞琛）　**Upper left**　Men's cap. (Photo by Wang Ruichen)
左中　男式夏凉帽。（图 / 王瑞琛）　**Middle left**　Men's summer hat. (Photo by Wang Ruichen)
左下　貂皮冬帽。（图 / 王瑞琛）　**Lower left**　Mink cap for winter. (Photo by Wang Ruichen)
右上　女冬便帽。（图 / 王瑞琛）　**Upper right**　Women's winter hat. (Photo by Wang Ruichen)
右中　女式马蹄形旗鞋。（图 / 王瑞琛）　**Middle right**　Qixie, Manchu women's horseshoe-shaped shoes. (Photo by Wang Ruichen)
右下　女式马蹄形旗鞋。（图 / 王瑞琛）　**Lower right**　Qixie, Manchu women's horseshoe-shaped shoes. (Photo by Wang Ruichen)

清著名宫廷画家郎世宁作品《松鹤图》。（图 / 王瑞琛）

Pine Tree and Cranes, painted by the famous royal painter Giuseppe Castiglione in the Qing Dynasty. (Photo by Wang Ruichen)

北京八达岭长城。（图／何世尧）

Badaling Great Wall of Beijing. (Photo by He Shiyao)

中国世界遗产影像志

WORLD HERITAGE IN CHINA

The Great Wall

长城

The Great Wall
长　城

公元前约 220 年，秦始皇下令将早期修建的一些分散的防御工事连接成一个完整的防御系统，用以抵抗来自北方的侵略。长城的修建一直持续到明代（1368 至 1644 年），终于建成为世界上最大的军事设施。长城在建筑学上的价值，足以与其在历史和战略上的重要性相媲美。

——世界遗产委员会评价

In 220 B.C., under Qin Shi Huang, sections of earlier fortifications were joined together to form a united defence system against invasions from the north. Construction continued up to the Ming Dynasty (1368 - 1644), when the Great Wall became the world's largest military structure. Its historic and strategic importance is matched only by its architectural significance.

——World Heritage Committee Evaluation

北京金山岭长城 。（图 / 杨大洲）
Jinshanling Great Wall of Beijing. (Photo by Yang Dazhou)

北京怀柔区箭扣长城。（图 / 翟东风）
Jiankou Great Wall in Huairou County of Beijing. (Photo by Zhai Dongfeng)

北京密云古北口长城。（图 / 李少白）
Gubeikou Great Wall of Miyun County of Beijing. (Photo by Li Shaobai)

北京慕田峪长城。（图 / 陈长芬）
Mutianyu Great Wall of Beijing. (Photo by Chen Changfen)

河北秦皇岛长城。（图 / 陈长芬）
Qinhuangdao Great Wall in Hebei Province. (Photo by Chen Changfen)

山西省朔州广武长城。(图 /Sophoto)
Guangwu Great Wall of Shuozhou, Shanxi Province. (Photo by Sophoto)

宁夏银川长城。（图 / 惠怀杰）

The Great Wall in Yinchuang, Ningxia Hui Autonomous Region. (Photo by Hui Huaijie)

甘肃日勒明长城（左侧）与汉长城（右侧）。（图 / 李少白）
The Great Wall of the Ming Dynasty (left) and the Han Dynasty (right) in Rile, Gansu Province. (Photo by Li Shaobai)

内蒙古包头巴彦淖尔市秦长城。（图 /Sophoto） The Bayannaoer Great Wall of the Qin Dynasty in Inner Mongolia.(Photo by Sophoto)

甘肃敦煌汉长城。（图 / 李少白）
Dunhuang Great Wall of the Han Dynasty in Gansu Province. (Photo by Li Shaobai)

内蒙古六苏木长城。（图 / 李少白）

Liusumu Great Wall in Inner Mongolia. (Photo by Li Shaobai)

甘肃省嘉峪关。（图/李江）

Jiayu Pass in Gansu Province. (Photo by Li Jiang)

河北山海关。（图 / 陈长芬）

Shanhai Pass in Hebei Province. (Photo by Chen Changfen)

陕西省榆林长城一角。（图 / 陈长芬）

(Part of) Yulin Great Wall in Shaanxi Province. (Photo by Chen Changfen)

1

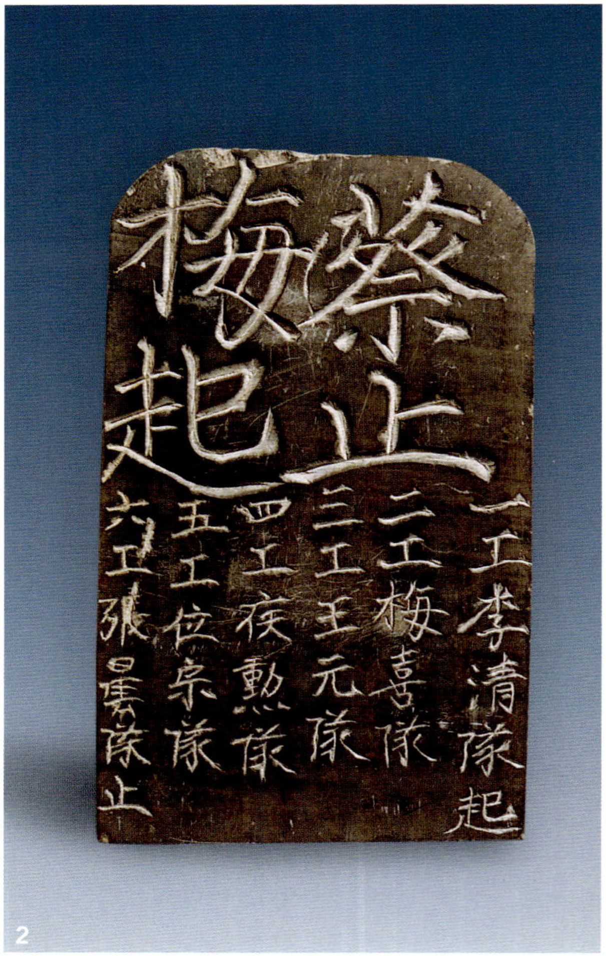

2

3

5

6

（组图 / 威廉 · 林赛）
(Photos by William Lindesay)

1. 长城工碑拓片

文物说明：长城工碑是记载长城修筑时间、地段、长度等信息的石碑。该石碑刻于 1578 年，现在依然在北京市怀柔区境内的长城上，尺寸 68X44 厘米 。/ 收藏意义：227 米长城修建的记录。/ 文物来源：该拓片拓印于 2002 年 9 月。/ 当前状况：作者藏品

Ink rubbing on paper of an inscribed stone tablet for the Great Wall

Description: This inscribed stone tablet is to record the detail information throughout the construction of the Great Wall, measuring 68 x 44 cm, dated 1578 A.D. and still extant in the stonework of the Ming Great Wall, Huairou District, Beijing.

Significance: Record of construction of 227-metre section of the Great Wall

Source: Rubbing made in September 2002.

Location: Author's collection, Beijing.

2. 长城工牌

文物说明：青石质小石碑，高 19 厘米、宽 11.5 厘米、厚 2 厘米。/ 收藏意义：稀有的长城建筑记工牌实物。/ 文物来源：雕刻于 1540 年 8 月。/ 当前状态：展示于嘉峪关长城博物馆。

Gong Pai for the Great Wall

Description: A small bluestone stele, 19 x 11 cm, 2 cm in thickness.

Significance: Rare on-site record of construction of the Great Wall.

Source: Inscribed in 1540.

Location: Exhibited in the Jiayuguan Great Wall Museum, Gansu.

3. 刻字的长城砖

文物说明：刻字的明代长城砖。/ 收藏意义：长城历史上数量最多的人工长城建筑材料。/ 文物来源：中国河北省境内的长城上。/ 当前状态：陈列于山海关长城博物馆。

Stamped brick from the Great Wall

Description: Stamped brick from Great Wall of the Ming Dynasty

Significance: The most widely produced building material component in the Great Wall history.

Source: On the Great Wall, Hebei Province.

Location: Shanhaiguan Great Wall Museum.

4. 木觚

文物说明：木觚（读音 gu), 七棱六面木质简牍，共 212 个汉字。/ 收藏意义：了解汉代长城前线的将士们对汉字书写的要求。/ 文物来源：在甘肃省嘉峪关市以西 100 公里处汉代烽燧中发现。 / 当前状态：陈列于嘉峪关长城博物馆。

Mu Gu

Description: A wooden border document with seven faces bearing a total of 212 Chinese characters.

Significance: Literacy, a new qualification required by Han army officers engaged in frontier defence work.

Source: Excavated at a watchtower on the Han Great Wall, 100 km west to Jiayuguan City, Gansu.

Location: Great Wall Museum of Jiayuguan.

5. 脊兽

文物说明：凤形脊兽，建筑构件，高 17 厘米。/ 收藏意义：鲜见的长城建筑构件。/ 文物来源：在河北省涞源县乌龙沟以西 2 公里的一处敌楼顶部发现。/ 当前状况：作者藏品。

Ji Shou

Description: A roof-guardian figurine of a phoenix; fired clay (brick), 17 cm in height.

Significance: A rare ornament on the Ming Great Wall.

Source: Upper level of a watchtower, 2 km west to Wulonggou, Laiyuan County, Hebei Province.

Location: Author's collection.

6. 手铳

文物说明：长 43.5 厘米、青铜质地的火器，是一种短枪的雏形。/ 收藏意义：在 15 世纪长城战事中经常使用的“热兵器”之一。/ 文物来源：明洪武十一年（1378 年）在山东临沂铸造。/ 当前状况：作者个人藏品

Shou Chong

Description: A blunderbuss or an early shotgun, 43.5 cm in length, cast in bronze, with leather gunpowder pouches.

Significance: Firearm type whose use proliferated across North China and throughout Great Wall theatre of war during the 15th century.

Source: Cast in 1378 at Linyi, Shandong Province.

Location: Author's collection.

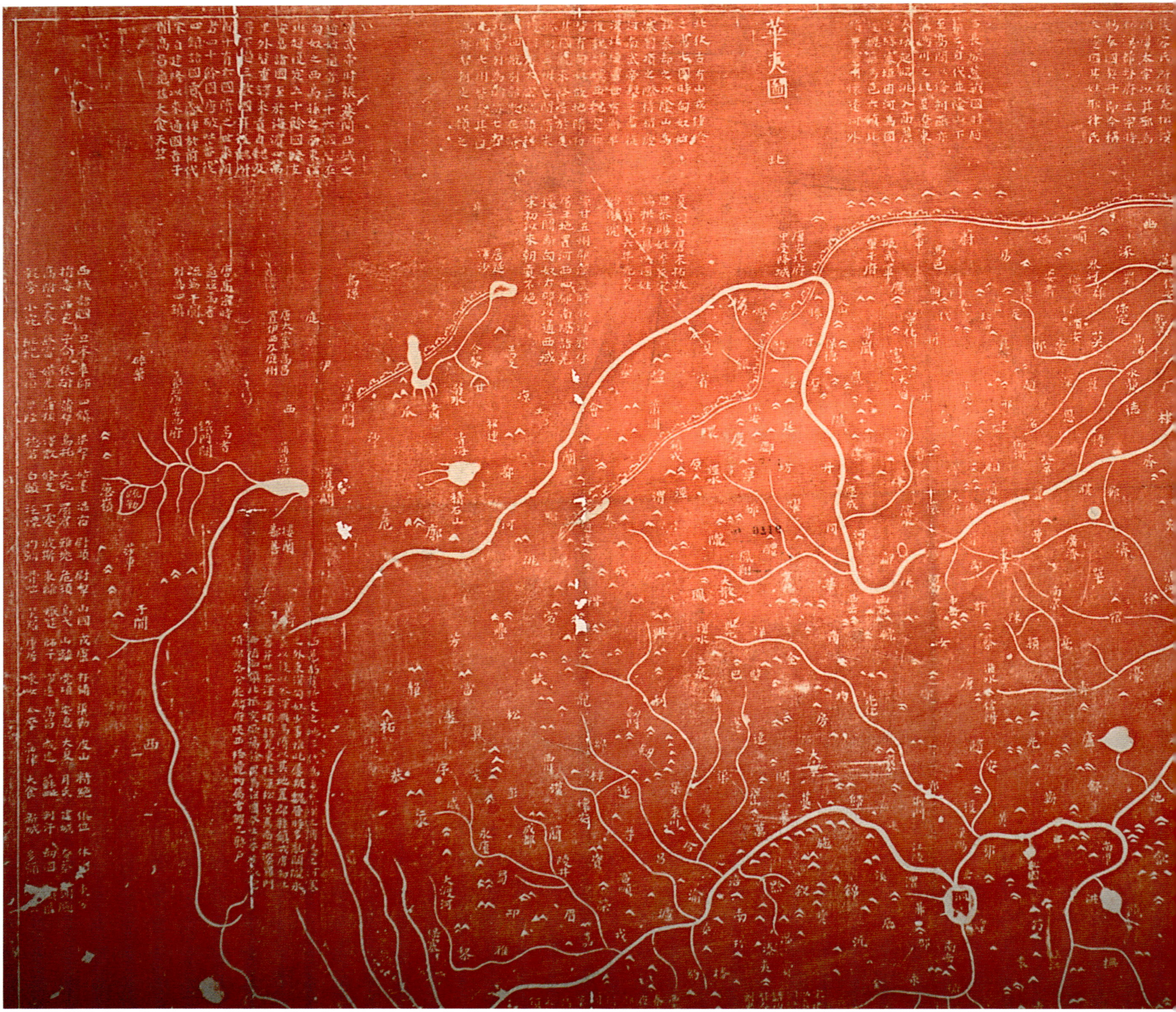
華夷圖

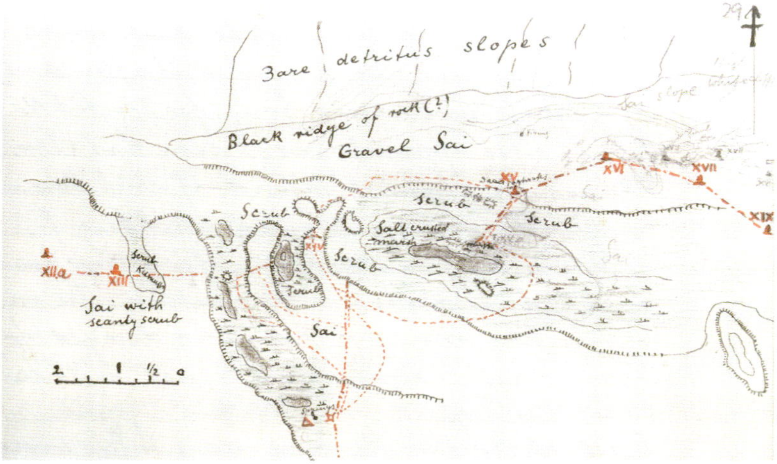

左图　《华夷图》拓片

文物说明：《华夷图》是中国最早标识万里长城的地图。/ 收藏意义：最早的长城石刻图形。/ 文物来源：以公元801年《海内华夷图》为蓝本，宋代时被镌刻在石板上。/ 当前状况：北京国家图书馆。原石刻保存于西安碑林博物馆。

The left　Ink rubbing of Hua Yi Tu

Description: Map of China and Barbarian Lands, first labeling the Great Wall.

Significance: Earliest extant image of the Great Wall.

Source: Based on a map drawn in 801 A.D., transferred to stone in the Song Dynasty.

Location: Original stele thought to be in collection of Forest of Steles Museum, Xi'an, Shaanxi Province. Map print from the stele collected in National Library of China, Beijing.

右图　斯坦因手绘汉长城地图

文物说明：手绘汉长城地图详细并精确地标出了汉长城烽燧和墙体。/ 收藏意义：第一张详尽的汉长城地图。/ 文物来源：1907 年 4 月由英国探险家、考古学家奥雷尔·斯坦因 (1863-1943) 绘制。/ 当前状况：现藏于英国牛津大学伯德利图书馆。

The right　Sketch map in ink of Western Han Great Wall by Stein.

Description: Sketch map in ink of Western Han Great Wall, showing positions of remnant wall, watchtowers and surrounding terrain.

Significance: First detailed large-scale map of Han Wall.

Source: Drawn by British explorer and archeologist Aurel Stein (1863-1943).

Location: Bodleian Library, Oxford.

（组图 / 威廉·林赛）

(Photos by William Lindesay)

中国世界遗产影像志

WORLD HERITAGE IN CHINA

秦始皇陵及兵马俑坑

Mausoleum of the First Qin Emperor

秦始皇陵 1 号坑军阵。（图 / 夏居宪）

Mausoleum of Emperor Qin Shi Huang and Terracotta Army Pit 1. (Photo by Xia Juxian)

Mausoleum of the First Qin Emperor
秦始皇陵及兵马俑坑

毫无疑问，如果不是 1974 年被发现，这座考古遗址中的成千上万件陶俑将依旧沉睡于地下。第一位统一中国的皇帝秦始皇，殁于公元前 210 年，葬于陵墓的中心，在他周围围绕着那些著名的陶俑。结构复杂的秦始皇陵是仿照其生前的都城——咸阳的格局而设计建造的。小陶俑形态各异，连同他们的战马、战车和武器，成为现实主义的完美杰作，同时也具有极高的历史价值。

——世界遗产委员会评价

No doubt thousands of statues still remain to be unearthed at this archaeological site, which was not discovered until 1974. Qin (210 B.C.), the first unifier of China, is buried, surrounded by the famous terracotta warriors, at the centre of a complex designed to mirror the urban plan of the capital, Xianyang . The small figures are all different; with their horses, chariots and weapons, they are masterpieces of realism and also of great historical interest.

——World Heritage Committee Evaluation

秦始皇陵园模拟图。（图 / 夏居宪）

Simulation of the Mausoleum of Emperor Qin Shi Huang. (Photo by Xia Juxian)

骊山北麓的秦始皇陵。（图 / 夏居宪）
The Mausoleum of Emperor Qin Shi Huang at the north foot of Mt. Li. (Photo by Xia Juxian)

左图　1号坑军阵前锋全景。（图 / 孙之常）

The left　Panorama of the military vanguard,Pit. No.1. (Photo by Sun Zhichang)

右上　2号坑战车俑组合。（图 / 孙之常）

Upper right　The chariot of Pit No.2. (Photo by Sun Zhichang)

右下　2号坑骑兵俑。（图 / 孙之常）

Lower right　The cavalry warriors of Pit No.2. (Photo by Sun Zhichang)

左图　3 号坑仪仗列俑。（图 / 孙之常）

The left　The honor guards of Pit No.3. (Photo by Sun Zhichang)

右图　3 号坑门厅战车组。（图 / 孙之常）

The right　War chariot in the hallway of Pit No.3. (Photo by Sun Zhichang)

（1号车）立车。（图/夏居宪）

(Chariot No.1) A carriage with a standing driver. (Photo by Xia Juxian)

（2号车）安车。（图/夏居宪）
(Chariot No.2) A carriage with a seated driver. (Photo by Xia Juxian)

带披膊的铠甲。（图 / 夏居宪）

Armor with shoulder pad. (Photo by Xia Juxian)

乐府钟。（图/夏居宪）

Yuefu bell. (Photo by Xia Juxian)

1 号坑发掘工作现场。（图 / 夏居宪）
Excavation of Pit No.1. (Photo by Xia Juxian)

上图　食官遗址发掘现场。（图 / 夏居宪）　**The upper**　Excavation of the food chamber. (Photo by Xia Juxian)
下左　铜车马出土原貌。（图 / 张平）　**Lower left**　Copper chariot upon excavation. (Photo by Zhang Ping)
下右　修陵人墓地发掘现场。（图 / 夏居宪）　**Lower right**　Excavation of the tomb of the builders. (Photo by Xia Juxian)

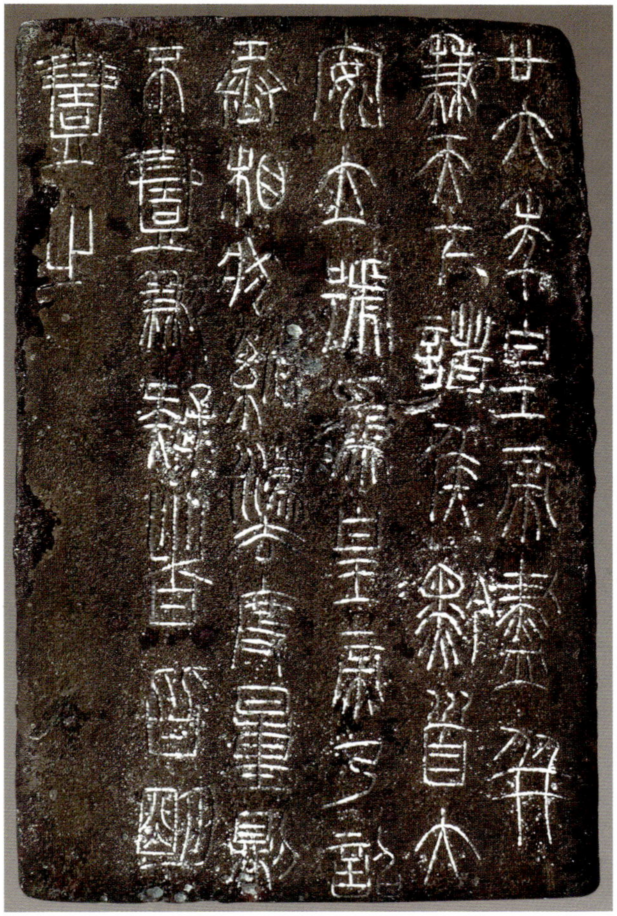

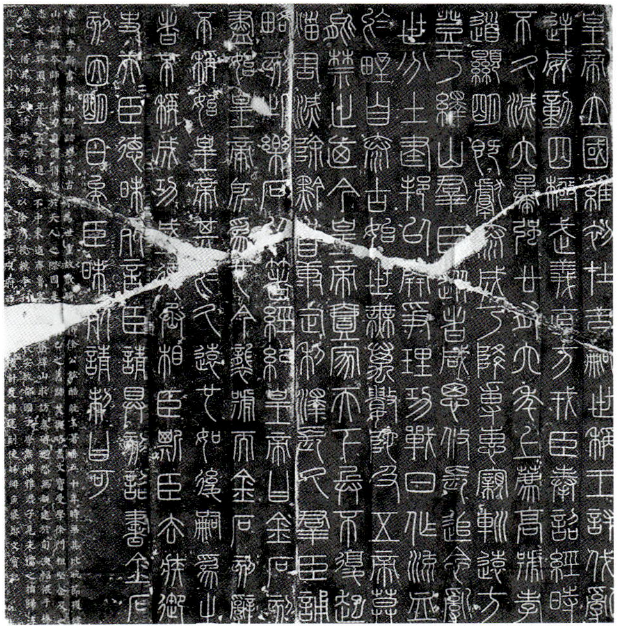

左图　秦咸阳宫殿壁画。（图 / 夏居宪）

The left　Fresco at the Qin palace in Xianyang. (Photo by Xia Juxian)

右上　秦诏板。（图 / 夏居宪）

Upper right　Bronze Imperial Edicts of Qin Dynasty. (Photo by Xia Juxian)

右下　峰山刻石。（图 / 夏居宪）

Lower right　Mt. Feng monument. (Photo by Xia Juxian)

中国世界遗产影像志

WORLD HERITAGE IN CHINA

北京皇家祭坛——天坛

Temple of Heaven: an Imperial Sacrificial Altar in Beijing

北京天坛祈年殿。（图 / 蒙紫）

Hall of Prayer for Good Harvest at the Temple of Heaven, Beijing. (Photo by Meng Zi)

Temple of Heaven: an Imperial Sacrificial Altar in Beijing

北京皇家祭坛——天坛

天坛，建于 15 世纪上半叶，座落在皇家园林当中，四周古松环抱，是保存完好的坛庙建筑群。无论在整体布局还是单一建筑上，都反映出天地之间（即人神之间）的关系，而这一关系在中国古代宇宙观中占据着核心位置。同时，这些建筑还体现出帝王在这一关系中所起的独特作用。

——世界遗产委员会评价

The Temple of Heaven, founded in the first half of the 15th century, is a dignified complex of fine cult buildings set in gardens and surrounded by historic pine woods. In its overall layout and that of its individual buildings, it symbolizes the relationship between earth and heaven - the human world and God's world - which stands at the heart of Chinese cosmogony, and also the special role played by the emperors within that relationship.

——World Heritage Committee Evaluation

圜丘。（图 / 周梅生）
Circular Mound Altar. (Photo by Zhou Meisheng)

天坛鸟瞰图。（图 / 张肇基）

An arial eye view of the Temple of Heaven. (Photo by Zhang Zhaoji)

鸟瞰斋宫。（图 / 张肇基）

An aerial view of Palace of Abstinence. (Photo by Zhang Zhaoji)

皇天上帝

皇穹宇内景。（图 / 李江）

The inside of Imperial Vault of Heaven. (Photo by Li Jiang)

上图　皇穹宇藻井。（图 / 姚天新）　**The upper**　The Circular Mound caisson of Imperial Vault of Heaven. (Photo by Yao Tianxin)
下图　祈年殿藻井。（图 / 姚天新）　**The lower**　Caisson of Hall of Prayer for Good Harvest. (Photo by Yao Tianxin)

左上　鼎炉。（图 / 姚天新）　**Upper left**　Tripod furnace. (Photo by Yao Tianxin)
右上　鼎。（图 / 姚天新）　**Upper right**　Tripod. (Photo by Yao Tianxin)
左下　香炉亭。（图 / 姚天新）　**Lower left**　Incense burner. (Photo by Yao Tianxin)
右下　祝版亭。（图 / 姚天新）　**Lower right**　Prayer Board Pavilion. (Photo by Yao Tianxin)

棂星门。棂星门是中国古代建筑的特殊形制。棂星为天田星，亦称灵星，祭天前先祭棂星。门柱为华表形式，代表最高等级，多用于帝王陵寝或坛庙建筑中，象征天门。（图 / 周梅生）

Lingxing Gate. Lingxing Gate is a special structure in ancient Chinese design. Lingxing-the Celestial Farmland-was worshiped prior to a sacrifice to heaven. The gatepost is in the form of an ornamental column that represents the highest rank; it was mainly used in such structures as imperial mausoleums and temples to represent the gate of heaven. (Photo by Zhou Meisheng).

中国 世界遗产 影像志

WORLD HERITAGE IN CHINA

北京皇家园林——颐和园

Summer Palace, an Imperial Garden in Beijing

鸟瞰颐和园。（图 / 马文晓）

Aerial view of the Summer Palace. (Photo by Ma Wenxiao)

中国 世界遗产 影像志

WORLD HERITAGE IN CHINA

Summer Palace, an Imperial Garden in Beijing

北京皇家园林——颐和园

北京颐和园，始建于 1750 年，1860 年在战火中严重损毁，1886 年在原址上重新进行了修缮。其亭台、长廊、殿堂、庙宇和小桥等人工景观与自然山峦和开阔的湖面相互和谐地融为一体，具有极高的审美价值，堪称中国风景园林设计中的杰作。

——世界遗产委员会评价

The Summer Palace in Beijing——first built in 1750, largely destroyed in the war of 1860 and restored on its original foundations in 1886 - is a masterpiece of Chinese landscape garden design. The natural landscape of hills and open water is combined with artificial features such as pavilions, halls, palaces, temples and bridges to form a harmonious ensemble of outstanding aesthetic value.

——World Heritage Committee Evaluation

鸟瞰南湖岛。（图 / 张肇基）

An aerial view of Nanhu Island. (Photo by Zhang Zhaoji)

昆明湖与万寿山。（图 / 茹遂初）
Kunming Lake and Wanshou Mountain.
(Photo by Ru Suichu)

谐趣园之夏。（图 / 茹遂初）
Garden of Harmonious Interest in Summer.
(Photo by Ru Suichu)

左图　颐和园长廊。（图 / 姚天新）

The left　The Long Corridor of the Summer Palace. (Photo by Yao Tianxin)

右图　颐和园长廊廊间的每根枋梁上都绘有彩画，共 14000 余幅，色彩鲜明，构图新颖，彩画的内容多为花鸟鱼虫以及中国古典四大名著中的情节。（图 / 李少白）

The right　Each ceiling beam between the sections of the Long Corridor is decorated with color paintings, numbering over 14,000 pieces altogether. The content of the color paintings mainly includes flowers, birds, fish, insects and details from the Four Ancient Chinese Classics. (Photo by Li Shaobai)

左上　石舫。（图 / 姚天新）　**Upper left**　Marble Boat. (Photo by Yao Tianxin)

右上　玉带桥。（图 / 茹遂初）　**Upper right**　Jade Ribbon Bridge. (Photo by Ru Suichu)

左下　铜牛。（图 / 姚天新）　**Lower left**　Copper Ox. (Photo by Yao Tianxin)

右下　排云殿。（图 / 姚天新）　**Lower right**　Paiyun Hall. (Photo by Yao Tianxin)

上图　清和田碧玉双碟衔环洗。（图 / 姚天新）　**The upper**　Hetian green jade brush rinser (the Qing Dynasty). (Photo by Yao Tianxin)
下左　清和田白玉盒。（图 / 姚天新）　**Lower left**　Hetian white jade box (the Qing Dynasty). (Photo by Yao Tianxin)
下中　清翡翠插屏。（图 / 姚天新）　**Lower centre**　Jadeite table screen (the Qing Dynasty). (Photo by Yao Tianxin)
下右　清和田碧玉杯。（图 / 姚天新）　**Lower right**　Hetian green jade cup (the Qing Dynasty). (Photo by Yao Tianxin)

上图　战国错金鸟尊。（图 / 姚天新）　**The Upper**　Inlayed gold bird-shape wine container of the Warring States Period. (Photo by Yao Tianxin)

下左　清乾隆粉彩山水人物瓶。（图 / 姚天新）　**Lower left**　Famille rose landscape figure vase. (Qianlong Period, the Qing Dynasty). (Photo by Yao Tianxin)

下中　清乾隆斗彩福寿纹方瓶。（图 / 姚天新）　**Lower centre**　Square vase with overglaze colours with the characters Of Fu (Blessing) and Shou (Longevity) (Qianlong Period, the Qing Dynasty). (Photo by Yao Tianxin)

下右　清乾隆绳纹圆口尊。（图 / 姚天新）　**Lower right**　Round Mouth wine container with rope veins. (Qianlong Period, the Qing Dynasty). (Photo by Yao Tianxin)

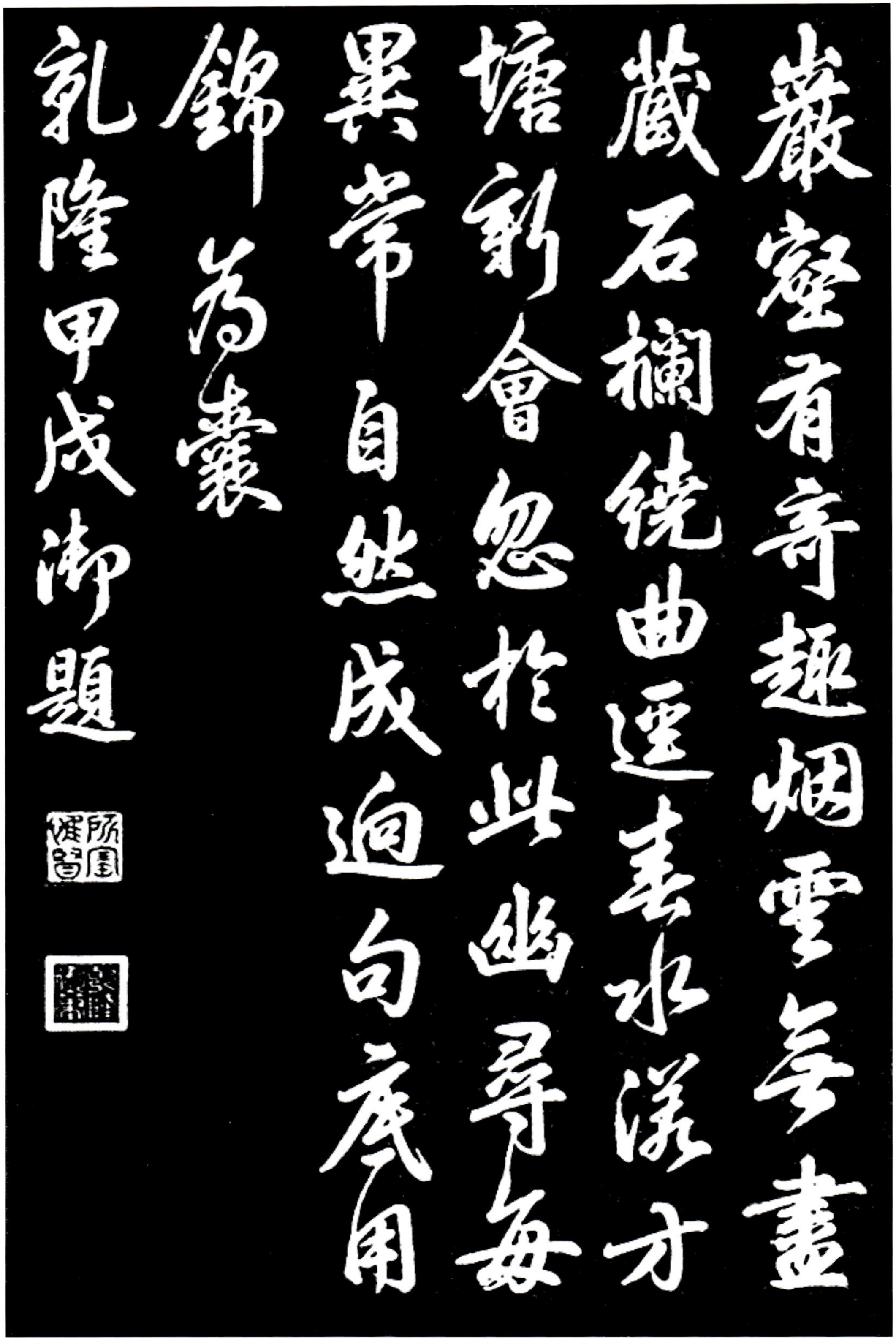

左图　谐趣园内寻诗迳乾隆皇帝手书诗碑拓片。（图 / 姚天新）

The left　Rubbing of the poem stele written by Emperor Qianlong in Looking-for-poem Path at the Garden of Harmonious Interest. (Photo by Yao Tianxin)

右图　清乾隆江南名胜图册。（图 / 姚天新）

The right　Atlas of Jiangnan scenic spots (Qianlong Period, the Qing Dynasty). (Photo by Yao Tianxin)

敷文書院

在鳳凰山之萬松嶺舊名萬松書院康熙五十五年
聖祖仁皇帝賜浙水敷文額因名敷文書院雍正十一年
世宗憲皇帝特賜帑金以資膏火
皇上御製題敷文書院七言律詩一首辛未敷文書院六韻五言排律
一首丁丑疊舊韻五言排律二首壬午乙酉

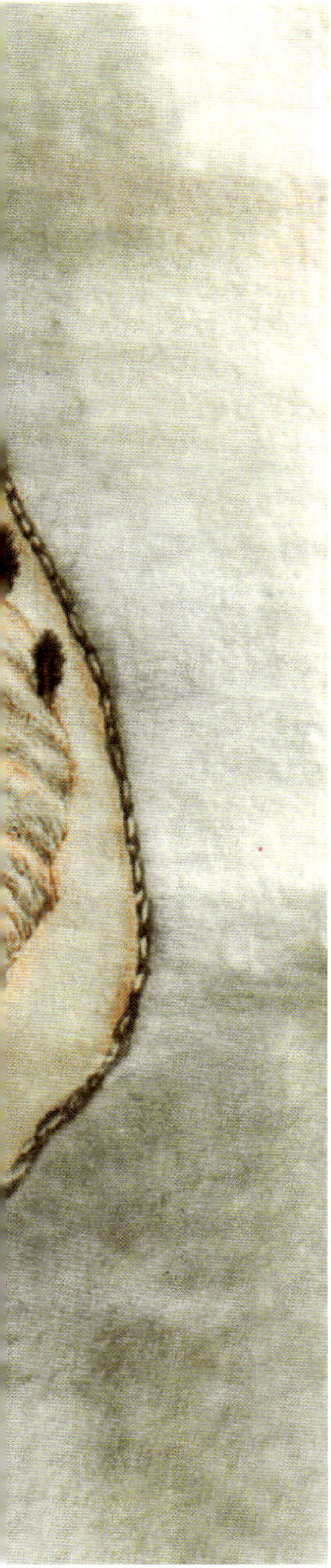

左图　清漪园时期藻鉴堂。（图 / 姚天新）

The left　Zaojiantang in the time of the Garden of Clear Ripples. (Photo by Yao Tianxin)

右上　治镜阁复原图。（图 / 姚天新）

Upper right　The restored image of the Mirror Pavilion. (Photo by Yao Tianxin)

右下　样式雷手绘图。（图 / 姚天新）

Lower right　Hand drawing by the Leis. (Photo by Yao Tianxin)

《皇家名胜图》。这幅图用散点透视的方法，集中展现了乾隆时期北京西北郊皇家苑囿中楼台耸翠、殿宇流丹的壮观景象。（图 / 姚天新）

Atlas of Imperial Scenic Spots. This drawing adopts the method of scattered point perspective and gives a collective representation of the magnificent views of the buildings in the imperial garden in Beijing's northwest suburbs in the Qianlong Period. (Photo by Yao Tianxin)

十七孔桥。（图 / 李少白）
17-Arch Bridge. (Photo by Li Shaobai)

中国世界遗产影像志

WORLD HERITAGE IN CHINA

Mountain Resort and Its Outlying Temples, Chengde

承德避暑山庄及其周围寺庙

湖区鸟瞰。湖区是避暑山庄的重要组成部分。（图 / 陈克寅）
An aerial view of the lake area, which claims a large area of the Mountain Resort. (Photo by Chen Keyin)

中国世界遗产影像志 WORLD HERITAGE IN CHINA

Mountain Resort and Its Outlying Temples, Chengde

承德避暑山庄及其周围寺庙

承德避暑山庄，是清王朝的夏季行宫，位于河北省境内，修建于公元 1703 年至 1792 年，是由众多的宫殿以及其他处理政务、举行仪式的建筑构成的一个庞大的建筑群。建筑风格各异的庙宇和皇家园林同周围的湖泊、牧场和森林巧妙地融为一体。避暑山庄不仅具有极高的美学研究价值，而且还保留着中国封建社会发展末期的罕见历史遗迹。

——世界遗产委员会评价

The Mountain Resort (the Qing Dynasty's summer palace), in Hebei Province, was built between 1703 and 1792. It is a vast complex of palaces and administrative and ceremonial buildings. Temples of various architectural styles and imperial gardens blend harmoniously into a landscape of lakes, pastureland and forests. In addition to its aesthetic interest, the Mountain Resort is a rare historic vestige of the final development of feudal society in China.

——World Heritage Committee Evaluation

避暑山庄鸟瞰图。（图 / 衣志坚）

An aerial view of Mountain Resort. (Photo by Yi Zhijian)

左图　须弥福寿之庙。（图 / 陈克寅）

The left　The Xumi Fushou Temple. (Photo by Chen Keyin)

右图　普乐寺。（图 / 陈克寅）

The right　Pule Temple . (Photo by Chen Keyin)

水心榭。建于康熙四十八年（1709年）。（图/陈克寅）
Pavilion in the Midst of Water. Built in the 48th year of Kangxi reign period (1709 A.D.). (Photo by Chen Keyin)

澹泊敬诚殿。澹泊敬诚殿为正宫区的主殿，是清代皇帝驻跸山庄时处理朝政、举行重大庆典活动及接见朝臣、少数民族王公大臣、外国使节之地。（图 / 陈克寅）

Hall of Frugality and Calm. It is the main hall in the palace area, the venue where the emperor handled administrative affairs and held grand ceremonies and gave audience to courtiers, nobility of the minority nationalities and foreign ambassadors during his majesty's stay in the Mountain Resort. (Photo by Chen Keyin)

烟波致爽殿。建于康熙四十九年（1710 年），是康熙、乾隆、嘉庆、咸丰驻跸时的寝宫。康熙曾说这里“四围秀岭、十里澄湖、致有爽气”，给人以旷然爽朗的感觉，因此题名“烟波致爽”。（图 / 陈克寅）

Yanbo Zhishuang Hall. It was built in the 49th year of Kangxi reign period (1710 A.D.). It is the residential hall where Emperors Kangxi, Qianglong, Jiaqing and Xianfeng lived during their stay in the resort. The hall got its name from Emperor Kangxi's comment that "the surrounding beautiful ranges and the large clean lake bring about coolness". (Photo by Chen Keyin)

宗印殿三世佛。此三世佛为横三世，即东方净琉璃世界的药师佛、中方娑婆世界的释迦牟尼佛和西方极乐世界的阿弥陀佛。（图 / 陈克寅）

The three Buddhas in Zongyin Hall. The three Buddhas are Medicine Buddha in the Eastern Pure and Glazed World, Sakyamuni in the Middle Whirling World and Maitreya Buddha in the Western Elysian World. (Photo by Chen Keyin)

左图　千手千眼观世音菩萨。（图 / 陈克寅）

The left　The thousand-hand-and-thousand-eye Guanyin Bodhisatta. (Photo by Chen Keyin)

右图　旭光阁藻井。采用三层重翘重昂九踩斗拱形式。井深七层，皆成圆形，如同伞盖。（图 / 陈克寅）

The right　The caisson in Morning Sunshine Tower. It adopts three-level-double-wing-seven-bracket structure. The caisson is nine layers deep and shaped like a circle in each layer and so looks like an umbrella. (Photo by Chen Keyin)

普陀宗乘之庙雪景。（图 / 陈克寅）

Putuo Zongcheng Temple in snow. (Photo by Chen Keyin)

乾隆戎装像。（图 / 陈克寅）

Emperor Qianlong dressed in military uniform. (Photo by Chen Keyin)

左上　康熙用过的弓和箭。弓胎长 164.4 厘米，榆木质，皮质弓弦，弦长 124.2 厘米。（图 / 陈克寅）

Upper left　The bow and the arrow used by Emperor Kangxi. The bow is 164.4 cm in length and made of elm while the string is 124.2 cm in length and made of leather. (Photo by Chen Keyin)

右上　皇帝龙袍。呈明黄色，上绣九条形态各异的龙纹。（图 / 陈克寅）

Upper right　The Emperor's dragon robe, brightly yellow in hue, with embroidery of nine dragons in different shapes. (Photo by Chen Keyin)

左下　乾隆御用马鞍。（图 / 陈克寅）

Lower left　The saddle used by Emperor Qianlong. (Photo by Chen Keyin)

右下　百蝶衣。慈禧所用，上绣百只形态各异的蝴蝶。（图 / 陈克寅）

Lower right　The hundred butterfly dress. It is wore by Dowager Cixi with embroidery of a hundred butterflies in different shapes. (Photo by Chen Keyin)

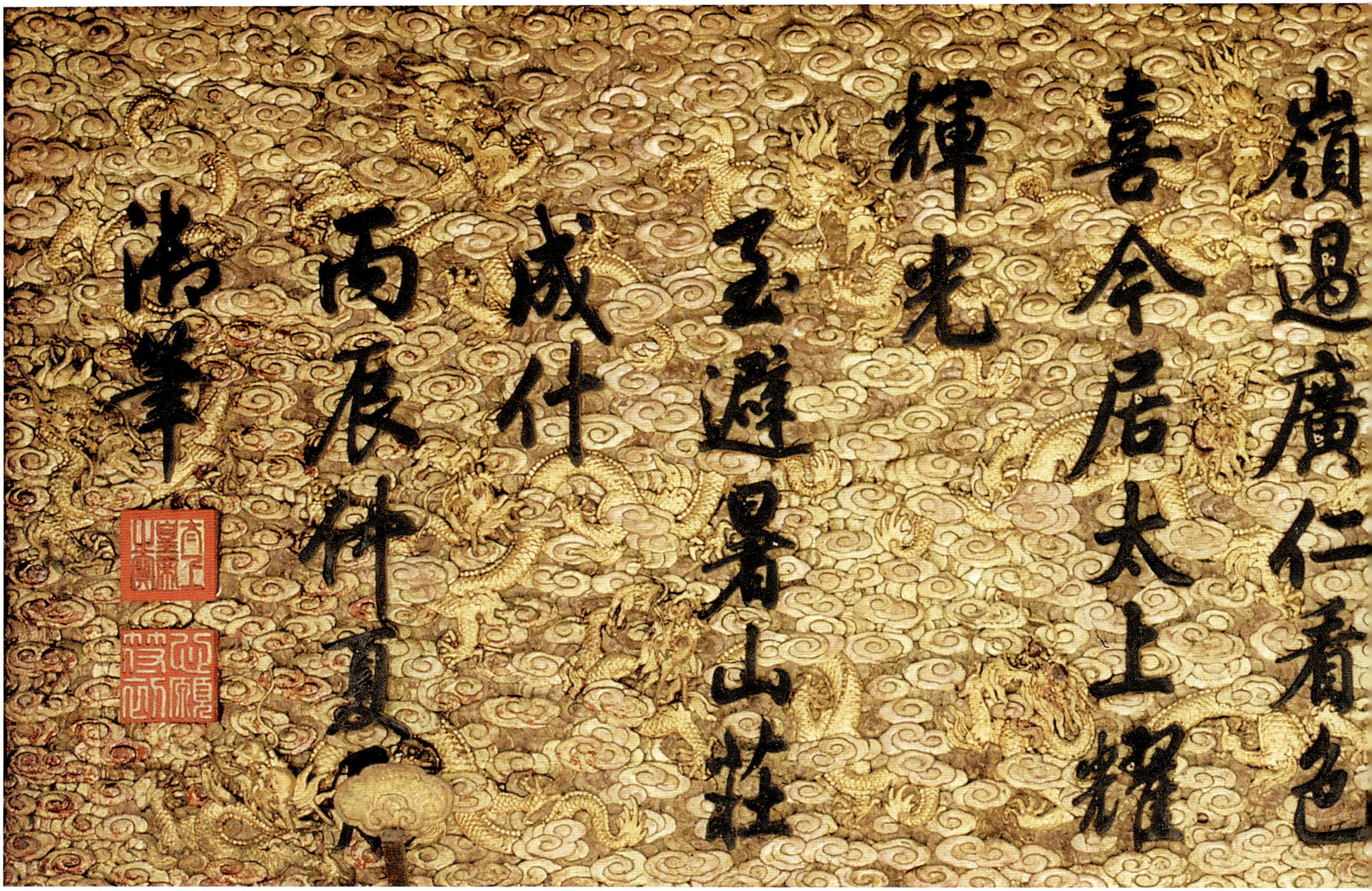
嶺過廣仁看色
喜今居太上耀
輝光
至避暑山莊
成什
丙辰仲夏
御筆

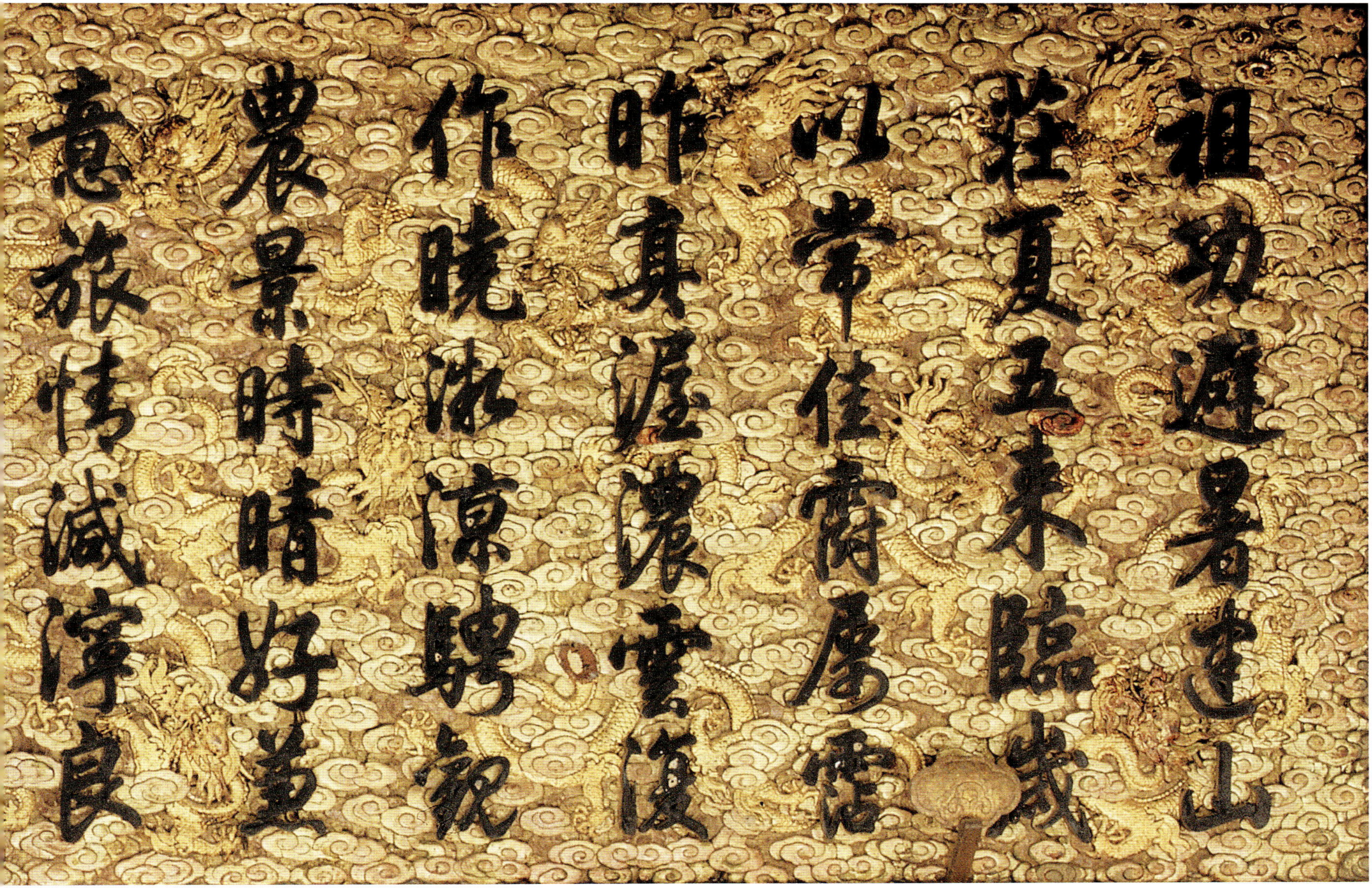

澹泊敬诚殿外悬挂的贴金云龙浮雕嵌黑字的乾隆皇帝手书诗匾。（图 / 陈克寅）

The board with poetry in Emperor Qianlong's handwriting hung outside Hall of Frugality and Calm. They are Yunlong relief overlaid with gold leaves. (Photo by Chen Keyin)

避暑山庄全图。（图 / 陈克寅）

A full view of Mountain Resort. (Photo by Chen Keyin)

中国
世界遗产
影像志

WORLD HERITAGE IN CHINA

明清皇家陵寝

Imperial Tombs of the Ming and Qing Dynasties

鸟瞰明十三陵。（图 / 马文晓）

An aerial view of the Ming Tombs. (Photo by Ma Wenxiao)

Imperial Tombs of the Ming and Qing Dynasties

明清皇家陵寝

明清皇家陵寝依照风水理论，精心选址，将数量众多的建筑物巧妙地安置于地下。它是人类改变自然的产物，体现了传统的建筑和装饰思想，阐释了中国封建社会的世界观与权力观。

辽宁的永陵、福陵和昭陵均修建于 17 世纪。清朝皇室为开创大清基业的先帝们修建的这些陵墓，体现了古老的中国风水理论。石像、雕刻以及龙纹砖上丰富的装饰都在述说着清朝墓葬建筑的演变。相对于 2000 年和 2003 年被列入世界遗产名录的明代皇陵来说，这三个墓葬群，不仅继承了前朝的文化传统，同时又融入了新的满族文明特色。

——世界遗产委员会评价

The harmonious integration of remarkable architectural groups in a natural environment chosen to meet the criteria of geomancy (Fengshui) makes the Ming and Qing Imperial Tombs masterpieces of human creative genius.The Ming and Qing Tombs are dazzling illustrations of the beliefs,world view,and geomantic theories of Fengshui prevalenrt in feudal China.They have served as burial edifices of illustrious personages and as the theatre for major events that have marked the history of China.

The Three Imperial Tombs of the Qing Dynasty in Liaoning Province include the Yongling Tomb,the Fuling Tomb,and the ZhaolingTomb,all built in the 17th century.Constructed for the founding emperors of the Qing Dynasty and their ancestors ,the tombs follow the precepts of traditional Chinese geomancy and fengshui theory.They festure rich decoration of stone carvings and tiles with dragon motifs,illustrating the development of the funerary architecture of the Qing Dynasty.It represents the addition of three Imperial Tombs of the Qing Dynasty in Liaoning to the Ming tombs inscribed in 2000 and 2003.The three tomb complexes, and their numerous edifices,traditions inherited from previous dynasties and features of Manchu civilization.

——World Heritage Committee Evaluation

清东陵 · 孝陵神道。（图 / 周梅生）

The Sacred Way of Xiaoling, one of the Eastern Qing Tombs. (Photo by Zhou Meisheng)

左图　明十三陵 · 思陵。（图 / 周梅生）

The left　Siling of the Ming Tombs. (Photo by Zhou Meisheng)

右上　明十三陵 · 神道华表。（图 / 周梅生）

Upper right　Ornamental column of the sacred way of the Ming Tombs. (Photo by Zhou Meisheng)

右中　明十三陵 · 长陵。（图 / 周梅生）

Middle right　Changling of the Ming Tombs. (Photo by Zhou Meisheng)

右下　明十三陵 · 康陵。（图 / 周梅生）

Lower right　Kangling of the Ming Tombs. (Photo by Zhou Meisheng)

左上　明十三陵 · 定陵地宫的石门。（图 / 李江）

Upper left　The stone gate of the underground palace of Dingling of the Ming Tombs. (Photo by Li Jiang)

右上　明十三陵 · 定陵地宫中殿。（图 / 李江）

Upper right　The main hall of the underground palace of Dingling of the Mng Tombs. (Photo by Li Jiang)

左下　明十三陵 · 定陵地宫的金钢墙。（图 / 李江）

Lower left　Diamond wall of the underground palace of Dingling of the Ming Tombs. (Photo by Li Jiang)

右下　明十三陵 · 定陵地宫后殿。（图 / 李江）

Lower right　The back hall of the underground palace of Dingling of the Ming Tombs. (Photo by Li Jiang)

左上　明十三陵·定陵凤冠。（图 / 李江）

Upper left Phoenix coronet of Dingling of the Ming tombs. (Photo by Li Jiang)

右上　明十三陵·定陵金冠。（图 / 李江）

Upper right Gold coronet of Dingling of the Ming Tombs. (Photo by Li Jiang)

左下　明十三陵·定陵的金托玉爵。（图 / 孙之常）

Lower left Jade Jue with gold support, Dingling of the Ming Tombs. (Photo by Sun Zhichang)

右下　明十三陵·定陵的嘉靖年制长明灯大缸。（图 / 孙之常）

Lower right Altar lamp vat made in Jiajing Period, Dingling of the Ming Tombs. (Photo by Sun Zhichang)

明显陵。（图 / 李江）
Xianling of the Ming Dynasty. (Photo by Li Jiang)

清东陵 · 孝陵石牌坊。（图 / 谭明）
Stone memorial gateway of XiaoLing , the Eastern Qing Tombs. (Photo by Tan Ming)

清西陵・泰陵石牌坊。（图 / 杨大洲）

TaiLing in the Western Qing Tombs. (Photo by Yang Dazhou)

清东陵 · 孝陵石牌坊“云龙戏珠”雕刻。（图 / 谭明）
The “dragon playing with pearl” carving on the stone memorial gateway of Xiaoling in the Eastern Qing Tombs. (Photo by Tan Ming)

左上　清东陵 · 定陵（咸丰）圣号碑。（图 / 李江）　**Upper left**　Sacred monument at Dingling (Emperor Xianfeng) , the Eastern Qing Tombs. (Photo byLi Jiang)

右上　清东陵 · 慈禧陵隆恩殿内景。（图 / 李江）　**Upper right**　The inner view of Long’en Hall in the tomb of Cixi , the Eastern Qing Tombs. (Photo by Li Jiang)

左下　清东陵 · 定东陵隆恩殿内景。（图 / 谭明）　**Lower left**　The inner view of Long’en Hall in Dingdongling , the Eastern Qing Tombs. (Photo by Tan Ming)

右下　清东陵 · 裕陵地宫。（图 / 谭明）　**Lower right**　The underground palace of Yuling , the Eastern Qing Tombs. (Photo by Tan Ming)

鸟瞰沈阳昭陵。（图 / 线云强）

An aerial view of Zhaoling in Shenyang. (Photo by Xian Yunqiang)

鸟瞰沈阳永陵。（图 / 线云强）

An aerial view of Yongling in Shenyang. (Photo by Xian Yunqiang)

鸟瞰沈阳福陵。（图 / 线云强）
An aerial view of Fuling in Shenyang. (Photo by Xian Yunqiang)

中国世界遗产影像志

大运河

WORLD HERITAGE IN CHINA

The Grand Canal

江苏淮安繁忙的运河。（图 / 倪峥嵘）

Busy transport on the Canal, Huai'an City, Jiangsu. (Photo by Ni Zhengrong)

大运河是位于中国东北和中东部平原的巨大水路系统，从北方的北京到南方的浙江。部分工程从公元前5世纪开始修筑，到公元7世纪（隋朝），它第一次被视为帝国统一的交通渠道。这项工程包含了大量的基础设施建设，创造了工业革命之前世界上规模最大、最广泛的土木工程项目。它构成了帝国内陆交通系统的脊梁，运送谷物和战略原料，提供大米养活居民。到公元13世纪，大运河包括了2000多公里的人工水道，连接起中国的五大水域。大运河对于保证国家的经济繁荣和稳定发挥了巨大的作用，直到今天仍然是一种重要的交通方式。

——世界遗产委员会评价

The Grand Canal is a vast waterway system in the north-eastern and central-eastern plains of China, running from Beijing in the north to Zhejiang province in the south. Constructed in sections from the 5th century B.C. onwards, it was conceived as a unified means of communication for the Empire for the first time in the 7th century A.D. (the Sui Dynasty). This led to a series of gigantic construction sites, creating the world's largest and most extensive civil engineering project prior to the Industrial Revolution. It formed the backbone of the Empire's inland communication system, transporting grain and strategic raw materials, and supplying rice to feed the population. By the 13th century it consisted of more than 2,000 km of artificial waterways, linking five of China's main river basins. It has played an important role in ensuring the country's economic prosperity and stability and is still in use today as a major means of communication.

——World Heritage Committee Evaluation

北京通惠河东便门处夕照。明永乐年间改建北京皇城，通惠河故道被围入宫墙之内，遂改以东便门外的大通桥为通惠河的新起点，即京杭大运河北端的终点。（图 / 张振华）

Dong Bian Gate at Tonghui River in Beijing at sunset. In the reconstruction of the Beijing during the Yongle reign of the Ming Dynasty, the old course of Tonghui River was enclosed within the palace wall, and thus Datong Bridge outside of Dong Bian Gate became the new starting point, which is the northern end of the Jing-Hang Grand Canal. (Photo by Zhang Zhenhua)

天津三岔口。南运河、北运河与海河交汇处。京杭大运河作为中国唯一南北走向的人工大河，纵向沟通了自西向东的五大天然河流——海河、黄河、淮河、长江、钱塘江。（图 / 张振华）

Sanchakou, Tianjin: the intersection of the South Canal, the North Canal and the Haihe River. As the only south-north manmade river in China, the Jing-Hang Grand Canal connects longitudinally five big natural rivers that flow from west to east, that is, the Haihe River, the Yellow River, the Huai River, the Changjiang River, and the Qiantang River. (Photo by Zhang Zhenhua)

江苏淮安水上立交大运河与淮河交汇处。（图 / 张振华）

The water interchange between the Grand Canal and the Yellow River at Huai'an, Jiangsu.(Photo by Zhang Zhenhua)

左上　山东位山引黄闸。大运河与黄河在北岸交汇处。（图 / 张振华）

Upper left　The gate for diverting water from the Yellow River,Weishan, Shandong. The intersection of the Grand Canal and the Yellow River at the north bank. (Photo by Zhang Zhenhua)

右上　大运河江苏镇江段与长江在南段交汇处。（图 / 张振华）

Upper Right　The intersection of the Grand Canal and the Changjiang River in Zhengjiang, Jiangsu. (Photo by Zhang Zhenhua)

左下　大运河江苏扬州段与长江在北岸交汇处。（图 / 张振华）

Lower left　The intersection of the Grand Canal and the Changjiang River on the north bank in Yangzhou, Jiangsu.(Photo by Zhang Zhenhua)

右下　大运河与钱塘江交汇处。（图 / 张振华）

Lower right　The intersection of the Grand Canal and the Qiantang River.(Photo by Zhang Zhenhua)

上图　流经山东济宁市区的大运河。（图 / 侯贺良）

The upper　The Grand Canal in Jining City, Shandong. (Photo by Hou Heliang)

下图　河南洛阳回洛仓遗址。作为隋唐大运河沿线的重要粮仓，它们有力地见证了隋唐时期中国南北漕运的兴旺发达。（图 / 王立力）

The lower　The site of Huiluo Granaries in Luoyang City, Henan. As major granaries by the Grand Canal in the Sui and Tang times, they provide powerful testimony to the thriving development of grain transfer operations during those dynasties. (Photo by Wang Lili)

上图　山东枣庄微山湖段运河航道。（图 / 张振华）

The upper　The course of the Great Canal in Weishan Lake, Zaozhuang City, Shandong. (Photo by Zhang Zhenhua)

下图　山东省汶上县南旺镇分水枢纽遗址。南旺枢纽是为了解决大运河跨越水脊难题而建设的大型综合性水利水运枢纽，是大运河上最具科技价值的节点。（图 / 刘军 / FOTOE）

The lower　The site of the water diversion hub at Nanwang Town, Wenshang County, Shandong Province. The Nanwang Hub,a large size comprehensive hydraulic and water transportation hub, was built to solve the difficult problem of the Grand Canal having to cross a water ridge. It is the most scientifically significant point on the Grand Canal. (Photo by Liu Jun / FOTOE)

上图　江苏扬州何园。又名为“寄啸山庄”。（图 / 高明义 /CFP）

The upper　He Garden in Yangzhou, Jiangsu. Also named “Jixiao Mountain Villa”. (Photo by Gao Mingyi/ CFP)

下图　江苏扬州个园。（图 / 建华 /FOTOE）

The lower　Geyuan Garden in Yangzhou, Jiangsu. (Photo by Jianhua/ FOTOE)

江苏扬州东关古渡。（图 / 张振华）

Dongguan Ancient Ferry,Yangzhou, Jiangsu.(Photo by Zhang Zhenhua)

江苏无锡水弄堂夜景。（图 / 张振华）
Night scene at Shuinong Hall in Wuxi, Jiangsu. (Photo by Zhang Zhenhua)

浙江嘉兴三塔。位于嘉兴西门外大运河畔，始建于唐代。原此处水深流急，行船易翻，遂建三塔以镇之，是京杭大运河嘉兴段的标志。（图 / 张振华）

Three Pagodas in Jiaxing in Zhejiang. First built in the Tang Dynasty, the pagodas are located by the Grand Canal outside the west gate of Jiaxing. The deep and rapidly flowing water here overturned boats frequently, so the three pagodas were built to impose order. They are the symbol of the Jiaxing section of the Jing-Hang Grand Canal.(Photo by Zhang Zhenhua)

舒羽

浙江杭州运河上的拱宸桥。（图 / 张振华）

The Gongchen Bridge on the canal in Hangzhou, Zhejiang. (Photo by Zhang Zhenhua)

流经浙江杭州市区的大运河。（图 / 韩丹）
The Grand Canal in the city of Hangzhou, Zhejiang province. (Photo by Han Dan)

《康熙南巡图》第七卷，清王翚作。描绘康熙南巡无锡至苏州的过程。（图 / 尹楠 /FOTOE）

The 7th volume of *Emperor Kangxi Making a Southern Tour* by Wang Cui of the Qing Dynasty. It describes the passage of Kangxi from Wuxi to Suzhou. (Photo by Yin Nan/FOTOE)

中国世界遗产影像志

WORLD HERITAGE IN CHINA

殷墟

Yin Xu

殷墟四合院建筑复原图。（图 / 郭平）

The Restored courtyard Building of Yin Xu. (Photo by Guo Ping)

Yin Xu

殷　墟

殷墟考古遗址靠近安阳市，位于北京以南约 500 公里处，是商代晚期（公元前 1300 至公元前 1046 年）的古代都城，代表了中国早期文化、工艺和科学的黄金时代，是中国青铜器时代最繁荣的时期。在殷墟遗址出土了大量王室陵墓、宫殿以及中国后期建筑的原型。遗址中的宫殿宗庙区（1000 米 ×650 米）拥有 80 处房屋地基，还有唯一一座保存完好的商代王室成员大墓“妇好墓”。殷墟出土的大量工艺精美的陪葬品证明了商代手工业的先进水平，现在它们是中国的国宝之一。在殷墟发现了大量甲骨窖穴。甲骨上的文字对于证明中国古代信仰、社会体系以及汉字这一世界上最古老的书写体系之一的发展有着不可估量的价值。

——世界遗产委员会评价

The archaeological site of Yin Xu, close to Anyang City, some 500 km south of Beijing, is an ancient capital city of the late Shang Dynasty (1300 B.C. - 1046 B.C.). It testifies to the golden age of early Chinese culture, crafts and sciences, a time of great prosperity of the Chinese Bronze Age. A number of royal tombs and palaces, prototypes of later Chinese architecture, have been unearthed on the site, including the Palace and Royal Ancestral Shrines Area, with more than 80 house foundations, and the only tomb of a member of the royal family of the Shang Dynasty to have remained intact, the Tomb of Fu Hao. The large number and superb craftsmanship of the burial accessories found there bear testimony to the advanced level of Shang crafts industry. Inscriptions on oracle bones found in Yin Xu bear invaluable testimony to the development of one of the world's oldest writing systems, ancient beliefs and social systems.

——World Heritage Committee Evaluation

殷墟宫殿宗庙遗址鸟瞰图。（图 / 郭平）

An aerial view of the remains of palaces and ancestral temples of Yin Xu. (Photo by Guo Ping)

上图　王陵遗址。（图 / 郭平）

The upper　The remains of royal mausoleum. (Photo by Guo Ping)

下图　殷墟祭坛基址。（图 / 郭平）

The lower　Foundation of the Sacrificial Altar of Yin Xu. (Photo by Guo Ping)

上图　殷墟车马坑展厅。（图 / 夏居宪）

The Upper　The Exhibition Hall of chariots and horses pit of Yin Xu. (Photo by Xia Juxian)

下图　宫殿宗庙遗址。（图 / 郭平）

The Lower　The remains of palaces and ancestral temples. (Photo by Guo Ping)

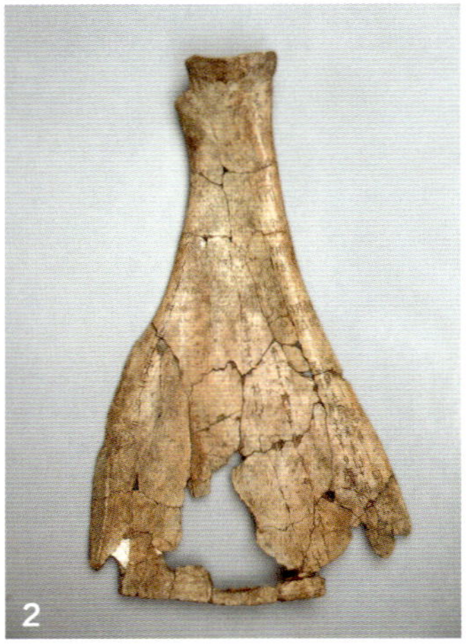

1. 甲骨文（龟甲）。（图 / 郭平）

1.Inscriptions on tortoise shells. (Photo by Guo Ping)

2-4. 甲骨文（牛甲）。（图 / 郭平）

2-4.Inscriptions on ox bones. (Photo by Guo Ping)

1

2

3

4

5

6

7

8

1. 商代青铜甗。（图 / 郭平）/ 2. 商代青铜爵。（图 / 郭平）/ 3. 商代青铜铙。（图 / 郭平）/ 4. 后母戊鼎。（图 / 郭平）
5. 商代妇好墓出土玉人。（图 / 孙之常）/ 6-7. 商代妇好墓出土的玉雕“阴阳人”，左阳右阴。（图 / 孙之常）/ 8. 商代玉龙。（图 / 郭平）

1. Bronze Zeng of the Shang Dynasty. (Photo by Guo Ping) / 2. Bronze Jue of the Shang Dynasty. (Photo by Guo Ping) / 3. Bronze Nao of the Shang Dynasty. (Photo by Guo Ping) / 4.Houmuwu Ding. (Photo by Guo Ping) / 5.Jade figures unearthed from the tomb of Fu hao of the Shang Dynasaty. (Photo by Sun Zhichang) / 6-7 the jade "hermaphrodite" unearthed from Fu hao’s tomb, the left being male while the right female. (Photo by Sun Zhichang) / 8. Jade Dragon of the Shang Dynasty. (Photo by Guo Ping)

中国
世界遗产
影像志

WORLD HERITAGE IN CHINA

元上都遗址

Site of Xanadu

鸟瞰元上都遗址。（图 / 和平）

An aerial view of the Site of Xanadu. (Photo by He Ping)

Site of Xanadu
元上都遗址

在长城以北的元上都遗址公园是由蒙古的中国宰相刘秉忠于 1256 年设计的，遗址包括了忽必烈传奇都城的遗迹。在面积超过 25000 公顷的范围内，该遗址展示了一次对蒙古游牧名族与汉文化进行融合的独一无二的尝试。忽必烈就是在这个基础上建立了统治中国超过一个世纪的元朝，并在此基础上于整个亚洲范围内拓宽其疆域。在此发生的宗教争论导致了藏传佛教在东北亚的传播，以至于今天这种宗教文化的传统依然被许多地方所沿袭。该遗址的设计基于中国背山面水的风水传统。该遗址以都城的遗迹为特色，这些遗迹包括了塔、宫殿、古墓、游牧民族的营地和铁幡竿渠及其他水利工程。

——世界遗产委员会评价

North of the Great Wall, the Site of Xanadu encompasses the remains of Kublai Khan's legendary capital city, designed by the Mongol ruler's Chinese advisor Liu Bingzhong in 1256. Over a surface area of 25,000 ha, the site was a unique attempt to assimilate the nomadic Mongolian and Han Chinese cultures. From this base, Kublai Khan established the Yuan Dynasty that ruled China over a century, extending its boundaries across Asia. The religious debate that took place here resulted in the dissemination of Tibetan Buddhism over north-east Asia, a cultural and religious tradition still practised in many areas today. The site was planned according to traditional Chinese Fengshui in relation to the nearby mountains and river. It features the remains of the city, including temples, palaces, tombs, nomadic encampments and the Tiefan'gang Canal, along with other waterworks.

——World Heritage Committee Evaluation

遗址卒域。（图 / 和平）

The domain of the heritage site. (Photo by He Ping)

元上都玉碑。（图 / 和平）

Jade monument in Xanadu. (Photo by He Ping)

元上都遗址。（图 / 王华）
Site of Xanadu. (Photo by Wang Hua)

1

1. 马头琴。（图 / 和平）

Matouqin (horse head string instrument). (Photo by He Ping)

2. 鎏金喇嘛。（图 / 和平）

Gilded Lama. (Photo by He Ping)

3. 鎏金罗汉。（图 / 和平）

Gilded Arhat. (Photo by He Ping)

4. 大威德金刚。（图 / 和平）

Yamantaka. (Photo by He Ping)

5. 转经筒（2 件）。（图 / 和平）

Prayer wheels. (Photo by He Ping)

6. 酥油灯。（图 / 和平）

Ghee lamp. (Photo by He Ping)

7. 鎏金贲巴壶。（图 / 和平）

Gilded Ben Pakistan pot/. (Photo by He Ping)

8. 马棒。（图 / 和平）

Horse bar. (Photo by He Ping)

9. 龙纹马汗刷。（图 / 和平）

Horse sweat brush with dragon veins. (Photo by He Ping)

10. 错银铁马蹬。（图 / 和平）

Iron stirrup inlaid with silver. (Photo by He Ping)

11. 布靴。（图 / 和平）

Cloth boots. (Photo by He Ping)

12. 货币。（图 / 和平）

Currency. (Photo by He Ping)

13. 信筒。（图 / 和平）

Mailbox. (Photo by He Ping)

2

3

4

5

6

7

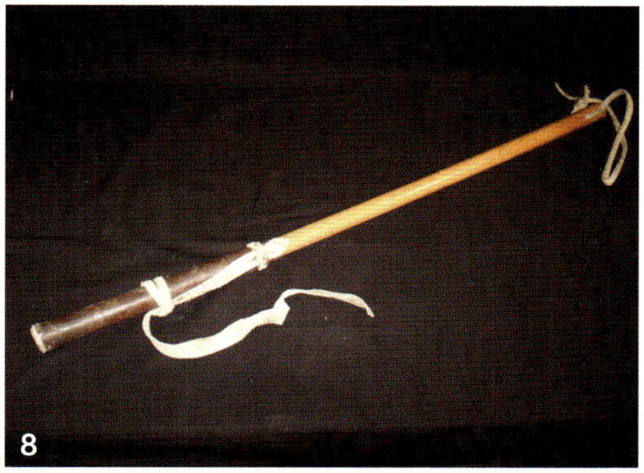
8

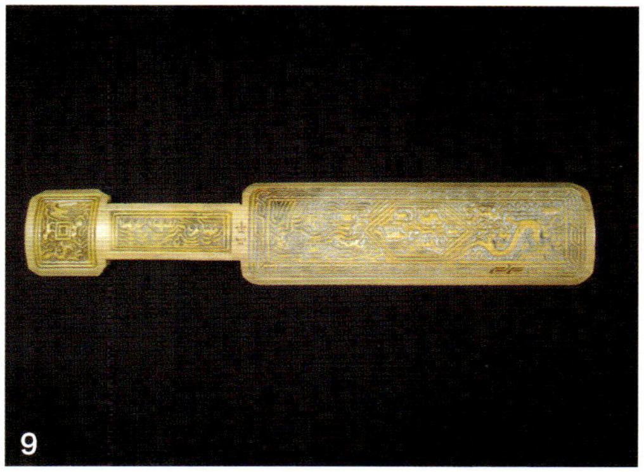
9

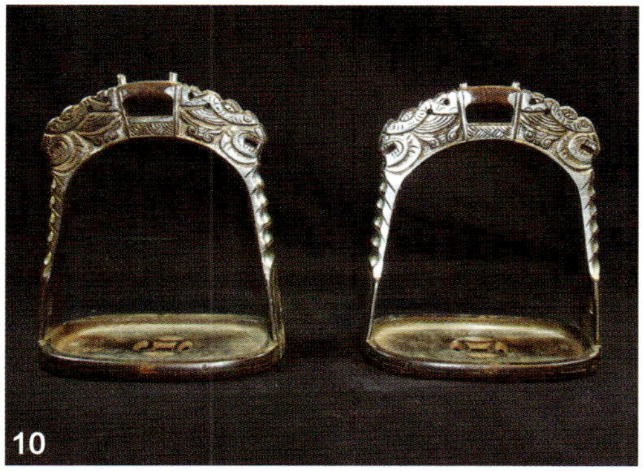
10

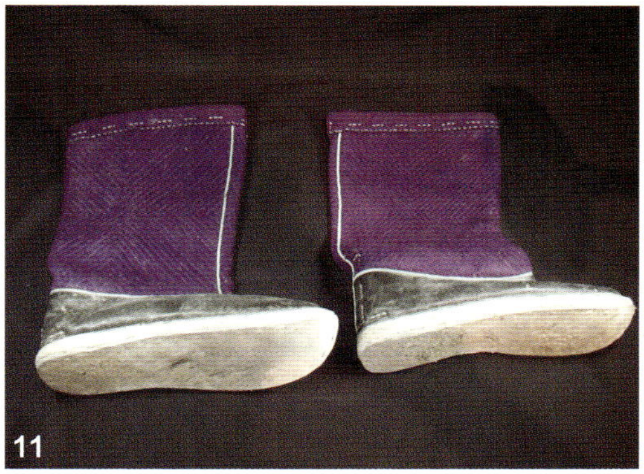
11

12

13

察哈尔套马比赛。（图 / 和平）

Participants take part in a lassoing competition in Chahar. (Photo by He Ping)

将军坟夜景。（图 / 鲜京尚 / 吉林省吉安市文物局提供）
Night scene at the general’s tomb. (Photo by Xian Jingshang/ provided by Ji’an Municipal Bureau of Cultural Relics, Jilin Province)

中国世界遗产影像志

WORLD HERITAGE IN CHINA

Capital Cities and Tombs of the Ancient Koguryo Kingdom

高句丽王城、王陵及贵族墓葬㊟

㊟ 高句丽是中国古代边疆的少数民族政权。

Note:Koguryo was an ethnic regime on the ancient Chinese frontier.

Capital Cities and Tombs of the Ancient Koguryo Kingdom

高句丽王城、王陵及贵族墓葬

该遗址包括五女山城、国内城和丸都山城3座城市遗址和40座墓葬：14座王陵以及26座贵族墓葬。它们都隶属于高句丽文化。从公元前37年至公元668年，高句丽王朝一直统治着中国北方的部分地区和朝鲜半岛北部地区。五女山城仅进行了部分考古挖掘工作。自从高句丽王朝迁都平壤后，位于现集安市境内的国内城，成为重要的陪都。丸都山城也曾是高句丽王朝的都城，现仍有许多历史遗存，包括一座大型宫殿遗址和37座墓葬。部分墓葬饰有精美的无梁穹顶，用以支撑其上方石砌或土夯的墓冢。

——世界遗产委员会评价

The site includes archaeological remains of three cities and 40 tombs: Wunu Mountain City, Guonei City and Wandu Mountain City, 14 tombs are imperial, 26 of nobles. All belong to the Koguryo culture, named after the Dynasty that ruled over parts of northern China and the northern half of the Korean Peninsula from 277 B.C. to A.D. 668. Wunu Mountain City is only partly excavated. Guonei City, within the modern city of Ji'an, played the role of a ‘supporting capital’ after the main Koguryo capital moved to Pyongyang. Wandu Mountain City, one of the capitals of the Koguryo Kingdom, contains many vestiges including a large palace and 37 tombs. Some of the tombs show great ingenuity in their elaborate ceilings, designed to roof wide spaces without columns and carry the heavy load of a stone or earth tumulus (mound), which was placed above them.

——World Heritage Committee Evaluation

鸟瞰辽宁省本溪五女山高句丽遗址。（图/线云强）
An aerial view of Koguryo site at Mt. Wunu, Benxi, Liaoning Province. (Photo by Xian Yunqiang)

上图　好太王陵。（图 / 周梅生）

The upper　The tomb of the Haotaiwang. (Photo by Zhou Meisheng)

下左　好太王碑。（图 / 周梅生）

Lower left　The Haotaiwang Monument. (Photo by Zhou Meisheng)

下右　好太王碑历史照片。（图 / 吉林省集安市文物局提供）

Lower right　An old photograph of Haotaiwang monument. (Photo provided by Ji'an Municipal Bureau of Cultural Relics, Jilin Province)

上图　丸都山城及洞沟墓葬群。（图 / 周梅生）

The upper　Wandu mountain city and Donggou tombs. (Photo by Zhou Meisheng)

下图　高句丽丸都山城宫殿遗址鸟瞰。（图 / 吉林省集安市文物局提供）

The lower　Bird's-eye view of Wandu palace site of Koguryo. (Photo provided by Ji'an Municipal Bureau of Cultural Relics , Jilin Province)

五盔坟五号壁画描绘的神农氏。（图 / 谷德平 / 吉林省集安市文物局提供）
Shennong in Fresco No.5 of Wu Kui Graveyard. (Photo by Gu Deping/provided by Ji'an Municipal Bureau of Cultural Relics Jilin Province)

中国
世界遗产
影像志
WORLD
HERITAGE IN
CHINA

民间文化遗产
Folk Cultural Heritage

曲阜孔庙、孔林和孔府 222
苏州古典园林 234
杭州西湖文化景观 244
澳门历史城区 256
福建土楼 268
丽江古城 280
平遥古城 292
皖南古村落——西递、宏村 300
开平碉楼与村落 308
青城山—都江堰 318
红河哈尼梯田 326
周口店『北京人』遗址 334
丝绸之路：长安—天山廊道的路网 342

杭州西湖。（图 / 何世尧）
West Lake (Photo by He Shiyao)

民间文化遗产

楼庆西　清华大学建筑学院教授

20 世纪 20 年代，我国考古学家在房山县的周口店发现了早期中国猿人的遗址，他们是距今 70–20 万年之间在这里生活的人类。1927 年，考古学家又在这里的山顶洞发现了距今 5 万年的人类遗址，考古学家称他们为“北京人”。这些猿人与“北京人”都是选择了自然山洞为生活场所，他们吃的是山林中野兽的肉，身上披的是野兽的皮，这时“北京人”已经知道用火。火使他们能够吃到熟食，之后经过漫长的岁月，开始用火烧土制成各种生活用的陶器，而正是山上的树木提供了烧火的燃料。北京西南山前的永定河与潮白河又为“北京人”提供了生活中必须有的水。周口店的遗址不但成了早期人类生活的场景，同时也展示了人类维持生活必须具备的山水环境，中国古代的堪舆学将它们总结成为“背山面水”，于是山水环境成为古代人居环境的风水宝地，成了中国古代长期遵循的模式。

云南南部红河哈尼族、彝族自治州的红河、元阳、绿春、金平县一带，这里有大片山林，不仅为人们提供了建屋原料和生活用燃料，而且还保护了丰富的山林水源。哈尼等民族的人民经过一代又一代的艰苦劳动，在山地上开辟出连绵数十里的水稻梯田，养育着世代百姓，他们又以木材作支架，用泥土筑墙，茅草、稻草作顶，建起了蘑菇式的住房，建筑出自己美丽家园，创造出一种特殊的“梯田文化”。

安徽古徽州一带，由于地少人多，迫使许多乡民离家出外谋生，历经拼搏，炼就了颇具实力的“徽商”。这些徽商不忘故土，纷纷回乡置买田产，兴建住宅与祠堂，为后代留下一座又一座古老的村落。地处黟县的西递村，黄山脚下田地之间一片粉墙黛瓦的房宅坐落在金色油菜花之中。另一座古村——宏村，拥有多处水塘，乡民将池水引经家家户户的宅前，有的还引入宅内的堂前屋下。这两座山水间的古村作为皖南村落的代表成为中国首先被列入世界文化遗产的民间建筑。

一方泥土养育一方百姓，同时也产生出一方的建筑。福建永定地区的客家人为了在乱世中求得家族的安全，采用当地的泥土、木材和河中的卵石筑造起一座座大型土楼，这些方形、圆形的，形如堡垒式的土楼坐落在山水之间，被外人惊奇地称为“天上落下来的飞碟，地下长出来的蘑菇”。

广东开平地区很早就有大批百姓走出国门去境外打工、经商，当他们有了成就之后也同安徽徽商一样，多回归故里建住房，盖碉楼，他们不仅带回了财富，也同时带回了在外面见识到的种种西方世界的建筑样式，于是在开平乡间出现了一批融合了中西建筑文化的碉楼，在广东田野间形成一种特殊的景观。这种有山有水与大自然环境融合的人居环境模式，不仅出现在农村，同时也在城市中得到体现。

云南的丽江就是这样一座处于山水环境中的古城，古城坐落在玉龙山下，三面环山，一条玉河水系贯穿古城。这里没有威严的城墙相围，没有经纬分明的街道，条条溪河流经住宅门前，城中心的四方街商业中心，每当人去街静的夜晚都能够用河中溪水来冲洗街面。人们站立城中，近山坡上的座座庙堂，远方白雪皑皑的雪山，使丽江成为一座兼有水乡之容、山城之貌的山水城市。

浙江杭州得天独厚地拥有一池西湖居于城之西部，湖外群山相绕，世世代代的杭州人历经艰辛，不断地经营着这山山水水，挖湖筑堤，盖房建桥，植树栽花，创造出一处又一处的文化景观，将杭州建设成为人间宜居的世外桃源。

上有天堂，下有苏杭。江苏苏州自古以来是鱼米之乡，经济发达，人文荟萃，吸引了四方商贾，也成了士官归隐良所。他们不但享受着这里城外有山，城里有水的环境之美，而且还将这山水环境引入到宅院之中，在自家院里挖池叠山，植树养花，创造出独具东方异彩的私家宅院，将山水人居环境发挥到极致。

中国之大，既有江南的青山绿水，又有西北的黄土高原，还有新疆的戈壁和西藏的雪原。东西南北自然环境相异，并非所有地域皆有山水相绕的风水环境。

山西平遥地处山西中部，这是完全按照中国传统礼制规划建造的一座古城，方形的城市平面四周有高崇的城墙与城楼，城内有严整的街道布局。这里是晋商发源地之一，最早的票号在这里诞生，一时商贾云集，讲究的商铺、宅第罗列街巷，市楼居中，衙署、庙堂布置有序。平遥成为体现汉民族地区封建礼制的典型城市。

澳门地处珠江三角洲西岸，是一座海中半岛式城市。16 世纪中叶，明朝廷划出半岛西南区供葡萄牙的商人居住与经商，由此而发展成为 19 世纪前中国对外的主要港口。由于中外人士的共处，使中西文化得以融合。在宗教信仰上，佛、道、伊斯兰、天主、基督诸教并行，这里既有传统的妈祖庙与佛寺，也有外来的基督与天主教堂，连同市内的总署大楼、会馆、图书馆都呈现出中西不同的建筑式样与风格，从而使澳门形成中西文化融合的适宜于中外人士共同生活的人居环境。

由于中国幅员辽阔，民族众多，各地方、多民族的百姓都会根据本地区的自然和人文条件去创建适宜的人居环境。现在已经成为世界文化遗产的乡村、城市只是其中很小的一部分。

在东西南北广阔的土地上，还保存着许许多多具有不同特征的古代城镇与乡村。在华北地区的黄土高原地带，连片的土山、土壁，常年的干旱少雨，粮食产量低，地上植被少，但是在长期的封建社会时期，普通百姓无法去选择自己的生活环境，他们只能用双手在土壁上挖窑洞，建住房，在山坡上经营自己的家园，筑选出一座座山寨。江苏吴江、昆山和浙江嘉兴、湖州一带河网密布，当地百姓就在这片片水域上，建造出一座座水乡。新疆吐鲁番地区几乎常年不降雨雪，夏季气温高达 40 余摄氏度，但是当地的各民族百姓用他们的智慧将遥远雪山上的溶水用坎儿井与水渠引到家宅门前，使干枯的土地得到滋润，家家户户门前都长着高高的杨树，院子里种的葡萄爬满屋顶，使吐鲁番的农村成为一片绿色海洋。

所有这些具有不同形态的乡村、城镇都是各族百姓在长期的劳动中创造出来的人居环境，它们记录着一个时代的政治、经济与文化，它们是中华民族数千年悠久文明的重要组成部分，都具有历史、艺术和科学的价值。这些乡村、城镇不仅是历代百姓生活的物质环境，而且也展示出在创造这类生活环境中所积累的经验与智慧，例如环境的选择与保护、城镇乡村的总体规划与布局、房屋的建造与保养等等，所有这些不仅仅是历史记忆，而且对于现代人居环境的营造也会有启示与借鉴意义。这应该就是将这些古代遗产作为世界性文化遗产加以长期保护的意义。

Folk Cultural Heritage

Lou Qingxi, professor of School of Architecture, Tsinghua University

In the 1920s Chinese archaeologists discovered a site of early Chinese Ape-man in Zhoukoudian, Fangshan District, who lived there between 700,000 and 200,000 years ago. In 1927, another site was discovered in Upper Cave in the same region. This latter group of Ape-man lived there 50,000 years ago and was named Peking Man by archaeologists. Both groups chose natural caves as their dwelling places, fed themselves with the meat of animals hunted from mountain forests and covered their bodies with animal skin. Peking Man already knew the use of fire. They cooked food with fire and many years later began to fire potteries for use. Mountain forests provided fuel while the Yongding and Chaobai Rivers running in front of the mountains to the southwest of Beijing provided water essential to their life. The two sites in Zhoukoudian not only represent the scene of early human life, but also indicate the necessity of a mountain-and-water environment for human life. In ancient geomancy this environment is summarized as "facing water with mountains behind" and a place fulfilling this description is deemed an ideal spot for habitation by ancient human beings. The mountain-and-water environment has become an established pattern to be followed by later generations in ancient China.

In Hani-Yi Autonomous Prefecture of Honghe, in the south of Yunnan Province, large areas of mountain forests have grown in counties like Honghe, Yuanyang, Lvchun and Jinping. The forests there not only provided people building materials and fuels for life but also conserved water rich in mountain forests. Generation after generation of Hani people and other ethnic groups cleared terraced fields to grow rice in mountains through hard toil. The fields usually stretched over ten kilometers long and fostered the hard-working people there. Local inhabitants constructed timber-framed, earthen-walled, thatch-or-straw-roofed houses shaped like mushrooms to live in. The beautiful farmland and houses here gave birth to the unique "terrace culture".

In ancient Huizhou of Anhui Province the conflict between a large population and a small area of land drove many people away to make their living elsewhere. Their struggles usually paid off and they became established businessmen known as "Hui Merchants". However, despite their success they remained attached to their home districts and often purchased plots of land there to build residences and ancestral memorials. Their efforts resulted in quite a number of ancient villages. A good case in point is Xidi Village in Yi County at the foot of Mount Huangshan. Here stand groups of whitewashed, black-tiled houses in the midst of yellow rape flowers. Another sample is Hongcun Village which abounds in ponds. Here villagers canalized water to the front of their houses or even inside. These two time-honored villages in the environment of mountain and water first entered the folk architecture section of world heritage as samples of villages in the south of Anhui Province.

There is a Chinese saying that the earth in a particular region fosters its inhabitants. Yet it also produces the architecture of that area. In order to guarantee the safety of their clans Hakka people of Yongding County, Fujian Province, constructed many Tulou buildings made up of local mud, timber and pebbles in streams. Those square or circular buildings shaped like blockhouses perch between mountains and rivers and are described by amazed visitors as "UFOs fallen from heaven, mushrooms springing from the earth."

In Kaiping Prefecture of Guangdong Province large numbers of people went abroad to work or do business a long time ago. Like Hui Merchants they would also return home and construct residences and blockhouses in their home town after they had established themselves in their career. They not only brought back riches, but also the architectural patterns of the West that they got to know during their stay there. As a result a group of blockhouses merging the architectural cultures of China and the West appeared in the countryside of Kaiping and has become a special sight in Guangdong.This settlement pattern of merging nature in a place with mountain and water not only emerged in the countryside, but was also practiced in urban areas.

Lijiang City of Yunnan Province is just such a time-honored city in mountain-and-water environment. This city sits at the foot of Mt. Yulong and is surrounded by mountains on three sides, with the Yu River (meaning Jade River) running through it. Unlike other cities, Lijiang has no imposing city walls and the streets here are not patterned as a checkerboard. Instead, streams run in front of each house in this city. In the center of the city there is the commercial center of Sifangjie Street. Every night when the streets are empty of people stream water will be drawn to flush the streets. Standing inside Lijiang, visitors can have a good view of the temples on slopes nearby and the snow-covered mountains afar, and the latter adorns Lijiang with features of both a mountain city and a city on water. In this sense Lijiang is really a city of mountain and water.

Hangzhou of Zhejiang Province is unique as a human settlement in possessing the West Lake embraced by mountains in the west. The inhabitants of Hangzhou spared no efforts in making good use of the mountains and the lakes. They dug the lake deeper and constructed dams around it; they built houses and bridges around or above it; they planted trees and flowers in the lake area. Hence they created one cultural view after another and turned Hangzhou into a land of idyllic beauty highly appealing to settlers.

As the Chinese saying goes, there is paradise in heaven and Suzhou and Hangzhou on earth. Suzhou of Jiangsu Province has been a fertile land of fish and rice since a very long time ago. The advanced economy and talents of this city not only drew merchants and businessmen here as permanent dwellers, but also drew scholars and officials to settle down here after their retirement. They not only enjoyed the beauty of this city which has mountains outside and water inside, but also created this mountain-and-water environment in their courtyards-they dug pools, piled up rocks and planted trees and flowers and successfully endowed their private houses with distinctive oriental charm. The mountain-and-water inhabitation environment finds its best incarnation here in this southern city.

Yet mountain and water inhabitation environment is not available everywhere in China. The vast land of China comprises not only the green mountains and clean waters of the South, but also the Loess Plateau in the northwest, as well as the Gobi deserts in Xinjiang and a land of snow in Tibet. Natural environments differ from place to place and so the mountain-and-water environment is not ubiquitous in China.

Ping Yao in the middle of Shanxi Province is an ancient city constructed in total accordance with traditional Chinese protocol. This is a square city surrounded by tall city walls and towers with a layout of well-planned streets. Ping Yao is the cradle of Shanxi commerce, and here the first draft bank was established. Historically, many businessmen gathered in this city and had their exquisite stores set up and mansions erected along the streets. In the center is the municipal hall surrounded by the administrative building of the government and temples set in good order. So Ping Yao has become a typical city representing feudal rites in areas occupied by the Han nationality.

Macao on the west shore of the Pearl River Delta is a peninsular city surrounded by sea. In the middle of the 16th century the government of the Ming Dynasty designated a special zone in the southwest section of the peninsula for Portuguese merchants to live and do business in. Macao became a major port for international business prior to the 19th century. The co-existence of Chinese and foreigners here led to the merging of Chinese and Western culture. In terms of religion, Buddhism, Taoism, Islam, Catholicism and Christianity all had their followers in this city. You may see traditional Mazu temples and Buddhist temples stand alongside Eastern and Catholic churches. The merging of culture is also evident in the architecture of this city-the municipal government building, guild halls and libraries all reveal the mixing of Sino-Western architectural patterns and styles. As a result Macao's living environment highlights the merging of Chinese and Western cultures and so is quite suited to both Chinese and foreigners.

In the vast territory of China, people of different nationalities and places created settlements based on natural environment and human conditions. Those villages and cities on the list of world cultural heritage only constitute a small portion, whereas a good number of ancient cities and villages with distinctive features are still well preserved but less well known. In the Loess Plateau region of north China, there are stretches of mounds and earth-cliffs. The dry weather all year round results in low grain yield and little vegetation. But in the long feudal period in Chinese history, the commoners had no choice but to adapt to their living environment. They could only dig caves on earth-cliffs and build cave-houses and toil with their hands in their hilly farmland. Fortified mountain villages came into being one by one in this region through their labor. In Wujiang and Kunshan of Jiangsu Province and Jiaxing and Huzhou of Zhejiang Province there are many rivers connected with each other. Local inhabitants founded their settlements in this region abounding with rivers. In the Turfan area of Xinjiang, there is scarcely any rainfall or snowfall the whole year around, and the temperature reaches over 40 degrees centigrade in summer. Yet the local people of various nationalities have the wisdom to use karez channels to conduct snow water from mountains to their houses to water the dry land. You may see tall poplar trees in front of their houses and grape vines springing from a courtyard and covering the whole housetop. Consequently the villages in Turfan have been turned into an ocean of green.

All those villages and cities differ from each other and yet they are all human settlements created in the process of long labor. They recorded the politics, economy and culture of a particular era and are important components in the long civilization of the Chinese people and have their historical, economical and cultural values. Those villages and cities provide not only the material living environment for people in different periods, but also reveal their accumulated experience and wisdom in creating these human settlements, such as the selection and protection of environment; the overall planning and designing of towns and villages; the construction and maintenance of houses, etc. Such experiences and wisdom are not only historical memories, but may also spark viewers' inspiration and serve as reference to them. This may explain why we make consistent efforts to protect these human settlements as world cultural heritage.

中国世界遗产影像志

WORLD HERITAGE IN CHINA

Temple and Cemetery of Confucius and the Kong Family Mansion in Qufu

曲阜孔庙、孔林和孔府

鸟瞰孔府。（图 / 侯贺良）

An aerial picture of the Kong Family Mansion. (Photo by Hou Heliang)

Temple and Cemetery of Confucius and the Kong Family Mansion in Qufu

曲阜孔庙、孔林和孔府

孔子是公元前 6 至 5 世纪最伟大的哲学家、政治家和教育家。孔子的庙宇、墓地和府邸位于山东省的曲阜。孔庙是公元前 478 年为纪念孔子而兴建的，千百年来屡毁屡建，到今天已经发展成超过 100 座殿堂的建筑群。孔林里不仅容纳了孔子的坟墓，而且他的后裔中，有超过 10 万人也葬在这里。当初小小的孔宅如今已经扩建成一个庞大显赫的府邸，整个宅院包括了 152 座殿堂。曲阜的古建筑群之所以具有独特的艺术和历史特色，应归功于 2000 多年来中国历代帝王对孔子的大力推崇。

——世界遗产委员会评价

The temple, cemetery and family mansion of Confucius, the great philosopher, politician and educator of the 6th - 5th centuries B.C., are located at Qufu, in Shandong Province. Built to commemorate him in 478 B.C., the temple has been destroyed and reconstructed over the centuries; today it comprises more than 100 buildings. The cemetery contains Confucius' tomb and the remains of more than 100,000 of his descendants. The small house of the Kong family developed into a gigantic aristocratic residence, of which 152 buildings remain. The Qufu complex of monuments has retained its outstanding artistic and historic character due to the devotion of successive Chinese emperors over more than 2,000 years.

——World Heritage Committee Evaluation

鸟瞰孔庙。（图 / 侯贺良）

An aerial picture of the Temple of Confucius. (Photo by Hou Heliang)

孔林明朝墓群。（图 / 侯贺良）

Tombs of the Ming Dynasty in Cemetery of Confucius. (Photo by Hou Heliang)

孔子墓。位于孔林中偏南地段。封土东西30米，南北28米，高5米。（图/孙隆椿）

Tomb of Confucius. It is located in the southern section of the cemetery. The mound is 30 meters long from east to west,28 meters long from north to south and 5 meters tall. (Photo by Sun Longchun)

左上　孔庙大成殿。大成殿为孔庙的正殿。（图 / 茹遂初）

Upper left　Dacheng Hall.It is the main hall of Temple of Confucius. (Photo by Ru Suichu)

右上　相传孔子当年讲学的杏坛。（图 / 茹遂初）

Upper right　Xing Tan Pavilion, which is said to be the venue where the Confucius lectured. (Photo by Ru Suichu)

左下　孔庙太和元气坊。（图 / 茹遂初）

Lower left　Taihe Yuanqi Gateway in Temple of Confucius. (Photo by Ru Suichu)

右下　孔庙至圣庙坊。（图 / 茹遂初）

Lower right　Gateway to the Temple of Saint. (Photo by Ru Suichu)

孔府大门。（图 / 茹遂初）

The Gate of the Kong Family Mansion. (Photo by Ru Suichu)

左上　孔府仪门。（图 / 茹遂初）

Upper left　Etiquette Door of the Kong Family Mansion. (Photo by Ru Suichu)

右上　孔府花园。（图 / 茹遂初）

Upper right　Garden in the Kong Family Mansion. (Photo by Ru Suichu)

左下　孔府前堂楼内景。（图 / 谭明）

Lower left　The inner view of the front Hall Building in the Kong Family Mansion. (Photo by Tan Ming)

右下　衍圣公会客吟诗的花厅。（图 / 茹遂初）

Lower right　Drawing Room where Yansheng Duke receives guests and composes poetry. (Photo by Ru Suichu)

明代衍圣公服刺绣装饰。（图 / 庞守义）

Embroidery ornaments on constume of Yansheng Duke in the Ming Dynasty. (Photo by Pang Shouyi)

中国世界遗产影像志

WORLD HERITAGE IN CHINA

苏州古典园林

Classical Gardens of Suzhou

退思园。（图 / 孙伟忠）

The Retreat and Reflection Garden. (Photo by Sun Weizhong)

Classical Gardens of Suzhou
苏州古典园林

没有任何地方比历史名城苏州的九大园林更能体现中国古典园林设计“咫尺之内再造乾坤”的理想。苏州园林被公认是实现这一设计思想的杰作。这些建造于 11 至 19 世纪的园林，以其精雕细琢的设计，折射出中国文化取法自然而又超越自然的深邃意境。

——世界遗产委员会评价

Classical Chinese garden design, which seeks to recreate natural landscapes in miniature, is nowhere better illustrated than in the nine gardens in the historic city of Suzhou. They are generally acknowledged to be masterpieces of the genre. Dating from the 11th-19th century, the gardens reflect the profound metaphysical importance of natural beauty in Chinese culture in their meticulous design.

——World Heritage Committee Evaluation

留园花窗。（图 / 吕大千）

The lattice window of the Lingering Garden. (Photo by Lv Daqian)

网师园。（图 / 陈健行）
The Net Mastu's Garden. (Photo by Chen Jianxing)

拙政园。（图 / 陈健行）

The Humble Administration’s Garden. (Photo by Chen Jianxing)

拙政园远香堂。（图 / 谭明）

Yuanxiang Hall of Humble Adminstrator's Garden. (Photo by Tan Ming)

1. 退思园漏窗。（图 / 谭明）/ 2. 狮子林漏窗。（图 / 谭明）/ 3. 沧浪亭漏窗。（图 / 谭明）/ 4. 留园太湖石。（图 / 谭明）
5. 留园奎宿峰。（图 / 谭明）/ 6. 留园冠云峰。（图 / 谭明）/ 7 – 9. 留园拼花石径局部。（图 / 谭明）

1.Latticed window in the Retreat and Reflection Garden. (Photo by Tan Ming) /2.Latticed window in the Lion Forest Garden. (Photo by Tan Ming) /3.Openwork window in the Canglang Pavilion. (Photo by Tan Ming) /4.Rock of Tai Lake in the lingering Garden. (Photo by Tan Ming) /5.Quisu Peak in the lingering Garden. (Photo by Tan Ming) /6.Guanyun Peak in the lingering Garden. (Photo by Tan Ming) /7-9. Jigsaw on the Mosaic path in the lingering Garden. (Photo by Tan Ming)

留园。（图 / 陈健行）

The lingering Garden. (Photo by Chen Jianxing)

中国 世界遗产 影像志

WORLD HERITAGE IN CHINA

杭州西湖文化景观

West Lake Cultural Landscape of Hangzhou

西湖。（图 / 卞志武）

West Lake. (Photo by Bian Zhiwu)

West Lake Cultural Landscape of Hangzhou
杭州西湖文化景观

自公元 9 世纪以来，西湖的湖光山色引得无数文人骚客、艺术大师吟咏兴叹、泼墨挥毫。景区内遍布庙宇、亭台、宝塔、园林，其间点缀着奇花异木、岸堤岛屿，为江南的杭州城增添了无限美景。数百年来，西湖景区对中国其他地区乃至日本和韩国的园林设计都产生了影响。在景观营造的文化传统中，西湖是对天人合一这一理想境界的最佳阐释。

——世界遗产委员会评价

The West Lake Cultural Landscape of Hangzhou, comprising the West Lake and the hills surrounding its three sides, has inspired famous poets, scholars and artists since the 9th century. It comprises numerous temples, pagodas, pavilions, gardens and ornamental trees, as well as causeways and artificial islands.These additions have been made to improve the landscape west of the city of Hangzhou to the south of the Yangtze river.The West Lake has influenced garden design in the rest of China as well as Japan and Korea over the centuries and bears an exceptional testimony to the cultural tradition of improving landscapes to create a series of vistas reflecting an idealised fusion between humans and nature.

——World Heritage Committee Evaluation

“三面云山一面城”。（图 / 韩丹）
Having mountains on three sides and city on one side. (Photo by Han Dan)

鸟瞰雷峰塔。（图 / 韩丹）

An aerial view of Leifeng Pagoda. (Photo by Han Dan)

小瀛洲。（图 / 何世尧）

Small Yingzhou. (Photo by He Shiyao)

灵隐寺飞来峰弥勒佛。（图 / 卞志武）

Sculpture of Maitreya Buddha at Feilai Feng, Lingyin Temple. (Photo by Bian Zhiwu)

西湖飞羽。（图 / 顾勇）

Flying feathers at West Lake. (Photo by Gu Yong)

中国世界遗产影像志

WORLD HERITAGE IN CHINA

Historic Centre of Macao

澳门历史城区

澳门历史城区鸟瞰图。（图 / 陈显耀）

An aerial view of the Historic Centre of Macao. (Photo by Chen Xianyao)

Historic Centre of Macao

澳门历史城区

澳门是一个繁华兴盛的港口，在国际贸易发展中有着重要的战略地位。从 16 世纪中叶开始，澳门处于葡萄牙统治之下，直到 1999 年中国对澳门恢复行使主权。澳门历史城区保留着葡萄牙和中国风格的古老街道、住宅、宗教和公共建筑，见证了东西方美学、文化、建筑和技术影响力的交融。城区还保留了一座堡垒和一座中国最古老的灯塔。此城区是在国际贸易蓬勃发展的基础上，中西方交流最早且持续沟通的见证。

——世界遗产委员会评价

Macao, a lucrative port of strategic importance in the development of international trade, was under Portuguese administration from the mid-16th century until 1999, when it came back under Chinese sovereignty. With its historic street, residential, religious and public Portuguese and Chinese buildings, the historic centre of Macao provides a unique testimony to the meeting of aesthetic, cultural, architectural and technological influences from East and West. The site also contains a fortress and a lighthouse, the oldest in China. It bears witness to one of the earliest and longest-lasting encounters between China and the West, based on the vibrancy of international trade.

——World Heritage Committee Evaluation

大三巴牌坊。（图 / 黄明辉）
The Ruins of the Cathedral of Saint Paul. (Photo by Wong Meng Fai)

正覺禪林

左图　妈阁庙。（图 / 黄明辉）

The left　A-Ma Temple. (Photo by Wong Meng Fai)

右上　旧城墙。（图 / 陈显耀）

Upper right　The old city wall. (Photo by Chen Xianyao)

右下　大炮台。（图 / 黄明辉）

Lower right　The Mount Fortress. (Photo by Wong Meng Fai)

左图　玫瑰堂。（图 / 陈显耀）

The left　St. Dominic's Church. (Photo by Chen Xianyao)

右上　仁慈堂。（图 / 陈显耀）

Upper right　Holy House of Mercy. (Photo by Chen Xianyao)

右下　圣母雪地殿。（图 / 陈显耀）

Lower right　Chapel of Our Lady Guia. (Photo by Chen Xianyao)

上图　主教坐堂。（图 / 陈显耀）　**The upper**　Cathedral of Bishop. (Photo by Chen Xianyao)
下图　圣老楞佐堂。（图 / 陈显耀）　**The lower**　St. Lawrence's Church. (Photo by Chen Xianyao)

上图　圣安多尼堂。（图 / 陈显耀）　**The upper**　Church of St. Anthony. (Photo by Chen Xianyao)
下图　圣若瑟修院及圣堂。（图 / 黄明辉）　**The lower**　St. Joseph's Seminary and Church. (Photo by Wong Meng Fai)

卢家大屋。（图 / 黄明辉）
The Lou Kau Mansion. (Photo by Wong Meng Fai)

中国世界遗产影像志

福建土楼

WORLD HERITAGE IN CHINA

Fujian Tulou

南靖县书洋镇下坂村裕昌楼水中倒影。（图 / 胡家新）

The water reflection of Yuchang Lou, Xiaban village, Shuyang town in Nanjing County. (Photo by Hu Jiaxin)

福建土楼位于福建省西南部内陆地区，距台湾海峡 120 多公里，由 46 座分布在稻田、烟草田和茶园中，建造于 12 世纪至 20 世纪的生土结构的房屋组成。土楼高数层，平面呈圆形或方形，大型的可容纳 800 人居住。建造土楼是防御的需要，土楼的功能类似于村落，一个家族的人都居住在一起，被称为“一个小的家族王国”或“熙熙攘攘的小城市”。它的特征是高大坚固的土墙，顶上铺有宽大的青瓦屋顶和出挑的屋檐，其最精细复杂的构造可追溯到 17-18 世纪。土楼被垂直分给各个家庭，在每层楼都有 2 间或 3 间房子，而与其简单的外表相比，土楼的内部相当舒适，且常常装饰华丽。

——世界遗产委员会评价

Fujian Tulou is a property of 46 houses built between the 12th and 20th centuries over 120 kilometers in south-west of Fujian province,inland from the Taiwan strait .Set amongst rice,tea and tobacco fields the Tulou are earthen houses.Several storeys high,they are built along an inward-looking,circular or square floor plan as housing for up to 800 people each. The were built for defence purposes around a central open courtyard with few windows to the outside and only one entrance. Housing a whole clan,the houses functioned as village units and were known as "a little kingdom for the family" or "bustling small city." They feature tall fortified mud walls capped by tiled roofs with wide over-hanging eaves.The most elaborate structures date back to the 17th and 18th centuries.The buildings were divided vertically between families with each disposing of twoor three rooms on each floor. In contrast with their plain exterior, the inside of the Tulou were built for comfort and were often highly decorated.

——World Heritage Committee Evaluation

永定客家土楼内舞龙舞狮表演。（匿 / 胡家新）

Dragon and lion dances at Yongding Hakka Tulou. (Photo by Hu Jiaxin)

（组图：福建土楼著名的六大土楼群）

(Photos: The six famous Tulou clusters of Fujian)

上图　洪坑土楼群。（图 / 胡家新）

The upper　Hongkeng Tulou cluster. (Photo by Hu Jiaxin)

中图　高北土楼群。（图 / 胡家新）

The centre　Gaobei Tulou cluster. (Photo by Hu Jiaxin)

下图　大地土楼群。（图 / 胡家新）

The lower　Dadi Tulou cluster. (Photo by Hu Jiaxin)

上图　初溪土楼群。（图 / 胡家新）

The upper　Chuxi Tulou cluster. (Photo by Hu Jiaxin)

中图　河坑土楼群。（图 / 胡家新）

The centre　Hekeng Tulou cluster. (Photo by Hu Jiaxin)

下图　田螺坑土楼群。（图 / 胡家新）

The lower　Tianluokeng Tulou cluster. (Photo by Hu Jiaxin)

（组图：福建土楼著名的“四楼”）
(Photos: The famous "Four Tulous" in Fujian)
衍香楼。坐落在永定县湖坑镇新南村，建于 1880 年，是最具书香气息的圆土楼。（图 / 胡家新）
Yanxiang Lou. Built in 1880 in Xinnan village, Yongding County. A round tulou with the strongest scholarly atmosphere. (Photo by Hu Jiaxin)

上图　和贵楼。坐落在南靖县梅林镇璞山村，建于 1732 年，是建在沼泽地上的方土楼，被誉为“天下第一奇楼”。（图 / 胡家新）

The upper　Hegui Lou. Built in 1732 in Pushan village, Nanjing County.A square tulou built in swampland known as"the most wonderful tulou under the sky". (Photo by Hu Jiaxin)

中图　振福楼。坐落在永定县湖坑镇西片村，建于 1913 年，是圆土楼融合近代西洋建筑艺术的杰作。（图 / 胡家新）

The centre　Zhenfu Lou. Built in 1913 in Xipian village, Yonding County.An outstanding round tulou combining with modern Western architectural art. (Photo by Hu Jiaxin)

下图　怀远楼。坐落在南靖县梅林镇坎下村，建于 1905 年，是建筑工艺最精美、保护最完好的双环圆土楼之一。（图 / 胡家新）

The lower　Huaiyuan Lou. Built in 1905 in Kanxia village, Nanjing County. One of the most exquisite and best-preserved double circular round tulou. (Photo by Hu Jiaxin)

福履同綏頌熾昌

振興有慶瞻輪奐

（拼图）福建土楼的传世楹联。（图 / 胡家新）

(Photo Collage) Ancient couplets from Fujian Tulou. (Photo by Hu Jiaxin)

永定县土楼遗址。（图 / 温学元）
The ruins of tulou, Yongding County. (Photo by Wenxueyuan)

中国世界遗产影像志

丽江古城

WORLD HERITAGE IN CHINA

Old Town of Lijiang

鸟瞰丽江古城。（图 / 卞志武）

An aerial view of the Old Town of Lijiang. (Photo by Bian Zhiwu)

Old Town of Lijiang
丽江古城

古城丽江，把经济和战略重地与崎岖的地势巧妙地融合在一起，真实、完美地保存和再现了古朴的风貌。古城的建筑历经数个世纪的洗礼，融汇了各个民族的文化特色而声名远扬。丽江还拥有古老的供水系统，这一系统纵横交错、精巧独特，至今仍在有效地发挥着作用。

——世界遗产委员会评价

The Old Town of Lijiang, which is perfectly adapted to the uneven topography of this key commercial and strategic site, has retained a historic townscape of high quality and authenticity. Its architecture is noteworthy for the blending of elements from several cultures that have come together over many centuries. Lijiang also possesses an ancient water-supply system of great complexity and ingenuity that still functions effectively today.

——World Heritage Committee Evaluation

丽江民居的屋顶装饰。（图 / 李建惠）
The rooftop decoration of the folkhouse in Lijiang. (Photo by Li Jianhui)

丽江黑龙潭。（图 / 倪益瑾）

Heilongtan (Black Dragon Pool) in Lijiang. (Photo by Ni Yijin)

上图　丽江古城四方街朝霞。（图 / 陆江涛）

The upper　The sunrise at Sifangjie Square in the Old Town of Lijiang. (Photo by Lu Jiangtao)

下图　丽江纳西族民居。（图 / 卞志武）

The lower　The folkhouse of Naxi people in Lijiang. (Photo by Bian Zhiwu)

上图　明代杨升庵撰《木氏谱序》。（图 / 车文龙）

The upper *The Prologue of Chieftain Mu* written by Yang Sheng'an in the Ming Dynasty. (Photo by Che Wenlong)

下图　丽江民房木雕。（图 / 卞志武）

The lower The wooden carving of Lijiang folkhouses. (Photo by Bian Zhiwu)

组图：绘制祭神用木牌画的老东巴。“东巴”纳西语意为“山乡”诵经者，即东巴教的“经师”，平时从事生产，受请即外出进行祭祀、婚丧、除病攘灾等宗教活动。他们是纳西族古代文化的创造者和传承者。过去纳西人尊东巴为“智者”。（组图 / 卞志武）

Group of Photos: An eldly Dongba painting on wooden pieces for ceremonies. Dongba, in Naxi language means the Chanting person in the mountains, who are the masters of Dongba religion. They live an ordinary life usually, but upon invitation, they will go out to hold religious ceremonies, marriages and funerals, cure illness and disperse disasters. They are the creaters and heirs of the ancient Naxi culture and were respected as Wise Men in the old times. (Photos by Bian Zhiwu)

纳西古乐。（图 / 车文龙）
Naxi ancient music. (Photo by Che Wenlong)

白沙壁画。（图 / 车文龙） Baisha Fresco. (Photo by Che Wenlong)

中国世界遗产影像志

平遥古城

WORLD HERITAGE IN CHINA

Ancient City of Ping Yao

乌瞰平遥古城。（图 / 周梅生）

An aerial view of Ping Yao. (Photo by Zhou Meisheng)

Ancient City of Ping Yao
平遥古城

平遥古城建于 14 世纪，是现今保存完整的汉民族城市的杰出范例。其城镇布局集中反映了五个多世纪以来，中国的建筑风格和城市规划的发展。特别值得一提的是，这里与银行业有关的建筑格外雄伟，因为 19 至 20 世纪初期平遥是整个中国金融业的中心。

——世界遗产委员会评价

Ping Yao is an exceptionally well-preserved example of a traditional Han Chinese city, founded in the 14th century. Its urban fabric shows the evolution of architectural styles and town planning in Imperial China over five centuries. Of special interest are the imposing buildings associated with banking, for which Ping Yao was the major centre for the whole of China in the 19th and early 20th centuries.

——World Heritage Committee Evaluation

平遥古城墙。（图 / 吕大千）
Ancient city wall in Ping Yao. (Photo by lv Daqian)

左上　平遥城隍庙。（图 / 李建惠）

Upper left　Temple of the City God, Ping Yao. (Photo by Li Jianhui)

右上　平遥市楼。（图 / 茹遂初）

Upper right　Market Tower on the South Avenue, Ping Yao. (Photo by Ru Suichu)

左下　平遥百川通票号旧址的后院。（图 / 茹遂初）

Lower left　The backyard of the former site of Baichuantong Exchange Shop, Ping Yao. (Photo by Ru Suichu)

右下　平遥民居的大门，门前的石柱为拴马桩。（图 / 茹遂初）

Lower right　A carved mounting stone in the ancient city of Ping Yao. (Photo by Ru Suichu)

左上　日升昌票号的议事厅。（图 / 茹遂初）

Upper left　Meeting Hall, Rishengchang Exchange Shop. (Photo by Ru Suichu)

右上　日升昌票号收银的柜台。（图 / 茹遂初）

Upper right　Cashiers' Office, Rishengchang Exchange Shop. (Photo by Ru Suichu)

左下　日升昌票号的金库。室内地面的方孔是进出地下金库的孔道。（图 / 茹遂初）

Lower left　Bank Vault, Rishengchang Exchange Shop. The rectangular hole on the floor inside the room is the entrance of the bank vault. (Photo by Ru Suichu)

右下　日升昌票号大掌柜办公的房间。墙上挂的画像为日升昌票号创始人、第一任大掌柜雷履泰。（图 / 茹遂初）

Lower right　Manager's Office, Rishengchang Exchange Shop. The man in the portrait on the wall is Lei Lvtai, the founder and first manager of the shop. (Photo by Ru Suichu)

镇国寺万佛殿五代时期的彩塑——释迦牟尼及弟子像。（图 / 茹遂初）

Color-painted statues of Shakyamuni and his desciples in the Wanfo Hall of Zhenguo Temple, made in the Five Dynasties. (Photo by Ru Suichu)

左上　双林寺菩萨殿主像千手观音。（图 / 茹遂初）

Upper left　The main statue, Thousand-hand Guanyin (Bodhisattva), in the Bodhisattva Shrine of Shuanglin Temple. (Photo by Ru Suichu)

右上　双林寺释迦殿影壁墙后的渡海观音像。（图 / 茹遂初）

Upper right　The Statue of Guanyin above the sea behind the screen wall of Shakya Shrine of Shuanglin Temple. (Photo by Ru Suichu)

左下　双林寺千佛殿自在观音像。（图 / 张国田）

Lower left　The Statue of Avalokitesvara in Qianfo Shrine of Shuanglin Temple. (Photo by Zhang Guotian)

右下　双林寺千佛殿佛传故事彩塑。（图 / 茹遂初）

Lower right　Colore-painted Buddhist stories in Qianfo Shrine of Shuanglin Temple. (Photo by Ru Suichu)

中国世界遗产影像志

WORLD HERITAGE IN CHINA

Ancient Villages in Southern Anhui — Xidi and Hongcun

皖南古村落——西递、宏村

宏村月沼。（图 / 周梅生）

The moon-shaped lake in Hongcun. (Photo by Zhou Meisheng)

Ancient Villages in Southern Anhui — Xidi and Hongcun
皖南古村落——西递、宏村

西递、宏村这两个传统的古村落在很大程度上仍然保持着在上个世纪已经消失或改变了的乡村的面貌。其街道规划、古建筑和装饰，以及供水系统完备的民居都是非常独特的文化遗存。

——世界遗产委员会评价

The two traditional villages of Xidi and Hongcun preserve to a remarkable extent the appearance of non-urban settlements of a type that largely disappeared or was transformed during the last century. Their street plan, their architecture and decoration, and the integration of houses with comprehensive water systems are unique surviving examples.

——World Heritage Committee Evaluation

西递马头墙。（图 / 李少白）
The horse-head gable in Xidi. (Photo by Li Shaobai)

西递全景。（图 / 周梅生）
The Pamorama of Xidi. (Photo by Zhou Meisheng)

西递胡文光刺史牌坊。（图 / 齐凤臣）

Cishi Archway (Memorial Archway of Hu Wenguang) in Xidi. (Photo by Qi Fengchen)

宏村承志堂商字木雕。（图 / 周梅生）
The woodcarving in the Chinese character of "Shang" (business) in Chengzhi Hall in Hongcun. (Photo by Zhou Meisheng)

中国世界遗产影像志

WORLD HERITAGE IN CHINA

Kaiping Diaolou and Villages

开平碉楼与村落

开平锦江里碉楼群。（图 / 何树炯）
Jinjiangli Diaolou cluster in Kaiping. (Photo by Ho Shukwing)

Kaiping Diaolou and Villages

开平碉楼与村落

开平碉楼与村落以广东省开平市用于防卫的多层塔楼式乡村民居——碉楼而著称，展现了中西建筑和装饰形式复杂而灿烂的融合，表现了 19 世纪末及 20 世纪初开平侨民在几个南亚国家、澳洲以及北美国家发展进程中的重要作用，以及海外开平人与其故里的密切联系。

——世界遗产委员会评价

Kaiping Diaolou and Villages feature the Diaolou, multi-storeyed defensive village houses in Kaiping, which display a complex and flamboyant fusion of Chinese and Western structural and decorative forms. They reflect the significant role of émigré Kaiping people in the development of several countries in South Asia, Australia and North America, during the late 19th and early 20th centuries.

——World Heritage Committee Evaluation

开平斜楼，自 1903 年建成后即倾斜，至今 111 年屹立不倒。（图 / 何树炯）
Kaiping tilted Tulou.It stays tilted for 111 years after it was built in 1903. (Photo by Ho Shukwing)

开平碉楼漩溪里拱券。（图 / 何树炯）

The arch of Xuanxili , Kaiping Diaolou. (Photo by Ho Shukwing)

民国廿二年

左图　开平马降龙骏庐壁画，漂洋过海的火船、欧美的洋楼射灯都描绘在住家的门口上。（图 / 何树炯）

The left　Fresco of Junlu,the fire ships coming across the sea and the spotlight of European and American buildings were painted on the door of the residence. (Photo by Ho Shukwing)

右上　开平立园炯庐，朱红的木门上大书“爱国”、“齐家”。充分表露了碉楼主人为国为家的情感。（图 / 何树炯）

Upper right　Liyuan Jionglu, Kaiping. On the red wood door were written "love the country" and "regulate the family",fully expressing the house-owner’s love of the country and the family. (Photo by Ho Shukwing)

右下　开平碉楼中的装饰灰雕画，经历 100 多年风雨，洗尽铅华，但仍渗透出当年华侨希望在家乡建造铁路的梦想。（图 / 何树炯）

Lower right　Plaster molding painting decorated on Kaiping Diaolou. After more than 100 years, the paintings still remind people the dream of the then overseas Chinese to build railway in their hometown. (Photo by Ho Shukwing)

开平赤坎古镇一景。（图 / 何树炯）
A glimpse at the ancient Chikan town in Kaiping. (Photo by Ho Shukwing)

中国世界遗产影像志

WORLD HERITAGE IN CHINA

青城山—都江堰

Mount Qingcheng and the Dujiangyan Irrigation System

都江堰鱼嘴。（图 / 王达军）

The Fish Mouth of Dujiangyan. (Photo by Wang Dajun)

Mount Qingcheng and the Dujiangyan Irrigation System
青城山—都江堰

都江堰灌溉系统始建于公元前 3 世纪，至今仍控制着岷江的水流，灌溉着成都平原肥沃的农田。青城山是中国道教的发源地，因许多古庙著称。

——世界遗产委员会评价

Construction of the Dujiangyan irrigation system began in the 3rd century B.C. This system still controls the waters of the Minjiang River and distributes it to the fertile farmland of the Chengdu plains. Mount Qingcheng was the birthplace of Taoism, which is celebrated in a series of ancient temples.

——World Heritage Committee Evaluation

鸟瞰青城山。（图 / 王达军）
An aerial view of Mt. Qingcheng. (Photo by Wang Dajun)

都江堰宝瓶口。（图 / 王达军）

Baopingkou(Mouth of Precious Bottle) at Dujiangyan. (Photo by Wang Dajun)

都江堰二王庙。（图 / 王达军）
Erwang(Two Kings) Temple at Dujiangyan. (Photo by Wang Dajun)

青城山山门。（图 / 王达军）
The mountain gate of Mt. Qingcheng. (Photo by Wang Dajun)

青城山上清宫。（图 / 王达军）

Shangqing Palace at Mt. Qingcheng. (Photo by Wang Dajun)

中国世界遗产影像志

红河哈尼梯田

WORLD HERITAGE IN CHINA

Cultural Landscape of Honghe Hani Rice Terraces

哈尼人水田中的朝阳。（图 / 李子青）

Hani paddy field under the morning sun. (Photo by Li Ziqing)

Cultural Landscape of Honghe Hani Rice Terraces
红河哈尼梯田

红河哈尼文化景观位于云南南部，面积 16603 公顷，以从高耸的哀牢山沿着斜坡顺延到红河沿岸的壮丽梯田而著称。在过去的 1300 多年间，哈尼族人民发明了复杂的沟渠系统，将山上的水从草木丛生的山顶送至各级梯田。他们还创造出一个完整的农作体系，包含牛、鸭、鱼类和鳝类，并且支持了当地主要的谷物——红米的生产。当地居民崇拜日、月、山、河、森林以及其他自然现象（包括火在内）。他们居住在分布于山顶森林和梯田之间的 82 个村寨里，这些村寨以传统的茅草“蘑菇房”为特色。为梯田建立的弹性管理系统，建立在特殊且古老的社会和宗教结构基础上，体现出人与环境在视觉和生态上的高度和谐。

——世界遗产委员会评价

The Cultural Landscape of Honghe Hani Rice Terraces, China covers 16,603-hectares in Southern Yunnan. It is marked by spectacular terraces that cascade down the slopes of the towering Ailao Mountains to the banks of the Hong River. Over the past 1,300 years, the Hani people have developed a complex system of channels to bring water from the forested mountaintops to the terraces. They have also created an integrated farming system that involves buffalos, cattle, ducks, fish and eel and supports the production of red rice, the area's primary crop. The inhabitants worship the sun, moon, mountains, rivers, forests and other natural phenomena including fire. They live in 82 villages situated between the mountaintop forests and the terraces. The villages feature traditional thatched "mushroom" houses. The resilient land management system of the rice terraces demonstrates extraordinary harmony between people and their environment, both visually and ecologically, based on exceptional and long-standing social and religious structures.

——World Heritage Committee Evaluation

元阳如万马奔腾状的梯田。（图 / 廖家祥）

Yuanyang terraces look like thousands of running horses. (Photo by Liao Jiaxiang)

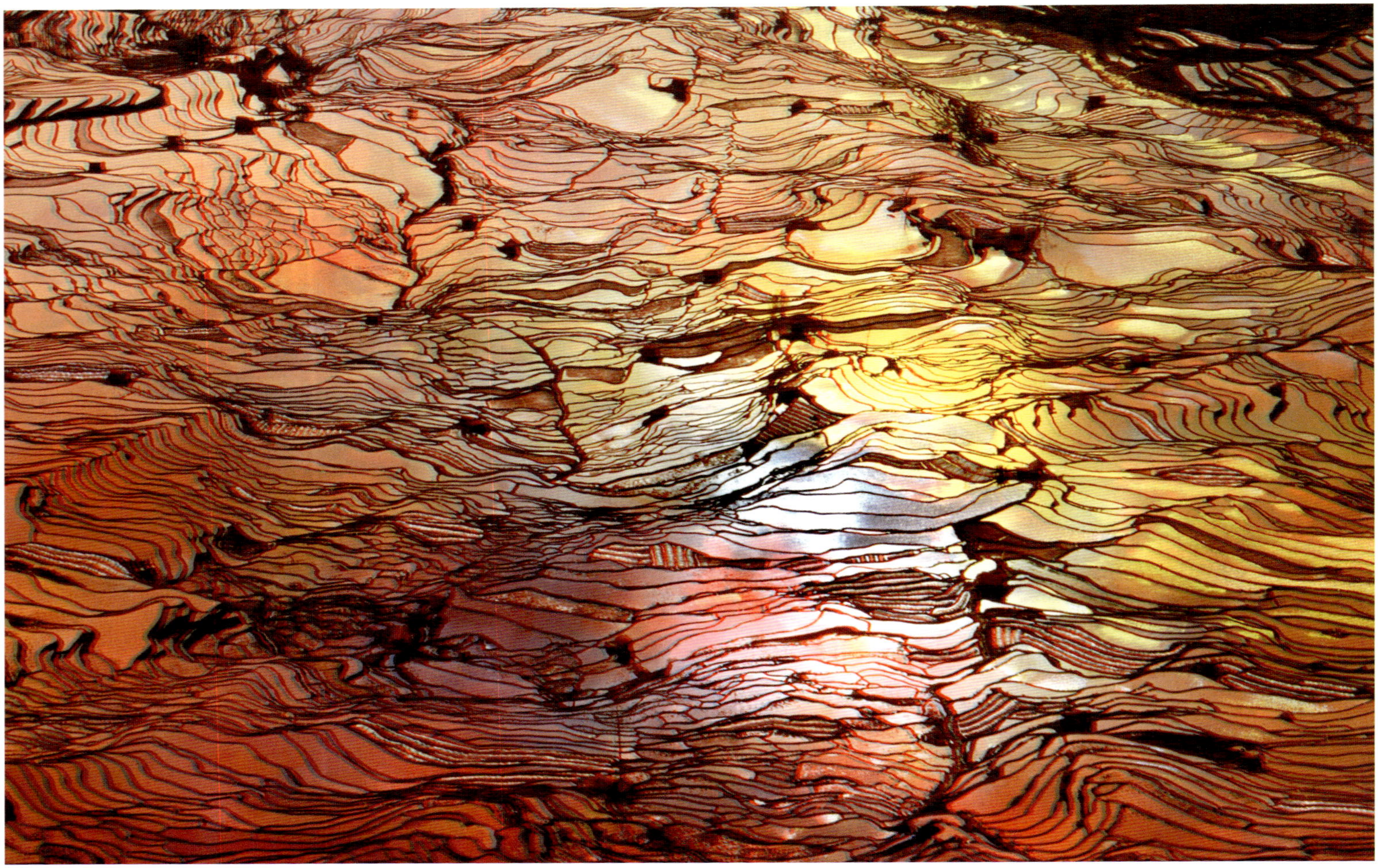

元阳县老虎嘴梯田之暮色。（图 / 陆江涛）

Night scene of Laohuzhui terraces of Yuanyang county. (Photo by Lu Jiangtao)

左上　元阳茶山哈尼族妇女在开挖梯田。（图 / 陆江涛）

Upper left　Hani women digging terraces at Chashan, Yuanyang County. (Photo by Lu Jiangtao)

右上　元阳县箐口村哈尼族传统纺线。（图 / 陆江涛）

Upper right　Hani traditional way of spinning, Qingkou village of Yuangyang County. (Photo by Lu Jiangtao)

左下　西河县甲寅乡镇泉水池边浣洗的妇女。（图 / 杨金海）

Lower left　Women washing at the pool, Jiayin village, Xihe County. (Photo by Yang Jinhai)

右下　元阳县箐口村哈尼族人在“昂玛突’祭祀神树中挂放鞭炮。（图 / 陆江涛）

Lower right　Hani villagers of Qingkou village, Yuanyang County , setting off firecrackers when worshipping their sacred tree. (Photo by Lu Jiangtao)

元阳梯田。（图 / 宋举浦）

Terraces in Yuanyang county. (Photo by Song Jupu)

猿人洞

中国世界遗产影像志

WORLD HERITAGE IN CHINA

周口店『北京人』遗址

Peking Man Site at Zhoukoudian

猿人洞。周口店北京猿人遗址的第 1 地点。（图 / 谭明）

Ape Man Cave. Locality 1 of Peking Man Site at Zhoukoudian. (Photo by Tan Ming)

Peking Man Site at Zhoukoudian

周口店“北京人”遗址

周口店“北京人”遗址位于北京西南 42 公里处，遗址的科学考察工作仍在进行中。到目前为止，科学家已经发现了中国猿人属“北京人”的遗迹，他们大约生活在中更新世时代，同时发现的还有各种各样的生活物品，以及可以追溯到公元前 18000 至 11000 年的新人类的遗迹。周口店遗址不仅是有关远古时期亚洲大陆人类社会的一个罕见的历史证据，而且也阐明了人类进化的进程。

——世界遗产委员会评价

Scientific work at the site, which lies 42 km south-west of Beijing, is still underway. So far, it has led to the discovery of the remains of Sinanthropus pekinensis, who lived in the Middle Pleistocene, along with various objects, and remains of Homo sapiens sapiens dating as far back as 18,000 - 11,000 B.C. The site is not only an exceptional reminder of the prehistorical human societies of the Asian continent, but also illustrates the process of evolution.

——World Heritage Committee Evaluation

周口店的动画演示猿人生活景象。（图 / 李江）
The motion pictures of Peking Man Site at Zhoukoudian demonstrating the life scene of ape man. (Photo by Li Jiang)

周口店“北京人”遗址正门的猿人雕像。（图 / 李江）
The Sculpture of Peking Man at the front gate of Peking Man Site at Zhoukoudian. (Photo by Li Jiang)

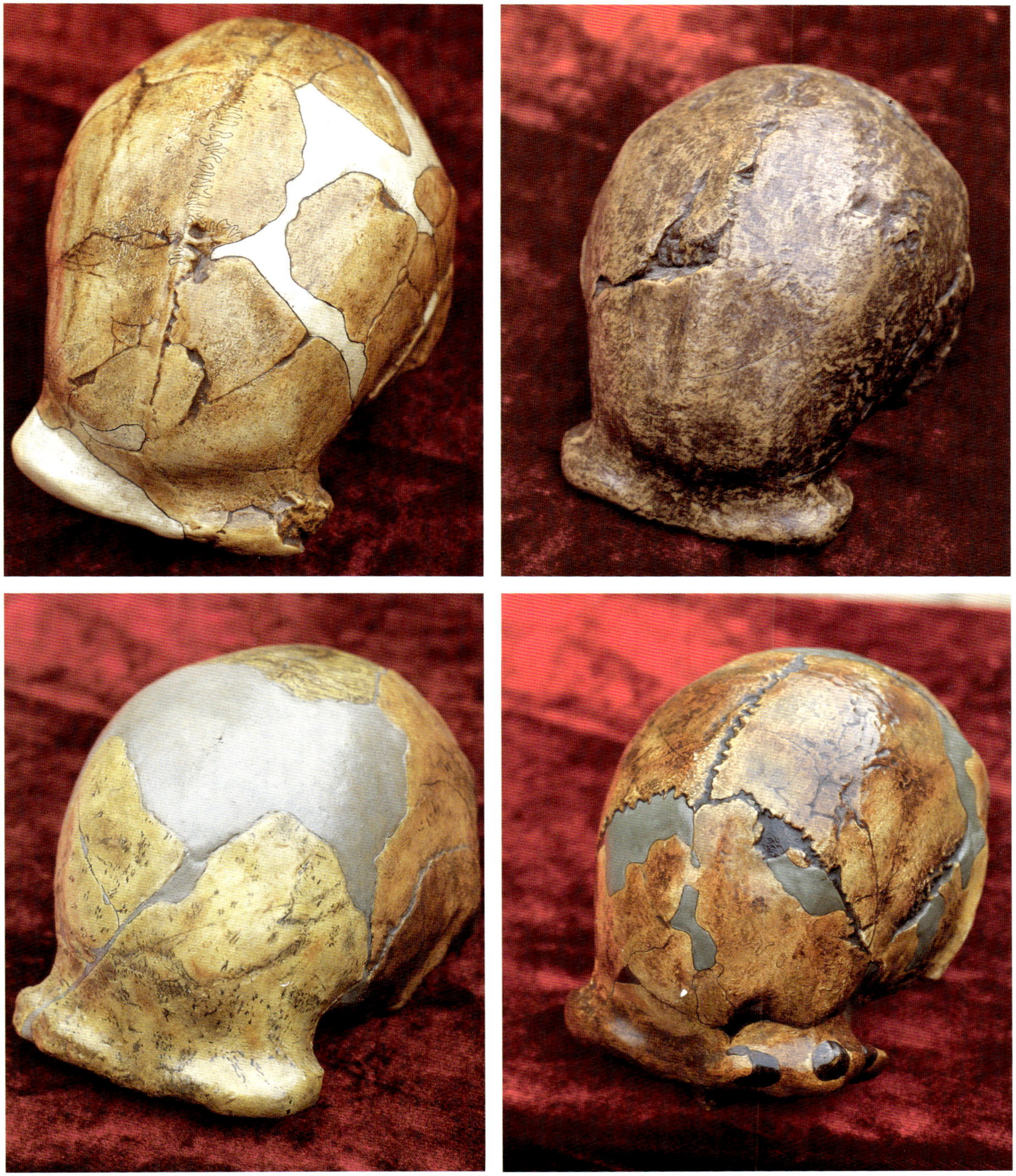

组图：北京猿人头盖骨。（图 / 李江）

Group of pictures: the skull of Peking Man. (Photo by Li Jiang)

北京猿人生活示意图。（图 / 李江）
Pictures illustrating the life of Peking Man. (Photo by Li Jiang)

中国世界遗产影像志

丝绸之路：长安—天山廊道的路网

WORLD HERITAGE IN CHINA

Silk Roads: the Routes Network of Chang'an-Tianshan Corridor

新疆塔克拉玛干沙漠的驼队。（图 / 郝沛）

The caravan on Taklimakan Desert, Xinjiang. (Photo by Haopei)

Silk Roads: the Routes Network of Chang'an-Tianshan Corridor

丝绸之路：长安—天山廊道的路网

该遗产涵盖 5000 公里漫长的丝绸之路网络，从中国汉唐时期的中都长安 / 洛阳至中亚的七河地区。丝绸之路形成于公元前 2 世纪至公元 1 世纪，一直使用到公元 16 世纪，联系了多个文明，促进了贸易、宗教信仰、科学知识、技术革新、文化实践和艺术等方面深刻的交流活动。丝绸之路网包含的 36 个组成部分包括多个帝国和汗国的首都及宫殿群、贸易据点、佛教窟庙、古代道路、驿馆、关隘、烽火台、部分长城、防御工事、墓葬及宗教建筑。

——世界遗产委员会评价

This property is a 5,000 km section of the extensive Silk Roads network, stretching from Chang'an/Luoyang, the central capital of China in the Han and Tang Dynasties, to the Zhetysu region of Central Asia. It took shape between the 2nd century B.C. and 1st century A.D. and remained in use until the 16th century, linking multiple civilizations and facilitating far-reaching exchanges of activities in trade, religious beliefs, scientific knowledge, technological innovation, cultural practices and the arts. The thirty-three components included in the routes network include capital cities and palace complexes of various empires and Khan kingdoms, trading settlements, Buddhist cave temples, ancient paths, posthouses, passes, beacon towers, sections of The Great Wall, fortifications, tombs and religious buildings.

——World Heritage Committee Evaluation

新疆库车克孜尔千佛洞。（图 / 郝沛）

The Kilzil Thousand Buddha Cave in Xinjiang. (Photo by Hao Pei)

唐大明宫含元殿复原图。含元殿是大明宫正殿。（图 / 茹遂初 /CFB）

The original design of Hanyuan Hall of Daming Palace of the Tang Dynasty. Hanyuan Hall was the main hall of Daming Palace. (Photo by Ru Suichu/CFB)

陕西西安大明宫国家遗址公园的紫宸殿遗址。（图 / 聂鸣 /FOTOE）
The ruins of Zichen Hall in Daming Palace National Relics Park in Xi’an, Shaanxi.(Photo by Nie Ming/ FOTOE)

陕西西安护国兴教寺。唐代著名高僧玄奘法师圆寂之地。（图 / 夏居宪）

The Huguo Xingjiao Temple in Xi’an, Shaanxi. The famous Buddhist master Xuanzang of the Tang Dynasty passed away here. (Photo by Xia Juxian)

上图　陕西西安荐福寺小雁塔。小雁塔所在的荐福寺是唐代长安三大译经场之一。（图 / 夏居宪）

The upper　The Little Wild Goose Pagoda at Jianfu Temple in Xi'an, Shaanxi. Jianfu Temple was one of the three main sites for translating scriptures in Chang'an during the Tang Dynasty. (Photo by Xia Juxian)

下图　陕西西安大慈恩寺大雁塔。唐代永徽三年（公元 652 年），玄奘为藏经典而修建。大雁塔是现存最早、规模最大的唐代四方楼阁式砖塔。（图 / 夏居宪）

The lower　The Big Wild Goose Pagoda at the Big Ci'en Temple in Xi'an, Shaanxi. It was built by Xuanzang in the 3rd year of the Yonghui era in the Tang Dynasty (652A.D.) to store scriptures. The Big Wild Goose Pagoda is the earliest and biggest surviving Tang brick pagoda in the quartet pavilion style. (Photo by Xia Juxian)

左图　隋唐洛阳定鼎门遗址博物馆。定鼎门作为洛阳城外郭城正门的时间长达 530 年，是中国古代延用时间最长的城门。（图 / 王立力）

The left　Sui-Tang Luoyang Dingding Gate Relics Museum. Having been the front gate of Outer Guocheng of Luoyang City for 530 years, Dingding Gate is the longest used city gate in ancient China. (Photo by Wang Lili)

右上　河南新安县汉函谷关。东汉王朝建都洛阳后，新安汉函谷关成为以洛阳为起点的丝绸之路上的必经之地和第一要塞。（图 / 王立力）

Upper Right　Hangu Pass of the Han Dynasty in Xin'an County, Henan. After Luoyang was made the capital of the Eastern Han Dynasty, Xin'an's Hangu Pass became the first fort that one needed to pass on the Silk Road that started in Luoyang. (Photo by Wang Lili)

右下　河南洛阳汉魏故城。它是世界上面积最大的古城，也是中国历史上建都时间最长的古城。（图 / 王立力）

Lower right　The ancient Luoyang Han-Wei City in Henan. It was the largest ancient city in the world, and served as capital for the longest time in Chinese history. (Photo by Wang Lili)

上图　甘肃麦积山石窟雕塑。（图 / 孙志军）

The upper　The sculpture in Mt. Maiji Grottoes in Gansu. (Photo by Sun Zhijun)

下图　麦积山石窟壁画。（图 / 孙志军）

The lower　The frescoes in Mt. Maiji Grottoes. (Photo by Sun Zhijun)

上图　麦积山石窟外景。（图 / 孙志军）

The upper　The exterior scenery of Mt. Maiji Grottoes. (Photo by Sun Zhijun)

左下　麦积山雕塑。（图 / 孙志军）

Lower left　Sculpture at Mt. Maiji. (Photo by Sun Zhijun)

右下　麦积山雕塑。（图 / 孙志军）

Lower right　Sculpture at Mt. Maiji. (Photo by Sun Zhijun)

甘肃炳灵寺石窟佛龛。（图 / 孙志军）
A Buddhist niche in Bingling Temple Grottoes, Gansu. (Photo by Sun Zhijun)

上图　炳灵寺第 169 窟女供养人像。（图 / 孙志军）

The upper　Image of a female donor in Grotto No. 169 at Bingling Temple. (Photo by Sun Zhijun)

下图　炳灵寺第 169 窟女供养人像。（图 / 孙志军）

The lower　Image of a female donor in Grotto No. 169 at Bingling Temple. (Photo by Sun Zhijun)

甘肃大方盘城与丝路古道。（图 / 孙志军）
The Big Square Pancheng and the ancient Silk Road in Gansu. (Photo by Sun Zhijun)

上图　甘肃敦煌境内汉代烽燧遗址。（图 / 孙志军）

The upper　The beacon tower site from the Han Dynasty in Dunhuang, Gansu. (Photo by Sun Zhijun)

下图　甘肃敦煌玉门关遗址。（图 / 孙志军）

The lower　The site of Yumen (Jade Gate) Pass in Dunhuang, Gansu. (Photo by Sun Zhijun)

上图　新疆北庭都护府石窟。（图 / 李学亮）

The upper　The stone grotto of Beiting Frontier Command in Xinjiang. (Photo by Li Xueliang)

下图　新疆北庭故城壁画。（图 / 李学亮）

The lower　The fresco of the old Beiting City in Xinjiang. (Photo by Li Xueliang)

上图　新疆吐鲁番高昌古城。（图 / 郝沛）

The upper　The ancient Gaochang City in Turpan, Xinjiang. (Photo by Hao Pei)

下图　新疆苏巴什佛寺遗址。（图 / 郝沛）

The lower　The site of Subhash Temple in Xinjiang. (Photo by Hao Pei)

新疆交河故城。（图 / 于云天）

The ancient Jiaohe City in Xinjiang. (Photo by Yu Yuntian)

（组图：大明宫文物）

1. 石雕佛头。（图 / 聂鸣 / FOTOE）/ 2. 石雕佛头。（图 / 聂鸣 / FOTOE）/ 3. 雕龙石柱。（图 / 聂鸣 / FOTOE）/ 4. 伎乐演奏陶俑。（图 / 聂鸣 / FOTOE）/ 5. 唐代胡人俑。（图 / 黄豁 / FOTOE）/ 6. 莲花纹方砖。（图 / 黄豁 / FOTOE）/ 7. 浮雕麒麟构件。（图 / 聂鸣 /FOTOE）

(Pictures of the relics of Daming Palace)

1.Stone carved Buddha Head. (Photo by Nie Ming/FOTOE) / 2.Stone carved Buddha head. (Photo by Nie Ming/FOTOE) / 3.Stone pillars carved with dragons. (Photo by Nie Ming/FOTOE) / 4.Jiyue playing pottery figurine. (Photo by Nie Ming/FOTOE) / 5.Figurine of a northern barbarian from the Tang Dynasty (Photo by Huang Huo/FOTOE) / 6.Square brick with lotus pattern. (Photo by Huang Huo/FOTOE) / 7.Kylin component in relief. (Photo by Nie Ming/FOTOE)

（组图：天山往事——古代新疆丝路文明展展品）

1. 唐黑人百戏俑。（图 / 孔兰平 / FOTOE ）/ 2. 唐女舞俑。（图 / 孔兰平 / FOTOE ）/ 3. 唐彩绘胡人头像。（图 / 孔兰平 / FOTOE ）/ 4. 南北朝联珠对凤锦覆面。（图 / 孔兰平 / FOTOE ）/ 5. 春秋战国时期牛角杯。（图 / 孔兰平 / FOTOE ）/ 6. 唐木质五弦琴、琴几。（图 / 孔兰平 / FOTOE ）/ 7. 春秋战国时期箜篌。（图 / 孔兰平 / FOTOE ）/ 8. 唐彩绘伏羲女娲麻布画。（图 / 孔兰平 / FOTOE ）/ 9. 唐木围棋盘。（图 / 孔兰平 / FOTOE ）/ 10. 战国虎纹圆金牌。（图 / 孔兰平 / FOTOE ）/ 11. 唐铜眼罩。（图 / 孔兰平 / FOTOE ）/ 12. 战国对熊方祭盘。（图 / 孔兰平 / FOTOE ）

(Pictures: Ancient stories of Mt. Tianshan-exhibits displayed at the exhibition of ancient Xinjiang Silk Road Civilization.)

1.Black acrobatics figurine of the Tang Dynasty. (Photo by Kong Lanping/FOTOE) / 2.Female dancer figurine of the Tang Dynasty. (Photo by Long Lanping/FOTOE) / 3.The painted head of a northern barbarian from the Tang Dynasty. (Photo by Kong Lanping/FOTOE) / 4.Brocade covering embroided with connected beads and a pair of phoenixes, from the Southern and Northern Dynasties. (Photo by Kong Lanping/FOTOE) / 5.Horn cup from the Spring and Autumn and Warring States Periods. (Photo by Kong Lanping/FOTOE) / 6.Wood Banjo and Qin table, from the Tang Dynasty. (Photo by Kong Lanping/FOTOE) / 7.Konghou from the Spring and Autumn and Warring Period (Photo by Kong Lanping/FOTOE) / 8.Color painting of Fuxi and Nuwo on linen from the Tang Dynasty. (Photo by Kong Lanping/FOTOE) / 9.Wood weiqi board from the Tang Dynasty. (Photo by Kong Lanping/FOTOE) / 10.Round gold plate decorated with tiger pattern from the Warring Period. (Photo by Kong Lanping/FOTOE) / 11.Copper patch from the Tang Dynasty. (Photo by Kong Lanping/FOTOE) / 12.Square Memorial Plate with a pair of bears from the Warring Period. (Photo by Kong Lanping/FOTOE)

号乃使博望侯張騫往西

甘肃敦煌莫高窟第 323 窟壁画《张骞出使西域》。（图 / 孙志军）

The fresco in Grotto No. 323 of Mogao Grottoes in Dunhuang, Gansu: Zhang Qian on his diplomatic mission to the Western Regions. (Photo by Sun Zhijun)

中国世界遗产影像志
WORLD HERITAGE IN CHINA

宗教文化遗产
Religious Cultural Heritage

拉萨布达拉宫历史建筑群 374
莫高窟 398
云冈石窟 422
龙门石窟 432
大足石刻 442
峨眉山—乐山大佛 450
登封『天地之中』历史建筑群 462
武当山古建筑群 472
五台山 482

龙门石窟奉先寺正壁卢舍那大佛。（图/谭明）
Losana Buddha on the front wall of Fengxian Temple, Longmen Grottoes. (Photo by Tan Ming)

宗教文化遗产

黄文昆　美术史学者

宗教，关乎人类对宇宙、世界和对人类自身的认识，寄托着人类的信仰和理想，是人们精神的动力、慰藉和依靠，数千年来引领着文明和文化的发展。在中国，宗教文化遗产十分丰富，与宗教有关的文物保护单位已有10处列入了《世界遗产名录》。

在中国历史上，影响最大的宗教当属佛教。佛教传自印度。印度的佛教形成于公元前6世纪，纪元前后传入中国，进入宫廷，也逐渐流传于民间。丝绸之路是其主要传播渠道，其次是海路。早在汉末、三国前后，佛教建筑已经分布在大江南北、黄河上下。史籍记载，印度和中亚、南亚诸国僧人不断来华，中国的信徒也纷纷西行求法。通过译经僧们的刻苦努力，中国上层社会支持并热心组织翻译活动，于是由抄本到刻印，逐渐形成流传有序、体系完整的中华藏经。在此基础上，中国佛教在2世纪以后的1800多年中几乎不间断地蓬勃发展，建树无穷，将佛教信仰延续至今。

在漫长的岁月里，佛教全方位地融入中国的政治、经济、文化、艺术等领域，自身也进行了适应性的改造和发展，以致到宋代与本土的儒教、道教相结合，出现“三教合一”的局面。中国历史文化的丰富遗产，佛教文化是其中的大宗。

由于民众的广泛信仰和国家的提倡，国内历代建造佛教寺院无数，但土木建筑经不起时光的侵蚀，昔日的荣华、遍及四方的功德，转眼成点点稀珍惊现于瓦砾。迄今，10世纪以前佛寺的殿宇楼阁因难以保护而几乎消损殆尽。

魏晋以降，社会大动荡、民族大融合，佛教得到长足的发展。人们在实践中总结经验，开始利用自然条件，采用溯源印度修造石窟寺的方法。中国的石窟寺最早出现在新疆，龟兹国（今库车、拜城一带）的石窟，以克孜尔、库木吐喇等窟群为代表，始建于公元3世纪，与中亚佛教一脉相承，大约延续到11世纪。东面的高昌国（吐鲁番地区），建窟寺于稍后。新疆以东，东晋十六国时期，自前秦建元二年（366年），和尚乐僔“杖锡西行”，在敦煌鸣沙山“造窟一龛”，此后，公元5世纪的头30年中，有后秦、西秦、北凉的帝王先后主持在上邽（今天水）麦积山、枹罕小积石山（今永靖炳灵寺）和凉州（今武威）南郊百里（据说在天梯山），成规模地修造石窟寺。北凉王沮渠蒙逊说得清楚：“以国城寺塔终非云固，古来帝宫终逢煨烬，若依立之效尤斯及，又用金宝终被毁盗，乃顾眄山宇可以终天。”（道宣《集神州三宝感通录》卷中）开窟造像，除了有西域的传承，更得山石坚固、体量宏伟等天然之利，还因为其地处偏僻、远离闹市纷尘，清幽之境宜于修行，也避开了许多人为的破坏。

“敦，大也；煌，盛也”（《汉书·地理志》），河西走廊西端的出口、面向西域的古镇、茫茫戈壁中的绿洲——敦煌，是一个梦幻般的地方，丝路上来往的行旅到这里歇息、补给，在这里学习语言，交流信息。西域以东开凿石窟最初就从这里开始。中国第一批列入世界文化遗产的敦煌莫高窟，保存公元5世纪至14世纪历经千年开凿的735个洞窟，其中有历代不同风格、内容极其丰富多彩的精美佛教壁画和塑像，不仅是举世闻名的古代艺术宝库，还具有极高的学术研究价值。20世纪初，莫高窟藏经洞发现敦煌遗书，五万卷文书引起世界学术界的极大兴趣，形成了百年来国际性的“敦煌学”研究热潮。

南北朝时期，曾经一统中国北方的北魏王朝，对于石窟寺的开凿倾注力量。鉴于曾经的太武帝废佛灭法，文成帝登基之后立即大力复兴佛教。和平元年（460年），沙门统昙曜奉敕在当时的国都平成（今大同）开山造像。有名的“昙曜五窟”，五座大像窟内，主尊高达13–17米，据信是象征北魏的五位皇帝，“雕饰奇伟，冠于一世”（《魏书·释老志》）。由于皇室、贵族的主持，云冈石窟规模宏大，气势非凡，后世典籍形容为“穷诸巧丽，骇动人神”（《续高僧传》），“凿石开山，因岩结构，真容巨壮，世法所希”（《水经注》），评价恰如其分。云冈的大工程延续了逾40年，以巨大的能量和示范作用推动全国佛教艺术的普及与发展。

公元5世纪末，北魏孝文帝厉行改革，推进汉化，迁都洛阳，政治文化中心转移到中原。洛阳南郊的龙门石窟代替云冈成为佛教造像艺术的中心。伊阙岩壁，石质优异，以古阳洞为起始，北魏、唐代两度高潮，伊水两岸窟龛密如蜂房。景明初（500年），宣武帝下令按照云冈模式为父母孝文帝、文昭皇后建造石窟（宾阳洞），费时23年，完美的雕塑造型成功表现出庄重而优雅的皇家气派。佛教达于鼎盛的唐朝，龙门石窟重建皇家石窟的辉煌，上元二年（675年）竣工的奉先寺大卢舍那像龛，蒙武后则天“助脂粉钱二万贯”，17.14 米高的主尊及菩萨、弟子、天王、力士组成的群像，以空前的规模和精湛的技艺，将佛教造像艺术推向了顶峰。

列入《世界遗产名录》的登封“天地之中”历史建筑群，其中的登封少林寺建于北魏，以后几度被毁几番重建。寺外西侧的塔林，是少林寺的祖茔，保存着唐、宋、金、元、明、清历代高僧的墓塔 230 余座，形式多样，历史价值很高。登封市西北、嵩山南麓峻极峰下的嵩岳寺塔，建于北魏正光四年（523 年），是现存最古老的砖塔，密檐式，十二边形，15 层，高约 41 米，形制独特，为中国建筑史上的稀珍。

山西五台山，原名清凉山，唐代以来被奉为文殊菩萨道场，五峰耸峙，其间塔刹寺庙数以百计，外围则有南禅寺和佛光寺，分别保存唐代建中三年（782 年）和大中十一年（857 年）的建筑以及塑像、壁画等文物，其中的两座大殿是现存中国木构建筑最早的实例。

“峨眉天下秀”。与五台山相呼应，另一处佛教名山四川峨眉山，被视为普贤菩萨道场。一并列入《世界遗产名录》的乐山名胜区，凌云山断崖上的乐山大佛，高 71 米，俯瞰三江合流，完成于唐贞元十九年（803 年），是现存最大的摩崖石刻造像，与高山浑然一体，当得起“夸父之巧，巨灵之工”这样的赞誉。

作为大乘佛教的一个支派，佛教密宗于公元 8 世纪正式传入中国，晚唐则有柳本尊在巴蜀大行其道。唐朝衰落之后，经济稳定、文化基础深厚的巴蜀地区在石窟寺的营建方面焕发出空前活力。在大足北山，我们欣赏到最完美的观音造型；在宝顶佛湾，赵智凤主持修造的密宗道场，气势恢宏，格局严谨，洋溢着生活气息。现存于重庆、四川的宋代石窟和摩崖造像犹如中国石窟艺术史上璀璨的明珠。

坐落在西藏拉萨红山（玛布日山）之上的布达拉宫，为公元 7 世纪吐蕃赞普松赞干布所建。据说唐贞观年间，在这里迎娶中国唐朝和尼泊尔国的公主。两位公主又建造了小昭寺和大昭寺。17 世纪中叶五世达赖重建布达拉宫，先后完成了白宫和红宫，这座依山垒筑的宫堡式建筑群，成为历世达赖喇嘛居住的地方、西藏地区宗教和政治的中心。西藏密宗根基厚重，佛学理论、修持仪轨以及佛寺建筑、造像、绘画都有独特的风格，体现着藏族人民的智慧与才能。

道教是中国本土的宗教，有着深厚的传统，其形成可上溯至汉魏。历史上道教与佛教有争斗也有融合，一般情况下并行不悖。佛教文化遗产之中往往有道教踪迹可寻，唐以后道教石窟亦多有开凿。五台山、峨眉山，原来都曾经是道教的基地。登封“天地之中”的中岳庙，祭祀嵩岳神祇，在唐代和明清备受皇室恩宠，经过大规模扩建、整修，成为中原最宏大壮观的道教建筑群。

四川青城山是道教的发源地，青翠四合，环境清幽，传说天师道始祖张道陵在此“羽化”，唐玄宗特颁诏令确认此山为道教圣地（《大唐开元神武皇帝书碑》）。湖北武当山，山高林密，雄浑壮阔，与青城山同为道教四大名山之一，且居首位。因为是“真武修仙”之处，永乐年间，明成祖“北修故宫，南建武当”，将这里建设成全国道教的中心。道教圣境当然还应该包括列为世界自然遗产的三清山风景名胜区。江西三清山因玉京、玉虚、玉华三峰高耸入云而得名，这里岩峰成林，植被葱茏，气象景观摄人心魄，无疑是道家修行的洞天福地。

入列《世界遗产名录》的中国文化保护项目，展现出丰厚的宗教文化内涵。不断发展中的宗教文化，数千年来助推历史的前进，促进艺术的繁荣。珍贵的遗产将在未来得到更大程度的国际关注与保护。

Religious Cultural Heritage

Huang Wenkun, Art historian

Religion is about human beings understanding of the universe, of the world and of humanity itself; it sustains the beliefs and ideals of mankind. As the spiritual motivation, solace and support of human beings, religion for thousands of years has guided the development of civilization and culture. Chinese history is rich in religious cultural heritage and 10 cultural protection sites connected to religion are listed on *the World Heritage List*.

In Chinese history, Buddhism was the most influential religion. Buddhism originated in India, where it took shape in the 6th century B.C., and it was introduced to China around the 1st centrury A.D. It first circulated in the imperial court, and later was gradually known in the society. The Silk Road was its main communication channel, with the sea route a secondary communication channel. As early as the late Han Dynasty and before and after the Three Kingdoms period, Buddhist buildings had been constructed on both sides of the Yangtze River and the upper and lower reaches of the Yellow River. According to historical records, monks from India, and from South and Central Asia continually arrived in China, and Chinese believers went westward in droves to seek scriptures. Due to the strenuous efforts of translators and with the Chinese upper society's support and warmhearted organization of translation activities, from copies to printed versions, the Chinese Tripitaka gradually took shape in an orderly and comprehensive fashion. On this basis, Chinese Buddhism, for more than 1,800 years after the 2nd century A.D., has undergone an almost constant thriving development, making great achievements and keeping Buddhist belief alive right up to the present.

Over a long history, Buddhism has been integrated into and has also been indispensable to Chinese politics, economy, culture and art, while at the same time Buddhism itself has been reformed so as to facilitate its adaptation to Chinese circumstances, and has developed so much so that by the time of the Song Dynasty it combined with Confucianism and Taoism to form a synthesis of the three teachings.

Buddhism culture is the staple of China's rich cultural heritage.

Countless Buddhist temples were built in successive dynasties, because Buddhism enjoyed wide faith among the people and was encouraged by the state. But buildings of earth and wood cannot stand the erosion of time, and past splendors and beneficence can soon be reduced to ruins, with only a little bit of rare treasure left to be discovered to the happy surprise of later generations. Almost all Buddhist temples built before the 10th century have practically all perished, given the difficulty in preserving them.

Beginning with the Wei and Jin dynasties, great social upheavals and ethnic integration fusion took place, and Buddhism underwent considerable development. People drew experience from practice and began to make use of the natural environment and adopt and apply the construction methods of cave temples that had originated in India. The earliest Chinese cave temples were built in Xinjiang. The stone caves in the Qiuci Kingdom (present day Kuche and Baicheng), represented by the cave clusters of Kyzyl and Kumu Tula, were built in the 3rd century, in conjunction with the spread of Buddhism in Central Asia, and continued until about the 11th century. Cave temples in Gaochang Kingdom in the east (present day Turfan area) were built slightly later. In the east of Xinjiang, at the time of the 16 states of Eastern Jin Dynasty, from the 2nd year of Jianyuan of the Former Qin (366 A.D.), the monk Lezun "went westward holding a tin stick" and "built a niche cave" at Mt. Mingsha in Dunhuang; after that, for the first 30 years of the 5th century, the emperors of the Later Qin, Western Qin and Northern Liang, one after another, presided over the building of cave temples in large scale at Mt. Maiji of Shanggui (present day Tianshui), Mt. Xiaojishi of Baohan (present day Bingling Temple in Yongjing), and Baili (said to be at Mt. Tianti) in the south suburb of Liangzhou (present day Wuwei). The king of Northern Liang, Juqu Mengxun, made it clear that "City wall, monasteries and pagodas are, in the end, not so very solid, and imperial palaces since ancient times have always been prone to destruction; structures built with precious metals and stones are also subject to looting, so cave edifices alone can last through the ages."(the middle volume of *Collection of Reasonings about the Triratna of the Divine Land by Daoxuan*) Cutting grottoes and carving statues, apart from being a tradition in the Western Regions, had also to do with the natural advantages of using solid and huge stones. As the area was out of the way and far from urban bustle, and the quiet environment was conducive to selfcultivation, avoiding much manmade damage.

"Dun means big; Huang means prosperous," according to *the geography section of The History of the Former Han*.(Yan Shigu's quotation of Ying Shao).Dunhuang, the exit at the west end of Hexi Corridor, the ancient town that faced the Western Regions, the oasis in the vast gobi, was a fantastic place where travelers along the Silk Road came for a rest and for supplies, studied languages and exchanged information. The cutting of stone caves in the east of the Western Regions started here first of all. The first group of Dunhuang Mogao grottoes to be listed on *the World Heritage List* include 735 grottoes that were cut during the nearly 1,000 years from the 5th century to the 14th century. Inside the grottoes are exquisite Buddhist frescoes and statues that are of different styles and different time periods, and are of diverse contents, rich and colorful. This is not only a world-famous treasure house of ancient art, but it also has very high value for academic research. At the beginning of the 20th century, the Dunhuang Manuscripts were discovered in the Mogao Caves where Buddhist sutras were stored. These 50,000 volumes of manuscripts aroused great interest in international academia, triggering an upsurge of "Dunhuang studies" across the world during the last hundred years.

At the time of the Southern and Northern Dynasties, the Northern Wei Dynasty that had united northern China devoted much effort to cut cave temples. After the past ban on Buddhism and the elimination of Buddhist doctrines by Emperor Taiwu, Emperor Wencheng, once on the throne, set to revive Buddhism vigorously. In the 1st year of Heping (460 A.D.), Tan Yao, Controller of Monks, was ordered by the emperor to cut grottoes and make statues in Pingcheng (present day Datong), then the capital. In the famous "five Tan Yao grottoes", that is, the five grottoes with big statues, the main statues, 13-17 metres tall, were thought to symbolize the five emperors of Northern Wei and were "cut and decorated so well that they are the best in the world" (*Book of Wei—Records of Buddhism and Taoism*). Because the project was hosted by the imperial family and the nobles, the Yungang Grottoes were grand in scale and showed extraordinary vigour, and later books described them as "extremely beautiful", "surprising both human and god" (*Biographies of Eminent Monks Continued*). "After cutting stone and opening the mountain, building the structure by making use of the cliff, the statues are great, lifelike and rarely seen" (*Shui Jing Zhu, or Commentary on the Waterways Classic*). These comments hit the mark. The project at Yungang lasted for more than 40 years, and it pushed foward the popularization and development of Buddhist art across the whole country with its great energy and exemplary demonstration.

At the end of the 5th century, Emperor Xiaowen of Northern Wei carried out drastic reforms, promoted sinicisation and moved his capital to Luoyang, thereby shifting the political and cultural centre to Zhongyuan, the Central Plains. Longmen Grottoes in the south suburb of Luoyang replaced Yungang as the centre of Buddhist statuary art. The Yique cliff face provided excellent stone, and beginning at Guyang Cave and reaching two peaks during the Northern Wei and the Tang Dynasties, there were created grottoes as dense as behives on both banks of the Yi River. In the early Jingming period (500 A.D.), Emperor Xuanwu gave an order to build his father Emperor Xiaowen and his mother Queen Wenzhao a grotto (Bingyang Cave) by modeling the Yungang pattern. It took 23 years. The perfect sculptures successfully reflected the solemn and elegant royal style. In the Tang Dynasty, when Buddhism reached its zenith, the Longmen Grottoes were rebuilt to reflect the briliance of royal grottoes, and in the 2nd year of Shangyuan (675 A.D.), when the Big Vairocana Statue Niche was completed, Empress Wu Zetian “donated 20,000 strings of cash, all her own money”. The statues, including the 17.14-metre-tall main statue, a Bodhisattva, heavenly kings and strong men, with their unprecedented scale and superb skill, pushed Buddhist statuary art to its peak.

Shaolin Temple, one of the historical buildings at Dengfeng, “the centre of heaven and earth” on *the World Heritage List*, was built in the Northern Wei Dynasty, and was destroyed several times and rebuilt several times. Ta Lin, or the Pagoda Forest on the west side outside the temple, was the ancestral graveyard of Shaolin Temple that preserves over 230 pagodas of eminent monks of the Tang, Song, Jin, Yuan, Ming and Qing dynasties. The pagodas of various styles have very high historical value. The pagoda of Songyue Temple is in the northwest of Dengfeng City, below Junji Peak and at the south foot of Mt. Song. It was built in the 4th year of Zhengguang in the Northern Dynasty (523 A.D.) and is the oldest surviving brick pagoda. It features dense eaves, a twelve-sided shape, 15 storeys, and is 41 metres tall. Unique in structure, it is a rare treasure in Chinese architectural history.

Mt. Wutai in Shanxi, formerly known as Mt. Qingliang, has since the Tang been seen as a ritual site associated with the Manjusri Bodhisattva. Among the five towering peaks are scattered hundreds of pagodas and temples, and Nanchan Temple and Foguang Temple at the periphery respectively preserve buildings built in the 3rd year of Jianzhong (782 A.D.) and the 11th year of Dazhong (857 A.D.) and such cultural relics as statues and frescoes. These two large temples are the earliest surviving examples of Chinese wood-structured building.

Mt. Emei has been described as "the greatest beauty under heaven". Echoing Mt. Wutai, Mt. Emei in Sichuan, another famous Buddhist mountain, has been considered the site associated with the Samantabhadra boddhisattva. The Leshan Giant Buddha carved at Lingyun Cliff appears on *the World Heritage List* together with Mt. Emei; it is 71 metres tall and looks down at the confluence of three rivers. Completed in the 19th year of Zhenyuan of the Tang Dynasty (803 A.D.), it is the biggest surviving stone statue. Blending into a harmonious whole with the mountain, it deserves the praise “ingenuity of Kuafu, exquisiteness of Juling”.

As a sect of Mahayana Buddhism, Esoteric Buddhism was formally introduced into China in the 8th century, and in the Late Tang Dynasty, Liu Benzun was very popular in Bashu in West

China. After the decline of the Tang Dynasty,the Bashu area, enjoying a stable economy and deep cultural foundations, launched with unprecedented vibrancy into building stone cave temples. At Beishan in Dazu, we can find the most perfect Guanyin statue; Baoding Buddha Bay, the home of Esoteric Buddhism, whose construction was presided over by Zhao Zhifeng, is magnificent in momentum, vigorous in pattern, and filled with the flavor of life. The grottoes and cliff figures of Song Dynasty that exist in Chongqing and Sichuan are just like the bright setting sun in the Chinese history of grotto art.

The Potala Palace at the Red Mountain (Mt. Maburi) in Lhasa, Tibet, was built by Songtsen Gampo, the King of Tubo, in the 7th century. It is said that during the Zhenguan period of the Tang Dynasty, two princesses of the Tang Dynasty and Nepal were married here. The two princesses built Ramoche Temple and Jokhang Temple. In the mid-17th century, the 5th Dalai Lama rebuilt the Potala Palace. The White Palace and the Red Palace were completed in turn. This architectural group in the style of a castle built on a hill was the residence for generations of Dalai Lamas, and it was the religious and political centre of Tibet.The Tibetan Tantra has thick roots, and its Buddhist theories, sadhana, temple architectures, statues and paintings all have unique style and represent the wisdom and talent of the Tibetan people.

Taoism, having originated in China proper, has a deep tradition. Its formation may be traced back to the Han and Wei dynasties. In history, Taoism and Buddhism both competed and blended. Under normal circumstances, they existed in parallel. In Buddhist cultural heritage may often be found the traces of Taoism. After the Tang Dynasty, many Taoist grottoes were also cut. Mt. Wutai and Mt. Emei had both once been the base of Taoism. Zhongyue Temple in Dengfeng, the "centre of heaven and earth" that enshrines the gods of Mt. Songshan, was very much favored by the royal family of Tang, Ming and Qing dynasties and was expanded and repaired on a grand scale to become the most grand and spectacular Taoist building cluster.

Mt. Qingcheng in Sichuan is the birthplace of Taoism. Verdant trees grow here, and the environment is quiet and beautiful. Legend has it that Zhang Daoling, the founding ancestor of Taoism, ascended to heaven and became immortal here. Emperor Xuanzong of the Tang Dynasty specifically issued an edict confirming the position of the mountain as the holy land of Taoism(*the monument written by Emperor Shenwu of Kaiyuan, the Tang Dynasty*). Mt. Wudang in Hubei, high and densely forested, vigorous and magnificent, is one of the four famous Taoist mountains, and is the first of the four. Because it was where "Zhenwu cultivated immortality," in the Yongle period Emperor Chengzu of the Ming Dynasty "constructed the Imperial Palace in the north and Wudang in the south" and made them the centres of Taoism of the country. The Taoist holy land also includes Mt.National Park, a world heritage site. Mt. Sanqingshan got its name for the three towering peaks of Yujing, Yuxu and Yuhua. Here the peaks have formed forest, the vegetation is verdant, and the meteorological scenery is breathtaking. This is doubtless a blessed place for Taoist cultivation.

The Chinese cultural protection projects listed on *the World Heritage List* reflect rich religious cultural connotations. The continuously developing religious culture has, for thousands of years, helped history to advance and has promoted artistic prosperity. These precious heritages are bound to receive more international attention and protection in the future.

布达拉宫。（图/扎西次登）

Potala Palace. (Photo by Zasits den)

中国世界遗产影像志

WORLD HERITAGE IN CHINA

Historic Ensemble of the Potala Palace, Lhasa

拉萨布达拉宫历史建筑群

Historic Ensemble of the Potala Palace, Lhasa
拉萨布达拉宫历史建筑群

布达拉宫自公元 7 世纪起就成为达赖喇嘛的冬宫，象征着藏传佛教及其在历代行政统治中的中心作用。布达拉宫，坐落在拉萨河谷中心海拔 3700 米的红色山峰之上，由白宫和红宫及其附属建筑组成。大昭寺也建造于公元 7 世纪，是一组极具特色的佛教建筑群。建造于公元 18 世纪的罗布林卡，曾经作为达赖喇嘛的夏宫，也是西藏艺术的杰作。这三处遗址的建筑精美绝伦，设计新颖独特，加上丰富多样的装饰以及与自然美景的和谐统一，更增添了其在历史和宗教上的重要价值。

——世界遗产委员会评价

The Potala Palace, winter palace of the Dalai Lama since the 7th century, symbolizes Tibetan Buddhism and its central role in the traditional administration of Tibet. The complex, comprising the White and Red Palaces with their ancillary buildings, is built on Red Mountain in the centre of Lhasa Valley, at an altitude of 3,700m. Also founded in the 7th century, the Jokhang Temple Monastery is an exceptional Buddhist religious complex. Norbulingka, the Dalai Lama's former summer palace, constructed in the 18th century, is a masterpiece of Tibetan art. The beauty and originality of the architecture of these three sites, their rich ornamentation and harmonious integration in a striking landscape, add to their historic and religious interest.

——World Heritage Committee Evaluation

鸟瞰布达拉宫。（图 / 田捷砚）
An aerial view of Potala Palace. (Photo by Tian Jieyan)

左上　红宫西有寂圆满大殿，亦称西大殿。（图 / 孙之常）

Upper left　West Main Hall at the Red Palace. (Photo by Sun Zhichang)

右上　白宫东有寂圆满大殿，亦称东大殿。（图 / 孙之常）

Upper right　East Main Hall at the White Palace. (Photo by Sun Zhichang)

左下　白宫西日光殿。（图 / 卞志武）

Lower left　West Sunlight Hall at the White Palace. (Photo by Bian Zhiwu)

右下　白宫东日光殿。（图 / 卞志武）

Lower right　East Sunlight Hall at the White Palace. (Photo by Bian Zhiwu)

左上　红宫屋顶上的金顶群。金顶群从东至西分别由八世、九世达赖喇嘛灵塔殿，主供佛殿，五世、七世、十世和十三世达赖喇嘛灵塔殿等七座金顶组成。（图 / 卞志武）

Upper left　Golden roofs above the Red Palace. From east to west these include the pagoda temples of the 8th, the 9th Dalai Lamas the Saint's Chapel, and the pagoda temples of the 5th, the 7th, the 10th and the 13th Dalai Lamas. (Photo by Bian Zhiwu)

右上　红宫屋顶上的金顶用铜质鎏金瓦铺成，上面还有宝瓶、共命鸟、鳌头、经幢、牦牛绒伞盖等鎏金装饰。（图 / 卞志武）

Upper right　The golden roof of the Red Palace is made of copper tile and decorated with such gilded objects as precious bottle, life-sharing birds, head of Ao (a huge legendary turtle), Sutra Pillar canopy of yakwool. (Photo by Bian Zhiwu)

左下　金顶斗拱有五层象鼻斗拱和七层猪鼻斗拱等形式，具有分散风力等作用，所以历史上从没有出现过狂风刮倒金顶的现象。（图 / 卞志武）

Lower left　The dougong (a system of brackets inserted between the top of a column and a crossbeam) at the golden roof, including such forms as five-layer trunk dougong and seven-layer trunk dougong, have the function of dispersing wind strength, which explains why even strong gales have not blown down the golden roof. (Photo by Bian Zhiwu)

右下　九世达赖喇嘛灵塔殿正门五解脱门板上的门环、环座及铁箍，铁棂花格的镂金纹等。（图 / 卞志武）

Lower right　The knocker, the base of the knocker and iron hoop, the golden carved lines of the iron bar tracery from the front door of the pagoda temple of the 9th Dalai Lama. (Photo by Bian Zhiwu)

红宫圣观音殿。（图 / 孙之常）

Guanyin Hall at the Red Palace. (Photo by Sun Zhichang)

上图　红宫法王洞内景。（图 / 孙之常）

The upper　The inside view of Dharma cave in the Red Palace. (Photo by Sun Zhichang)

下图　红宫法王洞内西侧的弥勒佛鎏金铜质塑像。（图 / 孙之常）

The lower　The gilded copper statue of Maitreya Buddha on the west side of Dharma cave in the Red Palace. (Photo by Sun Zhichang)

上图　清朝乾隆皇帝敕封八世达赖喇嘛的玉质文册。（图 / 孙之常）

The upper Jade album signed by Emperor Qianlong authorizing the 8th Dalai Lama. (Photo by Sun Zhichang)

下图　清朝道光皇帝赐给十一世达赖喇嘛的金册，长 23.2 厘米，宽 9.9 厘米，厚 0.2 厘米。全 13 页。封册用纯金制作，可以翻阅，中间用满、汉、藏、蒙四种文字刻“敕封十一世达赖喇嘛之册”。（图 / 卞志武）

The lower Gold album given by Emperor Daoguang authorizing the 11th Dalai Lama. It is 23.2 cm long, 9.9 cm wide and 0.2 cm thick. It consists of 13 pages and made of pure gold. It can be turned and read. In the middle are the characters "album for authorizing the 11th Dalai Lama" in Manchu, Chinese, Tibetan and Mongolian. (Photo by Bian Zhiwu)

左图　红宫殊胜三界殿内北侧正中的“当今皇帝万岁万万岁”牌位。（图 / 孙之常）

The left　The "long live our emperor" tablet in the middle at the north of the Shusheng Sanjie Temple in the Red Palace. (Photo by Sun Zhichang)

右图　清朝雍正皇帝敕封七世达赖喇嘛的金印。（图 / 孙之常）

The right　Gold seal from Emperor Yongzheng of the Qing Dynasty authorizing the 7th Dalai Lama. (Photo by Sun Zhichang)

左图　十三世达赖喇嘛灵塔殿内的珍珠曼陀罗是清朝慈禧太后送给十三世达赖喇嘛的，用 20 余万颗珍珠和珊瑚串制而成。（图 / 卞志武）

The left The pearl Datura in the pagoda temple of the 13th Dalai Lama was given by the Empress Dowager Cixi of the Qing. It is made up of 200,000 pearls and corals. (photo by Bian Zhiwu)

右上　银质净水瓶（图 / 孙之常）

Upper right Silver net bottle. (Photo by Sun Zhichang)

右中　唢呐（图 / 孙之常）

Middle right Suona horn. (Photo by Sun Zhichang)

右下　铜质鎏金，八瓣莲花大威德金刚雕塑（开放状）（图 / 卞志武）

Lower right In gilded copper, sculpture of Yamantaka sitting on 8-petaled lotus (in opening state). (Photo by Bian Zhiwu)

左上　白宫东日光殿藏宗喀巴唐卡。（图 / 孙之常）

Upper left Tsongkhapa Thangka at the East Sunlight Hall of the White Palace. (Photo by Sun Zhichang)

右上　白宫东日光殿内藏十一面千手千眼观世音菩萨像唐卡。（图 / 孙之常）

Upper right Thangka of Guanyin Bodhisattva with a thousand hands and a thousand eyes stored at the East Sunlight Hall of the White Palace. (Photo by Sun Zhichang)

左下　白宫东日光殿内藏大威德金刚像唐卡。（图 / 孙之常）

Lower left Thangka of Yamantaka stored at the East Sunlight Hall of the White Palace. (Photo by Sun Zhichang)

右下　白宫东日光殿永固福德宫藏上师供奉图唐卡。（图 / 孙之常）

Lower right Thangka of guru worshipping stored at the East Sunlight Hall of the White Palace. (Photo by Sun Zhichang)

红宫第二层迴廊南壁中部的展佛图。（图 / 孙之常）

Picture of Buddha in the middle of the south wall of the cloister on the second floor of the Red Palace. (Photo by Sun Zhichang)

红宫西有寂圆满大殿内东壁的五世达赖喇嘛赴京觐见清朝顺治皇帝图。（图 / 卞志武）

The picture of the 5th Dalai Lama meeting Emperor Qianlong of Qing Dynasty in Beijing, hung on the east wall at the West Main Hall in the Red Palace. (Photo by Bian Zhiwu)

从大昭寺鎏金屋顶上远眺布达拉宫。（图 / 谭明）
Looking at the Potala Palace from the gilded roof of Jokhang Temple. (Photo by Tan Ming)

左图　大昭寺。（图 / 卞志武）

The left　Jokhang Temple. (Photo by Bian Zhiwu)

右图　大昭寺殿内东侧正中释迦牟尼殿内的佛祖 12 岁等身佛像。（图 / 赵利山）

The right　Life-size statue of Sakyamuni at age 12 at the Shakyamuni Hall in Jokhang Temple. (Photo by Zhao Lishan)

罗布林卡。（图 / 卞志武）

Norbulingka. (Photo by Bian Zhiwu)

罗布林卡公园内的藏戏表演。（图 / 孙之常）
Performance of Tibetan opera at Norbulingka park. (Photo by Sun Zhichang)

左图　藏族做铜佛的老工匠。（图 / 翁乃强）

The left　Senior Tibetan craftsman making copper Buddha. (Photo by Weng Naiqiang)

右图　西藏的佛教信徒。（图 / 林晶华）

The right　Tibetan Buddhist follower. (Photo by Lin Jinghua)

布达拉宫之晨。（图 / 孙隆椿）

The morning of the Potala Palace. (Photo by Sun Longchun)

中国 世界遗产 影像志

莫高窟

WORLD HERITAGE IN CHINA

Mogao Caves

敦煌莫高窟九层楼。（图 / 吴健）

The Nine-layer Building at Dunhuang Mogao Caves. (Photo by Wu Jian)

莫高窟地处丝绸之路的一个重镇。它不仅是东西方贸易的中转站，同时也是宗教、文化和知识的交汇处。莫高窟的492个小石窟和洞穴庙宇，以其雕像和壁画闻名于世，展示了延续千年的佛教艺术。

——世界遗产委员会评价

Situated at a strategic point along the Silk Route, at the crossroads of trade as well as religious, cultural and intellectual influences, the 492 cells and cave sanctuaries in Mogao are famous for their statues and wall paintings, spanning 1,000 years of Buddhist art.

——World Heritage Committee Evaluation

初唐 · 敦煌莫高窟 112 窟伎乐天。（图 / 吴健）
Apsara at Cave No. 112 of Dunhuang Mogao Caves (the Early Tang Dynasty). (Photo by Wu Jian)

敦煌莫高窟外景。（图 / 周梅生）
Exterior of Dunhuang Mogao Caves. (Photo by Zhou Meisheng)

北京 · 敦煌莫高窟 275 窟交脚弥勒菩萨坐像。（图 / 文物出版社提供）
Sitting image of Cross-legged Maitreya Buddha at Cave No.275 of Dunhuang Mogao Caves (the Northern Liang Dynasty). (Photo provided by Cultural Relics Publishing House)

北魏·敦煌莫高窟第 259 窟禅定佛。（图 / 茹遂初）
Meditating Buddha at Cave No. 259 of Dunhuang Mogao Caves (the Northern Wei Dynasty). (Photo by Ru Suichu)

上图　西魏 · 敦煌莫高窟 285 窟强盗成佛图。（图 / 文物出版社提供）

The upper　Picture of bandit turning into buddha at Cave No. 285 of Dunhuang Mogao Caves (the Western Wei Dynasty). (Photo provided by Cultural Relics Publishing House)

下图　北周 · 敦煌莫高窟 428 窟萨埵太子本生。（图 / 孙志军）

The lower　Picture of prince making himself food for the tiger at Cave No. 428 of Dunhuang Mogao Caves (the Northern Zhou Dynasty). (Photo by Sun Zhijun)

上图　隋·敦煌莫高窟 407 窟三兔莲花飞天井心与千佛。（图 / 孙志军）

The Upper　Well-heart with three rabbits, lotus blossom, flying apsaras and thousand Buddhas, Cave No.407 of Dunhuang Mogao Grottoes · the Sui Dynasty. (Photo by Sun Zhijun)

下左　隋·敦煌莫高窟 420 窟胁侍菩萨。（图 / 文物出版社提供）

Lower left　Bodhisattva at Cave No. 420 of Dunhuang Mogao Caves (the Sui Dynasty). (Photo provided by Cultural Relics Publishing House)

下右　隋·敦煌莫高窟 419 窟胁侍菩萨。（图 / 文物出版社提供）

Lower right　Bodhisattva at Cave No. 419 of Dunhuang Mogao Caves (the Sui Dynasty). (Photo provided by Cultural Relics Publishing House)

初唐·敦煌莫高窟 217 窟无量寿经变。（图 / 茹遂初）

“Aparimitayur Sutra” at Cave No. 217 of Dunhuang Mogao Caves (the Early Tang Dynasty). (Photo by Ru Suichu)

初唐 · 敦煌莫高窟 321 窟飞天。（图 / 孙志军）
Flying Apsaras at Cave No. 321 of Dunhuang Mogao Caves (the Early Tang Dynasty). (Photo by Sun Zhijun)

中唐·敦煌莫高窟 158 窟西壁坛上佛涅槃像。（图 / 吴健）
Picture of Buddha Nirvana at Cave No. 158 of Dunhuang Mogao Caves (the Middle Tang Dynasty). (Photo by Wu Jian)

左图　盛唐·敦煌莫高窟 23 窟法华经变大千世界雨润万物生。（图 / 文物出版社提供）

The left　“Lotus Sutra” shows that everything grows in the boundless universe with the moistening of rain at Cave No. 23 of Dunhuang Mogao Caves (the High Tang Dynasty). (Photo by Cultural Relics publishing House)

右图　盛唐·敦煌莫高窟 171 窟观无量寿经变（部分）。（图 / 孙志军）

The right　(Part of) View of Aparimitayur Sutra at Cave No. 171 of Dunhuang Mogao Caves (the High Tang Dynasty). (Photo by Sun Zhijun)

左图　盛唐·敦煌莫高窟 45 窟龛内塑像。（图 / 孙之常）

The left　Statue at Cave No.45 of the Dunhuang Mogao Caves (the High Tang Dynasty). (Photo by Sun Zhichang)

右上　盛唐·敦煌莫高窟 328 窟菩萨。（图 / 文物出版社提供）

Upper right　Bodhisattva at Cave No. 328 of the Dunhuang Mogao Caves (the High Tang Dynasty). (Photo Provided by Cultural Relics Publishing House)

右下　盛唐·敦煌莫高窟 194 窟菩萨。（图 / 吴健）

Lower right　Bodhisattva at Cave No.194 of the Dunhuang Mogao Caves (the High Tang Dynasty). (Photo by Wu Jian)

晚唐·敦煌莫高窟 156 窟张议潮出行图（部分）。（图 / 茹遂初）

(Part of) "Zhang Yichao going on travels" at Cave No. 156 of Dunhuang Mogao Caves (the Late Tang Dynasty). (Photo by Ru Suichu)

晚唐 · 莫高窟 17 窟仕女图。（图 / 茹遂初）

Painting of a court lady at Cave No.17 of Dunhuang Mogao Caves (the Late Tang Dynasty). (Photo by Ru Suichu)

上图　五代 · 敦煌莫高窟 61 窟为莫高窟最大洞窟之一。（图 / 文物出版社提供）

The upper　Cave No. 61 is one of the biggest Caves in Dunhuang Mogao Caves (the Five Dynasties Period). (Photo Provided by Cultural Relics Publishing House)

下左　宋 · 敦煌莫高窟 55 窟观音普度救难经变图。（图 / 文物出版社提供）

Lower left　The fresco illustrating Avalokitesvara rescuing people who suffer from disasters **at** Cave No. 55 of Dunhuang Mogao Caves (the Song Dynasty). (Photo Provided by Cultural Relics Publishing House)

下右　元 · 敦煌莫高窟 3 窟千手观音。（图 / 文物出版社提供）

Lower right　Thousand-hand Guanyin at Cave No.3 of Dunhuang Mogao Caves (the Yuan Dynasty) (Photo Provided by Cultural Relics Publishing House)

西夏 · 莫高窟所属西千佛洞又称榆林窟。榆林窟 3 窟《玄奘取经图》。（图 / 吴健）

The Western Thousand Buddha Caves of Mogao Caves is also named Yulin Caves. The picture of *Xuan Zang on his pilgrimage for Buddhist scriptures* at Cave No.3 of Yulin Caves (the Western Xia Dynasty. (Photo by Wu Jian)

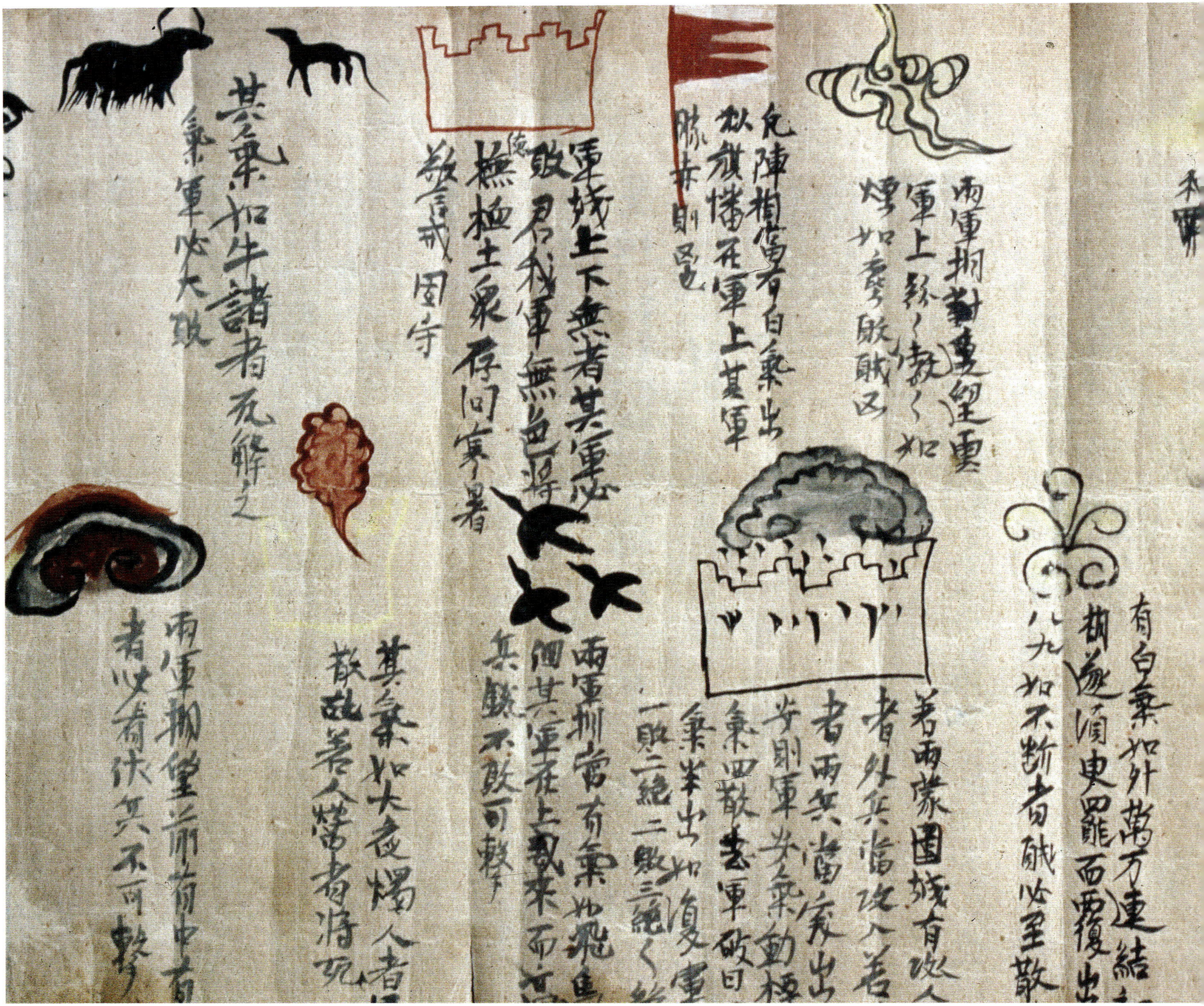
兩軍相對壘望雲
軍上紛〻紛〻如
煙如霧敗賊凶
凡陣相當有白氣出
狀如旗幟在軍上其軍
勝者則昌
軍城上下無者其軍必
敗君我軍無血
撫極土衆存問寡署
敬言戒固守
其氣如牛諸者充解之
氣軍必大敗
有白氣如外萬方連結
相隨須臾羅而復出
八九如不斷者有賊必至散
若兩軍圍城有攻人
者外兵當攻入若
者兩兵當安出
安則軍安氣動極
氣四散去軍破日
氣半出如復雲
一敗二絕二敗三絕
兩軍相當有氣如飛鳥
回其軍在上氣來而
其賊不敢可擊
其氣如火夜燭人者
敵戰善人當者將死
兩軍相望前有中有
者必有伏兵不可擊

敦煌莫高窟文书——《占云气书》。（图 / 茹遂初）
Dunhuang Mogao Caves document *The Book of Clouds*. (Photo by Ru Suichu)

中国世界遗产影像志

WORLD HERITAGE IN CHINA

云冈石窟

Yungang Grottoes

云冈石窟第 20 窟 · 释迦牟尼坐像（局部）。（图 / 孙之常）

(Part of)No. 20 grotto of Yungang Grottoes—the Shakyamuni Buddha. (Photo by Sun Zhichang)

Yungang Grottoes

云冈石窟

云冈石窟，位于山西省大同市，现存洞窟 252 座、石像 51,000 尊，代表了 5 世纪至 6 世纪时期中国高超的佛教艺术成就。“昙曜五窟”整体布局严整，风格和谐统一，是中国佛教艺术第一个巅峰时期的经典杰作。

——世界遗产委员会评价

The Yungang Grottoes, in Datong city, Shanxi Province, with their 252 caves and 51,000 statues, represent the outstanding achievement of Buddhist cave art in China in the 5th and 6th centuries. The Five Caves created by Tan Yao, with their strict unity of layout and design, constitute a classical masterpiece of the first peak of Chinese Buddhist art.

——World Heritage Committee Evaluation

云冈晚韵。（图 / 吴健）
Yungang Grottoes in the evening. (Photo by Wu Jian)

第 3 窟 · 灵岩洞。第 3 窟为云冈石窟最大的石窟。后室内有一佛二菩萨像，中间为阿弥陀佛，高 10 米，呈倚坐式，体态稳重、丰满，为隋唐时期的衣冠服饰和造像风格。(图 / 李建惠)

No. 3 grotto. Lingyan cave. The biggest cave of Yungang Grottoes. There are one Buddha statue and two Bodhisattva statues. Amitabha sitting in the middle is 10 metres tall. He looks dignified and plump, dressed in the style of the Sui and Tang Dynasties and reflecting the sculpture of Sui and Tang style. (Photo by Li Jianhui)

第 13 窟交脚弥勒像。(图 / 李建惠)
Cross-legged Maitreya at No. 13 grotto. (Photo by Li Jianhui)

第 18 窟佛与弟子。（图 / 张海雁）
The Buddha and his disciples in No. 18 grotto. (Photo by Zhang Haiyan)

上图　第 16 窟伎乐天。（图 / 张海雁）　**The upper**　Apsara in No.16 grotto. (Photo by Zhang Haiyan)
下图　第 10 窟前室。（图 / 张海雁）　**The lower**　The front chamber of No.10 grotto. (Photo by Zhang Haiyan)

第 6 窟前室壁画。（图 / 谭明）

The fresco in the front chamber of No.6 grotto. (Photo by Tan Ming)

中国世界遗产影像志

龙门石窟

WORLD HERITAGE IN CHINA

Longmen Grottoes

卢舍那大佛。亦称光明遍照佛，意即佛的智慧像日光一样普照一切。（图 / 王琛）
The Big Vairocana Buddha, also called Light All Buddha, means that the wisdom of the Buddha lights all, just like sunshine. (Photo by Wang Chen)

龙门地区的石窟和佛龛构成了北魏晚期至唐代（316至907年）期间最具规模和最为优秀的中国艺术藏品。这些艺术作品全部反映佛教宗教题材，代表了中国石刻艺术的最高峰。

——世界遗产委员会评价

The grottoes and niches of Longmen contain the largest and most impressive collection of Chinese art of the late Northern Wei and Tang Dynasties (316—907). These works, entirely devoted to the Buddhist religion, represent the high point of Chinese stone carving.

——World Heritage Committee Evaluation

龙门石窟群。（图 / 张嘉庆）
Longmen Grottoes. (Photo by Zhang Jiaqing)

莲花洞。因窟顶刻一朵精美的莲花而得名。主像释迦牟尼佛，两侧二弟子。（图 / 孙之常）

Lotus cave. It got its name because a lotus was carved at the top of the cave. The main statue is Shakyamuni Buddha, with two disciples standing on each side. (Photo by Sun Zhichang)

左图　万佛洞。主尊名阿弥陀佛，一手贴身斜举胸前，一手抚膝。这种手势说明阿弥陀佛在向弟子信徒说法，故称“说法印”。（图 / 孙之常）

The left　Ten-thousand Buddha Cave. The main statue is Amitabha, with one hand over his chest and the other hand on his knee, signifying that he is stating buddhist doctrines to his disciples; this is called "mudra of teaching". (Photo by Sun Zhichang)

右上　万佛洞。位于西山中部北端，是于公元 680 年为唐高宗、武则天祈福开凿的具有唐代皇家风范的石窟。因洞内南北两壁刻满 15000 尊小佛像而得名。（图 / 孙之常）

Upper right　Ten-thousand Buddha Cave. Situated at the north part of the middle of Mt. Xishan, it was cut in 680 A.D. to pray blessings for Emperor Gaozong and Wu Zetian. It was named such because of the 15,000 little Buddhas carved on the two walls of the cave. (Photo by Sun Zhichang)

右下　万佛洞洞口观世音菩萨。位于万佛洞洞口外南壁，造像高 85 厘米，比例匀称，造型优美，含蓄端庄，为唐刻观音的佳作。（图 / 孙之常）

Lower right　Guanyin at the entrance of Ten-thousand Buddha Cave. It is 85 centimetres tall and well-proportioned. It is an outstanding statue of Guanyin cut in the Tang Dynasty. (Photo by Sun Zhichang)

上图　宾阳中洞主佛。（图 / 孙之常）

The upper　The main Buddha statue in Middle Binyang Cave. (Photo by Sun Zhichang)

中图　宾阳中洞。北壁供养人图。（图 / 孙之常）

The centre　Middle Binyang Cave. Picture of provider on the north wall. (Photo by Sun Zhichang)

下图　宾阳中洞。南壁礼佛图。（图 / 孙之常）

The lower　Middle Binyang Cave. Buddha worship on the south wall. (Photo by Sun Zhichang)

上图 古阳洞杨大眼造像龛。（图 / 孙之常）

The upper Big-eye Yang statue niche on the north wall of Guyang Cave. (Photo by Sun Zhichang)

左下 古阳洞魏碑。（图 / 张嘉庆）

Lower left Wei Stele (tablet inscriptions of the Northern Dynasties) in Guyang Cave (Photo by Zhang Jiaqing)

右下 古阳洞窟顶。（图 / 孙之常）

Lower right the ceiling of Guyang Cave (Photo by Sun Zhichang)

看经寺窟顶供养飞天。（图 / 孙之常）
Supporting Flying Apsaras at the roof of Kanjing Temple. (Photo by Sun Zhichang)

中国世界遗产影像志

大足石刻

WORLD HERITAGE IN CHINA

Dazu Rock Carvings

宝顶山大佛湾北岩中部，大方便佛报恩经变相。（图 / 王涛）

The gratitude sutra of the great Convenient Buddha at the middle of the north cliff of Buddha Bay at Mt. Baoding. (Photo by Wang Tao)

大足地区的险峻山崖上保存着绝无仅有的系列石刻，时间跨度从公元 9 世纪到 13 世纪。这些石刻以其极高的艺术品质、丰富多变的题材而闻名遐迩，从世俗到宗教，鲜明地反映了中国这一时期的日常社会生活，充分证明了这一时期佛教、道教和儒家思想和谐相处的局面。

——世界遗产委员会评价

The steep hillsides of the Dazu area contain an exceptional series of rock carvings dating from the 9th to the 13th century. They are remarkable for their aesthetic quality, their rich diversity of subject matter, both secular and religious, and the light that they shed on everyday life in China during this period. They provide outstanding evidence of the harmonious synthesis of Buddhism, Taoism and Confucianism.

——World Heritage Committee Evaluation

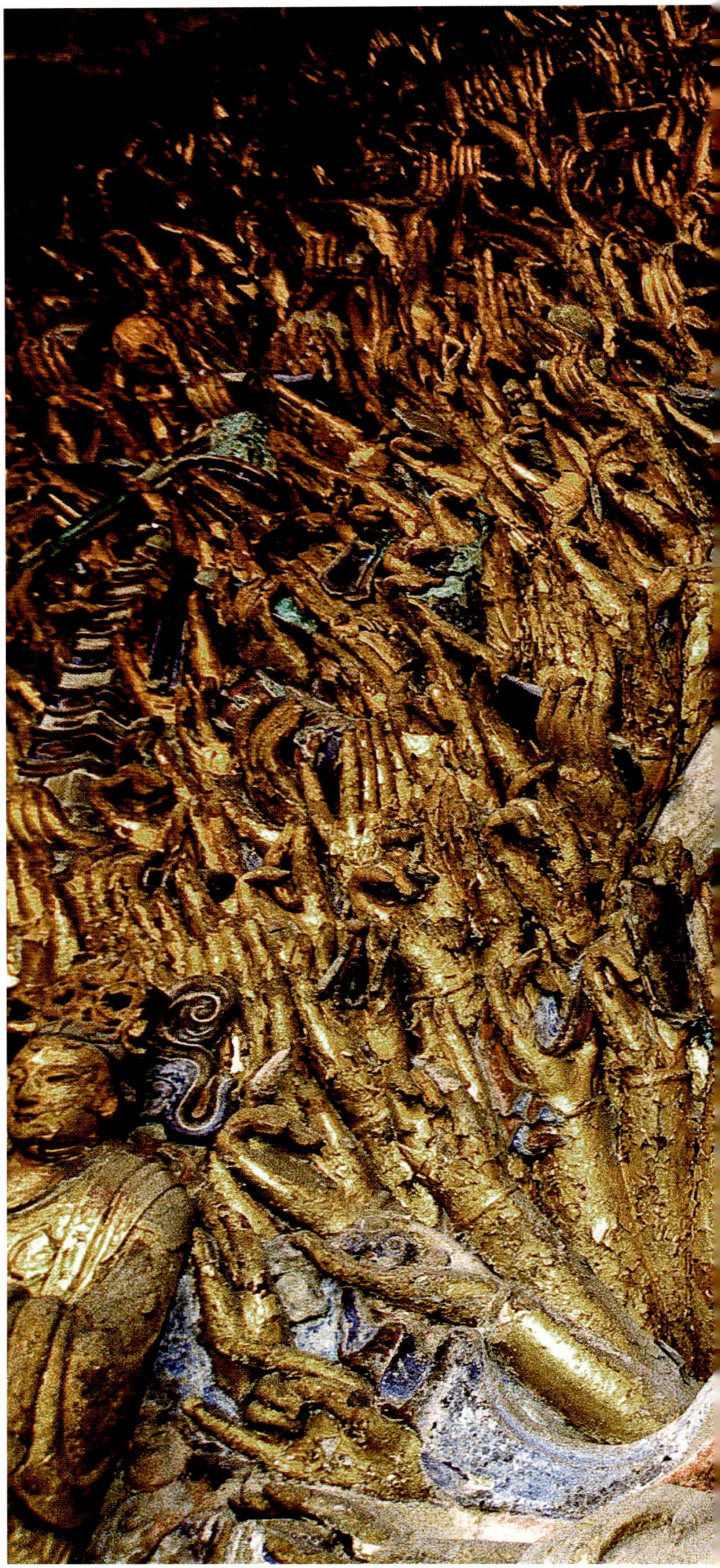

千手观音像——宝顶山第 18 号。（图 / 周千明）
No. 18 statue of Thousand-hand Guanyin at Mt. Baoding. (Photo by Zhou Qianming)

（拼图）北山·转轮经藏窟。（图/周千明）

(Photo Collage) The cave of Beishan Runner Sutra. (Photo by Zhou Qianming)

宝顶山第 29 号圆觉洞。正壁刻坐佛三尊，坐前刻跪像一尊，两壁刻菩萨十二尊。传说释迦牟尼佛的十二弟子修炼成功，在佛面前陈述个人修炼的情况。（图 / 谭明）

No.29 Yuanjue Cave at Mt. Baoding. This cave is magnificently carved and can be said to be the best of the Baoding stone carving art. On the front wall are carved three sitting Buddhas, with one kneeling statue in front of the sitting Buddhas and 12 Bodhisattvas on both walls. Legend has it that upon the success of their studies, the 12 disciples of Sakyamuni Buddha each stated their level of cultivation. (Photo by Tan Ming)

柳本尊正觉像。（图 / 钟敏）

The picture of the Patriarch Liu in Buddhahood. (Photo by Zhong Min)

中国世界遗产影像志

峨眉山—乐山大佛

WORLD HERITAGE IN CHINA

Mount Emei Scenic Area, including Leshan Giant Buddha Scenic Area

从金顶望云海。（图 / 李少白）

The sea of clouds viewed from Jinding. (Photo by Li Shaobai)

Mount Emei Scenic Area, including Leshan Giant Buddha Scenic Area

峨眉山—乐山大佛

公元 1 世纪，在四川省峨嵋山景色秀丽的山巅上，落成了中国第一座佛教寺院。随着四周其他寺庙的建立，该地成为佛教的主要圣地之一。许多世纪以来，文化财富大量积淀，最著名的要属乐山大佛，它是 8 世纪时人们在一座山岩上雕凿出来的，俯瞰着三江交汇之所。佛像身高 71 米，堪称世界之最。峨嵋山还以其物种繁多、种类丰富的植物而闻名天下，从亚热带植物到亚高山针叶林可谓应有尽有，有些树木树龄已逾千年。

——世界遗产委员会评价

The first Buddhist temple in China was built here in Sichuan Province in the 1st century A.D. in the beautiful surroundings of the summit Mount Emei. The addition of other temples turned the site into one of Buddhism's holiest sites. Over the centuries, the cultural treasures grew in number. The most remarkable is the Giant Buddha of Leshan, carved out of a hillside in the 8th century and looking down on the confluence of three rivers. At 71 m high, it is the largest Buddha in the world. Mount Emei is also notable for its exceptionally diverse vegetation, ranging from subtropical to subalpine pine forests. Some of the trees there are more than 1,000 years old.

——World Heritage Committee Evaluation

鸟瞰峨眉山。（图 / 田捷砚）

An aerial view of Mount Emei. (Photo by Tian Jieyan)

峨眉山金顶。（图 / 王达军）
Jinding of Mount Emei. (Photo by Wang Dajun)

金頂

左上　峨眉山明代铜印。（图 / 陈东林）　**Upper left**　The bronze seal of Ming Dynasty in Mount Emei. (Photo by Chen Donglin)
左下　峨眉山古贝叶经。（图 / 陈东林）　**Lower left**　Archaic Pattra-leaf Scripture of Mount Emei. (Photo by Chen Donglin)
右图　峨眉山万年寺砖殿普贤铜像。（图 / 陈东林）　**The right**　The bronze statue of Samantabhadra in Brick Shrine of Wannian Temple of Mount Emei .(Photo by Chen Donglin)

从金顶望云海。（图 / 李少白） The sea of clouds viewed from Jinding. (Photo by Li Shaobai)

乐山大佛。乐山大佛是世界上最高的石刻弥勒大佛。（图 / 王达军）

Leshan Giant Buddha, the tallest stone Buddha statue of Maitreya. (Photo by Wang Dajun)

中国世界遗产影像志

WORLD HERITAGE IN CHINA

Historic Monuments of Dengfeng in "The Centre of Heaven and Earth"

登封『天地之中』历史建筑群

少林寺塔林。（图 / 赵亚洲）

Shaolin Temple Pagoda Forest. (Photo by Zhao Yazhou)

Historic Monuments of Dengfeng in "The Centre of Heaven and Earth"
登封"天地之中"历史建筑群

位于中国河南省的嵩山，被认为是具有神圣意义的中岳。在海拔 1500 米的嵩山脚下，距河南省登封市不远，有 8 座占地共 40 平方公里的建筑群，其中包括三座汉代古阙，以及中国最古老的道教建筑遗址——中岳庙、周公测景台与登封观星台等。这些建筑物历经九个朝代修建而成，它们不仅以不同的方式展示了天地之中的概念，还体现了嵩山作为虔诚的宗教中心的力量。登封历史建筑群是古代建筑中用于祭祀、科学、技术及教育活动的最佳典范之一。

——世界遗产委员会评价

Mount Songshang is considered to be the central sacred mountain of China. At the foot of this 1500 metre high mountain, close to the city of Dengfeng in Henan province and spread over a 40 square—kilometre circle, stand eight clusters of buildings and sites, including three Han Que gates — remains of the oldest religious edifices in China, temples, the Zhougong Sundial Platform and the Dengfeng Observatory. Constructed over the course of nine dynasties, these buildings are reflections of different ways of perceiving the centre of heaven and earth and the power of the mountain as a centre for religious devotion. The historical monuments of Dengfeng include some of the best examples of ancient Chinese buildings devoted to ritual, science, technology and education.

——World Heritage Committee Evaluation

嵩岳寺塔是我国现存最古老的砖塔。（图 / 张伟民）
Pagoda of Songyue Temple. is the oldest existing brick pagoda. (Photo by Zhang Weimin)

左图　观星台。（图 / 赵亚洲）

The left　Stella Observatary. (Photo by Zhao Yazhou)

右上　嵩阳书院。（图 / 周梅生）

Upper right　Songyang Academy. (Photo by Zhou Meisheng)

右下　中岳庙天中阁。（图 / 周梅生）

Lower right　Tianzhong Pavilion of Zhongyue Temple. (Photo by Zhou Meisheng)

汉三阙（太室阙、少室阙、启母阙）。（图 / 赵亚洲）

The three Que from the Han Dynasty(Taishi Que, Shaoshi Que, Qimu Que). (Photo by Zhao Yazhou)

修禅。（图 / 曹茂赋）
Meditation. (Photo by Cao Maofu)

组图：少林寺僧练功。（图 / 姚丹）

Series Shaolin monks practising martial arts. (Photo by Yao Dan)

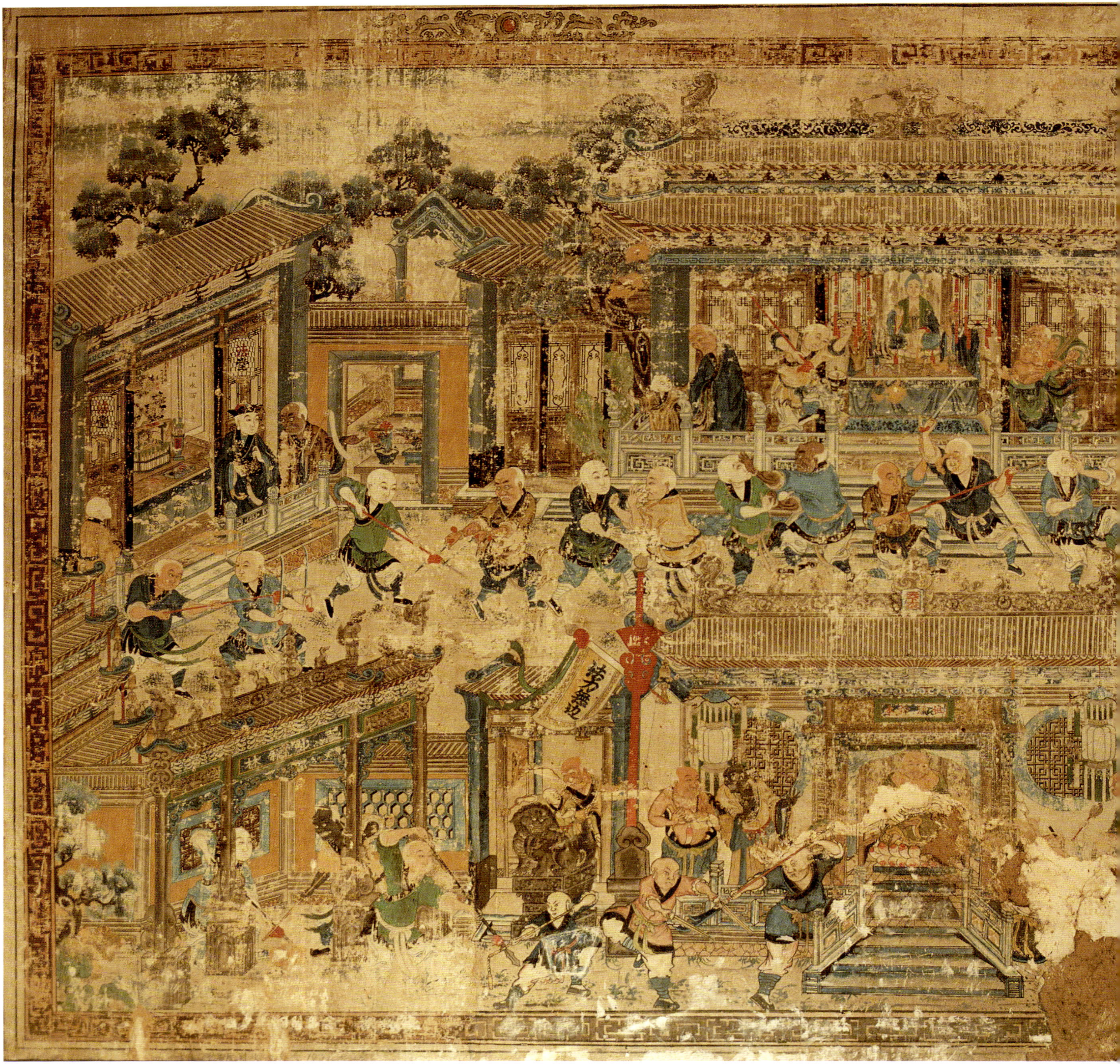

少林寺白衣殿内的武僧练功壁画。（图 / 吕大千）

Fresco of monks practising martial arts at Baiyi Hall of Shaolin Temple. (Photo by Lü Daqian)

中国世界遗产影像志

WORLD HERITAGE IN CHINA

武当山古建筑群

Ancient Building Complex in the Wudang Mountains

武当山紫禁城。（图 / 贾长江）

The Fobidden City of Mt. Wudang. (Photo by Jia Changjiang)

Ancient Building Complex in the Wudang Mountains
武当山古建筑群

这里的宫殿和庙宇构成了这一组世俗和宗教建筑的核心，集中体现了中国元、明、清三代的建筑和艺术成就。古建筑群坐落在沟壑纵横、风景如画的湖北省武当山麓，在明代期间（14 至 17 世纪）逐渐形成规模，其中的道教建筑可以追溯到公元 7 世纪，这些建筑代表了近千年的中国艺术和建筑的最高水平。

——世界遗产委员会评价

The palaces and temples which form the nucleus of this group of secular and religious buildings exemplify the architectural and artistic achievements of China's Yuan, Ming and Qing Dynasties. Situated in the scenic valleys and on the slopes of the Wudang mountains in Hubei Province, the site, which was built as an organized complex during the Ming Dynasty (14th - 17th centuries), contains Taoist buildings from as early as the 7th century. It represents the highest standards of Chinese art and architecture over a period of nearly 1,000 years.

——World Heritage Committee Evaluation

武当山金殿观日出。（图 / 吕大千）
Watching sunrise at the Golden Shrine of Mt. Wudang. (Photo by Lv Daqian)

龙头香。又名龙首石，建于元朝。位于南岩峭壁外的龙头香因其地势险要，被誉为“天下第一香。”（图 / 谭明）

Longtou Xiang. Also named Longtou (dragon head) Rock. Built in the Yuan Dynasty (1271-1368). Because of the dangerous geographical position, Longtou Xiang is called the "No.1 incense burner under the sun". (Photo by Tan Ming)

上图　武当山紫霄宫。（图 / 杨大洲）

The upper　Purple Cloud Palace at Mt. Wudang. (Photo by Yang Dazhou)

下图　武当山金殿。（图 / 王立力）

The lower　Golden Shrine at Mt. Wudang. (Photo by Wang Lili)

武当山太和宫皇经堂。（图 / 罗品禧）

Imperial Scriptures Hall in Taihe Palace at Mt. Wudang. (Photo by Luo Pinxi)

左上　在紫霄宫练习太极功夫的道人。（图 / 罗品禧）　**Upper left**　Taoist practising Taiji at Purple Cloud Palace. (Photo by Luo Pinxi)

右上　在树林练习太极功夫的道人。（图 / 罗品禧）　**Upper right**　Taoist practising Taiji in the woods. (Photo by Luo Pinxi)

左下　在紫霄宫练习太极功夫的道人。（图 / 罗品禧）　**Lower left**　Taoist practising Taiji at Purple Cloud Palace. (Photo by Luo Pinxi)

右下　太和宫习武的道人。（图 / 罗品禧）　**Lower right**　Taoist practising martial arts at Taihe Palace. (Photo by Luo Pinxi)

武当山金顶建筑。（图 / 罗品禧）
The buildings at the Golden Top of Mt. Wudang. (Photo by Luo Pinxi)

中国世界遗产影像志

五台山

WORLD HERITAGE IN CHINA

Mount Wutai

五台山。（图 / 齐凤臣）

Mount Wutai. (Photo by Qi Fengchen)

五台山由五座平顶的山峰构成，是一座佛教圣山。该山分布有 41 座寺院，其中包括佛光寺的东大殿，是现存的海拔位置最高的唐代木结构建筑，内有真人大小的泥塑雕像。该山的特色建筑还有明代的殊像寺，寺内 500 罗汉构成的巨型雕像群描绘了织入三维山水图画中的佛教故事。总体来说，该山的建筑提纲挈领地展示了佛教建筑发展的方式，这种方式影响了中国的宫殿建筑逾千年。五台山的字面意思是“五座台地构成的山”，是中国北方海拔最高的山，由陡坡和五座开阔且未长树木的山峰构成，外观独特，引人注目。从 1 世纪到 20 世纪早期该山不断有新寺庙出现。

——世界遗产委员会评价

With its five flat peaks, Mount Wutai is a sacred Buddhist mountain. The cultural landscape is home to forty-one monasteries and includes the East Main Hall of Foguang Temple, the highest surviving timber building of the Tang Dynasty, with life-size clay sculptures. It also features the Ming Dynasty Shuxiang Temple with a huge complex of 500 statues representing Buddhist stories woven into three-dimensional pictures of mountains and water. Overall, the buildings on the site catalogue the way in which Buddhist architecture developed and influenced palace building in China for over a millennium. Mount Wutai, literally, 'the five terrace mountain', is the highest in Northern China and is remarkable for its morphology of precipitous slopes with five open treeless peaks. Temples have been built on this site from the 1st century A.D. to the early 20th century.

——World Heritage Committee Evaluation

……五台山保存完好的十大黄庙之一和五大禅寺之一。（图 / 陈东林）

…temple. One of the ten Lama Temples and five Buddhist temples in Mount Wutai preserved in good shape. (Photo by Chen Donglin)

上图　龙泉寺。（图 / 陈东林）　**The upper**　Longquan Temple. (Photo by Chen Donglin)
中图　佛光寺东大殿。（图 / 陈东林）　**The middle**　The East Hall of Foguang Temple. (Photo by Chen Donglin)
下图　显通寺大雄宝殿。（图 / 陈东林）　**The lower**　The Main Hall of Xiangtong Temple. (Photo by Chen Donglin)

1

2

3

4

5

6

7

8

9

1. 镇风印（北魏）。（图 / 五台山） The Wind-checking Seal. (the Northern Wei Dynasty). (Photo by Mount Wutai)
2. 武则天铜像（唐）。（图 / 五台山） The bronze statue of Empress Wu Zetian. (the Tang Dynasty). (Photo by Mount Wutai)
3. 铜牛（宋）。（图 / 五台山） A Bronze Ox (the Song Dynasty). (Photo by Mount Wutai)
4. 铜铸十八臂观音（明）。（图 / 五台山） The 18-arm Guanyin in Bronze Cast. (the Ming Dynasty). (Photo by Mount Wutai)
5. 刘海戏金蟾（明）。（图 / 五台山） Liu Hai tricking the Gold Toad. (the Ming Dynasty). (Photo by Mount Wutai)
6. 金字经书（明）。（图 / 五台山） Scripture of Gilded Letters. (the Ming Dynasty). (Photo by Mount Wutai)
7. 乾隆御匾（清）。（图 / 五台山） A Board Granted by Emperor Qianlong. (the Qing Dynasty). (Photo by Mount Wutai)
8. 达摩祖师像（清）。（图 / 五台山） Statue of Bodhidharma. (the Qing Dynasty). (Photo by Mount Wutai)
9. 般若波罗蜜多心经（清）。（图 / 五台山） Prajna Paramita Heart Sutra. (the Qing Dynasty). (Photo by Mount Wutai)

佛光寺东大殿唐代彩塑像。（图 / 韩春宏）

Painted Statues of the Tang Dynasty in East Hall of Foguang Temple. (Photo by Han Chunhong)

佛光寺文殊殿明代壁画。（图 / 韩春宏）

Frescos of the Ming Dynasty in Manjusri Hall, Foguang Temple. (Photo by Han Chunhong)

中国世界遗产影像志
WORLD HERITAGE IN CHINA

自然遗产
Natural Heritage

泰　山 500
黄　山 510
庐山国家公园 518
新疆天山 530
武夷山 540
三清山国家公园 550
武陵源风景名胜区 558
九寨沟风景名胜区 566
黄龙风景名胜区 576
云南三江并流保护区 584
中国南方喀斯特 594
中国丹霞 602
澄江化石遗址 614
四川大熊猫栖息地 622

九寨沟诺日朗瀑布。（图／何世尧）
Nuorilang Waterfall in Jiuzhaigou Valley(Photo by He Shiyao)

自然遗产

刘嘉麒　中国科学院院士

自然界蕴藏着无穷无尽的奥秘，上至天文，下至地理，大至宇宙，小至核素……令人类的探索永无极致。在浩瀚无际的宇宙中，星球数以万计，直到现在，却只有地球拥有人类；在太阳系的八大行星中，地球最有生气，最有作为，是天之骄子！它朝气蓬勃，日夜运行，时而宁静，时而咆哮，蕴育着巨大的能量，是有生命的星体：岩浆是它的血液，地震是它的脉搏，火山是它的喉咙……在惊天动地的地质作用下，闹得天翻地覆，平地竖起高山，沧海变成桑田……塑造造了千姿百态的自然景观；构建了从地核、地幔到地壳，从岩石圈、水圈、生物圈、到大气圈的参天大厦，屹立于星球之林，遨游在广袤太空，养育着千奇百怪数以亿计的生灵。这些生灵来自自然，依存自然，又回归自然。自然是人类的载体。

中华大地几乎囊括了自然界的各种景观。从浩瀚的海洋到世界屋脊——青藏高原，从芦苇荡漾的湖泊、湿地到干旱荒芜的沙漠、雅丹，千山万水，峡谷洞天……保留了漫长历史的自然遗迹，展现出各种各样的美景奇观。仅就已列入世界自然遗产的 14 个具代表性的景观看，已显示出我国自然遗产的多样性、特殊性和珍贵性。

三山五岳首当其冲，被誉为“五岳之首”的泰山，代表着其它四岳兄弟：华山、衡山、恒山和嵩山，兼具自然与文化的双重身份，最早被列入世界遗产。它以雄伟壮丽的身姿和悠久的历史文化挺拔于齐鲁大地，屹立于亚洲东方，既似中华民族的象征，又如神州的守护神；它主要由古老的太古代变质岩组成，已知最老年龄达 27 亿年之久，有可能超过 30 亿年，是中国已列入世界自然遗产中资历最长者，当之无愧地被拥为“五岳独尊”。

“五岳归来不看山，黄山归来不看岳。”黄山展示了无比的神奇与魅力，可谓大自然的骄子。约 2 亿年前形成的花岗岩构筑了黄山的主体，在自然营力的雕琢下，形成了波澜起伏的山峦和气冲霄汉的峰林，在那险峻的山峰和陡峭的岩壁上，辅以挺拔的苍松和翠绿的草丛，显得格外妩媚壮丽。

江西的三清山犹如黄山的孪生兄弟，其机体也由中生代的花岗岩组成，是典型的花岗岩地貌景观。它险峻的玉京、玉华、玉虚三座山峰，犹如道教供奉的玉清、上清、太清三位天尊耸立在怀玉山之巅，故而得名三清山。

与三清山同在赣北的庐山和闽北的武夷山，不仅山清水秀，生态环境优越，是避暑胜地，更有深厚的科学内涵和文化底蕴。庐山是研究中国第四纪冰川的胜地，留下了许多科学工作者考察的足迹，吸引了历代文人墨士到那里吟诗作画，唐代诗人李白的《望庐山瀑布》写过“日照香炉生紫烟，遥看瀑布挂前川。飞流直下三千尺，疑是银河落九天。”

可见，每座山都是一幅美妙的画卷，每个景都蕴涵着生动的诗篇。人们常把美景比作画，其实景比画更美。山是画的狼毫，水是诗的墨汁，山在水里，水在山中，山水相映，触景生情，令历代文人多感叹，引无数英雄竟折腰。

如果说构筑黄山、三清山的花岗岩和构筑峨眉山的玄武岩，是地下岩浆的产物，那么，以砂岩形成的丹霞地貌、武陵源景观，由碳酸盐构筑的喀斯特地貌及九寨沟、黄龙景观，则是水的功劳。砂岩和碳酸盐都是沉积岩，是在有水的环境下形成的，从河湖到海洋，水域越大，形成的岩体也越大。当这些沉积岩出露到地表以后，水又不断侵蚀、雕琢这些岩石。可见，无论是丹霞还是喀斯特，成也有水，“败”也有水。

发源于青藏高原的怒江、澜沧江和金沙江，展示了水的神奇和力量，它们横空出世，一泻千里，在似刀切的横断山山谷中，平行排列（最近间距仅 19 公里），齐头并进达 170 余公里才各奔东西，成为缅甸萨尔温江、印支半岛湄公河和中国扬子江的上游，形成世界上罕见的“江水并流而不交汇”的“三江并流”奇特自然地理景观，是中国境内面积最大的世界遗产地，拥有丰富的地质地貌景观和生物物种，被誉为“世界生物基因库”和“天然高山花园”。

以广东丹霞山为代表的丹霞地貌，是以砂岩为载体，以红色为特征的高山峡谷，悬崖峭壁，石柱险峰等地貌景观，广泛分布于广东丹霞山、湖南崀山、福建泰宁、江西龙虎山、浙江江郎山、贵州赤水等地，染红了大半个中国。这是由中国学者用汉字命名的专业地貌术语，得到了国际同行的认同，并广泛应用于国际学术交流，是中国学者对地貌学的一个重要贡献，也体现了中国丹霞在全球地貌中的特殊地位。

湖南武陵源的擎天石柱、石塔、石林、奇峰及峡谷、沟壑……是砂岩型的另一种特殊地貌景观，在全球几乎只有那里的张家界、天子山、索溪峪有这种景观，所以，有的国际地貌学家建议，就把这种地貌叫张家界地貌。

中国的喀斯特地貌别有洞天，其分布之广，类型之多，规模之大，形态之特殊，全球少见，在整个云贵高原和西南地区，到处可以发现。为此，联合国教科文组织用“中国南方喀斯特”这样的“大包装”，把中国的喀斯特地貌囊括到世界自然遗产中，其典型代表有云南昆明的石林，重庆武隆的天生桥，贵州荔波的喀斯特原始森林、水上森林和“漏斗”森林……溶洞曲径通幽，暗河可以行舟，宽阔之处形成的天下第一洞——芙蓉洞，高达30–50米，阔约上万平方米，宛然是个天然大厦，洞壁上生长的各种姿态卷曲石、方解石和石膏晶花，更是令人眼花缭乱……从地上到地下，从整体到局部，全方位地展现出无数的神奇和奥秘。

位于四川北部的九寨沟、黄龙洞，是隐藏在深山幽谷中的闺秀。由当年名不见经传的九个藏族村寨组成的九寨沟，如今已扬名天下，成为世界瑰宝。那里虽处于青藏高原的东缘，海拔三四千米，却山川锦绣，生机盎然。从高山冰川到森林草原，从瀑布山泉到湖泊河滩，演绎着春、夏、秋、冬四季景观：冬有冰雪皑皑，夏有湖水湛蓝，春来山花烂漫，秋至层林尽染……最精彩的是九寨沟中的108个海子（小湖泊），一个海子一个姿态，一个姿态一个惊叹。与九寨沟毗邻的黄龙景区几乎全由钙华铺就，钙华滩、钙华扇、钙华台、钙华湖、钙华泉、钙华瀑布、钙华洞穴……一应俱全，其规模宏大、类型繁多、形态奇妙、色彩斑斓、环境特殊，堪称天然钙华博物馆。如果说石灰岩是形成喀斯特的母体，那么，钙华就是石灰岩吐出的乳汁。通常，钙华多形成于火山、温泉发育地区，而黄龙地区能在“冷”环境下形成如此壮观的钙华，实在罕见。

自然景观独一无二，不可复制，不能再生。它不仅陶冶情操让人们赏心悦目，具有不可估量的观赏价值，更具有丰富的科学内涵和研究价值。被列入世界自然遗产的“云南澄江化石遗址”和“四川卧龙大熊猫保护基地”，从不同角度揭示了生物和人的生存演变及其与自然的关系。云南澄江化石再现了5亿多年前寒武纪生物大爆发的场面，在同一时代，同一地点发现多种不同门类生物集聚在一起，这对于达尔文的生物进化论是一个重要挑战，启迪人们思考生物的进化可能是多途径的。大熊猫是当今世界最稀缺、最珍贵的动物之一，要保护它就要了解它生存的环境，揭开大熊猫故乡——卧龙的迷。

从开天辟地的远古时期，到生机盎然的新生代，地球已度过约46亿年，岩石是它的密码，化石是它的档案，每个景点都有每个景点的故事，每处遗迹都是一部神秘的天书。它们记载了地球的前世今生，诠释了大自然的变化万千。

Natural Heritage

Liu Jiaqi, academician of the Chinese Academy of Sciences

Nature abounds with mysteries: from astronomy to geography, from boundless universe to tiny atoms..Due to the existence of those mysteries mankind is forever in exploration. The vast universe contains thousands of planets and the earth is the only one occupied by human beings; among the eight planets of the solar system, the earth is the most energetic and most promising, uniquely blessed by heaven. It is full of vitality, and revolves day and night; sometimes it is tranquil, sometimes it roars. It harbors boundless energy as well as life: Flowing lava is its blood; earthquakes show its pulse while volcanoes are its throat…

Powerful geological processes have brought about numerous changes on earth—such as mountains rising from level ground and oceans turning into farmland. As a result, the earth has gradually come into being, from core to mantle to crust, from lithosphere and hydrosphere to biosphere and atmosphere, and natural views of all sorts are fashioned on the surface of this globe. The earth now stands tall among planets, moving in the vast universe and sustaining countless creatures of all sorts. These creatures come from nature, depend on nature, and return to nature in the end. Nature is the supporter of mankind.

We can see nearly every kind of topography in China: from vast ocean to the roof of the world—the Qinghai-Tibet Plateau, from lakes and wetland abounding with swaying reeds to dry and barren desert and Danxia landforms, from endless mountains and rivers to numerous canyons and caves. In the vast land of China the remains of nature's long process of change are preserved, and various beauties and wonders are on display. The fourteen representative natural views listed on the world natural heritage list are sufficient to illustrate the diversity, particularity and rarity of the natural heritage of China.

Let's begin with the well-known three mountains and five mounts. Mount Taishan is acclaimed as "the head of the five mounts" and well represents the other four, namely Mount Hua, Mount Heng (衡), Mount Heng (恒), and Mount Song. It is distinguished for its imposing and magnificent posture as well as its long history and culture and so enjoys double identity as heritage of both nature and culture. It is justifiably the first one listed on the world heritage. This renowned mount in Shandong Province rises in the east of Asia and may be taken as the symbol of the Chinese as well as the patron god of China. Its body is mainly made up of metamorphic rocks of the Achaean era and the oldest rock is as old as 2.7 billion years (and possibly over 3 billion years old) and is undoubtedly the most senior one among those entering the world heritage. So Mount Taishan fully earns its distinction as "pre-eminent among the five famous mounts" and its supreme status has not only drawn millions of pilgrims, but also emperors of different dynasties, who ascended the peak of Mount Taishan, called Yuhuangding, to worship this grand mount. Confucius once ascended Yuhuangding and claimed that from the summit the whole world was tiny; Du Fu, the celebrated Tang poet, once composed memorable lines in his tour of Mount Taishan, wondering "how I long to reach the mountaintop of this paragon, surrounding mountains will appear so small then." Today's visitors to Mount Taishan will identify with the insights of both observers.

Though the three famous mountains that complement the five famous mounts may be understood differently by Chinese, most people think they refer to Mount Huangshan, Mount Lushan and Mountain Yandang. All of them possess matchless glamour and are deemed paragons of nature.

The body of Mount Huangshan is made up of granite formed

about 200 million years ago. In the long process the forces of nature have wrought this mount into undulating mountain ranges and peaks towering into clouds. The precipitous peaks and steep cliffs adorned by straight pine trees and green grass are charming and magnificent; the fine ecosystem of this mount is visible under blue sky most of time and but buried occasionally in a fantastic cloud plain. One cannot help comparing Mount Huangshan to a natural painting or a piece of fairyland fascinating to mortal beings. No wonder Xu Xiake, the traveler-geographer of the Ming Dynasty, left us famous lines remarking that he "will no longer be tempted by ordinary mountains after visiting the five famous mounts, and unimpressed by the beauty of the five famous mounts after touring Mount Huangshan."

Mount Sanqingshan in Jiangxi Province is also made up of granites of Mesozoic time and takes on the typical granite topography. So it may be taken as the twin brother of Mount Huangshan. The three precipitous peaks of this mount (Yujing, Yuhua and Yuxu) are just like statues of the three celestial beings worshipped in Taoism (namely Yuqing, Shangqing and Taiqing) standing on the peak of Mount Huaiyu, and so it won the name Sanqing.

Mount Lushan (which is also located in the north of Jiangxi Province) and Mountain Wuyi in the north of Fujian Province are not only well-known for their superior ecosystems (which render both places summer resorts), the landscape of green mountains and clean water, but also for their profound scientific connotations and cultural deposits. Mount Lushan is a famous spot for studying the fourth glacial period of China and many scientists have gone there to do field work. Many men of letters have also been drawn there and left many poems and paintings about this mount. The most famous poem is *Cataract on Mount Lushan* by the celebrated Tang poet Li Bai, "The sunlit Censer peak exhales a wreath of cloud, Like an upturned stream the cataract sounds loud. //Its torrent dashes down three thousand feet from high, //As if the Silver River fell from azure sky." And in another poem about Mount Lushan, the same poet writes, "The hanging stream falls three thousand feet, and night and day the torrent dashes miles and miles. Like lightning the flow runs, a vague rainbow appearing now and then." Those well-turned lines are still passed down generation after generation.

Every mountain is a beautiful painting while every view evokes beautiful lines. We always compare beautiful sceneries to paintings, but they are even more beautiful than paintings. Mountains are the paintbrushes, while water is the ink for writing the poems. Mountains are reflected in water, and water abounds in mountains. The mountains and water co-exist and complement each other, inspiring famous lines from men of letters and winning the admiration of countless heroes.

If we say Mount Huangshan and Mount Sanqingshan of granite and Mount Emei of basalt are ultimately the result of lava from underground, Danxia landforms of sandstone and the Wulingyuan landscape and Karst landform of carbonate rocks together with the landscapes of Jiuzhaigou and Huanglong show us the contributions of water. Sandstone and carbonate are both sedimentary rocks formed in a water environment. From rivers and lakes to seas and oceans, the larger the body of water, the larger the rock formed. When those sedimentary rocks emerge above water, water begins to play the role of a powerful geologic agent, corroding and carving those rocks. Therefore, whether in Danxia landform or Karst landform, water plays its role in their formation as well as their corrosion.

Universal order finds expression in everything and nature is a harmonious chain of being. Nujiang River, Lancang River and Jinsha River rising in the Qinghai-Tibet Plateau, the water tower of the world, illustrate the magic and power of water. They suddenly rise in the snowland, run parallel in the deeply-cleft canyons of Hengduan Mountains for distances of up to 170 kilometers, though in some places they are as little as 19 kilometers apart. Then the three magnificent rivers take their own courses and flow into the Salween River in Burma, the Mekong River of Indochina and the Yangtze River in China respectively. This is the singular natural philosophical landscape of "the parallel flowing of three rivers"-the three rivers run parallel without converging-a rare view in the world. This area is the largest among the world heritage zones in China and abounds in geomorphologic landscape and species and so has been called the "the Biological Gene Pool" and "natural Alpine Garden".

The Danxia landform represented by Mount Danxia of Guangdong Province is constituted by sandstone and is red in hue, and the particular landscapes include canyons in high mountains, precipices and cliffs, stone pillars and steep peaks. This landform is widely distributed in Mount Danxia of Guangdong Province, Mount Lang in Hunan Province, Taining in Fujian Province, Mount Longhu in Jiangxi Province, Mount Jianglang in Zhejiang Province and Chishui of Guizhou Province; so half of China is dyed red. Danxia is a Chinese professional term in geomorphology named by Chinese scientists and has won international peer recognition and is widely used in international academic exchange. This fact reveals the special position of Chinese Danxia landform in world morphology.

Another special landform of sandstone is epitomized in towering stone pillars, towers, forests, peaks, canyons and gullies of Wulingyuan, Hunan Province. This landscape exists exclusively in Zhangjiajie, Tianzishan, and Suoxiyu of this region, so some foreign geomorphology specialists propose that this should be called Zhangjiajie landform.

The Karst landform of China is unique in the whole world in its wide distribution, large diversity, high scale and singularity in shape. It is ubiquitous in the whole Yunnan-Guizhou Plateau and the southwest of China. So UNESCO uses the umbrella name of "the Karst landform in South China" to cover various Karst landscapes in China in the world natural heritage. The representatives of this landform include: the stone forest in Kunming, Yunnan Province, the natural bridge in Wolong, Chongqing; the Karst primeval forest, water forest, and funnel forest in Libo, Guizhou Province. In those spots, the karst caves usually lead to an enchanting view; the underground river can bear canoes; Cave Furong, the No. 1 Cave of China, formed in a spacious area, is 30 to 50 meters tall with an area of about ten thousand square meters. It is just like a dazzling natural mansion with curling stones in various shapes, and calcite and crystallized plaster flowers on its interior. In every quarter, no matter whether above or below ground, no matter whether you view the cave as a whole or partially, you will discover countless wonders and mysteries in this gigantic mansion.

Jiuzhaigou and Huanglong are hidden in high mountains and deep valleys in the north of Sichuan Province like two young ladies free from gazers' eyes. Jiuzhaigou, made up of nine Tibetan villages that originally were little known to the outside, is now deemed a treasure in the world and enjoys much popularity.

Though it is located on the east border of the Qinghai-Tibet Plateau and 3,000 to 4,000 meters above sea level, the mountains and rivers there are full of vigor and vitality and extremely beautiful. From mountain glaciers to forests and grasslands, from cataracts and springs in the mountains to lakes and shoals in the valleys, you can see views of the four seasons: the snow-capped areas reflects winter, the azure blue water in the lakes resembles autumn, the blooming flowers encapsulate spring while the deep-dyed woods remind you of fall. The most wonderful part of Jiuzhaigou has to be the 108 small lakes, each with a unique shape winning admiration from amazed visitors. Huanglong is adjacent to Jiuzhaigou, and the whole area here is paved with travertine, no matter whether it is shoals, fans, terraces, lakes, springs, cataracts or caves. The grand scale, large diversity, unique shapes of those various bright-colored travertine landforms in a unique environment render this area a natural museum of travertine. If we say limestone is the mother body of Karst landforms, travertine ought to be regarded as milk produced by this mother. Travertine usually appears in volcano or hot spring areas and so the spectacular travertine topography in the cool environment of Huanglong is really rare.

Natural views are unique and cannot be copied or reproduced. They are not only spellbinding and breed fine sentiments due to their invaluable visual effects, but also have rich scientific connotations and research value. Yunnan Chengjiang Fossil Site and Sichuan Wolong Ginat Panda Sanctuaries on the list of world natural heritage are two examples revealing the process of survival evolution of species and man and their relationships to nature. The fossils in Chengjiang portray the scene of biological outbreak in the Cambrian period over 500 million years ago. The assemblage of creatures of different orders in the same place in the same era poses a serious challenge to Darwin's theory of evolution. This phenomenon inspires us to assume that the evolution of species may be performed through different channels. Giant panda is one of the scarcest and rarest animals in current world, and protecting this endangered species involves understanding the living environment of giant Panda and solving the mystery of Wolong-the habitat of giant Panda.

The earth has undergone 4.6 billion years from its birth in ancient times to the Cenozoic era of life today. Rocks are the key to decode this globe, while fossils are its files. Every spot has its own story and every relic is a mysterious book of nature for us to read. These sites record the history of this planet from prehistoric times to the present age and interpret the metamorphosis of nature. What we seek to do today is to adorn the beautiful land and add more beauty to it.

中国世界遗产影像志

泰山

WORLD HERITAGE IN CHINA

Mount Taishan

泰山日出。（图 / 宫正）

Sunrise in Mount Taishan. (Photo by Gong Zheng)

中国世界遗产影像志

WORLD HERITAGE IN CHINA

Mount Taishan 泰　山

近两千年来，庄严神圣的泰山一直是帝王朝拜的对象。山中的人文杰作与自然景观完美和谐地融合在一起。泰山一直是中国艺术家和学者的精神源泉，是古代中国文明和信仰的象征。

——世界遗产委员会评价

The sacred Mount Taishan ('shan' means 'mountain') was the object of an imperial cult for nearly 2,000 years, and the artistic masterpieces found there are in perfect harmony with the natural landscape. It has always been a source of inspiration for Chinese artists and scholars and symbolizes ancient Chinese civilizations and beliefs.

——World Heritage Committee Evaluation

泰山之巅。（图 / 侯贺良）

The top of Mount Taishan. (Photo by Hou Heliang)

泰山十八盘。（图 / 侯贺良）

The Eighteen Hairpin Bends of Mount Taishan. (Photo by Hou Heliang)

上图　泰山大观峰上唐代摩崖《纪泰山铭》石刻。（图 / 谭明）

The upper　The cliff inscription *Ji Taishan Ming* of the Tang Dynasty on Daguan Peak, Mount Taishan. (Photo by Tan Ming)

下图　经石峪。（图 / 谭明）

The lower　Jingshi Valley. (Photo by Tan Ming)

泰山晚霞奇观。（图 / 张仁东）

Rosy clouds at dusk , Mount Taishan. (Photo by Zhang Rendong)

宋代壁画《泰山神启跸回銮图》局部。（图 / 侯贺良）

God of Mount Taishan Starting and Ending his Cruise of the Mountain(part) of the Song Dynasty. (Photo by Hou Heliang)

中国世界遗产影像志

黄山

WORLD HERITAGE IN CHINA

Mount Huangshan

黄山夜色。（图 / 张永富）

Mount Huangshan at night. (Photo by Zhang Yongfu)

黄 山

黄山被誉为“震旦国中第一奇山”，在中国历史上的鼎盛时期，通过文学和艺术的形式（例如 16 世纪中叶的“山”、“水”风格）受到广泛的赞誉。今天，黄山以其壮丽的景色——生长在花岗岩石上的奇松和浮现在云海中的怪石而著称，对于从四面八方来到这个风景胜地的游客、诗人、画家和摄影家而言，黄山具有永恒的魅力。

——世界遗产委员会评价

Huangshan, known as 'the loveliest mountain of China', was acclaimed through art and literature during a good part of Chinese history (e.g. the Shanshui 'mountain and water' style of the mid-16th century). Today it holds the same fascination for visitors, poets, painters and photographers who come on pilgrimage to the site, which is renowned for its magnificent scenery made up of many granite peaks and rocks emerging out of a sea of clouds.

——World Heritage Committee Evaluation

黄山佛光。（图 / 张永富）
Buddhist Halo of Mount Huangshan. (Photo by Zhang Yongfu)

黄山天都峰。（图 / 张永富）
Tiandu Peak of Mount Huangshan. (Photo by Zhang Yongfu)

黄山之石。（图 / 陈勃）

Rocks of Mount Huangshan. (Photo by Chen Bo)

黄山迎客松。（图 / 张永富）

The Guest-Greeting Pine Tree of Mount Huangshan. (Photo by Zhang Yongfu)

中国
世界遗产
影像志

WORLD HERITAGE IN CHINA

庐山国家公园

Lushan National Park

庐山含鄱口日出。（图 / 游云谷）

The Sunrise at Hanbokou in Mount Lushan. (Photo by You Yungu)

Lushan National Park

庐山国家公园

江西庐山是中华文明的发祥地之一。这里的佛教和道教庙观，与体现儒家思想的典型建筑（最杰出的大师曾在此授课）一起，完全融汇在美不胜收的自然景观之中，赋予无数艺术家以灵感，而这些艺术家开创了中国文化中对于自然的审美方式。

——世界遗产委员会评价

Mount Lushan, in Jiangxi, is one of the spiritual centres of Chinese civilization. Buddhist and Taoist temples, along with landmarks of Confucianism, where the most eminent masters taught, blend effortlessly into a strikingly beautiful landscape which has inspired countless artists who developed the aesthetic approach to nature found in Chinese culture.

——World Heritage Committee Evaluation

庐山瀑布云。（图 / 欧阳萍）

The cataract clouds of Mount Lushan. (Photo by Ouyang Ping)

庐山如琴湖。(图 / 倪益瑾)

Ruqin Lake of Mount Lushan. (Photo by Ni Yijin)

庐山三叠泉。（图 / 李子青）
Three Tiled Springs of Mount Lushan. (Photo by Li Ziqing)

左上　白鹿洞书院内朱熹塑像。（图 / 宫正）

Upper left　The Statue of Zhu Xi in White Deer Cavern Academy. (Photo by Gong Zheng)

右上　古刹西林寺和东林寺古塔。（图 / 李子青）

Upper right　The ancient pagodas of the time-honored Xilin and Donglin Temples. (Photo by Li Ziqing)

左下　庐山—牯岭别墅度假区。（图 / 刘力群）

Lower left　Guling Villa Resort,Mount Lushan. (Photo by Liu Liqun)

右下　庐山仙人洞。（图 / 宗玉珍）

Lower right　The Immortal Cavern of Mount Lushan. (Photo by Zong Yuzhen)

明画家沈周绘《庐山高图》。(图 / 李子青)

Lofty Mount Lu painted by Shen Zhou of the Ming Dynasty. (Photo by Li Ziqing)

明代著名画家唐寅绘《匡庐图》。（图 / 李子青）

Mount Lu painted by the famous painter Tang Yin of the Ming Dynasty. (Photo by Li Ziqing)

北宋书法家米芾书白居易《大林寺桃花》。（图 / 李子青）
The Handwriting of Mi Fu, calligrapher of the Northern Song Dynasty, *The Peach Blossoms in Dalin Temple,* composed by Bai Juyi. (Photo by Li Ziqing)

人間四月
芳菲盡山
寺桃花始
盛開長恨

中国世界遗产影像志

新疆天山

WORLD HERITAGE IN CHINA

Xinjiang Tianshan

天山博格达峰与天池。（图 / 李学亮）

Bogda Peak and Tian Chi (Heaven's Pool). (Photo by Li Xueliang)

新疆天山包括四个区域——托木尔、喀拉峻—库尔德宁、巴音布鲁克及博格达，总面积 606,833 公顷。它们是中亚地区天山山系的组成部分，也是世界上最大的山系之一。新疆天山具有独特的地理风貌以及美丽的风景区，包括皑皑白雪、雪山、冰川覆盖的雪峰、寥无人迹的森林草地，清澈的河流、湖泊和红色地层的峡谷。这些景色与邻近的广袤沙漠地貌形成强烈的对比，展示炎热和寒冷、干燥和湿润、荒寂和繁茂两种环境的巨大视觉差异。遗产地的地貌和生态系统从上新世纪保存至今，是持续的生物和生态演化历程的杰出范例。遗产地延伸至塔克拉玛干沙漠——世界上面积最大、海拔最高的沙漠之一，以巨大的沙丘地貌和严重的沙尘暴闻名于世。而且，新疆天山还是一些特有的遗存植物物种（有些是稀有、濒危物种）的重要繁衍地。

——世界遗产委员会评价

Xinjiang Tianshan comprises four components — Tomur, Kalajun-Kuerdening, Bayinbukuke and Bogda — that total 606,833 hectares. They are part of the Tianshan mountain system of Central Asia, one of the largest mountain ranges in the world. Xinjiang Tianshan presents unique physical geographic features and scenically beautiful areas including spectacular snow and snowy mountains glacier-capped peaks, undisturbed forests and meadows, clear rivers and lakes and red bed canyons. These landscapes contrast with the vast adjacent desert landscapes, creating a striking visual contrast between hot and cold environments, dry and wet, desolate and luxuriant. The landforms and ecosystems of the site have been preserved since the Pliocene epoch and present an outstanding example of ongoing biological and ecological evolutionary processes. The site also extends into the Taklimakan Desert, one of the world's largest and highest deserts, known for its large dune forms and great dust storms. Xinjiang Tianshan is moreover an important habitat for endemic and relic flora species, some rare and endangered.

——World Heritage Committee Evaluation

天山南坡丹霞地貌。（图 / 李学亮）
Danxia landscape at the south slope of Tianshan. (Photo by Li Xueliang)

托木尔冰川。（图 / 郝沛）

Tomur glacier. (Photo by Hao Pei)

天山雪莲。（图 / 晏先）
Tianshan snow lotus. (Photo by Yan Xian)

巴音布鲁克九曲十八弯。（图 / 郝沛）

Bayinbuluke Nine Curves and Eighteen Bends. (Photo by Hao Pei)

天山喀拉峻草原马群。（图 / 李学亮）

Horses at Tianshan Kalajun grassland. (Photo by Li Xueliang)

中国世界遗产影像志

武夷山

WORLD HERITAGE IN CHINA

Mount Wuyi

画面右侧为武夷山著名的大王峰，左侧远山为玉女峰，中间为铁板嶂，九曲溪把玉女峰和大王峰分隔。（图 / 胡国钦）

On the right is the famous Dawang Peak of Mt. Wuyi; the distant mountain on the left is Yunu Peak, and in the middle is Tiebanzhang. Nine Bend River separates Yunv Peak and Dawang Peak. (Photo by Hu Guoqin)

Mount Wuyi 武夷山

武夷山脉是中国东南部最负盛名的生物多样性保护区，也是大量古代孑遗植物的避难所，其中许多生物为中国所特有。九曲溪两岸峡谷秀美，寺院庙宇众多，但其中也有不少早已成为废墟。该地区为唐宋理学的发展和传播提供了良好的地理环境，自 11 世纪以来，理教对东亚地区文化产生了相当深刻的影响。公元前 1 世纪时，汉朝统治者在程村附近建立了一处较大的行政首府，厚重坚实的围墙环绕四周，极具考古价值。

——世界遗产委员会评价

Mount Wuyi is the most outstanding area for biodiversity conservation in south-east China and a refuge for a large number of ancient, relict species, many of them endemic to China. The serene beauty of the dramatic gorges of the Nine Bend River, with its numerous temples and monasteries, many now in ruins, provided the setting for the development and spread of neo-Confucianism, which has been influential in the cultures of East Asia since the 11th century. In the 1st century B.C. a large administrative capital was built at nearby Chengcun by the Han Dynasty rulers. Its massive walls enclose an archaeological site of great significance.

——World Heritage Committee Evaluation

武夷九曲大拐弯。（图 / 胡国钦）

The Big Bend Of Nine Bend River in Mt. Wuyi. (Photo by Hu Guoqin)

武夷山九曲溪。（图 / 胡国钦）
Nine Bend River of Mt. Wuyi. (Photo by Hu Guoqin)

左上　武夷宫。（图 / 胡国钦）

Upper left　Wuyi Palace. (Photo by Hu Guoqin)

右上　登天游峰必经之亭。（图 / 胡国钦）

Upper Right　The pavilion on the way to Tianyou Peak. (Photo by Hu Guoqin)

左下　九曲溪。（图 / 胡国钦）

Lower left　Nine Bend River. (Photo by Hu Guoqin)

右下　晒布岩。又名仙掌峰，是武夷山典型的丹霞奇峰。（图 / 胡国钦）

Lower right　Shaibu Cliff, also named Xianzhang Peak, is a Danxia Peak typical of Mt. Wuyi. (Photo by Hu Guoqin)

左上　珍稀动物金斑喙凤蝶。（图 / 胡国钦）

Upper left　Teinopalpus aureus, a kind of precious butterfly. (Photo by Hu Guoqin)

右上　国家一级保护植物南方红豆杉。（图 / 胡国钦）

Upper right　Southern Chinese yew, the national first class protection plant. (Photo by Hu Guoqin)

左下　断尾小猴。（图 / 胡国钦）

Lower left　King of stump-tailed monkey. (Photo by Hu Guoqin)

右下　锦鸡。（图 / 胡国钦）

Lower right　Golden pheasant. (Photo by Hu Guoqin)

武夷锦绣禅茶园。（图/胡国钦）
Jinxiu Zen Tea Park at Mt. Wuyi. (Photo by Hu Guoqin)

中国世界遗产影像志

WORLD HERITAGE IN CHINA

三清山国家公园

Mount Sanqingshan National Park

三清山日出。（图/舒剑）

Sunrise in Mount Sanqingshan. (Photo by Shu Jian)

Mount Sanqingshan National Park
三清山国家公园

总面积 22,950 平方公顷的三清山国家公园，坐落于江西省东北地区的怀玉山脉西部。它以造型奇特、险峻陡峭的石柱与山峰为特征的自然景观被列入世界遗产名录：有许多貌似人形与动物轮廓的 48 座花岗岩山峰和 89 座花岗岩石柱，而高 1,817 米、自然风景优美的怀玉山则以丰富的花岗岩造型、多种植被、远近变化的景观和十分特殊的气候奇观而著称。这个地区属于亚热带季风气候与海洋气候的交汇区，形成了亚热带景观的温带森林岛屿，拥有大片的森林，众多的瀑布、湖泊和泉水，其中一些瀑布高达 60 米。

——世界遗产委员会评价

A 22,950 ha property located in the west of the Huaiyu mountain range in the northeast of Jiangxi Province (in the east of central China) has been inscribed for its exceptional scenic quality,marked by the concentration of fantastically shaped pillars and peaks:48 granite peaks and 89 granite pillars,many of which resemble human or animal silhouettes.The natural beauty of the 1,817 metre high Mount Huaiyu is further enhanced by the juxtaposition of granite features with the vegetation and particular meteorological conditions which make for an ever-changing and arresting landscape with bright on clouds and white rainbows.The area is subject to a combination of subtropical monsoonal and maritime influences and forms anisland of temperate forest above the surrounding subtropical landscape. It also features forests and numerous waterfalls,some of them 60 metres in height,lakes and springs.

——World Heritage Committee Evaluation

三清山司春女神。（图 / 舒剑）
Oriental Spring Goddess of Mount Sanqingshan. (Photo by Shu Jian)

三清山之树。（图 / 陈长芬）

Trees on Mount Sanqingshan. (Photo by Chen Changfen)

三清山云海。（图 / 舒剑）

The sea of clouds in Mount Sanqingshan. (Photo by Shu Jian)

中国
世界遗产
影像志

WORLD HERITAGE IN CHINA

Wulingyuan Scenic and Historic Interest Area

武陵源风景名胜区

天子山之晨光初照。（图 / 茹遂初）

Tianzishan at Dawn. (Photo by Ru Suichu)

Wulingyuan Scenic and Historic Interest Area
武陵源风景名胜区

武陵源景色奇丽壮观，位于中国湖南省境内，连绵26,000多公顷，景区内最独特的景观是3,000余座尖细的砂岩柱和砂岩峰，大部分都200余米高。在峰峦之间，沟壑、峡谷纵横，溪流、池塘和瀑布随处可见，景区内还有40多个石洞和两座天然形成的巨大石桥。除了迷人的自然景观，该地区还因庇护着大量濒临灭绝的动植物物种而引人注目。

——世界遗产委员会评价

A spectacular area stretching over more than 26,000 ha in China's Hunan Province, the site is dominated by more than 3,000 narrow sandstone pillars and peaks, many over 200 m high. Between the peaks lie ravines and gorges with streams, pools and waterfalls, some 40 caves, and two large natural bridges. In addition to the striking beauty of the landscape, the region is also noted for the fact that it is home to a number of endangered plant and animal species.

——World Heritage Committee Evaluation

张家界石峰。（图 / 李建惠）
Rock peaks in Zhanjiajie. (Photo by Li Jianhui)

张家界景点之“梦笔生花”。（图 / 杨树田）

"Meng Bi Sheng Hua", a famous scenic spot in Zhangjiajie. (Photo by Yang Shutian)

武陵源天子山之春。(图 / 何世尧)

Spring of Tianzishan, Wulingyuan. (Photo by He Shiyao)

中国 世界遗产 影像志

WORLD HERITAGE IN CHINA

Jiuzhaigou Valley Scenic and Historic Interest Area

九寨沟风景名胜区

九寨沟火花海。（图 / 王达军）
Spark Lake of Jiuzhaigou Valley. (Photo by Wang Dajun)

Jiuzhaigou Valley Scenic and Historic Interest Area
九寨沟风景名胜区

九寨沟位于四川省北部，连绵超过 72,000 公顷，曲折狭长的九寨沟山谷海拔 4,800 多米，因而形成了一系列多种森林生态系统。壮丽的景色因一系列狭长的圆锥状喀斯特地貌和壮观的瀑布而更加充满生趣。山谷中现存约 140 种鸟类，还有许多濒临灭绝的动植物物种，包括大熊猫和四川扭角羚。

——世界遗产委员会评价

Stretching over 72,000 ha.in the northern part of Sichuan Province, the jagged Jiuzhaigou valley reaches a height of more than 4,800 m, thus comprising a series of diverse forest ecosystems. Its superb landscapes are particularly interesting for their series of narrow conic karst land forms and spectacular waterfalls. Some 140 bird species also inhabit the valley, as well as a number of endangered plant and animal species, including the giant panda and the Sichuan takin.

——World Heritage Committee Evaluation

九寨沟长海。（图 / 王达军）
Long Lake of Jiuzhaigou Valley. (Photo by Wang Dajun)

九寨沟树正群海。（图 / 王达军）

Shuzheng Lakes of Jiuzhaigou Valley. (Photo by Wang Dajun)

九寨沟五花海之鳄鱼嘴。（图 / 王达军）

Crocodile Mouth in Five Flower Lake of Jiuzhaigou Valley. (Photo by Wang Dajun)

冬天的诺日朗瀑布。（图 / 周梅生）

Nuorilang Waterfall in Winter. (Photo by Zhou Meisheng)

中国世界遗产影像志

黄龙风景名胜区

WORLD HERITAGE IN CHINA

Huanglong Scenic and Historic Interest Area

黄龙钙华彩池。（图 / 卞志武）

Calcareous Multicolored Pond in Huanglong. (Photo by Bian Zhiwu)

中国
世界遗产
影像志

WORLD HERITAGE IN CHINA

Huanglong Scenic and Historic Interest Area

黄龙风景名胜区

黄龙风景名胜区，位于四川省西北部，是由众多雪峰和中国最东边的冰川组成的山谷。除了高山景观，人们还可以在这里发现各种不同的森林生态系统，以及壮观的石灰岩构造、瀑布和温泉。这一地区还生存着许多濒临灭绝的动物，包括大熊猫和四川疣鼻金丝猴。

——世界遗产委员会评价

Situated in the north-west of Sichaun Province, the Huanglong valley is made up of snow-capped peaks and the easternmost of all the Chinese glaciers. In addition to its mountain landscape, diverse forest ecosystems can be found, as well as spectacular limestone formations, waterfalls and hot springs. The area also has a population of endangered animals, including the giant panda and the Sichuan golden snub-nosed monkey.

——World Heritage Committee Evaluation

黄龙五彩池冬景。（图 / 杨元惺）

Multi-Colored Pond at Huanglong in winter. (Photo by Yang Yuanxing)

黄龙争艳池。（图 / 王达军）

Flamboyant Pond at Huanglong. (Photo by Wang Dajun)

钙华滩流金沙铺地。（图 / 卞志武）
Golden Sand Pavement. (Photo by Bian Zhiwu)

黄龙五彩池。（图 / 王达军）
Multi-Colored Pond in Huanglong. (Photo by Wang Dajun)

中国世界遗产影像志

WORLD HERITAGE IN CHINA

Three Parallel Rivers of Yunnan Protected Areas

云南三江并流保护区

金沙江第一拐。（图 / 陆江涛）

The first turn in Jinsha River. (Photo by Lu Jiangtao)

中国世界遗产影像志

WORLD HERITAGE IN CHINA

Three Parallel Rivers of Yunnan Protected Areas
云南三江并流保护区

三江并流自然景观位于云南省西北山区的三江国家公园内，包括八大片区，面积 170 万公顷，是亚洲三条著名河流的上游地段，金沙江（长江上游）、澜沧江（湄公河上游）和怒江（萨尔温江上游）三条大江在此区域内并行奔腾，由北向南，途径 3,000 多米深的峡谷和海拔 6,000 多米的冰山雪峰。这里是中国生物多样性最丰富的区域，同时也是世界上温带生物多样性最丰富的区域。

——世界遗产委员会评价

Consisting of eight geographical clusters of protected areas within the boundaries of the Three Parallel Rivers National Park, in the mountainous north-west of Yunnan Province, the 1.7 million hectare site features sections of the upper reaches of three of the great rivers of Asia: the Yangtze (Jinsha), Mekong (Lancang) and Salween (Nujiang) run roughly parallel, north to south, through steep gorges which, in places, are 3,000 m deep and are bordered by glaciated peaks more than 6,000 m high. The site is an epicentre of Chinese biodiversity. It is also one of the richest temperate regions of the world in terms of biodiversity.

——World Heritage Committee Evaluation

德钦云岭澜沧江峡谷。（图 / 陆江涛）

Lancang River Gorge in Deqin Yunling Ranges. (Photo by Lu Jiangtao)

三江并流（沿约北纬 27 度 20 分鸟瞰），从左至右分别为怒江、澜沧江、金沙江。（图 / 李丽川）

Three Parallel Rivers (an aerial view along approximately 27°20//N).The three rivers are Nujiang, Lancang and Jinsha River from left to right. (Photo by Li Lichuan)

迪庆州德钦县卡瓦格博羊年祭典。（图 / 陆江涛）

The sacrificial rites in Sheep Year of Kawagebo in Deqin County, Diqing Autonomous Region. (Photo by Lu Jiangtao)

迪庆州德钦县书松尼姑寺分发午餐。（图 / 陆江涛）

Shusong Nunnery in Shusong, Deqin County distributing lunches. (Photo by Lu Jiangtao)

迪庆小中甸草原上的狼毒草，这是香格里拉独有的一道草原景观。（图 / 陆江涛）
Euphorbia herb in Xiaozhongdian prairie, Diqing Autonomous Region. A unique prairie scene in Shangri-la. (Photo by Lu Jiangtao)

中国
世界遗产
影像志

WORLD HERITAGE IN CHINA

South China Karst

中国南方喀斯特

贵州荔波喀斯特 · 拉桥峰丛。（图 /Sophoto）

Laqiao Peak Cluster, Libo Karst of Guizhou Province. (Photo by Sophoto)

South China Karst
中国南方喀斯特

中国南方喀斯特地区主要分布在云南、贵州和广西等省份，占地面积超过 50 万平方公里。中国南部喀斯特地貌丰富多样，富于变幻，举世无双。这处遗产呈连续性分布，主要可分为三个区域：荔波喀斯特、石林喀斯特和武隆喀斯特。中国南方喀斯特地形是全球湿润热带及亚热带喀斯特地形的典型代表。石林喀斯特被誉为自然奇观，是世界级参照标准。石林包括由含白云石的石灰石构成的乃古石林和在湖泊中生成的苏依山石林。同其他喀斯特地形相比，石林喀斯特的石峰更加丰富多彩，形状和颜色也更富于变化。荔波喀斯特的特点是锥形和塔形地貌，构成了独特、美丽的风景，同样是同类型喀斯特地貌的世界级标准。武隆喀斯特因其巨大的石灰坑、天然桥梁和天然洞穴而列入世界遗产。

——世界遗产委员会评价

The South China Karst region extends over a surface of half a million km^2 lying mainly in Yunnan, Guizhou and Guangxi provinces. It represents one of the world's most spectacular examples of humid tropical to subtropical karst landscapes. The stone forests of Shilin are considered superlative natural phenomena and a world reference with a wider range of pinnacle shapes than other karst landscapes with pinnacles, and a higher diversity of shapes and changing colours. The cone and tower karsts of Libo, also considered the world reference site for these types of karst, form a distinctive and beautiful landscape. Wulong Karst has been inscribed for its giant dolines (sinkholes), natural bridges and caves.

——World Heritage Committee Evaluation

云南石林。（图 / 杨新民）
Yunnan stone forest. (Photo by Yang Xinmin)

上图　贵州荔波喀斯特・小七孔鸳鸯湖。（图 /Sophoto）　**The upper**　Little Seven-hole Mandarin Duck Lake, Libo karst of Guizhou Province. (Photo by Sophoto)
下图　重庆武隆。（图 /Sophoto）　**The lower**　Chongqing Wulong. (Photo by Sophoto)

重庆武隆天坑。（图 / 卞志武）

Wulong Sinkhole, Chongqing. (Photo by Bian Zhiwu)

云南石林。（图 / 何世尧）

Yunnan stone forest. (Photo by He Shiyao)

中国 世界遗产 影像志

中国丹霞

WORLD HERITAGE IN CHINA

China Danxia

广东丹霞山长老峰。（图 / 杨志）

The Zhanglao Peak of Mt. Danxia in Guangdong Province. (Photo by Yang Zhi)

China Danxia
中国丹霞

中国丹霞是中国境内由陆相红色砂砾岩在内生力量（包括隆起）和外来力量（包括风化和侵蚀）共同作用下形成的各种地貌景观的总称。这一遗产包括中国西南部亚热带地区的 6 处遗址。它们的共同特点是壮观的红色悬崖以及一系列侵蚀地貌，包括雄伟的天然岩柱、岩塔、沟壑、峡谷和瀑布等。这里跌宕起伏的地貌，对保护包括约 400 种稀有或受威胁物种在内的亚热带常绿阔叶林和许多动植物起到了重要作用。

——世界遗产委员会评价

China Danxia is the name given in China to landscapes developed on continental red terrigenous sedimentary beds influenced by endogenous forces (including uplift) and exogenous forces (including weathering and erosion). The inscribed site comprises six areas found in the subtropical zone of south-west China. They are characterized by spectacular red cliffs and a range of erosional landforms, including dramatic natural pillars, towers, ravines, valleys and waterfalls. These rugged landscapes have helped to conserve subtropical broad-leaved evergreen forests, and host many species of flora and fauna, about 400 of which are considered rare or threatened.

——World Heritage Committee Evaluation

江西龙虎山仙桃峰。（图 / 杨志）
Xiantao Peak at Mt. Dragon and Tiger in Jiangxi Province. (Photo by Yang Zhi)

湖南崀山·八角寨。(图 / 杨志)
Bajiao Village, Mt. Langshan in Hunan Province. (Photo by Yang Zhi)

福建泰宁大金湖 · 赤壁丹霞。（图 / 杨志）

Chibi Danxia of Dajin Lake of Taining, Fujian Province. (Photo by Yang Zhi)

贵州赤水·佛光岩。(图/杨志)
Foguang Cliff·of Chishui, Guizhou Province. (Photo by Yang Zhi)

浙江江郎山远眺。(图 / 杨志)
Distant view of Mt. Jianglangshan, Zhejiang Province. (Photo by Yang Zhi)

中国世界遗产影像志

WORLD HERITAGE IN CHINA

澄江化石遗址

Chengjiang Fossil Site

云南省澄江县帽天山古生物化石馆外景。（图 / 潘泉）

Exterior view of Mt. Maotian Fossil Museum. (Photo by Pan Quan)

Chengjiang Fossil Site
澄江化石遗址

占地面积 512 公顷的云南省澄江化石地拥有保存极好的生物群，提供了寒武纪早期海洋生物群落最完全的记录，展示了种类繁多的生物体、脊椎动物和无脊椎动物的软硬组织解剖。这里的化石记录了一个复杂的海洋生态系统的早期形成。遗产地保存了至少 16 个门类中多种不可思议的生物群落，多达 196 个物种，是距今 5.3 亿年前寒武纪早期地球上生命的快速多样化的见证。几乎今天所有主要动物类群都产生于寒武纪早期，澄江化石遗址，为科学研究古生物学提供了独特的窗口。

——世界遗产委员会评价

A hilly 512 ha site in Yunnan province, Chengjiang's fossils present the most complete record of an early Cambrian marine community with exceptionally preserved biota, displaying the anatomy of hard and soft tissues in a very wide variety of organisms, invertebrate and vertebrate. They record the early establishment of a complex marine ecosystem. The site documents at least sixteen phyla and a variety of enigmatic groups as well as about 196 species, presenting exceptional testimony to the rapid diversification of life on Earth 530 million years ago, when almost all of today's major animal groups emerged. It opens a palaeobiological window of great significance to scholarship.

——World Heritage Committee Evaluation

帽天山古生物化石发现地。（图 / 孙隆椿）
Site where Mt. Maotian Fossils were discovered. (Photo Sun Longchun)

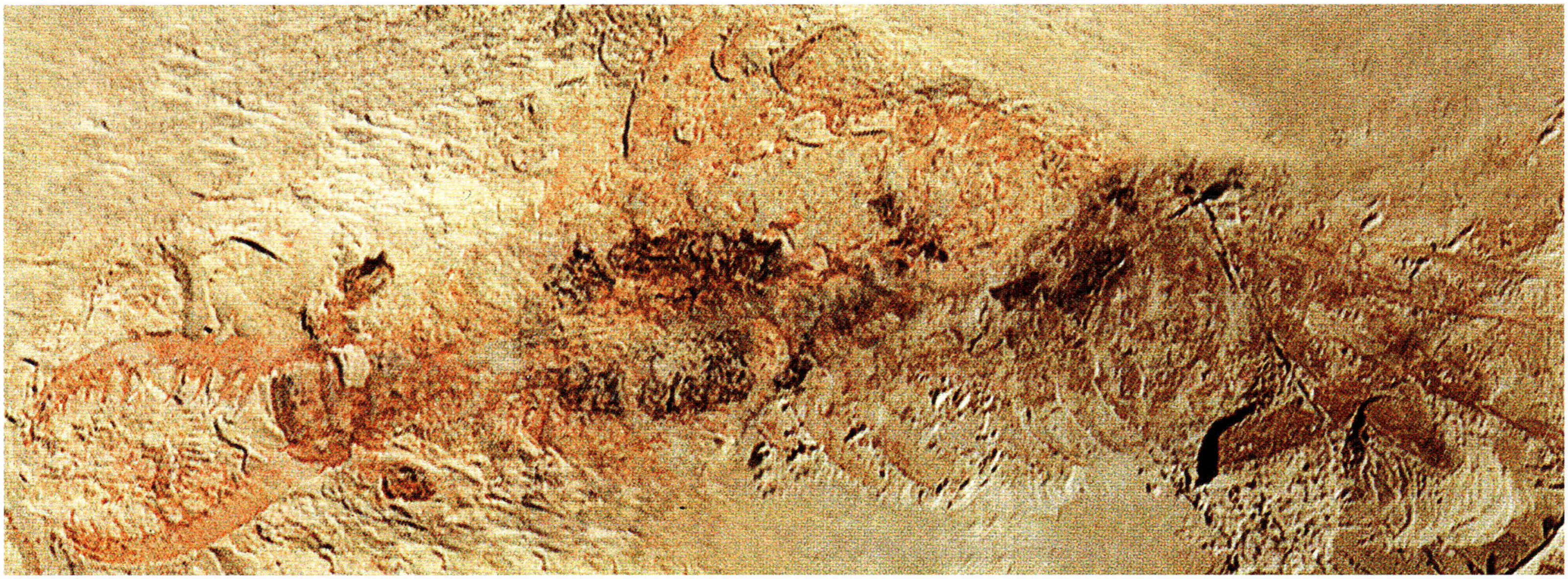

上图　奇虾复原图。(图 / 云南省澄江县帽天山化石馆提供)

Upper　Restored image of anomalocaris. (Photo provided by Mt. Maotian Fossil Museum of Chengjiang,Yunnan Province)

下图　奇虾化石。(图 / 云南省澄江县帽天山化石馆提供)

Lower　Anomalocaris fossil. (Photo provided by Mt. Maotian Fossil Museum of Chengjiang,Yunnan Province)

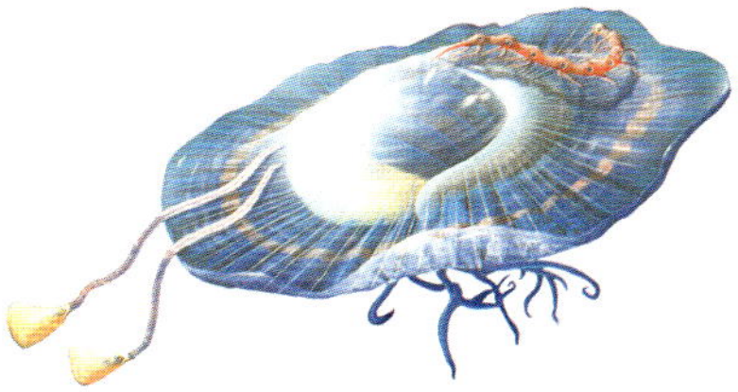

1

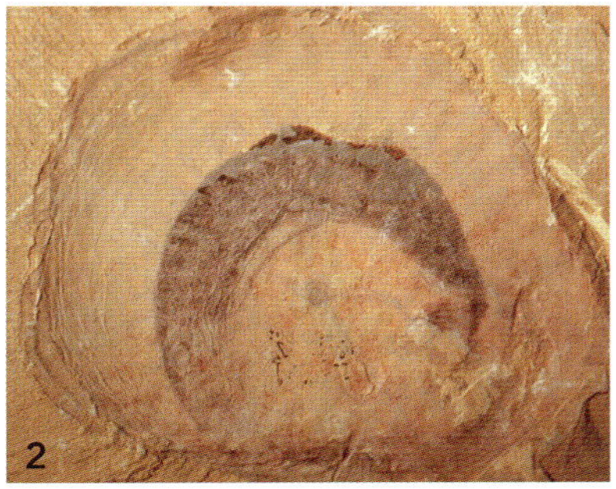

2

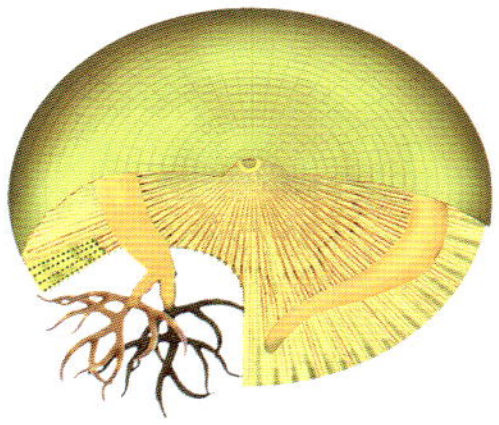

3

4

5

6

7

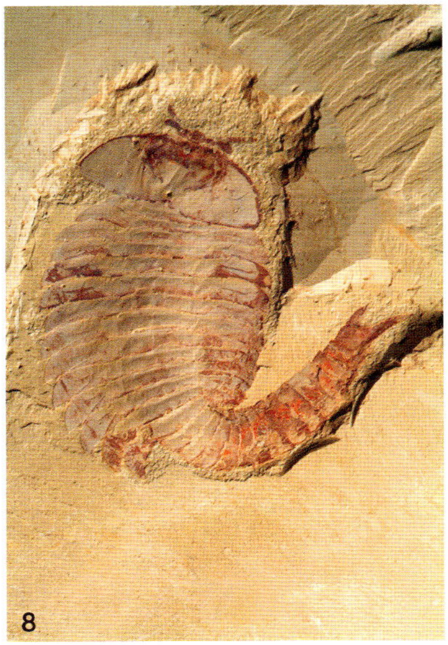

8

(组图/云南省澄江县帽天山化石馆提供)

(Photos provided by Mt. Maotian Fossil Museum of Chengjiang,Yunnan Province)

1　依尔东钵化石复原图

Restored image of Yi Er Dong Bo fossil

2　依尔东钵化石。

Yi Er Dong Bo fossil

3　轮盘水母化石复原图

Restored image of Roulette jellyfish fossils

4　轮盘水母化石。

Roulette jellyfish fossils

5　栉水母化石复原图。

Restored image of Ctenophora fossil.

6　栉水母化石。

Ctenophora fossil.

7　延长抚仙湖虫化石复原图

Restored image of Fuxianhuia fossils

8　延长抚仙湖虫化石。

Fucianhuia fossils

澄江动物群复原景观。（图 / 云南省澄江县帽天山化石馆提供）　Reconstruction of Chengjiang fauna. (Photo by Yunnan Chengjiang Mt. Maotian Fossils Museum)

中国世界遗产影像志

WORLD HERITAGE IN CHINA

四川大熊猫栖息地

Sichuan Giant Panda Sanctuaries — Wolong, Mt Siguniang and Jiajin Mountains

四川卧龙大熊猫。（图 / 何世尧）

Giant panda in Wolong, Sichuan province. (Photo by He Shiyao)

Sichuan Giant Panda Sanctuaries — Wolong, Mt Siguniang and Jiajin Mountains

四川大熊猫栖息地

四川大熊猫栖息地面积 924,500 公顷，目前全世界 30% 以上的濒危野生大熊猫都生活在那里，包括邛崃山和夹金山的七个自然保护区和九个景区，是全球最大、最完整的大熊猫栖息地，为第三纪原始热带森林遗迹，也是最重要的圈养大熊猫繁殖地。这里也是小熊猫、雪豹和云豹等全球严重濒危动物的栖息地。栖息地还是世界上除热带雨林以外植物种类最丰富的地区之一，生长着属于 1,000 多个属种的 5,000 到 6,000 种植物。

——世界遗产委员会评价

Sichuan Giant Panda Sanctuaries, home to more than 30% of the world's pandas which are classed as highly endangered, covers 924,500 ha. with seven nature reserves and nine scenic parks in the Qionglai and Jiajin Mountains. The sanctuaries constitute the largest remaining contiguous habitat of the giant panda, a relict from the paleo-tropic forests of the Tertiary Era. It is also the species' most important site for captive breeding. The sanctuaries are home to other globally endangered animals such as the red panda, the snow leopard and clouded leopard. They are among the botanically richest sites of any region in the world outside the tropical rainforests, with between 5,000 and 6,000 species of flora in over 1,000 genera.

——World Heritage Committee Evaluation

大熊猫栖息地四川四姑娘山。（图 / 何世尧）

Mt. Siguniang, agiant panda habitat. (Photo by He Shiyao)

大熊猫爬树。（图 / 何世尧）

Giant panda climbing a tree. (Photo by He Shiyao)

卧龙大熊猫繁殖基地。（图 / 卞志武）
Giant panda breeding base in Wolong.
(Photo by Bian Zhiwu)

明清故宫（北京故宫、沈阳故宫）

Imperial Palaces of the Ming and Qing Dynasties in Beijing and Shenyang

1

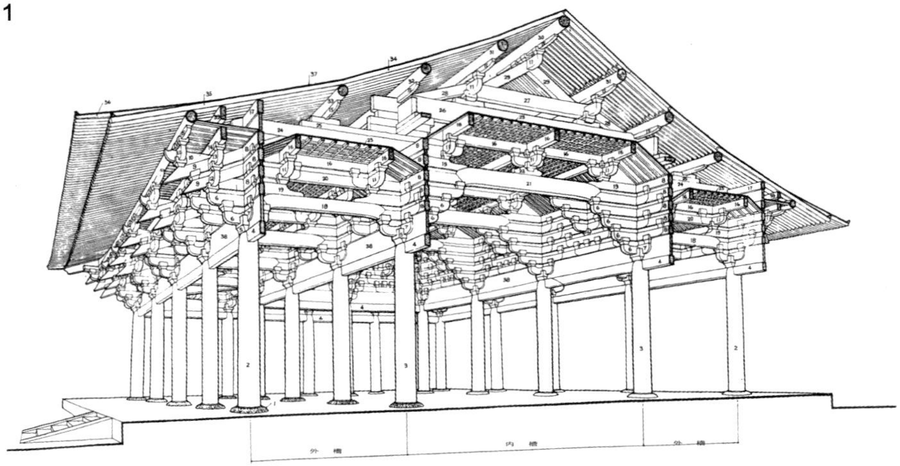

1.柱基 2.檐柱 3.内槽柱 4.兰额 5.栌斗 6.华栱 7.泥道栱 8.柱头方 9.下昂 10.耍头 11.令栱 12.瓜子栱 13.慢栱 14.罗汉方 15.替木 16.平棊方 17.压槽方 18.明乳栿 19.半驼峰 20.素方 21.四椽明栿 22.驼峰 23.平闇 24.草乳栿 25.缴背 26.四椽草栿 27.平梁 28.托脚 29.叉手 30.脊槫 31.上平槫 32.中平槫 33.下平槫 34.椽 35.檐椽 36.飞子（复原） 37.望版 38.栱眼壁 39.牛脊方

2

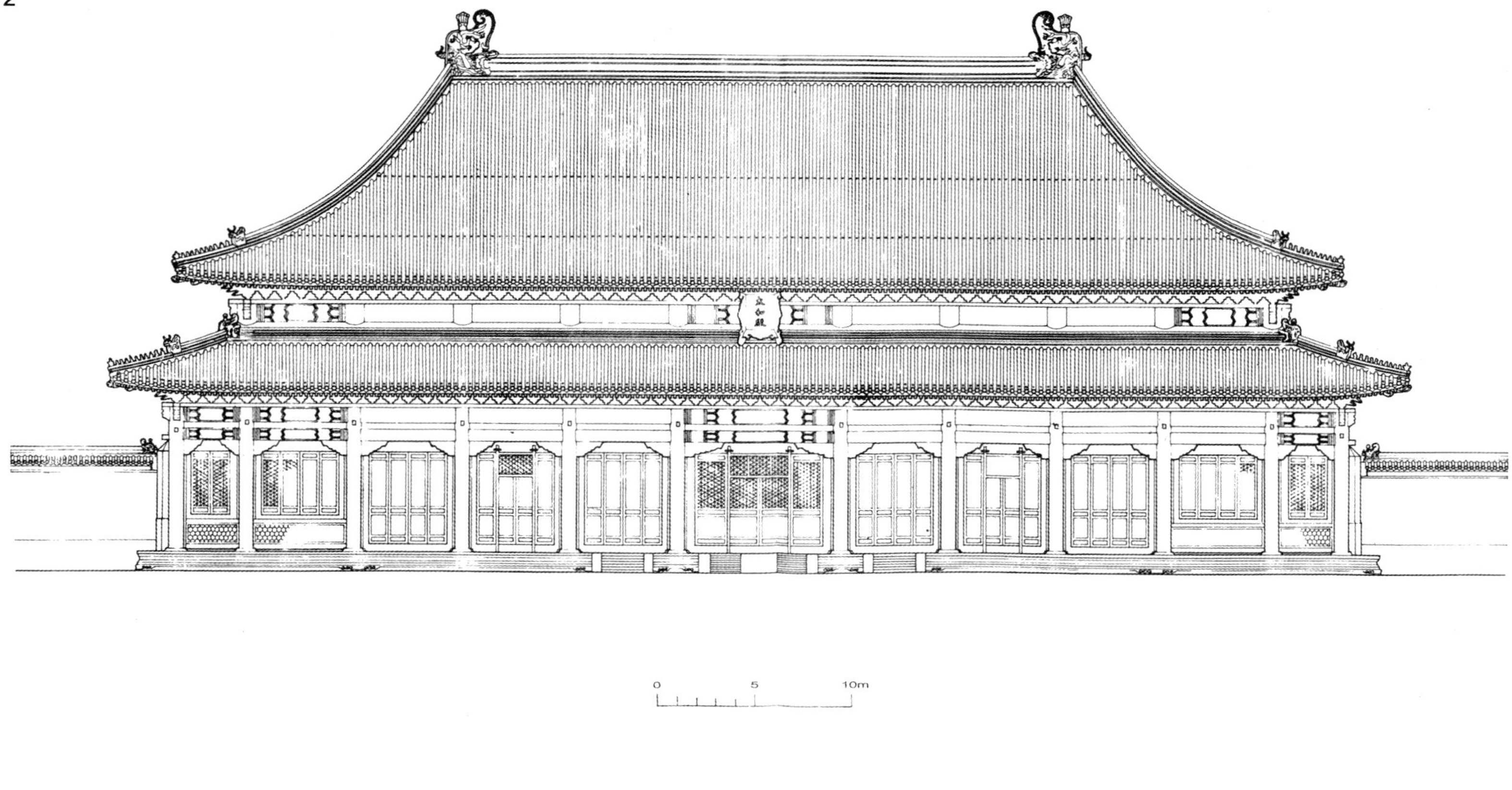

3

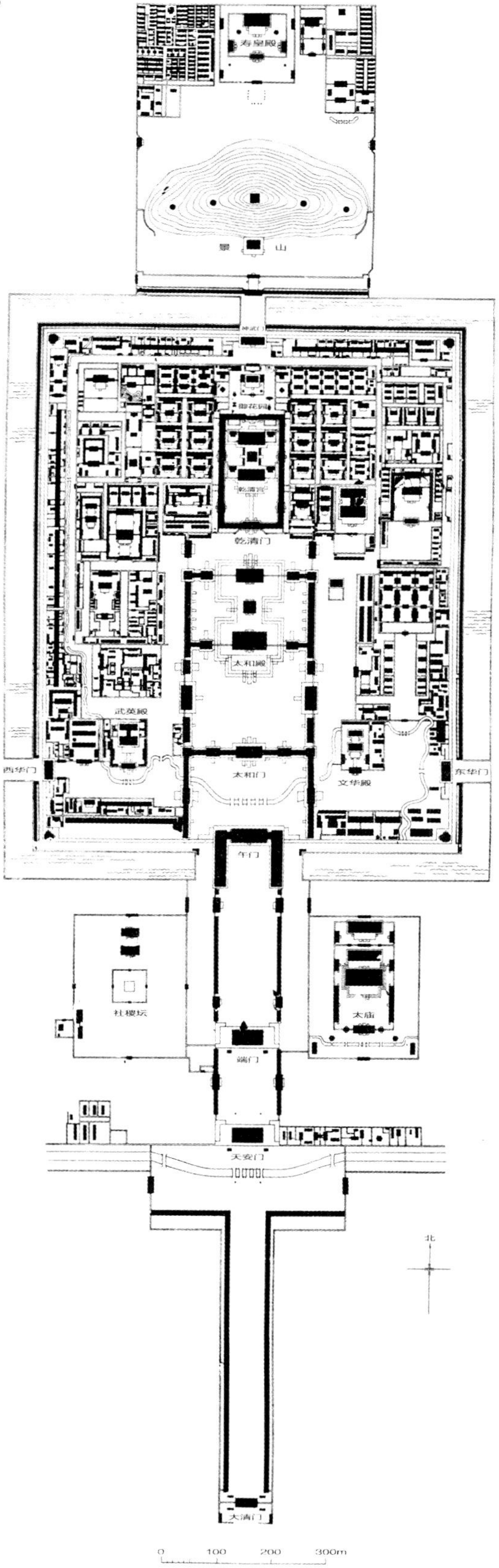

4

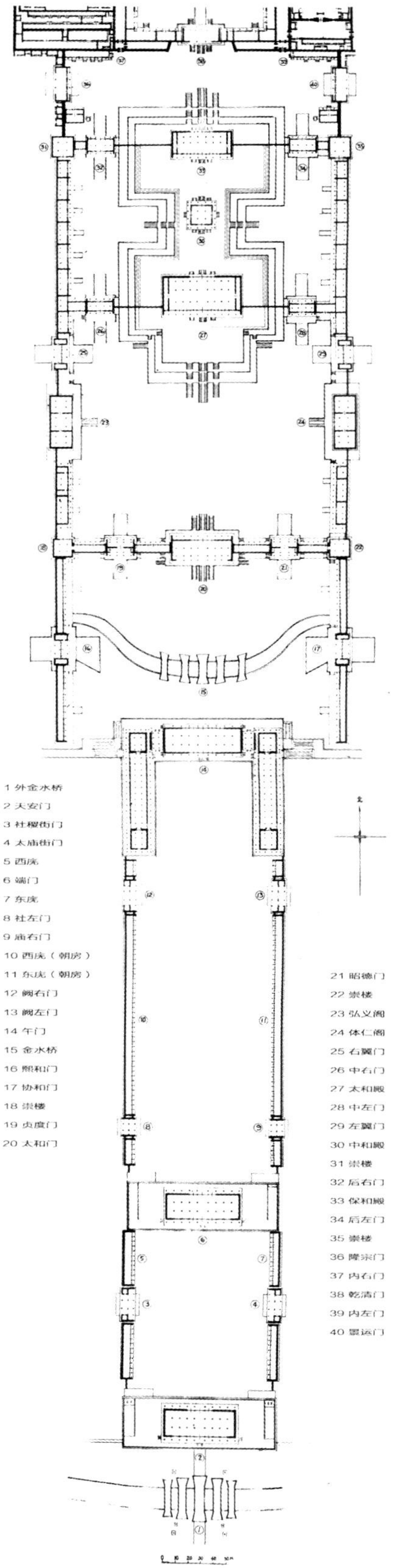

1　北京故宫太和殿梁架结构示意图。（图 / 故宫博物院）
Diagram of the bean structure of Hall of Supreme Harmony. (Photo by Palace Museum)

2　北京故宫太和殿正立面图。（图 / 故宫博物院）
The front view of Hall of Supreme Harmony. (Photo by Palace Museum)

3　北京故宫总平面图。（图 / 故宫博物院）
The general plan of the Imperial Palace, Beijing. (Photo by Palace Museum)

4　北京故宫外三殿平面图。（图 / 故宫博物院）
The plan of the three outer halls of the Imperial Palace, Beijing. (Photo by Palace Museum)

北京皇家祭坛——天坛

Temple of Heaven: an Imperial Sacrificial Altar in Beijing

1　北京天坛祈年殿正立面图。（图 / 天坛公园管理处）

Facade of the Hall of Prayer for Good Harvest, the Temple of Heaven, Beijing. (Photo by the Temple of Heaven Park)

2　北京天坛总平面图。（图 / 天坛公园管理处）

General plan of the Temple of Heaven, Beijing. (Photo by the Temple of Heaven Park)

3　明代大祀殿图。（图 / 天坛公园管理处）

Plan of the Hall of Great Sacrifice of Ming Dynasty. (Photo by the Temple of Heaven Park)

4　北京天坛祈年殿总平面图。（图 / 天坛公园管理处）

General plan of the Hall of Prayer for Good Harvest, the Temple of Heaven, Beijing. (Photo by the Temple of Heaven Park)

5　北京天坛圜丘及皇穹宇平面图。（图 / 天坛公园管理处）

Plan of the Circular Mound Altar and the Imperial Vault of Heaven, the Temple of Heaven, Beijing. (Photo by the Temple of Heaven Park)

1

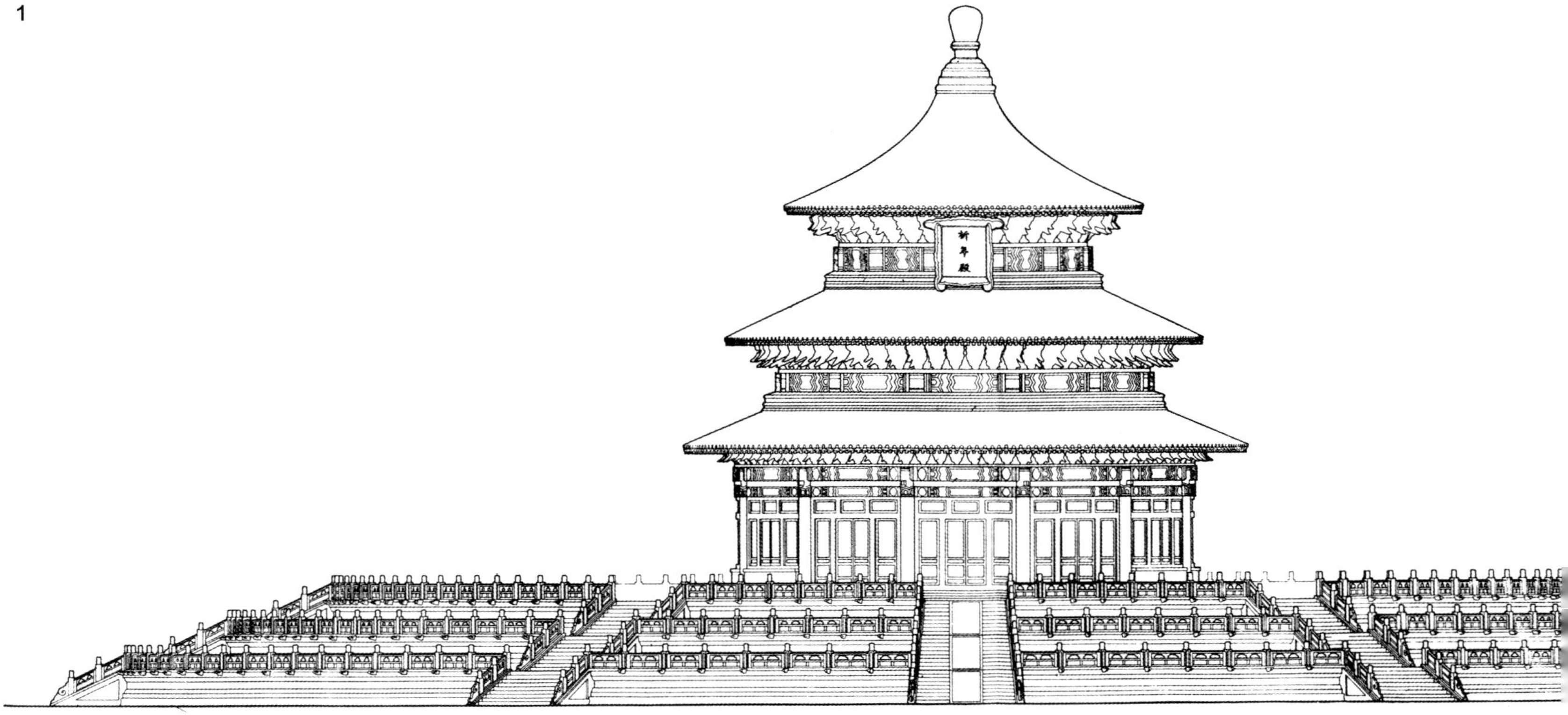

2

北京天坛平面图

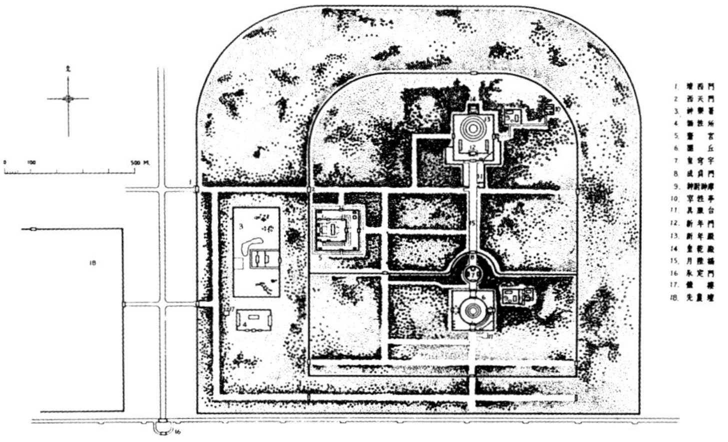

3

圖總壇郊舊

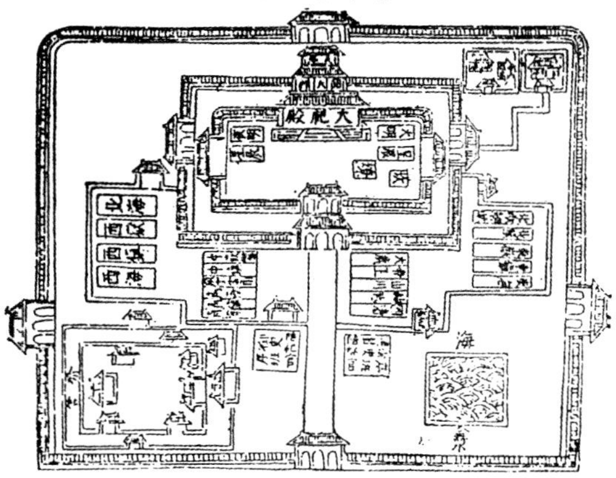

明代大祀殿图

4

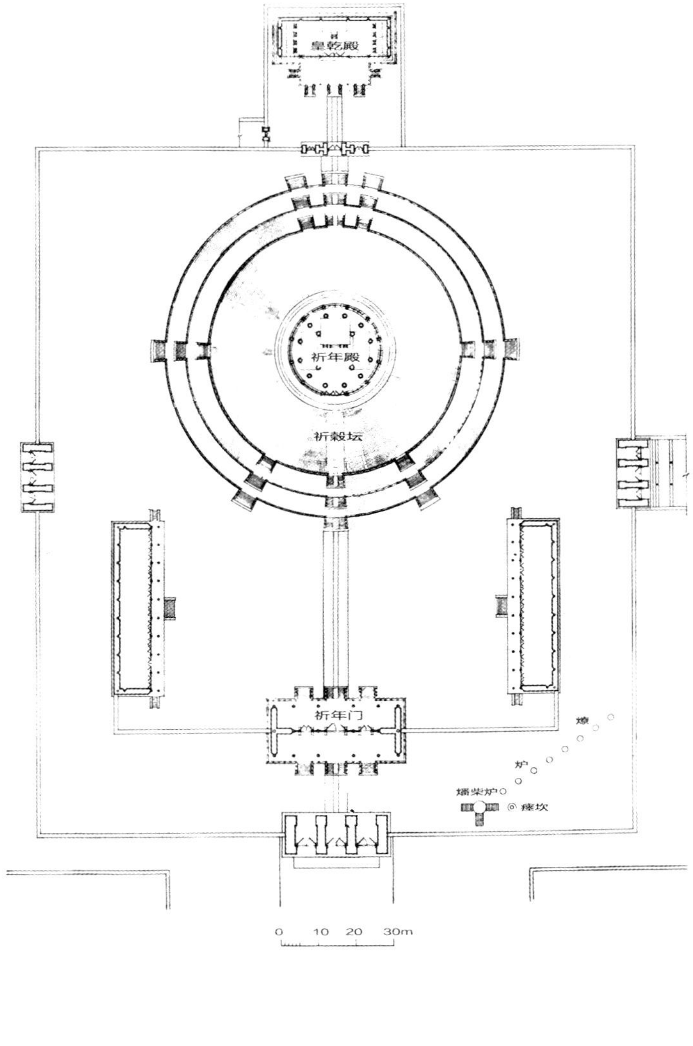

5

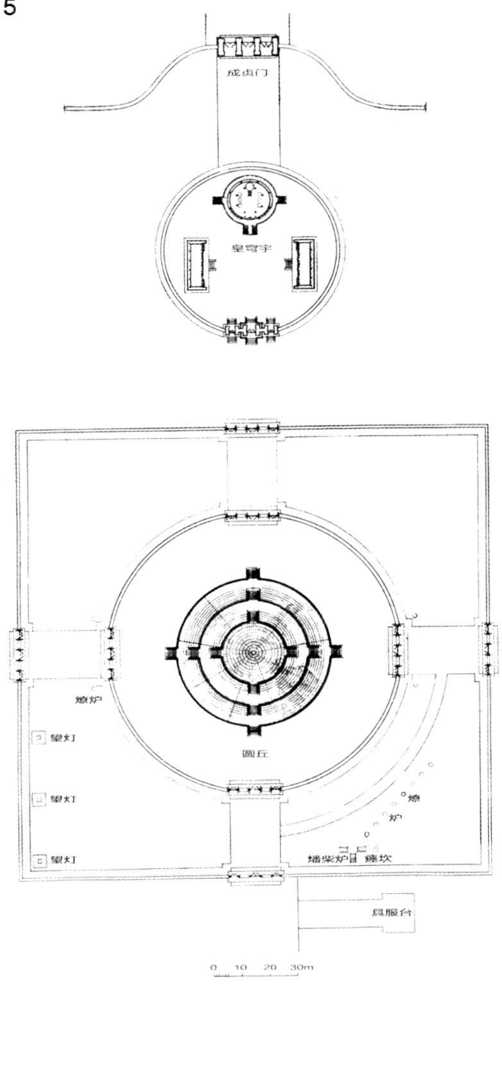

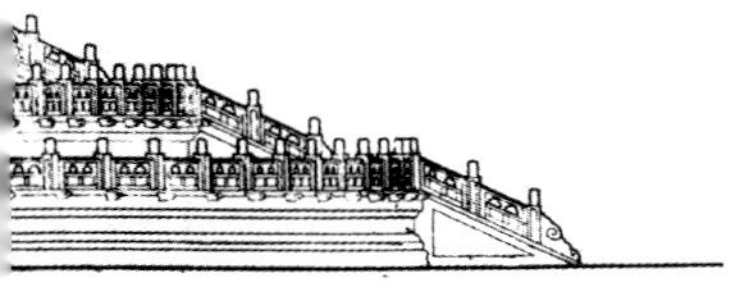

秦始皇陵及兵马俑坑

Mausoleum of the First Qin Emperor

1　陕西临潼县秦始皇陵平面图。（图 / 秦始皇帝陵博物院）

The plan of Emperor Qinshihuang Mausoleum in Lintong County, Shannxi Province. (Photo by Emperor Qinshihuang's Mausoleum Site Museum)

2　兵马俑坑位置平面示意图。（图 / 秦始皇帝陵博物院）

Layout of the Terracotta Army Pit. (Photo by Emperor Qinshihuang's Mausoleum Site Museum)

3　二号坑形制与军阵平面示意图。（图 / 秦始皇帝陵博物院）

The shape and battle array of No.2 Pit. (Photo by Emperor Qinshihuang's Mausoleum Site Museum)

4　一号坑东端试掘方军阵示意图。（图 / 秦始皇帝陵博物院）

Sketch map of battle array upon trial excavation at the east side of No.1 Pit. (Photo by Emperor Qinshihuang's Mausoleum Site Museum)

1

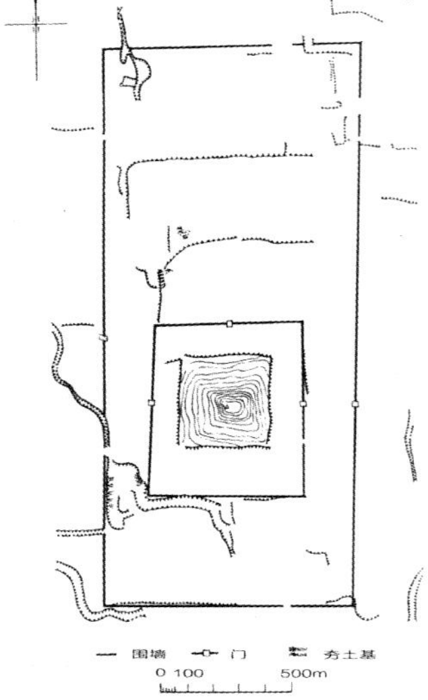

一号坑东端试掘方军阵示意图

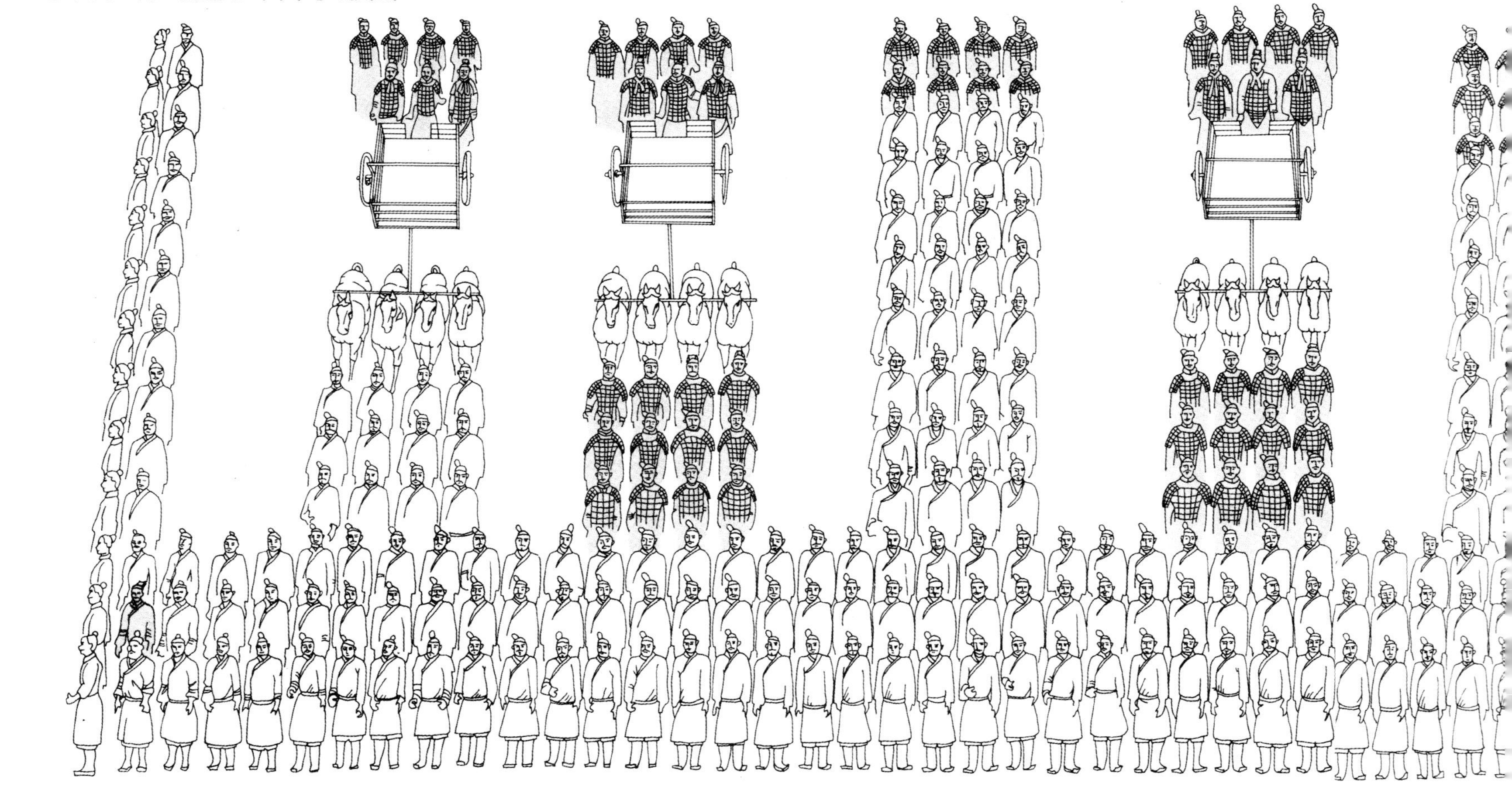

2

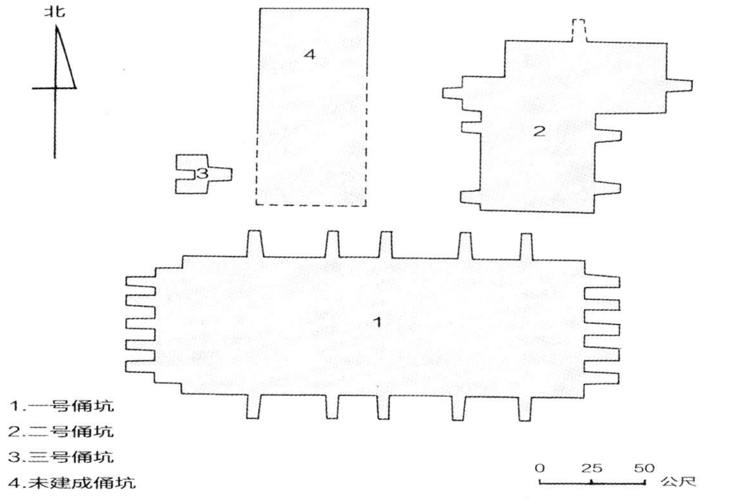

1.一号俑坑
2.二号俑坑
3.三号俑坑
4.未建成俑坑

3

二号坑形制与军阵平面示意图

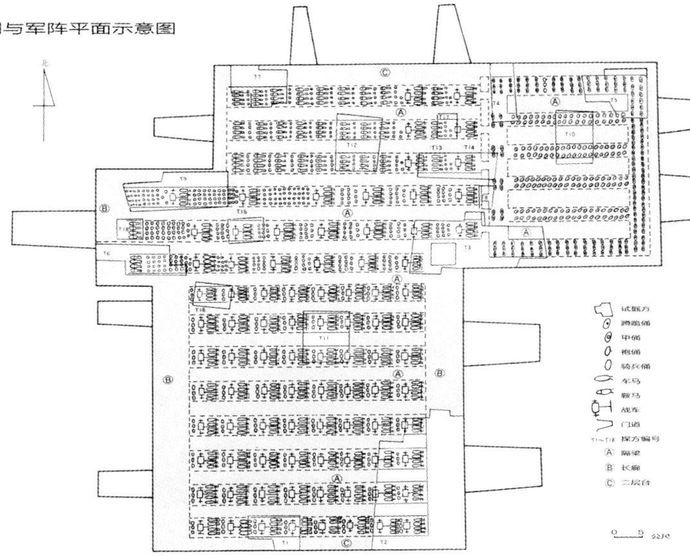

4

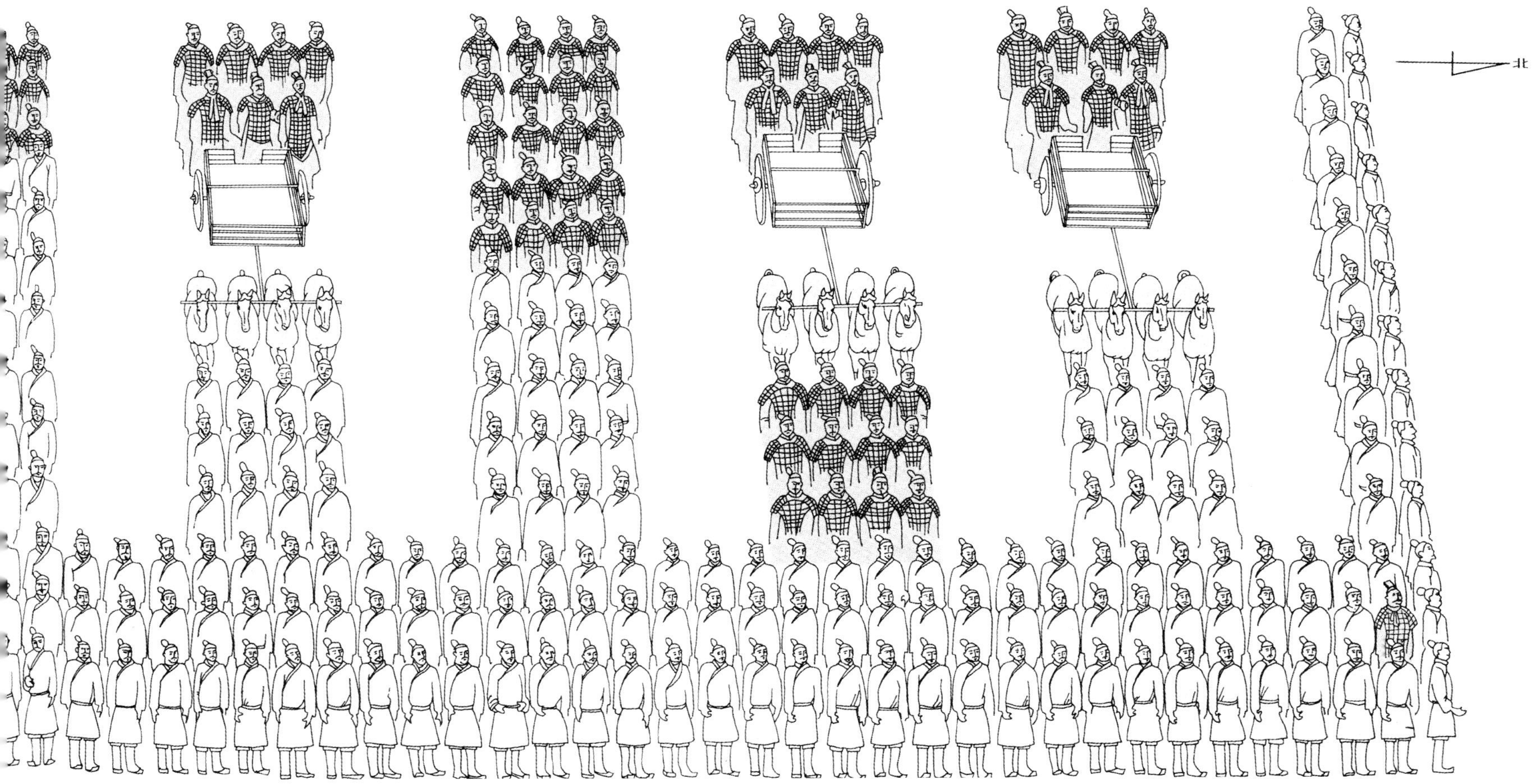

一号铜车(立车)结构图

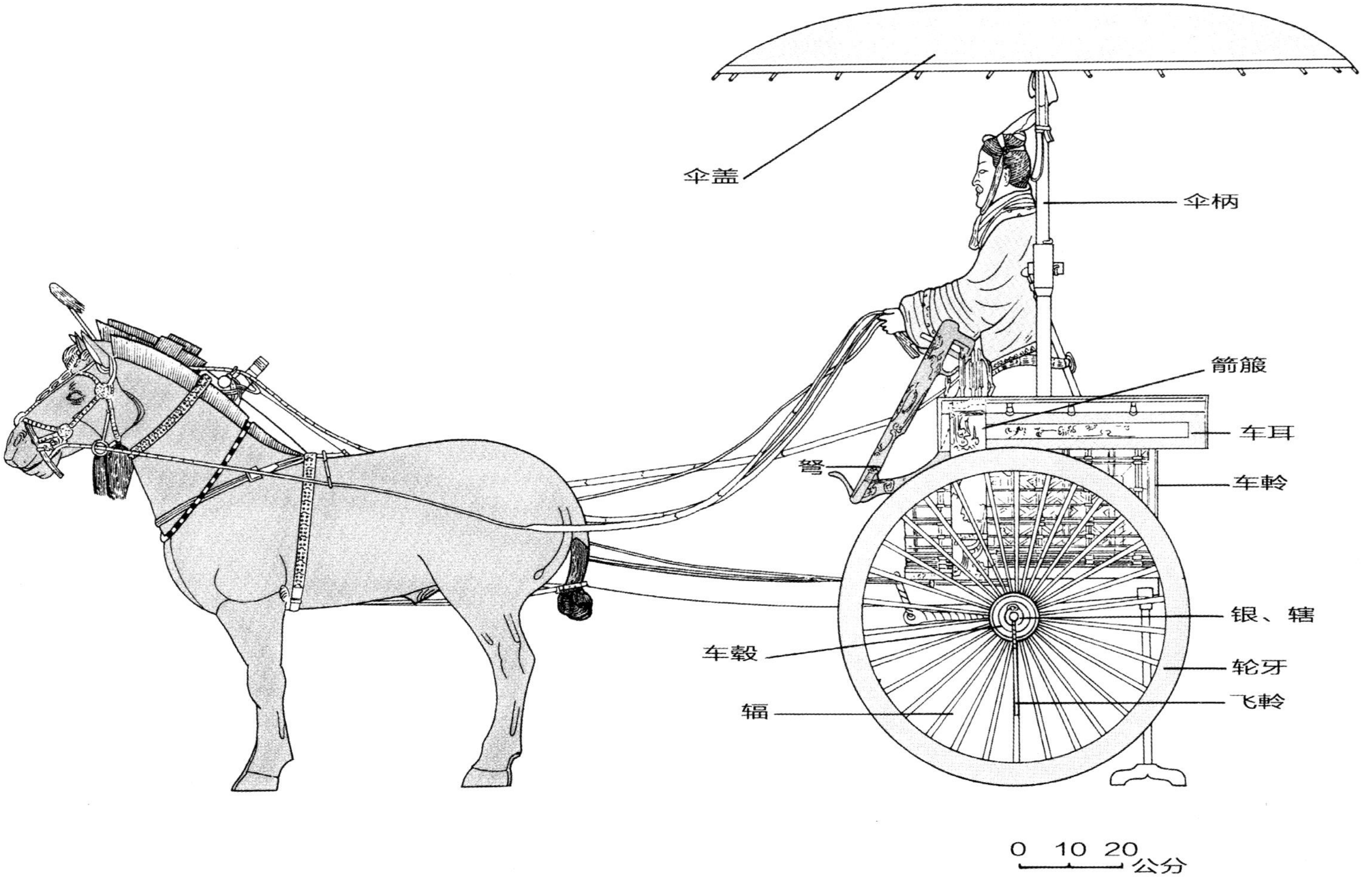
伞盖
伞柄
箭箙
车耳
辔
车軨
银、辖
车毂
轮牙
辐
飞軨
0 10 20
公分

中级军吏俑服饰部位名称图例
长冠
冠带
壅领
披膊
前胸甲
背甲
联甲带
长襦
絮衣
翘尖履
履缘
正面
侧面
背面
轻装步兵俑
轻装立射俑
圆髻铠甲步兵俑
介帜铠甲步兵俑
将军俑

安车御官俑

侧面　正面　背面

安车车与纹饰

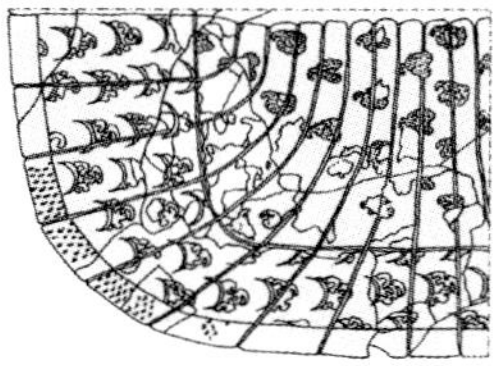

蓬盖纹饰

车后室门内侧纹饰

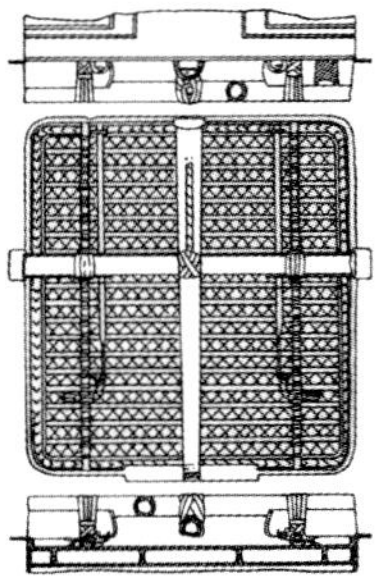

车后室底部仰、前、后视结构图

二号铜车（安车）结构图

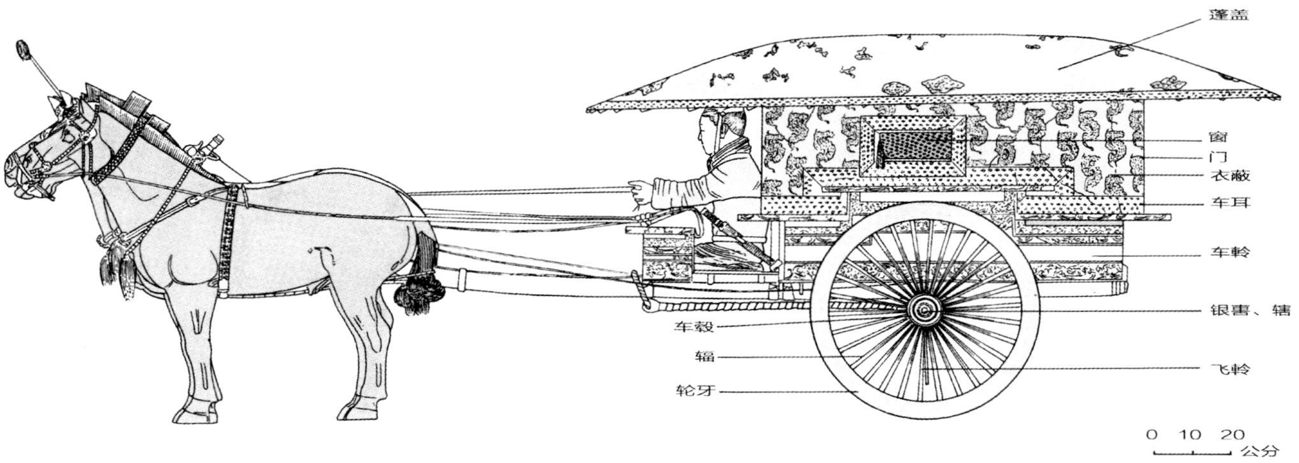

中级军吏俑

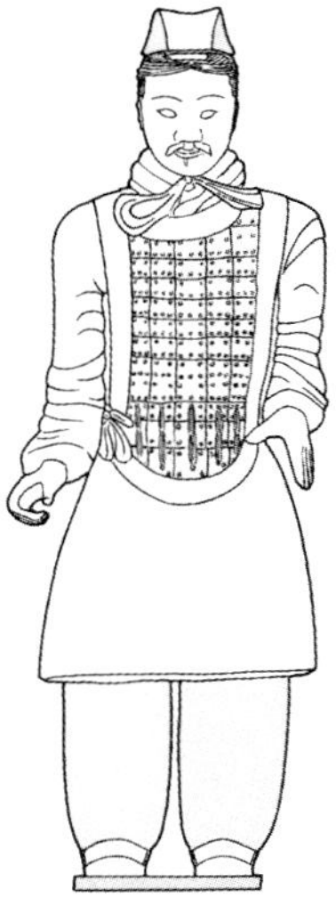

铠甲下级军吏俑

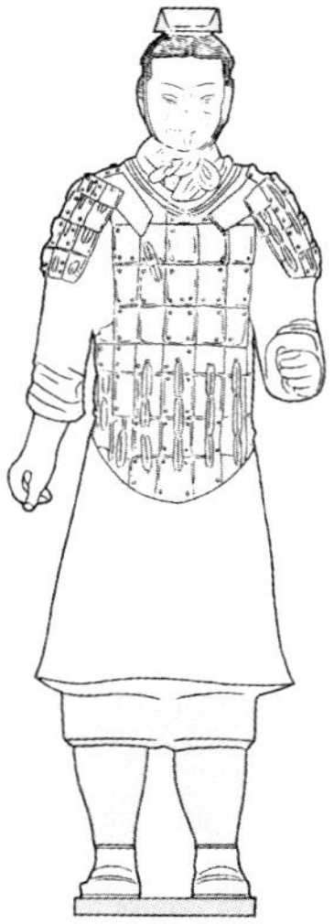

轻装下级军吏俑

跪射铠甲步兵俑

战车甲士俑

指挥车御手俑

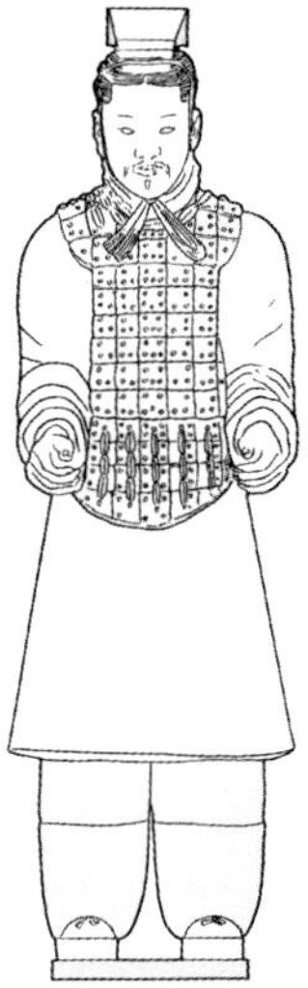

骑兵俑

曲阜孔庙、孔林和孔府

Temple and Cemetery of Confucius and the Kong Family Mansion in Qufu

1

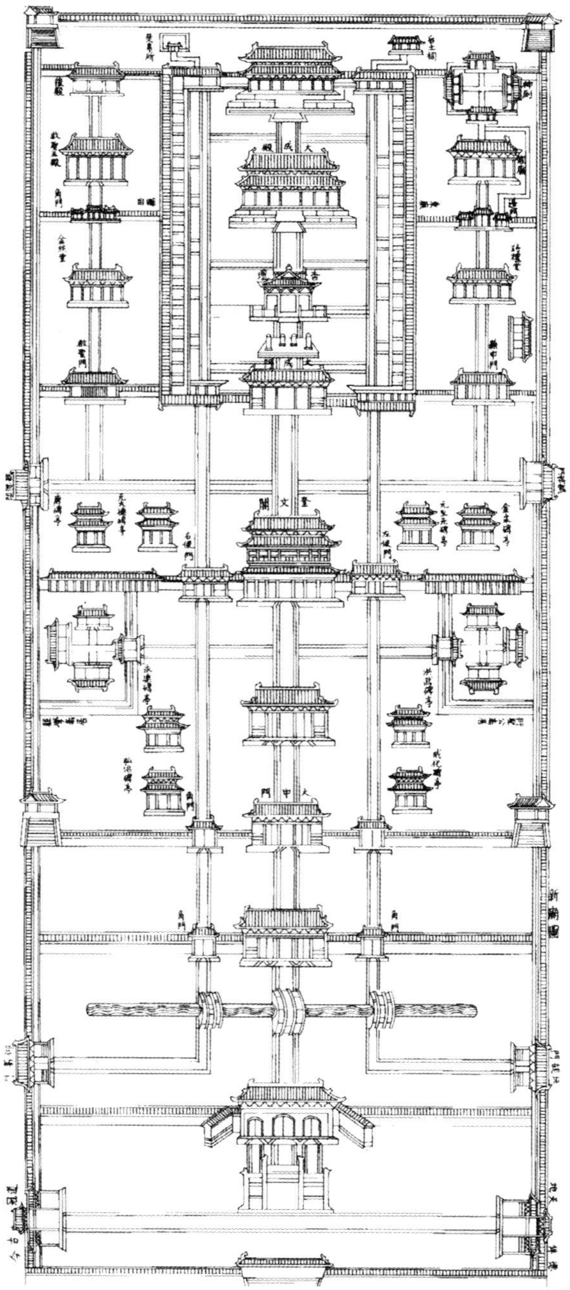

2

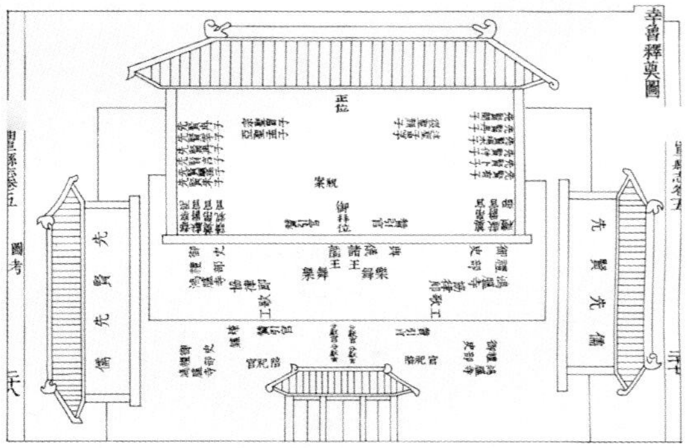

3

4

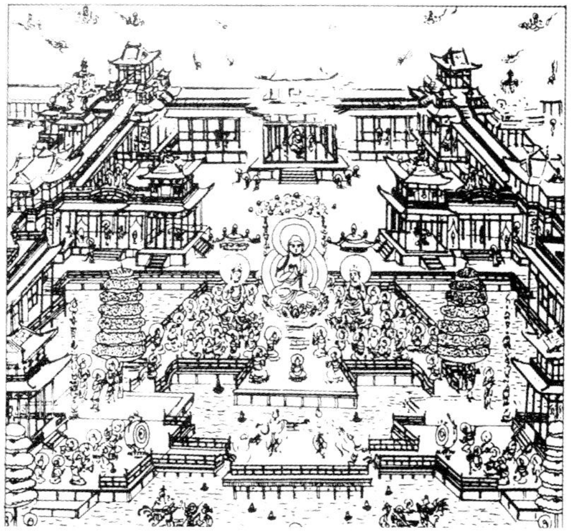

1　明代孔庙平面图。

The plan of Temple of Confucius of Ming Dynasty.

2　曲阜孔庙大成殿释奠仪位置图（乾隆《曲阜县志》）。

The location for Shidian Ritual in Dacheng Hall, Temple of Confucius in Qufu (from *Annals of Qufu* County in Emperor Qianlong's Reign)

3　孔庙图。（摹自《阙里志》明正德本）。

Map of Temple of Confucius. (copied from *Quelizhi* Zhengde version of Ming Dynasty)

4　孔庙奎文阁侧立面。

Side view of Kuiwen Pavilion, Temple of Confucius.

5　1940 年的孔府平面图（选自《孔孟圣迹图鉴》）。

The plan of the Kong Family Mansion in 1940. (from *Shengji Tujian of Confucius and Mencius*)

6　元代孟庙图（摹自洪武六年图碑）。

Temple of Mencius in Yuan Dynasty. (copied from the stele erected in the sixth year of Hongwu Period)

7　元代颜庙图（摹自《陋巷志》）。

Temple of Yanzi in Yuan Dynasty . (copied from *Annals of Alleys*)

8　清乾隆时之曾庙（摹自乾隆《曲阜县志》）。

Temple of Zengzi during Emperor Qianlong's Reign (copied from *Annals of Qufu County*)

5

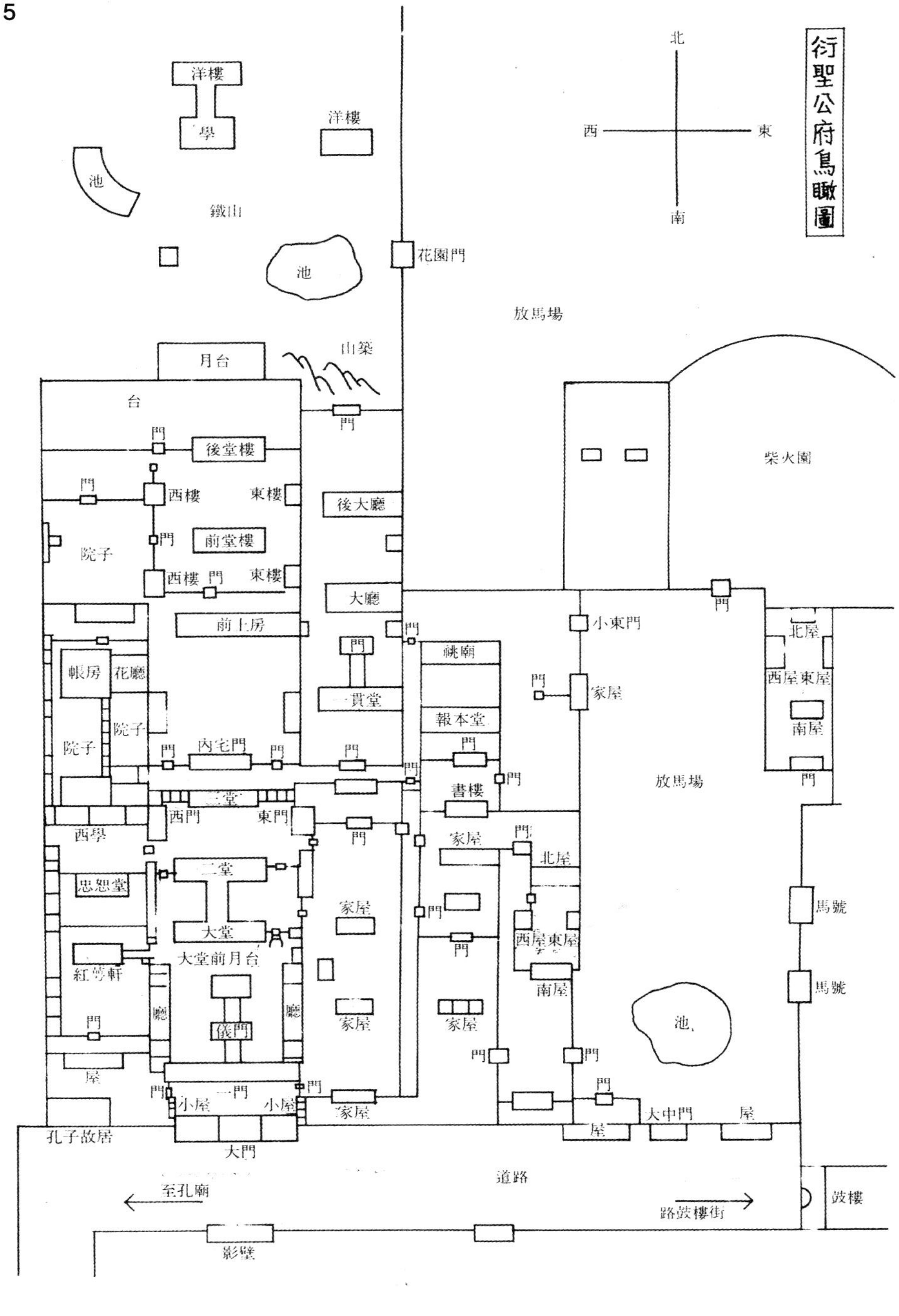
衍聖公府鳥瞰圖
北
南
西
東
洋樓
學
洋樓
池
鐵山
池
花園門
放馬場
山築
月台
台
門
後堂樓
門
西樓
東樓
後大廳
院子
門
前堂樓
西樓
門
東樓
大廳
前上房
門
門
帳房
花廳
祧廟
院子
一貫堂
報本堂
院子
門
內宅門
門
門
門
書樓
門
二堂
西門
東門
門
西學
家屋
門
三堂
北屋
忠恕堂
家屋
門
大堂
西屋
東屋
紅萼軒
大堂前月台
門
南屋
門
廳
廳
家屋
家屋
儀門
門
門
門
屋
門
一門
門
門
小屋
小屋
家屋
大中門
屋
孔子故居
大門
屋
道路
至孔廟
路鼓樓街
鼓樓
影壁
柴火園
門
小東門
門
家屋
北屋
西屋
東屋
南屋
門
放馬場
馬號
馬號
池

6

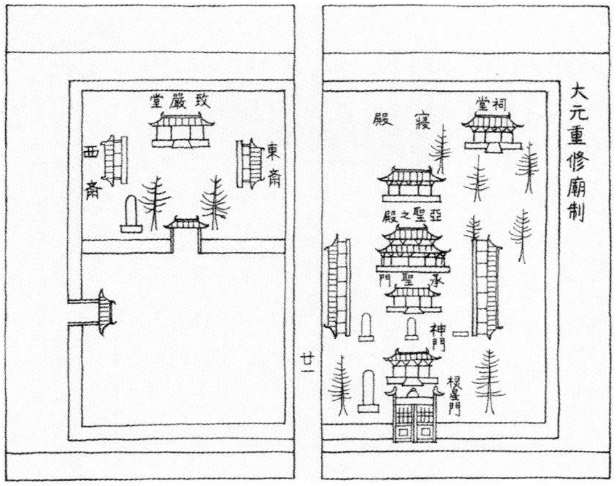
大元重修廟制
致嚴堂
西齋
東齋
寢殿
祠堂
亞聖之殿
承聖門
神門
櫺星門
廿一

7

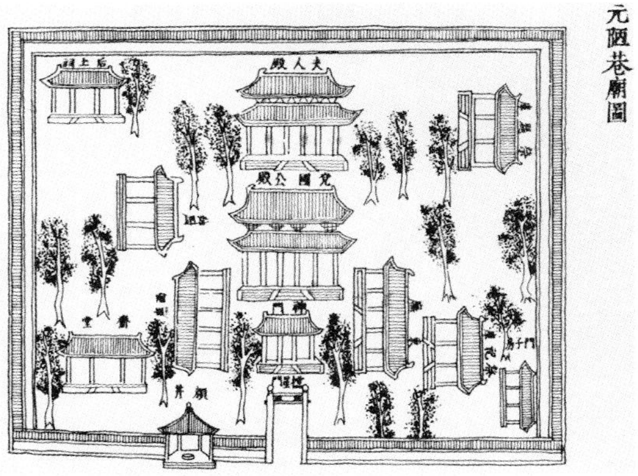
元顏巷廟圖

8

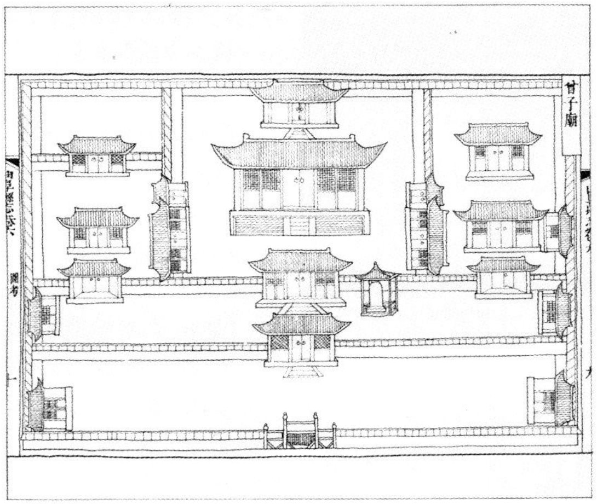

苏州古典园林

Classical Gardens of Suzhou

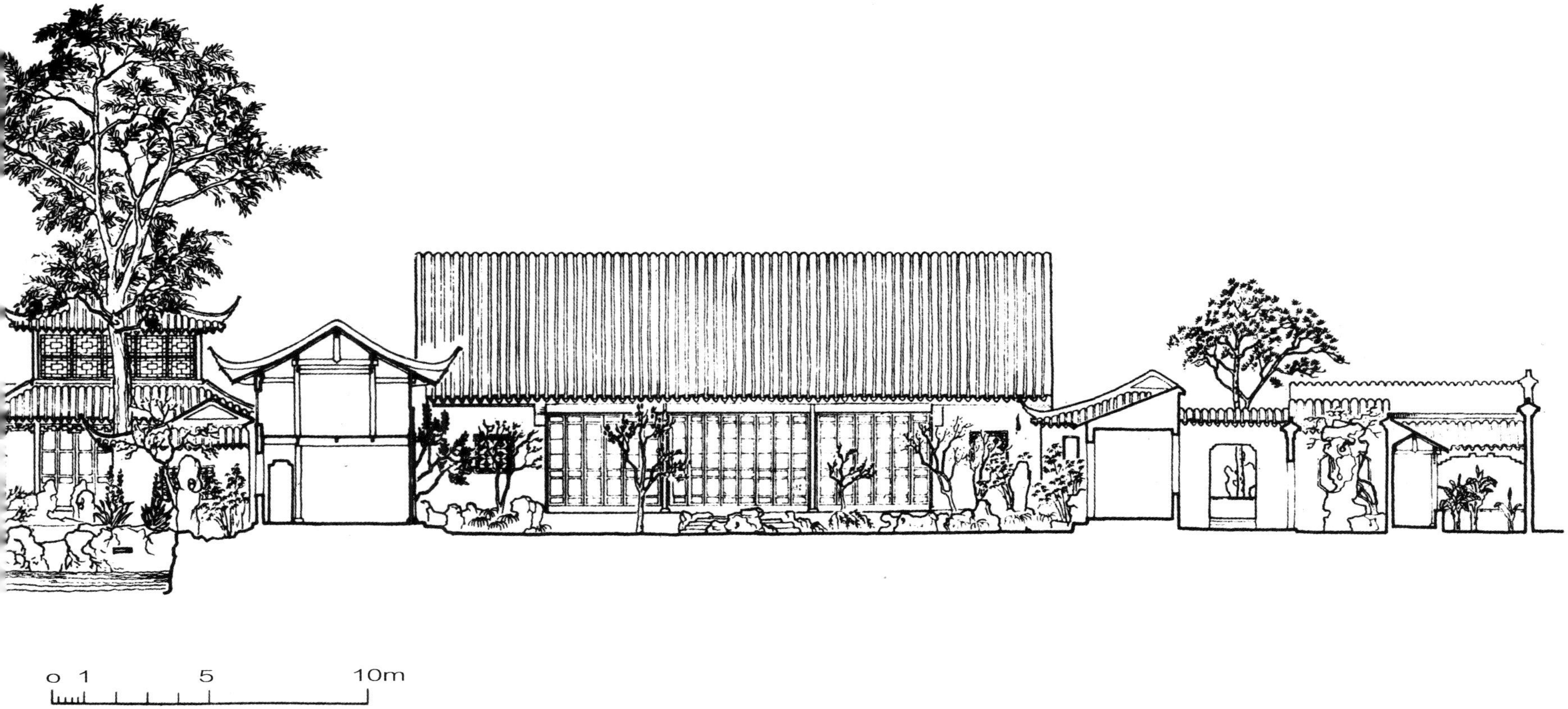

江苏苏州市寒碧庄（今留园）剖面图。（图 / 刘敦祯）

The section plan of Hanbi Villa of Suzhou (the present Lingering Garden). (Photo by Liu Dunzhen)

寒碧山莊圖
丁巳四月下浣

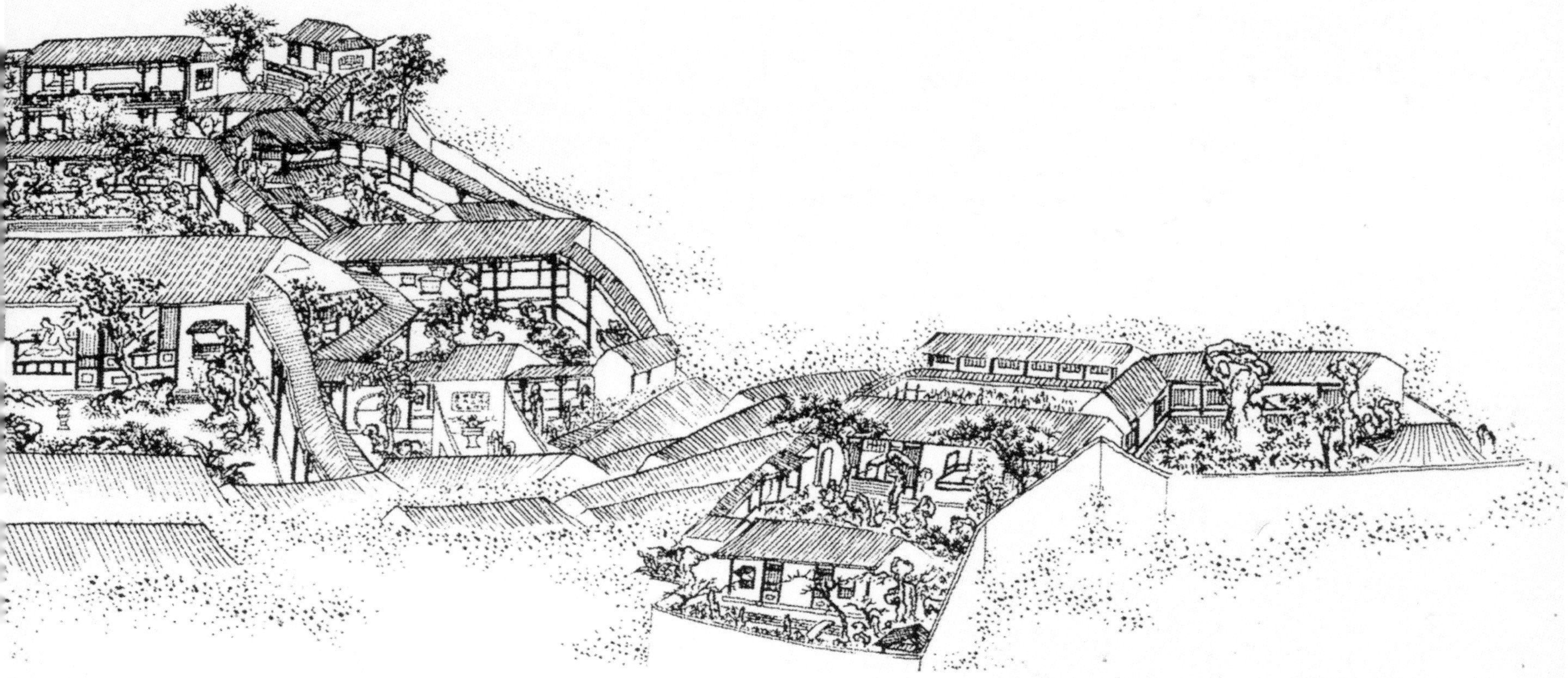

清中叶刘懋功《寒壁山庄图》（摹本）。
(a copy of)The Picture of *Hanbi Mountain Villa* by Liu Maogong of the Mid-Qing Dynasty. (Photo by CPPH)

1

2

3

4

1　怡园园景鸟瞰图。（图 / 刘敦祯）

An aerial view of Yiyuan Garden. (Photo by Liu Dunzhen)

2　留园石林小院剖视图。（图 / 刘敦祯）

Cross-sectional plan of Stone Forest Chamber in Lingering Garden. (Photo by Liu Dunzhen)

3　网师园中部鸟瞰图。（图 / 刘敦祯）

An aerial view of the middle section of the Net masters Garden. (Photo by Liu Dunzhen)

4　拙政园小沧浪水院剖视图。（图 / 刘敦祯）

Cross-sectional plan of Small Gentle Waves Chamber in Humble Adminstrator's Garden. (Photo by Liu Dunzhen)

福建土楼

Fujian Tulou

1 福建土楼发展演变示意图。（图 / 黄汉民） Sketch map of the evolution of Fujian Tulou. (Photo by Huang Hanmin)
2 怀远楼。（图 / 黄汉民） Huaiyuan Lou. (Photo by Huang Hanmin)
3 福建土楼的防伪功能。（图 / 郭育诚） Defense function of Fujian Tulou. (Photo by Guo Yucheng)
4 福裕楼。（图 / 黄汉民） Fuyu Lou. (Photo by Huang Hanmin)
5 济安楼会盟立约序。（图 / 黄汉民） Preface to the Agreement of Ji’an Lou Alliance. (Photo by Huang Hanmin)

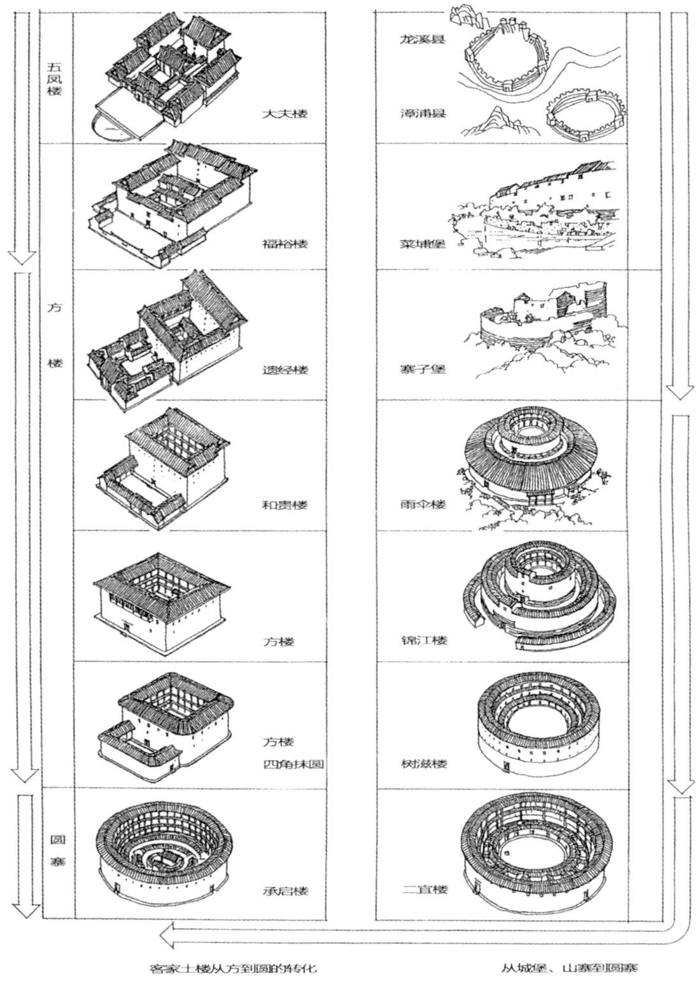

1

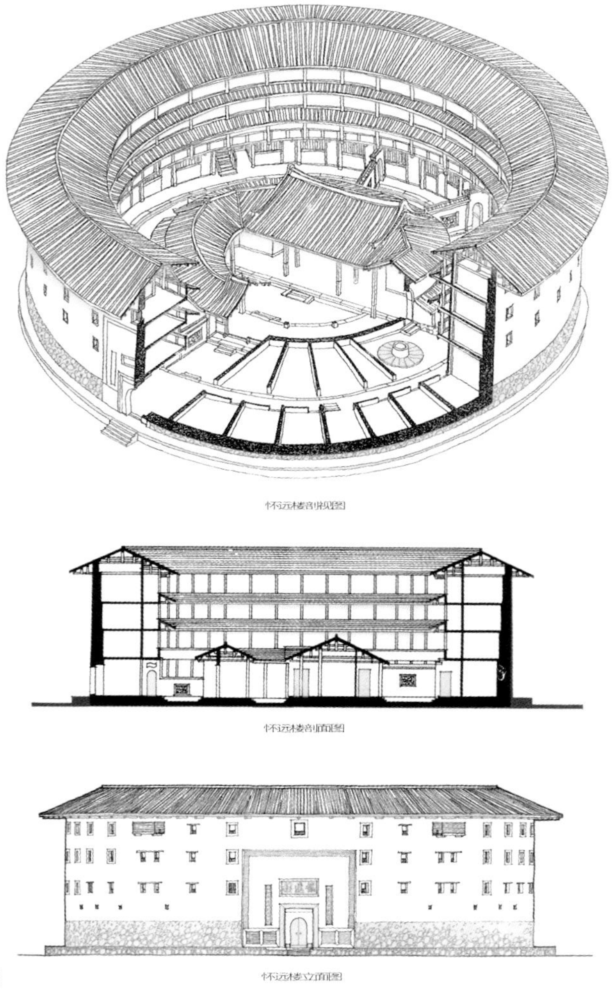

2

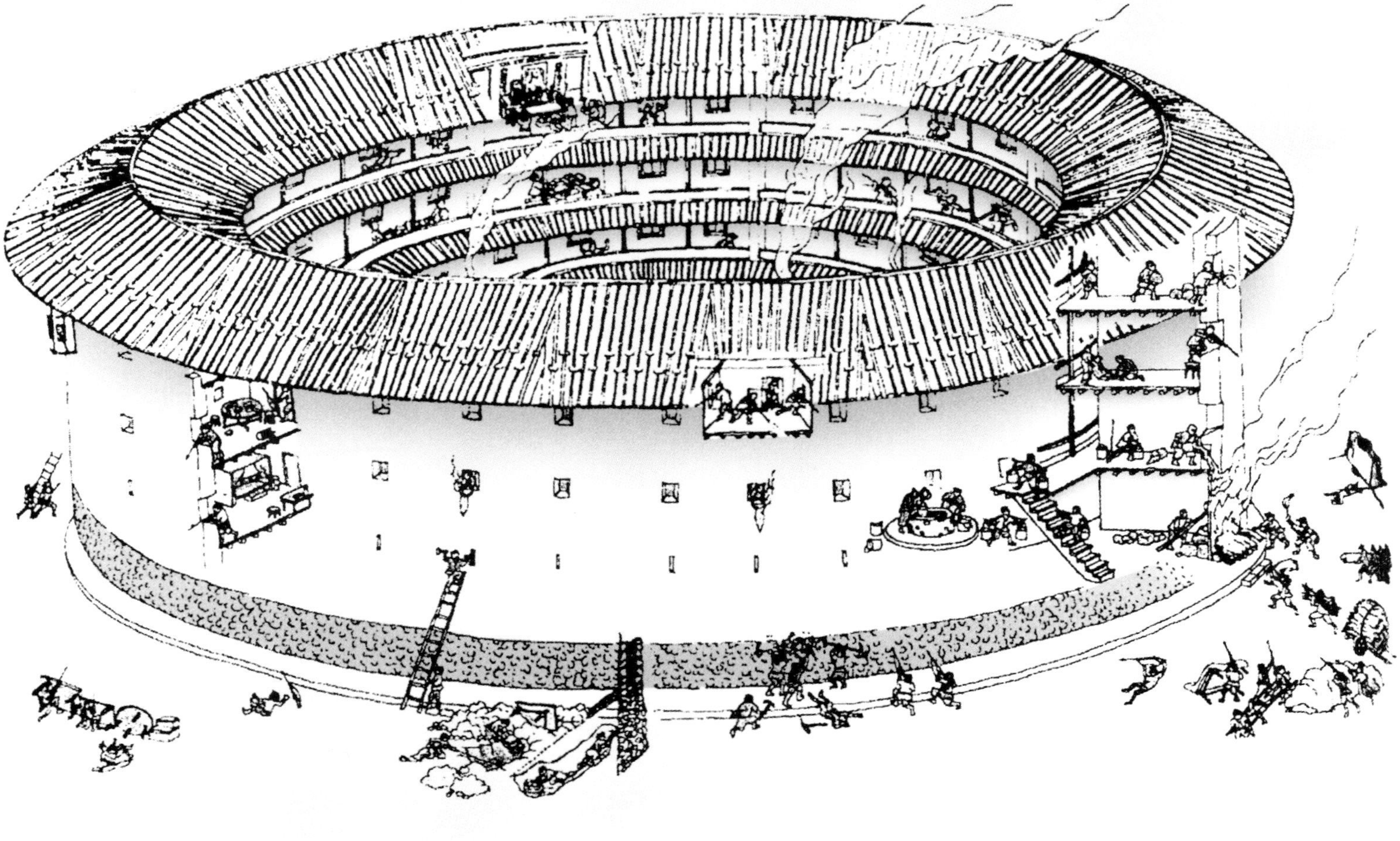

3

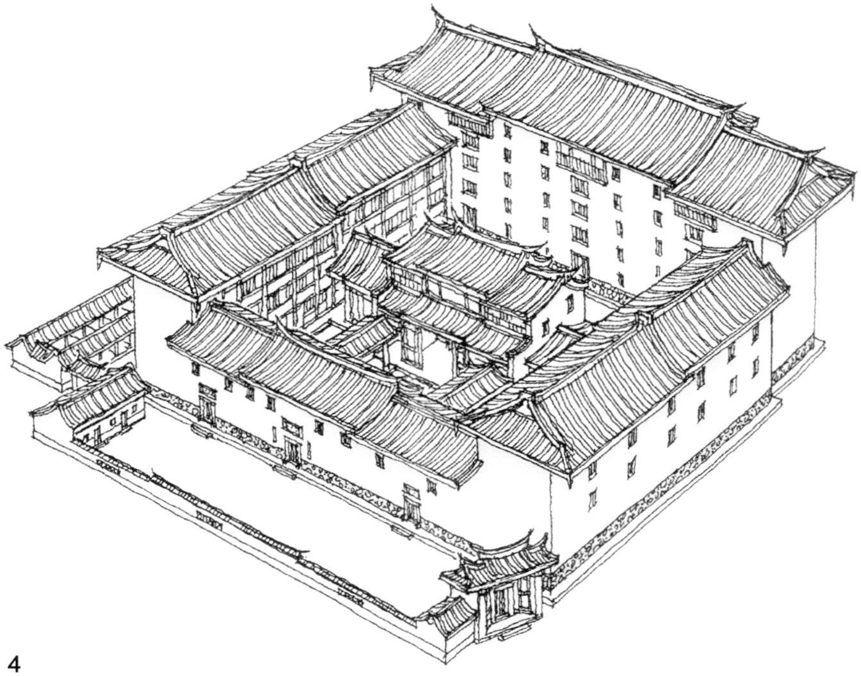

4

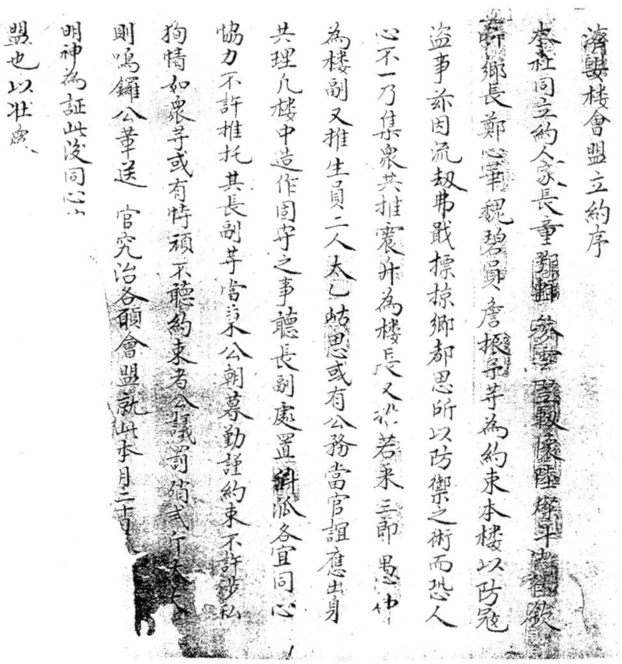

濟雲楼會盟立約序
[illegible]社同立約人家長童[illegible]
[illegible]鄉長鄭[illegible]親碧員詹[illegible]等為約束本楼以防寇
盗事亦因流劫弗戢摽掠鄉都思所以防禦之術而恐人
心不一乃集衆共推寰升為楼長又[illegible]若朱三郎思仲
為楼副又推生員二人太乙[illegible]思或有公務當官謳應出身
共理凡楼中造作固守之事聽長副處置[illegible]派各宜同心
協力不許推托其長副等當[illegible]公朝暮勤謹約束不許[illegible]私
狗情如衆等或有恃頑不聽約束者公議罰[illegible]
則鳴鑼公革送 官究治各願會盟就此本月二十[illegible]
明神為証此後同心[illegible]
盟也以壯[illegible]

5

拉萨布达拉宫历史建筑群

Historic Ensemble of the Potala Palace, Lhasa

1

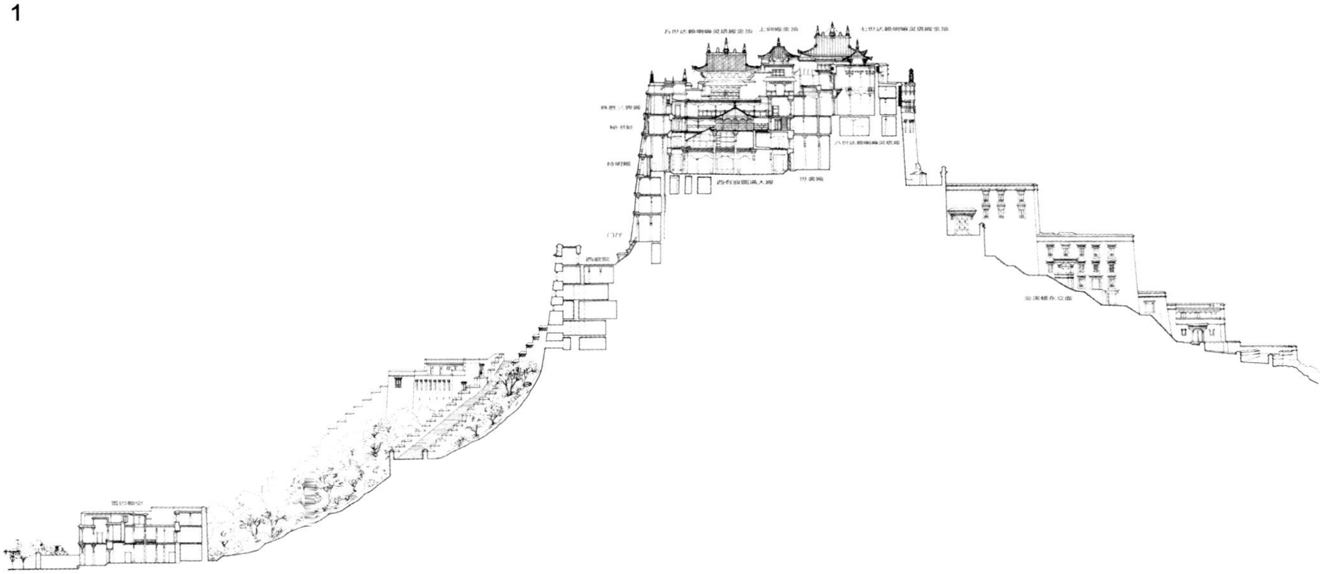

2

3

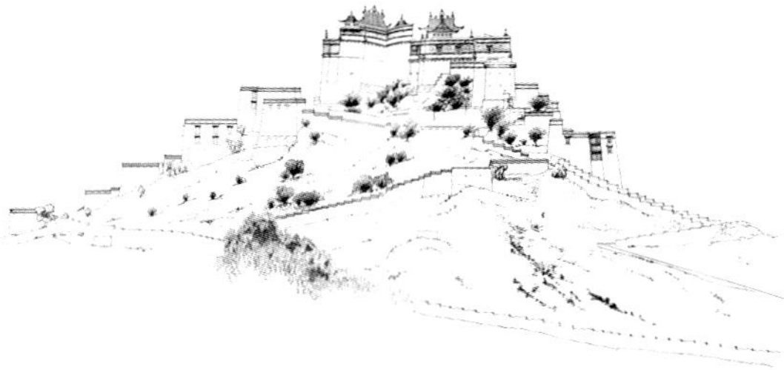

4

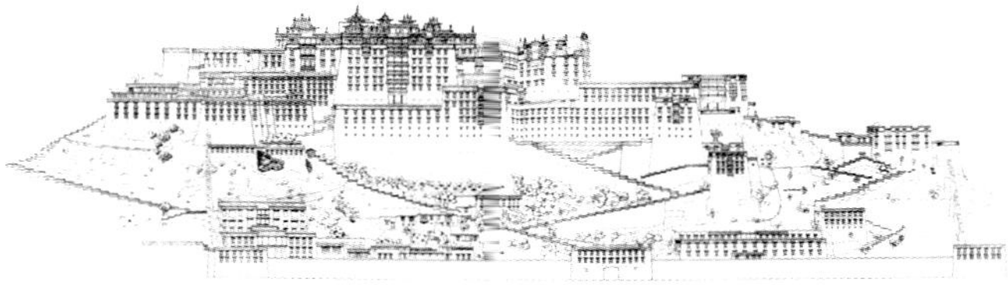

5

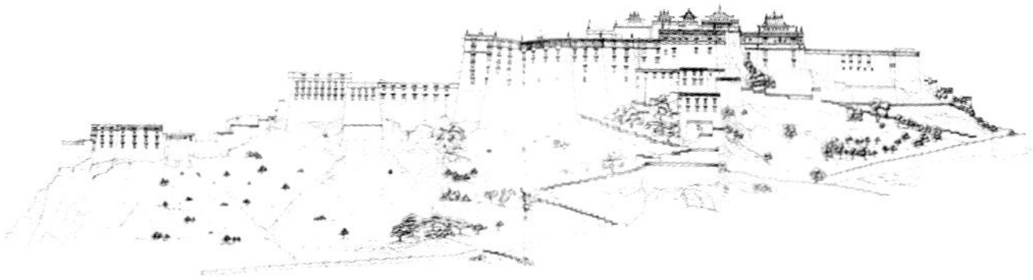

1　雪巴勒空至西有寂圆满大殿剖面图。（图 / 姜怀英）　Section plan of Sholpa Department to West Main Hall. (Photo by Jiang Huaiying)

2　布达拉宫东立面图。（图 / 姜怀英）　East elevation of Potala Palace. (Photo by Jiang Huaiying)

3　布达拉宫西立面图。（图 / 姜怀英）　West elevation of Potala Palace. (Photo by Jiang Huaiying)

4　布达拉宫南立面图。（图 / 姜怀英）　South elevation Potala Palace. (Photo by Jiang Huaiying)

5　布达拉宫北立面。（图 / 姜怀英）　North elevation of Potala Palace. (Photo by Jiang Huaiying)

1

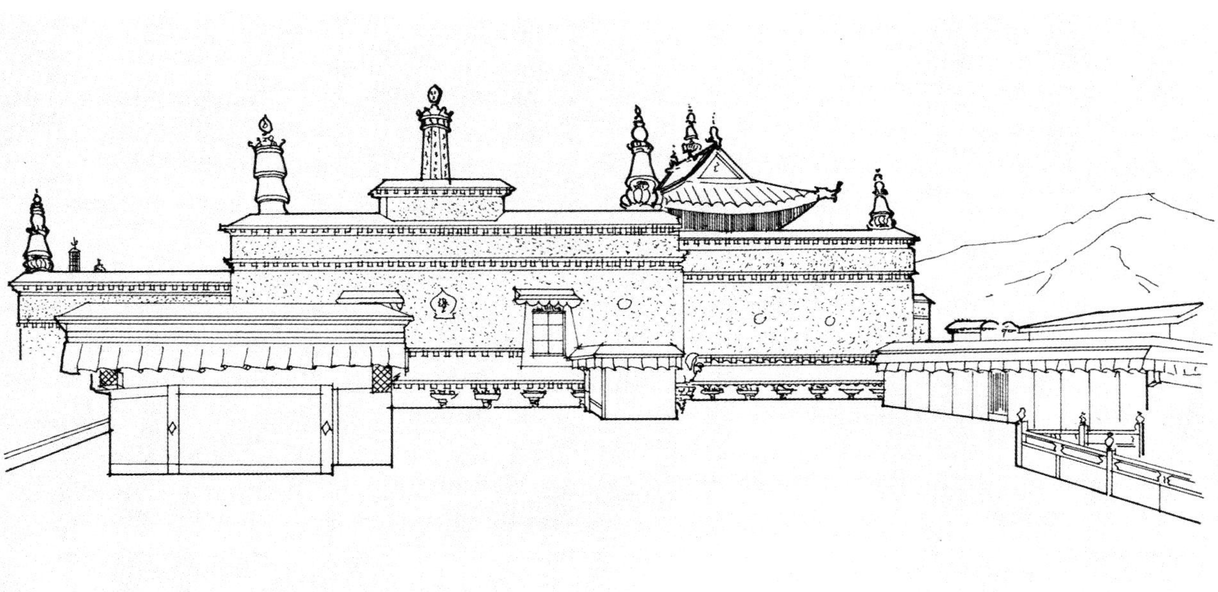

2

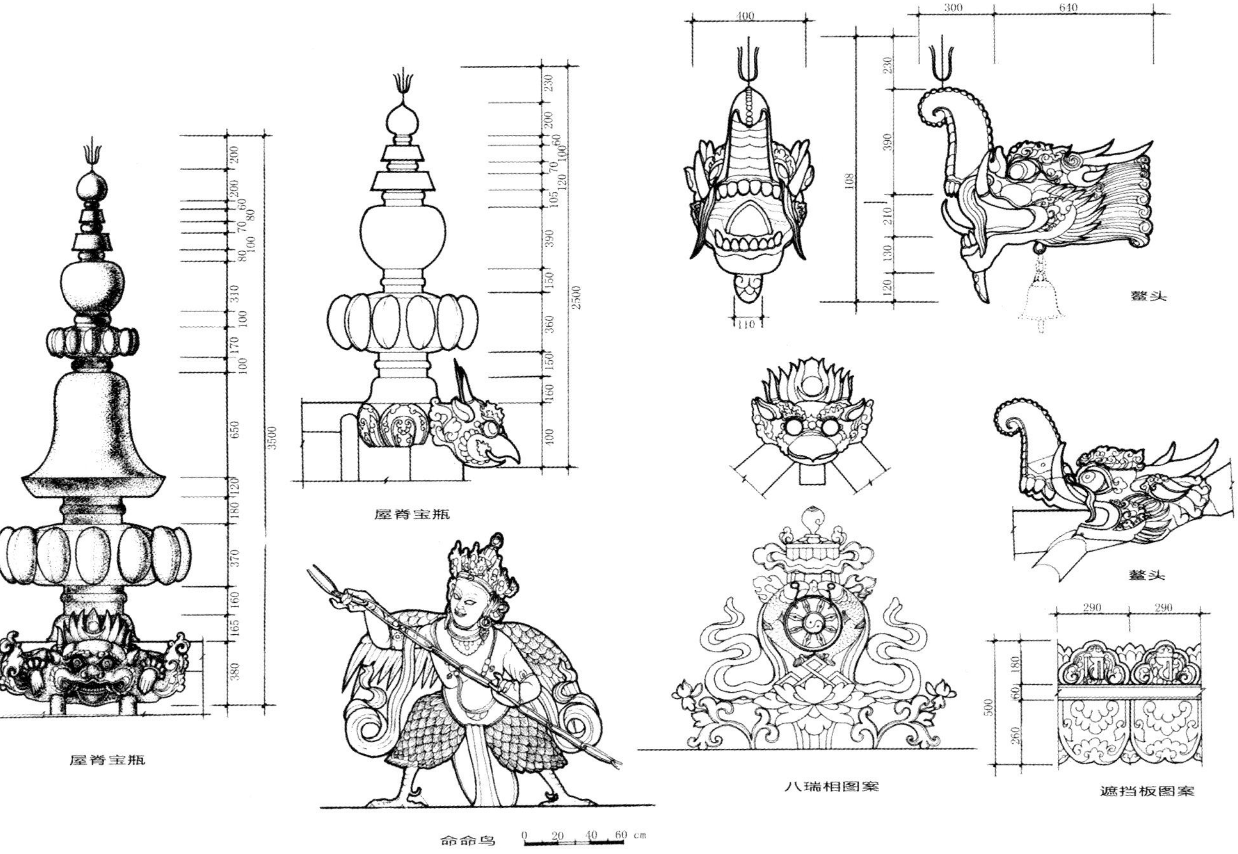

1　白宫顶部与红宫金顶衔接透视图。（图 / 姜怀英）

Perspective drawing of the connection between the roof of the White Palace and the golden roof of the Red Palace. (Photo by Jiang Huaiying)

2　红宫十三世达赖喇嘛灵塔殿金顶装饰详图。（图 / 姜怀英）

Detailed picture of the decoration of the golden roof of Pagoda Temple of the 13th Dalai Lama at the Red Palace. (Photo by Jiang Huaiying)

龙门石窟

Longmen Grottoes

奉先寺 正壁立面图

右天王像 右菩萨像 右弟子像 坐佛像 左弟子像 左菩萨像 左天王像

北壁 立面图

正壁主像 等值线图

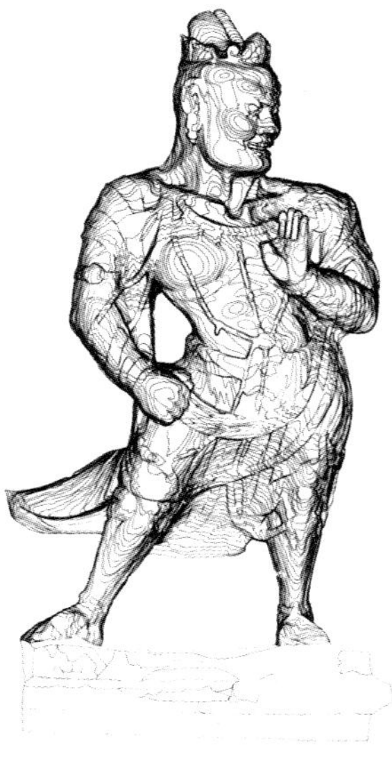

北壁力士 等值线图

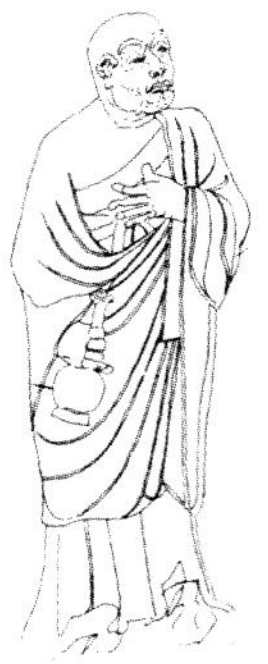
1 北壁西起第3身

2 北壁西起第4身

3 北壁西起第5身

4 北壁西起第6身

5 北壁西起第7身

6 北壁西起第8身

7 北壁西起第9身

8 正壁北起第1身

9 正壁北起第2身

10正壁北起第3身

11 正壁北起第4身

12 正壁北起第5身

13 正壁北起第6身

14 正壁北起第7身

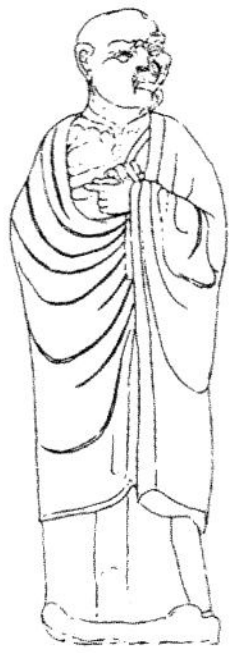
15正壁北起第8身

16正壁北起第9身

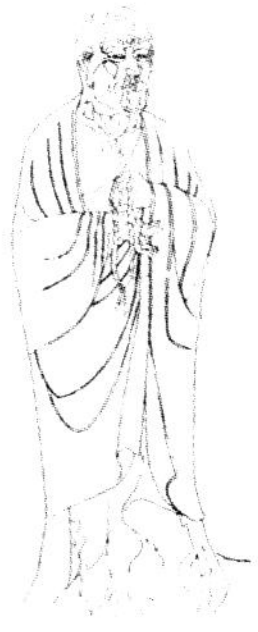
17 南壁东起第3身

18 南壁东起第4身

19 南壁东起第5身

20 南壁东起第6身

21 南壁东起第7身

（组图：龙门石窟）

(Photos by Longmen Grottoes)

莫高窟

Mogao Caves

1　甘肃敦煌莫高窟窟型。（图 / 敦煌研究院）
The grotto shape of Dunhuang Mogao Caves. (Photo by Dunhuang Research Acadamy)
2　甘肃敦煌莫高窟第 420 窟实测图。（图 / 敦煌研究院）
Measured drawing of Grotto No. 420 of Mogao Caves. (Photo by Dunhuang Research Acadamy)
3　莫高窟总立面图。（图 / 孙儒）
General elevation of Dunhuang Mogao Caves. (Photo by Sun Ru)

莫高窟总立面图

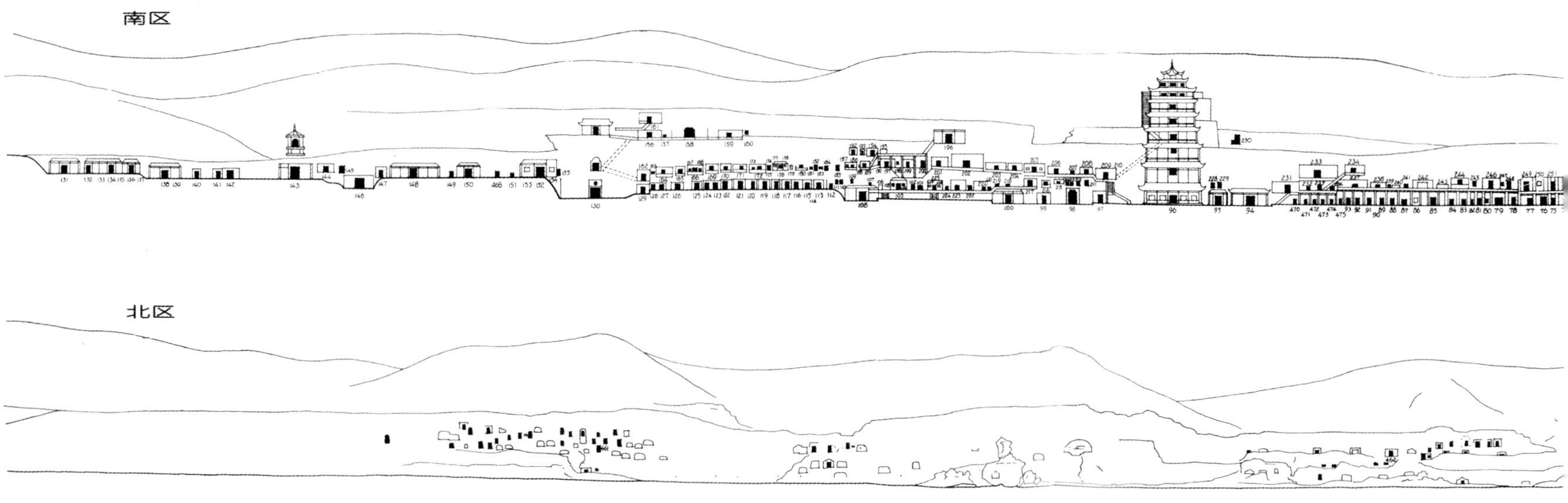

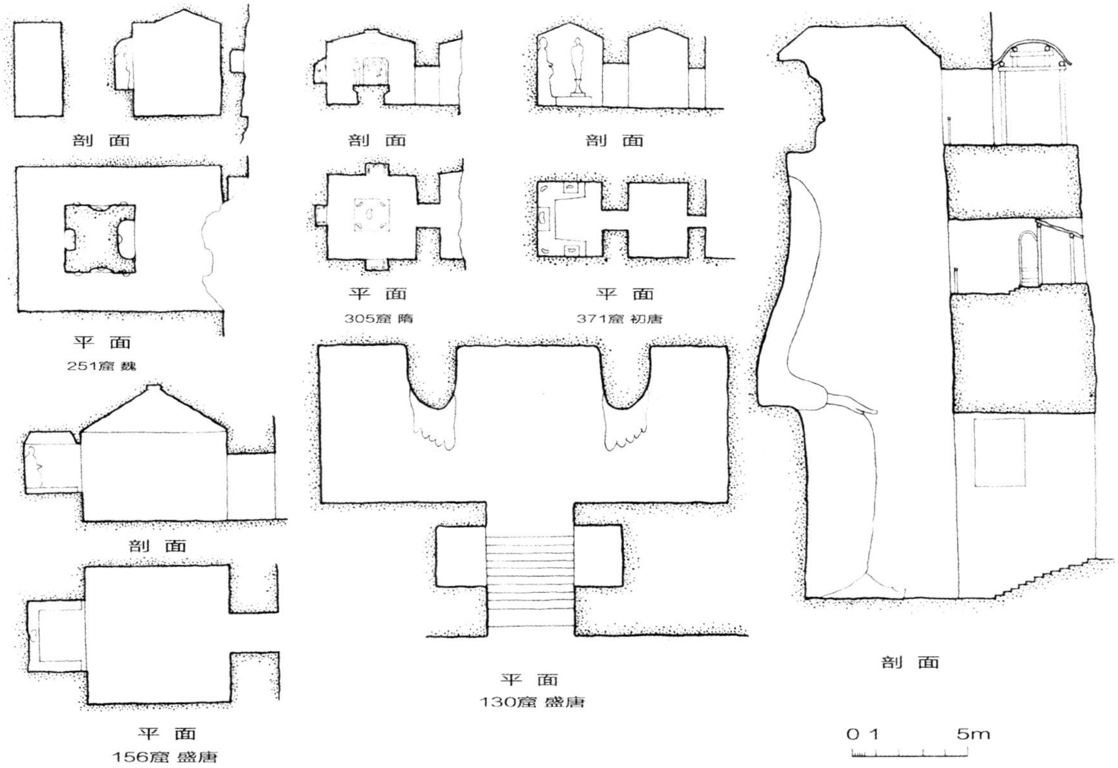
剖 面
平 面
251窟 魏
305窟 隋
371窟 初唐
130窟 盛唐
156窟 盛唐
0 1 5m

1

第420窟实测图

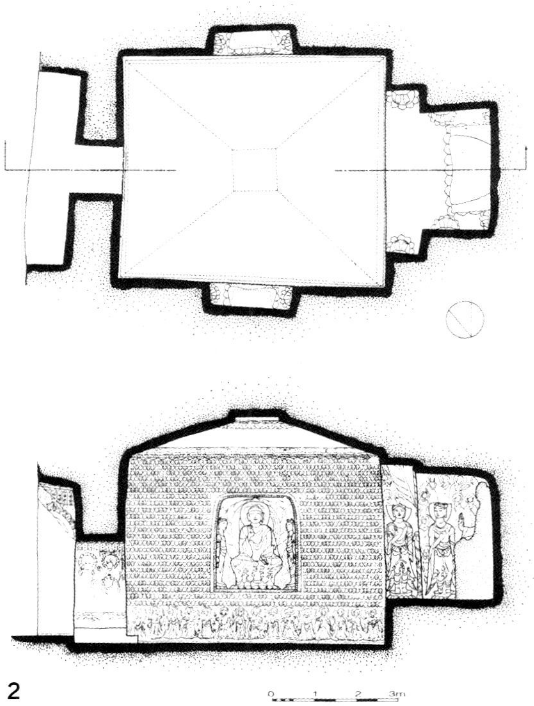
0 1 2 3m

2

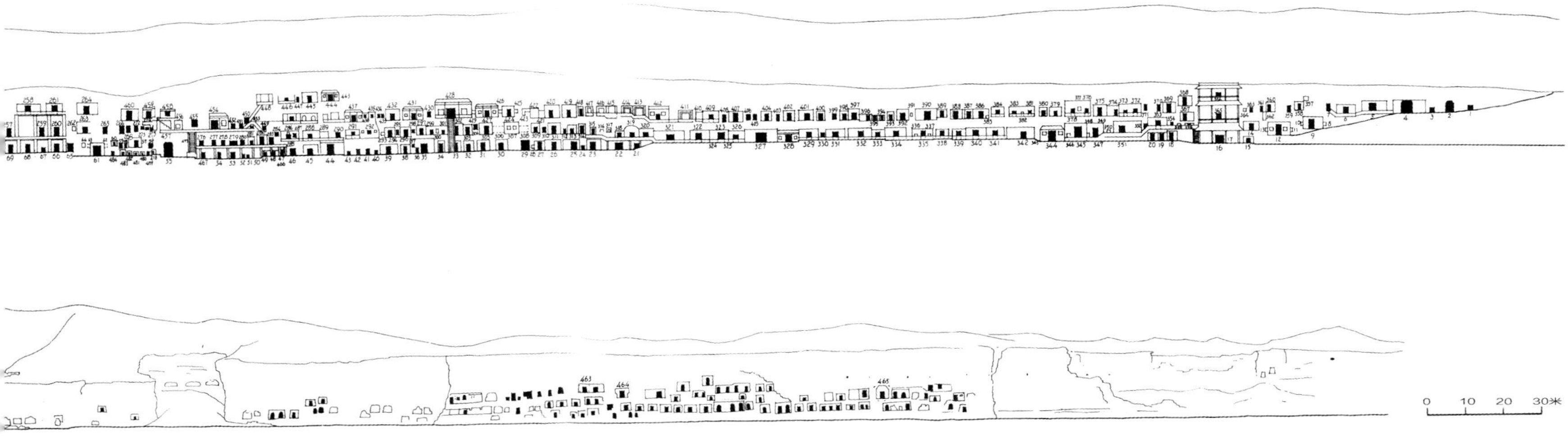
463
464
465
0 10 20 30米

1

2

3

1　甘肃敦煌莫高窟 321 窟壁画“飞天”。（图 / 敦煌研究院）

The flying Apsaras fresco of Caves No. 321 of Mogao Caves. (Photo by Dunhuang Research Acadamy)

2　甘肃敦煌莫高窟唐代壁画中的住宅。（图 / 敦煌研究院）

The dwelling house in the Tang Dynasty fresco of Mogao Caves. (Photo by Dunhuang Research Acadamy)

3　甘肃敦煌莫高窟 445 窟弥勒经变中耕获图。（图 / 敦煌研究院）

A picture of tilling and harvesting in Caves No. 445 of Mogao Caves. (Photo by Dunhuang Research Acadamy)

1　甘肃敦煌县莫高窟 332 窟东壁初唐阿弥陀净土变（摹本）。（图 / 敦煌研究院）

Amitabha pure land change of the early Tang Dynasty on the east wall of Cave No. 332 of Mogao Caves (copy). (Photo by Dunhuang Research Acadamy)

2　奈良国立博物馆藏平安后期（12 世纪前半叶）。（图 / 敦煌研究院）

Late period of Pingan (early part of the 12th century) stored in Nara National Museum. (Photo by Dunhuang Research Acadamy)

3　元兴寺极乐坊藏镰仓前期（13 世纪前半叶）阿弥陀。（图 / 敦煌研究院）

Amitabha of early Kamakura period stored at the Room of Bliss in Yuanxing Temple. (Photo by Dunhuang Research Acadamy)

4　知恩院藏镰仓后期（13 世纪后半叶）阿弥陀净土变（摹本）。（图 / 敦煌研究院）

Amitabha pure land change of the late Kamakura period (late 13th century) preserved in Chion Temple (copy). (Photo by Dunhuang Research Acadamy)

明清故宫（北京故宫、沈阳故宫）

北京故宫

依照中国古代星象学说，紫微垣（即北极星）位于中天，乃天帝所居，天人对应，所以故宫又称“紫禁城”。紫禁城位于北京市市中心，天安门广场北 1 公里、景山南门对面。为明清两代的皇宫，有 24 位皇帝相继在此登基执政。始建于 1406 年，迄今已 600 余年。故宫是世界上现存规模最大、最完整的古代木构建筑群，占地 72 万多平方米，建筑面积约 15 万平方米，拥有殿宇 9000 多间。故宫黄瓦红墙，白玉雕栏，规划严整，巍峨壮丽，是中国古建筑的精华。

建筑布局

故宫严格地按《周礼·考工记》中“前朝后寝，左祖右社”的帝都营建原则建造。整个故宫，在建筑布置上一砖一瓦都在表现着皇权至上、唯帝王独尊的设计理念，同时达到左右均衡和形体变化的艺术效果。

为了突出帝王至高无上的权威，故宫有一条贯穿宫城南北的中轴线，在这条中轴线上，按照“前朝后寝”的古制，布置着帝王发号施令、象征政权中心的三大殿（太和殿、中和殿、保和殿）和帝后居住的后三宫（乾清宫、交泰殿、坤宁宫）。在其内廷部分（乾清门以北），左右各形成一条以太上皇居住的宫殿——宁寿宫，和以太宫太妃居住的宫殿——慈宁宫为中心的次要轴线，这两条次要轴线又和外朝以太和门为中心，与左边的文华殿、右边的武英殿相呼应。两条次要轴线和中央轴线之间，有斋宫及养殿，其后即为嫔妃居住的东西六宫。

主要建筑

四大门

故宫有四个大门：东华门，西华门，神武门和午门。

午门　为正门，俗称“五凤楼”，是皇帝下诏书、下令出征的地方。午门当中的正门平时只有皇帝才可出入，皇帝大婚时皇后进一次，殿试考中状元、榜眼、探花的三人可从此门走出一次。文武大臣进出东侧门，宗室王公出入西侧门。

神武门　为后门，明朝时为“玄武门”，是一座城门楼形式的建筑，用最高等级的重檐庑殿式屋顶构建，但它的大殿只有五开间加围廊，没有左右向前伸展的两翼，所以在形制上要比午门低一个等级。神武门现为故宫博物院正门。

东华门与西华门　两门遥相对应，形制相同，平面矩形，红色城台，白玉须弥座，当中辟三座券门。城台上建有城楼，黄琉璃瓦重檐庑殿顶。城楼面阔五间，进深三间，四周出廊。

三大殿

太和门内，在 3 万多平方米开阔的庭院中，是外朝的中心：太和殿、中和殿、保和殿，统称三大殿。三大殿都建在汉白玉砌成的 8 米高的台基上，远望犹如神话中的宫阙琼楼。

太和殿　俗称“金銮殿”，是皇帝举行大典的地方，在宫中等级最高，体量最大，亦最富丽堂皇，是我国现存的一座最大的古代木结构殿宇。有直径达 1 米的木柱 92 根，其中 6 根围绕御座的是沥粉金漆的蟠龙柱。御座设在殿内高 2 米的基座上，前有造型美观的仙鹤、炉、鼎，后有精雕细刻的围屏。整个大殿装饰得金碧辉煌，威严华丽。

中和殿　是皇帝去太和殿举行大典前稍事休息和演习礼仪的地方，位于太和殿后。中和殿四面出廊，金砖铺地，黄琉璃瓦单檐四角攒尖顶，正中有鎏金宝顶。四脊顶端聚成尖状，上置铜胎鎏金球形的宝顶。

保和殿　在中和殿后，黄琉璃瓦重檐歇山式屋顶。屋顶正中有一条正脊，前后各有两条垂脊，在各条垂脊下部再斜出一条岔脊，连同正脊、垂脊、岔脊共九条。保和殿是每年除夕皇帝赐宴外藩王公的场所，也是科举考试举行殿试的地方。

内　庭

故宫建筑的后半部叫内廷，以乾清宫、交泰殿、坤宁宫为中心，东西两翼有东六宫和西六宫，是皇帝平日办事后妃居住生活的地方。前半部建筑庄严雄伟，以象征皇帝的至高无上；后半部内廷则富有生活气息，建筑多是自成院落，有花园、书斋、馆榭、山石等。

乾清宫　内廷正殿，高 20 米。殿的正中有宝座，内有“正大光明”匾。两头有暖阁。清康熙前这里为皇帝居住和处理政务之处，清雍正后皇帝移居养心殿，但仍在此批阅奏报、选派官吏和召见臣工。

坤宁宫　是明朝及清朝雍正帝之前的皇后寝宫，两头有暖阁。清代改为祭神场所。雍正后，西暖阁为萨满的祭祀地。其中东暖阁为皇帝大婚的洞房，康熙、同治、光绪三帝，均在此举行婚礼。

交泰殿　在乾清宫和坤宁宫之间，含“天地交合、安康美满”之意。四角攒尖，镀金宝顶，龙凤纹饰。明清时，该殿是皇后生日举办寿庆活动的场所。清代的“宝玺”（印章）也收藏在这里。

御花园

在坤宁北。原名宫后苑，占地 11000 多平方米，有建筑 20 余处。主体建筑钦安殿为重檐盝顶式，坐落于紫禁城的南北中轴线上，以其为中心，向前方及两侧铺展亭台楼阁。园中青翠的松柏和修竹点缀着玲珑的山石，形成四季长青的园林景观。

遗产价值

北京故宫的宫殿建筑，是我国现存最大、最完整的古建筑群。宫殿沿着一条南北向的中轴线排列，左右对称，规划严整，气魄宏伟，极为壮观。北京故宫和故宫博物院是世界上极少数同时具备艺术博物馆、建筑博物馆、历史博物馆、宫廷文化博物馆等特色，并且是符合国际公认的“原址保护”、“原状陈列”基本原则的博物馆和文化遗产。

沈阳故宫

2004 年，沈阳故宫作为明清故宫的扩展项目入选《世界遗产名录》。

沈阳故宫位于今沈阳市沈河区明清旧城中心，是后金入关前的沈阳（盛京）皇宫和清朝迁都北京后的盛京行宫（或称奉天行宫），始建于 1625 年，初成于 1636 年。1644 年清迁都北京后，经过整修，又成为皇帝巡幸东北时的行宫。现存古建筑 100 多座，总占地面积 60000 多平方米。沈阳故宫主体部分，是清太宗皇太极时期 (1627–1643 年) 的皇宫，具有浓厚的满族特色和中国东北地域建筑特色。

建筑布局

与北京故宫相比，沈阳故宫建筑风格具有独特的满、蒙、藏特色。东路为清太祖努尔哈赤时期建造的大政殿与十王亭——十王亭建筑群布局仿照八旗行军帐殿（大幄次）的布局。中路为清太宗皇太极时期续建的大内宫阙，包括大清门、崇政殿、凤凰楼以及清宁宫、关雎宫、麟趾宫、衍庆宫、永福宫等，其特点是“宫高殿低”，居住部分位于高台之上，俯瞰理政的正殿区域，这是来源于满族人喜居于台岗之上的生活习惯。西路是乾隆时期增建的文溯阁、嘉荫堂和仰熙斋等，西路以及中路的东西二宫则是完全的汉式建筑。整座皇宫楼阁林立，殿宇巍峨，雕梁画栋，富丽堂皇。

主要建筑

大政殿　俗称八角殿。始建于 1625 年，是盛京皇宫内最庄严最神圣的地方。八角重檐攒尖式，八面出廊，其下为须弥座台基。殿顶满铺黄琉璃瓦，镶绿剪边，正中相轮火焰珠顶，宝顶周围有八条铁链各与力士相连。殿前两明柱各有金龙盘绕，殿内为梵文天花和降龙藻井。殿内设有宝座、屏风及熏炉、香亭、鹤式烛台等。大政殿用于举行大典，如皇帝即位、颁布诏书、宣布军队出征、迎接将士凯旋等。1644 年福临在此登基继位，是为顺治元年。

十王亭　位于大政殿两侧八字形依次排列，是满族八旗制度在宫殿建筑上的反映，此建筑布局为中国古代宫廷建筑所仅见。其东侧五亭由北往南依次为左翼王亭、镶黄旗亭、正白旗亭、镶白旗亭、正蓝旗亭；西侧五亭依次为右翼王亭、正黄旗亭、正红旗亭、镶红旗亭、镶蓝旗亭。是清初八旗各主旗贝勒、大臣议政及处理政务的所在。

大清门　是盛京皇宫（今沈阳故宫博物院）的正门，俗称午门，建于天聪六年（1632 年）之前，为盛京皇宫中皇太极续修的早期建筑之一。它是一座面阔五间的硬山式建筑，房顶满铺琉璃瓦，饰以绿剪边，尤其是大清门山墙的最上端，南北突出的四个墀头，三面皆用五彩琉璃镶嵌而成，纹饰为凸出的海水云龙及象征吉祥的各种动物，做工精巧，栩栩如生。

崇政殿　在中路前院正中，俗称"金銮殿"，是沈阳故宫最重要的建筑。整座大殿全是木结构，面阔五间，进深三间。前后出廊硬山式，辟有隔扇门，前后出廊，围以石雕栏杆。殿顶铺黄琉璃瓦，镶绿剪边，正脊饰五彩琉璃龙纹及火焰珠。此殿为清太宗皇太极陛见臣下、宴请外国使臣以及处理大政的常朝之处。1636 年，后金改国号为"清"的大典就在此举行。"东巡"诸帝于此举行"展谒山陵礼成"等庆贺典礼。

凤凰楼　建造在崇政殿北首 4 米高的青砖台基上，有三层，顶铺黄琉璃瓦，镶绿剪边。此楼为盛京最高建筑，故有"盛京八景"之一"凤楼晓日"、"凤楼观塔"等称呼。凤凰楼上藏有乾隆御笔亲题的"紫气东来"匾。

清宁宫　为五开间前后廊硬山式。是清太宗皇太极和皇后居住的"中宫"。室门开于东次间，屋内西侧形成"筒子房"格局，东梢间为帝后寝宫。宽大的支摘窗式样朴素，棂条皆以"码三箭"式相交。宫门不用隔扇式，正对宫门竖立祭天的"索伦竿"，此均源自满族民间的传统风格。殿顶铺黄琉璃瓦镶缘剪边，前后皆方形檐柱，柱头饰兽面，檀枋施彩绘等，则是吸收汉、藏民族建筑艺术。

文溯阁　建于乾隆四十七年（1782 年），专为存放《文溯阁四库全书》而建，另有《古今图书集成》亦存于阁内。现为沈阳故宫西路的主体建筑，建筑形式仿照浙江宁波的天一阁，面阔六间，二楼三层重檐硬山式，前后出廊，上边盖黑色琉璃瓦加绿剪边，前后廊檐柱都装饰有绿色的地仗。所有的门、窗、柱都漆成绿色，外檐彩画也以蓝、绿、白相间的冷色调为主，这与其它宫殿红金为主的外檐彩饰迥然不同。其彩绘题材也不用宫殿中常见的行龙飞凤，而是以"白马献书"、"翰墨卷册"等与藏书楼功用相谐的图案，给人以古雅清新之感。

其帐幄式建筑造型及其布局，是满族人从狩猎发展而来的八旗制度在宫殿建筑上生动而具体的再现，为中国古代宫殿建筑所仅见。沈阳故宫的建筑风格与结构不仅体现地域特点，而且表达了民族融合的思想，与清王朝执政思想是统一的。此外，沈阳故宫所用材料的等级介于皇家与富豪之间，这与其统治地位相符，反映了清王朝初期创业时的景象，对研究古代建筑与文化有非常高的价值。

遗产价值

沈阳故宫博物院不仅以其多民族风格的宫苑建筑成为著名的旅游胜地，更以其丰富的院藏文物珍宝而享誉中外。其中，尤以明清宫廷文物弥足珍贵，堪称国宝。院藏文物珍宝展是集故宫院藏服饰、珐琅器、书画、雕刻品、漆器、瓷器等门类藏品之精粹。这些文物集中体现了中国劳动人民高超的工艺水准和清代宫廷的艺术风格，反映了中国明清时期生产工艺的水平，具有重要的观赏价值和研究价值。

沈阳故宫收藏和陈列的明清历史文物、艺术珍品及工艺美术品中，有许多中西文化交流的工艺品，如钟表、玻璃器皿可谓独具特色。这些技艺精湛的工艺品，充分显示了外国匠师们的创造智慧与艺术才能，同时也是 17–18 世纪中西方文化交流、贸易往来的历史见证。

长　城

不到长城非好汉，屈指行程二万。

——毛泽东

长城又称“万里长城”，是古代中国在不同时期为抵御塞北游牧部落联盟侵袭而修筑的规模浩大的军事工程的统称。2012 年 6 月 5 日，国家文物局在北京居庸关长城宣布，历经近五年的调查认定，中国历代长城总长度为 21196.18 千米，分布于北京、天津、河北、山西、内蒙古、辽宁、吉林、黑龙江、山东、河南、陕西、甘肃、青海等 15 个省市自治区，包括长城墙体、壕堑、单体建筑、关堡和相关设施等长城遗产 43721 处。这是中国首次科学、系统地测量历代长城的总长度。

不同时期的长城

春秋战国时期，各国诸侯为了防御别国入侵，修筑烽火台，并用城墙连接起来，形成了最早的长城。据历史文献记载，中国历史上有二十多个诸侯国家和封建王朝修筑过长城，总长度在 10 万里以上，其中秦、汉、明三个朝代所修长城的长度都超过了 1 万里。中国大部分省、市、自治区都有古长城、烽火台遗迹。

秦长城　中国北方的长城，肇始于战国时期的秦、赵、燕三国。

秦国自商鞅变法开始，便极力推行富国强兵策略。秦始皇为了修筑长城动用了 30 万人，创造了人类建筑史上的奇迹。长城的修建客观上起到了防止匈奴南侵、保护中原经济文化发展的积极作用。孙中山先生曾评价：“始皇虽无道，而长城之有功于后世，实与大禹治水等。”

赵国于武灵王二十六年（公元前 300 年）下令筑长城，自代并阴山而西，直抵大河，以防匈奴南下掳掠。

燕国是战国七雄中最弱的一个，直到燕昭王即位（公元前 311 年）以后，发愤图强，“燕亦筑长城，自造阳至襄平，置上谷、渔阳、右北平、辽西、辽东郡以拒胡。”

汉长城　自文帝到宣帝，修成了一条西起大宛贰师城，东至黑龙江北岸，全长近 1 万公里的长城，古丝绸之路有一半的路程与这条长城并行，是历史上最长的长城。不过直到西汉前期，战国秦、赵、燕长城仍在发挥军事防御作用，虽然它的防御能力已大不如战国时期了。直到汉武帝把匈奴赶到漠北以后，修复蒙恬所筑秦长城和修建外长城，这条战国秦、赵、燕长城才被放弃，它的军事防御作用随之终结。

唐长城　2011 年 11 月 6 日，享有“唐长城”之誉的牡丹江边墙与秦长城一样被正式列入中国长城世界文化遗产名录。

牡丹江边墙是渤海时期为防御北方黑水靺鞨而修筑的一条防御体系，是和中国长城具有同等性质的军事防御工程。

明长城　明代，为了防御鞑靼、瓦剌的侵扰，从没间断过对长城的修建，从洪武至万历，其间经过 20 次大规模的修建，筑起了一条西起甘肃嘉峪关，东至辽东虎山，全长 6350 公里的边墙。明朝在“外边”长城之外，还修筑了“内边”长城和“内三关”长城。“内边”长城以北齐所筑为基础，起自内蒙古与山西交界处的偏关以西，东行经雁门关、平型诸关入河北，然后向东北，经涞源、房山、昌平，直达居庸关，然后又由北向东，至怀柔的四海关与“外边”长城相接，以紫荆关为中心，大致成南北走向。“内三关”长城在很多地方和“内边”长城并行，有些地方两城相隔仅数十里。

现存重点遗址

八达岭长城　各地的长城景观中，北京八达岭长城建筑得特别坚固，保存也最完好。八达岭长城位于北京延庆县，是明长城最具代表性的一段，居庸关的前哨，海拔高度 1015 米。地势险要，历来是兵家必争之地，是明代重要的军事关隘和北京的重要屏障。

慕田峪长城　慕田峪长城位于怀柔区境内，是北京新十六景之一。西接居庸关长城，东连古北口，著名的长城景观箭扣、牛角边、鹰飞倒仰等位于慕田峪长城西端，是万里长城的精华所在。

司马台长城　独具“险、密、奇、巧、全”五大特点的司马台长城，位于北京市密云县东北的古北口镇境内，距北京 120 公里。它东起望京楼，西至后川口，全长 5.4 公里，整段长城构思精巧，结构新颖。著名长城专家罗哲文教授盛赞：“中国长城是世界之最，而司马台长城又堪称中国长城之最。”司马台长城是我国唯一保留明代原貌的古建筑遗址。

古北口长城 古北口长城是中国长城史上最完整的长城体系，由北齐长城和明长城共同组成，包括卧虎山、蟠龙山、金山岭和司马台四个城段。古北口是山海关、居庸关两关之间的长城要塞，为辽东平原和内蒙古通往中原地区的咽喉，尤其在辽、金、元、明、清这五朝，大大小小争夺古北口的战役从未停止过。

山海关长城 山海关长城是万里长城的入海处。现属山海关境内的长城全长 26 公里，由关城、东罗城、西罗城、南翼城、北翼城、威远城和宁海城七大城堡构成，四周有长 4769 米、高 11.6 米、厚 10 余米的城墙，墙体高大坚实，气势宏伟。在东、西、南、北建有四个城门，城东南隅、东北隅建有角楼，城中间建有雄伟的钟鼓楼。整座建筑规模雄宏，防御工程坚固。

嘉峪关长城 嘉峪关长城是明长城西端的终点，河西第一隘口，也是丝绸之路上的重要一站。建于明洪武五年（1372 年），面积超过 33500 平方米，是迄今为止保存最完整的一座关城。由内城、外城和城壕组成完整的防御体系。关城四隅有角楼，高两层，形如碉堡。

居庸关长城 有“天下第一雄关”之称的居庸关是万里长城上历史最悠久、最著名的关隘之一，其建筑规模之大，文化内涵之深，堪称我国万里长城关城建设之最。居庸关位于北京城西北 48 公里处的关沟峡谷之中。这里两山夹峙，山形陡峭，一水中流。

遗产价值

长城是世界古代史上最伟大的军事防御工程，它并非简单孤立的一线城墙，而是由点到线、由线到面，把长城沿线的烽燧、隘口、军堡、关城和军事重镇连接成一张严密的网，形成一个完整的防御体系。军堡、关城和军事重镇这个体系具有战斗、指挥、观察、通讯、隐蔽等多种功能，并配置有长驻军队的点线结合防御工程整体。

在冷兵器时代，长城防御体系的军事作用是卓有成效的。秦时，“北筑长城而守藩篱，却匈奴七百余里，胡人不敢南下而牧马。”（《新书·过秦》）汉武帝时，“建塞徼，起亭燧，筑外城，设屯戍以守之，然后边境得用少安。”（《汉书·匈奴传》）由此可见，修筑长城不仅是一种积极防御的措施，也是一种积蓄力量、继续进取的谋略。这是长城存在的根本意义。

长城的主体工程是绵延万里的高大城墙，大都建在山岭最高处，沿着山脊把蜿蜒不尽的山势勾画出清晰的轮廓，塑造出奔腾飞跃、气势磅礴的巨龙，从而成为中华民族的象征。在万里城墙上，分布着千百座雄关、隘口，成千上万座敌台、烽火台，打破了城墙的单调感，使高低起伏的地形更显得雄奇险峻，充满巨大的艺术魅力。

秦始皇陵及兵马俑坑

秦始皇陵位于陕西临潼县城东 5 公里，距西安 36 公里。不仅是中国历史上第一座皇帝陵，也是最大的皇帝陵。1974 年以来，在陵园东 1.5 公里处发现从葬兵马俑坑 3 处，出土陶俑 8000 余件、战车百乘以及数万件实物兵器等文物。1980 年又在陵园西侧出土青铜铸大型车马两乘。秦始皇陵兵马俑坑的发现引起全世界的震惊和关注，是世界上最大的地下军事博物馆，被称为“世界第八大奇迹”。

建筑布局

“秦皇扫六合，虎视何雄哉！刑徒七十万，起土骊山隈。” 这脍炙人口的诗句出自大诗人李白笔下，它讴歌了秦始皇的辉煌业绩，描述了营造骊山墓工程的浩大气势。的确，陵园工程之浩大、用工人数之多、持续时间之久都是前所未有的，由此开创了历代封建统治者奢侈厚葬之先例。 陵园工程的修建伴随着秦始皇一生的政治生涯：当他 13 岁刚刚登上秦国国王宝座时，陵园营建工程就开始了。

秦始皇陵及兵马俑坑坑是秦始皇陵的陪葬坑。据史书记载，陵园由丞相李斯主持规划设计，大将章邯监工，修筑时间长达 38 年。当时，秦朝总人口约 2000 万，而筑陵劳役达 72 万之多。修陵冢所用黄土，取自今陵园以南 2000 米的三刘村到采石场之间，该地有高 5–25 米的多级黄土崖。陵园所用大量石料取自渭河北岸的仲山、峻峨山，全靠人力运至临潼，工程艰难可想而知。

陵区分陵园区和从葬区两部分。陵园区占地近 8 平方公里，建外城、内城两重，封土呈四方锥形。整个陵园坐西向东，以封土为中心可分为四个层次，即地下宫城（地宫）为核心部位，其它依次为内城、外城和外城以外，主次分明。占地面积 56.25 平方公里，城内面积约 2.13 平方公里。陵园的城垣由内外两重构成，两座城垣都呈南北向长方形，相互套合，呈南北长东西窄的’回’字形。城墙总长约 12 公里，与西安的明代城墙长度相近。

出土经过

1974 年 3 月，陵东的西杨村村民杨志发打井时，一锄头下去，刨出一个陶制武士头。经考古工作者发掘，终于发现了使全世界为之震惊的秦始皇陵兵马俑坑。

1974–1977 年陕西省考古工作者在临潼县西杨村西南的发掘现场共发现三座秦俑坑，三坑皆为土木混合结构的地穴式坑道建筑。1974 年 3 月发现的 1 号坑最大，平面呈长方形，面积达 14260 平方米。坑内由战车组成的 40 路纵队，除位于边沿、担负侧翼与后卫的武士分别面向南、北、西方外，其余 38 路武士及战车一律面朝东方。按已发掘部分的排列密度推算，1 号坑埋藏兵马俑总数达 6000 余件。

1976 年发现的 2 号坑位于 1 号坑东端北侧 20 米处，平面略呈曲尺形，面积约 6000 平方米。据已发掘的资料推算，此坑埋藏兵马俑约 1400 余件，木质战车 89 辆。3 号坑位于 1 号坑西端北侧 25 米处，东距 2 号坑约 120 米，平面呈凹字形，面积约 520 平方米。坑内埋藏木质战车 1 辆，陶马 4 匹，武士俑 68 件。武士俑作环绕四壁、面朝内相向排列。

从各坑的形制结构及兵马俑的装备情况判断，1 号坑象征由步兵和战车组成的主体部队，2 号坑为步兵、骑兵和车兵穿插组成的混合部队，3 号坑是统领 1、2 号坑的军事指挥所。

陶俑与铜车马

秦陵兵马俑坑出土的陶俑均具有浓厚的军事色彩，因此，都应属于武士俑。从服装上看，可分为战袍武士俑和铠甲武士俑，从身份和地位上可分为军吏俑和士兵俑两大类。其中，军吏俑按级别又可分为高级军吏俑（俗称将军俑）、中级军吏俑和下级军吏俑。按兵种可分为步兵俑、车兵俑、骑兵俑、弩兵俑。仅从冠和铠甲来划分，高级军吏俑头戴鹖冠，身穿鱼鳞甲；中级军吏俑头戴单板长冠，身穿花边铠甲；下级军吏俑头戴单板长冠，身穿无花边铠甲。士兵头上无冠，有甲衣甲片者地位较高，但所有甲衣一律不带花纹。从上述分类看，秦朝军队是一个兵种齐全、等级森严的铁军。

铜车马出土于秦陵西侧 20 米处，1980 年局部试掘铜车马坑时，在一木椁内出土一前一后纵置的两辆大型铜车马，出土时已残破，经修复后恢复原状。 铜车马主体为青铜所铸，一些零部件为金银饰品。秦代的金属加工技术有了辉煌的成就，在秦陵铜车马的制造上集中体现出来。秦陵铜车马共有 3000 多个零件，秦代工匠巧妙地运用了铸造、焊接、镶嵌、销接、活铰连接、子母扣连接、转轴连接等各种工艺技术，将其结合为一个整体，达到了非常高的工艺水平。

遗产价值

秦始皇陵及兵马俑坑所折射的历史层面既多又广，在建筑史、服饰史、制度史尤其是王陵制度史等方面，具有独特的认识价值。

秦始皇陵及兵马俑坑震撼世人的首推其卓越的艺术成就。几千件魁伟英武的大型陶塑艺术作品，以整体形象排列在将近两万平方米的空间里，体现出古代艺术家驾驭宏大艺术题材、追求整体气韵和艺术创造的卓越才能，其磅礴的气势几乎使所有不同肤色的参观者都从心灵深处产生强烈震撼。秦俑千人千面、呼之欲出的人物塑像从形体把握、神韵处理、色彩运用、细部刻画等方面表现出作者的艺术素养和艺术成就。作品写实主义的风格不仅给我们留下了一个高超的古代艺术范本，同时也留下了许多关于那个时代的极富价值的历史记录。

秦始皇陵及兵马俑坑文物的出土也较大幅度地改写了人们对秦代的科技水平的认识，以大量的实证材料形象地展现了秦代生产力的发展水平。就科技史而言，秦俑坑发现的许多资料都是令世人震惊的。此外，俑坑数千兵马俑所展示的军事内容无疑是军事史研究的最重要的、最形象的资料之一，许多资料使人们对古代军事领域的认识更进一步。

北京皇家祭坛——天坛

祭天作为人类祈求神灵赐福禳灾的一种文化行为，曾经是中国古代先民生活中的重要内容。我国从传说中的“三皇五帝”时代至清末，一直举行祭天典礼，绵延上下五千年，可谓渊远流长。

天坛是明永乐十八年（1420 年）仿南京形制建天地坛，合祭皇天后土，当时是在大祀殿行祭典。嘉靖九年（1530 年）嘉靖皇帝听大臣言：“古者祀天于圜丘，祀地于方丘。圜丘者，南郊地上之丘，丘圜而高，以象天也。方丘者，北郊泽中之丘，丘方而下，以象地也。”于是决定天地分祭，在大祀殿南建圜丘祭天，在北城安定门外另建方泽坛祭地。嘉靖十三年（1534 年）圜丘改名天坛，方泽改名地坛。大祀殿废弃后，改为祈谷坛。嘉靖十七年（1538 年）祈谷坛被废，于嘉靖十九年（1540 年）在坛上另建大享殿，二十四年（1545 年）建成。清乾隆十六年（1751 年）更名祈年殿。以后多次修缮、扩建。

建筑布局

在整个北京城里，北有地坛祭地，南有天坛祭天，东有日坛祭太阳，西有月坛祭月亮，其中天坛最为光彩夺目，气宇非凡。

天坛是圜丘、祈谷两坛的总称，是明清两代皇帝“祭天”、“祈谷”的场所。有坛墙两重，形成内外坛，坛墙南方北圆，象征天圆地方。主要建筑在内坛，圜丘坛在南、祈谷坛在北，二坛同在一条南北轴线上，中间有墙相隔。圜丘坛内主要建筑有圜丘坛、皇穹宇等，祈谷坛内主要建筑有祈年殿、皇乾殿、祈年门等。著名的祈年殿在最北方，这是天坛内最宏伟、最华丽的建筑，也是想象中离天最近的地方。明嘉靖二十四年（1545 年）改为三重顶圆殿，殿顶覆盖上青、中黄、下绿三色琉璃瓦，寓意天地万物。清乾隆十六年（1751 年）改三色瓦为统一的蓝瓦金顶，定名“祈年殿”，是孟春（正月）祈谷的专用建筑。

天坛的总体设计，从它的建筑布局到每一个细节处理，都强调了“天”的意念。它有 300 多米长的高出地面的甬道，人们登临其上，环顾四周，首先看到的是广阔的天空和那象征“天”的祈年殿，一种与天接近的感觉油然而生。

主要建筑在内坛的南北中轴线上，圜丘坛在南，祭天；祈谷坛在北，祈谷。两坛由一座长 360 米、宽近 30 米、南低北高的丹陛桥（也称海墁大道或神道）相连。坛内主要建筑有祈年殿、皇乾殿、圜丘、皇穹宇、斋宫、无梁殿、长廊、双环万寿亭等，还有回音壁、三音石、七星石等名胜古迹。

主要建筑

圜丘坛　天坛是祈谷、圜丘两坛的总称，有两重坛墙环绕，将坛域分为内、外坛两部分，均为南方北圆。

圜丘坛是举行冬至祭天大典的场所，主要建筑有圜丘、皇穹宇及配殿、神厨、三库及宰牲亭，附属建筑有具服台、望灯等。圜丘明朝时为三层蓝色琉璃圆坛，清乾隆十四年（1749 年）扩建，并改蓝色琉璃为艾叶青石台面，汉白玉柱、栏。

皇穹宇　皇穹宇位于圜丘坛以北，是供奉圜丘坛祭祀神位的场所，存放祭祀神牌的地方。初为重檐圆攒尖顶建筑。清乾隆十七年（1752 年）改建为鎏金宝顶单檐蓝瓦圆攒尖顶。砖木结构，殿内没有横梁，全靠八根檐柱、八根金柱和众多的斗拱支托屋顶，巧妙地运用了力学原理。三层天花藻井，层层收进，极有特色，为古建筑中少有。殿檐覆盖蓝色琉璃瓦，檐顶有镏金宝顶，殿墙是正圆形磨砖对缝的砖墙，远远望去，就像一把金顶的蓝宝石巨伞。

回音壁　站在圜丘台中间的圆心石上轻轻唤一声，就立即从四面八方传来回声，好似众人齐鸣，一呼百应。封建帝王附会说这是皇天上帝在向凡人发出“圣谕”。其实，这种现象是声波被阻的回音。

祈谷坛　是举行孟春祈谷大典的场所，建于明朝永乐十八年（1420 年）。主要建筑有祈年殿、皇乾殿、东西配殿、祈年门等，附属建筑有内外壝墙、具服台、丹陛桥，内坛墙上东南西北各设天门，西外坛墙设祈谷坛门，内坛东部有七星石。祈谷坛的祭坛为坛殿结合的圆形建筑，是根据古代“屋下祭帝”的说法建立的。三重蓝琉璃瓦，圆形屋檐，攒尖顶，宝顶鎏金。

祈年殿　祈年殿是一座宏伟而又极具民族风格的独特建筑，展现了中国古人独特的天文理念和缜密的建筑思维，表达了古代中国人对天的崇敬和对五谷丰登的企盼。殿高 33 米，直径 24.2 米，宏伟壮观，气度非凡，是昔日北京的最高建筑之一。圆形三重檐攒尖屋顶向上层层收缩，都是用蓝色琉璃瓦覆盖，以此来象征“天”。顶部是鎏金宝顶，抬头仰视，便是龙凤藻井，中心是龙凤成祥的图案。而巨大的三层殿顶全靠殿内 28 根落地柱支撑，中间的 4 根柱名为“龙井柱”，东南西北方向分别代表了春夏秋冬；而龙井柱外围的 12 个红漆金柱所分割出来的 12 个开间，则分别代表了一年的 12 个月份；外面两环的 24 个开间又分别代表了一年的 24 个节气；同时，28 根大柱，也代表了天上的 28 个星宿。

丹陛桥　是连接祈谷坛南砖门及南天门（成贞门）的甬道，也是连接祈坛和圜丘坛的轴线，长 360 米，宽 30 米。丹陛桥上有三条石道，中为神道，东为御道，西为王道。北高南低，北端高 4 米，南端高 1 米。北行令人步步登高，如临天庭。

斋宫　位于祈谷坛内坛西南隅。宫内建有无梁殿、寝殿、钟楼、值守房和巡守步廊等礼仪、居住、服务、警卫专用建筑，均采用绿色琉璃瓦，以两重宫墙、两道御沟围护。斋宫布局严谨，环境典雅，是中国古代祭祀斋戒建筑的代表作。

神乐署　位于天坛西外坛，为明清时期演习祭祀礼乐的场所，被誉为明清两朝最高的礼乐学府。六楹五开间，东西向设穿堂门，殿内面积达 600 平方米。现开辟为“中和韶乐”展演区，举办古代祭祀乐舞展演，同时作为中和韶乐乐器钟、磬的主要展馆。

遗产价值

天坛是世界上最大的祭天建筑群。天坛建于 15 世纪上半叶，是保存完好的坛庙建筑群。无论在整体布局还是单一建筑上，都反映出天地之间的关系，而这一关系在中国古代宇宙观中占据着核心位置。同时，这些建筑还体现出帝王在这一关系中所起的独特作用。

天坛从选位、规划、建筑设计以及祭祀礼仪和祭祀乐舞，无不依据中国古代《周易》阴阳、五行等学说，成功地把古人对“天”的认识、“天人关系”以及对上苍的愿望表现得淋漓尽致。

北京天坛建筑处处展示中国古代特有的寓意、象征的艺术表现手法。圜丘的尺度和构件的数量集中并反复使用“九”这个数字，以象征“天”和强调与“天”的联系。

北京天坛集古代哲学、历史、数学、力学、美学、生态学于一炉，是古代坛庙建筑的精品，被誉为是中国古代建筑技术与艺术完美结合的金字名片，成为北京的象征。

北京皇家园林——颐和园

颐和园是中国现存规模最大、保存最完整的皇家园林，中国四大名园（另三座为承德避暑山庄、苏州拙政园、苏州留园）之一。位于北京市海淀区，距北京城区 15 公里，占地约 290 公顷。颐和园主要由万寿山和昆明湖两大部分组成，水面（昆明湖）面积约 220 公顷，占全园面积的四分之三。园内建筑以佛香阁为中心，共有亭、台、楼、阁、廊、榭等不同形式的建筑 3000 多间。整个景区规模宏大，是集中国园林建筑艺术之大成的杰作。

建筑布局

颐和园，原名清漪园，始建于清乾隆帝十五年（1750 年），历时 15 年竣工，是清代北京著名的“三山五园”（香山静宜园、玉泉山静明园、万寿山清漪园、圆明园、畅春园）中最后建成的一座。乾隆十五年（1750 年），乾隆皇帝为孝敬其母孝圣皇太后，动用 448 万两白银在这里改建为清漪园，以此为中心把两边的四个园子连为一体，形成了从现清华园到香山长达二十公里的皇家园林区。咸丰十年（1860 年），清漪园被英法联军焚毁。光绪十四年（1888 年），慈禧太后以筹措海军经费的名义动用 500–600 万两白银，由雷廷昌主持重建，改称颐和园。到光绪二十六年（1900 年），颐和园又遭“八国联军”的破坏，许多珍宝被劫掠一空。光绪二十九年（1903 年）修复。1924 年，颐和园辟为对外开放公园。1949 年之后，政府不断拨款修缮。1961 年 3 月 4 日，颐和园被公布为第一批全国重点文物保护单位，1998 年 11 月被列入《世界遗产名录》。

颐和园景区大致可分为万寿前山、昆明湖、后山后湖三部分。前山以佛香阁为中心，组成巨大的主体建筑群，华丽雄伟，气势磅礴。碧波荡漾的昆明湖平铺在万寿山南麓，约占全园面积的四分之三。湖中有一座南湖岛，由美丽的十七孔桥和岸上相连。湖西部有一西堤，堤上修有六座造形优美的桥。后山后湖碧水萦回，古松参天，环境清幽。

颐和园的建筑风格吸收了中国各地建筑的精华。东部的宫殿区和内廷区，是典型的北方四合院风格，一个一个的封闭院落由游廊联通；南部的湖泊区是典型的杭州西湖风格，一道“西堤”把湖泊一分为二，十足的江南格调；万寿山的北面，是典型的西藏喇嘛庙宇风格，有白塔，有碉堡式建筑；北部的苏州街店铺林立，水道相通，又是典型的水乡风格。

颐和园集传统造园艺术之大成，借景周围的山水环境，饱含中国皇家园林的恢弘富丽气势，又充满自然之趣，高度体现了“虽由人作，宛自天开”的造园准则。万寿山、昆明湖构成其基本框架，百余座建筑物点缀其间，大小院落 20 余处，古树名木 1600 余株。其中佛香阁、长廊、石舫、苏州街、十七孔桥、谐趣园、大戏台等都已成为家喻户晓的代表性建筑。

主要建筑

万寿山 万寿山为燕山余脉，高 58.59 米，海拔 108.94 米，前临昆明湖。明弘治七年（1494 年），孝宗的乳母助圣夫人罗氏在山前建园静寺。乾隆十五年（1750 年），为庆祝皇太后六十寿辰于园静寺旧址建大报恩延寿寺。次年将山改名为万寿山，并将开拓昆明湖的土方按照原布局的需要堆放在山上，使东西两坡舒缓而对称，成为全园的主体。建筑群依山而筑，从山脚的“云辉玉宇”牌楼，经排云门、二宫门、排云殿、德辉殿、佛香阁直至山顶的智慧海，形成一条层层上升的中轴线。现存的万寿山建筑是英法联军烧毁后慈禧太后重新建造的。

昆明湖 昆明湖是颐和园的主要湖泊，占全园面积的四分之三。南部的前湖区碧波荡漾，烟波浩淼；湖中有一道西堤，堤上桃柳成行；十七孔桥横卧湖上，湖中三岛上也有形式各异的古典建筑。由于岛堤分隔，湖面出现层次，避免了单调空疏。西堤以及堤上的六座桥是有意识地摹仿杭州西湖的苏堤和“苏堤六桥”，使昆明湖益发神似西湖。西堤一带碧波垂柳，自然景色开阔。湖岸和湖堤绿树成荫，水光潋滟，呈现出一派富于江南情调的近湖远山的自然美。

佛香阁 佛香阁是一座宏伟的塔式宗教建筑，为全园建筑布局的中心。清乾隆时（1736–1795 年）在此筑九层延寿塔，至第八层奉旨停修，改建佛香阁。咸丰十年(1860年)毁于英法联军。光绪时(1875–1908年)在原址依样重建，供奉佛像。该阁仿杭州的六和塔建造，兴建在20米的石造台基上，阁高41米，八面，三层，四重檐。阁内有八根铁梨木大柱，直贯顶部，下有20米高的石台基。结构相当复杂，为古典建筑精品。

颐和园长廊　回廊和角亭建筑是园林的常用形式。颐和园长廊东起邀月门，西至石丈亭，中间穿过排云门，两侧对称点缀着留佳、寄澜、秋水、清遥四座重檐八角攒尖亭，象征春夏秋冬四季。全长728米，共273间，有548根柱子。长廊以其精美的建筑、曲折多变的造型和极为丰富的彩画而久负盛名，是我国现存古建筑中最长的廊。廊间的每根枋梁上都绘有彩画，共14000余幅。

四大部洲　在万寿山后山中部，有一组汉藏式的建筑群。占地20000平方米，因山顺势，就地起阁。前有须弥灵境(现改为平台)，两侧有3米高的经幢，后有寺庙群主体建筑香岩宗印之阁。四周是象征佛教世界的四大部洲，即：东胜身洲、西牛货洲、南赡部洲、北俱卢洲和用不同形式的塔台修建成的八小部洲。南、西南、东北、西北还有代表佛经“四智”的红、白、黑、绿四座喇嘛塔，塔上有十三层环状“相轮”，表示佛经“十三天”。塔型别致，造型端庄美观。四大部洲和八小部洲中间有两个凹凸不平的台殿，一个代表月台，一个代表日台，象征着日月环绕佛身。

大戏楼　大戏楼在德和园内，与承德避暑山庄里的清音阁、紫禁城内的畅音阁，合称清代三大戏台。德和园大戏楼是为慈禧六十寿辰修建的，专供慈禧看戏。高21米，在颐和园中仅次于最高的佛香阁。戏楼共三层，后台化妆楼二层。顶板上有七个“天井”，地板中有“地井”。舞台底部有水井和五个方池。演神鬼戏时，可从“天”而降，也可从“地”而出，还可引水上台。

遗产价值

颐和园作为一个大型皇家园林，在世界造园史上有自己独特的理念和艺术成就，它模拟大自然的美景，经过加工、提炼和创造，把自然美和人工美统一起来，使有限的空间得到无限延伸，形成赏心悦目变换丰富的“可望、可行、可游、可居”的特殊环境。颐和园是中国封建王朝最后建造的世上首屈一指的皇家园林，它杰出的园林艺术价值和重要的科学文化历史价值，使它成为中外最著名的游览胜地之一，成为人类的共同文化财富。

承德避暑山庄及其周围寺庙

承德避暑山庄是中国现存最大的古典皇家园林，由皇帝宫室、皇家园林和宏伟壮观的寺庙群组成，又名“承德离宫”或“热河行宫”。占地 564 万平方米，环绕山庄婉蜒起伏的宫墙长达万米，是中国现存最大的古典皇家园林。与北京紫禁城相比，避暑山庄以朴素淡雅的山村野趣为格调，取自然山水之本色，吸收江南塞北之风光，成为与北京的颐和园、苏州的拙政园、苏州的留园并称的中国四大名园。

建筑布局

当年康熙皇帝在北巡途中，发现承德这片地方地势良好，气候宜人，风景优美，又直达清王朝的发祥地——北方，是满清皇帝家乡的门户，还可俯视关内，外控蒙古各部，于是选定在这里建筑行宫。康熙四十二年（1703 年）开始在此大兴土木，至康熙五十二年（1713 年）建成三十六景。乾隆六年（1741 年）到乾隆五十七年（1792 年）又继续修建，新增加三十六景和山庄外的外八庙，界墙内面积达到 564 公顷，别成一处皇家园林巨构。

山庄融南北建筑艺术精华，园内建筑规模不大，殿宇和围墙多采用青砖灰瓦、原木本色，淡雅庄重，简朴适度，与京城故宫的黄瓦红墙、描金彩绘、堂皇耀目呈鲜明对照。山庄的建筑既具有南方园林的风格、结构和工程做法，又多沿袭北方常用的手法，成为南北建筑艺术完美结合的典范。

避暑山庄分宫殿区、湖泊区、平原区、山峦区四大部分。

宫殿区位于湖泊南岸，地势平坦，是皇帝处理朝政、举行庆典和生活起居的地方，占地 10 万平方米，由正宫、松鹤斋、万壑松风和东宫四组建筑组成。湖泊区在宫殿区的北面，湖泊面积包括洲、岛约占 43 公顷，有八个小岛屿，将湖面分割成大小不同的区域，层次分明，洲岛错落，碧波荡漾，富有江南特色。东北角有清泉，即著名的热河泉。平原区在湖区北面的山脚下，地势开阔，有万树园和试马埭，是一片碧草茵茵，林木茂盛，茫茫草原风光。山峦区在山庄的西北部，面积约占全园的五分之四，这里山峦起伏，沟壑纵横，众多楼堂殿阁、庙宇寺观点缀其间。整个山庄东南多水，西北多山，是中国自然地貌的缩影。

主要建筑

避暑山庄是中国三大古建筑群之一，它的最大特色是山中有园，园中有山，大小建筑有 120 多组，其中康熙以四字组成“康熙三十六景”，乾隆以三字组成“乾隆三十六景”，合而成为“避暑山庄七十二景”。其中最著名的有：

松鹤斋　康熙时，皇太后来避暑山庄，居住在西峪的松鹤清樾。乾隆十四年 (1749 年)，乾隆帝在正宫东面另建一组八进院落的建筑，题名松鹤斋，以供皇太后居住。当年，松鹤斋内“常见青松蟠户外，更欣白鹤舞庭前”，庭院中并有驯鹿悠游其间。绥成殿后依次有照房 15 间、门殿 3 间、大殿 7 间，名为乐寿堂，后改名为“悦性居”，都是皇太后的寝宫。

正宫　是宫殿区的主体建筑。建于康熙五十年至五十二年，乾隆十九年（1754 年）重新修缮，改建，占地 1 万平方米。包括九进院落，由丽正门、午门、阅射门、澹泊敬诚殿、四知书屋、十九间照房、烟波致爽殿、云山胜地楼、岫云门以及一些朝房、配殿和回廊等组成。分为“前朝”、“后寝”两部分。前朝是皇帝处理军机政务的办公区，后寝是皇帝和后妃们日常起居的生活区。主殿叫“澹泊敬诚”，是用珍贵的楠木建成，因此也叫楠木殿。是皇帝治理朝政的地方，各种隆重的大典也都在这里举行。

东宫　在松鹤斋的东面，地势比正宫和松鹤斋低。东宫的前面宫墙上另辟大门，称德汇门，为重台城门，形制与丽正门相仿。进入德汇门后，中轴线上的主体建筑依次有门殿七间、正殿十一间，以及清音阁、福寿阁、勤政殿、卷阿胜境殿等。1933 年，日寇入侵承德，为庆祝“胜利”将东宫烧毁，现仅存基址。其中清音阁俗称大戏楼，与现存故宫畅音阁、颐和园中德和园大戏楼形式相近。阁高三层，外观雄伟。

万壑松风殿 万壑松风的主殿。康熙帝经常在这里接见官吏，批阅奏章，读书写字。1722 年，康熙发现皇四子和硕雍亲王胤禛之第四子弘历（乾隆帝）聪明伶俐，十分喜爱，于是传旨，命将弘历送入宫中。这年的夏天，弘历由父母带领，随祖父前往承德避暑山庄。康熙将避暑山庄的侧堂“万壑松风”赐给弘历居住，平时进宴或批阅奏章，都要乾隆侍奉在旁，朝夕教诲。弘历继位后，将这座殿宇题名为“纪恩堂”。乾隆三十年，乾隆写《避暑山庄纪恩堂记》，以纪念康熙皇帝对他的垂爱及养育之恩。

普宁寺 因寺内有木雕大佛，又称大佛寺，建于清乾隆二十年至二十三年（1755–1758 年）。此寺仿西藏三摩耶庙形式而建。按佛教教义关于世界构造的模型布局，中央的大乘阁象征须弥山，四周的殿宇象征四大部洲。其中安远庙是仿新疆伊犁固尔扎庙修建；普陀宗乘之庙和须弥福寿之庙，前者依拉萨布达拉宫、后者仿扎什伦布寺修建。全寺占地约 2.3 万平方米，主要建筑有钟鼓楼、碑亭、天王殿、大雄宝殿、大乘阁等。

普乐寺 位于避暑山庄东北，俗称圆亭子。建于清乾隆三十一年（1766 年），占地面积 2.4 万平方米，建筑布局分前后两部分。前部分有山门、钟鼓楼、天王殿、宗印殿；后半部分为坛城。在高大的石坛城上，建圆形旭光阁，重檐伞式攒尖黄琉璃瓦顶，阁中置一立体曼陀罗，内供铜欢喜佛。北阁与北京天坛祈年殿形制类似。

普陀宗乘之庙 位于避暑山庄正北。普陀宗乘是藏语布达拉宫的汉译，故又称小布达拉宫。建于清乾隆三十二年（1767 年），历经四年完工。此庙是外八庙最大的一处，占地面积约 22 万平方米。庙内共有大小建筑约 60 处，多是平顶白墙。主体建筑大红台是一座暗红色的方形建筑，其中心的万法归一殿顶部全部被鎏金铜瓦所覆盖。这里是举行重大的宗教仪式或清帝接见重要的少数民族部落首领及王公大臣们的场所。普陀宗乘之庙古木参天，环境清幽，景致殊佳。

殊像寺 位于避暑山庄之北，东临普陀宗乘之庙，建于乾隆三十九年，仿山西五台山殊像寺而建，形制以汉族庙宇建筑为主。殊像寺内的喇嘛均为满族，供奉的主神为文殊菩萨，当时民间认为乾隆皇帝是文殊菩萨转世，所以该寺又有“乾隆家庙”之称。

遗产价值

避暑山庄是中国清朝皇帝为了实现安抚、团结中国边疆少数民族、巩固国家统一的政治目的而修建的一座夏宫。避暑山庄兴建后，清帝每年都有大量时间在此处理军政要务，接见外国使节和边疆少数民族政教首领，使这里成为中国清朝的第二个政治中心。

避暑山庄是帝王范囿与皇家寺庙建筑经验的结晶。园林建造实现了“宫”与“苑”形式上的完美结合和“理朝听政”与“游息娱乐”功能上的高度统一，具有鲜明的政治功用。

避暑山庄及周围寺庙，继承和发展了中国古典园林“以人为之美入自然，符合自然而又超越自然”的传统造园思想，把中国古典哲学、美学、文学等多方面文化的内涵融入其中，使其成为中国传统文化的缩影，并创造性地运用了各种造园素材、造园技法，使其成为自然山水园与建筑园林化的杰出代表。

明清皇家陵寝

明清皇家陵寝分布于北京、河北、辽宁、安徽、江苏、湖北等地，主要建筑有：明皇家陵寝明皇陵、明孝陵、明祖陵、明十三陵、明显陵；清皇家陵寝之清永陵、清福陵、清昭陵、清东陵和清西陵。这些陵寝保存完整，体现了中国封建社会的最高丧葬礼制和千百年封建社会的宇宙观、生死观、道德观和习俗，也体现了当时中国最高水平的规划思想和建筑艺术。

陵寝建筑是中国古代建筑的重要组成部分，陵寝的规制因受当时社会思想、经济实力、帝王意识、审美标准等诸多因素的影响而各具特色。中国古代的陵寝制度经过一千多年的发展演变，至明清两代开始进入一个高潮时期。

明太祖朱元璋对前代陵寝制度作了重大改革：将覆斗式封土改为圆式宝顶，增加祭奠设施，改方形院落为多进长方形院落，创立了一个崭新的陵寝制度。清代陵寝不仅承袭了明代体制，而且作了进一步改革和完善，从而把中国古代陵寝营建活动推向了最后的顶峰。

首先，清代陵寝更加注重环境质量。不仅要对水文、地质、气候等诸因素进行严格的考察，而且更注重山川形势，要求所选的环境能够充分体现“天人合一”的理念。其次，清代陵寝更加强调建筑与环境的和谐统一。在建筑序列配置上与周围的山川形势互相呼应，以营造一个合乎理想的陵寝氛围。其三，清代陵寝更加注重建筑质量，不仅坚固宏大，而且富丽堂皇。

明孝陵

明孝陵坐落在南京市紫金山南麓独龙阜玩珠峰下，东毗中山陵，南临梅花山，是南京最大的帝王陵墓，亦是中国古代最大的帝王陵寝之一。

明孝陵是明朝开国皇帝朱元璋和皇后马氏的合葬陵墓，因皇后谥“孝慈”，故名孝陵。作为明陵之首的明孝陵壮观宏伟，代表了明初建筑和石刻艺术的最高成就，直接影响了明清两代500多年帝王陵寝的形制。依历史进程分布于北京、湖北、辽宁、河北等地的明清帝王陵寝，均按南京明孝陵的规制和模式营建。

明孝陵经历了600多年的沧桑巨变，许多建筑物的木结构部分已不存在，但陵寝的格局仍保留了原有的恢弘气势，地下墓宫完好如初，保持了陵墓原有建筑的真实性和空间布局的完整性。

建筑布局

明孝陵山环水绕，人文与自然景观浑然天成。陵园规模宏大，格局严谨。

明孝陵的神道石刻是中国帝王陵中唯一不呈直线，而是环绕梅花山形成一个弯曲的形状，形似北斗七星，神道长达2400米左右。沿神道依次有下马坊、禁约碑、大金门、神功圣德碑碑亭、御桥、石像路、石望柱、武将、文臣、棂星门等。过棂星门折向东北，便进入陵园的主体部分。这条正对独龙阜的南北轴线上依次有金水桥、文武方门、孝陵门、孝陵殿、内红门、方城明楼、宝顶等建筑。陵寝建筑都是按中轴线配制，体现了中国传统建筑的风格。在建筑设计上，明孝陵首创了在封土及宝城前建筑方城和明楼的布局格式，使后寝部分显得气势雄伟，凌驾于其它区域之上。大金门、碑楼、享殿、方城等大型建筑，普遍使用石质须弥座作为基座，使建筑显得厚实、坚固、庄重、高贵。大型建筑的顶部则根据建筑本身在陵寝中所处主次位置，覆盖尺寸不一、釉色各异的琉璃构件，显示出富贵、华丽、崇高和威严。

遗产价值

明孝陵有30多处不同风格、用途各异的建筑物和石雕艺术品，整体布局宏大有序，单体建筑厚重雄伟，细部装饰工艺精湛.明孝陵所处的地理环境山清水秀，起伏跌宕，“北斗七星”布局使其富有传统文化内涵。其神道的特色在于人工建设与自然形势的完美结合，完全依山势地形作蜿蜒曲折的布置，这其中包含了深刻的中国传统思想文化和鲜明的个性特征。神道石刻则风格多样，造型厚重简朴，融整体宏大与局部精细为一体，代表了中国明初石雕艺术的最高水平。

明孝陵是明初政治思想、社会文化、审美意识、建筑技术和国家财力的体现，它既继承了汉、唐、宋帝陵制度中的优秀成分，又创建了新的帝陵制度。陵寝布局设计和建筑形式，具有鲜明的时代风格和典范意义。

明十三陵

明十三陵坐落在北京西北郊昌平区境内的燕山山麓，距北京约 50 公里，总面积 120 余平方公里。自永乐七年（1409 年）五月始作长陵，到明朝最后一帝崇祯葬入思陵止，共 230 多年间，先后修建了 13 座金碧辉煌的帝王陵墓、7 座妃子墓、1 座太监墓。共埋葬了 13 位皇帝、23 位皇后、2 位太子、30 余名妃嫔、1 位太监。是当今世界上保存完整、埋葬皇帝最多的墓葬群。十三陵建造的顺序依次为长陵、献陵、景陵、裕陵、茂陵、泰陵 、康陵、永陵、昭陵、定陵、庆陵、德陵、思陵，其中最著名的要数长陵和定陵。这是两处体系完整、规模宏大、气势磅礴的陵寝建筑群。

建筑布局

明十三陵既是一个统一的整体，各陵又自成一个独立的单位，陵墓规格大同小异。每座陵墓分别建于一座山前。除思陵偏在西南一隅外，其余均成扇面形分列于长陵左右。在中国传统风水学说的指导下，十三陵从选址到规划设计，都十分注重陵寝建筑与大自然山川、水流和植被的和谐统一，追求形同“天设地造”的完美境界，用以体现“天人合一”的哲学观点。明十三陵作为中国古代帝陵的杰出代表，展示了中国传统文化的丰富内涵。这种依山建陵的布局曾经受到英国著名史家李约瑟高度评价，他说：皇陵在中国建筑形制上是一个重大的成就，它整个图案的内容也许就是整个建筑部分与风景艺术相结合的最伟大的例子。

石牌坊 是陵区前的第一座建筑物，结构为 5 楹、6 柱、11 楼，全部用汉白玉雕砌，在额枋和柱石的上下，刻有龙、云图纹及麒麟、狮子等浮雕。整个牌坊结构恢宏，雕刻精美，反映了明代石质建筑工艺的卓越水平。

碑亭 碑亭位于神道中央，是一座歇山重檐、四出翘角的高大方形亭楼，为长陵所建。亭内竖有龙首龟趺石碑一块，高 6 米多，上题“大明长陵神功圣德碑”，碑文长达 3500 多字，是明仁宗朱高炽撰文、明初著名书法家程南云所书。碑亭四隅立有 4 根白石华表，其顶部均蹲有一只异兽，名为望天吼。华表和碑亭相互映衬，显得十分庄重浑厚。在碑亭东侧，原建有行宫，为帝后前来祀陵时的更衣处，现已无存。

神路石雕群 从碑亭北的两根六角形的石柱起，到龙凤门止的千米神道两旁，整齐地排列着 24 只石兽和 12 躯石人，造型生动，雕刻精细。石兽共分 6 种，每种 4 只，均呈两立两跪状。石人分勋臣、文臣和武臣，各 4 尊，为皇帝生前的近身侍臣，均为拱手执笏的立像，威武而虔诚，用以象征皇帝生前的威仪，表示皇帝死后在阴间也拥有文武百官及各种牲畜可供驱使，仍可主宰一切。

棂星门 棂星门又叫龙凤门。由四根石柱构成三个门洞，门柱类似华表，柱上有云板、异兽。在三个门额枋上的中央部分，还分别饰有一颗石雕火珠，因而该门又称“火焰牌坊”。龙凤门西北侧，原建有行宫，是帝后祭陵时的歇息之处。

重点陵寝

明长陵 明长陵位于天寿山主峰南麓，是明朝第三位皇帝成祖文皇帝朱棣（年号永乐）和皇后徐氏的合葬陵寝。在十三陵中建筑规模最大，营建时间最早，地面建筑也保存得最为完好。高耸的明楼，是长陵的标志。它是十三陵中的祖陵，也是陵区内最主要的旅游景点之一。长陵的陵宫建筑占地约 12 万平方米，平面布局呈前方后圆形状。第一进院落，前设陵门，其制为单檐歇山顶的宫门式建筑；第二进院落，前面设祾恩门，面阔五间，进深二间，正脊顶部距地面高 14.57 米。中路台阶间的御路石上雕刻有浅浮雕图案，工艺十分精美。院内北面正中位置，建有高大巍峨的祾恩殿，面阔九间，进深五间，殿内总面积 1956.44 平方米，是我国罕见的大型殿宇之一。大殿构件全部为楠木制成，60 根巨型立柱支撑殿顶。殿内装修虽不尚华丽，但十分古朴典雅。

明定陵 明定陵是明代第 13 位皇帝神宗显皇帝朱翊钧（年号万历）的陵墓，这里还葬有他的两个皇后。主要建筑有祾恩门、祾恩殿、宝城、明楼和地下宫殿等。占地 18 万平方米，是十三陵中唯一一座被发掘了的陵墓。明定陵地面建筑的总布局呈前方后圆形，前有宽阔院落三进，后有高大宝城一座。陵正门前方是三座汉白玉石桥，过了桥是高大的碑亭，亭周围有祠祭署、宰牲亭、定陵监等建筑物 300 多间。新中国成立后，为进行历史科学研究，试掘了定陵。墓中有各种珍贵物品 3000 余件。

明昭陵 明昭陵位于大峪山东麓，是明朝第 12 代皇帝穆宗庄皇帝朱载垕（年号隆庆）及其 3 位皇后的合葬陵寝。昭陵是十三陵中第一座大规模修葺复原的陵园，也是陵区正式开放的旅游景点之一。昭陵陵园建筑面积为 35000 平方米，留存后来的建筑有完整的祾恩门、祾恩殿及其东西配殿、方城、明楼、宝顶等。明朝灭亡后，昭陵遭受严重破坏。乾隆年间，清政府为缓和民族矛盾，重新修葺明十三陵，对昭陵的明楼、祾恩门、祾恩殿进行了修复。这次修缮，虽然使陵园制度稍趋完备，但却改变了原有建筑的规制。明楼变得由繁而简，祾恩门和祾恩殿则缩小了尺寸。为了恢复昭陵原貌，从 1987 年 4 月正式启动昭陵复原修缮工程，明楼、祾恩殿、祾恩门、两庑配殿、神功圣德碑亭、宰牲亭、神厨、神库等建筑均得以复原。

明显陵

明正德十六年（1521 年）三月，明武宗朱厚照无嗣崩殂，根据太祖朱元璋“兄终弟及”的遗训，袭封为兴献王不久的朱厚熜被迎往北京入继大统，是为明世宗。朱厚熜即帝位后，自立统嗣体系，不顾朝臣反对，追尊生父朱祐熜为皇帝。朱祐熜被追尊为皇帝后，原有兴献王坟也相应按帝陵规制升级改建。嘉靖二年（1523 年）四月，兴献王坟原覆黑瓦换为黄琉璃瓦，并修筑神路桥等。嘉靖三年（1524 年）三月，王坟正式更名为显陵。

显陵位于湖北省钟祥市城东 7.5 公里纯德山，是明世宗嘉靖皇帝的父亲恭睿皇帝和母亲章圣皇太后的合葬墓，始建于明正德十四年（1519 年）。陵墓面积 1.83 平方公里，是我国中南地区唯一的一座明代帝王陵墓，也是中国明代帝陵中最大的单体陵墓。其“一陵两冢”的陵寝结构，为历代帝王陵墓中绝无仅有。

建筑布局

明显陵的建筑格局，从整体看，宛如一个巨大的“宝瓶”，分内外围城，外围城高 6 米，宽 1.8 米，长 3500 余米，红墙黄瓦，随山势起伏，雄伟壮观。外围城南端为两重陵门，称新、旧红门。门前左右各立下马碑 1 通，碑上刻字为权臣严嵩手笔。门内石板铺成的神道，直抵内城。中部立棂星门，六柱三门，方形石柱，柱脚以抱鼓石支撑，柱顶各置独角神兽一只。棂星门前神道两侧，列立狮子、獬豸、骆驼、卧象、麒麟、立马、卧马等石兽 8 对和文臣、武将各 2 躯，全用整块汉白玉雕琢而成。茔城分前后两圈城墙，中以瑶台相接，平面形状如哑铃，城墙周设堞垛。茔城前砌方形城台，下设券顶甬道，上建明楼。陵园内各建筑物的基础，大部分采用须弥座式的石雕台基。祾恩殿前的云龙丹陛、散水螭首及回廊栏杆等构件的雕刻技法尤为精湛，是明代石刻艺术的经典作品。

显陵在规划布局上，利用中国传统的风水理论，将陵区四周的山川水系作为建筑构成的主体要素，根据“负阴抱阳”、“背山面水”的原则，将松林山左峰作为依托玄宫（皇帝棺椁停放的地下宫殿）的祖山，左有山脉作为陵区两侧环护的砂山，前沿的天子岗作为陵寝的案山，形成了一个与自然高度和谐的局部小环境。

在建筑布局上，充分利用松林山间的台地依次安排下马碑、门、亭、望柱、石像生、坊、桥等，顺山势引导至享殿、明楼和宝城。疏密有间，层层递进，给人以封建礼制的秩序感。建筑掩映于山环水抱之中，相互映衬，如同“天设地造”，构成了一个建筑艺术与环境美学相结合的杰作。在建筑手法上显陵也有独特之处，如一座陵墓二座地下宫殿、金瓶形的外罗城、九曲回环的御河、龙形神道和内外明塘等都是明陵中仅见的孤例。

清东陵

清东陵位于河北省遵化市西北部的昌瑞山下，在这里共建有 15 座陵寝（皇帝陵 5 座、皇后陵 4 座、妃园寝 5 座、公主园寝 1 座），埋葬帝、后、妃及皇子、公主等共 161 人。清东陵是中国现存规模最为宏大、体系最为完整、保存最为完好的帝王陵墓建筑群。

清东陵的 15 座陵寝是按照“居中为尊”、“长幼有序”、“尊卑有别”

的传统观念设计排列的。入关第一帝世祖顺治皇帝的孝陵位于南起金星山、北达昌瑞山主峰的中轴线上，其位置至尊无上，其余皇帝陵寝则按辈分高低分别在孝陵的两侧呈扇形东西排列开来。孝陵之左为圣祖康熙皇帝的景陵，次左为穆宗同治皇帝的惠陵；孝陵之右为高宗乾隆皇帝的裕陵，次右为文宗咸丰皇帝的定陵。形成儿孙陪侍父祖的格局，其统绪嗣承关系十分明显，表达了国祚绵长、江山万代的愿望。

清东陵的经营跨越了两个半世纪的时空，几乎与清王朝相始终，葬有许多对清代历史有着重要影响的、声名显赫的人物，蕴含着丰富的历史信息，不仅是研究清代陵寝规制、丧葬制度、祭祀礼仪、建筑技术与工艺的不可多得的实物资料，而且也是研究清代政治、经济、军事、文化、科学、艺术的典型例证。

建筑布局

清东陵的陵墓从规划建制到建筑造型均仿照明朝，采用集中陵区的手法安排总入口，从石牌坊和正红门开端，经统一的神道石像生、碑亭及华表，然后分达各陵区。其布局顺序为：五孔石券桥、牌楼、碑亭、三孔券桥，大月台、宫门、隆恩殿及左右配殿，而后为石平桥、月台、琉璃门、五供、方城（上立明楼）、月牙城、宝城、宝顶。皇帝、皇后、亲王、公主、嫔妃次第安排，陵制级别相当严格，形成了一套程式化的形制。清代帝王在选勘陵址时，以中国传统的“风水学”理论为依据，刻意追求“龙穴砂水无美不收，形势理气诸吉咸备”的山川形势，以达到“天人合一”的意象。清东陵正是这种理念的最佳体现。

清东陵的建筑恢宏、壮观、精美。在 580 多单体建筑组成的庞大古建筑群中，有中国现存面阔最宽的石牌坊，五间六柱十一楼的仿木结构巧夺天工；中国保存最完整的长 6000 多米的孝陵主神路，随山势起伏极富艺术感染力；乾隆裕陵地宫精美的佛教石雕，令人叹为观止；慈禧陵三座贴金大殿，其豪华装修举世罕见，“凤上龙下”石雕匠心独运……

整座东陵在木构和石构两方面都有精湛的技巧，可谓集清代宫殿建筑之大成，其中孝陵的石像生最多，共达 18 对，造型多朴实浑厚；乾隆的裕陵规模最大、最为堂皇，而慈禧的普陀峪定东陵则是首屈一指的精巧建筑。清东陵 15 座陵园中，只开放了裕陵和东、西太后陵及香妃墓等 4 处供游客参观。

清西陵

清西陵位于河北省易县城西 15 公里的永宁山下，在北京西南方 120 公里，是清代帝王陵寝之一，与河北省遵化县东陵东西相望而称西陵。清西陵 4 座皇帝陵、3 座皇后陵、3 座妃园寝、4 座王爷、公主、阿哥园寝共 14 座陵寝和两座附属建筑（永福寺、行宫），是中国陵寝建筑艺术的重要组成部分。

清西陵始建于雍正八年（1730 年），历经 18 世纪中叶——19 世纪初，余绪延至民国年间。四座帝陵建筑规模宏大，布局合理，宫殿辉煌，石雕精美，形式多样，内涵丰富，保存完整；后妃及亲王、公主、阿哥等园寝严格按照封建等级制度的规格建造，虽历经沧桑，现大部分保存完好。

清西陵以大量的实物形象和文字史料，从不同侧面展示了 18 世纪 30 年代——20 世纪初期中国陵寝建筑艺术风格及皇家宗教信仰的重大发展、变化，对中国古代陵寝建筑艺术的创新与发展有重要贡献，具有清代以前各代陵寝建筑不可替代的历史、艺术、科学和鉴赏价值。

建筑布局

清西陵东起梁各庄，西到紫荆关，南抵大雁桥，北接奇峰岭，占地约 100 平方公里，内有帝陵 4 座，即：雍正泰陵、嘉庆昌陵、道光慕陵、光绪崇陵；后陵 3 座，以及妃嫔、公主、亲王的园寝 7 座，而以泰宁山主峰下的泰陵为中心，其他陵园则分布东、西两侧。

清西陵的南端入口建有石牌坊，其后依次有大红门、圣德神功碑楼、七孔桥、石像生、龙凤门、神道碑楼，然后是清西陵的主陵——泰陵的隆恩门、隆恩殿、方城明楼、宝顶等。这些建筑物以一条南北贯穿、长 2.5 公里的神道串联起来，入口的石牌坊，东陵只有 1 座，西陵则建有 3 座；东陵的石像生、龙凤门是位于七孔桥之后，而西陵则在之前。

慕陵是道光皇帝和孝穆、孝全两位皇后的陵墓。该陵不置方城明楼，规模较小，但其隆恩殿以香气清远的楠木构筑，且只施雕镂而不著彩绘，在红墙黄瓦、金碧辉煌的建筑群中显得朴实典雅。殿内藻井刻满许多腾云驾雾的飞龙，其用意在藉引龙上天、吞云吐雾而不喷水，以保持陵墓内部干燥。

盛京三陵

盛京，即今天的沈阳，满语称“谋克敦”，汉译为“兴盛之城”。它是中国最后一个封建王朝——清朝的肇兴之地，在这里修建有清朝开国之君及其父祖们的三座陵墓，即清永陵、清福陵、清昭陵，因位处盛京，故称“盛京三陵”。

重点陵寝

福陵 福陵又称“东陵”，是清太祖努尔哈赤及其孝慈高皇后叶赫纳喇氏的陵墓。始建于1629年（天聪三年），1651年基本建成。后经清顺治、康熙、乾隆多次修建，形成了规模宏大、设施完备的古代帝王陵墓建筑群。

福陵建筑格局因山势形成前低后高之势，其南向四周围以红墙，正中是正红门，自南而北地势逐渐升高，门外的两旁对立着石狮、华表、石牌坊和刻有满、蒙、汉、回、藏五种文字的下马碑。正红门是很长的一段神路，路的两侧有坐狮、立马、卧驼、坐虎等四对石兽。尽头是利用天然山势修筑的一百零八级砖阶，以象征三十六天罡和七十二地煞。砖阶之上是重檐歇山式碑楼，黄琉璃瓦顶，内立康熙帝用汉、满两种文字书写的“大清福陵神功圣德碑”。再向北便是城堡式的方城，南面的正中是隆恩门，上建三层歇山式的门楼建筑。方城的四角各有一座角楼，城内正中是坐落在须弥座式大台基上的隆恩殿，殿内供奉着木主神牌。殿的后边有洞门，洞门之上建有重檐歇山式的大明楼，中间立有“太祖高皇帝之陵”的石碑。方城内的建筑，屋顶都铺有黄琉璃瓦，廊柱是朱红地仗，梁枋间都是“和玺”壁画。

昭陵 是清太宗皇太极及其皇后的陵墓，在盛京三陵中规模最大，结构最完整。因坐落在沈阳市北端，故又称北陵。昭陵始建于清崇德八年（1643年），与福陵同年竣工，后又经康熙、嘉庆增建，陵区占地面积近48万平方米，现存古建筑38座（组）。昭陵建在平地上，四周护以缭墙，很像一座小城。主体建筑都建在中轴线上，由南向北依次为：神桥、牌楼、正红门、碑亭、隆恩门、隆恩殿、明楼、宝顶。方城中心的隆恩殿以雕刻精美的花岗岩台阶为底座，黄琉璃瓦顶，再加上画栋雕梁，金匾红墙，前有隆恩门，后有明楼，左右有配殿，四隅有角楼，犹如众星拱月一般，显得异常雄伟庄严。方城北端为宝城，略如月牙形，城内称宝顶，其下即地宫墓室。登上宝顶四望，绿树环合，景色清幽，宛若置身于城市山林之中。

现在昭陵已辟为北陵公园。

永陵 永陵在盛京三陵中规模最小，占地仅1.1万多平方米，但列三陵之首。永陵始建于1598年，是满清皇族的祖陵。陵墓内葬着努尔哈赤的六世祖猛哥帖木儿、曾祖福满、祖父觉昌安、父亲塔克世及伯父礼敦、叔父塔察篇古以及他们的福晋。陵宫由下马碑、前宫院、方城、宝城、省牲所、冰窖、果楼等部分组成。启运山如屏风矗立背后，苏子河如玉带飘过陵前，河对岸的烟囱山与启运山遥相呼应，使地处群山环绕中的永陵显得十分壮阔。

永陵前院正门名正红门或前宫门，是硬山式琉璃瓦顶建筑，面阔三楹，进深二间，每间置二扇木栅栏门，上覆红漆。这种木栅栏在清代帝、后陵寝中唯永陵所独有，是建州女真人“树栅为寨”的古老生活遗俗。前院正中东西并列四座单檐歇山式四祖碑亭，按中长次右、左老右少的位序依次为肇、兴、景、显四祖碑亭。方城内正殿称享殿，是供奉四祖神位及祭祀的场所。

遗产价值

盛京三陵是明清帝王陵墓的重要组成部分，无论是古建筑的营建法式和完备的建筑规制，还是的祭祀典制、管理陵墓的职官体制等都与明清帝王陵墓一脉相承。同时，清盛京三陵还是中国东北少数民族帝王在兴起过程中一个特定历史时期的产物，因此，它又保留了大量该时期一个民族从思想理念到审美情趣以及建筑水平、风俗习惯等诸多的文化信息。盛京三陵每座陵墓自成体系，虽规模较小，但规制完备，礼制设施齐全，陵寝建筑规制将中国古代环境地理学中宗教、信仰、习俗同周围自然环境相结合，使其达到建筑选址、规划、设计的统一，并成为中国古代建筑形式、雕刻、绘画以及综合理念的历史依据和现代鉴赏者的实物资料。

大运河

中国是世界上开凿运河时间最早的国家，公元前 486 年，中国春秋时期的吴王夫差在扬州开邗沟，筑邗城，兴建第一条运河。后经历代修建，形成从南到北全长 1794 公里的大运河，穿越北京、天津、河北、山东、江苏、浙江、安徽等省市。

大运河是世界建造时间最早、使用最久、空间跨度最大的人工运河，是中华民族留给世界的宝贵遗产。

历史渊源

从吴王夫差开凿运河算起，运河的历史已经将近 2500 年。公元前 495 年夫差为了征服越国，开凿了由苏州至无锡、常州的运河，从奔牛入长江。公元前 486 年，吴王夫差为了伐齐争霸中原，开掘扬州至淮阴一段被称为“邗沟”的水道，沟通了江淮水系。这就是中国乃至世界最早的运河。

公元 7 世纪，隋结束内乱实现了统一，隋炀帝为使江汉平原及江南富庶地区的物资能源源不断地运往洛阳，于公元 605 年下令开凿洛阳至淮安的“通洛渠”，沟通了黄、淮水系；开凿洛阳经临清至涿州的“永济渠”，沟通了黄、海水系；开挖镇江至杭州的“江南运河”，形成了南北大运河。

到 13 世纪，元朝为使水路不再绕道洛阳，先后开挖了“洛州河”、“会通河”，把天津到清江之间的天然河道、湖泊连接起来；清江以南浚修邗沟和江南运河，直达杭州，形成了南北便捷的水路运输大通道。1293 年，著名科学家郭守敬修通了直通大都城内积水潭的河道。至此，北起北京，南达杭州，全长 1794 公里的京杭大运河形成。

遗产构成

大运河包括横贯中国中东部地区的隋唐大运河、京杭大运河和浙东运河，在春秋战国、隋朝及元朝时期都曾经历过大规模修建。

隋唐大运河

隋唐大运河以洛阳为中心，南起余杭（杭州），北至涿郡（北京），隋朝开凿全长 2700 公里，跨越地球十多个纬度，纵贯中国最富饶的东南沿海和华北大平原，经过浙江、江苏、安徽、河南、山东、河北、天津、北京八个省市，通达黄河、淮河、长江、钱塘江、海河五大水系，是中国古代南北交通的大动脉，在中国的历史上产生过巨大的作用，是中国古代劳动人民创造的一项伟大的水利建筑工程，也是世界上开凿最早、规模最大的运河。后经元朝取直疏浚，全长 1794 公里，成为现今的京杭大运河。

京杭大运河

京杭大运河是世界上里程最长、工程最大、最古老的运河之一，与长城并称为中国古代的两项伟大工程。按地理位置分为七段：

通惠河　自北京昌平区白浮村神山泉经昆明湖至积水潭、中南海，出崇文门向东，在今天的朝阳区杨闸村向东南折，至通州区张家湾村入潞河，长 82 公里。

北运河　北京通州区到天津段称北运河，长 186 公里。

南运河　天津到山东临清段称南运河，长 400 公里。

鲁运河　临清到台儿庄段称鲁运河，长约 500 公里。

中运河　台儿庄到江苏淮安段称中运河，长 186 公里。

里运河　淮安到瓜洲段称里运河，全长约 180 公里。

江南运河　镇江到浙江杭州段称江南运河，长约 330 公里。

目前，京杭大运河季节性的通航里程已达 1100 多公里。江苏邳县以南的 660 多公里航道，500 吨位的船只可以畅行无阻。

浙东运河

浙东运河，得名自唐宋的浙江东道，是中国浙江省境内的一条运河，以历史文化名城绍兴为中心点，西起萧山西兴，跨曹娥江，经过绍兴市，东至宁波甬江，全长239公里。运河最初开凿的部分位于绍兴市（越国都城）境内的山阴古水道，始建于春秋时期。西晋时，会稽（绍兴）内史贺循主持开挖西兴运河，此后与曹娥江以东运河形成西起西小江，东到东小江的完整运河。南宋初建都绍兴，浙东运河绍兴段成为当时的皇家御河，也是重要的通商航道。

遗产点分布

依据历史分段和命名习惯，大运河共包括十大河段。遗产分别选取了各河段的典型河道段落和重要遗产点，包括河道遗产27段，总长度1011公里，相关遗产共计58处。遗产类型包括闸、堤、坝、桥、水城门、纤道、码头、险工等运河水工遗存，以及仓窖、衙署、驿站、行宫、会馆、钞关等大运河的配套设施和管理设施，和一部分与大运河文化意义密切相关的古建筑、历史文化街区等。

作为京杭大运河的最南端以及浙东运河的起点，杭州是中国大运河的一个重要节点。杭州市列入大运河首批遗产点段共有11处，包括富义仓、凤山水城门遗址、桥西历史街区、西兴过塘行码头、拱宸桥、广济桥等6个遗产点，以及杭州塘段、江南运河杭州段、上塘河段、杭州中河—龙山河、浙东运河主线等5段河道。

扬州城区段有反映扬州古港、水利和城池建筑的遗址如水斗门、东关古渡和古湾头闸，有古代帝王巡视扬州留下的遗迹如瓜州古渡锦春园，有体现“富比王侯”的扬州盐商住宅群落何园、个园等等。

在淮安段，有运河鼎盛时期的漕运总督府旧址、古老的码头，以及展示漕运历史的漕运博物馆，还有运河、古黄河、淮河交汇形成的蔚为壮观的水上立交以及大运河孕育的大批历史名人留下的人文景观。

大运河洛阳段重要文化遗产点包括：含嘉仓遗址、回洛仓遗址、天津桥遗址、洛河市区段以及瀍河部分河道。

大运河山东段横跨该省5个地级市，包括8段运河15处遗产点。该段的遗产点涵盖了各类水工设施遗存，初步再现了传统运河工程的技术发明创造性和技术体系的典范性。其中南旺枢纽是为了解决大运河跨越水脊难题而建设的大型综合性水利水运枢纽，是大运河上最具科技价值的节点。

天津段有全长71公里的河道遗产入选，其中北运河部分自武清区筐儿港减河与北运河连接处至三岔河口，长48公里；南运河部分自三岔河口至西青区杨柳青镇，长23公里。

在北京段，共有两处河道和两处遗产点入选。其中，河道分别为通惠河北京旧城段——西城区什刹海和东城区玉河故道、通惠河通州段；遗产点分别为万宁桥和东不压桥。

遗产价值

大运河是世界上最长的、最古老的人工水道，也是工业革命前规模最大、范围最广的土木工程项目，它促进了中国南北物资的交流和领土的统一管辖，反映出中国人民高超的智慧、决心和勇气，以及东方文明在水利技术和管理能力方面的杰出成就。历经两千余年的持续发展与演变，大运河直到今天仍发挥着重要的交通运输、行洪、灌溉、输水等作用，自古至今在保障中国经济繁荣和社会稳定方面发挥了重要作用。

殷 墟

殷墟是中国商代后期都城遗址，位于河南省安阳市殷都区小屯村周围，横跨洹河两岸，殷墟王陵遗址与殷墟宫殿宗庙遗址、洹北商城遗址等共同组成了规模宏大、气势恢宏的殷墟遗址。商代从盘庚到帝辛（纣），在此建都达 273 年，是中国历史上可以肯定确切位置的最早的都城。

殷墟是中国历史上第一个文献可考，并为考古学和甲骨文所证实的都城遗址，因而殷都安阳排在中华古都之首。殷墟古称“北蒙”，甲骨卜辞中又称为“商邑”、“大邑商”。自公元前 1300 年盘庚迁殷，到公元前 1046 年帝辛亡国，经历了盘庚、小辛、小乙、武丁、祖庚、祖甲、廪辛、康丁、武乙、文丁、帝乙、帝辛共 8 代 12 位国王 273 年的统治。这里一直是中国商代后期的政治、经济、文化和军事中心。商灭亡后，这里逐渐沦为废墟。

建筑布局

殷墟的总体布局以小屯宫殿宗庙区为中心，沿洹河两岸呈环形放射状分布，是一座开放形制的古代都城，距今已有 3300 多年历史。

洹北商城

1999 年 1 月，安阳殷墟遗址东北部地下约 2 米的深处，新发现一座规模巨大的商代城址。

该城址平面略呈方形，南北长2200米，东西宽2150米，总面积约4.7平方公里，方向北偏东 13 度。城址的南北中轴线南段，已确认分布有宫殿宗庙建筑群。地下文物表明，这座城址的年代略早于作为商王朝晚期都邑的传统概念上的“殷墟”，分布上与旧的“殷墟”范围略有重叠，但整体在洹河北岸，学术界将其命名为“洹北商城”。

洹北商城遗址和宫殿宗庙区遗址、王陵区遗址共同构成了殷墟申报遗址的范围，真正体现了世界遗产原真性、完整性、价值性的要求，内容更加丰富，增加了殷墟申遗的砝码。

宫殿宗庙遗址

50 余座建筑遗址分宫殿、宗庙、祭坛（甲、乙、丙）3 组，宏伟壮观。另外还发现铸铜遗址等。宫殿区出土大量的甲骨文、青铜器、玉器、宝石器等珍贵文物。殷墟文物有的是华夏之最，有的是世界之冠，蕴藏着殷代先民们的创造、智慧和卓越的技能。

这些宫殿宗庙建筑，以黄土、木料作为主要建筑材料，其建筑多坐落于厚实高大的夯土台基上。房基置柱础，房架多用木柱支撑，墙用夯土版筑，屋顶覆以茅草，造型庄重肃穆、质朴典雅，具有浓郁的中国宫殿建筑特色，代表了中国古代早期宫殿建筑的先进水平。

著名的妇好墓是 1928 年以来殷墟宫殿宗庙区内最重要的考古发现之一，也是唯一能与甲骨文联系并断定年代、墓主人及其身份的商代王室成员墓葬。殷墟宫殿宗庙区还分布着为数众多的甲骨窖穴。自 19 世纪末甲骨文发现以来，这里共出土甲骨约 1.5 万片。

王陵遗址

殷墟王陵遗址与宫殿宗庙遗址隔河相对，是商王的陵地和祭祀场所，也是中国已知最早的完整的王陵墓葬群，面积达 11.3 公顷。王陵遗址共发现有 12 座王陵大墓和 2500 多座祭祀坑。王陵大墓多为“亚”“中”“甲”字形大墓，这些大墓墓室宏大，形制壮阔。面积最大的达 1803 平方米，深达 15 米。墓内椁室、棺木极尽奢华，随葬器物精美。坑内埋葬着数千具祭祀牺牲的遗骨，这些人牲大部分被砍杀，多为青壮年，还有女性和未成年的儿童，每坑 8–10 人不等。仅 1976 年发掘清理的 191 座祭祀坑就发现祭祀人牲 1178 人，这些祭祀坑的存在成为商代残酷人祭制度的历史见证。殷墟王陵的埋葬制度、分布格局、随葬方式、祭祀礼仪等，集中反映了商代晚期的社会组织、阶级状况、等级制度、亲属关系，代表了中国古代早期王陵建设的最高水平。它的发现确证了殷墟商代都城的历史地位，成为探索中华文明起源的重要基石。

祭祀场

在商代，每当祭祀时商王都会把人像牲畜一样供奉给祖先和神灵，这种制度被学者们称之为“人牲制度”。被杀的人牲绝大多数为战俘，少数为奴隶。商王和贵族奴隶主在祭祀祖先、祈祷神灵佑护、建筑宫室和祈雨时都要用人牲，因此这里就成为了商王祭祀祖先的一个大型公共祭祀场所。在王陵大墓的周围，共发现2000余座祭祀坑，埋葬着大量祭祀牺牲的遗骸。据不完全统计，殷墟甲骨文中有关人祭的甲骨有1350片，卜辞1992条，共用人牲13052人。

科学技术水平

殷墟时期，以青铜器为标志的自然科学技术在很多领域达到了世界先进水平。考古发掘表明，殷墟时期的手工业空前发达，不仅门类齐全，而且工艺水平极高。一些主要的手工业生产部门，如青铜冶铸、制玉、制陶、制骨、制车、纺织等都已达到了相当大的规模。

殷墟时代在科学技术其它领域也取得了巨大成就。

这里出土的甲骨文记载，殷人已能够准确地记录日食、月食和星象；殷历法采取阴阳合历，将一年分为12个月，并采取增加闰月的方法，解决了与回归年实际太阳日的矛盾。

在数学方面，殷人已有了个、十、百、千、万等数字概念，并采用了十进位制。

在医学方面，商代晚期已能认识人类的十多种疾病，除用药物治疗外，还能应用针砭、按摩等治疗方法，达到了较高水平。

青铜器

中国青铜文化源远流长，具有浓郁的民族特色和艺术风格。殷墟出土的四千余件青铜器，包括礼器、乐器、兵器、工具、生活用具、装饰品、艺术品等，形成了以青铜礼器和兵器为主的青铜文明，达到中国青铜时代发展的巅峰。殷墟出土的青铜马车，已经使用了大量青铜构件，独辕双套双轮，结构精致复杂，体现出高超的机械、青铜铸造等复合技术。殷墟青铜礼器的大量出现，证明中国青铜文化已发展到了最高的阶段。其夸张而神秘的风格，蕴含着深厚粗犷的原始张力和艺术的魅力，反映了殷商先民特有的宗教情感和审美观念。殷墟在青铜冶铸方面辉煌的成就使其成为世界古代青铜文明的中心之一。

司母戊鼎是中国商代后期王室祭祀用的青铜方鼎，1939年3月19日在河南省安阳市武官村一个农户家的田中出土，因其腹部铸有“司母戊”三字而得名，是商朝青铜器的代表作。大鼎器型高大厚重，气势宏大雄伟，纹饰华丽，工艺高超。高133厘米，口长110厘米，口宽78厘米，重832.84千克。鼎腹长方形，上竖两只直耳（发现时仅剩一耳，另一耳是后来据另一耳复制补上），下有四根圆柱形鼎足，是目前世界上发现的最大的青铜器。该鼎是商王武丁的儿子为祭祀母亲而铸造的。

石器、玉器

商代文明不仅以庄重的青铜器闻名，也以众多的石器与玉器著称。商代晚期玉器以安阳殷墟妇好墓出土玉器为代表，共出土玉器755件，按用途可分为礼器、仪仗、工具、生活用具、装饰品、艺术品和杂器七大类。其中动物、人物玉器大大超过几何形玉器，玉龙、玉凤、玉鹦鹉神态各异，形神毕肖。玉人或站、或坐、或跪，姿态多样，栩栩如生。

学者们认定，殷墟出土的玉器，其原料大都为新疆的和田玉、辽宁岫玉。由此可见，早在3000多年前的商代，就已经有通往新疆的“金石之路”了，这比始于公元前2世纪的“丝绸之路”还要早1200多年。

殷墟玉器的发现，不仅使我们对商代玉雕艺术有了比较全面的了解，而且对研究我国玉雕史、艺术史以及商代的社会、经济和文化等方面的有关问题均有重要的参考价值。

遗产价值

殷墟发掘，确证了中国商王朝的存在，重新构建了中国古代早期历史的框架，使传统文献记载的商代历史成为信史。以宫殿宗庙建筑和王陵大墓为代表的商代建筑，树立了中国古代早期宫殿建筑和皇家墓葬的典范。在殷墟出土的1.5万片甲骨上，发现了目前中国文字体系最早的证据，至今仍为世界上四分之一的人口使用。以青铜器、玉器为代表的殷墟文物和以人祭、人殉、车马殉葬、兽祭等为代表的殷墟丧葬习俗，为商代晚期文化传统提供了独特的证据。

元上都遗址

《马可·波罗游记》中这样记载元上都：

内有大理石宫殿，甚美。其房舍内皆涂金，绘重重鸟兽花木，工巧之极。技术之佳，见之足以娱乐人心目。

元上都遗址位于内蒙古自治区锡林郭勒盟正蓝旗旗政府所在地东北约 20 公里处、闪电河北岸，是中国元代都城遗址。由我国北方骑马民族创建的这座草原都城，被认定是中原农耕文化与草原游牧文化奇妙结合的产物，史学家称誉它可与意大利庞贝古城媲美。

历史渊源

1256 年忽必烈奉蒙哥汗旨意，命刘秉忠"于岭北滦水之阳，筑城堡，营宫室"。刘秉忠勘址金莲川，历时三年建成，是一座集游牧文化特色与中国传统建筑风格于一身的草原都城。

1259 年，蒙哥汗率军伐宋，卒于四川钓鱼山，忽必烈果断地与南宋议和，从鄂州前线北撤。次年 3 月，忽必烈以开平为根据地，联络蒙古各宗王。10 月，忽必烈于开平即汗位，建元中统。随即率军北上，夺取都城和林，迫使阿里不哥下野西退。开平自此一跃而为首都，置中书省，总理全国政务。蒙元史的发展，从此步入一个崭新的历史阶段。

1263 年，经扩建改造的开平正式封号为上都，设上都总管府。次年，改燕京为中都。1267 年，又在中都东北建新城。1272 年，改中都为大都。自此，元朝实行两都制，以大都为首都，以上都为夏都。元朝的主要机构在上都均有分衙或下属官署，上都仍是全国重要的政治中心。

建筑布局

上都地理位置特殊，"控弦西北，东际辽海，南面而临制天下，形势尤重于大都"。上都距原蒙古汗国的政治、军事中心和林较近，是沟通南北东西的重要枢纽，对联络、控制拥有强大势力的漠北蒙古宗亲贵族，在政治、军事上均占有举足轻重的地位。它不仅是对付蒙古宗王反叛势力的前沿阵地，也是便于运筹帷幄的最高决策场所。因而元朝前几位皇帝，如忽必烈、铁穆耳、海山等即位的忽里台都在上都举行。

元上都的总体格局在采用中国古代传统城市布局的同时，兼顾了蒙古民族游牧生活的穹庐毡帐，城市布局并不是十分规整，每一群建筑都各有围墙，体现出一种离宫别馆式的建筑风格。

据记载，元上都曾拥有 11 万人口，城垣周长超过 8 公里。城内有官署约 60 所，各种寺庙堂观 160 余处。驿道四通八达，为漠北与中原的交通枢纽。全城由宫城、皇城、外城三重城墙和关厢组成。城墙用黄土夯筑，宫城、皇城城墙则用砖、石包砌。外城方形，每面长 2200 米，开 4 门，有瓮城。城内用土墙隔为两部分，北面是御园，南面是官署和作坊区。都城周边地区则是许多祭祀遗址和墓葬区。

主要建筑

皇城　皇城在外城东南角，平面近方形。城内有"四横三纵"共 7 条主要街道，建筑错落分布，带有离宫色彩。皇城城墙外砌砖石，寺庙、国学和部分大型建筑都在皇城内。外城北部是皇家苑囿和金顶大帐"棕毛殿"的建筑所在。城外东、南、西有关厢，其范围很大，建筑遗迹甚多，百姓民居和商肆店铺工匠仓库主要集中在关厢地带。

宫城　宫城是全城的核心，有东华、西华、御天三门，城墙用砖包镶，四角有楼，其中南边的御天门最为重要，它与皇城南门明德门在一条中轴线上，是出入的主道。城内有官署约 60 所，各种寺庙 160 余处，有大明、仪天、宝云、宸丽、慈福、鸿禧、睿思等殿；大安、延春、连香、紫檀、凝晖等阁；绿珠、瀛州两堂以及振堂等重要建筑。其中大安阁是宫城内最主要的建筑，也是上都城的象征。城内除中央及北城墙中部的大型宫殿位于中轴线以外，大部建筑未采用对称的布局，殿、亭、阁、榭各具特色，形状大小各异，色彩风格不同。

外城　外城全用土筑，周长约 9–10 公里。在皇城西北面，北部为皇帝观赏的御苑，南部为官署、寺观和作坊所在地。城外东、南、西三处关厢地带，为市肆、民居、仓廪所在。城西有离宫西内，周围建筑以行宫和营帐为主。还有一处方圆 25 公里的大御花园。北郊则有很多寺庙、宫观等建筑。1358 年红巾军攻克上都，焚毁宫阙衙署，结束了它作为一代陪都的历史。

祭祀、墓葬区　在元上都遗址周边地区分布有一系列附属文物遗存，主要有羊群庙祭祀遗址、砧子山墓葬区、卧牛石墓葬区、一棵树墓葬区、东凉亭遗址等。

羊群庙祭祀遗址，位于元上都西北 35 公里处，由四处祭祀地点组成，是元代上层贵族为祭祀其祖先而建立的祭祀场所。四处祭祀遗址均由石围墙、祭台、汉白玉石雕像和供祀建筑遗存组成。

元上都墓葬区现已发现砧子山、卧牛石和一棵树三处。其中砧子山墓葬区位于元上都遗址东南约 8 公里砧子山的东南和西北两侧山坡上，墓地分布范围较大，共有 500 余座墓葬，多数都有石砌的方形茔墙。共发掘清理了 73 座墓葬。卧牛石墓葬区位于元上都遗址古城西偏北约 20 公里处的向阳山坡上，共清理发掘墓葬 15 座。该墓葬地表均用自然石块叠砌一凸字形墓茔，多为火葬墓，其形制有砖椁墓、木椁墓和竖穴土坑墓三类。卧牛石墓地墓葬形制规整，保存较好，墓葬内随葬品较为丰富，是元代居住在元上都的汉人墓葬。一棵树墓葬区位于元上都古城西北约 12 公里处的山湾阳坡，共发掘墓葬 26 座，随葬品丰富，发掘清理出金器、银器、瓷器及其他铜铁器多件。

遗产价值

元上都遗址的位置和环境，显示出来自于蒙古族和汉族两者在价值观及生活方式上的共同影响。城市遗址展现了两个民族结合的城市规划模式。通过蒙古族和汉族在思想上和制度上的融合，元朝才得以将它的统治扩展到当时已知世界的极大一部分范围。元上都遗址是一个包含了不同民族团体的融合型城市规划的独特范例。

元上都遗址非凡地见证了元朝的征服者忽必烈汗的最高统治，这种统治包括对被征服者文化、政体的吸收和改变，也包括征服者保持和维系原有文化传统的决心和努力。

元上都遗址的位置、环境以及它的城市模式证实了游牧与农耕文化的并存与融合。汉地结合园林和景观的城市规划对于元朝蒙古人的生活方式在元上都是必要的，也因此产生了一个城市布局的杰出范例，展现了人类历史上的一个重要阶段。

元王朝曾是横跨欧亚的强大帝国，征服 40 国，拥有 3000 万平方公里的疆域，在人类历史上产生了广泛而深远的影响，作为元王朝的都城理所当然成为当时世界的政治文化中心。这份厚重的文化遗产不仅是属于中华民族的，也是属于世界的。

元上都在中外外交史上具有重要影响。元代中外交往频繁，上都地区当时商贾工匠云集，不但有从中原来的商人，也有从中亚和欧洲来的商人，他们运来各种金属器皿、日用品和奢侈品，转而运走上都地区的畜产品，从而促进了以元上都为中心的蒙古地区的经济繁荣。

元上都在元代科技史上的地位更不容忽视。早在蒙哥汗时期，开平就设有天文观测所——承应阙。波斯科学家札马鲁丁曾受蒙哥汗委托筹建天文台，在此研制了许多大型天文仪器并制定了“万年历”。1262 年，忽必烈在上都召见了著名科学家郭守敬，并采纳了他对北方水利资源和华北平原水利灌溉建设的六条建议。

高句丽王城、王陵及贵族墓葬

高句丽是中国古代边疆的少数民族政权，汉元帝建昭二年（公元前 37 年）由扶余人朱蒙在西汉玄菟郡高句丽县（今辽宁省新宾县境内）建国，后建都于纥升骨城（今辽宁省桓仁县境内五女山城）。西汉元始三年（公元 3 年），迁都国内城，同时筑尉那岩城（均在今吉林省集安境内），至北魏始光四年（公元 427 年）迁都平壤。公元 668 年，高句丽政权被唐与朝鲜半岛的新罗联军所灭。

高句丽政权曾是中国东北地区影响较大的少数民族政权之一，在东北亚历史发展过程中发生过重要作用，创造了灿烂的古代文明，在吉林、辽宁等地留下了丰富的历史遗迹和文物。

主要建筑

20 世纪 90 年代以来，中国考古工作者在集安、桓仁陆续发掘了多处高句丽王城和贵族墓葬遗迹，对部分遭受自然损害的王陵进行了维修，高句丽丰富的文化内涵、轮廓逐渐清晰。遗产地主要包括五女山城、国内城、丸都山城、12 座王陵、26 座贵族墓葬、好太王碑和将军坟一号陪冢。其中王城、王陵和贵族墓弥足珍贵，具有重要的历史文化价值。

王　城

国内城、丸都山城（始名尉那岩城）是高句丽早中期（公元 1–5 世纪）的都城，其特点是平原城与山城相互依附共为都城。在东北亚地区中世纪世代城址中，国内城与丸都山城是都城建筑的杰作。国内城是为数不多的地表保存有石筑城墙的平原城类型都城遗址，保存下来的城墙依然坚实牢固而又不失美观庄严。丸都山城的布局因山形走势而巧妙构思、合理规划，完美地实现了自然风貌与人类创造的浑然一体。通过考古发掘揭露的宫殿址遗迹，仍可显示原有建筑的恢弘气势。国内城与丸都山城是高句丽政权延续使用时间最长的都城，它们可以见证已经被历史长河湮没了的高句丽创造的辉煌文明。

在王城中，五女山山城是中国古代东北地区少数民族高句丽创建的第一个都城。作为鸭绿江两岸现存百余座高句丽山城中建造最早的一座，它的规模宏大，体系完备，保存也较为完整。城内分布多处高句丽早期的重要建筑遗址及生活、军事遗迹，文化内涵十分丰富。五女山山城承袭了中国北方民族构筑山城的传统，但在选址布局、城墙筑法、石料加工等方面，具有很大的突破和创新。在中国古代东北民族建筑史上，具有里程碑意义。

王陵和贵族墓

位于集安市的高句丽古墓群，是奴隶制国家高句丽王朝的遗迹。在集安市周围的平原上，分布了 1 万多座高句丽时代的古墓，这就是闻名海内外的“洞沟古墓群”。其中太王陵、将军坟和千秋墓等规模宏大，从侧面反映出高句丽的历史发展进程。古墓群中以将军坟、太王陵为代表的十几座大型高句丽王陵以及大量的王室贵族壁画墓，是高句丽建筑的一个缩影。尤为重要的是，地方文化底蕴与周边特别是中国中原文化因素的有机交融在它们身上得到充分的展现，是高句丽文化昭示后人的经典之作。

好太王碑　据史料记载，好太王碑建于东晋安帝义熙十年（公元 414 年），迄今已有 1590 年的历史。它是用一块完整的巨大角砾凝灰岩石柱稍加修凿而成。碑高 6.39 米，四面幅宽不等，在 1.34–2 米之间。碑体重约 37 吨，碑身略呈方柱形，无碑额。整座石碑未借助任何外力，直接矗立在一块不规则的花岗岩石板上。

好太王名谈德，于公元 391 年 18 岁时即位，39 岁死亡。好太王在位的 22 年间是高句丽历史上的空前繁荣发展时期，好太王碑是长寿王为纪念其父的功业而树立的。主要记述了好太王碑是高句丽第 20 代王长寿王为其父高句丽第 19 代王好太王立的纪功碑，记载了高句丽民族起源和建国的神话传说，前三王的承继关系；好太王一生东征西战，广开土境的赫赫战功；好太王守墓烟户的数量、来源以及有关的守墓制度。高句丽历史上目前已知的有文字文物仅存三件，好太王碑是其中记叙内容最为丰富的一件，对研究高句丽的政治、军事、文化、制度、传统和它与新罗、百济及日本列岛的关系都有很重要的意义。

太王陵　太王陵是高句丽第 19 代王——国冈上广开土境平安好太王的陵墓，始建于公元 391 年，是现存高句丽王陵中唯一确知年代、葬者的典型墓葬。太王陵为方坛阶梯石室墓，正方形，边长 66 米，残高 14.8 米，由数级阶坛砌成。每级阶坛由数层修琢工细的长方石条垒砌。墓室四壁用修整光滑的石块平砌，上覆一巨石为顶。整座墓陵规模庞大，结构古朴。

太王陵旁原有墓庵一座，供奉广泽尊王守陵。墙壁上诗画琳琅满目，其中清代道光四年（1824 年）副贡柯琮琪的诗句“年年谒祖到清溪，携酒牵羊一路挤。回忆古藤身化处，旧庵隐约夕阳西。”描述了当时祭祀太王陵的情景。

高句丽壁画墓　高句丽壁画墓位于吉林省集安市。高句丽民族骁勇善战，在早期壁画中有不少表现军队与战争的场面。更多的绘画内容为宫殿、亭阁、马厩、水井、卫兵、侍女、牛马鸡狗、花草树木、日月星辰等图案。此外，这类壁画还绘有极具中原文化特征的伏羲、女娲、黄帝、神农、仙人、僧侣、道士等，表现出丰富的儒、佛、道文化。由于高句丽留下的文字很少且散见于中国古籍，因此，内容丰富的高句丽古墓壁画成为专家学者研究高句丽历史、文化、风俗等的重要考古资料。

高句丽墓葬八卦图　这幅八卦图出现在吉林省集安市高句丽贵族墓葬“五盔坟”4 号墓室北壁的左下角。壁上绘有一个道士形象的人：他跣足端坐于莲台上，左腿盘屈，右腿立起，披发低首，身着绿色羽衣，一只手在地上绘着一幅八卦图。在高句丽贵族墓室壁画中画有这样一个年代最早、且极具个性的八卦图实图，对中国易学史与东北文化史的研究有极为重要的意义。

将军坟　在吉林省集安市区东北 5 公里的龙山脚下，有一座形似埃及金字塔的巨型石墓，这就是有“东方金字塔”之称的“将军坟”。这座方坛阶梯墓是高句丽第 20 位王“长寿王”的陵寝。

将军坟建于公元 5 世纪初，以 1100 余块修凿工整的长方型花岗岩石条垒筑而成，中间以卵石和沙砾填充。为了防止自身重量压迫使条石外移，四面各放置三块巨大的护坟石。除北面失落一块外，其余各面护坟石至今保存完整。将军坟高 12.4 米，陵墓外形为 7 级阶梯，墓室开口在第 5 级阶梯中部。

文献记载中的“长寿王”“体貌魁杰、志气豪迈”，他继承了父亲“好太王”的基业，继续开拓疆土，并为了向朝鲜半岛南部发展，他把都城迁到了平壤。高句丽政权在“长寿王”时期达到了鼎盛，成为东北亚地区最强大的国家之一。

千秋墓　位于集安城西 3.5 公里处麻线河东岸 200 米的坡地上。形制浩大，宛若山岳，因墓上发现有“千秋万岁”字样的汉字铭文砖而名之为“千秋墓”。千秋墓为方坛阶梯石室墓，近正方形，边长 80–85 米，残高 15 米。墓顶较平坦，约 20 米见方，乱石中埋有数块经加工的大石条。墓上现存有大量的筒瓦和板瓦残片及文字砖残段。千秋墓修筑方式与将军坟相同，但工程巨大数倍于将军坟，堪称高句丽墓葬之冠，是一座高句丽的王陵。

遗产价值

高句丽曾经创造了辉煌的历史。其主要的历史遗迹大量地存续于中国的吉林省和辽宁省，成为该段历史无可替代的实物见证。高句丽创造了具有民族特色的文化，但中后期受中原文化影响很深，儒、佛、道文化盛行；特别是高句丽坚固的山城、雄伟的陵墓、辉煌的古墓壁画，成为华夏文明的重要组成部分。高句丽壁画墓被誉为“东北亚艺术宝库”，记载了中国古代东北少数民族的特殊文化。

曲阜孔庙、孔林和孔府

在山东省的西南部，有一个孔姓人口占五分之一的县级市，她就是有着数千年悠久历史的“东方圣城”——曲阜。“千年礼乐归东鲁，万古衣冠拜素王”。曲阜之所以享誉全球，是与孔子的名字紧密相连的。孔子是世界上最伟大的哲学家之一，中国儒家学派的创始人。在2000多年的历史长河中，儒家文化逐渐成为中国的正统文化，并影响到东亚和东南亚各国，成为整个东方文化的基石。

主要建筑

公元前478年，孔子死后第二年，为了“岁时奉祀”，鲁哀公将孔子生前所居之堂立为“庙”。当时只有“庙屋三间”，内藏孔子生前所用的衣、冠、琴、车、书等。其后，随着历代王朝层层加谥孔子，孔庙不断得到维修扩建，至明、清时期形成了现在的规模。

孔　庙

孔庙建筑规模宏大，雄伟壮丽，是我国最大的祭孔场所。庙内共有九进院落，以南北为中轴，分左、中、右三路，纵长630米，横宽140米，有殿、堂、坛、阁等460多间，总面积约16000平方米；门坊54座，“御碑亭”13座。孔庙主要建筑有金、元碑亭；明代奎文阁、杏坛、德侔天地坊；清代重建的大成殿、寝殿等。

奎文阁　又名藏书楼，是一座专门收藏历代帝王御赐书籍、墨迹的楼阁。它三重飞檐，四层斗拱，丹墙黄瓦，具有独特的建筑艺术风格，是一座仅次于大成殿的高大建筑。

十三碑亭　位于奎文阁和大成门之间的院落里，南面8座，北面5座，俗称“御碑亭”。计有唐、宋、金、元、明、清六代巨碑50余通。在书法艺术上，真草隶篆，座座不同，风格笔法，各有千秋。

大成殿　孔庙的正殿，也是孔庙的核心。唐代称文宣王殿。清雍正二年（1724年）重建，九脊重檐，黄瓦覆顶，雕梁画栋，八斗藻井饰以金龙和玺彩图，双重飞檐正中竖匾，上刻清雍正皇帝御书“大成殿”三个贴金大字。殿高24.8米，长45.69米，宽24.85米，座落在2.1米高的殿基上，为全庙最高建筑，也是中国三大古殿之一。殿内正中供孔子塑像，左右配享颜子、曾子、子思和孟子塑像，俗称“四配”。两侧又有塑像12尊，他们是闵损、冉耕、冉雍、宰予、端木赐、冉求、仲由、言偃、卜商、颛孙师、有若和朱熹，为“十二哲”。这16位学者是儒家学派公认的正宗继承人。

孔　林

孔林位于曲阜县城北2公里处，占地3000余亩，是我国规模最大、持续年代最长、保存最完整的一处氏族墓葬群和人工园林。园中古木参天，浓荫如盖，相传孔子的弟子，各以其故乡的树木种植于孔林之内，因而树种极多。林中墓冢累累，碑碣林立，除孔子、孔鲤、孔及这祖孙三代墓葬和建筑外，还有孔令贻、孔毓垢、孔闻韶、孔尚任墓等。洙水桥北不远处为享殿，是祭孔时摆香坛的地方。享殿之后，正中大墓为孔子墓地，墓前有明人黄养正篆刻“大成至圣文宣王墓”巨碑。东边为其子“泗水侯”孔鲤墓；前为其孙“沂国述圣公”孔子思墓。孔子墓前东侧有三亭，是宋真宗、清圣祖和清高宗来此祭孔时停留之处，叫作“驻跸亭”。

孔　府

孔府西与孔庙为邻，是孔子世袭“衍圣公”的世代嫡裔子孙居住的地方，仅次于明、清皇帝宫室的最大府第。孔府占地240多亩，有厅、堂、楼、轩等各式建筑463间，分为中、东、西三路。东路为家庙，西路为学院，中路为主体建筑。中路以内宅为界，前为官衙，设三堂六厅；后为内宅，设前上房、前堂楼、后堂楼、后五间。最后是孔府花园。

孔府大堂是当年衍圣公宣读圣旨、接见官员、申饬家法族规、审理重大案件，以及节日、寿辰举行仪式的地方。正中太师椅上，赫然披铺一张斑斓虎皮，十分惹人注目。

二堂也叫后厅，是衍圣公会见四品以上官僚及受皇帝委托考试礼学、乐学童生的地方，室内正中上、下挂着“钦承圣绪”和“诗书礼乐”

的大匾，两旁立着几块石碑。其中慈禧太后手书的“寿”字，是清光绪二十年（1894 年）衍圣公孔令贻专程赴京为慈禧太后祝寿时赏给他的御礼。

三堂之后，便是孔府的内宅部分。正北迎面是七间正厅，名前上房，是孔府主人接待至亲和近支族人的客厅，也是他们举行家宴和婚丧仪式的主要场所。室内家具精美，文物古玩琳琅满目。

文物收藏

孔庙、孔林、孔府的历史、科学、艺术价值集中体现在它所保存的文物上。孔府收藏的大批历史文物中，最著名的是“商周十器”，亦称“十供”，形制古雅，纹饰精美，原为宫廷所藏青铜礼器，清乾隆三十六年由清廷赏赐孔府。此外，300 多座、1300 多间金、元、明、清古建筑反映了各个时期的建筑规制和特点；1000 多件汉画像石、孔子圣迹图、石仪、龙柱等反映了石刻艺术的变化和发展；5000 多块西汉以来的历代碑刻既是中国书法艺术的瑰宝，也是研究中国古代政治、思想、经济、文化、艺术的宝贵资料；十余万座历代墓葬是研究墓葬制度的重要实物；17000 余株古树名木是研究古代物候学、气象学、生态学的活标本。十余万件馆藏文物中，以元明衣冠、孔子画像、衍圣公及夫人肖像、祭祀礼器最为著名，其中元明衣冠是中国罕见的传世同类文物，对于研究古代服饰、纺织工艺具有重要价值；30 余万件孔府明清文书档案是中国最为丰富的私家档案，是研究明清历史尤其是经济史的重要资料。

遗产价值

孔庙、孔府集中地体现了中国近 1000 年来的建筑风格，特别是明清时期中国古代建筑达到了前所未有的水平。建筑多以木材作为整体的构架，用各种形式的斗拱支撑结构，庭院式的布局注重对称。孔庙、孔府的建筑群凝聚了历代建筑的精华，极具建筑艺术之美。同时在建筑的布局、规划和装饰等方面，也反映出儒家思想的精髓。而这些正是体现了讲究造型和整体布局的空间处理方式，使建筑又蕴含了孔子思想中万物和谐共处的意念。特别是孔庙， 突出地体现着儒家的建筑取向，堪称为“和” 的建筑美学观的杰作和典范，是一座屹立于世界东方的崇高的文化和艺术殿堂。“孔林”中生长的 17000 余株古树名木不仅见证了“三孔”的发展历史，同时也是研究古代物候学、气候学和生态学的宝贵素材。

苏州古典园林

苏州地处长江下游的太湖之滨，自然条件和地理环境十分优越。自公元前 514 年春秋吴国在此建立都城以来，这里一直是江南地区的政治、经济和文化中心，工商繁荣，人文荟萃，尤其在园艺、建筑、工艺美术和绘画方面，水平高超，名家辈出，从而为苏州古典园林的产生和发展提供了充分的条件。

苏州古典园林的历史可上溯至公元前六世纪春秋时吴王的苑囿，私家园林最早见于记载的是东晋（约公元 4 世纪）的辟疆园。历代造园兴盛，名园日多。明清时期，苏州成为中国最繁华的地区，私家园林遍布古城内外。16 世纪 –18 世纪全盛时期，有园林两百余处，现在保存完好的尚有数十处，在世界造园史上有其独特的历史地位和价值。

景观特色

苏州园林是文化意蕴深厚的“文人写意山水园”。造园者造园时多以画为本，以诗为题，通过凿池堆山、栽花种柳，创造出具有诗情画意的景观，被称为是“无声的诗，立体的画”。

苏州园林充分体现了“自然美”的主旨，在设计构筑中，采用因地制宜，借景、对景、分景、隔景等种种手法来组织空间，造成园林中曲折多变、小中见大、虚实相间的景观艺术效果。通过叠山理水，栽植花木，配置园林建筑，形成充满诗情画意的文人写意山水园林，在都市内创造出人与自然和谐相处的“城市山林”。

苏州园林的重要特色之一，是它不仅是历史文化的产物，同时也是中国传统思想文化的载体。表现在园林厅堂的命名、匾额、楹联、书条石、雕刻、装饰，以及花木寓意、叠石寄情等，不仅是点缀园林的精美艺术品，同时储存了大量的历史、文化、思想和科学信息、物质内容和精神内容。其中有反映和传播儒、释、道等各家哲学观念、思想流派，借助古典诗词文学，对园景进行点缀、生发、渲染，使人于栖息游赏中，化景物为情思，产生意境美，获得精神上的满足。而园中汇集保存完好的中国历代书法名家手迹，又是珍贵的艺术品，具有极高的文物价值。

主要景观

明清两朝，苏州造园活动达到高潮。最盛时期，苏州的私家园林和庭院达到 280 余处，至今保存完好并开放的有：始建于宋代的沧浪亭、网师园，元代的狮子林，明代的拙政园、艺圃，清代的留园、耦园、怡园、曲园、听枫园等。其中，拙政园、留园、网师园、环秀山庄因其精美卓绝的造园艺术和个性鲜明的艺术特点于 1997 年底被联合国教科文组织列为“世界文化遗产”。沧浪亭、狮子林、拙政园和留园分别代表着宋、元、明、清四个朝代的艺术风格，被称为苏州“四大名园”。

拙政园　典雅、淡秀的拙政园位于苏州古城东北街 178 号，占地面积 78 亩。这是一座始建于 15 世纪初的古典园林，具有浓郁的江南水乡特色，经过几百年的苍桑变迁，至今仍保持着平淡疏朗、旷远明瑟的明代风格，被誉为“中国私家园林之最”。

全园分东、中、西、住宅四部分。中部山水明秀，厅榭典雅，花木繁茂，是全园的精华所在。西部水廊逶迤，楼台倒影，清幽恬静。东部平岗草地，竹坞曲水，空间开阔。

留园　地处阊门外留园路。以其布局严谨、风格高雅、景观丰富，曾被评为“吴中第一名园”。

留园厅堂敞丽，装饰精美，利用许多建筑群将全园空间巧妙分隔，组合成若干各具特色的景区，这些景区用曲廊联系，全园曲廊长达七百余米，随形而变，因势而曲，或蟠曲于山腰，或蜿蜒于水际，逶迤相续，始终不断，使园景堂奥深远，无穷变化，有步移景异之妙。

网师园　网师园是苏州园林中极具艺术特色和文化价值的中型古典山水宅园代表作品。始建于南宋淳熙年间，至清乾隆时定名为“网师园”。园中布局分为宅第和园林两部分，东部为宅第，中部为主园，西部为内园。宅第为苏州典型的清代官僚住宅，前后三进。屋宇高敞，有轿厅、大厅、花厅，内部装饰雅洁，外部砖雕工细，堪称封建社会仕宦宅第的代表作。主园建筑物较多，组成庭院两区。全园布局外形整齐均衡，内部因景划区，境界各异。

沧浪亭 地处城南三元坊。在现存苏州园林中，历史最为悠久。全园布局自然和谐，堪称构思巧妙、手法得宜的佳作。全园景色简洁古朴，落落大方。不以工巧取胜，而以自然为美。沧浪亭园外景色因水而起，颇富山岛水乡诗意。而园内布局以山为主，建筑亦大多环山，并以长廊相接。沿池筑一复廊，蜿蜒曲折，将临池而建的亭榭连成一片，使园外之水与园内之山相映成趣、相得益彰，自然地融为一体，是为借景的典范。

狮子林 为苏州四大名园之一，至今已有650多年的历史。狮子林既有苏州古典园林亭、台、楼、阁、厅、堂、轩、廊之人文景观，更以湖山、奇石、洞壑而著名于世，素有“假山王国”之美誉。狮子林假山共有21个洞口，横向极尽迂回曲折，竖向力求回环起伏。元代诗人谭惟则有句：“人道我居城市里，我疑身在万山中”，是狮子林非常生动的写照。

环秀山庄 环秀山庄又名颐园，是以假山为主的一处古典园林。设计巧妙得宜，湖山、池水、树木、建筑，得以融为一体；假山一座、池水一湾，更是独出心裁。园虽小，却极有气势。特别是戈氏所叠假山，堪称一绝，占地不过半亩，然咫尺之间，千岩万壑，环山而视，步移景易。主峰突兀于东南，次峰拱揖于西北，池水缭绕于两山之间。山有危径、洞穴、幽谷、石崖、飞梁、绝壁，境界多变，一如天然。主峰高7.2米，涧谷长12米，山径长60余米，盘旋上下，如高路入云，气象万千。

遗产价值

苏州古典园林宅园合一，可赏，可游，可居，这种建筑形态的形成，是在人口密集和缺乏自然风光的城市中，人类依恋自然、追求与自然和谐相处、美化和完善自身居住环境的一 种创造。拙政园、留园、网师园、环秀山庄这四座古典园林，建筑类型齐全，保存完整，系统而全面地展示了苏州古典园林建筑的布局、结构、造型、风格、色彩以及装修、家具、陈设等各个方面的内容，是明清时期江南民间建筑的代表作品，反映了这一时期中国江南地区高度的居住文明，曾影响到整个江南城市的建筑格调，并带动民间建筑的设计、构思、布局、审美以及施工技术向其靠拢，从而反映了中国古代江南民间起居休亲的生活方式和礼仪习俗，是了解和研究古代中国江南民俗的实物资料。

杭州西湖文化景观

“西湖文化景观”肇始于公元 9 世纪，成形于 13 世纪，兴盛于 18 世纪，由真实、完整地保存至今的西湖自然山水、景观整体格局、系列题名景观“西湖十景”、10 处相关重要历史文化遗存和 240 公顷的西湖龙井茶园共 5 种类型的景观要素组成，分布于杭州城市西部的西湖及其周边群山共 43.3 平方公里的范围内。

景观特色

“西湖文化景观”，一是由苏堤、白堤和小瀛洲、湖心亭、阮公墩共同组成“两堤三岛”景观格局，于公元 9–19 世纪逐渐形成；二是由西湖水域与环湖的南山与北山峰峦系列、西湖东侧的城市沿湖景观共同组成的城湖空间关系——“三面云山一面城”，成形于 12 世纪，维系至今。

湖区以苏堤和白堤的优美风光著称。苏堤和白堤横贯于西湖，把西湖分隔为西里湖、小南湖、岳湖、外湖和里湖五部分。每当晨光初启，宿雾如烟，湖面腾起薄雾时，便出现“六桥烟柳”的优美风景。孤山是西湖中最大的天然岛屿，苏堤、白堤越过湖面，小瀛洲、湖心亭、阮公墩三个人工小岛鼎立于外西湖湖心，夕照山的雷峰塔与宝石山的保俶塔隔湖相望，由此形成了“一山、二塔、三岛、三堤、五湖”的基本格局。

主要景观

“杭州西湖文化景观”的题名景观主要是“西湖十景”，包括：苏堤春晓、曲院风荷、平湖秋月、断桥残雪、花港观鱼、柳浪闻莺、三潭印月、双峰插云、雷峰夕照、南屏晚钟。这一系列景观涉及了关于季节、时段、气象、动植物的景观特色，以及园林、宅院、佛寺、亭台楼阁等极为丰富的景观元素，并各有侧重地表现出或生动、或静谧、或隐逸、或禅境等的审美主题。

孤山　孤山是西湖中最大的岛屿。东西分别以白堤和西泠桥与湖岸相连，岛上名胜古迹甚多。主要景观包括中山公园、浙江省博物馆、文澜阁、西泠印社、放鹤亭、秋瑾墓、俞楼、慕才亭（苏小小墓）等。

中山公园原为清代行宫御花园，1927 年为纪念孙中山先生，公园命名为“中山公园”。放鹤亭在孤山东北角，为纪念宋代以“梅妻鹤子”闻名的林逋而建。浙江省博物馆在孤山南麓，现有各类文物藏品十余万件。文澜阁在浙江省博物馆内西北角，清乾隆年间，为存放《四库全书》，仿北京故宫文渊阁样式改建。西泠印社于 1904 年创办于孤山西南麓，因地近西泠桥而命名，是中国近代著名的金石书画艺术团体。

白堤与苏堤　白堤东起断桥，经锦带桥向西，在“平湖秋月”与孤山相接，长约 1 公里。两侧广种桃柳，是欣赏西湖全景和周边诸山的最佳观赏点。

苏堤旧称苏公堤，南起南屏山麓南山路，北至岳王庙东，横贯湖中，堤长 2797 米，宽 30–40 米。据南宋咸淳《临安志》：“元祐中，东坡既奏开浚湖水，因以所积葑草筑为长堤，起南讫北，横跨湖面，绵亘数里，夹道杂植花柳，中为六桥，行者便之。”后几经培植修葺，现已成为西湖最著名的景点之一。

断桥　断桥位于白堤东首，民间故事《白蛇传》中，断桥为白素贞与许仙邂逅之处，因而在西湖诸桥中最负盛名。

古时桥上有门，门上有檐，下雪时中间一段的雪都在门檐上，桥上只有两头有雪，远远望去桥像断了一样，所以称作断桥。断桥是通往孤山的必经之路，每值雪后，人们纷纷去断桥欣赏西湖雪景，孤山与里西湖银装素裹，格外动人，因有“断桥残雪”一景。

虎跑泉　虎跑泉是一处以“泉”为主题的观泉、听泉、品泉、试泉的泉源景观，又是以性空、济公、弘一法师传奇故事为特色的人文景观，位于西湖之南的大慈山定慧禅寺内。民间传说唐代性空大师游历此山，发现这里风景虽美，但却没有水源，于是决定去往别处。忽然有神人告诉他，即将有两只老虎来此挖泉。翌日，果然有两虎刨山出泉，从此，“龙井茶叶虎跑泉”成为“西湖双绝”。

灵隐寺　该寺佐证了佛教、特别是禅宗文化对西湖景观的直接影响，至今仍为西湖佛寺之冠，是我国东南沿海地区最重要的佛教活动场所之一，其两石塔、两经幢刻造精细，仿造木构建筑逼真，具有珍贵的文物价值。

飞来峰　飞来峰造像是中国东南地区规模最大的佛教摩崖造像群，是中国汉族地区供奉藏传佛教造像最多的佛教石窟。它保存了晚唐以后佛教造像艺术发展演变的重要环节，填补了中国石窟艺术史上五代至元代的空缺，在我国石窟艺术史上占有重要的地位，是我国石窟艺术的瑰宝。

遗产价值

西湖文化景观由中国古代的二位大文豪白居易和苏轼开创和营造，突出体现了“天人合一”的哲学理念，蕴含了中国儒家、道家、释家三大传统文化与信仰要素，突出承载了中国传统的崇佛文化、隐逸文化、茶禅文化、忠孝文化和藏书文化，见证了13–14世纪两个高度发达的亚洲文明——草原文明的蒙元文化与农耕文明的赵宋文化在中国东部江南地区的碰撞，体现了中国农耕文明发达时期文人士大夫在景观设计上的创造性精神，虽经千百年历史演变，都基本上获得了完整和真实的保存和延续，在公元9–20世纪的中国及其周边地区的景观设计史和文化交流史上具有重要地位。

同时，“西湖景观”与中国著名的四大古典爱情传说中的《白蛇传》和《梁山伯与祝英台》直接相关，在中国传统文学艺术领域和广大的民间生活中均拥有极为广泛的影响。

澳门历史城区

澳门历史城区保存了澳门四百多年中西文化交流的历史精髓。它是中国境内现存年代最远、规模最大、保存最完整和最集中、以西式建筑为主、中西式建筑互相辉映的历史城区，是西方宗教文化在中国和远东地区传播历史重要的见证，更是四百多年来中西文化交流互补、多元共存的结晶。澳门历史城区或澳门历史古城区（旧称澳门历史建筑群），是由 22 座位于澳门半岛的建筑物所组成，以旧城区为核心的历史街区。

历史渊源

16 世纪中叶，因应中外贸易的新形势，明朝政府划出澳门半岛西南部一片地段，供以葡萄牙人为主的外国商人居住和进行贸易，澳门由此发展成 19 世纪前中国主要的对外港口，也是亚洲地区重要的国际港口。贸易活动的兴盛吸引了世界各地的人纷至沓来，一个融合欧、亚、非、美四洲人民的“华洋杂居”的国际城市由是诞生。葡萄牙人将这个用城墙围起的城市命名为“天主圣名之城”，今天的“澳门历史城区”就是它的核心部分。

四百多年间，在这块城区内，来自葡萄牙、西班牙、荷兰、英国、法国、意大利、美国、日本、朝鲜甚至非洲地区等不同地方的人，带着不同的文化思想、不同的职业技艺、不同的风俗习惯，在澳门历史城区内盖房子、建教堂、修马路、筑炮台甚至修建坟场，展开多姿多彩的生活，包括各类文化活动。在这种机遇下，澳门得风气之先，成为中国境内接触近代西方器物与文化最早、最多、最重要的地方，是当时中国接触西方文化的桥头堡。与此同时，居住在澳门的外国人，也以各种方式，向世界各国介绍在澳门见到的中国文化思想与生活习俗。澳门，也是一道外国认识中国的门户。

随着外国人的定居，他们把自己的建筑传统越洋带到澳门，使澳门成为近代西洋建筑传入中国的第一站。尤其是葡萄牙人在澳门的建筑物，无不显露出与葡萄牙本土建筑的密切关系。事实上，文艺复兴后的一些主要建筑形式、风格，结合亚洲其它地区不同的建筑元素在澳门产生了新的变体，形成独树一帜的建筑风格。

景观特色

澳门历史城区因为中西文化共融的缘故，城区当中的大部分建筑都具有中西合璧的特色。城区内的建筑大部分至今仍完好地保存或保持着原有的功能，包括中国最古老的教堂遗址和修道院、最古老的基督教坟场、最古老的西式炮台建筑群等。

明末清初，大量天主教传教士以澳门为传教基地，积极从事远东地区的传教和建设工作，开创了许多“中国第一”，如中国第一所西式大学（圣保禄学院）、中国第一所西式医院（白马行医院）、第一座西式剧院、第一座现代化灯塔、第一所以西方金属制版和印刷拉丁文字的印刷厂（圣保禄学院附属印刷所）、中国第一份外文报纸（《蜜蜂华报》）(*A Abelha da China*) 等等。由耶稣会在澳门开办的圣保禄学院（现已不存）及圣若瑟修院，为天主教在远东和中国的传教事业培养了大量人才，同时也培养了大批中国籍的传教士。

主要景观

“澳门历史城区”是一片以澳门旧城区为核心的历史街区，其间以相邻的广场和街道连接而成，包括妈阁庙前地、亚婆井前地、岗顶前地、议事亭前地、大堂前地、板樟堂前地、耶稣会纪念广场、白鸽巢前地等多个广场空间，以及妈阁庙、港务局大楼、郑家大屋、圣老楞佐教堂、圣若瑟修院及圣堂、岗顶剧院、何东图书馆、圣奥斯定教堂、民政总署大楼、三街会馆（关帝庙）、仁慈堂大楼、大堂（主教座堂）、卢家大屋、玫瑰堂、大三巴牌坊、哪吒庙、旧城墙遗址、大炮台、圣安多尼教堂、东方基金会会址、基督教坟场、东望洋炮台（含东望洋灯塔及圣母雪地殿圣堂）等历史建筑。

玫瑰圣母堂　玫瑰圣母堂又称板樟堂或多明我堂，始建于 1687 年，是天主教的明我会教士初到澳门时设立的，至今已有四百多年的历史。

教堂艺术特色比较浓厚。圣堂内的天花板装饰非常漂亮，皇冠图案色彩典雅，精美绝伦。层叠的壁柱间隔扭曲的麻花柱，弯曲的线脚烘托断山花，形成华美的巴洛克风格，是澳门最美丽的祭坛之一。

岗顶前地 岗顶前地古称磨盘山，该地段虽然不大，但自然环境清幽典雅，人文宗教景观荟萃，著名的建筑物有：圣奥斯定教堂、岗顶剧院（伯多禄五世剧院）、圣若瑟修院、何东图书馆等，再加上由碎石铺成的波浪图案路面，散发着浓郁的欧陆情调，置身其中，让人感到无尽的悠闲舒适。

议事亭前地 为民政总署大楼前的广场，两侧建筑建于 19 世纪末 20 世纪初。右侧主要建有具西方古典主义特色的邮政局大楼，新古典主义的仁慈堂大楼；左侧是一列三层带有行人走廊的新古典主义楼宇，建筑色彩多样，显现出浓浓的南欧风情。

圣保禄教堂前壁 大三巴牌坊是圣保禄教堂的前壁遗迹，1835 年 1 月圣保禄教堂失火，整幢教堂几乎付之一炬，所幸教堂前壁幸免于难，成为今日的大三巴牌坊。当年的圣保禄教堂建筑，具有卓尔不群的气势和显赫的地位，它不仅是远东最大的天主教堂，也是远东第一所西方大学。

遗产价值

澳门历史城区是中国现存最古老的西式建筑遗产，是东西方建筑艺术的综合体现。历史城区见证了西方宗教文化在中国以至远东地区的发展，也见证了中国向西方传播民间宗教的历史渊源。同时也是中西文化多元共存的独特反映，是中国历史城市中极具特色的组合。

福建土楼

福建土楼以土、木、石、竹为主要建筑材料，利用将未经烧焙的按一定比例的沙质黏土和黏质沙土拌合而成、用夹板夯筑而成的两层以上的房屋，是中原汉民即客家先民沿黄河、长江、汀江等流域历经多次辗转迁徙后，将远古的生土建筑艺术发扬光大并推向极致的特殊产物，福建土楼以分布广、数量多、品类丰富、保存完好而著称。分布范围以福建西南地区尤为集中，总数达 3 万多座，因其大多数为福建客家人所建，故又称“客家土楼”。

历史渊源

福建土楼是客家文化的象征，它以历史悠久、种类繁多、规模宏大、结构奇巧、功能齐全、内涵丰富著称，具有极高的历史、艺术和科学价值，被誉为“世界上独一无二的、神话般的山区建筑模式”。

福建土楼产生于宋元，成熟于明末、清代和民国时期。土楼中最古老和最年轻的圆楼均在永定初溪，直径 66 米的集庆楼已届 600 岁“高龄”，直径 31 米的善庆楼则仅有 30 年历史。

福建土楼的形成与历史上中原汉人几次著名大迁徙有关。西晋永嘉年间即约在公元 4 世纪时，北方战祸频仍，天灾肆虐，当地民众大举南迁，拉开了千百年来中原汉人不断举族迁徙入闽的序幕。进入闽南的中原移民与当地居民相互融合，形成了以闽南话为特征的福佬民系；辗转迁徙后经江西赣州进入闽西山区的中原汉人则构成福建另一支重要民系——以客家话为特征的客家民系。

福建土楼所在的闽西南山区，正是福佬与客家民系的交汇处，地势险峻，人烟稀少，一度野兽出没，盗匪四起。聚族而居既是根深蒂固的中原儒家传统观念要求，更是聚集力量、共御外敌的现实需要。福建土楼依山就势，布局合理，吸收了中国传统建筑规划的“风水”理念，适应聚族而居的生活和防御的要求，巧妙地利用了山间狭小的平地和当地的生土、木材、鹅卵石等建筑材料，是一种自成体系，具有节约、坚固、防御性强等特点，又极富美感的生土高层建筑类型。这些独一无二的山区民居建筑，将源远流长的生土夯筑技术推向极致。

景观特色

福建土楼的造型、装饰和建造工艺世所罕见，俗称“生土楼”。它是以生土作为主要建筑材料，掺上细沙、石灰、竹片、木条等，经过反复揉、舂、压建造而成。土木结合、外闭内敞、规模宏大、造型优美、品类多样、就地取材、构思精巧、聚族而居等是土楼建筑的主要特征。其独特的建设形式、高超的工程技术和丰富的文化内涵、众多家庭聚族而居于一楼的均等居住形式，使之不同于世界其他任何建筑，可谓天下一绝。

福建土楼主要有三种典型风格，即五凤楼、方楼、圆楼。从整体看，以三堂屋为中心的五凤楼含有明确的主次意识，它是汉族文化发源地的黄河中游流域古老院落式布局的延续发展。方楼的布局与五凤楼相近，但其坚厚土墙从上堂屋扩大到整体外围，防御性大大加强。圆楼不但强化了防御功能，而且尊卑主次严重削弱。

土楼建筑的另一特色是结构极为规范，房间的规格大小一致。大多数土楼均只有一个大门供人出入。且由于墙壁较高较厚，既可防潮保暖，又可隔热纳凉。

福建土楼千姿百态，种类繁多，分方楼、圆楼两大体系二十多种建筑形式，被誉为“没有大门的中国客家土楼博物馆。”在众多土楼中，最具代表性的是圆楼。

圆楼是当地土楼群中最具特色的建筑，一般从一个圆心出发，依不同半径一层层向外展开，如同湖中的水波，环环相套，非常壮观。其最中心处为家族祠院，向外依次为祖堂、围廊，最外一环住人。整个土楼房间大小一致，面积约 10 平方米；使用共同的楼梯，各家几乎无秘密可言。土楼中最美的圆形土楼首推振成楼，它是世界上神话般的居民建筑，有“土楼王子”之称。

主要景观

成为世界文化遗产的 46 座福建土楼由六群四楼组成，福建永定县占三群两楼，南靖县和华安县占三群楼，包括分布在永定县的初溪土楼群、洪坑土楼群、南靖县的田螺坑土楼群、河坑土楼群、华安县的大地土楼群等，主要分布在福建西部和南部的崇山峻岭中，以其独特的建筑风格和悠久的历史文化著称于世。

初溪土楼群 初溪土楼群位于永定县下洋镇初溪村，由五座圆楼和数十座方楼组成，如图案般舒展有致。最有特色的客家民居建筑有继善楼、反围龙式的积善堂和善庆楼等。善庆楼是一座堂前向外周匝式的反围龙式建筑，其建筑结构在传统客家围龙屋建筑中别具一格，在粤东客家地区极为少见。

洪坑村土楼群 洪坑村建于不同时代、形态各异、规模不一的客家土楼以及宗祠、寺庙、学堂等沿溪而建，错落有致，布局合理，与青山、绿水、村道、小桥、田园完美结合，融为一体。洪坑村土楼为林氏民居，现有建于16世纪中叶（明代）至现代的圆形土楼、方形土楼、宫殿式土楼、五凤式土楼、府第式土楼等各种类型的土楼数十座，为中国传统的生土民居建筑艺术和传统文化提供了特殊的见证。

高北土楼群 高北土楼群位于永定县高头乡高北村，是永定土楼的代表作。全村几十座土楼，依山傍水，高低错落。建于明代的无石基的五云楼诉说着土楼悠久的历史，雅致的侨福楼展示了旅居海外拳拳赤子爱国爱乡的诚挚情怀。. 众土楼和大自然融为一体，呈现一派美妙无比的田园风光。

田螺坑土楼群 田螺坑土楼群位于南靖县书洋镇上坂寮村的一条狭长小山沟里，在高耸入云的半山腰处，由五幢土楼组成田螺坑土楼群。四座圆楼簇拥着一座方楼，像是一朵怒放的梅花，美妙绝伦，璀璨夺目。公路随着山势蜿蜒而下，随着观看角度的变化，田螺坑景观魔术般地不断变幻，圆楼时而在前时而退后，方楼时而隐蔽时而暴露。

河坑土楼群 河坑土楼群位于南靖县书洋镇曲江村河坑自然村，整个土楼群以“法天象地”作为规划布局理念，方、圆土楼一次规划分批建设，在不足1平方公里范围内集中排布14座大型土楼，是福建土楼中排布最密集的土楼群落，反映出由土楼形成的村落与自然环境融为一体的独特特征。其中七座明清时期建造的方形土楼和七座近代建造的圆形土楼构成两组地上“北斗七星”的星象奇观。

大地土楼群 大地土楼群位于福建漳州市华安县仙都镇大地村，由“土楼之王”二宜楼、“福建土楼博物馆”南阳楼、“宜居典范”东阳楼三座土楼和周边的玄天阁、嘉应庙、慈西庵、茶香街等景点组成，是世界文化遗产“福建土楼”的重要组成部分。三座土楼依山而建，选址、造型、格局处处体现“天人合一”，神形兼备，不愧为堪舆风水的经典之作。

遗产价值

土楼作为福建客家人引为自豪的建筑形式，是福建民居中的瑰宝。同时又揉进了人文因素，堪称“天、地、人”三方结合的缩影。因此，一部土楼史，便是一部乡村家族史。土楼的子孙往往无须族谱便能侃侃道出家族的源流。此外，就地取材，用最平常的土料筑成高大的楼堡，化平凡为神奇，又体现了客家人征服自然过程中伟大的创造力和超人的智慧。

厚重的福建土楼，承载着厚重的传统文化。发人深省的楹联匾额，与楼共存的私塾学堂，教化育人的壁画彩绘，无不激荡着历朝历代土楼人家“修身齐家”的理想和“止于至善”的追求。位于永定洪坑土楼群的振成楼有副名联备受称道：

振作哪有闲时，少时壮时老年时，时时须努力；

成名原非易事，家事国事天下事，事事要关心。

丽江古城

丽江古城又名大研镇，位于中国西南部云南省的丽江市，坐落在丽江坝中部，与同为第二批国家历史文化名城的四川阆中、山西平遥、安徽歙县并称为“保存最为完好的四大古城”。

丽江古城是一座没有城墙的古城。光滑洁净的青石板路，完全手工建造的土木结构的房屋，无处不在的小桥流水。探寻它的过去，人们发现这片曾被遗忘的“古纳西王国”，远古以来已有人类生息繁衍。今日的主人纳西民族，则是古代南迁羌人的后裔。在千百年的漫长岁月里，他们辛勤劳作，筑起自己美好的家园。

丽江由于地处中国西南横断山区，气候垂直分布明显，虽处高原，终年看见雪山，但雨量充沛，干湿季分明。秋天是丽江最美的季节，秋高气爽的天空，色彩缤纷的树木和花朵，映衬着远处的玉龙雪山，令人心旷神怡。

古城布局

四方街是丽江古街的代表，位于古城的核心位置。不仅是大研古城的中心，也是滇西北地区的集贸和商业中心。

依山傍水的丽江大研镇，既无高大围城，也无轩敞大道，但它古朴如画，处处透出自然和谐。镇内屋宇因地势和流水错落起伏，人们以木石与泥土构筑起美观适用的住宅，融入了汉、白、藏民居的传统，形成独特风格。当地常见的是“三坊一照壁”式民宅，每房三间两层，朝南的正房供长辈居住，东西厢房一般由下辈住用。许多庭院门楼雕饰精巧，院内以卵石、瓦片、花砖铺设地面。正面堂屋一般有六扇格子门窗，窗心的雕刻大多是四季花卉或吉祥鸟兽。堂前廊檐大多比较宽，是一处温馨惬意的活动空间。

景观特色

有别于中国任何一座王城，丽江古城未受“方九里，旁三门，国中九经九纬，经途九轨”的中原建城影响。城中无规矩的道路网，无森严的城墙，古城布局中的三山为屏、一川相连；水系利用中的三河穿城、家家流水；街道布局中的“经络”设置和“曲、幽、窄、达”的风格；建筑物的依山就水、错落有致，共同构成古城建筑的基本特色。

丽江古城的民居建筑是纳西族建筑艺术和建筑风格的集中体现。其在布局、结构和造型方面按自身的具体条件和传统生活习惯，结合了汉、白、藏族民居的传统，并在房屋抗震、遮阳、防雨、通风、装饰等方面进行了大胆创新发展，形成了自己独特的风格，是研究中国建筑史、文化史不可多得的重要遗产。

主要景观

束河古镇　束河，纳西语称“绍坞”，意为“高峰之下的村寨”，是纳西先民在丽江坝子中最早的聚居地之一，也是茶马古道上保存完好的重要集镇，被视为是纳西先民从农耕文明向商业文明过渡的活标本。

白沙古镇　位于丽江坝子北部，玉龙雪山脚下，是最靠近雪山的古城镇，“世界文化遗产丽江古城”的重要组成部分。作为木氏家族的发源地，木氏家族在白沙建起的这个镇子被认为是最具有纳西遗风的古镇，是最原生态的纳西村落。以琉璃殿、大宝积宫内的“白沙壁画”为代表的丽江壁画，融合了藏传佛教、汉传佛教、道教以及东巴教等多种宗教，反映出汉、藏、白、纳西等民族传统绘画风格，是明代纳西族社会大开放的产物。

古街　四方街围着一个大约 4000 平方米的梯形小广场，五花石铺地，街道两旁的店铺鳞次栉比。其西侧的制高点是科贡坊，为风格独特的三层门楼。西有西河，东为中河。西河上设有活动闸门，可利用西河与中河的高差冲洗街面。从四方街四角延伸出四大主街：光义街、七一街、五一街，新华街，又从四大主街岔出众多街巷，如蛛网交错，四通八达，从而形成以四方街为中心、沿街逐层外延的缜密而又开放的格局。

古桥　在丽江古城区内的玉河水系上，飞架有 354 座桥梁，其密度为平均每平方公里 93 座。形式有廊桥（风雨桥）、石拱桥、石板桥、木板桥等。较著名的有锁翠桥、大石桥、万千桥、南门桥、马鞍桥、仁寿桥，均建于明清时期。大石桥为古城众桥之首，位于四方街东向100米，由明代木氏土司所建。该桥系双孔石拱桥，拱圈用板岩石支砌，桥长十余米，桥宽近4米，桥面用传统的五花石铺砌，坡度平缓，便于两岸往来。

木府　木府原系丽江世袭土司木氏衙署，“略备于元，盛于明”。历经战乱动荡，1998年春重建，并在府内设立了古城博物院。

修复重建的木府占地46亩，坐西向东，沿中轴线依地势建有忠义坊、万卷楼、护法殿、戏台、家院、走廊、宫驿等15幢仿古建筑。

五凤楼　五凤楼原名“法云间”，位于黑龙潭公园北端，始建于明万历二十九年（1601年）。楼高20米，楼台三叠，屋担八角，三层共24个飞檐，恰似五只彩凤展翅来仪，故名“五凤楼”。全楼共有32根柱子，其中四根中柱各高12米，柱上部分用斗架手法建成。天花板上绘有太极图、飞天神王、龙凤呈祥等图案，线条流畅，色彩绚丽，具有汉、藏、纳西等民族的绘画艺术风格。

东巴文化

纳西族自远古时期就创造了一种独特的民族文化，因其主要保存于纳西族宗教东巴教中而得名。东巴文化主要包括东巴文字、东巴经、东巴绘画、东巴音乐、东巴舞蹈、东巴法器和各种祭祀仪式等。

东巴文字　东巴文字属原始象形文字，共有1400个单字，至今仍在流传使用，被誉为世界上唯一活着的象形文字，被视为全人类的珍贵文化遗产，从19世纪70年代起引起国际学术界的关注。中国学者编著的《纳西象形文字谱》、《么些象形文字字典》等，代表了东巴文字研究领域的较高水平。

纳西古乐　在纳西族的音乐文化中，有一种驰名中外的纳西古乐。据考证，这种古乐起源于14世纪，它是云南省最为古老的音乐，也是中国或世界最古老的音乐之一。纳西古乐由白沙细乐、洞经音乐和皇经音乐组成（皇经音乐现已失传），融入了道教法事音乐，儒教典礼音乐，甚至唐宋元的词、曲牌音乐等，形成了它独特的旋律神韵，被誉为“音乐化石”。纳西古乐最具欣赏性的元素是其“稀世三宝”：第一件宝贝是古老的曲子，第二件是古老的乐器（乐师们手上所持乐器，皆有上百年历史），第三件是古老的艺人。

东巴仪式　纳西族东巴教是纳西族原始宗教向人为宗教过渡的一种宗教。多达30余种的东巴教仪式是纳西东巴文化的主要载体，即用象形文字记载在东巴经书里的内容，通过各种宗教仪式表现出来，并以宗教仪式世代传承。这些仪式力图诠释人与自然和人与社会的矛盾，与纳西族先民生产生活息息相关，蕴藏着丰富的文化内涵。

东巴绘画　东巴绘画，大体分为木牌画、纸牌画、卷轴画三种，其中以卷轴书最负盛名。“神路图”是东巴画中的代表，长14米，宽30米，整幅画分为三段，分别表现天堂、人间、地狱。线条粗犷，造型质朴。此外还有明清寺庙壁画，或称“白沙壁画”。出于汉族画家之手，用笔精细流畅，人物性格鲜明、生动、自然。

东巴木雕　东巴木雕主要以杜鹃木为材料。雕刻家们在这种木头上，用线刻、浮雕、立体雕的手法，雕刻出圆形、方形、立体的图案。这些图案或具象，或抽象，都非常古朴美丽，民族风味甚浓。线刻有的取材于日常生活，表现弹琴、挑担、犁田、种地的画面和热带植物花鸟等，有的取材于英雄故事。

遗产价值

丽江古城已有800多年的发展历史，聚居在这里的纳西族与其他少数民族一道创造了光辉灿烂的民族文化。不论是古城的街道、广场牌坊抑或是水系、桥梁还是民居装饰、庭院小品、楹联匾额、碑刻条石，无不渗透着纳西人的文化修养和审美情趣，无不充分体现出地方民族宗教、美学、文学等多方面的文化内涵、意境和神韵。尤其是内涵丰富的东巴文化、白沙壁画等传统文化艺术更是为人类文明史留下了灿烂的篇章。

平遥古城

平遥古城位于山西省中部，是一座具有2700多年历史的文化名城。平遥古城历尽沧桑、几经变迁，成为国内现存最完整的一座明清时期中国古代县城的原型。平遥古城素有“中国古建筑宝库”之称，文物古迹保存之多、品位之高，实为国内所罕见，对研究中国古代城市变迁、城市建筑、人类居住形式和传统文化的发展具有极为重要的历史、艺术、科学价值。

历史渊源

平遥古城始建于西周宣王时期（公元前827–782年）。自公元前221年中国实行“郡县制”以来，平遥一直作为“县治”的所在地延续至今。这是中国最基层的一级城市。保存的古城墙是明洪武三年（1370年）扩建后的原状，城内现存六大寺庙建筑群和县衙署、市楼等历代古建筑均是原来的实物。城内有大小街巷100多条，也是原来的历史形态，街道两旁的商业店铺基本上是17–19世纪的建筑。城内有3797处传统民居，其中400多处保存价值较高，地方风貌独特。

古城布局

平遥古城是一座完全按照中国汉民族传统城市规划思想和布局程式修建的县城。在封闭的城池里，以市楼为中心，有4条大街、8条小街及72条小巷经纬交织在一起，它们功能分明，布局井井有条。城内古居民宅全是清一色青砖灰瓦的四合院，轴线明确，左右对称，特别是砖砌窑洞式的民宅更加具有很浓的乡土气息。这些古色古香的建筑原汁原味地勾勒出明、清时期市井繁华的风貌。迄今为止，古城的城墙、街道、民居、店铺、庙宇等建筑仍然基本完好，原来的形式和格局大体未动，它们同属平遥古城现存历史文物的有机组成部分。

平遥城有古城门六道，东西各二。鸟瞰平遥古城，形同一只伏地欲行的乌龟，头南尾北，东西四门好比龟之四足，民间因有"龟城"之说。南门之外，古有中都河水蜿蜒而过，从而引发了古代文人“龟前戏水，山水朝阳，城之修建，以此为用”的遐想。乌龟是吉祥、长寿的象征，“龟城”之说源于古人对“四灵”的崇拜，“龟城”寓意固着金汤，长治久安。

景观特色

平遥古城文物古迹保存之多、品位之高实为国内所罕见。其中有始建于西周、扩建于明洪武三年（1370年）的国内保存最完整的古城墙；有始建于北汉天会七年（公元963年）现存最珍贵的木结构建筑镇国寺万佛殿；有始建于北齐武平二年（公元571年）被誉为“中国古代彩塑艺术宝库”的宋元明清彩塑2052尊的双林寺；有中国宋金时期文庙的罕见实物——文庙大成殿；有被誉为“天下第一号”、“汇通天下”的“日升昌”票号；有始建于唐显庆二年，国内古建筑中罕见的“悬梁吊柱”奇特结构清虚观；有遍布古城内外1000通碑刻及年代不一、形式多样、色彩缤纷的各种琉璃实物等。

主要景观

城隍庙　位于城东南的城隍庙街，由城隍庙、财神庙、灶君庙三组建筑组成。城隍神是古代汉民族宗教文化普遍崇祀的重要神祇之一，有道是：“皇帝有难上天坛，县官有难到此来”。历史上尤其是明代，城隍受封的官职高于县令，明太祖诏令各地必需要建城隍庙，与县衙署对称设置，“阴阳各司其职”，这是古代“人神共治”思想的明确反映。

古城墙　人称平遥有三宝，古城墙是其中之一。建城之初，此城墙仅为夯土筑成，规模较小，到明洪武三年（1370年）才扩建成现在的规模。这座周长约6公里的古城墙，有3000个垛口、72座敌楼，据说这象征孔子三千弟子及七十二贤人。此外，清朝后期，在古城东南角还曾修建了一座象征古城文运昌盛的魁星阁，由此可见以孔子为代表的儒家思想影响之深远。

镇国寺　出古城北门向东北有镇国寺，它是古城的第二“宝”。该寺的万佛殿建于五代（10世纪）时期，目前是中国排名第三位的古老木结构建筑，距今已有1000多年的历史。殿内的五代彩塑是不可多得的雕塑艺术珍品。

双林寺 古城的第三宝是位于城西南方向、重建于北齐武平二年（公元 571 年）的双林寺。在该寺的十余座大殿内有元代至明代的彩色泥塑两千多尊，被人们誉为“彩塑艺术的宝库”。

财神庙 平遥古城内有一座保存相当完好的财神庙。财神庙规模不大，一进院落，占地仅 833 平方米。庙门为砖券洞，前出廊。门洞上建乐楼，东西两廊建厢楼。正面高台基上建献殿，后建窑洞式财神殿，供奉比干、关羽、赵公明三神像。整座庙宇布局严谨，形态庄重。

日升昌 “日升昌”钱庄坐南朝北，南北长 65 米，东西宽 20 米，总建筑面积为1300平方米。钱庄内三进院落，布局讲究，式样别致，高墙、大院、深宅，给人以外雄内秀的感觉。

遗产价值

平遥古城众多的文化遗存，不仅代表了中国古代城市在不同历史时期的建筑形式、施工方法和用材标准，也反映了中国古代不同民族、不同地域的艺术进步和美学成就。

平遥古城的规划设计，完全遵循中国传统儒家思想为主导的礼制而行，整体建筑以南北大街为中轴线，左城隍庙，右县衙署；左文庙，右武庙；左道观，右寺院；是严格对称布局。街道两旁的民居建筑，多为儒家传统所提倡的和谐、厚朴、严整、宁静的四合院形式，它是我国现今保存最为完好的汉族传统城镇的典范。

平遥古城是按照汉民族传统规划思想和建筑风格建设起来的城市，集中体现了 14–19 世纪前后汉民族的历史文化特色，对研究这一时期的社会形态、经济结构、军事防御、宗教信仰、传统思想、伦理道德的人类居住形式有重要的参考价值。

平遥古城在 19 世纪中后期，是中国金融业最为发达的城市之一，是当代最有影响的票号总部所在地和金融业总部机构最集中的地方。

中国第一家钱庄——日升昌，创建于道光四年(1824 年)，百年沧桑，业绩辉煌，执全国金融之牛耳，分号遍布全国 30 余座城市、商埠重镇，远及欧美、东南亚等国，以“汇通天下”著称于世。她的诞生与发展，有力地促进了全国金融流通，加速了资本周转，对当时民族工商业的发展作出了杰出的贡献，掀开了中国金融史的光辉一页。

皖南古村落——西递、宏村

西递、宏村古民居位于中国东部安徽省黟县境内的黄山风景区。西递和宏村是安徽南部民居中最有代表性的两座古村落，它们以世外桃源般的田园风光、保存完好的村落形态、工艺精湛的徽派民居和丰富多彩的历史文化内涵而闻名天下。

历史渊源

皖南山区的黟县是一个人口仅十来万的小县，西递、宏村就坐落在这里。唐朝大诗人李白曾赞美道：“黟县小桃源，烟霞百里间。地多灵草木，人尚古衣冠。”道出了皖南乡村的独特意境。

西递始建于北宋皇祐年间（1049–1054 年），距今已有近千年的历史。整个村落呈船形，四面环山，两条溪流从村北、村东经过村落在村南会源桥汇聚。村落以一条纵向街道和两条沿溪的道路为主要骨架，构成东向为主、向南北延伸的村落街巷系统。巷道和建筑的设计布局协调，村落空间变化灵活，建筑色调朴素淡雅。

宏村始建于南宋绍兴元年（1131 年）。村落面积约 19 公顷，原为汪姓聚居之地，现存明清时期古建筑 137 幢。宏村的古建筑均为粉墙青瓦，排列规整。其中最为宏大、最为精美的代表作是承志堂，被誉为“徽派木雕工艺陈列馆”。各种木雕层次丰富，繁复生动，经过百余年时光的消磨，至今仍金碧辉煌。

景观特色

西递、宏村古村落的科学价值，特别反映在聚落规划、村落防火、人居环境、文化生态、文化景观、文化整合等方面。如传统古村落通常是“滚雪球”式的发展，即随着村庄的扩大，道路、水系无序状态非常突出，而皖南不少古村落的发展具有明显的规划性——道路纵横有序，水系来去有常。从文化生态角度看，皖南古村落与皖南自然环境具有制约、适应、再现和选择关系。从文化景观角度看，皖南古村落观照了中国传统文化的内向型气质、和谐型风格和伦理型内核。从文化整合角度看，皖南古村落是徽商经济实力和徽人思想观念的外在表现。

西递、宏村的村落选址、布局和建筑形态，都以周易风水理论为指导，体现了天人合一的中国传统哲学思想和对大自然的向往与尊重。那些典雅的明、清民居建筑群与大自然紧密相融，创造出一个既合乎科学，又富有情趣的生活居住环境，是中国传统民居的精髓。西递、宏村独特的水系是实用与美学相结合的水利工程典范，尤其是宏村的牛形水系，深刻体现了人类利用自然、改造自然的卓越智慧。

徽派民居的主要特点

尊重自然山水大环境 古徽州对村落选址的地形、地貌、水流风向等因素都有周到的考虑，往往都是依山傍水，环境优美，布局合理，交通顺畅，建筑融汇于山水之间。

富于美感的外观整体性 群房一体，独具一格的马头墙，采用高墙封闭，马头翘角，墙面和马头高低进退错落有致，青山、绿水、白墙、黛瓦是徽派建筑的主要特征之一，在质朴中透着清秀。

较灵活的多进院落式布局 建筑平面布局的单元是以天井为中心围合的院落，高宅、深井、大厅，按功能、规模、地形灵活布置，富有韵律感。

精美的细部装饰 徽文化中“三雕”（砖雕、石雕、木雕）艺术令人叹为观止，砖雕门罩、石雕漏窗、木雕楹柱与建筑物融为一体，是徽派建筑的一大特色。

主要景观

承志堂 承志堂位于宏村上水圳中段，建于清咸丰五年（1855 年），是清末大盐商汪定贵住宅。整栋建筑为木结构，内部砖、石、木雕装饰富丽堂皇，占地面积约 2100 平方米，建筑面积 3000 余平方米，是一幢保存完整的大型民居建筑。全宅有 9 座天井，大小房间 60 间。

南湖书院 明末，宏村人在南湖北畔建六所私塾，又称“依湖六院”，以供子弟授业解惑。清嘉庆十九年（1814 年），将依湖六院合并重建，取名“以文家塾”，亦名“南湖书院”，是一所具有传统徽派建筑风格的古书院，由志道堂、文昌阁、启蒙阁、会文阁、望湖楼、祗园六部分组成。

瑞玉庭　建于清咸丰年间，距今约 1400 余年历史。原主人出身于徽商世家，建筑充分体现其经营之道和思想境界：门罩上一块元宝式的砖雕，刻着“富贵”二字；天井有四水归堂，天井四周的雀翅上描金雕刻有四季花鸟图，取意万象更新、四季发财。

桃李园　建于清咸丰年间，由正屋和庭院组成，系西递徽商胡元熙的旧居兼私熟蒙馆。正屋为三间三进二楼结构，前两进为两小套背向三间屋。

二进楼上设有独特的“楼上井”，使整幢房屋光线充足，空气畅通。而且，楼上木雕扶栏板特凿孔洞，以供小姐相亲之用。

西园、东园　西园是一所较为典型的园林式建筑。一字排开三幢楼房，用一个狭长的庭院将其连成一个整体，而庭院中又用墙体分隔成前、中、后三院，并饰以拱形门洞，镶以长方形漏窗，园中栽种花卉、翠柏，敷设花台、假山、浴池、盆景，所有的设计与摆设无一不在显示主人的修养与品味。

从西园到东园仅数步之遥，“东园”系西园主人胡文照的父亲为让儿子读书所造。东园小小的厅堂仅十个足掌的宽度，寓意十年寒窗。西厢门镶嵌着“冰裂图”，寓意冰冻三尺非一日之寒，而对面的东厢门镶嵌着“五蝠图”，寓意只有苦心读书，才能苦尽甘来，收获幸福。

遗产价值

包括西递、宏村在内的皖南古村落是指安徽省长江以南山区地域范围内，具有共同地域文化背景的历史传统村落，具有强烈的徽州文化特色。皖南山区历史悠久，文化积淀深厚，保存了大量形态相近、特色鲜明的传统建筑及其村落。皖南古村落不仅与地形、地貌、山水巧妙结合，而且加上明清时期徽商的雄厚经济实力对家乡的支持，文化教育日益兴旺发达，还乡后以雅、文、清高、超脱的心态构思和营建住宅，使得古村落的文化环境更为丰富，村落景观更为突出。

西递、宏村古村落与其他村落形态最大的不同在于，它们的建设和发展在相当程度上脱离了对农业的依赖。古村落居民的意识、生活方式及情趣方面，大大超越了农民思想意识和一般市民阶层，而是保留和追求与文人、官宦阶层相一致，因此具有浓郁的文化气息。

西递、宏村古村落是随着明清时期徽商的兴盛而发展起来的，能够在有限地建筑空间内最大程度地体现其构思的精巧以及工艺的高超，实为别具匠心的建筑形式。后来徽商逐渐衰败没落，而这种徽派民居的建筑特色却依附在古民居村落里保留下来，因此，具有重要的历史价值和建筑价值。

开平碉楼与村落

开平碉楼位于广东省开平市，是中国乡土建筑的一个特殊类型，是一种集防卫、居住和中西建筑艺术于一体的多层塔楼式建筑。根据现存实证，开平碉楼最迟在明代后期（16 世纪）已经产生，到 19 世纪末 20 世纪初发展成为表现中国华侨历史、社会形态与文化传统的一种独具特色的群体建筑形象。现存碉楼 1833 座，被誉为“华侨文化的典范之作”、“令人震撼的建筑艺术长廊”。

历史渊源

开平碉楼的兴起，与开平的地理环境和过去的社会治安密切相关。开平地势低洼，河网密布，而过去水利失修，每遇台风暴雨，洪涝灾害频发，民众深受其害。加上其所辖之境，原为新会、台山、恩平、新兴四县边远交界之地，向来为“四不管”之地，因此土匪猖獗，社会秩序混乱。在这种情况下，当地乡民为求自保，便设计出碉楼以作防护的设施。

民国十一年（1922 年）12 月，众匪来劫开平中学，恰被鹰村碉楼探照灯照射，四处乡团及时围堵，截回校长及学生 17 人。此事轰动全县，海外华侨闻讯也十分惊喜，觉得碉楼在防范匪患中起了重大作用，因此便纷纷携款回乡，资助家乡修建碉楼。由此一来，开平碉楼如雨后春笋般发展起来，最多时达到 3000 多座，现存也有 1400 多座。

景观特色

开平碉楼的建筑风格和装饰艺术千姿百态，令人叹为观止。在碉楼的总体造型、建筑构件和表现手法上，中国传统的建筑艺术与西方建筑风格熔为一体；而西方建筑风格又有多种类型，古希腊的柱廊、古罗马的券拱和柱式、伊斯兰的叶形券拱和铁雕、哥特时期的券拱、巴洛克建筑的山花、新文艺运动的装饰手法以及工业派的建筑艺术表现形式等等，都融进了开平的乡土建筑之中，它不单纯是某一时期某一国家某一地域建筑艺术的引进，而是中外多种建筑风格“碎片”的组合，多种建筑类型相互交融的产物。

中国领土上西洋特色的建筑，大都是洋人用坚船利炮“打”进来的，带有西方殖民者硬性移植的色彩，而开平碉楼却充分体现了华侨主动吸取外国先进文化的一种自信、开放、包容的心态，他们把自己的所见所闻，加上自己的审美情趣，融注在千辛万苦建成的碉楼上。人们在修筑这数千座碉楼的时候，不经意地便创造出一种绝世艺术，一种别具特色的文化。

开平碉楼尽管在用材、建筑、装饰形式上各有差异，但碉楼门窗窄小，铁门钢窗，顶层四边均设有枪眼，这是共同的特色。

广东开平的碉楼，记载着一个个华侨家庭或家族的兴衰，至今还维系着源于当地而延伸到世界各地的乡情和传统。

以开平为中心出现的碉楼群，是中国乡村民众主动接受西方建筑艺术并与本土建筑艺术融合的产物，充分体现了他们面对外国先进文化时的一种自信、开放、包容的心态。他们把自己的所见所闻，加上自己的审美情趣，融合在碉楼上，使之成为留置于故土的一片精神守望地。不同的旅居地、不同的审美观，造就了开平碉楼的千姿百态。

华侨是文化的传播者。中外多种文化交融和碰撞是华侨文化发展的必然产物。它所带来的文化冲突，广泛触及中国传统社会的方方面面和各个阶层。开平碉楼与民居非常突出地体现了中国华侨文化的深刻性和普遍性。同时，它寄寓了中国人的传统环境意识，是人与自然的完美结合。

主要景观

锦江里碉楼群 锦江里隶属开平市蚬冈镇。清朝光绪年间（1875–1908 年），由黄氏家族按规划建成此村，并在日后次第建成瑞石楼、升峰楼和锦江楼 3 座碉楼。其中，民国七年（1918 年）村民在村后中部集资兴建了锦江楼。锦江楼是典型的众楼，楼高 5 层 17.36 米，钢筋混凝土结构，顶层为悬挑出来的平台，女儿墙外有中西融合的灰塑图案，正中为一悬山顶的楼屋。建筑形体简洁，朴实无华，是防御性显著的碉楼。瑞石楼位于锦江楼的东侧，坐落在村落民居的主轴线上，是典型的居楼式碉楼。瑞石楼在立面上运用西洋式窗楣线脚、柱廊造型，大量的灰塑图案中，融入了中国传统的福、禄、喜、寿等内容，在西洋的外表下蕴涵着浓郁的传统文化气息。整体建筑呈现出中世纪意大利城堡风格。升峰楼建于民国十七年（1928 年），为赴美经商致富的黄峰秀所建。楼高 7 层 12.34 米，钢筋混凝土结构，造型精致秀丽，充满南亚印度建筑的情调，是典型的居楼。

自力村碉楼群 自力村隶属开平市塘口镇，东距开平市区 12 公里，是由安和里（俗称犁头咀）、合安里（俗称新村）和永安里（俗称黄泥岭）三条方姓自然村组成。清道光十七年（1837 年）犁头咀首先立村。该村民居格局与周围自然环境协调一致，村落布局为零星状。自力村碉楼建筑精美，保存完好，布局和谐，错落有致，四周良田万顷，稻香阵阵，踏着田间小道，穿过绿树修竹直入村内，顿生世外桃源之感。呈现眼前的 9 座碉楼 6 座庐，中西合璧，各具特色，堪称"碉楼建筑中的精品"。

马降龙碉楼群 马降龙碉楼群位于开平市百合镇百合墟东南面，为黄、关两姓家族于清朝末年和民国初年兴建。现有村民 171 户、506 人，其中 80% 为侨户，海外侨胞多于国内人口，主要分布在美国、加拿大、澳大利亚等国。

马降龙村背靠气势磅礴的百足山，面临清澈如镜的潭江水，5 个自然村像一条珠链，错落有致地分布在青山绿水之间。身临其境，翠竹扑面，绿树成荫，鸟语花香，生态环境十分优美。13 座碉楼造型别致，保存完好，掩映于村后茂密的竹丛中，与周围民居、自然环境融为一体，登高远眺，疑为天上人间。

迎龙楼 迎龙楼坐落在开平市赤坎镇三门里村，是开平市现存最早的碉楼，为关氏家族于明朝嘉靖年间兴建。占地面积 152 平方米，建筑面积 456 平方米，砖木结构，楼高 3 层 11.4 米，为全村制高点。楼顶为传统硬山顶式，风格朴拙，造型简洁。其方形的建筑形体没有受到外来因素的影响，是开平碉楼中传统模式的代表。

方氏灯楼 方氏灯楼坐落在开平市塘口镇塘口墟北面的山坡上，民国九年（1920 年）由方氏家族共同集资兴建，原名"古溪楼"。楼高 5 层 18.43 米，钢筋混凝土结构。顶层为西洋式穹窿顶的亭阁，楼内配备值班预警的西方早期发电机、探照灯、枪械等设备，是典型的更楼。

加拿大村 "加拿大村"原名耀华坊，位于赤坎镇灵源村，为旅加华侨出资兴建。村场由加国知名建筑师规划；村中有 10 座古民居、1 座碉楼，多建于 20 世纪 20–30 年代。建筑风格融合了中国传统灰塑、罗马柱、圆拱、花雕等建筑艺术，为典型的中西合璧式建筑。

遗产价值

开平 1833 座碉楼融合了不同国家的建筑元素，风格各异、错落有致，从它们的材料、功能、结构上，可以看出当时华侨受西方个性张扬、观念自由的影响很深，当年开平的农民主动到西方学习当时西方的物质文化、制度文化、观念文化，带回家乡来，最后产生了碉楼这种遗产，成为当时华侨文化的结晶。

同时，开平碉楼也反映了中国乡村社会在近代的转型。从碉楼的建筑风格和楼里的陈设都可以看出，村民们的意识、观念、生活方式等正从传统的农业社会向近现代社会转变。也即是说，开平碉楼与村落的背后，蕴涵着丰富的华侨历史信息，记载着近代社会转型中本地华侨在特定的历史时期对其居住国、家乡乃至整个中国社会的贡献。这段历史，在遥远的中国乡村奇迹般地完整保存下来，这在世界历史领域都是罕见而弥足珍贵的。

青城山—都江堰

青城山——都江堰地处横断山北段川西高山峡谷区域内，地质构造复杂，是四川盆地向青藏高原过渡带，山峦起伏，坡陡谷深，气候温暖湿润，地质历史悠久，生物种类繁多，是全世界亚热带山地生物多样性保护最完整的地区。

都江堰风景名胜资源丰富，得天独厚，既有大型水利工程都江堰，又有“人间仙境”龙池国家森林公园，还有道教名山青城山。

水利工程都江堰

主要景观

水利工程景观 都江堰渠首三大主体工程修建在岷江出山口处。这里群山环抱，大江中流，气势恢宏，景色绝佳。由于都江堰管理需要，各时期兴建的建筑群落如二郎庙、伏龙观、水利厅衙门均是精美的古建筑遗产；玉垒关、观澜亭以及索桥、南桥则是古代建筑艺术的精华。这些点面的建筑艺术与岷江、与都江堰工程、与河流共同构成了文化遗产的主体。

宝瓶口引水口 李冰根据水流及地形特点，在坡度较缓处，凿开一道底宽 17 米的楔形口子。峡口枯水季节宽 19 米，洪水季节宽 23 米。据《永康军志》载：“春耕之际，需之如金，号曰’金灌口’”。因此宝瓶口古时又名金灌口。宝瓶口是内江进水咽喉，是内江能够“水旱从人”的关键水利设施。由于宝瓶口自然景观瑰丽，有“离堆锁峡”之称，属历史上著名的“灌阳十景”之一。

飞沙堰 飞沙堰溢洪道位于金刚堤尾部、离堆前端，长约两百米，高约两米，历史上用笼篼卵石堆砌而成，如今为混凝土所代替。当内江水量较小的时候，飞沙堰拦水进入宝瓶口，像一道河堤；当洪水季节水量较多时，多余的水就自动排泄到外江。飞沙堰看上去十分平凡，却是保证成都平原不受水灾的关键设施。因为它不仅能在洪水期泄洪，还利用水漫过飞沙堰流入外江水流的漩涡作用，有效地减少了泥沙在宝瓶口前后的淤积。

鱼嘴分水堤 鱼嘴是都江堰最典型、最重要的工程。鱼嘴修筑在岷江出山口的自然弯道上，利用弯道环流的原理，可以在洪水季节和枯水季节，自动调节内外两江进水量比例。一方面避免内江下游遭受洪水侵害，另一方面确保灌区在春耕时节有足够的用水。鱼嘴的另一个重要作用是有效地解决了泥沙排放的问题。

伏龙观 伏龙观建在离堆之上，三面悬绝，一面用 42 级宽三丈一尺五寸石阶和开阔的大坝相连，使伏龙观显得特别雄伟庄严。原有殿宇两重，清同治间建成李冰殿，共有主殿三重。1959 年整修时，将玉皇殿、喜雨楼合并，改建为钢筋混凝土砖木排架。前殿陈列着 1974 年修建外江节制闸时从河床中挖出的李冰石刻像，高 2.9 米，重 4.5 吨。石像造于东汉灵帝初年,距今已逾1800年,是我国现存最早的圆雕石像，非常珍贵。

二王庙 二王庙古建筑群坐落在今都江堰西门外的玉垒山麓，是为纪念都江堰的开凿者、秦蜀郡太守李冰及其子二郎而修建的。二王庙初建于南北朝，现存建筑系清末民初重建，山门“二王庙”三个金字为爱国将领冯玉祥将军题写。庙内有李冰和二郎的塑像，石壁上嵌有李冰以及后人关于治水的格言，被称为治水三字经。

道教名山青城山

青城山是邛崃山脉南段的东支，地质构造复杂。这里属中亚热带四川盆地湿润气候区，夏无酷暑，冬少严寒，雨量多，湿度大，常为云雾笼罩，满山林木葱茏，四季青翠。山上花卉资源丰富，观果、观叶植物繁多，盛产野生药材。在追求质朴、崇尚自然的道家眼中，这样的自然环境无疑是一处洞天福地。

青城山因其秀丽的自然风光和众多道教建筑而成为天下名山，也是中国道教的发源地之一。东汉顺帝汉安二年（公元 143 年），传说道教天师张道陵晚年显道于青城山，选中青城山的深幽涵碧，结茅传道，青城山遂成为道教的发祥地，被列为“第五洞天”。全山的道教宫观以天师洞为核心，包括建福宫、上清宫、祖师殿、圆明宫、老君阁、玉清宫、朝阳洞等数十座古建筑至今完好保存。同时，文人墨客们留下了珍贵的“墨宝”，为这座名山增添了丰富的人文景观，对于深入研究中国古代的道教哲学思想，有着重要的学术价值和艺术价值。

主要景观

祖师殿 祖师殿位于天师洞右后侧山腰间。又名真武宫，创建于唐代。该殿环境清幽，殿内有真武祖师、吕洞宾、铁拐李等神仙塑像及八仙图壁画、诗文刻石等。

上清宫 上清宫位于青城山第一峰、距峰顶约 500 米的半坡上。始建于晋代，现存庙宇为清同治年间所建，上有“天下第五名山”、“青城第一峰”等摩崖石刻。宫内祀奉道教始祖李老君，有老子塑像和《道德经》五千言木刻。

天师洞 天师洞始建于隋朝大业年间，三面环山，一面临涧，古树参天，十分幽静。现存殿宇建于清末，规模宏伟，雕刻精细，并有不少珍贵文物和古树。相传东汉末年张道陵曾在此讲经传道，今洞中有张道陵及其三十代孙“虚靖天师”像。观内正殿为“三清殿”，殿后有黄帝祠和天师洞等古迹。天师洞右下角有一小殿，名三皇殿，内有轩辕、伏羲、神农石像。

遗产价值

都江堰是当今世界年代久远、以无坝引水为特征的宏大水利工程，它不仅是中国水利工程技术的伟大奇迹，也是世界水利工程的璀璨明珠。它充分利用当地西北高、东南低的地理条件，根据江河出山口处特殊的地形、水脉、水势，因势利导，无坝引水，自流灌溉，使堤防、分水、泄洪、排沙、控流相互依存，共为体系，保证了防洪、灌溉、水运和社会用水综合效益的充分发挥。它最伟大之处是建堰两千两百多年来经久不衰，迄今依然发挥着巨大的不可替代的作用。都江堰的创建，以不破坏自然资源、充分利用自然资源为人类服务为前提，变害为利，使人、地、水三者高度和谐统一，开创了中国古代水利史上的新纪元。

青城山道教对中国道教具有不可估量的影响。现在，青城山仍是弘扬中国道教文化的主要场所。青城山道教古建筑群至今保存完好，弥足珍贵。

红河哈尼梯田

云南省红河州地处哀牢山南部，这里聚居着哈尼、彝、傣、苗、瑶、壮、汉 7 个民族，经过千百年各族人民的辛勤劳动，他们依山开垦了 36 万多亩的梯田，用双手绘就了一幅多姿多彩的边地民俗风情画廊，被誉为“最神奇的大地雕塑”。

红河哈尼梯田是以哈尼族为主的各族人民利用当地“一山分四季，十里不同天”的地理气候条件创造出来的农耕文明奇观，据载已有 1300 多年的历史。这里的梯田规模宏大，绵延整个红河南岸的元阳、绿春、金平等县，仅元阳县境内就有 19 万亩。这里水源丰富，空气湿润，雾气变化多端，将山谷和梯田装扮得含蓄而灵动。

历史渊源

一座座的“田山”，仿佛就是一部非文字的巨型史书，直观地展示了哈尼先民在自然与社会双重压力下顽强抗争、繁衍生息的漫长历史。哈尼族古老的《天地人的传说》中说：大鱼创造了宇宙天地和第一对人，男人叫直塔，女人叫塔婆；塔婆生下二十二个娃，其中老三是龙，龙长大以后到海里当了龙王，为感激塔婆的养育之恩，他向塔婆敬献了三竹筒东西，其中一筒里盛有稻谷种子。也就是说，哈尼人认为，自开天辟地以来便有了稻子，说明哈尼人是最早驯化野生稻的民族之一，水稻种植是哈尼人古老的生产内容。千百年来，哈尼族将哀牢山区三江流域的野生稻驯化为陆稻，又将陆稻改良为水稻，在得天独厚的生态环境中，使三江流域成为人类早期驯化栽培稻谷的地区之一。

哈尼梯田成因

哈尼梯田之所以如此壮丽和独特，首先是大自然特殊的地理结构和自然因素造成的。哀牢山大面积的高山森林和植被的垂直变化使得当地森林和土地拥有强大的蒸腾作用和巨大的贮水功能，形成了森林——水源——梯田的自然系统。

元阳县共居一山的 7 个民族大致说来是按海拔高低分层而居的：海拔 144–600 米的河坝区，多为傣族居住；600–1000 米的峡谷区，多为壮族居住；1000–1400 米的下半山区，多为彝族居住；1400–2000 米的上半山，多为哈尼族居住；2000 米以上的高山区，多为苗、瑶族居住；汉族多居住在城镇和公路沿线。哈尼族居住的上半山，气候温和，雨量充沛，年均气温在 15 摄氏度左右，全年日照 1670 小时，非常适宜水稻生长。

哈尼族先民自隋唐之际进入这片地区后就开垦梯田种植水稻，在此 1300 多年间，哈尼族发挥了巨大的天才创造力，在大山上挖筑了成百上千条水沟干渠。条条沟渠如银色的腰带，将座座大山紧紧缠绕，大大小小沟箐中流下的山水被悉数截入沟内，汩汩山水顺着水沟流入高层梯田，高层梯田注满后再流入下层梯田。再满再流，直至汇入河谷江河。由此而来，每一条水沟都是一条山泉，每一块梯田都相当于一道水渠，水水相连，沟沟相通，年年月月演奏着大山永不停歇的生命之歌。

景观特色

元阳哈尼族梯田生态系统呈现以下特点：每一个村寨的上方，必然矗立着茂密的森林，提供着水、用材、薪炭之源，其中以神圣不可侵犯的寨神林为特征；村寨下方是层层相叠的千百级梯田，那里提供着哈尼人生存发展的基本条件：粮食；中间的村寨由座座古意盎然的蘑菇房组合而成，形成人们安度人生的居所。这一结构被文化生态学家盛赞为森林、水系、村寨和梯田四度同构的人与自然高度协调的、可持续发展的、良性循环的生态系统，这就是千百年来哈尼人民生息繁衍的美丽家园。

元阳县境内全是崇山峻岭，梯田落差极大，最大落差有 1500 多米，坡面长度更是达到了几公里。以一座山坡而论，梯田最高级数达 3000 级，这在中外梯田景观中是罕见的。随着山势的起伏，每块梯田都显示出与众不同的颜色，远远望去，层次分明。错落在一坡坡梯田间的，是大大小小的村落。最值得看的是老虎嘴一带，那里的梯田立体感最强，坡度最陡，所以颜色的层次感也最强烈。而龙树坝的梯田，却完全是另一番景象，少了几分壮阔，多了一些小巧与艳丽。

主要景观

元阳哈尼梯田主要有三大景区：坝达景区有 14000 多亩梯田，老虎嘴景区有近 6000 亩梯田，多依树景区有上万亩梯田。梯田都修筑在山坡上，坡度在 15° – 75° 之间。

坝达景区　坝达景区又叫麻栗寨景区，位于县城南部 43 公里，新街东部 15 公里。该景区梯田面积大，线条美，立体感强，景色十分壮观。从海拔 1100 米的麻栗寨河起，连绵不断的成千上万层梯田，直伸延至海拔 2000 米的高山之巅，把麻栗寨、坝达、上马点、全福庄等哈尼村寨高高托入云海中。站在麻栗寨茶厂观看梯田，近万亩梯田宛如一片坡海，泛着粼粼波光，奔来眼底，令人作武陵桃园之想。每到下午 4 点以后，白茫茫的坡海随着夕阳西下，逐渐变成粉红色、红色。继而再变成粉红色、白色。哈尼族村落风光旖旎，民风敦厚，村民待客十分热情。

老虎嘴景区　老虎嘴梯田位于元阳县城 50 公里处。这片梯田分布于深谷间，状如一巨大的花蕊，3000 多亩梯田形状各异，如万蛇静卧于花蕊间。老虎嘴梯田是元阳哈尼梯田最具有代表性、最为壮观的地方，站在高高的老虎嘴上俯瞰，如潮似海，无边无沿；仔细观看，隐约有两匹骏马扬蹄奔腾，又似一只千年乌龟静卧山间，仿佛讲述着哈尼先民开垦梯田的沧桑历史。往西望去，无数级梯田由南向北从深谷伸高，在夕阳余辉下，红白黑相映，光彩夺目。往东遥望，数千亩梯田攀附在七座半圆型山梁上，形成立体的海洋。

其实，站在老虎嘴的任何一个地方看下面的梯田，都是一幅水灵灵的江南水墨画卷，都是一曲动人心魄的田野长歌。

多依树景区　多依树景区位于县城东部55公里，新街东部25公里。景区以 5 个哈尼族村寨、4 个彝族村寨为主，包含爱村、大瓦遮等连片的 6000 多亩梯田，展示云海、梯田、山寨的奇丽风光、哈尼、彝族的多元文化和省级自然保护区内的 16000 多公顷原始森林。

景区梯田三面临山，一面傍谷，状如一个大海湾。布满临山三面的无数村落，一座座蘑菇房如整装待发的帆船。站在高高的黄草岭村后山观赏，整块梯田上半部稍缓，如万蛇蠕动；下半部较陡，直入深谷，致使白花花的“大海湾”如一个巨大的瀑布从南向北倾泻，壮观无比。

遗产价值

农业经济是梯田的最基本价值。梯田开发最初与人口增加以及便于耕作、灌溉和水土保持需要紧密相关。千百年来，面对高山峡谷的生存空间，哈尼人创造、总结出一套垦种梯田的成功经验。他们根据不同的地形、土质修堤筑埂垄，利用“山有多高，水有多高”的自然条件，把终年不断的山泉溪涧通过水笕沟渠引进梯田。

哈尼民族创造出自己的文化，并由此带来巨大的内在凝聚力，哈尼梯田就是这个文化的象征与符号，是一个民族生存的奇迹。哈尼梯田不是景观，但却有一种沁人心脾的力量，因为它表明我们还有传统，它见证了中国历史发展阶段中最重要的农业时代的文明。

周口店“北京人”遗址

周口店“北京人”遗址，位于北京市区西南48公里房山区周口店村的龙骨山。这里地处山区和平原交接处，东南为华北大平原，西北为山地。周口店附近的山地多为石灰岩，在水力作用下，形成许多大小不等的天然洞穴。山上有一东西长约140米的天然洞穴，俗称“猿人洞”。1929年中国古生物学家裴文中在此发现原始人类牙齿、骨骼和一块完整的头盖骨，并找到了“北京人”生活、狩猎及使用火的遗迹，证实50万年以前北京地区已有人类活动。这一发现奠定了周口店遗址在全世界古人类学研究中特殊的、不可替代的地位。

生活环境

在灰烬中发现的敲破的烧骨，表明“北京人”已经知道熟食。在严峻的自然条件下，“北京人”依靠群体的力量维系着艰难的生存。季节变化、自然灾害、猛兽侵袭、疾病困扰，无一不给他们带来巨大的威胁。从化石测知的数十个“北京人”个体的年龄得知，他们的死亡率极高，大多数人在14岁前就已夭亡了，可见他们的生活条件相当恶劣。

“北京人”从居住地附近的河滩、山坡上挑选石英、燧石、砂岩石块，采取以石击石的方法打制出各种不同用途的工具，用来满足他们生活生产的需要。科学家根据出土动植物化石推知，昔日周口店一带森林茂密，水草丰盛，气候一度比今日华北温暖。随着全球性气候波动，这里在几十万年间也曾发生冷暖、干湿的频繁交替。所幸“北京人”学会了用火，这大大提高了他们适应环境的能力。

体貌特征

“北京人”在人类进化历程中已走过很长的路，但其外貌仍保留了不少原始状态，如头骨低平、眉嵴突出、面部短而吻部前伸；脑容量平均仅1000多毫升，大约只及现代人的三分之二；身材粗短，男性高约156厘米，女性约144厘米；腿短臂长，头部前倾，四肢骨已与现代人接近，能够步履稳健地直立行走。

“北京人”头盖骨（额骨）化石，是1966年在我国著名古人类学家裴文中先生主持下发掘出土的一块额骨化石，也是目前保存在国内的唯一一件“北京人”头盖骨（额骨）化石真品，与失踪的“北京人”头盖骨化石属于同一时期。

“北京人”头部保存的原始性质和爪哇人相似，因而它们同属于直立人发展阶段。“北京人”的门齿呈铲形，有宽鼻子和低而扁平的面孔，下颌骨内面靠前部有下颌圆枕，表明他们具有明显的现代蒙古人种特征。“北京人”的下肢骨髓腔较小，管壁较厚，但在尺寸、形状、比例和肌肉附着点方面都已和现代人相似，这证明他们已经善于直立行走。“北京人”的上肢骨除了髓腔较小、管壁较厚外，和现代人的接近程度更甚于下肢骨，说明他们的上肢已能进行与现代人十分相似的活动。

考古发现

“北京人”用石器揭开了人类历史的序幕

早在旧石器时代的初期，“北京人”已懂得选取岩石，制作石器，表明“北京人”已经学会使用原始的工具从事劳动，这是人和猿的根本区别所在。“北京人”的文化遗物包括石制品、骨角器和用火遗迹。遗址中出土了数以万计的石制品，原料均来自于遗址附近。在世界已知的同时期遗址中，从数量到质量，还没有发现有堪与相匹的同类石器文化遗存。

把人类用火的历史又提前了几十万年

在“北京人”居住过的洞穴里，发现厚度达4–6米、色彩鲜艳的灰烬，表明“北京人”已懂得使用火、支配火，并学会保存火种的方法，是人类由动物界跨入文明世界的重要标志。在周口店第一地点发现的用火遗迹，把人类用火的历史提前了几十万年。

为研究北京生态环境变迁史提供了依据

通过对“北京人”及其周围自然环境的研究，表明50万年前北京的地质地貌与现在基本相似，在丘陵山地上分布有茂密的森林群落，其中栖息着种类丰富的动物种群。但也曾出现过面积广阔的草原和沙漠，其中有鸵鸟和骆驼栖息的遗迹，表明在这段漫长的岁月里，北京地区曾经历过温暖湿润和寒冷干燥的气候过程。

发掘过程

周口店最早发现的地点是第六地点，是瑞典科学家安特生于 1918 年发现的。

1921 年，安特生与美国古生物学家格兰阶、奥地利古生物学家斯丹斯基，一道发现了周口店第一地点，同年发现了周口店第二地点。1927 年步达生将周口店发现的三枚人的牙齿正式命名为中国猿人北京种。这一年周口店遗址正式开始发掘，中国地质学家李捷参加发掘工作，并发现了周口店第三和第四地点。1929 年裴文中发现了第五、七、八地点，找到了“北京人”第一个头盖骨。同年将已发现的地点以“北京人”遗址为第一地点，其余依序编号至第九地点。

1930 年在周口店遗址还发现了距今约两万年前的山顶洞人化石和文化遗物，但随之而来的连年战乱，使自 1927 年以来发现的“北京人”和山顶洞人的化石标本全部遗失，迄今下落不明，这一事件成为 20 世纪考古史上的世界之谜。中华人民共和国成立后，恢复了对周口店遗址的发掘研究，获取了大量的宝贵资料。1953 年在周口店“北京人”遗址附近建成了周口店遗址博物馆，对公众开放。

重要遗址

第一地点

周口店遗址第一地点，又称“猿人洞”，原是一个天然的石灰岩溶洞，东西长 140 米，南北宽最宽处 40 米，西部最窄处 2 米，高度 40 米。从大约 50 万年起，北京猿人在这里断断续续生活了 20 万年 –40 万年，北京猿人的遗骨、遗物、遗迹和洞顶塌落的石块和洞外流入的泥沙等，在洞内一层又一层填充起来，形成厚达 13 层的堆积层。

1921 年和 1923 年瑞典地质学家安特生与奥地利古生物学家斯丹斯基发现并进行了试掘，1927 年发现了一颗保存很好的人类下臼齿化石，被葛利普教授命名为“北京人”，并沿用至今。1929 年 12 月 2 日裴文中发现了第一颗保存完整的人类头盖骨化石。1949 年，中断了 11 年的发掘工作又得以恢复，1951 年 –1980 年又先后进行了几次发掘。该地点先后进行了 23 年的发掘，共出土约 203 件北京猿人的化石，其中包含完整和比较完整的头盖骨 6 个，发现用火堆积遗存 3 处，并发现石制品十万多件，同时出土了 98 种哺乳动物化石。

第二地点

周口店遗址第二地点是安特生、格兰阶和斯丹斯基于 1921 年发现的，也是周口店遗址最早发现的两个地点之一。该遗址距离第一地点大约 200 米，高约 15 米，厚 2 米，地层为棕红色粘土层。杨钟健先生最先作了研究，编为周口店第二地点。共发现哺乳动物化石 22 种，爬行类和鸟类各 1 种。时代为中更新世。

第四地点

周口店遗址第四地点位于龙骨山南坡，距周口店第一地点西约 70 米。该地点高出周口店河 46 米，洞口向南，发现时洞顶已经大部分塌落，基本上属于露天堆积。1927 年由步林和李捷发现，十年后的 1937 年，相关人员对该地点进行了发掘，发现 40 多种哺乳动物化石。1973 年初，在顾玉珉主持下，对第四地点进行发掘，被挖掘的堆积物厚度达 6.5 米，发现了较丰富的石制品、用火遗迹和 1 枚人牙化石，经鉴定这枚牙齿为距今约 20–10 万年的早期智人的一颗左上前臼齿化石。

遗产价值

周口店遗址是世界上迄今为止人类化石材料最丰富、最生动、植物化石门类最齐全、而研究又最深入的古人类遗址。“北京人”的发现，为人类进化理论提供了有力实证，是中国科学家为世界考古史做出的伟大贡献。“北京人”及其文化的发现与研究，解决了 19 世纪爪哇人发现以来的关于“直立人”是猿还是人的争论。事实证明，“直立人”是人类历史的最早期，处于从猿到人进化过程最重要的环节，他们是“南猿”的后代，后来“智人”的祖先。“北京人”具有“直立人”的典型形态标准，而“北京人”对火的使用，更加完备了其作为人的特征。“北京人”的发现，为中国古人类及其文化的研究奠定了基础，是当之无愧的人类远古文化宝库。

丝绸之路：长安—天山廊道的路网

丝绸之路是古代中国一条东西方之间经济、政治、文化交流的主要通道。西汉时期以都城长安（今西安）为起点，东汉时期以都城洛阳为起点，跨越陇山山脉，穿过河西走廊，通过玉门关和阳关，抵达新疆，沿绿洲和帕米尔高原通过中亚、西亚和北非，最终抵达非洲和欧洲。它的最初作用是运输中国古代出产的丝绸。因此，当德国地理学家斐迪南·弗赖赫尔·冯·李希霍芬（Ferdinand Freiherr von Richthofen）最早在 19 世纪 70 年代将之命名为“丝绸之路”后，这个名称即被广泛接受。

历史渊源

丝绸之路通常是指欧亚大陆北部的商路，与南方的茶马古道形成对比。西汉武帝时张骞首次开通丝绸之路，罗马人通过安息帝国、贵霜帝国和阿克苏姆帝国取得中国的丝绸。西汉末年，在匈奴的袭扰下，丝绸之路中断。

公元 73 年，东汉班超又重新打通隔绝 58 年的西域，并将这条路线首次延伸到了欧洲。通过这条贯穿亚欧的大道，中国的丝、绸、绫、缎、绢等丝制品，源源不断地运向中亚和欧洲，从而促进了亚欧各国和中国的友好往来，成为沟通东西方文化的友谊之路。

遗迹分布

丝绸之路沿线包括中心城镇遗迹、商贸城市遗迹、交通遗迹、宗教遗迹和关联遗迹等 5 类代表性遗迹共 33 处，中国境内有 22 处考古遗址、古建筑等遗迹，其中包括河南 4 处、陕西 7 处、甘肃 5 处、新疆 6 处。哈萨克斯坦、吉尔吉斯斯坦境内各有 8 处和 3 处遗迹。

唐长安城大明宫遗址

大明宫，唐帝国的政治中心，是中国古代乃至世界上面积最大的宫殿建筑群。位于唐京师长安城（今陕西西安）城北的龙首原，始建于公元 634 年，原名永安宫，是唐长安城的三座主要宫殿（大明宫、太极宫、兴庆宫）中规模最大的一座，占地 350 公顷，拥有 50 多座殿堂和阁楼，被誉为丝绸之路上的东方圣殿。自唐高宗起，唐朝的帝王们大都在这里居住和处理朝政，作为国家的统治中心，历时 200 余年。唐末战乱，大明宫于唐朝末年毁于战火。

大雁塔

大雁塔被视为古都西安的象征。唐代永徽三年（公元 652 年），玄奘为藏经典而修建，塔身七层，通高 64.5 米。大雁塔作为现存最早、规模最大的唐代四方楼阁式砖塔，是佛塔这一印度佛寺的建筑形式随着佛教传播而向东传入中原地区并融入汉文化的典型物证，是凝聚了汉族劳动人民智慧结晶的标志性建筑。

大雁塔所在的大慈恩寺由唐代皇室敕令修建，是唐长安城内最著名、最宏丽的佛寺，由玄奘法师主持，是唐代长安三大译经场之一，在佛教传播史上具有重要地位。

汉魏洛阳城遗址

汉魏洛阳城遗址是东汉、曹魏、西晋、北魏的都城遗址，在今河南省洛阳市东约 15 公里处。西周初在此筑城，称“成周”。因在洛水之北，故称洛阳。东周、东汉、曹魏、西晋、北魏等朝代先后以此为国都，都城史长达 540 年以上。该故城是中国所有都城遗址中，历代定都总时间最长、规模最大且保存较为完整的古城遗址，对后来都城的建筑形制、设计规划，影响达千年之久。

现内城城垣，东北西三面遗存 1 万多米，最高处达 9 米，主要有宫城正门阊阖门遗址和宫城正殿太极殿遗址，北魏皇家寺院永宁寺遗址，中国第一座官办佛建寺院白马寺，汉魏时期国立大学太学遗址，汉魏时期皇家礼制祭祀建筑明堂、辟雍遗址，中国古代最早的天文观测台灵台遗址，以及曾出土大量国宝的东周王陵金村大墓等。

玉门关遗址

玉门关，位于甘肃敦煌市西北 90 公里处。始置于汉武帝开通西域道路、设置河西四郡之时，因西域输入玉石时取道于此而得名。西汉时为通往西域各地的门户，元鼎至元封年间（公元前116年－前105年）修筑酒泉至玉门间的长城，玉门关随之设立，成为汉代重要的军事关隘和丝路交通要道。

麦积山石窟

麦积山石窟，因山形酷似农家麦垛状故名。石窟窟龛凿于高20–80米、宽200米的垂直崖面上。现存有窟龛194个，其中东崖54窟，西崖140窟，泥塑、石胎泥塑、石雕造像7800余尊，最大的造像东崖大佛高15.8米，壁画1000余平方米。

东崖的石窟以涅槃窟、千佛廊、散花楼上的七佛阁等最为精美；西崖聚集着万佛堂、天堂洞、121窟、123窟、127窟、165窟等最有价值的洞窟。窟内现存泥塑30多件。麦积山第四窟的建筑是全国各石窟中最大的一座摹仿中国传统建筑形式的洞窟，是研究北朝木构建筑的重要资料，如实地表现了南北朝后期已经中国化了的佛殿的外部和内部面貌，在石窟发展史上具有重要的意义。

炳灵寺石窟

炳灵寺石窟，位于甘肃省临夏回族自治州永靖县西南约40公里处的积石山的大寺沟西侧的崖壁上，西晋初年（约公元3世纪）开凿。现存有窟龛183个，共计石雕造像694身，泥塑82身，壁画约900平方米，分布在大寺沟西岸长约200米、高60米的崖面上。石窟以位于悬崖高处的唐代“自然大佛”（169窟）以及崖面中段的众多中小型窟龛构成其主体。

交河故城

交河故城位于新疆吐鲁番市西约11公里处的亚尔孜沟内，是公元前2世纪至公元5世纪由车师人开创和建造的，在南北朝和唐朝达到鼎盛。是世界上最大最古老、保存最完好的生土建筑城市，也是我国保存两千多年最完整的都市遗迹，唐西域最高军政机构安西都护府最早就设在交河故城。

古城遗址保存相当完好，古城南北长1600余米，东西最宽处约300米，分为寺院、民居、官署等部分。古城总面积47万平方米，现存建筑遗迹36万平方米。城内建筑物大部分为唐代所建，建筑布局独具特色。该城保留着宋代以前我国中原城市的建筑特点。

克孜尔石窟

克孜尔石窟又称克孜尔千佛洞或赫色尔石窟，位于新疆拜城县克孜尔镇东南明屋塔格山的悬崖上，南面是木扎特河河谷。

克孜尔石窟是中国开凿最早、地理位置最西的大型石窟群，大约开凿于公元3世纪，在公元8–9世纪逐渐停建，延续时间之长在世界各国也是绝无仅有的。石窟有4个石窟区，正式编号的石窟有236个，大部分塑像都已被毁，还有81窟存有精美壁画，为古代龟兹国的文化遗存。

遗产价值

丝绸之路是东西方之间融合、交流和对话之路，近两千年以来为人类的共同繁荣做出了重要的贡献。它形成于公元前2世纪，兴盛于公元6–14世纪，沿用至16世纪，分布于今中国、哈萨克斯坦和吉尔吉斯斯坦境内。丝绸之路见证了亚欧大陆经济、文化、社会发展之间的交流，尤其是游牧与定居文明之间的交流；它在长途贸易推动大型城镇和城市发展方面是一个出色的范例；它与张骞出使西域等重大历史事件直接相关，深刻反映出佛教、摩尼教、拜火教、祆教等宗教和城市规划思想在古代中国和中亚地区的传播。丝绸之路是亚欧大陆的交通动脉，是中国、印度、希腊三种主要文化交汇的桥梁。

拉萨布达拉宫历史建筑群

布达拉宫

举世闻名的布达拉宫，耸立在西藏拉萨市红山之上。“布达拉”系“舟岛”的梵文音译，又译作“普陀罗”或“普陀”，原指观世音菩萨所居之岛。拉萨布达拉宫俗称第二普陀山。布达拉宫号称“世界屋脊上的明珠”，它的宫殿布局、土木工程、金属冶炼、绘画、雕刻等方面均闻名于世，体现了以藏族为主，汉、蒙、满各族能工巧匠高超的技艺和藏族建筑艺术的伟大成就。

历史沿革

布达拉宫始建于公元7世纪。相传松赞干布迁都拉萨后，为迎娶唐朝的文成公主，特别在红山之上修建了共1000间宫殿的3座9层楼宇，取名“布达拉宫”。楼群一侧为藏王的寝宫，中间宫殿的顶部建有佛塔，另一侧是后宫。在后宫与中间宫殿之间架起四层楼高的铜铁铸空中廊桥。1645年（藏历木鸡年），五世达赖喇嘛为巩固政教合一的甘丹颇章地方政权，由第司索朗绕登主持，重建布达拉“白宫”及宫墙、城门、角楼等，并把政权机构由哲蚌寺迁至此处。1690年（藏历铁马年），第司桑杰嘉措为五世达赖喇嘛修建灵塔，扩建了“红宫”。吐蕃王朝灭亡之后，古老的宫堡大部分毁于战火，加上雷击等自然灾害，布达拉宫的规模日益缩小。17世纪重建后，布达拉宫成为历代达赖喇嘛的冬宫，同时也是西藏政教合一的统治中心。此后，历世达赖喇嘛增建了五个金顶和一些附属建筑。特别是1936年（藏历火鼠年）十三世达赖喇嘛的灵塔殿建成后，形成了布达拉宫今日的规模。

主要建筑

外观共13层的布达拉宫，整体建筑主要由东部的白宫、中部的红宫及西部白色的僧舍组成，包括山下印经院和后花园宗角禄康等附属建筑。三大建筑耸立在红山之上，圣洁而雄伟，被当地藏民称之为“白色宫殿”。

白宫　白宫位于第4层中央的东有寂圆满大殿（措庆夏司西平措），是布达拉宫白宫最大的殿堂，面积717平方米。这里是达赖嘛嘛坐床、新政大典等重大宗教和政治活动的场所。第5、6两层是摄政的办公和生活用房。最高处第7层有两套达赖喇嘛冬季的起居宫，由于这里终日阳光普照，故称东、西日光殿。西日光殿（尼悦索朗列吉）是原殿，东日光殿（甘丹朗色）是后来仿造的，两者布局相仿，分别是十三世和十四世达赖的寝宫，也是他们处理日常事务的地方。殿内包括朝拜堂、经堂、习经室和卧室等，陈设十分豪华。

红宫　红宫最主要的建筑是历代达赖喇嘛的灵塔殿，共有5座，分别是五世、七世、八世、九世和十三世灵塔殿。各殿形制相同，但规模不等。其中最大的是五世达赖灵塔殿（藏林静吉）。殿高3层，由16根大方柱支撑，中央安放五世达赖灵塔，两侧分别是十世和十二世达赖的灵塔。五世达赖灵塔殿的享堂西大殿（措钦鲁，亦名司西平措）是红宫中最大的殿堂，高6米多，面积达725.7平方米。在红宫的西部是十三世达赖灵塔殿（格来顿觉），建于1936年，是布达拉宫最晚的建筑。殿内除了灵塔，还供奉着一尊银造的十三世达赖像和一座用20万颗珍珠、珊瑚珠编成的法物“曼扎”。

红宫中的法王殿（曲结哲布）和圣者殿（帕巴拉康）相传都是吐蕃时期遗留下来的建筑。法王殿正处在布达拉宫的中央位置，它的下面就是玛布日山的山尖。据说这里曾经是松赞干布的静修之所，现供奉着极为珍贵的松赞干布、文成公主、尺尊公主和禄东赞等人的塑像。

建筑特色

布达拉宫依山而建，现占地41万平方米，建筑面积13万平方米。宫体主楼13层，高115米，全部为石木结构。殿宇嵯峨，气势雄伟，有横空出世、气贯苍穹之势。坚实敦厚的花岗石墙体，松茸平展的白玛草墙领，金碧辉煌的金顶，具有强烈装饰效果的巨大鎏金宝瓶……绚丽多彩，交相映辉，体现出藏族古建筑迷人的特色。

宫殿的设计和建造根据高原地区阳光照射的规律，墙基宽而坚固，墙基下面有四通八达的地道和通风口，各大厅和寝室的顶部都有天窗，便于采光，调节空气。宫内的柱梁上有各种雕刻，墙壁上的彩色壁画面积达 2500 多平方米。

布达拉宫的建筑艺术，是数以千计的藏传佛教寺庙与宫殿相结合的建筑类型中最杰出的代表，在中国乃至世界都是绝无仅有的例证。

布达拉宫位于拉萨市西北郊区约 2 公里处的小山上，在当地信教人民的心目中，此山犹如观音菩萨居住的普陀山，建筑由东部的白宫、中部的红宫组成。布达拉宫重重叠叠，迂回曲折，同山体融合在一起，高高耸立，巍峨壮观。宫墙红白相间，宫顶金碧辉煌，具有强烈的艺术感染力。它是拉萨城的标志，也是独一无二的雪域高原上的人类文化遗产。

布达拉宫整体建筑为石木结构，宫殿外墙厚达 2–5 米，基础直接埋入岩层。墙身全部用花岗石砌筑，高达数十米。每隔一段距离，中间即灌注铁汁，进行加固，同时提高了墙体抗震能力。屋顶和窗檐为木结构，飞檐外挑，屋角翘起。铜瓦鎏金，闪亮的屋顶采用歇山式和攒尖式，具有汉族建筑风格。屋檐下的墙面装饰有鎏金铜饰，形象都是佛教法器式八宝，有浓重的藏传佛教色彩。

布达拉宫过去曾是政教合一的统治中心，与西藏历史上的重要人物松赞干布、文成公主、尺尊公主和历代达赖喇嘛等有着十分密切的关系，因而具有重大的历史意义和宗教意义。在萨松朗杰殿中供奉有用藏、汉、满、蒙四种文字书写的康熙皇帝长命牌位和乾隆皇帝画轴，表现了历代达赖同中央政府的隶属关系。整座布达拉宫堪称是一座建筑艺术与佛教艺术的博物馆，这是中华各民族团结进取和国家统一的象征。

文物收藏

300 余年来，布达拉宫收藏和保存了极为丰富的历史文物，如释迦牟尼的舍利子，108 函 2500 余卷经书，特别是金字缮写的甘珠尔、天竺等地的贝叶经，以及明清以来中央政府关于西藏的各种封敕达赖喇嘛的金册、玉册、金印和乾隆皇帝御赐为遴选达赖转世灵童而设的金本巴瓶。还有布达拉宫内设置的 8 座灵塔，其中最大的一座为五世达赖喇嘛修建，耗费黄金 3721 千克，上万颗宝石；灵塔包以金皮，镶嵌大量珠宝。还有藏族匠师制作的各种金银器物，镶嵌珠宝的法器、供器和民族工艺品等，琳琅满目。布达拉宫还珍藏着大量书籍，从佛教经典到医学、天文历算，无所不有。这些文物对于研究西藏的政治、经济、历史、文化等都具有重大的意义和价值。

“唐卡”是藏语音译，是最富有藏族特征的一个画种：用彩缎装裱，画在绢、布或纸上的卷轴画。主要以宗教人物、宗教历史事件、教义为内容，也涉及到西藏天文历算、藏医藏药等题材。布达拉宫保存有近万幅唐卡，最大的可达几十平方米。

保护与维修

中华人民共和国成立后，布达拉宫的保护管理一直得到政府的高度重视。1988 年国务院决定拨出巨款对布达拉宫进行大规模的维修，并于次年 10 月隆重开工。在藏汉族工程技术人员的协作下，工程历经 5 年胜利竣工。时隔不到 10 年，布达拉宫二期维修工程从 2002 年开始实施，主要对布达拉宫地垄进行加固，对各殿堂房顶虫蛀木材加以更换和对壁画进行修复。当年一同实施的还有罗布林卡和萨迦寺的维修。截至 2008 年夏初，布达拉宫主体古建筑地垄加固和红宫、白宫等 17 处古建筑维修已基本完成，珍宝馆土建工程也已告竣，壁画修复工程和雪城内部分建筑屋顶“阿嘎”土的夯打和珍宝馆院内环境整治等项目亦相继竣事。今天的布达拉宫，以她崭新的姿容，屹立在雪域高原的圣山之上。

遗产价值

现存布达拉宫的设计、布局、材料、工艺、装饰等均保存了自 7 世纪创建以来历次重大增扩建和重建的历史原状。众多的建筑虽属历代不同时期建造，但都十分巧妙地利用了山形地势特点，使整座建筑显得非常雄伟壮观，协调完整。宫宇叠垒，迂回曲折，与山体有机地融合，这是布达拉宫给人最为直接的感受，也是它最突出的特点。布达拉宫不但在整体建筑艺术上有着创造性的突破，而且在建筑艺术的美学成就上也达到了无可比拟的高度。

大昭寺

2000 年 11 月，联合国教科文组织将大昭寺作为布达拉宫的扩展项目列入《世界遗产名录》，成为世界文化遗产。（罗布林卡在 2001 年也被列入）。

大昭寺，又名“祖拉康”、“觉康”（藏语意为佛殿），位于拉萨老城区中心，是一座藏传佛教寺院。始建于唐贞观二十一年（公元647年），是藏王松赞干布为纪念尺尊公主入藏而建，距今已有1300多年的历史，在藏传佛教中拥有至高无上的地位。

建筑特色

大昭寺是西藏现存最辉煌的吐蕃时期的建筑，也是西藏最早的土木结构建筑，并且开创了藏式平川式的寺庙布局规式。大昭寺融合了藏、唐、尼泊尔、印度的建筑风格，成为藏式宗教建筑的千古典范。大昭寺建筑面积达25100余平方米，有20多个殿堂。主要有弥勒佛殿、观音菩萨殿、祖孙三法王殿和度母殿等。主殿高4层，整个建筑金顶、斗拱为典型的汉族风格，碉楼、雕梁则是西藏样式。主殿第2、3层檐下有排列成行的103个木雕伏兽和人面狮身，寺内有长近千米的藏式壁画《文成公主进藏图》和《大昭寺修建图》。

常言：“先有大昭寺，后有拉萨城”。大昭寺在拉萨市具有中心地位，不仅是地理位置上的，也是社会生活层面的。环大昭寺内中心的释迦牟尼佛殿一圈称为“囊廓”，环大昭寺外墙一圈称为“八廓”，大昭寺外辐射出的街道叫“八廓街”即八角街。以大昭寺为中心，将布达拉宫、药王山、小昭寺包括进来的一大圈称为“林廓”。这从内到外的三个环型，便是藏民们行转经仪式的路线。

文物收藏

在大昭寺数以万计的文物典藏中，释迦牟尼12岁等身鎏金铜像最为精美与尊贵，据称，该佛像同2500年前的佛祖没有任何区别，见像如见佛。最早从古印度流入中国，后经唐文成公主带入西藏，遂被供奉于大昭寺至今。拉萨之所以有“圣地”之誉，与这座佛像有关。

大昭寺内另一件无比珍贵的文物是檀木雕刻和释迦牟尼殿前的8根檀木木柱，这些木雕和木柱均出自公元7世纪，经历了1400年的风雨剥蚀，至今完好无损，敲一下，会发出清脆的金属声。

遗产价值

大昭寺不仅仅是一座供奉众多佛像、圣物以使信徒们膜拜的殿堂，它还是佛教中关于宇宙的理想模式——坛城（曼陀罗）这一密宗义理立体而真实的再现。寺前终日香火缭绕，信徒们虔诚的叩拜在门前的青石地板上留下了等身长头的深深印痕。万盏酥油灯长明，记录着朝圣者永不止息的足迹，也留下了岁月的永恒。

在大昭寺的正门入口处前面，有三根石柱，一根石柱上用汉藏两种文字镌刻着公元823年签订的唐蕃会盟书，见证了汉藏人民的深厚友情；另一根石柱上则刻着种痘文（为纪念清朝乾隆年间中央政府向西藏人民传授种痘方法以防治天花所立），见证了中央政府对西藏人民的关怀。从大昭寺金顶俯瞰大昭寺广场，右边远处山上是布达拉宫，近处的柳树是“公主柳”，相传为文成公主所栽，昭示着汉藏人民的友情千秋万代，根深叶茂。

罗布林卡

罗布林卡，藏语意为“宝贝园林”，位于西藏拉萨西郊。始建于18世纪40年代（达赖七世时），是历代达赖喇嘛消夏理政的地方，也是一座典型的藏式风格园林。经过200多年的扩建，全园占地36万平方米，园内有植物100余种，不仅有拉萨地区常见花木，而且有取自喜马拉雅山南北麓的奇花异草，还有从内地移植或从国外引进的名贵花卉，堪称高原植物园。

主要建筑

罗布林卡由格桑颇章、金色颇章、达登明久颇章几组宫殿建筑组成，每组建筑又分为宫区、宫前区和林区三个主要部分。以格桑颇章为主体的建筑群，位于第二重围墙内南院的东南部；以措吉颇章（湖心亭）为主体的建筑群，位于格桑颇章西北约120米处，是罗布林卡中最美的景区；以金色颇章为主体的建筑群，位于罗布林卡西部。各组建筑均以木、石为主要材料建成，规划整齐，具有明显的藏式建筑风格。其突出的特点是：高处筑台，低处挖池，任其自然，以取景为胜。园中树木茂密，湖心宫、龙王亭、金色林卡等建筑掩映其间，幽曲动人。清新的空气，安谧的环境，具有一种西藏园林特有的朴实自然的情趣，是西藏人造园林中规模最大、风景最佳、古迹最多的园林。

文物收藏

罗布林卡的文物，总体上说可以分为两大类，一类是西藏本土制造的宗教文物，另一类是历朝中央政府和皇帝赏赐和馈赠给西藏地方上层的各类珍品，西藏本土制造的宗教文物，以金铜造像最为著名。制作精细、比例匀称、色彩鲜明艳丽，佛像上的镀金厚重，镀金面光洁度高，佛冠、耳坠、臂钏、手镯、飘带等饰物，一律用绿松石镶嵌。这些明显特征，说明 18 世纪中叶以后，西藏本土佛像铸造技术已步入了独立发展的成熟阶段。

除佛像、佛塔外，唐卡收藏也是一大亮点。罗布林卡珍藏了大量 18 到 20 世纪勉唐画派、钦则画派和嘎赤画派的各类作品，这些作品人物刻画逼真细腻，栩栩如生，弥足珍贵。

还有，主要殿堂内墙壁上的壁画亦堪称精美绝伦，是藏族文化宝库中不可多得的艺术珍品。

遗产价值

罗布林卡是西藏最大的藏式人工园林，融汇了藏、汉两族的建筑风格，是藏式园林建筑的代表作。其中收藏的大量艺术珍品不仅具有极高的文化艺术价值，也是千余年来藏汉等民族友好交往的见证。

莫高窟

敦煌是古代丝绸之路上的重镇，敦煌莫高窟所藏的艺术珍品是中外文化交流的瑰宝，中国人为有莫高窟而骄傲。

莫高窟位于甘肃敦煌市东南25公里的鸣沙山东麓崖壁上，南北长约1600米。据记载，前秦建元二年（公元366年），僧人乐僔路经此山，忽见金光闪耀，如现万佛，于是便在岩壁上开凿了第一个洞窟。此后法良禅师等又陆续在此建洞修禅。这里曾经有“漠高窟”之称，意为“沙漠的高处”。后简写为“莫高窟”。

历史沿革

自汉代以来，敦煌即成为汉族和许多少数民族聚集杂居的地方，各民族文化在这里交汇、融合；敦煌又是西出西域、东入中原的咽喉要道，自古以来，笃信佛教的地方官吏、豪门贵族以及贫苦百姓都捐出银两用以凿窟、塑像、绘画，而来往于丝绸古道的商人、使者、僧侣等更是为了祈佑自己能平安穿过沙漠戈壁，或死后能进入天国，争相雇佣大批工匠在鸣沙山崖壁上开凿窟龛，塑像绘佛，供奉自己心中的佛国偶像。从东晋十六国时期开始，又历经北魏、西魏、北周、隋、唐、五代、宋、西夏、元等朝代的千年接力创作，留给后人的是一座五彩缤纷的佛教文化艺术宝库。

北朝时期

北魏、西魏和北周时，统治者崇信佛教，石窟建造得到王公贵族们的支持，因而发展速度较快。开凿于北朝时期的洞窟共有36个，其中年代最早的第268窟、第272窟、第275窟有可能建于北凉时期。北朝时期窟形有中心塔柱窟、殿堂窟和禅窟。这一时期的塑像多为一佛二菩萨组合，也有交脚菩萨、思惟菩萨，和天王、禅僧，后来又加上了二弟子；影塑有飞天、供养菩萨和千佛。

塑像人物神情端庄宁静，风格朴实自然，至北周一改前朝的“秀骨清像”，强调“丰硕壮实”。壁画前期多以土红色为底色，色调热烈浓重，线条流畅，形象挺拔，各种故事画生动异常，有西域佛教的特色。西魏以后，地色多为白色，色调趋于雅致，风格洒脱，具有中原文化风貌。

隋唐时期

隋唐时期，随着丝绸之路的繁荣，莫高窟进入兴盛时期。现存隋唐洞窟300多个，主要为殿堂窟，在正壁开佛龛，也有四壁三龛窟，以后出现了中心佛坛窟和涅槃窟、大像窟等。中心塔柱窟在这一时期逐渐消失。

唐代壁画绚丽多彩，尊像画、经变画臻于极致。塑像造型朴厚丰满，风格更加中原化，并出现了前代所没有的高大塑像。群像组合多为7尊或9尊，完美的造型与壁画相得益彰。

五代、宋时期

五代和北宋时期的洞窟现存100多个，多为改建、重绘前朝窟室，形制主要是佛坛窟和殿堂窟。从晚唐到北宋，统治敦煌的归义军节度使张氏和曹氏家族崇信佛教，设置画院，主持莫高窟的开凿与修建，因此供养人画像在这一阶段大量出现且内容十分丰富。塑像和壁画都沿袭了晚唐的风格，但愈到后期，其形式愈显程式化，内容有所丰富，但不复有唐代的创作活力和激情。

西夏和元代

莫高窟现存西夏和元代的洞窟，壁画雕塑基本仍沿袭前朝风格。一些西夏中期的洞窟出现了回鹘王的形象，而到了西夏晚期，壁画中增加了密宗的内容。元代洞窟只有8个，全部是新开凿的，其中展示了线描造型的最高水平，还出现了湿壁画技法。也有藏传密宗的洞窟，壁画和雕塑与中原风格大异其趣。元代以后，明朝封关，莫高窟也停止了兴建并逐渐淡出人们的视野。

敦煌艺术

敦煌石窟艺术是集建筑、雕塑、绘画于一体的立体艺术，古代艺术家继承中原汉民族文化，吸取、融化西域佛教艺术的影响，发扬当地文化传统，创造出大量具有敦煌地方特色的中国佛教艺术品，为研究中国古代政治、经济、文化、艺术、宗教、民族关系及中外友好往来等提供了珍贵资料，是全人类共同的文化宝藏和精神财富。

彩塑艺术

莫高窟所处山崖石质疏松，不适合制作石雕，所以莫高窟的造像大都在石胎上施加泥塑，衬以木骨。塑造的佛教尊像，有单身像和群像等多种组合。群像一般以佛居中，两侧侍立弟子、菩萨等，少则 3 身，多则达 11 身。彩塑形式有圆塑、浮塑、影塑等。这些塑像构思精巧逼真，想象力丰富，艺术造诣极高，而且经过彩绘，与壁画融为一体。

彩塑佛像、菩萨像、弟子像以及天王、力士等，由于制作年代不同，风格也迥然有异，尤其是北朝的“秀骨清像”、“曹衣出水”和唐代的“吴带当风”等风格，充分体现了当时的艺术家们超凡的想象力和高超的创作水平。

壁画艺术

莫高窟壁画绘于洞窟的四壁、窟顶和佛龛内，内容博大精深，主要有尊像、佛教故事、经变、佛教史迹、神怪、供养人、装饰图案等七类题材，此外还有很多表现当时耕作、狩猎、纺织、交通、战争、建设、经商、音乐、舞蹈、婚丧嫁娶等社会生活各方面的画作，是东晋十六国至元代千余年的民俗风貌和历史变迁的艺术再现，为中国美术史研究提供了重要实物。

敦煌壁画形象逼真，尤其是“飞天”图案，被唐朝人誉为“天衣飞扬，满壁风动”，成为敦煌壁画的象征，而如反弹琵琶的伎乐仙女更是佛国世界里的艺术精灵。艳丽的色彩，飞动的线条，在古代画师对理想天国热烈而动情的描绘里，我们似乎感受到了她们在大漠绿洲纵横驰骋的不竭激情……

建筑艺术

现存 492 个洞窟中保存有绘画、彩塑，按石窟建筑和功用分为中心柱窟、殿堂窟（包括中心佛坛窟）、大像窟、涅槃窟、禅窟、影窟和瘗窟等形制。窟型最大者高 40 余米，宽约 30 米。从早期石窟保留至今的中心塔柱式这一外来形式的窟型中，反映出古代艺术家在接受外来艺术的同时，加以消化、吸收，使其成为我国的民族形式。不少洞窟是现存古建筑的杰作，多个洞窟外保存有较为完整的唐代、宋代木质结构窟檐，是不可多得的木结构古建筑实物资料，具有极高的研究价值。石窟保护区域内还有许多佛塔，其中有五代、宋代和西夏的珍贵实物建筑遗存。

遗产价值

自从 1900 年莫高窟藏经洞中发现了 5 万多卷宗教文书和世俗文书，敦煌艺术震惊了世界，“敦煌学”已成为世界性的显学。

莫高窟共有洞窟 492 个，壁画 45000 多平方米，彩塑 2400 余身，飞天 4000 余身，唐宋木结构建筑 5 座，莲花柱石和铺地花砖数千块，是一处由建筑、绘画、雕塑组成的博大精深的综合艺术殿堂，内容涉及古代社会的艺术、历史、经济、文化、宗教等领域，是世界上现存规模最宏大、保存最完好的佛教艺术宝库，被誉为“东方艺术明珠”，具有珍贵的历史、艺术、科学价值，是中华民族的历史瑰宝，也是人类优秀的文化遗产。

云冈石窟

北魏著名地理学家郦道元在《水经注》中记录了云冈石窟的壮景：

凿石开山，因岩结构，真容巨壮，世法所希。山堂水殿，烟寺相望，林渊锦镜，缀目新眺。

历史沿革

云冈石窟位于山西省大同市西郊武州山南麓，始建于北魏时代，是中国第一处由皇室显贵主持开凿的大型石窟。石窟依山开凿，东西绵延 1 公里。整个窟群分东、中、西三部分。东部的石窟多以佛塔为主，又称塔洞；中部“昙曜五窟”是云冈开凿最早、气魄最大的窟群；西部窟群开凿略晚，大多是北魏迁都洛阳后的作品。共有窟龛 252 个，造像超过 51000 尊。最大的佛像高达 17 米，最小的佛像仅有几厘米高。其中的昙曜五窟，布局设计严谨统一，是中国佛教艺术第一个巅峰时期的经典之作。

云冈石窟与甘肃敦煌莫高窟、河南洛阳龙门石窟、甘肃天水麦积山石窟并称为中国四大石窟；而云冈石窟与莫高窟、龙门石窟和重庆大足石刻则是中国境内被列入联合国教科文组织世界文化遗产名录的四座石窟。

云冈石窟艺术

造型特色

云冈石窟是中土第一座大型皇家佛教石窟寺，也是中国早期石窟艺术的代表作品。云冈石窟艺术以皇家风范、雄浑壮丽、题材多样、雕刻精美、内涵丰富而驰名中外；以融会东西、贯通南北的鲜明的民族化进程为特色，在中国石窟艺术中独树一帜。石窟以大量的实物形象和文字史料，从不同侧面展示了公元 5–6 世纪中国石窟艺术风格及北方地区宗教信仰的重大发展变化，对中华佛教艺术的创新与发展有着重大贡献，具有其他早期石窟不可替代的历史、艺术、科学的鉴赏价值。

精品洞窟

云冈石窟现存主要洞窟 45 个，其中第 1–20 窟为开凿较早、规模较大，且最受人关注的洞窟，其中首推最早建成的昙曜五窟，被称为“精品中的精品”。

昙曜五窟即现在的第 16–20 窟。洞窟呈椭圆形平面设计，窟内雕造大像，主尊形体占去窟内大部分空间，气象庄严。据说五尊大像象征北魏的五位皇帝。

第 16 窟　一个以伎乐驰名的洞窟，中间巨佛高 13.5 米，昂首挺胸，气度非凡，有“美男子”之称。其他佛像，或英俊清秀，或肃穆端庄，或披千佛袈裟而立，或合十而坐。周壁风化较甚，有部分佛龛、千佛保存。

第 17 窟　形制较特殊，洞窟地面低于洞外地面。主尊为交脚菩萨，高 15.6 米，面部、双臂及背光的大部分已崩塌，腿部雕刻尚未完工。戴宝冠，身上饰瓔珞、臂钏，胸前佩蛇纹饰带。

第 18 窟　洞窟外观与第 20 窟基本相同，有一门及明窗。窟内主尊立佛高 15.5 米，头顶素面高肉髻，面相浑圆，大眼，高鼻，垂耳，面带微笑。身着贴身的半披肩千佛袈裟，沿着袈裟衣纹贴满了小坐佛。左右侧壁各有一立佛像，高约 9 米，其容貌与主尊十分相似，着通肩袈裟。经过风化的壁面残存一些菩萨弟子的头部和身躯，宛如由壁面浮出，极为生动。

第 19 窟　昙曜五窟中最大的洞窟。主洞平面为椭圆形，穹窿顶，开有门和明窗。主尊坐佛高约 17 米，占据窟内主要空间。素面高肉髻，面相丰圆，与第 20 窟大佛相似。窟内壁面刻千佛，前部左右两侧各一尊立佛像，其一左手抚小孩头顶，或为释迦牟尼为其子授记形象。窟外两侧各凿出耳洞，内各有一尊高 8 米的坐佛。

第 20 窟　露天大佛结跏趺坐，被称为云冈石窟的象征。佛像高

13.7 米，胸以上因石质坚硬，保存完好。造型古朴硕大，两肩宽厚，袈裟右袒，面形丰圆，薄唇高鼻，神情肃穆。背光的火焰纹和坐佛、飞天等浮雕十分华美，把主佛衬托得更加刚健雄浑。

伎乐天

云冈石窟第 12 窟也叫音乐窟，洞窟内雕刻着许多伎乐天。她们手中拿的乐器有十多种，像箜篌、筚篥、曲项琵琶等，是早期从中亚传到中国的，而排箫、古琴、古筝、埙则是中国的传统乐器。这些雕刻为研究中外音乐史和舞蹈史提供了珍贵的资料，是古代多元文化结合的产物，各民族深厚悠久的民间乐舞艺术在此积淀。经调查统计，石窟中目前有 22 个洞窟雕刻乐器图像，尚存各种乐器雕刻 27 个种类 500 余件，乐队组合 60 余组。

遗产价值

云冈石窟的造像气势宏伟，内容丰富多彩，被誉为中国古代雕刻艺术的宝库。窟中菩萨、力士、飞天形象生动活泼，塔柱上的雕刻精致细腻。

云冈石窟按照开凿的时间可分为早、中、晚三期，不同时期的石窟造像风格各有特色。早期的“昙曜五窟”气势磅礴，具有浑厚、纯朴的西域情调。中期石窟则以精雕细琢、装饰华丽著称于世，显示出复杂多变、富丽堂皇的北魏时期艺术风格。晚期窟室规模虽小，但人物形象清瘦俊美，比例适中，是中国北方石窟艺术的榜样和“瘦骨清像”的源起。上承秦汉现实主义艺术之风气，下开隋唐浪漫主义色彩之先河。

龙门石窟

龙门石窟是中国四大石窟之一（其余三处为甘肃敦煌莫高窟、山西大同云冈石窟、甘肃天水麦积山石窟），位于洛阳市城南 13 公里处。东西两山对峙，伊河水从中间穿流而过，古称“伊阙”。隋炀帝迁都洛阳后，将皇宫的正门正对伊阙，而皇帝又以真龙天子自居，自此，伊阙便被人们习惯地称为龙门。唐代大诗人白居易说：“洛都四郊，山水之胜，龙门首焉”。

历史沿革

龙门石窟经历北魏、东魏、北齐、隋、唐等朝代，雕凿断断续续达 400 年之久，其中北魏和唐代大规模营建有 140 多年，因而在龙门的所有洞窟中，北魏洞窟约占 30%，唐代占 60%，其他朝代仅占 10% 左右。据统计，东西两山现存窟龛 2345 个、佛塔 70 余座，造像 11 万余尊。最大的佛像卢舍那大佛，通高 17.14 米。并有碑刻题记超过 2860 块，其中久负盛名的“龙门二十品”和褚遂良的《伊阙佛龛碑》，分别是魏碑体和唐楷的典范。

龙门石窟艺术

造型特色

龙门石窟是北魏、唐代皇家贵族发愿造像最集中的地方，是皇家意志和行为的体现，具有浓厚的国家宗教色彩。石窟中保留着大量的宗教、美术、建筑、书法、音乐、服饰、医药等方面的实物资料，因此，它是一座大型石刻艺术博物馆。两朝的造像反映出迥然不同的时代风格。北魏造像在这里不再是像云冈石窟造像那样粗犷、威严、雄健的风格，而生活气息逐渐变浓，趋向活泼、清秀、温和。这些北魏造像，脸部瘦长，双肩瘦削，胸部平直，衣纹的雕刻使用平直刀法，坚劲质朴。这些形制瑰异、琳琅满目的石刻艺术品，是中国传统文化与域外文明交汇融合的珍贵记录。

与北魏时期人们崇尚以瘦为美的艺术风格不同，唐代人以胖为美，所以唐代佛像脸部浑圆，双肩宽厚，胸部隆起，衣纹的雕刻使用圆刀法，自然流畅。龙门石窟的唐代造像继承了北魏的优秀传统，又发扬了汉民族的文化传统，创造了雄健生动而又纯朴自然的写实风格，体现了大唐帝国强大的物质力量和精神力量，显示了唐代雕刻艺术的最高成就。

精品洞窟

奉先寺　全称奉先寺大卢舍那像龛，是龙门石窟规模最大、艺术最为精湛的一组摩崖群雕，因为它隶属于当时的皇家寺院奉先寺而简称“奉先寺”。此窟开凿于唐高宗初年。洞中佛像形态丰腴安祥，生动感人，具有唐代佛像艺术的鲜明特点。这里共有 9 躯大像，中间主佛为卢舍那大佛，为释迦牟尼的报身佛。佛像通高 17.14 米。在雕塑家的手中，佛像集高尚的情操、丰富的感情、开阔的胸怀和典雅的外貌于一身，因此，具有极大的艺术魅力。

潜溪寺　潜溪寺是龙门西山北端第一个大窟，约建于唐代初期。窟顶藻井为一朵浅刻大莲花。主佛阿弥陀佛端坐在须弥座上，面容丰满，胸部隆起，衣纹斜垂座前，身体各部比例匀称，神情睿智，整个姿态给人以静穆慈祥之感。主佛左侧为年长的弟子迦叶，右侧为年轻的弟子阿难。两弟子旁边分别为观音菩萨和大势至菩萨。阿弥陀佛与两侧的菩萨共称为“西方三圣”，即掌管西方极乐世界的三位圣人，是佛教净土宗信仰的对象。

宾阳洞　“宾阳”，意为迎接出生的太阳。宾阳三洞开凿于北魏时期，因这一时期历史的变故，导致计划中的三所洞窟仅完成了宾阳中洞，南洞和北洞直到初唐才完成主要造像。

宾阳中洞内为马蹄形平面，穹窿顶，中央雕刻重瓣大莲花构成的莲花宝盖，莲花周围是八身伎乐天和两身供养天人。它们衣带飘扬，迎风翱翔在莲花宝盖周围，姿态优美动人。洞中三壁的三铺大型造像，代表着北魏雕塑艺术的最高水平；前壁精美的浮雕不幸遭到破坏和盗凿。

宾阳南洞的几尊主要的佛像都是在初唐完成的。洞中主佛为阿弥陀佛，面相饱满，双肩宽厚，体态丰腴，体现了唐朝以丰腴为美的风格。

万佛洞　是龙门石窟造像组合最完整的洞窟。洞内主佛为阿弥陀佛，端坐于双层莲花座上，面相丰满圆润，两肩宽厚，简洁流畅的衣纹运用了唐代刀法圆润的雕刻手法。洞内南北两壁整齐地刻有 15000 尊小佛像，每尊只有 4 厘米高。在南北两壁的基坛上各刻有六位伎乐人，舞伎在悠扬的乐曲声中翩翩起舞，体态轻盈，婀娜多姿。

莲花洞　与古阳洞相同，均为利用天然溶洞凿建的石窟，此窟因窟顶雕有一朵高浮雕的大莲花而得名，建于北魏晚期。莲花周围的飞天体态轻盈，细腰长裙，姿态自如。洞内主尊为佛立像着褒衣博带式袈裟，衣褶简洁明快。二弟子是浅浮雕，左侧弟子迦叶深目高鼻，胸部肋骨突起，手持锡杖，似一西域苦行僧。窟内满布龛像，其中最小的佛像仅 2 厘米高，仍生动细致，栩栩如生。

古阳洞　在龙门山的南段，开凿于北魏太和年间（公元 477–499 年），规模巨大，是龙门石窟造像群中开凿最早、最具学术价值的洞窟。著名的魏碑书法典范“龙门二十品”中，十九品出自此窟。洞窟平面呈马蹄形。主像释迦牟尼佛，着双领下垂式袈裟，面容清瘦，眼含笑意，安祥地端坐在方座上。

药方洞　因窟门刻有诸多古代药方而得名。洞门两侧刻有药方 150 多种，药方涉及内科、外科、小儿科、五官科等。这些药方不仅可以治疗常见的疾病，而且还能治疗疑难杂症，如“疗噎方”可以治疗食道癌等。药方洞的药方是中国现存最早的石刻药方，对研究中国医药学有着重要的意义。

遗产价值

龙门地区的石窟和佛龛展现了中国北魏晚期至唐代（公元 493—907 年）期间，最具规模和最为优秀的造型艺术。这些佛教题材的艺术作品，代表了中国石刻艺术的最高峰。

龙门石窟所处地理位置优越，自然景色幽美，是许多石窟难以比拟的。龙门石窟以大量的实物形象和文字资料从不同侧面反映了中国古代政治、经济、宗教、文化等许多领域的发展变化，对中国石窟艺术的创新与发展做出了重大贡献。龙门石窟的历史、艺术和科学鉴赏价值，使其成为石窟艺术系列中的代表作之一，对于研究中国古代的政治、经济、宗教、地理、民俗、艺术、医药以及中外文化交流等都提供了重要资料。

大足石刻

大足石刻位于重庆市，以大足县、潼南县、铜梁县、壁山县为范围，保存有数量可观的中国唐、宋时期的石刻造像。大足石刻是大足县境内主要为摩崖造像形式的石窟艺术的总称。大足石刻群有石刻造像 70 多处，总计十万多躯，其中以宝顶山和北山两处最为著名，其以佛教造像为主，是中国晚期石窟造像艺术的典范，规模之宏大、艺术之精湛、内容之丰富，可与敦煌莫高窟、云冈石窟、龙门石窟齐名。

历史沿革

大足县，从唐光启元年（公元 885 年）始到南宋灭亡一直是昌州州治所在地。大足石刻中的“五山”摩崖造像即在这近 400 年间完成。

现存大足石刻作品中，最早的是开凿于初唐永徽元年的尖山子摩崖造像，其后两百多年间仅新开凿圣水寺摩崖造像一处。这两处初、中唐造像总共不过 20 龛。直到公元 885 年昌州迁治大足后，摩崖造像方渐大兴。

唐景福元年（公元 892 年），昌州刺史兼静南军节度使韦君靖，在县城北龙岗山（今北山）营建“粮贮十年，兵屯数万”的永昌寨的同时，首先在北山凿造佛像。此后，州、县官吏和当地士绅、平民、僧尼等相继效法，直到公元 907—965 年间（五代十国时期。四川为蜀国，史称前蜀、后蜀）营造佛像不断，形成大足石刻史上第一个造像高潮。

大足石刻艺术

大足石刻注重雕塑艺术自身的审美规律和形式规律，在立体造型技法上，运用写实与夸张互补的手法，对不同的人物赋予不同的性格特征。强调善恶、美丑的强烈对比，表现的内容贴近生活，既有很强的艺术感染力，又有极大的社会教化作用。在布局上，是艺术、宗教、科学、自然的巧妙结合。在审美上，融神秘、自然、典雅三者于一体，充分体现了中国传统文化重鉴戒的审美要求。

宝顶石刻　宝顶山摩崖石刻（石窟）距大足县城东北 15 公里，由宋蜀中名僧赵智凤建于南宋淳熙六年至淳祐九年（1179—1249 年），历时 70 多年。石刻共 13 处，造像数以万计，以大佛湾和小佛湾为主。巨型雕刻 360 余躯，以六道轮回、广大宝楼阁、华严三圣像、千手观音像等。

南山石刻　南山造像开凿于南宋绍兴年间（1131—1162 年），崖面长 86 米，高 3.5–10.2 米。其中造像五龛窟，主要有三清古洞、后土圣母龛、龙洞、真武大帝龛等道教题材。如 5 号三清古洞，共刻像 421 尊，以道教最高神“三清”为主，配刻以“四御”及圣母、王母等群神，生动地反映了 12 世纪道教已由早期的老君、“三官”崇拜演变为神系、神阶明确的“三清”、“四御”信仰的历史事实。在中国宋代道教石窟中，此窟雕刻最为精美；就内容而言，是最完备而有系统地反映宋代道教神第的实物资料，有着极高的宗教、历史、艺术价值。

北山石刻　北山摩崖石刻（石窟）位于大足县城北 2 公里处，开凿于唐昭宗景福元年（892 年），历经五代、两宋，相继在佛湾、营盘坡、观音坡、北塔寺、佛耳岩等处造像近万躯。在长 300 多米、高 7 米的崖壁上，有碑碣 6 通，题记和造像铭记 55 则，经幢 8 座，阴刻“文殊师利问疾图”一幅，石刻造像 264 龛窟。佛湾造像雕刻精细，体态俊逸，风格独特。“韦君靖碑”、“蔡京碑”、“古文孝经碑”为世所独存，既是书法珍品，又可补史料之遗缺，价值极高。佛湾石刻分南北两个区域，南区大多是晚唐、五代时期的作品，北区大多为两宋作品。晚唐时期的作品人物造型端庄丰满，气质浑厚，衣饰简朴，线条流畅。五代时期的作品玲珑精巧，多彩多姿，衣着服饰由简到繁，逐渐摆脱了外来文化影响，具有石刻造像过渡期的特征。两宋时期的作品，多为该时代佛教雕塑的代表作，具有极高的艺术水平。

石篆山石刻　石篆山摩崖造像为典型的释、道、儒“三教”合一造像区，在石窟中较为罕见。其中，第 6 号为孔子及十哲龛，正壁刻儒家创始人孔子坐像，两侧壁刻孔子最著名的十大弟子。第 7 号为三身佛龛。三身佛结跏趺坐于莲座上，座下皆压一蟠龙。毗卢佛居中，头戴高花冠，冠中有一金轮，身着对襟宽袖佛袍，双手在胸前结印。

卢舍那佛居左，释迦牟尼佛居右，均头顶有螺纹高肉髻，身着袈裟，右手举胸前做说法状。第 8 号为老君龛，正中凿中国道教创始人老子坐像，左右各立七尊真人、法师像。据造像记知，以上三龛造像均为大庄园主严逊出资开凿，同出著名雕刻家文惟简等之手。

石门山石刻 石门山摩崖造像为佛教、道教合一造像区，尤以道教造像最具特色。如第 2 号玉皇大帝龛外的千里眼像，眼如铜铃，似能目及千里；顺风耳面貌丑怪，张耳作聆听状；二像肌肉丰健，筋脉显露，手法夸张。第 7 号独脚五通大帝，左脚独立于一风火轮上，广额深目，口阔唇厚，袍带飞扬，有来去如风之势。第 10 号三皇洞现存造像 35 身，儒雅清秀，衣纹折叠舒展，手法写实“人味”多于“神味”。第 12 号东岳大帝宝忏变相龛刻像 98 身，以东岳大帝、淑明皇后居中，反映出两宋时期东岳世家在道教神系中的突出地位。佛教题材主要有药师佛龛、水月观音龛、释迦佛龛、十圣观音窟、孔雀明王经变窟、诃利帝母龛等。其中尤以第 6 号十圣观音窟最为精美。

遗产价值

以北山、宝顶山、南山、石篆山、石门山（简称“五山”）摩崖造像为代表的大足石刻是中国石窟艺术重要的组成部分，也是世界石窟艺术中公元 9 世纪末—13 世纪中叶间最为壮丽辉煌的一页。“五山”摩崖造像以规模宏大、雕刻精美、题材多样、内涵丰富、保存完好而著称于世；以集佛、道、儒“三教”造像之大成而异于前期石窟；以鲜明的民族化、生活化特色，在中国石窟艺术中独树一帜；以大量的实物形象和文字史料，从不同侧面展示了公元 9 世纪末—13 世纪中叶间中国石窟艺术风格及民间宗教信仰的重大发展、变化，对中国石窟艺术的创新与发展有重要贡献，是一处独具特色的世界文化遗产。

峨眉山—乐山大佛

峨眉山月半轮秋，
影入平羌江水流。
夜发清溪向三峡，
思君不见下渝州。
——李白《峨眉山月歌》

峨眉山，位于中国四川省峨眉山市境内，景区面积 154 平方公里，最高峰万佛顶海拔 3099 米，是一个集自然风光与佛教文化为一体的中国国家级山岳型风景名胜区。

峨眉山在东汉以前就有轩辕问道、葛由入山、楚狂归隐等神仙故事流传，成为人们向往的仙道之地。后来峨眉山被列为三十六洞天之第七洞天，成为了著名的道教胜地。经魏晋发展，至唐王朝峨眉山道教进入全面发展的鼎盛时期。

被道书《仙鉴》称为“仙宗十友”的唐代诗人陈子昂、李白，先后亲临峨眉山寻仙访道。李白青年时登临峨眉山，在山中住了相当长的时间，他在《登峨眉山》一诗中写道：“蜀国多仙山，峨眉邈难匹。周流试登览，绝怪安可息。”李白不仅称赞峨眉是蜀中仙山之冠，而且还描述了峨眉道教的兴旺。今天，峨眉山上的一些寺庙和地名仍然保持了道家的名称，如纯阳殿、遇仙寺、仙峰寺等，唯有九老洞的财神赵公明仍享受着僧俗的香火。

到了宋代，由于宋太祖及其后继者不遗余力地支持佛教的发展，峨眉山最终确立了“普贤道场”的地位，成为全国的佛教圣地。明清两代由于有朝廷的支持，峨眉山大批建筑拔地而起，使得佛教以压倒之势占据了山中宗教统治地位。

主要景观

九老洞　九老洞是峨眉山最大的洞穴，全长约 1500 米。九老洞得名于“九老”在洞中修仙的传说。近人林散之诗《九老洞》有句：“松翠自波涛，半空起层台。此中有驯猿，时时清啸哀。老僧唤之来，饲之以青梅。相依两摩挲，情好如婴孩。”

金顶　金顶为峨眉山主峰，海拔 3099 米，是峨眉游山的终点，名胜云集。华藏寺高耸于岩顶，建于唐朝，屋顶为锡瓦覆盖。在金顶可观看峨眉四大奇观——日出、云海、佛光、圣灯。

报国寺　报国寺是步入峨眉的门户，举行各种佛事活动的中心。该寺创建于明万历年间，曾名“会宗堂”，寺内供奉佛教始祖释迦牟尼的右胁侍普贤菩萨、道教创始人的化身广成子、春秋名士陆通，取儒、道、释三教会宗合祀之意。全寺占地近 4 万平方米，主要建筑有山门、弥勒殿、大雄殿、七佛殿、普贤殿、藏经楼等，自前至后沿中轴线次第排开，逐渐升高。

清音阁　清音阁，又称卧云寺，位于峨眉山牛心岭下黑白二水汇流处，海拔 710 米。寺内供有释迦牟尼佛和文殊、普贤菩萨像。阁下有双飞亭，左右各有桥，如鸟翼展飞，故名双飞桥，亭下黑、白二水汇流处有一巨石，高丈许，形如牛心，故名“牛心石”。“戊戌六君子”之一的刘光弟撰书一联：“双飞两虹影，万古一牛心”。

峨眉四大奇观

云海　峨眉云海是由低云组成，峰高云低，云海中浮露出许多岛屿，云腾雾绕，宛若佛国仙乡；白浪滔滔，这些岛屿化若浮舟，又像是“慈航普渡”。近代诗人赵朴初诗句“天著霞衣迎日出，峰腾云海作舟浮”，是这一景致的绝妙写照。

日出　峨眉山矗立在四川盆地的西部边缘，鸟瞰纵横千里的“天府平原”，游人登山观日出，视野开阔，涤荡胸襟。伴随着旭日东升，朝霞满天，万道金光射向大地，峨眉山宛若从头至脚逐渐披上金色的大氅，呈现出全部的秀美身姿。南宋诗人范成大唱咏道：“云物为人布世界，日轮同我行虚空”。

佛光　佛光，又称峨眉宝光。佛家称为普贤菩萨眉宇间放出的光芒。

实际上，佛光是光的自然现象，是阳光照在云雾表面产生的衍射和漫反射作用形成的。谭钟岳诗云：“非云非雾起层空，异彩奇辉迥不同。试向石台高处望，人人都在佛光中。”

圣灯　金顶无月的黑夜，摄身岩下有时忽见一光如萤，继而数点，渐至无数，在黑暗的山谷飘忽不定，佛家称为“圣灯”。著名气象学家竺可桢将“佛灯”列为庐山三大疑案之一，千百年来人们对此做着各种推断和解析，但是，至今仍是一个未解之迷。释心诚《圣灯》诗云：“飞自峭崖东，飘来点点红。回翔分远近，掩映入空蒙。焰冷千年火，光摇半壁风。夜深人静后，挂满梵王宫。”

乐山大佛

位于凌云山东麓的栖鸾峰，古称“弥勒大像”、“嘉定大佛”，始凿于唐开元初年（公元713年），历时90年才得以完成。佛像依山临江，是世界现存最大的一尊摩崖石像，有“山是一尊佛，佛是一座山”的称誉。大佛为弥勒倚坐像，坐东向西，面相端庄，通高71米。坐像雕刻细致，线条流畅，身躯比例匀称，气势恢宏，体现了盛唐文化的宏大气派，具有很高的艺术价值和丰富的文化内涵，是中华民族的文化瑰宝，是世界历史文化的宝贵遗产。

1400年来，大佛饱受自然风雨侵蚀，以致佛身千疮百孔，面目全非。中华人民共和国成立后，曾在1962–1963年、1972–1975年、1982–1991年、1994年、1996年、2001年、2010年，先后7次、投入资金近5亿元对乐山大佛及周边环境进行维修与改造，使其呈现出了崭新的容貌，有效地保护了乐山大佛的真实性和完整性。

遗产价值

考古资料表明，早在一万年以前，这一区域内已有古代先民的活动。进入文明社会，有文献、史迹可考的人文历史已有2000多年。在如此漫长的历史时期，古代先民创造了光辉的历史文化，留下了丰富的历史遗产。佛教的传入、寺庙的兴建和繁荣，又使峨眉山这座雄而秀的“蜀国仙山”增添了神秘的色彩；宗教文化——特别是佛教文化，构成了历史文化的主体。所有的建筑、造像、法器、礼仪、音乐、绘画等无不展示出峨眉山宗教文化的浓郁气息和鲜明色彩。全山现有寺庙30余处，其中飞来殿、万年寺无梁砖殿均为国家一、二级保护单位。建筑富有地方传统民居风格，装修典雅，朴实无华，无论选址、设计和营造都别具匠心，既有庙堂之庄严，又富景观之美丽。其技艺之高，堪称中国名山风景区寺庙建筑艺术的典范。

登封“天地之中”历史建筑群

在中国人的早期宇宙观中，中国是位居天地中央之国，而国之中央则在中国登封的嵩山。中国早期王朝将登封作为建都之地，以象征皇权神授。以“天地之中”理念为动力，中国古代礼制、天文以及儒教、佛教、道教等文化流派均热衷于在嵩山建立核心基地，逐渐成为中华文明的核心。历代礼制、宗教、科技和教育等建筑的代表作品汇聚于此并得到了真实保留，因此具有很高的价值。

主要景观

太室阙　位于登封市城东太室山黄盖峰下，中岳庙天中阁前600余米处的中轴线上。太室阙始建于汉安帝元初五年（公元118年），以青灰色块石砌筑，分为东西两阙，间距6.75米，相对如门，是太室祠的象征性大门。阙身平面呈长方形，上有出檐的四阿顶，为石质仿木结构，东西两阙分别由母阙和子阙组成。太室阙是古代祭祀太室山神的重要实物见证，是中国古代祭祀礼制建筑的典范，对研究建筑史、美术史和东汉社会情况具有重要的参考价值。

少室阙　位于登封市城西6公里嵩山南麓十里铺村西，为汉代少室山庙的神道阙。少室山庙和太室山庙始建于秦，汉安帝时在庙前建阙。阙后有一东西长60余米、南北宽40余米的平台，当为少室山庙旧址。据杨炯撰《唐少姨庙碑记》，少室庙唐代改称少姨庙，其神为妇人像。相传少姨为涂山氏之妹。元代时又把“少姨”作为蚕神嫘祖来奉祀。元代杨奂游中岳时曾在少姨庙即兴赋诗曰：“路旁双阙老，蔓草入荒祠；时见山家女，烧香乞蚕丝。”

启母阙　位于登封市城西北2公里嵩山南麓万岁峰下，为汉代启母庙前的神道阙。启母阙北190米有一处开裂巨石，即“启母石”。据《淮南子》载：大禹治水三过家门而不入，其妻涂山氏化为巨石，石破北方而生启，故后世流传有“闻鼓饷夫”的故事。今存启母庙阙铭，有一部分内容写中国古代一次触目惊心的特大洪水，鲧因用堵的方法进行治理失败而丧生，禹吸取教训改用疏通河道排洪泄水的方法，取得成功。铭文间隙处及其它石块上浮雕人物画像、幻术、骑马出行等画像70余幅。

观星台　位于登封市东南13公里告成镇北周公庙内。现存建筑自南向北有照壁、大门、仪门、周公测景（影）台石表、周公庙卷棚、大殿、观星台、帝尧殿等。观星台建于元至元年间（1271~1294年），是我国现存时代最早、保护较好的天文台，在世界上也属最早的天文建筑之一。

周公测景（影）台　俗称无影台，是一座纪念性的石表，为我国古代立八尺表（土圭）测日影的遗制。相传周文王次子周公（姬旦），为营建洛阳曾来此测验日影。唐开元十一年（公元723年）天文官南宫说仿周公土圭之制，刻立八尺石表。周公测景台用青石制作，分台座和石柱两部分。石柱为表，台座为圭，表的顶端为屋宇式盖顶，南面刻有“周公测景台”字样。登封观星台的主要作用在于测量太阳的影长，以掌握与农业有关的四时节气变化。

中岳庙　始建于公元前2世纪的中岳庙是国内现存规模最大、规格最高、保存最完整的一组道教古建筑群。其飞甍映日，杰阁联云，雕梁画栋，金碧辉煌，整个庙宇的布局形制都与北京故宫相似。庙内的秦汉古柏、北魏碑刻、宋代铁人等真实反映了道教文化发展的悠久历程和丰富内涵，见证了印刻“天地之中”信仰的道教文化发展史。

嵩阳书院　嵩阳书院始建于北魏太和八年（公元484年），宋代成为全国四大书院之首，是中国最早的书院之一，也是程朱理学的策源地和传播中心。名儒司马光、范仲淹、程颐、程颢等相继在此讲学，一时声名大振。经金、元、明、清多次增补修建，规模逐渐形成，布局日趋严整。现今书院保持了清代建筑布局，中轴建筑共分五进院落，由南向北依次为大门、先圣殿、讲堂、道统祠和藏书院，中轴线两侧有配房和西院敬义斋等，共有古建筑25座108间。其规划布局和实物留存独具特色，对研究中国古代书院建筑、教育制度以及儒家文化具有不可替代的标本意义。

少林寺建筑群

少林寺建筑群主要包括三部分：常住院（即人们通称的少林寺）、塔林、初祖庵。少林寺主体为常住院，中轴线建筑共七进，由南向北依次是山门、天王殿、大雄宝殿、法堂、方丈院、立雪亭、千佛殿。

常住院　常住院始建于北魏太和十九年（公元 495 年），寺内现存明、清建筑 30 余座，每座建筑都承载着令人荡气回肠的历史故事。五百罗汉朝毗卢、少林拳谱、十三棍僧救秦王壁画等文物，都是中外文化交流、融合、创新与发展的极为珍贵的实物资料。

初祖庵　初祖庵是天地之中历史建筑群建筑之一，位于嵩山少林寺西北 2 公里五乳峰下的阜丘山上，是南天竺（印度）僧菩提达摩的后辈为纪念他在少林寺达摩洞面壁九年而建的一组小建筑群。

塔林　少林寺塔林位于河南省登封市嵩山少林寺的西侧，这里是少林寺历代德高望重的僧侣的坟墓。塔的造型有四角、六角、柱体、锥体、直线形、抛物线形、瓶形、圆形以及独石雕刻等，其中以唐贞元七年的“法玩塔”、北宋宣和三年的“普通塔”、金正隆二年的“西堂塔”、元初至元二十七年的“中林塔”、明万历八年的“坦然塔”和清康熙五年的“彼岸塔”最为著名，是塔林中最具代表性的塔。少林寺塔林是中国佛教道场中现存规模最大、数量最多的塔群。现存唐、宋、元、明、清时期的砖石墓塔 241 座和现代塔两座，整个塔林占地约 14000 平方米。少林寺塔林是综合研究中国古代砖石建筑和雕刻艺术的宝库。

遗产价值

登封“天地之中”八处 11 项历史文化遗产，是最具代表性、最有科学、技术、艺术、历史价值的古代建筑，历经汉、魏、唐、宋、元、明、清几个朝代，绵延不绝，构成了一部中国中原地区 2000 多年形象直观的建筑史。

少室阙、启母阙，是中国最古老的国家级祭祀礼制建筑典范；中岳庙和太室阙，是中国古代礼制建筑格局最全面的代表；嵩阳书院作为中国最早的传播儒家理学、祭祀儒家圣贤和举行考试的书院，是已经消失了的书院文化的载体；嵩岳寺塔、少林寺建筑群和会善寺，是不同时期佛教在中国发展的纪念碑。千余年来，它们影响了广大范围内的宗教建筑形制。这组建筑类型之多、规格之高、历时之久、内涵之丰富、影响之深远，为世所罕见。它们是中国古代礼制、宗教、科技和教育等建筑类型的杰出代表。

武当山古建筑群

武当山位于湖北省西北部丹江口市西南，又名太和山、玄岳山，是我国著名的道教圣地。

在方圆 400 多公里的区域内，有七十二峰、二十四洞、三潭、九泉、十池、九井、十石、九台等风景名胜，有“五里一庵，十里一宫” 的道观殿堂。明代旅行家徐霞客曾评价此山：“玄岳出于五岳之上”。

武当山悠久的历史与道教关系极为密切。《图经》：“武当，神仙窟宅，自黄老设教，神仙至人栖之者众”。自周朝至东汉末期，武当山已是修仙炼丹家和隐士的向往之地。东汉末道教诞生后，武当山逐步成为我国道教活动的主要场所。三国、魏晋南北朝时期，到武当山修道者明显增多。武当山已有“太和”、“仙室”等富有道教色彩的名称。唐朝统治者自称是老子（李耳）的后裔，大力扶持道教，使之成为三教之首。唐贞观年间（公元 627—649 年）在此建有规模宏大的道教建筑群。宋元两代进行了进一步扩大修建，明朝达到修建的鼎盛时期。

景观特色

武当建筑充分利用了峰峦的高大雄伟和崖洞的奇峭幽邃，将每个宫观都建造在峰峦岩洞间的合适位置，使它们与周围林木、岩石、溪流和谐一体，相映成辉。建筑设计的规划或宏伟壮观，或小巧精致，或深藏山坳，或濒临险崖，将古建筑群与大山的内在美结合成一种独特的人文景观，构成一种奇妙的审美感知，使之达到建筑与自然的高度和谐。

武当山建筑从净乐宫到天柱峰，皇家共建有 33 组建筑群，这些建筑群根据其赋予的等级，严格按典章制度安排。大型道宫也采取皇家特有的建筑规格，在建筑组合上强调主轴线，“皇权中轴”的指导思想十分明确。

武当山古建筑群类型多样，用材广泛，各项设计、构造、装饰、陈设，不论木构宫观、铜铸殿堂、石作岩庙，以及铜铸、木雕、石雕、泥塑等各类神像都达到了极高的技术与艺术水平。同时，这里还衍生出武当道教、武当道乐和武当武术等文化范畴的精髓，为中华民族的传统文化增添了新的内容。

主要景观

金殿　武当山金殿俗称“金顶”，位于武当山主峰天柱峰的顶端。为明代铜铸仿木结构宫殿式建筑，殿面宽与进深均为三间，四周立柱 12 根。殿内于后壁屏风前设神坛，塑真武大帝坐像。神坛上方高悬鎏金巨额，书“金光妙相”四字，为康熙皇帝手笔。殿体各部分件采用失蜡法铸造，遍体鎏金，无论瓦作、木作构件，皆结构严谨，合缝精密，虽经 500 多年风雨侵蚀，至今仍辉煌如初，从而显示出中国古代铸造业发展的极高水平。

紫禁城　建于永乐十七年（1419 年）。“紫”取自“紫气东来”，“禁”指皇家禁地，由此可见紫禁城除保护金殿外，还有政治寓意。又名皇城，高达数丈，周长超过 344 米，环绕天柱峰巅，由每块重达千斤的条石依崖砌成。远看美丽迷人的光晕围绕金殿，十分奇妙壮观。进入南天门，就是灵官殿长廊，幽暗阴森，冷气袭人。登上一段石级，是一块小平场，上有锡铸的灵官殿，玲珑古朴，为稀世文物。

紫霄宫　位于武当山东南的展旗峰下，是武当山保存最完好的一座宫殿，其主体建筑至今已历近 600 年。建筑布局充分利用地势特点，在纵向陡峭横向宽敞的地形上，沿轴线构筑建筑，层层递进，逐次升高，形成三进院落。主次分明，庄严肃穆，极具皇家道场气派。

南岩宫　坐落在武当山南岩（又名紫霄岩、独阳岩）绝壁之上，上接碧霄，下临绝壑，周围峰岭奇峭，林木苍翠，是武当山三十六岩中景色最美之处。南岩宫建筑群始建于唐代，宋、元、明、清均有增修扩建，共有殿宇 640 余间。南岩宫建筑群在总体布局上匠心独运，巧借地势，依山傍岩；在手法上打破了传统的完全对称的布局和模式，座座宫室镶嵌于悬崖峭壁之上，虽系人工，宛若天成，使其与环境风貌达到了高度的和谐统一，营造了“天人合一”的至高意境。

复真观　又名太子坡。这里的古建筑群基本上是按照真武修炼的故事来精心设计的，利用狮子峰的特殊地形，古代建筑大师们顺依山势的回转建起犹如波浪起伏的夹道墙，被称为“九曲黄河墙”。进二道山门豁然显出一宽阔院落，漫步走进，只见小院重叠、幽静雅适。前有依岩而建的“五云楼”，中有“皇经堂”、“藏经阁”，后有高台之上的“太子殿”。整体布局左右参差，高低错落，谐调而完美，充分体现出道教“清静无为”的思想内涵。

磨阵井　又名纯阳宫，建于清康熙年间，为一座四合院式道院。布局精巧，结构紧凑。现存山门、大殿、配殿、姥姆亭、北道院等建筑 52 间。大殿内壁画《真武修真图》形象地叙述了真武修真、得道成仙的故事，画风古朴。院内一口古井，旁立一根铁杵，传说当年真武太子在此受紫元君化身姥姆以“铁杵磨绣针，功到自然成”的哲理点化，最终修道成仙。

遗产价值

武当山古建筑中的宫阙庙宇集中体现了中国元、明、清三代世俗和宗教建筑的艺术成就，代表了近千年的中国建筑艺术的最高水平。

武当山古建筑现存四座道教宫殿、两座宫殿遗址、两座道观及大量神祠、岩庙，在布局、规制、风格、材料和工艺等方面都保存了原状。建筑主体以宫观为核心，分布在盆地或台地之上，庵堂神祠分布于宫观附近地带，岩庙则占踞险峰，形成“五里一庵十里宫，丹墙翠瓦望玲珑”的巨大景观。这些庙堂道观在建筑艺术、建筑美学上达到了极为完美的境界，有着丰富的中国古代文化和科技内涵，是研究明初政治和中国宗教历史以及古建筑的实物资料。

五台山

佛教传入五台山，始于东汉。史籍记载，永平十年（公元 67 年）12 月，汉明帝派往西域求法的使者同两位印度高僧迦叶摩腾和竺法兰来到洛阳，次年，来到五台山。由于汉明帝的支持，他二人获得建寺的权利。寺院落成后，以其山形命名为灵鹫寺。从那时起，五台山开始成为中国佛教的中心，五台山的大孚灵鹫寺与洛阳白马寺同为中国最早的寺院。五台山也是中国唯一一处青庙（汉传佛五台山是中国唯一一处青庙（汉传佛教）、黄庙（藏传佛教）交相辉映的佛教道场。

主要景观

五座山峰

东台　又称望海峰，台顶如鳌鱼脊，耸立于台怀镇东北 10 公里处，海拔 2795 米。台顶面积最小，仅 7 万平方米。台上曾建有望海楼，据传登楼能远眺东海日出。今楼已毁，但登此台晨观日出，眺望群山秀色，欣赏云海变幻，依然壮丽非凡。现仅存北宋宣和年间（1119—1125 年）创建的笠子塔。从形制来看，该塔应为一座覆钵式的喇嘛塔。

西台　又称挂月峰，距台怀镇 23 公里，海拔 2773 米，面积约 28 万平方米。台地的周围群山拱围，岩石幽深，峰顶旧建法雷寺，供奉文殊乘狮像。

南台　又称锦绣峰，距台怀镇南面 25 公里，海拔 2485 米，台顶面积约 14 万平方米。山峰峭拔，烟光凝翠，景色甚佳。顶上建有普济寺，内供智慧文殊像。农历四月，北面四台还是冰天雪地，南台山腰却已百花怒放。

北台　又称叶斗峰，约距台怀镇 25 公里，为五台之最高峰，海拔 3058 米，顶天立地，有“华北屋脊”之称。台顶建有灵应寺，内供无垢文殊像。

中台　又称翠石峰，距台怀 10 公里，台顶面积约 15 万平方米。与四台相比，中台的主要特点是大。峰的西北面有太华池，北有甘露泉，东南有玉龙池，池旁有三株泉，是南北五溪流水的发源地。台顶有演教寺，内供文殊像。还有明朝建的祈光塔，四角各有小塔，象征东西南北中五台。

十大寺院

佛光寺　位于五台县的佛光新村。寺内现存正殿即原东大殿，建于唐大中十一年（公元 857 年），稍晚于唐建中三年（公元 782 年）所建南禅寺正殿，在全国现存的木结构建筑中居第二位。佛光寺的唐代建筑、唐代雕塑、唐代壁画、唐代题记，历史价值和艺术价值颇高，被称为“唐代四绝”。

显通寺　显通寺位于五台山内台怀镇北侧。寺内的七处九会殿，是明代万历三十四年（1606 年）神宗命妙峰法师用磨砖砌成的一座华严道场。该寺初建于东汉永平年间（公元 58—75 年），原名大孚灵鹫寺，后北魏孝文帝再建，名花园寺。唐太宗时重修，名华严寺。明太祖朱元璋重修后赐额“大显通寺”。后来历经扩建修葺，形成今日规模。寺宇面积 8 万平方米，各种建筑 400 余间。特色明显，保存完好。

塔院寺　位于五台山台怀镇显通寺南侧，原是五台山显通寺的塔院。明代时重修舍利塔，独成一寺，因院内有大白塔，故名塔院寺。耸入云天的大白塔，是寺内的主要标志，在五台山群寺簇拥下极其壮观。

菩萨顶　位于五台山台怀镇显通寺北侧灵鹫峰上，是五台山规模最大的黄教寺院。寺院创建于北魏孝文帝年间，历代曾多次重修。明永乐以后，蒙藏喇嘛教徒进驻五台山，遂成为五台山黄庙之首。全寺占地 45 亩，顺山就势建筑殿宇，布局严谨。寺前有石阶 108 级。山门内有天王殿、钟鼓楼、大雄宝殿等建筑。各殿均用三彩琉璃瓦覆盖。

殊像寺　位于普陀宗乘庙西面，狮子沟北麓。乾隆二十六年（1761

年），乾隆帝陪皇太后到山西五台山文殊菩萨道场——殊像寺进香，见文殊妙相庄严，令人起敬，“默识其像以归”。回到京师，太后即令人按五台山文殊模样雕刻石像供于香山宝相寺。乾隆三十九年（1774年），乾隆帝敕命内务府仿五台山殊像寺规制，按香山文殊相貌在承德修建此庙。因该庙喇嘛皆为满族，故清廷称此庙为家庙。

碧山寺　位于台怀镇东北 2 公里北台山麓，始建于明英宗年间，是五台山最大的十方禅寺。所谓“十方”，是指凡出家僧人和四方居士到此，都可以免费食宿，如果从这里启程时缺少路费，寺内还会周济一些，所以很多朝山教徒都把这里作为必朝之地。

金阁寺　金阁寺位于山西五台山南台之北，中台之南，除五座台顶的寺庙建筑外，金阁寺所处的地势最高，海拔 1900 米。金阁寺与中国密宗的传播和密宗创始人之一的不空法师有着极其密切的关系。

南山寺　始建于元代，整个寺院共有七层，分为三大部分，下三层名为极乐寺，中间一层名为善德堂，上三层称作佑国寺。

寺内的石雕和泥塑最有特点，内容包括佛教传说、道教典故以及林木花草等图案，刀工细致，构图精妙，堪称五台山一绝。

龙泉寺　龙泉寺位于五台山台怀镇南 5 公里九龙岗山腰，故又名“九龙岗”。龙泉寺原为杨家将家庙，寺旁有泉曰“龙泉”，寺因此而得名。 始建于宋代，民国初期重建，占地 15950 平方米，殿堂僧舍 165 间。现存影壁、台级、牌坊和三座院落。

普济寺　普济寺距台怀镇南面 25 公里，海拔 2485 米，台顶面积约 14 万平方米。山峰陡峭，繁花似锦，因之取名为“锦绣峰”。顶上建有普济寺，内供智慧文殊像。

遗产价值

五台山历史悠久，在长达 15 个世纪的发展中逐渐形成了规模庞大、宏伟壮观、古朴庄严且与自然环境和谐统一的寺庙建筑群。其寺庙建筑的规制和时间跨度，都堪称亚洲之最、世界之最。这些寺庙的规模大小不一、形制布局各有特色，充分体现了“天人合一”的理念，并将儒家的“中庸之道”、老子的“万物负阴抱阳”的哲学思想发挥到了极致，为研究中国佛教发展史提供了特殊的见证，具有独特的内涵和价值，在世界文化之林中独树一帜。

泰　山

泰山，古名岱山，又称岱宗，位于山东省中部，前邻孔子故里曲阜，背依泉城济南，东西长约 200 公里，南北宽约 50 公里，面积达 426 平方公里。主峰玉皇顶在泰安市北，海拔约 1545 米。绵亘于泰安、济南、莱芜三市之间，贯穿山东中部，主脉、支脉、余脉涉及周边十余县。自然景观雄伟壮美，有数千年中华文化的渗透和积累，被誉为中华民族精神文化的缩影。

风景名胜

泰山风景以壮丽著称。累叠的山势，厚重的形体，苍松巨石的烘托，云烟岚光的变化，使它在雄浑中兼有明丽，静穆中透着神奇，成为我国山水名胜的集大成者。

泰山风景名胜以泰山主峰为中心，呈放射状分布，由自然景观与人文景观融合而成。风景区内共有山峰 156 座，崖岭 138 座，名洞 72 处，奇石 72 块，溪谷 130 条，瀑潭 64 处，名泉 72 眼，古树名木万余株，寺庙 58 座，古遗址 128 处，碑碣 1239 块，摩崖刻石 1277 处。主要分布在岱阳、岱顶、岱阴及灵岩。

主要景点

十八盘　泰山有 3 个十八盘。自开山至龙门为“慢十八”，再至升仙坊为“不紧不慢又十八”，又至南天门为“紧十八”，共计 1600 余阶。“紧十八”西崖有巨岩悬空，侧影似佛头侧枕，俗名迎客佛。泰山十八盘是泰山登山盘路中最险要的一段，倾角 70° – 80° ，为泰山的主要标志之一。此处两山崖壁如削，陡峭的盘路镶嵌其中，远远望去，恰似天门云梯。

南天门　在十八盘尽处，旧称三天门、天门关，海拔 1460 米。飞龙岩与翔凤岭之间的低坳处，双峰夹峙，仿佛天门自开。门为阁楼式建筑，石砌拱形门洞，额题“南天门”。红墙点缀，黄色琉璃瓦盖顶，气势雄伟。

岱庙　号称华夏名山第一庙。岱庙始建于秦汉，宋代扩修，是历代帝王的泰山行宫。天贶殿，位于仁安门北，是岱庙主体建筑，建于宋大中祥符二年（1009 年）。大殿建于长方形石台之上，三面雕栏围护，长 48.7 米，宽 19.73 米，高 22.3 米。规模宏大，辉煌壮丽，与北京故宫太和殿，曲阜大成殿齐名。

四大奇观

泰山日出　这是泰山最壮观的奇景之一，也是泰山的重要标志。岱顶观日历来为游人所向往，也使许多文人墨客为之引亢高歌。当黎明时分，游人站在岱顶举目远眺东方，一线晨曦由灰暗变成淡黄，又由淡黄变成橘红。漫天彩霞与地平线上的茫茫云海融为一体，犹如巨幅油画从天而降。浮光耀金的海面上，日轮掀开了云幕，撩开了霞帐，像一个飘荡的宫灯，冉冉升起在天际，须臾间，金光四射，群峰尽染……

云海玉盘　泰山云雾可谓呼风唤雨，变幻无穷：有时白云滚滚，如浪似雪；有时乌云翻滚，形同翻江倒海。站在岱顶俯瞰下界，可见片片白云与滚滚乌云融为一体，汇成滔滔奔流的“大海”，令人心潮起伏，恍若置身世外。

晚霞夕照　当夕阳西下，漫步泰山极顶，仰望西天，那五颜六色的云朵，烂若丹霞，皎如素雪，满天的霞光映照在“大海”之中，壮丽而富情趣，不由让人陶陶然。

黄河金带　晚霞夕照与黄河金带的神奇景色，与季节和气候有着很大的关系。时值秋季，天高气爽，放眼四望“江山如此多娇”的壮美景色尽收眼底。

四大禅院

灵岩寺　坐落于泰山西北麓，位于济南市长清区万德镇境内。始建于东晋，距今已有 1600 多年的历史。该寺历史悠久，佛教底蕴深厚，自唐代起就与浙江国清寺、南京栖霞寺、湖北玉泉寺并称“海内四大名刹”，并位列其首。

普照寺　泰山普照寺位于岱麓凌汉峰下，秀峰环抱，翠柏掩映，亭台楼阁，气象峥嵘。传为六朝时建，历代皆有拓修。寺院以大雄宝殿、摩松楼为主体建筑，形成三进式院落。两侧配以殿庑、禅房和花园等。内有筛月亭，亭下置石桌，敲击有钟磬声。冯玉祥隐居泰山时，于亭上题联云：“曲径云深宜种竹，空亭月朗正当楼”。后院为菊林院，有松一株，冠大如棚，清光绪间明士何焕章游山至此，题“一品大夫”。现辟为纪念馆。有联云：“松曰好青，竹曰好绿；天吾一砖，地吾一瓦。”

竹林寺　在泰山西溪谷中。寺周翠竹环抱，松柏簇拥，风景十分秀美，向有“小径沿山，清流夹道，蟠曲羊肠，景随步换”之誉。始建年代无考，自唐后屡兴屡废。据记，元代元贞年间名僧法海重修，声名远播，以至“东振齐鲁，北抵幽燕，西逾赵魏，南距大河，莫不闻风趋赴”。后竹林寺在一场火灾中焚毁，现又在原址上仿唐代风格重新修建。

玉泉寺　玉泉寺位于岱顶北，有公路与泰安城相通。寺东南有莲花峰、香炉峰、周明堂故址、天井湾；西为摩天岭；南临卖饭棚子；北依返倒山、长城岭。群山环抱，密林掩映，高崖飞涧，人迹罕至。由北魏僧人创建，金代僧人善宁重建，元代僧普谨增建七佛阁，后屡兴屡废。

遗产价值

泰山与中国的其他四座名山——南岳衡山、西岳华山、北岳恒山、中岳嵩山合称“五岳”，泰山有“五岳之首”、“天下第一山”之誉。古代先民往往把雄伟奇特的东岳视为神灵，把山神作为祈求风调雨顺的对象来崇拜，于是，地处东方的泰山便成了“万物孕育之所”、“神灵之宅”。自古以来，中国人就崇拜泰山，有“泰山安，四海皆安”的说法。相传远古时即有72位君主来到泰山巡狩祭祀，秦始皇登峰遇雨，留下五大夫松的传说；汉武帝八至泰山，惊叹“高矣！极矣！大矣！特矣！壮矣！赫矣！骇矣！惑矣！”在泰山封禅和祭祀，并且在泰山上下建庙塑神，刻石题字。古代的文人雅士更对泰山仰慕备至，纷纷前来游历，作诗撰文。泰山宏大的山体上留下了20余处古建筑群，2200余处碑碣石刻。

黄　山

黄山，原名黟山，因峰岩青黑苍黛故名。相传轩辕黄帝曾在此炼丹，笃信道教的唐玄宗，遂于天宝六年改名为“黄山”。明朝地理学家徐霞客曾两次登临黄山，赞叹：“薄海内外，无如徽之黄山。登黄山，天下无山，观止矣！”1990 年 12 月，黄山风景名胜区作为一项文化与自然双重遗产被联合国教科文组织列入《世界遗产名录》，2004 年 2 月成为世界地质公园。

黄山雄踞风景秀丽的安徽南部，是我国最著名的山岳风景区之一。南北长约 40 公里，东西宽约 30 公里，山脉总面积 1200 平方公里，核心景区面积约 160.6 平方公里，地跨市内黟县、休宁县和黄山区、徽州区，面积 1078 平方公里。

黄山经历了漫长的造山运动和地壳抬升，以及冰川和自然风化作用，才形成其特有的峰林结构。黄山群峰林立，素有“三十六大峰，三十六小峰”之称。主峰莲花峰海拔高达 1864.8 米，与平旷的光明顶、险峻的天都峰一起，雄居景区中心，周围还有 77 座千米以上的山峰，群峰叠翠，有机地组合成一幅波澜壮阔、气势磅礴、令人叹为观止的立体画卷。

黄山山体主要由燕山期花岗岩构成，垂直节理发育，侵蚀切割强烈，断裂和裂隙纵横交错，长期受水溶蚀，形成瑰丽多姿的花岗岩洞穴与孔道，使之峡谷交错，关口处处。前山岩体节理稀疏，岩石多球状风化，山体浑厚壮观；后山岩体节理密集，多为垂直状风化，山体峻峭，形成了“前山雄伟，后山秀丽”的地貌特征。

生物资源

黄山是一座天然动植物公园，名花古木，珍禽异兽，种类繁多。黄山自然环境条件复杂，生态系统稳定平衡，植被垂直分带明显，群落完整。高山沼泽和高山草甸是绿色植物荟萃之地。森林覆盖率为 56%，植被覆盖率达 83%。黄山野生植物有 1452 种。黄山上属国家一类保护的有水杉 1 种，二类保护的有银杏等 4 种，三类保护的 8 种；有石斛等 10 个物种属濒危物种。首次在黄山发现或以黄山命名的植物有 28 种，尤以名茶“黄山毛峰”、名药“黄山灵芝”驰名中外。黄山动物种类 300 多种，有梅花鹿、黑麂、毛冠鹿、苏门羚、长尾雉等 14 种国家级保护的野生动物。

风景名胜

六大景区

玉屏景区　以玉屏楼为中心，莲花峰和天都峰为主体，沿途有“蓬莱三岛”、“百步云梯”、“一线天”、“新一线天”、“鳌鱼洞”等奇妙景观。天都峰位于玉屏峰南，相距 1 公里，是黄山三大主峰中最为险峻的山峰，海拔 1830 米。古诗赞曰：“任它五岳归来客，一见天都也叫奇。” 天都峰顶有“登峰造极”石刻，使人有“海到尽处天是岸，山登绝顶我为峰”之感。

北海景区　是黄山景区的腹地，在光明顶与始信峰、狮子峰、白鹅峰之间，是一片海拔 1600 米左右的高山开阔地带，面积 1316 公顷。该景区以峰为体，汇集了峰、石、矼、坞、台和松、云奇景，构成一幅幅伟、奇、幻、险的天然图画，是黄山的风景窗口。

温泉景区　古称桃源仙境。景区以揽胜桥为中心向四周辐射，桃花溪和逍遥溪贯穿其中。由此到慈光阁，仅 25 分钟步程。慈光阁，原为慈光寺，古称朱砂庵。始建于明朝嘉靖年间，万历三十八年钦赐“护国慈光寺”。

白云景区　位于黄山西部，面积 1655 公倾。景区以钓桥庵为中心，景致清幽，峰峦叠峙。集松、石、泉于一体，独具黄山山水之胜。

松谷景区　黄山素有“前山险，后山秀”之说，后山即指黄山北大门的松谷景区。该景区位于黄山北坡，是狮子峰、骆驼峰、书箱峰、宝塔峰之间的山谷合称。游览松谷景区可以观赏到仙人观海、关公挡曹等怪石巧石，翡翠池、五龙潭等水景，芙蓉居、松谷禅林等古建筑。

云谷景区 位于黄山东部，海拔高度仅890米，是一处地势较低、略显开阔的谷地。明代文士傅严漫游至此，应掷钵禅僧之求，手书“云谷”二字，此后禅院改名“云谷寺”。云谷主要景点有云谷山庄、古树、怪石、“九龙瀑”和“百丈泉”等。

黄山四绝

黄山四绝，是指黄山的四种独特景观，分别为：奇松、怪石、云海、温泉。

奇松即黄山松，是由黄山独特的地貌、气候而形成的中国松树的一种变体。所“绝”之处，在于它根不着土，却能寄生在坚硬的石头上，从石缝中吸取所需要的养分和水，且能生长得苍翠欲滴，生机勃勃，可见其生命力之旺盛。黄山“四绝”之一的怪石，以奇取胜，以多著称。“云海”为黄山一绝，自古黄山云成海。黄山是云雾之乡，以峰为体，以云为衣，一年四季皆可观，尤以冬景最佳。黄山“四绝”之一的温泉（古称汤泉），源出海拔850米的紫云峰下，水质以含重碳酸为主，可饮可浴。传说轩辕黄帝就是在此沐浴七七四十九日返老还童、羽化飞升的，故又称之为“灵泉”。

遗产价值

黄山以博大的胸怀，将各历史时期、各社会阶层的各种文化意识和行为融为一体，在其自然景物与环境之间，形成了特定的黄山文化，是中国著名山水画派的发祥地之一。

黄山的历史文化沉积丰厚，历代遗留的寺庙、亭阁、盘道、古桥和摩崖石刻共200多处，散布在奇峰秀水之间，增添了不少高贵气息和典雅氛围。

庐山国家公园

“横看成岭侧成峰，远近高低各不同。不识庐山真面目，只缘身在此山中。”

苏东坡的这首《题西林壁》将庐山远观和近看的景象淋漓尽致地表现出来。由此可见，文化一旦以一种独特的方式融汇在自然之中，它便能够充实和强化自然美，并产生画龙点睛的妙趣，使其更生动，更具魅力。庐山便是这样一座千古文化名山。

身处庐山之中，感受它的温差，感受它的云山雾绕，感受它的变幻莫测，感受它的千姿百态，你将被这美景所震撼。

庐山是一座历史悠久的文化名山，名胜古迹遍布。千百年来，无数文人墨客、名人志士在此留下了浩如烟海的丹青墨迹和脍炙人口的篇章。相传夏禹王疏九江来过庐山，秦始皇南巡时也曾登临；陶渊明、李白、杜甫、白居易、范仲淹、苏轼、陆游、王阳明等历代大文豪都曾纷纷赋诗填词，岳飞、文天祥、李时珍、徐霞客等亦曾到此游历。据统计，现存历代名人歌颂庐山的诗词达4000多首。其中苏轼写庐山云雾：“不识庐山真面目，只缘身在此山中”；李白写马尾瀑：“飞流直下三千尺，疑是银河落九天”；毛泽东写吕洞宾修仙而居的仙人洞：“天生一个仙人洞，无限风光在险峰”，等等，均是情景交融的千古绝唱。

山上的历代名家书法、碑刻均有很高的艺术价值，是我国旅游文化的瑰宝。

生物资源

庐山生物资源丰富，生态系统完整。这里气候夏季凉爽，云雾频繁，植物显示出中国第三纪植被特征。庐山植物生长茂盛，植被丰富，随着海拔的增高，地表水热状况垂直分布，由山麓到山顶分别生长着常绿阔叶林，常绿及落叶阔叶混交林。植物有210科、735属、1720种，分为温带、热带、亚热带、东亚、北美和我国7个类型，是一座天然植物园。庐山有鸟类171种，在鄱阳湖国家级候鸟保护区越冬的候鸟达100余万只，其中有世界最大的白鹤群，占世界白鹤总数的95%。

风景名胜

庐山长约25公里，宽约20公里，最高峰汉阳峰海拔1474米，牯岭街1167米。巍巍的庐山，远看：一山飞峙大江边；近看：千峰携手紧相连；横看：铁壁铜墙立湖岸；侧看：擎天一柱耸云间。

主要景点

庐山主要风景名胜有牯岭镇、仙人洞、五老峰、三叠泉、东林寺等。风景名胜区面积302平方公里，外围保护地带500平方公里。庐山有独特的第四纪冰川遗迹，有河流、湖泊、坡地、山峰等多种地貌类型，有地质公园之称。庐山独特的庐山文化，具有重要的科学价值与美学价值。

牯岭镇 是庐山上一座奇特的山城，有“云中花园城市”之称。出镇往西，可到西湖。西湖又名花径湖，其状如提琴，又因山泉声响如琴音，故又名“琴湖”。这是庐山第二人工湖，面积10万平方米，湖心亭榭临湖而立，风景极佳。

仙人洞 沿锦绣谷小道西行约500米即可到达仙人洞。洞系自然风化而成，高6米，宽12米，深14米。洞顶为参差如手指的岩石覆盖，形似佛手，故又名“佛手岩”。洞中有清泉自洞顶石缝流出，名“一滴泉”。“山高水滴千年不断，石上清泉万石长流”一联，是其真实写照。至清代，佛手岩才成为道家的洞天福地，改称“仙人洞”。现存“称师亦称祖，是道仍是儒”的吕仙塑像和神龛是20世纪70年代重建的。

五老峰 从山麓海会寺仰望五老峰，似五位老人并坐，故有此名。如果从不同的角度去看五老峰，就会发现这几个峰峦，或像迎风啸吟的诗仙，或像雄心未已的暮年壮士，或像豪情奔放的学者，或像阅尽沧桑的老僧，或像垂钓鄱阳湖的鹤发渔翁。当年，大诗人李白睹此不禁感慨：“庐山东南五老峰，青天削出金芙蓉”。

三叠泉 三叠泉又名三级泉、水帘泉，古人称“匡庐瀑布，首推三叠”，誉为“庐山第一奇观”。由大月山、五老峰的涧水汇合，从大月山流出，经过五老峰背，由北崖悬口注入大盘石上，又飞泻到二级大盘石，再喷洒至三级盘石，形成三叠。抛珠溅玉的三叠泉宛如白鹭千只，上下奋飞；又如万斛明珠，自九天飞洒。风物之美，直如仙境。

东林寺　东林寺位于庐山西麓，是我国佛教净土宗的发源地。东晋太元十一年（公元 386 年），名僧慧远在此建寺讲学，倡导“弥陀净土法门”，并创设莲社。东林寺在唐时达到极盛，有殿、厢、塔、室共 300 余间。扬州高僧鉴真东渡日本之前，曾来过东林寺，后偕东林寺僧智恩同渡日本，慧远和东林净土宗的教义也随之传入日本，至今日本东林教仍以庐山东林寺慧远为始祖。

遗产价值

庐山是中国古代教育基地和宗教中心。白鹿洞书院创建于公元 940 年，居中国古代四大书院之首。宋代理学大师朱熹在此提出的教育思想成为中国古代教育的准则，在世界教育史上也有重要影响。

白鹿洞原是唐代洛阳人李渤年轻时隐居求学之地。南唐升元年间，在此处“建学置田”，正式称之为“庐山国学”，此为白鹿洞开办学校之始。北宋初年，各地设置书院，庐山国学乃改称为白鹿洞书院，从此规模逐步扩大，成为全国四大书院之一。

公元 391 年，佛教领袖慧远建立东林寺，是中国最早的寺庙园林。慧远在庐山活动了 36 年，创建净土法门，使庐山成为中国南方的佛教中心。公元 5 世纪时，南朝道士陆修静在庐山开创道教南天师派。唐代马祖道一在山上开创佛教临济宗和沩仰宗，影响极大。宋代，庐山有寺庙多达 361 座。明清以后，伊斯兰教、基督教、天主教也在庐山建堂传教。经过 1600 多年的发展，庐山已形成一山兼聚五教的罕见现象。

新疆天山

新疆天山，指中国境内的东天山，长达 1760 公里，占天山总长度的三分之二以上，横亘新疆全境，是准噶尔盆地和塔里木盆地的天然地理分界，也是新疆地理的独特标志。

新疆天山属全球七大山系之一，是世界温带干旱地区最大的山脉链，也是全球最大的东西走向的独立山脉。新疆天山世界自然遗产地，由昌吉回族自治州的博格达、巴音郭楞蒙古自治州的巴音布鲁克和阿克苏地区的托木尔、伊犁哈萨克自治州的喀拉峻—库尔德宁等四个区域组成，总面积达 5759 平方公里。

生物资源

尽管天山山系中众多山峰终年为冰雪覆盖，但是在 3000 米雪线以下，动植物资源却异常丰富。托木尔峰和博格达峰的山麓和河谷地区，满山遍野长满了云杉和塔松，四季常青。托木尔峰南北坡的茂密森林，是新疆主要木材产区之一。云杉林中，到处可见野蔷薇、党参等生长，各种药用植物达 80 多种；亚高山草甸带，一片片金莲花迎风开放，花枝招展；雪线附近的乱石堆中，凌寒怒放的雪莲散发着清香，为这一片冰天雪地的世界带来了勃勃生机。天山地区也是优良牧草的基因库，已发现的禾本科植物就达 55 种，对发展畜牧业具有重要作用。

天山之中还有许多珍禽异兽，海拔 3000 米以下的峰峦、山地的密林深处和草原之中，是各种飞禽走兽栖息、繁衍的天然场所。天山的旱獭、水獭、盘羊、雪豹、猞猁、天山鹿、天山羚羊等是受保护的珍贵野生动物。

风景名胜

著名雪峰

在天山山系中，海拔在 5000 米以上的山峰大约有数十座，除最高峰托木尔峰外，主要还有中哈边界的汗腾格里峰、博格达峰、瓦斯基配卡维里山、德拉斯克巴山等。这些高耸入云的山峰，终年为冰雪覆盖，远远望去，闪耀着银辉的雪峰雄伟壮观，顶天立地，充满着千年不解的神秘。

博格达峰　博格达峰，海拔 5445 米，是天山东部博格达山的最高峰。山峰 3800 米以上是终年不化的积雪区，白雪皑皑，茫茫无际，故有“雪海”之称。整个博格达山脉共有 300 多条冰川，而博格达峰区占了四分之一以上。博格达峰北坡的一条冰川，面积约 11 平方公里，是博格达峰区最大的一条冰川。这条冰川夏季消融强烈，融水汇成许多冰川河道，迭宕奔腾，咆哮而下，震耳欲聋。

在阜康市境内的博格达峰半山腰，有一个半月形的天然高山湖泊，人称“天池”。湖水清澈，晶莹如玉。其主湖外，在东西两侧还有两处水面，东侧为东小天池，古名“黑龙潭”，位于天池东 500 米处，传说是西王母沐浴梳洗的地方，故又名“梳洗涧”、“浴仙盆”。

托木尔峰　“明月出天山，苍茫云海间”。托木尔峰，这是比博格达峰更加雄奇伟岸的天山雪峰，它的峰尖直插云霄，被称作“天山最高峰”。“托木尔”维吾尔语意为“铁”，即“铁峰”，位于阿克苏地区温宿县境内的中国与吉尔吉斯斯坦国境线附近，中哈界峰汗腾格里峰西南 20 公里处。周围有 6000 米以上的高峰十余座。托木尔峰地区的冰川面积达 2800 多平方公里，是中国最大的现代冰川区。其主峰及周围共 10 万公顷山地于 1980 年被列为自治区级自然保护区，主要保护高山冰川及下部森林、生物群落及生态环境。峰区以北为西汉乌孙故地，是天马、汗血马的原产地。

主要景点

天池石门　石门是进入天池风景区的天然山口，两侧宽约百米，最窄处仅十余米。石门两峰夹峙，一线中通，是河道切割形成的峡谷，故又称“石峡”。石壁巍峨，高达数十米，长约 100 米，天开奇绝，犹如打开的两扇门板。石色赭暗，如同铁铸，故称“铁门关”。石门内三工河穿流而过，水旋路转，河水湍急，浪花飞溅。正可谓：“鬼斧神工刀劈就，一线通途上青天。”

王母脚盆　“王母脚盆”又称“小龙潭”，位于“五十盘天”第三盘的右下方，海拔1660米，由天池湖水从地下渗漏入池，水似琼浆玉液，犹如王母的冰肌玉肤，传说是“王母娘娘的洗脚盆”。池周围塔松竞秀，倒映湖中，极其清幽深邃。

西小天池瀑布　过了西小天池不远，路右侧的瀑布即为“西小天池瀑布”，瀑布凌空，垂挂数十米，犹如一卷垂落的银帘，银帘的后面，隐现着王母娘娘梳洗的倩影。近代方志学家王树楠有诗诵道：“半亭飞瀑挂瑶虹，万仞层冰镂玉龙。晴霭断桥笼弱柳，怒涛深涧响寒松。”今于原址重建“闻涛亭”：八角、两层、红柱、黄琉璃瓦。规制崇宏，颇有气象。

鳄鱼吐珠　翻过东小天池南面的山头，即达大天池北岸。天池北岸是一座巨大的天然堤坝，由古冰川终碛垄及山体崩落物迭加堆积而成，高289米，整个大坝似一条鳄鱼尾巴，故称“鳄鱼坝”。大坝东首建有人工水闸，名“鳄鱼闸”。天池水下泻，形成一条十多米高的瀑布，称“鳄鱼吐珠”，水溅“黑龙峡”谷地，汇成山涧溪流，北流不远形成一潭，即东小天池。“鳄鱼吐珠”、“冰潭银帘”和“悬泉飞瀑”合称“天池三瀑”。

西王母祖庙　位于天池东岸，博格达峰的西北方向，海拔2000米左右，它是新疆最古老、海拔最高的道观之一。传说王母娘娘在此修道成仙，故称之为西王母祖庙。

遗产价值

新疆天山是我国西北干旱地区典型的山岳型自然景观，它包括高山冰雪带、台原草被带、中山峡谷森林带、低山草原带和戈壁、沙漠带等十分明显的自然景观垂直带谱。具有重要的干旱区山地生物多样性价值、地方特有植物种子资源遗传价值、濒危野生动物栖息地科学价值，以及以远古瑶池神话及宗教、民族风情为内涵的多元文化保存价值。

武夷山

武夷山座落于福建省北部武夷山市西南，全景区面积 60 平方公里，属典型的丹霞地貌，素有“碧水丹山”、“奇秀甲东南”之美誉。武夷山有黄山之奇，华山之险，庐山飞瀑之胜，桂林山水之秀，博采众长，小巧玲珑，具有综合性特点。

武夷山常绿阔叶林是中国中亚热带常绿阔叶林分布最为典型、物种最丰富和森林生态系统保存最完整的。武夷山集山岳、河川风景于一身，不仅“奇、秀、美、古”兼而有之，而且在山与水的紧密结合、人文与自然和谐统一上达到绝妙的境界。清澈碧绿的九曲绕山而行，曲折萦回。发育典型的丹霞山临水而立，千姿百态。又有 3000 余年的古文化遗存洒落在溪畔峰麓、岩壁洞穴。自然山水之中溶注着浓郁的文化气息。

在中国文化史上的地位，武夷山与泰山各有千秋。泰山孕育孔子，孔子集前古学术思想之大成，开创儒学，成为中国文化传统的主要骨干。武夷山造就了朱熹，朱熹集孔子以下学术思想之大成，构建了完整的儒学思想体系——朱子理学，成为中国封建社会后期 700 余年间的正统思想。因而国内外学者普遍认为，在中国文化史、传统史、思想史、教育史和礼教史上影响最大的，前推孔子，后推朱熹。

风景名胜

主要景区

天游峰景区　天游峰是一条由北向南延伸的岩脊，东接仙游岩，西连仙掌峰，削崖耸起，壁立万仞，高耸群峰之上。每当雨后乍晴，晨曦初露之时，白茫茫的烟云，犹如大海的波涛，汹涌澎湃。站在一览台上观望云海，宛如置身蓬莱仙境之中，故名“天游”。峰上名木古树众多，常绿阔叶林郁郁葱葱。明代著名地理学家徐霞客赞道：“不临溪而能尽九溪之胜，此峰固应第一也。”

峰顶胡麻涧旁的石壁上，有历代摩崖石刻近百处。其中最大的一幅为“第一山”，系道光壬辰冬武显将军徐庆超题写。

九曲溪景区　自古山以水秀，而武夷之水精华在九曲溪。九曲溪全长约 7.5 公里，溪水碧清，曲曲弯弯，如玉带盘绕群峰。山回溪折，折复绕山，环结成“曲曲山回转，峰峰水抱流”的九曲之胜。山与水的完美结合是九曲溪最突出的特色。曲折萦回的九曲溪贯穿于丹崖群峰之间，如玉带串珍珠，将“三十六峰”，“九十九岩”连为一体，构成 " 一溪贯群山，两岸列仙岫 " 的独特自然美景。

武夷山中最著名的一些山峰和高插于悬崖峭壁上的神秘悬棺都列在九曲溪边。景区内还有遇林亭宋代瓷窑遗址、武夷宫等游览景点，极具人文价值。

大红袍景区　大红袍景区位于武夷山风景区的中心部位，景区著名大峡谷“九龙窠”内。这是一条受东西向断裂构造控制发育的深长谷地，沟壑深切，两侧长条状单面山高耸、石骨嶙峋的九座危峰，分南北对峙骈列，独特的节理发育，使峰脊高低起伏，有如九条巨龙欲腾又伏。峡口矗立着一座浑圆的峰岩，像一颗龙珠居于九龙之间，势如九龙戏珠，高远眺望，惟妙惟肖。谷地中、崖壁上，劲松苍翠，修竹相扶，绿意葱葱。久负盛名的武夷茶王“大红袍”就生长在峡谷的最底部。六株古茶树枝繁叶茂，已有 300 余年的历史，其成品的色、香、味均在乌龙茶之首，故有“茶王”的美誉。

主要景点

武夷大峡谷　武夷大峡谷拥有青龙大瀑布景区及大峡谷漂流两大游览项目。青龙大瀑布位于武夷山大峡谷公园西侧，瀑布周围森林茂密，水源十分丰富。深谷绝壁上，堪称“华东第一漂”的大峡谷漂流河床属桐木溪的一段，该溪为九曲溪的源头之一，是武夷山最清澈最纯净的水源。

龙井山　龙井山位于武夷山自然风景区东南面 8 公里，北距武夷山市区 12 公里处。峡谷内一年四季花木繁茂，鸟类繁多，自然生态均衡，被一些科考人员称为“绿色之肺”。

史书记载，自宋代以来，龙井山祈雨堂就是当地百姓祈雨求福的地方，已成为武夷山东部最热闹、最有影响力的祈雨场所，至今还有当年祈雨所用的起水方井遗存。主要景点有：龙井瀑布、龙王岩、深山大湖、观景台、祈雨堂等。

黄岗山 黄岗山海拔约2160米，是中国东南最高峰，号称“华东大陆屋脊”。由于山势陡峭，群峰林立，该地区常年云雾缭绕，雨量充沛，气候温暖，形成了我国东南大陆面积最大，保存最完整的中亚热带森林生态系统。黄岗山顶属武夷山自然保护区的核心区。由于保护区的特殊性质，并未完全对外开放。

水帘洞 武夷山水帘洞为武夷山著名的七十二洞之一，位于章堂涧之北。朱熹名句“问渠那得清如许，为有源头活水来”的篆体刻字掩映于丹崖之上。或称“唐曜洞天”，古来道观多构建于此。洞室宽敞明亮，设石桌石凳，供人休憩。设石栏护卫，凭栏可赏洞外飘洒飞散的水帘。

武夷宫 武夷宫又名会仙观、冲佑观、万年宫，坐落于大王峰南麓，前临九曲溪口，是历代帝王祭祀武夷君的地方，也是宋代六大名观之一。后几经兵燹荼毒，虽屡有修葺，但终未能恢复到昔日面貌。2008年，武夷宫主殿得以重修，而且，全面恢复武夷宫的计划也在逐步进行着。

武夷山架壑船棺 武夷山架壑船棺、虹桥板是古越人丧葬遗存，距今已有3000多年历史。所谓船棺，其实就是一种形似小船的棺柩。船棺外形分两类：一类为两头翘起如船形；一类方形其状如盒，俗称“函”。它们停放在离地面几十米的峭壁上，千年不毁，故人们把它们看成宝物，誉之为“敞艇”、“仙舟”、“仙人屋”、“金棺材”、“沉香船”等。“虹桥板”，是用来支架船棺或架设栈道的木板，是架壑船棺的附属物。船棺中随葬品极为古朴，且品种丰富。棺中棉布残片是中国迄今发现最早的棉纺织品实物，是研究我国先秦历史和已消逝的古闽族文化极为珍贵的资料。

遗产价值

武夷山是座历史文化名山。早在新石器时期，古越人就已在此繁衍生息。如今悬崖绝壁上遗留的“架壑船”和“虹桥板”，就是古越人留下来的遗迹。西汉时，汉武帝曾遣使者到武夷山用干鱼祭祀武夷君。唐代，唐玄宗大封天下名山大川，武夷山也受到封表，并刻石记载，还明令保护山林，不准砍伐。唐末五代初，杜光庭在《洞天福地记》里把武夷山列为天下三十六洞天之一。宋绍圣二年（1095年），祈雨获应，又封武夷君为显道真人。

三清山国家公园

三清山位于中国江西省上饶市玉山县与德兴市交界处，为怀玉山脉主峰。因玉京、玉虚、玉华“三峰峻拔，如道教三清尊神（玉清元始天尊、上清灵宝天尊、太清道德天尊）列坐其巅”而得其名。三峰中以玉京峰为最高，海拔 1819.9 米，是江西省第五高峰，也是信江的源头。三清山是道教名山，风景秀丽，被誉为中国最秀丽的山峰。

三清山神奇壮丽的景观是与适宜的地质、气候分不开的，是地壳运动对地质作用长期变迁的产物。三清山在地质史上经历了 14 亿年的沧桑巨变。在距今二三千万年前，相继发生喜马拉雅期的造山运动，即新构造运动，山岳大幅抬升，伴随水力侵蚀作用的强烈下切，使地势高低差悬殊。由于三清山的地质环境正处于造山运动既频繁又剧烈的地段，所以断层密布，节理发育，尤其是垂向的断层和节理特别发育。山体不断抬升，长期风化侵蚀，加上重力崩解作用，形成了峰插云天、谷陷深渊的奇特地貌。三清山风景区的形成，可说是天工造物，是大自然的杰作。

生物资源

春来繁花似锦、姹紫嫣红；夏近绿荫飘浮、清爽宜人；秋去红叶尽染、色彩斑斓；冬至雪盖冰挂、玉树琼花。这正是三清山优越生态环境条件下充满生机与灵气的生态景观的真实写照。

三清山的生物世界经历了两亿多年的演化更替，孕育了现代三清山独特的中亚热带东方湿润常绿阔叶林生态系统，拥有高等植物 2373 种、野生动物 1728 种。在第四纪时期，三清山没有受到山岳冰川的侵袭，成为许多古老植物的避难所，使世界珍稀古老植物群落和物种的多样性得以遗存，也使三清山成了世界上不可多得的原生态生物乐园。在东亚—北美间断分布植物中，中国有 117 属，三清山有 68 属，占中国该类型属数的 58%。因此，三清山除了地质科学和地貌科学的重要价值外，还拥有突出的生物学和生态学价值。

道教文化

三清山道教文化肇始于晋代葛洪，因而葛洪在三清山拥有特殊地位。东晋升平年间，他与李尚书上三清山结庐炼丹，著书立说，宣扬道教教义，遂成了三清山的“开山始祖”、三清山道教的第一位传播者。

三清山得“道”弥彰。至唐朝时，道教被朝廷奉为国教，三清山的道教也随之兴盛起来。三清山上第一座道教建筑——老子宫观（此观被称为“三清福地”）在葛洪炼丹处拔地而起，三清山道教地位得以进一步巩固。自宋代尤其是明代以来，三清宫等道教建筑依山水走向，顺八卦方位，将自然景观与道家理念合而为一，方圆数十里道风浓郁，道境昭然。今人考三清宫为明代失踪皇帝——建文帝朱允炆藏身之所。三清山地当浙赣之交，东达沪杭，南通闽粤，西迎荆楚，北望苏皖，接黄山而携龙虎，近武夷而处其中。

风景名胜

景观特色

三清山山体南北长 12.2 公里，东西宽 6.3 公里，平面呈荷叶形，由东南向西北倾斜。由于处在造山运动频繁而剧烈的地带，因此三清山断层密布，山体不断抬升，又经长期风化侵蚀和重力的崩解作用，形成奇峰矗天、幽谷千刃的山岳绝景奇观。三清山东险、西奇、北秀、南绝，美在古朴自然，奇在形神兼备。仙灵众相，维妙维肖，遨游于清虚之境，出没于云雾之中，古为道家秘境。历代宫观建筑与雄险奇秀的自然景观融为一体，异彩纷呈，钟灵毓秀，故有“天下第一仙峰，世上无双福地”之誉。

主要景观

司春女神　司春女神位于南清园东北部，三清山标志性景观。整座山体造型就像一位秀发披肩的少女，天地造化，鬼斧神工。传说女神为西王母第 23 女，名瑶姬。世人认为她是春天的化身，因而又称之为“司春女神”。

三清奇松　三清奇松，是三清山景色中一大特色，主要的种类有台湾松和华东黄杉，大多数都生长在三清山千米的悬崖峭壁上面，风姿绰约，极具特色，与三清山奇峰构成一道靓丽的风景，自来为游客所称道。

奇峰怪石　三清山奇峰怪石众多，其中引人入胜的要数三清山十大绝景，最标志性的景观要数女神峰和巨蟒峰，造型奇妙，惟妙惟肖。这些奇峰怪石的形成是由于花岗岩体经历了日晒雨淋，风化剥蚀，使那些石头粗坯受到了无数次的精雕细刻而形成的。还有玉女开怀、老道拜月、猴王观宝、观音赏曲、三龙出海、神龙戏松等数千座怪石，就像天然的石雕博物馆。

云海仙境　云海是三清山风景中最为奇特的绝景。三清山秀峰叠峙，危崖突兀，幽壑纵横。气流在山峦间穿行，上行下跃，环流活跃。漫天的云雾和层积云，随风飘移，时而上升，时而下坠，时而回旋，时而舒展，构成一幅奇特的千变万化的云海大观。三清山景区群峰耸立，峡谷纵横，每当云海涌来时，整个三清山景区就被分成诸多云的海洋，给人仙境般的感觉。

三清山杜鹃　每年四五月份，三清山杜鹃花就开了，届时，满山遍野的高山杜鹃如团团彩云，沿途数里，香气袭人，使三清山成了花的世界。这里的杜鹃品种有云锦、猴头、紫丁香、鹿角、马银花、映山红等 19 种。女神峰至玉台一带的杜鹃林，大的高达数米，直径 40 余厘米，树龄逾 1700 年，实属罕见。相伴而生的还有高山玉兰，花朵大如手掌，花色有嫩黄，浅红，或生长于流泉之畔，或斜倚于峰壁之间，淡雅高洁，惹人喜爱。

遗产价值

三清山地处欧亚板块东南部，具有 10 亿年几乎连续的地质演化史，包含了许多世界上重大地质事件的地层学证据，容纳了东亚所能见到的多种生态系统，具有独一无二的花岗岩地质地貌，是国际上研究地球历史和古板块构造的最佳地区。由于没有受到第四纪冰川的直接覆盖和影响，三清山保存了大量东亚—北美间断分布孑遗物种，是第四纪冰期生物的避难所，对研究植物物种洲际间断分布和孑遗植物具有国际意义。

三清山由于花岗岩地貌多样性和生物多样性以及独特的气候景观，形成了奇峰怪石、急流飞瀑、云海雾涛、古树名花等景观，从多学科、多层面展示了独特花岗岩石柱与山峰，丰富的花岗岩造型石与多种植被、远近变化的景观及震撼人心的气候奇观相结合，创造了世界上独一无二的景观美学效果，呈现了引人入胜的自然美。

武陵源风景名胜区

武陵源风景名胜区位于中国中部省份湖南省的西北部，由张家界市的张家界森林公园、索溪峪自然保护区和天子山自然保护区组合而成，总面积约500平方公里。最近又发现了杨家界新景区。亿万年前，武陵源是一片汪洋大海，大自然不停地搬运、雕琢，变幻出今日武陵源砂岩峰林峡谷的地貌。

武陵源在区域构造体系中，处于新华夏第三隆起带。在漫长的地质历史时期内，大致经历了武陵—雪峰、印支、燕山、喜山及新构造运动。武陵—雪峰运动奠定了本区基底构造；印支运动塑造了本区的基本构造地貌格架，而喜山及新构造运动是形成武陵源奇特的石英砂岩峰林地貌景观的最基本的内在因素之一。

生物资源

武陵源是“天然去雕饰”的人间仙境，也是资源丰富的绿色植物宝库和野生动物乐园。武陵源有十分丰富的植物资源。境内森林覆盖率已达74.75%，并保存着两处原始次森林，为我国重要的古老孑遗生物的生长地区。境内有高等植物3000余种，首批列入国家重点保护的珍稀濒危种子植物有珙桐等35种。在众多的植物中，武陵松分布最广，数量最多，形态最奇，有“武陵源里三千峰，峰有十万八千松”之美誉。

武陵源有宝贵的野生珍稀动物，较多的是猕猴，其次是被当地人叫作“娃娃鱼”的大鲵。

风景名胜

景观特色

武陵源有“五绝”：奇峰、怪石、幽谷、秀水、溶洞。

武陵源独特的石英砂岩峰林为国内外所罕见，成为它奇绝超群的胜景。在360多平方公里的面积中，有山峰3000多座，垂直400米以上的石峰有1000余个。这里的峰石与别处不同，直立而密集，那些突兀耸立的岩壁、峰石，如帛，如笋，一扇扇，一根根，连绵不绝，气势恢宏而磅礴。

这里的溶洞不但数量多，规模大，而且极富特色。有名可数的有黄龙洞、观音洞、响水洞、龟栖洞、飞云洞及金螺洞等。

与自然风光相映成趣的，是纯朴的田园风光。一块块梯田，一间间房舍点缀在青山绿水间，与武陵源的大山、密林浑然一体，构成一幅原始苍茫的风景画卷。

主要景区

张家界风景区　张家界地貌奇特，有石峰2000多座，形态各异。树木茂盛，森林覆盖率达88%，四周山地环抱，坡陡沟深。区内景点众多，尤以黄狮寨、砂刀沟、金鞭岩、金鞭溪等最为著名。

香芷溪峰高天远，涧深水清，斜阳古道，鸟叫蝉鸣，似世外桃源；龙泉峡绝壁罗列，是天然的屏障，宛若壮观的古城墙；百猴谷是猕猴和白鹭的家园，成队的猕猴出没于悬崖沟谷之间，成群的白鹭栖息于苍枝绿叶之中……

黄石寨，海拔1200米，占地面积250亩，是张家界流水侵蚀、峰林景观地貌的典型代表，为张家界森林公园最大最集中的观景台。

天下第一桥，属张家界精华景点。大自然的鬼斧神工，将一块厚约5米的天然石板，横空“架”在两座山峰之上，把东西两峰连接起来。桥高350米，桥长20米，宽仅1.5–3米不等，但较平坦，可通行人。

“千里相会”，位于张家界国家森林公园内，有两座石峰紧密相连，恰如相拥相抱的一对夫妻。相传东海龙宫小龙女与峨眉山后生苦苦相恋，惹恼龙王，遂将他二人点化成石。

迷魂台位于张家界国家森林公园砂刀沟一带，一座座岩峰石柱如桌、如椅、如楼、如阁，其形态妙不可言。每当雨后初晴，轻云淡雾缭绕于群峰之间，时隐时现，变幻莫测，使游人难辨天上人间，故有迷魂台一名。

索溪峪风景区　索溪峪自然风景区有“峰两千，水八百”之称。区内有2000多座山峰，还有19道沟壑和6条溪流。这里山与水交映，描绘出一幅“山因水更奇，水因山更秀”的奇妙画卷。

百瀑溪是索溪峪中最为壮观的景色。这里到处都是瀑布，水流纵横飞泻，汇集之处，自然形成一条名副其实的“百瀑溪”。

索溪峪中有大型石灰岩溶洞 100 多个，可供游览的有十多个，而最具特色的当属黄龙洞，号称“地下明珠”。洞中有宫，宫中有河，规模宏大，气象万千。

“十里画廊”最壮观的景致莫如仙女拜观音，它被列为索溪峪六大奇观之一。过东风桥 400 余米，回首东望，一群仙女面对端坐的观音，极尽虔诚膜拜之态。三座御香炉，烟云缭绕，把一幅虔拜图衬托得惟妙惟肖。

黄龙洞总面积为 300 多亩，垂直高差达 140 余米。大小支洞总长度为 14 公里。洞内石钟乳、石柱、石幔、石花、石瀑，琳琅满目，绚丽多姿。而在所有的钟乳石之中又以“定海神针”最为称奇，它高 27 米，两端粗，中间细，通体透明，直抵宫顶。整个大洞犹如一株盘根错节的古木，分布开来，正所谓洞中有洞，天外有天，山重水复，无所不奇。

天子山风景区　天子山风景区位于武陵源北，与张家界、索溪峪山水相依，是武陵源三大风景区之一，总面积 67 平方公里。景观奇特，惊险万端，以峰高、峰大、峰多著称。

在天子山主峰举目远眺，方圆百里，尽收眼底。这里的石峰，形态之奇，令人叹为观止：“御笔峰”鬼斧神工，“仙人桥”天造地设，“仙女献花”天工造化，“屈子行吟”形神兼备……

天子山被誉为“秀色天下绝，山高人未识”的自然风景处女地，它有一座天桥，两口天池，三座古庙，四个天门，五处飞泉，六个洞府，七个风景区，84 座天然观景台。集奇、险、秀、幽、野于一体，像一首抒情诗，如一幅风景画，披着神秘的面纱，讲述着动人的故事。

将军岩是天子山绝景之一。酷似人形的天然巨石高 90 余米，耸立于数百米巨峰之巅，威风凛凛。云雾弥漫，看不清他的面容，但见身披金甲，背手而立，俨然一位指挥千军万马的将军。

遗产价值

武陵源风景区保持着较原始的生态系统，3000 多座形状奇异的山峰，800 多条沟谷，还有变幻的云海、神秘的溶洞、奔泻的瀑布，集中国名山的雄、奇、险、秀、幽、野于一身，有“天下奇峰归武陵”的美誉。武陵源风景名胜区独特的石英砂岩峰林为国内外罕见，具有不可比拟、不可替代、不可分割等特点而成为奇艳超群的景观；武陵源的水景类型齐全，包括溪、泉、湖、潭、瀑等，异彩分呈，有“秀水八百”的美称；武陵源森林茂盛，武陵松分布广泛，数量极多，有“十万八千松”之称。

九寨沟风景名胜区

九寨沟风景区地处四川省北部的万山丛中，因周围有九个藏族村寨而得名。总面积约 620 平方公里，大约有 52% 的面积被茂密的原始森林所覆盖。自然景色兼有湖泊、瀑布、雪山、森林之美。沟中地僻人稀，景物特异，富于原始自然风貌。有长海、剑岩、诺日朗、树正、扎如、黑海六大景区，以翠海、叠瀑、彩林、雪峰、藏情“五绝”而驰名中外。

生物资源

原始森林覆盖了九寨沟一半以上的面积。林中植物种类繁多，现有天然森林近 3 万公顷，植物两千余种。多种野生动物繁衍栖息于此，其中包括脊椎动物 170 种、鸟类 141 种，属国家保护的有 17 种。林地上积满厚厚的苔藓，散落着鸟兽的羽毛，充满原始森林的野趣和风貌。

九寨沟为多种自然要素交汇地区，山地切割较深，高差悬殊，植物垂直带谱明显，植物资源丰富，植被类型多样，隐藏着不同气候带的地带性植被类型。植物区系成分十分丰富，几乎包括了所有大的世界分区。许多古老、孑遗植物保存良好，对于研究植物系统演化及植物区系的演变均有一定的科学价值。

风景名胜

景观特色

奇特的水体景观 九寨沟以水景著称。山、水、林诸多景物中，尤以水景最为奇丽。在狭长的山沟谷地中，有色彩斑斓、清澈如镜的一百多个湖泊散布其间，泉、瀑、河、滩将无数碧蓝澄澈的湖泊连缀一体，千姿百态，如诗如画。九寨沟以高原钙华湖群、钙华瀑群和钙华滩流等水景为主体的奇特风貌，其水景规模之巨、景型之多、数量之众、形态之美、环境之佳等指标综合鉴定，位居中国风景名胜区水景之冠。

优美的综合环境 九寨沟以明朗的高原风光为基调，融翠湖、叠瀑、秋林、雪峰于一体，历来被当地藏民视为“神山圣水”。沟内山、水、林、石均为藏民所崇拜和保护的对象。风景名胜区对外开放后，被游人称为“人间仙境”、“童话世界”。

保存完好的冰川遗迹 九寨沟的山水形成于第四纪古冰川时期，现保存着大量的第四纪古冰川遗迹。其角峰峥嵘，刃脊崔嵬，冰斗、U字谷十分典型，悬谷、槽谷独具风韵。槽谷伸至海拔 2800 米的地方。谷地古冰川侧碛、终债垄发育，成为我国第四纪冰川保存良好的地方之一。

主要景区

树正沟 树正沟是九寨沟秀丽风景的大门。全长 13.8 公里，有四十余座湖泊（海子），约占九寨沟景区全部湖泊的 40%。四十多座湖泊，犹如四十多面晶莹剔透的宝镜，顺沟叠延五、六公里。水光潋滟，碧波荡漾，芦苇摇曳，鸟语花香。

则查洼沟 则查洼沟作为九寨沟风景区“Y”字形构造的左支旅游线路，它是九寨沟内四条游览路线距离最长、海拔最高的一条游览路线。具有多个景点，风光优美。

日则沟 日则沟风光线全长 18 公里，是九寨沟风光线中的精髓。其间有落差最大的瀑布、聚宝盆似的滩流、古木参天的原始森林。各个景点排列有序，高低错落，转接自然，给人以强烈的美的感受。

主要景点

翠海 水是九寨沟的精灵，而九寨沟的海子（湖泊）更具特色，湖水终年碧蓝澄澈，明丽见底，而且随着光照变化、季节推移，呈现不同的色调与水韵。百余座湖泊，个个古树环绕，奇花簇拥，宛若镶上了美丽的花边。湖泊都由激流的瀑布连接，犹如用银链串起来的一块块翡翠，各具特色，变幻无穷。

叠瀑　九寨沟是瀑布王国。这里几乎所有的瀑布全都从密林里狂奔而出，就像一台台绿色织布机永不停息地编织着各种规格的白色丝绸。其中诺日朗瀑布是全国最宽的瀑布，它从高高的山岩上急泻而下，似巨幅幕帘凌空飞落，雄浑而壮丽。

九寨沟最为奇特的瀑布当属日则沟的珍珠滩瀑布。它处在一面峭壁上方，千万年流水融成的许多圆形坑洞，经急速的流水冲进又反弹而出形成许多飞溅的水珠，经阳光反射，就像一颗颗五彩的珍珠。

彩林　被誉为九寨沟五绝之一的彩林，覆盖了景区一半以上的面积，两千余种植物争奇斗艳，绚丽斑斓；三万顷苍苍莽莽的原始森林，随着季节的变化，呈现出种种奇丽风光。金秋时节，林涛树海换上了美艳无比的盛装，那深橙的黄栌、金黄的桦叶、绛红的枫树、殷红的野果，深浅相间，错落有致，令人眼花潦乱，美不胜收。

雪峰　九寨沟三条沟谷，层峦叠嶂，山势挺拔，眺望远方，皑皑雪峰，尽收眼底。登上尕尔纳山，极目远眺，山峦逶迤，谷壑深幽，天象奇观，一览无余。

遗产价值

九寨沟是大自然的杰作。在数十平方公里的风景区内，景点之多、景观之美、观光内容之丰富，实属罕见，达到人类风景美学法则的最高境界。

九寨沟的奇山异水，立体交叉，四维渗透，融色美、形美、声美于一体，构成了一幅多层次、多方位的天然画卷。

黄龙风景名胜区

相传很久以前，曾有“黄龙真人”于黄龙沟玉翠峰隐居修道，所建前、中、后三座寺庙，千百年来一直香火旺盛。其中后寺传至今日，仍为道家神庙，殿内依旧供奉着黄龙真人图像。每逢农历六月黄龙寺传统庙会，方圆数百里的藏、羌、回、汉各族群众便会聚于此，或进香朝山、入寺祈祷；或游乐赏景、唱歌跳舞……

黄龙风景名胜区位于四川省阿坝藏族羌族自治州松潘县境内，海拔在3000米以上，是中国地势最高的风景名胜区之一。风景区由黄龙景区和牟尼沟景区两部分组成。地表钙华是黄龙景观的最大特色，面积700平方公里。主要景观集中于长约3.6公里的黄龙沟，沟内遍布碳酸钙华沉积，并呈梯田状排列，仿佛是一条金色巨龙，并伴有雪山、瀑布、原始森林、峡谷等景观。以其雄、峻、奇、野的风景特色，享有“世界奇观”、“人间瑶池”的美誉。

生物资源

从黄龙沟底部（海拔2000米）到山顶（海拔3800米）依次出现亚热带常绿与落叶阔叶混交林、针叶阔叶混交林、亚高山针叶林、高山灌丛草甸等。包括大熊猫、金丝猴在内的十余种珍贵动物活动其间，使黄龙景区的特殊岩溶地貌与珍稀动植物资源相互交织，浑然天成。

风景名胜

主要景区

红星岩景区　红星岩景区位于漳腊盆地东侧、岷山山脉西坡，该景点海拔较高，以第四纪冰川作用形成的大量奇峰异石地貌景观和冰川堰塞湖为其显著特色，人迹罕至，颇具神秘色彩。位于海拔4300米的“红星海”，湖面呈不对称的五角星型，宁静秀丽，周围繁花似锦。在其悬崖中部绝壁上有一眼红色岩洞，像鲜血染红的一般，其成因至今未知。风起云涌之时，岩洞隐没在云雾里，时隐时现，诡谲奇幻。

雪宝顶景区　雪宝顶，系岷山山脉主峰，海拔5588米，位于松潘县城东50公里。《松潘县志》载诗云：“岩悬势天穹，精莹凝太空，高凌世界外，寒沍群山中。”五岳，人称为万山之父，而此雪宝顶横空出世，玉笋攀天，高峭、伟岩、晶莹、挺拔，纵使五岳，也拜服其下。

雪宝顶山终年积雪，山腰岩石嶙峋，沟壑纵横，湖泊星罗棋布。较大的海子有108个，尤以东南圆海、西南方海、西北半圆海和东北三角海最为著称。雪宝顶山麓花草遍布，灌木丛生，松柏参天。青羊、山鹿、獐子等珍贵动物在此栖息、繁衍，一派生机盎然的景象。

四沟景区　距黄龙沟约12公里，为一条开阔的古冰川沟谷。沟口一带为平坦开阔的洪积阶地，古色古香的深山小镇黄龙乡即在此。景区地形复杂多变，既有高耸入云的奇峰，又有开阔的河滩地带。原始森林和冰川、地震遗迹，历经亿万年沧桑变迁，至今仍然保持着当时原貌，与美丽的田园风光相互映衬，自成奇趣。

分水岭之上，为广阔的高山草甸牧场。从这里，可俯视九寨沟源头多姿的冰川堰塞湖及无垠的原始森林。古时候川西北著名的“龙安马道”就经过这里，因此沟内至今仍留有宽阔的马道。

丹云峡景区　丹云峡以俊秀的峡谷风光，成为黄龙的“五绝”之一。它拥有丰富的树种、灌木和花草，是植物的天堂。这里冬天一片雪白，夏天山林翠绿，春天漫山遍野的红杜鹃、秋天一路枫叶红遍峡谷，那情景仿佛夕阳之下的火烧云从天而降，丹云峡因此而得名。山生云，树生风，丹云峡几乎每天都有云雾从林中升起，缭绕山间，时隐时现，游人至此，宛若走进了神话世界。

牟尼沟景区　在牟尼沟风景区原始大森林中，有一股巨大的水流自104米高的台阶式钙华岩体上汹涌咆哮着直泻而下，气势极为壮观，它就是我国最大的钙华瀑布——扎嘎大瀑布。扎嘎瀑布海拔3270米，瀑高93.2米，宽35米。上游是湖泊，下游为一串阶梯式河床。上百个层层叠叠的钙华环型瀑布玉串珠连，经三级钙华台阶跌宕而下，冲击成巨大钙华化面而形成朵朵巨大白花，瀑声如雷，动人心魄。

主要景点

黄龙沟 位于岷山主峰雪宝顶，下临涪江源流——涪源桥，是一条长7.5公里、宽1.5公里的缓坡沟谷。沟内布满乳黄色岩石，远望好似蜿蜒于密林幽谷中的黄龙，黄龙沟一名即由此而来。明代在此修建了黄龙寺，用以奉祀黄龙。黄龙沟以它“奇、绝、秀、幽”的自然景观而蜚声中外，它酷似中国人心目中“龙”的形象，因而历来被喻为“人间瑶池”、“中华象征”。黄龙沟连绵分布钙华段长达3600米，彩池多达3400余个。

迎宾池 进入黄龙景区，首先看到的便是一组精巧别致、水质明丽的池群——迎宾池。池子大小不一，形状奇特，色彩艳丽。四周山岳环峙，林木葱茏，山间野花竞放，彩蝶飞舞。山间石径曲折盘旋，点缀着观景亭阁，倍增情趣。

黄龙寺 距沟口约3.5公里。据《松潘县志》载：“黄龙寺，明兵马使马朝觐建，亦名雪山寺，相传黄龙真人养道于此，故名。有前中后三寺，殿阁相望，各距五里。”

沟内原有前、中、后三座寺庙，前寺现仅存遗址；中寺共五殿，占地约5100平方米，现存观音殿及殿内十座罗汉塑像，位于黄龙沟尽头，海拔3558米，占地约2100平方米，庙宇建筑基本保存完好。相传黄龙助禹治水有功，后人为祭祀他，便在此修庙立碑。现寺内正殿塑有身披玄色道袍、神态安祥的黄龙真人坐像。

五彩池 在长达2.5公里的脊状坡地上，阳光下伴着湍急的水波，整个沟谷金光闪闪，看上去恰似一条巨大的黄龙从雪山上飞腾而下。随着流速缓急、地势起伏以及枯枝乱石的阻隔，水中富含的碳酸钙开始凝聚，发育成固体的钙华埂，使流水潴留成层叠相连的大片彩池群，描绘出了黄龙奇观的第一幅天然图画。碳酸钙沉积过程中，又与各种有机物、无机物结成不同质的钙华体，还有光线照射的种种变化，形成池水同源而色泽不一的景致，人们便称其为“五彩池”。

遗产价值

黄龙风景名胜区处于三大地质构造单元的结合部，地理状况特别复杂。整个风景区总面积1340平方公里，区内雪峰林立，瀑布悬流，资源丰富，保存完好，具有重要的科学价值和美学价值。

黄龙自然风景区的自然遗产以巨型地表钙华景观为最著，规模宏大，类型繁多，结构奇巧，色彩艳丽，在中国风景名胜区中独树一帜，成为一绝。黄龙是以绚丽的高原风光和特异的民族风情为综合景观的基调。高山摩天、峡谷纵横、林海苍苍、碧水荡荡，其间镶嵌着精巧的池、湖、滩、瀑、泉、洞等各类钙华景观，点缀着神秘的寨、寺、耕、牧、歌、舞等各族乡土风情，呈现出一派神奇无穷的天然画境。过渡状态的地理结构，造成自然环境上的复杂性，蕴涵着不少未解之谜，为各学科提供了探索自然奥秘的广阔天地。同时黄龙地区海拔3000米以上广泛发育着清晰的第四纪冰川遗迹，对研究现代冰川和古冰川遗迹及其与钙华之间的关系等，均具有重要的科研价值。

云南三江并流保护区

三江并流是指金沙江、澜沧江和怒江三条发源于青藏高原的大江在云南省境内自北向南并行奔流 170 多公里，穿越担当力卡山、高黎贡山、怒山和云岭等崇山峻岭，形成世界上罕见的“江水并流而不交汇”的奇特自然地理景观。其间澜沧江与金沙江距离最短，直线距离为 6.6 公里，澜沧江与怒江的最短直线距离不到 19 公里。

三江并流地区是世界上蕴藏最丰富的地质地貌博物馆。4000 万年前，印度板块与欧亚板块碰撞，引发了横断山脉的急剧挤压、隆起、抬升和切割，高山与大江交替展布，形成世界上独有的三江并流景观。区内汇集了高山峡谷、雪峰冰川、高原湿地、森林草甸、淡水湖泊、稀有动物、珍贵植物等奇异风景。这一珍贵、罕见的地质地貌遗迹，是大自然留给人类的共同财富，具有十分重要的世界意义和保护价值。

生物资源

三江并流是世界生物多样性最丰富的地区之一，这里集中了北半球南亚热带、中亚热带、北亚热带、暖温带、温带、寒温带、温带、寒带的多种气候和生物群落，是地球最直观的体温表和中国珍稀濒危动植物的避难所。这里有高等植物 210 余种，哺乳动物 173 种，鸟类 417 种，爬行类 59 种，两栖类 36 种，淡水鱼 76 种，凤蝶类昆虫 31 种，而这些动物总数均达到中国总数的 25% 以上。大多数稀有濒危动物都生活在这一区域的西部地区，如滇金丝猴、羚羊、雪豹、孟加拉虎、黑颈鹤等；珍稀濒危植物有秃杉、桫椤、红豆杉等。

主要景观

三大江

金沙江　长江上游自青海省境内的巴塘河口至四川省宜宾市一段为金沙江，长 2308 公里，东岸云南省中甸县大小雪山丫口有秀丽的林海雪原景观。到丽江石鼓境内急转向北，深切高原，造成著名的虎跳峡，其间水流湍急，悬崖飞瀑，谷深达 3000 米以上，比大名鼎鼎的美国科罗拉多大峡谷还高 600 多米。1935 年 5 月，中国工农红军长征途中曾强渡皎平渡口。

澜沧江　上源扎曲、吉曲均出青海省唐古拉山，在西藏自治区昌都地区汇合，东南流贯云南西部，到西双版纳傣族自治州南部出国境，称湄公河。澜沧江流域及毗邻地区，江河纵横，地形复杂，山川挺拔，气候多样，造就了高山峡谷、江河、湖泊、植物、花卉、珍稀动物等极其丰富的自然景观。云南省少数民族有一半以上世代聚居于此，构成了区域内绚丽多彩的人文景观。

怒江　又称潞江，源出青藏边境唐古拉山南麓，出国境流入缅甸后称“萨尔温江”。怒江奔腾于高黎贡山和碧罗雪山之间，两岸山岭海拔均在 3000 米以上，最高为 5060 米。两岸多危岩，所谓“水无不怒石，山有欲飞峰”，是对它的生动写照。峡谷内植物繁茂，花俏草绿，一派烂漫缤纷景象。

八大片区

高黎贡山区　是“三江并流”区域内植物物种多样性的集中展示区。其中东西绵延的常绿阔叶林，是现今我国乃至东亚保存最完好的一片，也是特有植物类群最丰富的地区，它包括了“怒江第一湾”及周边地区为代表的怒江深切河曲地质景观，其中的石月亮景点是怒江流域高山喀斯特溶洞景观的典型代表。

梅里雪山区　区内保存着大量的古深海大洋地质、生物遗迹和冰川、造山运动遗迹和广泛的冰川及冻土地貌发育，是“三江并流”遗产地比较集中的地质遗迹展示区。滇金丝猴作为“三江并流”区域最具有典型意义的旗舰物种，在保护区内最为集中。在卡瓦格博峰周边，针阔混交林、湿性常绿阔叶林原生状态保存良好，代表了澜沧江干热河谷典型的多样性自然地理特征。

哈巴雪山区　区内拥有我国纬度最南的现代海洋性冰川、金沙江流域典型完整的高山垂直带自然景观。在很小的空间范围内，集中了从亚热带干暖河谷到高山寒带的各植被类型。寒温性针叶林是哈巴雪山自然保护区山地生态系统中最重要的生态系统类型，是世界遗产提名地最典型的高山针叶林保护区域。

千湖山区 位于迪庆州香格里拉县小中甸乡，是金沙江流域原始植被、高原湖泊的集中展示区之一。

据不完全统计，大小不一的高原湖泊有100多座，其中以碧古天池和三碧海为代表，具有独特的高原森林湖泊景观价值。

红山区 包含了金沙江流域典型的高原夷平面、高山喀斯特等地貌特征完整的古冰川遗迹和丰富的植物生态系统、高原湖泊等多种景观类型，其中，以尼汝南宝草场、小雪山丫口高原地质景观最具典型意义，是具有极高保护价值和开发潜力的原始景观资源研究展示区域。

云岭片区 位于怒江兰坪县境内澜沧江与其支流通甸河之间。该保护区森林覆盖率高达76%，大多保持原始状态，生物多样性相当丰富。区内野生动物分布广泛，据初步调查，共记录到哺乳动物28种，隶属7目13科。

老君山区 是“三江并流”范围内金沙江流域下游，主要包含了金沙江流域的“高原冰蚀湖群”、高山丹霞地貌集中发育区和金沙江流域景区展示和规范化保护管理示范区。这里有杜鹃纯林生态系统，是金沙江流域杜鹃花种类最丰富的分布区。杜鹃林与高山湖泊共同构成了精彩的景观画卷。丽江老君山分布着中国面积最大、发育最完整的丹霞地貌奇观，它镶嵌在莽莽原始森林的万绿丛中，璀璨夺目。

老窝山区 位于澜沧江流域下游，迪庆藏族自治州维西傈僳族自治县，是澜沧江流域的景观资源类型补充片区，以高山湖泊、高原草甸和野生花卉资源为保护重点，主要景点包括新化湖、老窝山高山冰积湖群、澜沧江二级支流拉洛河、红岩洞溶洞、栗地坪野生花卉等，其自然景观仍处在原始未开发阶段。

遗产价值

“三江并流”区域是地质多样性最丰富的地区之一。从大地演化的蛇绿岩、枕状溶岩、古生化至第四世纪的地质岩层记录到陆内造山带变质变形的冰川雪峰、溶洞河流、喀斯特地貌等地貌景观几乎无所不有，是科考、研究、探险的圣地。区内壮观的雪山冰川，险峻的峡谷急流，开阔的高山草甸，明澈清净的高山湖泊，秀美的丹霞峰丛和喀斯特台地，构成了遗产地丰富而多元的风景轮廓。同时也是生物多样性最丰富的地区之一。这里集中了北半球南中北亚热带、暖温带、温带、寒温带、寒带的多种气候和生物群落，这在中国乃至北半球和全世界都是唯一的。此外，还孕育了数千年来的“江边文化”。金沙江上游的石鼓镇、澜沧江上游的叶枝镇作为历史文化名镇的代表，已成为三江并流区域和“茶马古道”上的亮点。这些特色鲜明的民族文化和独树一帜的自然景观共同构成这一区域最为宝贵的历史文化遗产。

中国南方喀斯特

中国南方喀斯特覆盖了五万平方公里，主要位于云南省、贵州省和广西壮族自治区，有着多样的喀斯特地形地貌。遗产地包含荔波喀斯特，石林喀斯特和武隆喀斯特三个类别。中国南方喀斯特展示了一个由多湿的热带至亚热带的喀斯特地貌，而石林是世界范围内一个伟大的自然现象和一个世界性的地标。

中国南方喀斯特经历了长期的地质年代，是地球重要而典型的自然地理特征和喀斯特地貌形态，既保留了地质历史时期古喀斯特遗迹，又代表了重要的和正在进行的喀斯特过程。由于很少受到冰期的影响，无论是现代的成熟喀斯特地貌还是历史上形成的古喀斯特地貌的地质历史都很完整。受青藏高原隆起等影响，演化至今的“中国南方喀斯特”已完整形成了一个热带、亚热带喀斯特上升发育区的结构系统和演化序列，对研究现代区域水文及长江三峡的形成等都提供了宝贵的地貌证据，在世界上也是少有的。石林喀斯特（云南）被挑选作为中国南方喀斯特所发现的各种石林地貌的经典样板，石林县的石林表明了这些跨越两亿七千万年的喀斯特地貌演变的事件性特征。

对于喀斯特地形的研究，中国早在 17 世纪的明朝晚期就已经开始了，这比外国早两百年左右。中国著名的地理学家徐霞客曾于 1637–1639 年用两年的时间遨游广西、贵州、云南，对中国西南石灰岩分布地区进行了详细的调查和考察。他写的《徐霞客游记》一书，对石灰岩地区的地貌形态作了详尽细致而又朴实生动的描述，被认为是世界上研究喀斯特地貌最早的一本科学著作。

喀斯特景观主要有地表喀斯特和地下喀斯特两种类型。

地表喀斯特包含溶沟和石芽、天坑和竖井、溶蚀洼地和溶蚀谷地、干谷、峰林、峰丛、孤峰、天生桥及地表钙华堆积等，其中云南地区的石林就是发育比较好的形态高大的石芽群，它的形成条件是厚层、质纯、产状平缓、垂直节理稀疏和湿热的气候环境；峰丛地貌被誉为喀斯特地貌的博物馆；钙华沉积是大自然赐予人类的一幅壮丽美景。

地下喀斯特包含溶洞、溶蚀地貌——石锅和边槽、堆积地貌等。其中堆积地貌是溶洞景观中的精华部分，在我国西南地区的溶洞中可以欣赏这些神奇的洞天世界。重力水的堆积是溶洞堆积地貌的主要形成方式，由水滴雕琢而成的石钟乳、石笋、石柱、石幔、边石堤等千姿百态，绚丽多彩。另外，在溶洞中还有许多奇特的景观，有的似莲花开放，有的如树枝伸展，还有一些石葡萄、石珊瑚等则更是惟妙惟肖，活灵活现。

遗产地分布

中国几乎所有的省区都有喀斯特分布，但以广西、云南、贵州等省区为多。中国整个西南地区石灰岩连成一片，分布最广，面积共达 55 万平方公里。其中尤以广西地区出露的面积最大，达 12 万平方公里，约占广西全区总面积的 60%。贵州和云南东南部石灰岩的分布面积也约占该地区总面积的 50%。此外，广东、浙江、江苏以及四川盆地和鄂西山区等地都有大面积的石灰岩分布。

2006 年，由云南石林的剑状、柱状和塔状喀斯特、贵州荔波的森林喀斯特、重庆武隆的以天生桥、地缝、天洞为代表的立体喀斯特共同组成的“中国南方喀斯特”，成为中国政府当年申报世界自然遗产的唯一项目。此次申报的“中国南方喀斯特”形成于 50 万年 –3 亿年间，总面积达 1460 平方公里，其中提名地（核心区）面积 480 平方公里，缓冲区面积 980 平方公里。

云南石林

石林地处滇东高原腹地，位于石林彝族自治县境内，距昆明市 70 余公里。石林冬无严寒，夏无酷暑，四季如春，是一个集自然风光、民族风情、休闲度假、科学考察为一体的著名大型综合旅游区。石林以喀斯特景观为主，以“雄、奇、险、秀、幽、奥、旷”著称，具有世界上最奇特的喀斯特地貌（岩溶地貌）景观，在世界地学界享有盛誉。

石林形成于 2.7 亿年前，经漫长地质演化和复杂的古地理环境变迁，才形成了现今极为珍贵的地质遗迹，它涵盖了地球上众多的喀斯特地貌类型，分布世界各地的石林仿佛汇集于此，其石牙、峰丛、溶丘、溶洞、溶蚀湖、瀑布、地下河错落有致，是典型的高原喀斯特生态系统立体全景图。

石林景区面积达1100平方公里，保护区为350平方公里。进入景区，仿佛步入时间的隧道，让人充分领略到大自然的鬼斧神工。悠游海底迷宫，峭壁万仞，石峰嶙峋，像千军万马，又似古堡幽城，如飞禽走兽，又像人影仙踪，千姿百态，栩栩如生。

石林的魅力不仅在于自然景观，还在于独具特色的石林撒尼土著风情。最有影响的是“一诗”、“一影”、“一歌”、“一节”。彝文记录的古老的撒尼叙事长诗《阿诗玛》被译成20多种文字在国内外发行；改编成中国第一部彩色立体声电影《阿诗玛》，享誉海外；每年农历六月二十四日的彝族火把节是撒尼人传统的节日，摔跤、斗牛、火把狂欢等场面蔚为壮观，被誉为“东方狂欢节”。

贵州荔波

贵州省荔波县属黔南布依族苗族自治州，与广西接壤。茂兰国家级喀斯特森林自然保护区就位于荔波县的东南部，它由东南部的喀斯特森林区、甲良镇洞庭五针松保证点及小七孔喀斯特森林科学游览区三部分组成，总面积21285公顷。其中核心区5827公顷，缓冲区8910公顷，实验区4588公顷。

荔波喀斯特原始森林、水上森林和“漏斗”森林，合称“荔波三绝”。它们是石头上长出的森林。

漏斗森林为森林密集覆盖的喀斯特峰丛漏斗，其树木密集，四周群山封闭，底部有漏斗型的落水洞，状若巨大的绿色窝穴。漏斗底部至锥峰一般高差150–300米，万物都保持着原始自然的特色。洼地森林为森林广泛覆盖的喀斯特锥峰洼地，常有农田房舍分布其间，构成山清水秀的田园森林风光。盆地森林为森林覆盖较广的喀斯特盆地（谷地），四周森林茂密的孤峰及峰丛巍然耸立。盆地开阔平坦，良田纵横，形成了蔚然壮观的盆地森林景观。

重庆武隆

武隆县地处重庆市东南边缘、乌江下游，东邻彭水，南接贵州省道真县，自古有“渝黔门屏”之称。武隆的景区包括天下第一洞芙蓉洞、亚洲最大的天生桥群、全世界罕见而稀有的喀斯特系统形成的后坪天坑。

芙蓉洞　芙蓉洞是一个大型石灰岩洞穴，全长2400米，洞体高大，宽、高多在30–50米之间，其中辉煌大厅底面积在1.1万平方米以上。洞内各种次生化学沉积形态（即钟乳石类）琳琅满目，丰富多彩。主要景点约30处，其中十多处在国内外均可堪称最佳景点。

天生桥　武隆天生桥是全国罕见的地质奇观，属典型的喀斯特地貌。景区以天龙桥、青龙桥、黑龙桥三座气势磅礴的石拱桥称奇于世，属亚洲最大的天生桥群。

天坑群　后坪天坑群位于重庆长江三峡腹地的武隆后坪乡境内，属武陵山系，总面积为15万平方米的五个天坑，藏于原始森林和竹林中，绝壁千丈，神秘莫测。

遗产价值

喀斯特是世界最卓越的自然景观之一，以石灰岩和白云岩为主的碳酸盐岩为物质基础而形成。中国是世界喀斯特比例最高的国家，碳酸盐岩出露面积达1.25×106平方公里，喀斯特发育极为典型。从发育条件、发育程度以及景观美感度等方面评价，又以中国南方喀斯特最佳，其独特的地质地貌及演化过程、生态系统和生物多样性，以及所形成的美学、民族文化等方面的综合自然景观都具有显著的全球价值，长期以来得到了国内外学者的广泛重视和认同。

中国丹霞

丹霞夹明月，华星出云间。
上天垂光彩，五色一何鲜。
——曹丕《芙蓉池作诗》摘句

1928 年，获美国哥伦比亚大学地质学硕士学位的矿床学家冯景兰，在我国广东省仁化县丹霞山注意到了分布广泛的第三纪（6500 万年 –165 万年前）红色砂砾岩层。在丹霞山地区，厚达 300–500 米的岩层被流水、风力等风化侵蚀，形成了堡垒状的山峰和峰丛、千姿百态的奇石、石桥和石洞。冯景兰意识到这是一种独特的地貌景观，并把形成这种地貌的红色砂砾岩层命名为丹霞层。而“丹霞”一词源自曹丕的《芙蓉池作诗》：“丹霞夹明月，华星出云间”。丹霞，指天上的彩霞。

1938 年，构造地质学家陈国达把这种红色岩层上发育的地貌称为“丹霞地形”，并把这种地形作为判断丹霞地层的标志。20 世纪 40–70 年代末，原中山大学地理系吴尚时、曾昭璇教授将红层地貌作为独立的岩石地貌类型进行了系统的研究，并使“丹霞地貌”这一名词得以广泛传播。20 世纪 80 年代以后，科学工作者先后对我国 21 个省区近 400 处丹霞地貌进行了实地考察，并把丹霞地貌研究推向全国。

丹霞地貌最突出的特点是“赤壁丹崖”广泛发育，形成了顶平、身陡、麓缓的方山、石墙、石峰、石柱等奇险的地貌，形态各异的山石形成一种观赏价值很高的风景地貌，是名副其实的“红石公园”。

在地质和地貌学层面上分析，这种形成于西太平洋活性大陆边缘断陷盆地极厚沉积物上的地貌景观，是由红色砂岩和砾岩组成，反映了一个干热气候条件下的氧化陆相湖盆沉积环境。到目前为止，在中国已发现丹霞近 800 多处，广泛分布在热带、亚热带湿润区、温带湿润——半湿润区、半干旱、干旱区和青藏高原高寒区。据国际研究资料，世界上红层广泛分布在除南极之外的各大洲，发育了与中国丹霞相同或相似的地貌类型，因此，丹霞是一个具有全球意义的特殊自然地理现象和红层地貌类型。

中国丹霞地貌主要分布于 26 个省区。广东省韶关市东北的丹霞山以赤色丹霞为特色，由红色沙砾陆相沉积岩构成，是世界“丹霞地貌”命名地，在地层、构造、地貌、发育和环境演化等方面的研究在世界丹霞地貌区中最为详尽和深入。在此设立的“丹霞山世界地质公园”，总面积 319 平方公里，2004 年经联合国教科文组织批准为中国首批世界地质公园之一。

福建泰宁、武夷山、连城、永安，甘肃张掖，江苏新沂马陵山，湖南怀化、通道侗族自治县东北部万佛山、邵阳新宁县崀山，江西龙虎山、鹰潭、弋阳、上饶、瑞金、宁都，青海坎布拉，广东仁化丹霞山、坪石镇金鸡岭、南雄县苍石寨、平远县南台石和五指石，浙江永康、新昌，广西桂平的白石山、容县的都峤山，四川江油的窦圌山、都江堰市的青城山，重庆綦江的老瀛山，陕西凤县的赤龙山以及河北承德等地，是中国丹霞地貌的典型区域。

遗产地分布

贵州赤水

赤水丹霞地处四川盆地和云贵高原结合部的中国最大的丹霞分布区。高原的剧烈抬升与流水的强烈下切造成了地形的巨大反差。这里发育了最为典型的阶梯式河谷与最为壮观的丹霞瀑布群，成为青年早期高原峡谷型丹霞的代表。

赤水丹霞结合了瀑布、湿地、翠林等其他大自然的美景，森林覆盖率超过 90%。而大面积古植被和 2359 种动植物和珍稀濒危动植物一起，更成为赤水丹霞最独特的特征。赤水丹霞地貌，以其艳丽鲜红的丹霞赤壁、拔地而起的孤峰窄脊、仪态万千的奇山异石、巨大的岩廊洞穴和优美的丹霞峡谷与绿色森林、飞瀑流泉相映成趣，有“很高的旅游观赏价值。

福建泰宁

泰宁盆地记录了白垩纪以来华南板块东部大陆边缘活动带的演化历史。独特的崖壁洞穴群、密集的深切峡谷曲流和原始的沟谷生态构成罕见的自然特征，成为青年期低海拔山原峡谷型丹霞的代表；峡谷急流与密集峰丛紧密结合，不但保持了生态环境的原生性、生物和生态的多样性，而且造就了异常优美的山水景观。

湖南崀山

崀山以圆顶密集式丹霞峰丛——峰林为特点，如万笋插天，若万马奔腾；巷谷、线谷和天生桥规模宏大，丹霞喀斯特独特。植被“生态孤岛效应”和生境狭窄特有现象突出，是丹霞植物群落演替系列最完整的地区和动植物协同进化的代表地。其丹霞景观具有罕见自然美和原始属性，是一座天然的丹霞地貌博物馆，被誉为“丹霞之魂”、“国之瑰宝”。

广东丹霞山

丹霞山发育在南岭褶皱带中央的构造盆地中，具有单体类型的多样性和地貌景观的珍奇性，是中国丹霞地貌的命名地及主要类型和基本特征的模式地；是发育到壮年中晚期簇群式峰丛峰林型丹霞的代表。这里热带物种成分最多，沟谷雨林特征最突出，是丹霞生物谱系、丹霞“孤岛效应”与“热岛效应”研究的模式区域。

江西龙虎山

龙虎山所在的信江盆地，突出的侵蚀残余峰丛、峰林、孤峰、残丘组合特征，表明这里属于老年早期疏散峰林宽谷型丹霞的代表。区内保留了难得的低海拔中亚热带常绿阔叶林，是重要的珍稀濒危物种重要的栖息地；悬崖洞窟中众多的古代悬棺群，与中国道教祖庭的文化景观等巧妙结合，构成一幅多姿多彩的山水画卷。

浙江江郎山

江郎山在浙江省江山市城南 25 公里的江郎乡，所在的峡口盆地是一个位于深断裂上的构造盆地。坚硬的方岩组火山碎屑构成的红层，是江郎山孤石撑天地的物质保障。抗侵蚀性不同的岩石由于受到差异性侵蚀而形成地貌上突出的孤峰。其峭壁上有明代理学家湛若水摩崖题刻的“壁立万仞”四字。江郎山聚岩、洞、云、瀑于一山，奇险陡峻，蔚为壮观。唐代大诗人白居易赞曰：“安得此身生羽翼，与君来往醉烟霞”。徐霞客三次游江山时也写到江郎山，他把江郎山与雁荡山、黄山和鼎湖峰进行比较，极力地赞叹江郎山“奇”、“险”、“神”的迷人风景。

遗产价值

中国丹霞集地质多样性、地貌多样性、生物多样性及景观珍奇性于一体，是全球红层类特殊地貌景观，具有赤壁丹崖、群峰耸峙、峡谷深切、风景优美等主要特征。

中国丹霞是目前唯一以丹霞系列提名的世界自然遗产提名地，系列总体的科学价值、美学价值和生态价值胜过所有目前已有的世界自然与混合遗产中以丹霞（红层）地貌为申报要素的遗产地，为任何一个现有遗产地所不可替代；世界红层的遍在性和形成时间、空间分布的差异性表明中国丹霞是世界红层地貌和丹霞发育中不可缺少的重要环节；中国丹霞相对现有世界遗产，是山—水—林配置最好的丹霞（红层）地貌区，具有更突出的丹霞地貌科学价值和美学价值，具有更加良好的生态环境价值；以丹霞为载体形成的丹霞文化更注重天人和谐，反映了一种世界意义的地貌文化的突出普遍价值。

澄江化石遗址

1984年夏天，中国科学院南京地质古生物研究所的侯先光来到澄江，寻找曾经生存于寒武纪的高肌虫化石。在离帽天山不远的洪家冲，侯先光一钉锤下去，揭开了一个沉睡了5.3亿年的惊天秘密。

澄江帽天山化石带，呈带状蜿蜒分布，长20公里，宽4.5公里，埋藏深度在50米以上。遗址占地512公顷，是目前保存最完整的寒武纪早期海洋古生物化石群，展现了门类广泛的无脊椎与脊椎生命体的硬组织及软组织解剖构造。澄江化石群记录了早期复杂海洋生态系统的形成，它为古生物学的学术研究打开了一扇明亮的窗户。

在漫长的地质历史时期中，动物尸骸、尤其是无脊椎动物的软体部分，极易腐烂，只有在极其特殊的自然环境下，才能得以保存为化石。地质学家和古生物学家们对云南澄江的地层取样研究后认为：在寒武纪早期，滇东、滇中、黔西、两广一带是海域，澄江为海域在滇中隆起的扬子江浅海区，靠海岸较近，因此容易聚集泥质的沉积物。这时期气候温暖，海水矿物质丰富，海绵、蠕虫、节肢动物、腕足动物等底栖动物，水母状动物等浮游动物，多门类的游泳动物与藻类植物大量出现。后来这些海栖动物和植物突然被洪水或其他意外性涌来的泥质沉积物埋藏，隔绝了空气，天长日久便形成化石。

生物资源

澄江生物群出现于寒武纪生物大爆发时期，除了低等植物藻类外，大量代表现生各个动物门类的动物同时出现。共169属191种，其中动物159属180种，植物藻类3属3种。

澄江生物群以软躯体化石的罕见保存为特色，已发现的澄江生物群化石分属海绵动物、腔肠动物、鳃曳动物、叶足动物、腕足动物、软体动物、节肢动物等多个动物门以及一些分类位置不明的奇异类群。此外，还有多种共生的海藻。动物化石群中的水母化石填补了中国古生物研究的空白。寒武纪早期水母化石的发现，在国际上也属首次。

除水母化石外，还有海绵、蠕虫、腕足类、腹足类，软舌螺，金碧虫和其他类型的节肢动物等，其软件结构及骨骼保存得非常完善，并以种类之多，保存之完整、生动，可与世界著名的澳大利亚晚前寒武纪的埃迪卡拉动物群、加拿大中寒武纪的布尔吉斯页岩动物群相媲美。而且这一发现，填补了布尔吉斯、埃迪卡拉这两个动物群之间演化的一个重要环节，对回答生命演化中一些基本问题产生重要影响。

主要化石景观

澄江帽天山动物化石群由于门类多、层次分明、分布广泛，加之保存完整，因而被誉为世界古生物之最，其与澳大利亚埃迪卡拉动物群、加拿大布尔吉期页岩动物群同被世界古生物学列为地球早期生命起源和演化实例的三大奇迹。

云南虫　云南虫是人类的远祖，属脊索动物门。脊索动物是脊椎动物的祖先。

帽天山的第一块云南虫化石是侯先光研究员1991年发现的。侯先光发现这块化石后，由于对某些性质难以解释，就把它作为分类位置不明确的动物里面。1995年陈均远教授等专家学者经过研究，在英国《自然》杂志上发表文章，提出云南虫是脊索动物的论证。这个观点把脊索动物起源从布尔吉斯页岩的“皮凯亚虫”向前推进了1500万年。

抚仙湖虫　它是昆虫的远祖。1993年瑞典古生物学家伯格琼斯发现时认为它是囊虫动物或者扁虫动物。1996年陈均远等专家经过反复研究后认为，它是直虾类的祖先。

纳罗虫　海底爬行泥食性动物。是侯先光于1984年7月1日在帽天山上发现的第一块纳罗虫化石，从此揭开了帽天山神秘的面纱。1985年，侯先光与导师张文堂合作，在《古生物学报》上发表论文《纳罗虫在亚洲大陆的新发现》，将其正式命名为“澄江动物群”。

怪诞虫　头大，是寒武纪最著名的动物。

罗哩山虫　它是侯先光等人1989年采集命名的。

云南火把虫　这种动物可能是食肉或者食腐类动物。

奇虾　奇虾是寒武纪海洋的霸主，古生物中的强盗。

昆明鱼　昆明鱼是澄江化石群中最古老的脊椎动物，被称为“天下第一鱼”。

遗产价值

澄江生物群是以全景式写照，生动的再现了 5.3 亿年前的“寒武纪大爆发”发生的真实过程，他充分显示了寒武纪早期生物多样性。几乎所有现生动物的门类和许多灭绝的生物在完全没有祖先痕迹可寻的前提下奇迹般地出现在寒武纪的原始海洋中，从而将大多数现生动物门类的进化历史追溯到了寒武纪的开始阶段。

澄江生物群给我们提供了一个完整的最古老的海洋生态群落图，这种生态群落之前我们的认识几乎是一片空白。发现该化石群后，我们不仅能知道在寒武纪大爆发时产生了哪些动物，我们还能初步了解不同动物的生活方式和食性。澄江生物群或许还能帮助我们了解寒武纪生物大爆发中生物演化的原因，以及诱发这种大爆发的原由。

四川大熊猫栖息地

四川大熊猫栖息地位于中国四川省境内，包括卧龙、四姑娘山和夹金山脉，面积9245平方公里，地跨成都市、雅安市、阿坝藏族羌族自治州、甘孜藏族自治州四个地级行政区的12个县或县级市。目前全世界30%以上的野生大熊猫生活在那里，是全球最大最完整的大熊猫栖息地。

四川大熊猫栖息地主要位于大渡河与岷山之间、成都平原与青藏高原之间的邛崃山脉，南北长180公里，东西宽40–70公里，涵盖成都、雅安、阿坝、甘孜4市州12县。该范围涵盖9个风景名胜区和7个自然保护区，面积9510平方公里，其中核心区面积5370平方公里，缓冲区为4140平方公里，被列入世界自然遗产的四川大熊猫栖息地面积9245平方公里。

自1998年四川率先在全国实施天然林保护工程以来，四川大熊猫的栖息地面积逐年扩大。在汶川地震发生前，大熊猫栖息地面积已达177万公顷，成为1206只野生大熊猫的乐园。通过对大熊猫栖息地灾后恢复重建，四川省不仅使被损毁的大熊猫栖息地得以恢复，同时新增4万公顷大熊猫栖息地，将大熊猫自然保护区扩充至37个，并建成土地岭、泥巴山野生大熊猫遗传基因交流的一条走廊，使大熊猫在栖息地和自然保护区内得到了很好的保护。

自然保护区和风景名胜区

四川大熊猫栖息地由中国四川省境内的7个自然保护区和9个风景名胜区组成。

自然保护区

卧龙国家级自然保护区　位于汶川县境内，成立于1963年，主要保护大熊猫及森林生态系统。

蜂桶寨国家级自然保护区　位于宝兴县境内，成立于1975年，主要保护大熊猫及森林生态系统。

小金四姑娘山国家级自然保护区　位于小金县境内，成立于1996年，主要保护野生动物及高山生态系统。

喇叭河省级自然保护区　位于天全县境内，成立于1963年，主要保护大熊猫、牛羚等珍稀动物。

黑水河省级自然保护区　位于芦山县和大邑县境内，成立于1993年，主要保护大熊猫及森林生态系统。

金汤—孔玉省级自然保护区　位于康定县境内，成立于1995年，主要保护珍稀动物及生态环境。

草坡省级自然保护区　位于汶川县境内，成立于2000年，主要保护大熊猫及生态环境。

风景名胜区

青城山—都江堰国家级风景名胜区　位于都江堰市境内，成立于1982年。

天台山国家级风景名胜区　位于邛崃市境内，成立于1989年。

四姑娘山国家级风景名胜区　位于小金县境内，成立于1994年。

西岭雪山国家级风景名胜区　位于大邑县境内，成立于1994年。

鸡冠山—九龙沟省级风景名胜区　位于崇州市境内，成立于1986年。

夹金山省级风景名胜区　位于宝兴县境内，成立于1995年。

米亚罗省级风景名胜区 位于理县境内，成立于1995年。

灵鹫山—大雪峰省级风景名胜区 位于芦山县境内，成立于1999年。

二郎山省级风景名胜区 位于天全县境内，成立于2000年。

遗产提名地

中国四川大熊猫栖息地有三个遗产提名地：卧龙、四姑娘山、夹金山脉。

卧　龙

传说是龙王云游至此，因留恋这里的美丽风光而化作群山俯卧在这里，于是，这方神奇的土地有了一个形象的名字——“卧龙”。

自然保护区位于阿坝州汶川县境内，离成都市区仅120公里左右，距都江堰50多公里。卧龙处于邛崃山脉东麓，青藏高原向四川盆地过渡地带的高山峡谷区，5000米以上的高山就有101座，最高峰四姑娘山海拔6250米。这里峰峦重叠，云雾缭绕，原始森林、次生灌木林、箭竹林郁郁葱葱。卧龙地势较高而且湿润，十分适宜大熊猫的主要食物——箭竹和桦桔竹的生长，是大熊猫生存和繁衍的理想地区。核桃坪大熊猫饲养繁殖场和全世界唯一的大熊猫研究中心，是观赏、了解大熊猫的好地方。

目前该地拥有全国十分之一的野生大熊猫、一半以上的圈养大熊猫，是世界名副其实的“大熊猫之乡”。

四姑娘山

四姑娘山地处小金县与汶川县交界处，由横断山脉中四座毗连的山峰组成，根据当地藏民的传说，为四个美丽的姑娘所化，因而得名。

四姑娘山海拔6250米，终年积雪，直插蓝天，蔚为壮观。

溪沟呈南北向穿行于峡谷之中，纵深十至数十公里。其中四姑娘山双桥沟纵深30余公里，峡谷时宽时窄，宽阔处可达数公里，斜坡上覆以广阔的草坪，溪流蜿蜒其间。

四姑娘山是一片神奇美丽的土地，气候特殊，垂直高差显著，动植物资源十分丰富。山麓森林茂密，绿草如茵，清澈溪流潺潺不绝，直是一派秀美的南欧风光，人称“中国的阿尔卑斯”。

夹金山

夹金山位于小金县南部，由木城沟和木尔寨沟两个原始生态区构成。2000年12月国家林业局批准成立“夹金山国家森林公园”，夹金山脉现有野生大熊猫约240只，约占四川总数的四分之一和全国总数的四分之一。自1955年起，雅安市夹金山脉地区向国家先后提供活体大熊猫，占国家调用的全国野生大熊猫总数中的46%和我国赠予外国的“国礼”大熊猫的78%，是国际上野生大熊猫的最大供给地。夹金山脉大熊猫栖息地还是大熊猫、金丝猴等82种脊椎动物与珙桐等105种高等植物的模式标本产地。

遗产价值

大熊猫动物群的形成经历了第三纪热带环境、第四纪热带——亚热带环境和现代山地亚热带——亚高山寒温带环境的演化，是地球发展最新阶段——第四纪的地质——生物过程的突出例证，在哺乳动物分类与进化以及古环境变迁研究上，具有十分重要的价值。

Imperial Palaces of the Ming and Qing Dynasties in Beijing and Shenyang

The Imperial Palace of Beijing

According to ancient Chinese astrology, the North Star (called ziwei in Chinese) is located in the center of the sky where the emperor of heaven resides. Correspondingly, the Imperial Palace of Beijing is also called "Purple Forbidden City". It is situated in the center of Beijing, one kilometer to the north of Tian'anmen square and opposite the south gate of Jingshan Park. It was the imperial palace of the Ming and Qing dynasties, and 24 emperors ascended to the throne here. First built in 1406 A.D., it now is over 600 years old. It is the largest and most complete ancient wooden structure complex still surviving in the world. The total area of the Imperial Palace is 720,000 square meters, and the area occupied by buildings (totaling 9,000 bays) is about 150,000 square meters. The well-planned, towering and grandiose Forbidden City with yellow tiles and red walls and white jade railings is the paragon of ancient Chinese architecture.

Architectural Arrangement

The Imperial Palace strictly follows the construction rules for imperial palaces laid down in *Rituals of Zhou: Construction Works* (《周礼 · 考工记》), "the court in the front and the palaces in the back, the Imperial Shrine of Family (Chinese: 太庙 ; pinyin: Tàimiào) on the left and the Imperial Shrine of State (Chinese: 太社稷 ; pinyin: Tàishèjì) on the right". The whole palace epitomizes the design concept of supreme royal power and the paramount position of the emperor, even down to every brick and tile. The architecture also achieves the artistic effect of balance from left to right and variety in shape.

In order to highlight the paramount authority of the emperor, there was a central axis from north to south in the Imperial Palace. Along this axis stand three halls (the Hall of Supreme Harmony, the Hall of Central Harmony and the Hall of Preserving Harmony) and three palaces (the Palace of Heavenly Purity, the Hall of Union and the Palace of Earthly Tranquility) . The three halls symbolize the center of the regime where the emperor issued orders, while the three palaces are the residence of the emperor and empress. In the Inner Court (the section to the north of Gate of Heavenly Purity) there are two minor axes on the right and left respectively centered by the Palace of Tranquil Longevity (residence of the father of the emperor) and the Palace of Earthly Tranquility (the residence of the wives of ex-emperors) . The two minor axes also match the Outer Court centered by the Gate of Heavenly Harmony with the Hall of Literary Glory on the left and the Hall of Military Excellence on the right. Between the two minor axes and the central axis are the Hall of Abstinence and the Hall of Mental Cultivation. The eastern six palaces and the western six palaces behind the two buildings are the residences of the concubines of the emperor. The central axis not only goes through the Imperial Palace, but also reaches the Yongding Gate of the capital to the south and the Drum and Bell Towers to the north. So the central axis cuts through the whole city and renders the capital an imposing and well-designed city.

Main Buildings

The Four Splendid Gates

The Imperial Palace has four entrances: the East Glorious Gate, the West Glorious Gate, the Gate of Divine Might, and the Meridian Gate.

The Meridian Gate is the front gate, usually called "the Five Phoenix Tower" by the common people. It is from this gate that the emperor issued decrees and gave the order of war. The central gateway of this gate was normally only used by the emperor; the empress used it on the occasion of her wedding, and also could be used once by the top three examinees in the imperial examination. The east gateway was for the civil and military officials while the west gateway was for members of the royal family.

The Gate of Divine Might is the back gate of the Imperial Palace and was named "Xuanwu Gate" in the Ming Dynasty. It is a tower-shaped building with highest-scale double eave and hip roof. But the hall of this gate is more compact, without protruding wings on the left and right. So it was a grade lower than the Meridian Gate in shape and structure. This gate now serves as the front gate of the Palace Museum.

The East Glorious Gate and the West Glorious Gate These two gates echo each other in location and structure. Both are rectangular edifices with a base of white marble and three circular arch shaped gateway; they have double eaves and hip roof covered by yellow glazed tiles. The gates are five bays wide and three bays deep and surrounded by corridors.

Three Prominent Halls

The courtyard occupying an area of 30,000 square meters beyond the Gate of Supreme Harmony contains the center of the Outer Court: the Hall of Supreme Harmony, the Hall of Central Harmony and the Hall of Preserving Harmony (generally called three grand halls) . They are all built on 8-meter-tall terraces made up of white marble; from a distance they could be palaces in heaven.

The Hall of Supreme Harmony was where the emperor held important ceremonies. It is the highest-scaled architecture and the largest in size as well as the most richly decorated building. It is also the largest ancient wooden structure hall surviving in China. There are 92 1-meter-in-diameter wooden columns supporting this structure and 6 of them surrounding the throne are called dragon pillars coated with lek powder and lacquer. The throne is set on a two-meter-tall pedestal inside the hall with beautiful bronze ware such as crane, incense-burner and tripod (鼎) in front and an exquisitely carved folding screen in the back. The whole hall is decorated in magnificent style.

The Hall of Central Harmony behind the Hall of Supreme Harmony is the place where the emperor took rest and rehearsed rituals before great ceremonies. It has corridors on the four sides. The floor of this hall is paved with "golden bricks" (a kind of specially baked paving brick from Suzhou) . It is a single-eave pavilion roofed structure covered by yellow blazed tiles on the top. In the center of the roof where four ridges converge is a gilt bronze-bodied dome in the shape of a ball.

The Hall of Preserving Harmony is behind the Hall of Central Harmony. It is a double-eave hip and gable roofed structure covered by yellow blazed tiles. There is a main ridge in the middle of the roof and two diagonal ridges in front of and behind the main ridge. Under each diagonal ridge is a bifurcation ridge. So all together there are nine ridges on the roof. This hall is the place where the emperor gave banquets to rulers of vassal states and held the imperial examination.

The Inner Court

The back part of the Imperial Palace is called the Inner Court. The Palace of Heavenly Purity, the Hall of Union and the Palace of Earthly Tranquility are the center of the Inner Court while there are the eastern six palaces and western six palaces to the east and west. The Inner Court is the place where the emperor handled national affairs and the royal household resided. While buildings in the Outer Court featured magnificence and grandeur to highlight the supremacy of the emperor, the Inner Court in the back had a strong flavor of life. This is manifested in that the structures are located in self-contained courtyards with gardens, studies, pavilions and rocks.

The Palace of Heavenly Purity is the main hall of the Inner Court with a height of 20 meters. In the center of the hall is a throne and a tablet with four Chinese characters " 正大光明 " (meaning "fair and square") . On both ends of the hall are warm rooms. Before and during Emperor Kangxi's reign this was the place where the emperor lived and handled state affairs. From the time of Emperor Yongzheng's reign the monarchs moved to the Hall of Mental Cultivation. Yet this palace remained a place for the emperor to read memorials from officials and appoint and receive officials.

The Palace of Earthly Tranquility was the empress's residence in Ming and Qing dynasties before Emperor Yongzheng's reign. On both ends of the palace there are also warm rooms. In the Qing Dynasty this palace was converted into a venue for offering sacrifices to gods. After the time of Emperor Yongzheng the warm room on the west end served as a venue for shamans to worship. The warm room on the east end used to be the bridal room for the emperor's wedding with the empress. Emperors Kangxi, Tongzhi and Guangxu all had their wedding ceremonies here.

The Hall of Union is between the Palace of Heavenly Purity and the Palace of Earthly Tranquility. And the name of this hall means "the bridal of heaven and earth brings happiness and health". It is a four-corner-pavilion-roofed structure with a gilt dome with dragon and phoenix patterns. During the Ming and Qing dynasties this was the place where the empress celebrated her birthdays. The seal of the Qing Dynasty was also harbored here.

From the time of Emperor Yongzheng the Hall of Mental Cultivation became the actual residence of the emperors in the Imperial Palace. During Emperor Tongzhi's reign, two empress dowagers, Cixi and Ci'an, attended to state affairs behind a bamboo curtain in the east warm room of this hall.

The Imperial Garden

The Imperial Garden is at the north of the Palace of Earthly Tranquility. It used to be called "the Garden in the Back of the Palace" and occupies an area of over 11,000 square meters. There are over 20 buildings in the garden and the main building here is Hall of Imperial Peace, a double-eave Lu-topped structure located along the north-south main axis of the Imperial Palace. With this building as the center, pavilions and towers stretch to the front and left and right. In the garden green pine trees and cypresses and bamboos adorn the exquisite rocks and form an evergreen garden view.

Significance of the Heritage

The palace architecture of Palace Museum is the largest and most complete surviving ancient architecture complex in China. All the palaces are arranged symmetrically along the central north-south axis and so the whole complex of buildings appears magnificent and splendid. Beijing Imperial Palace and the Palace Museum are among the few museums and cultural heritages that share the characteristics of art museum, architecture museum, history museum and palace culture museum and are in accordance with the internationally recognized norms of "site protection" and "display of original appearance."

Shenyang Palace Museum

In 2004, Shenyang Palace Museum was entered in *the World Heritage List* as an extension project of the Imperial Palace of Ming and Qing dynasties.

Located at the old city centre of Ming and Qing dynasties in predent-day Shenhe District of Shenyang City, Shenyang Palace Museum, whose construction began in 1625 and completed in 1636, was the imperial palace in Shenyang before the Late Jin Dynasty conquered the Ming Dynasty and became the Shengjing temporary Imperial Palace after the Qing Dynasty made Beijing its new capital. After the Qing Dynasty moved its capital to Beijing, Shenyang Imperial Palace went through an expansion and became the temporary palace for the emperor when he made an inspection tour to the Northeast. The over 100 remaining ancient buildings take an area of more than 60,000 square metres. The main body of Shenyang Palace Museum, having been the imperial palace during the period of the Qing emperor Huang Taiji (1627 – 1643) , has strong Manchu characteristics as well as the characteristics of local northeastern construction.

Architectural Arrangement

Compared with Beijing Palace Museum, Shenyang Palace Museum reflects unique Manchu, Mongolian and Tibetan architectural features. The east section consists of Dazheng Hall, that is, the main hall, and Shiwang (ten princes) Pavilion, which were modelled after the layout of Dawoci, the march house account of the "Eight Banners" (military-administrative organizations of the Man nationality in the Qing Dynasty) . The middle section consists of the imperial palaces built in the period of Emperor HuangTaiji, including Daqing Gate, Chongzheng Hall, Phoenix Building, and Qingning Palace, Guanju Palace, Linzhi Palace, Yanqing Palace, and Yongfu Palace. This section is characterised by "tall palace and low hall", with the residential houses built at high platform to overlooking the main hall area of administration, which had to do with the living habit of Manchu who loved to live over platforms and hillocks. The west section is made up of Wensu Chamber, Jiayin Chamber and Yangxi Room built under Emperor Qianlong. The East and West palaces in west section and middle section are completely of Han style. In the whole palace museum are a forest of buildings and pavilions that are towering, magnificent and with richly decorated interior of carved beams and painted rafters.

Main Buildings

Dazheng Hall Popularly know as Bajiao (octagonal) Hall. First built in 1625, it was the most sacred place in Shengjing Imperial Palace. It is an octagonal eaves pavilion with 8 sides and corridors, and stands on sumeru platform. The roof is covered with yellow glazed tiles and edged with green trim. Around the Baoding (precious top) are 8 iron chains connected each with a strong man. The two columns in front of the hall are decorated with golden dragons, while inside the hall are sanskrit ceiling and dragon caisson. In the hall are displayed throne, screen, cense burner, incense pavilion, crane candlestick. Dazheng Hall was where great ceremonies were held, such as the enthronement of emperors, issuing imperial edict, announcing the battles and welcoming triumphant army coming back. In 1644 when Fulin was enthroned here was the first year of Emperor Shunzhi.

Shiwang(ten princes) Pavilions Arranged in sequence on the two sides of Dazheng Hall, Shiwang Pavilions are the reflection of the Manchu Eight Banners political system in the construction of palace. It is the only one of its kind in ancient Chinese imperial architecture. From north to south on the east side are in sequence the pavilion of the Left Wing Prince, pavilion of Xianghuang Banner, pavilion of Real White Banner, pavilion of Real Blue Banner; and on the west side are in sequence pavilion of the Right Wing Prince, pavilion of Real Yellow Banner, pavilion of Real Red Banner, pavilion of Xianghong Banner and pavilion of Xianglan Banner. This is where the princes, baylors (a rank of the Manchu nobility below that of the Prince) and ministers discussed and handled political affairs.

Daqing Gate Popularly known as the Meridian Gate, Daqing Gate was the front gate of Shengjing Imperial Palace (the present Shenyang Palace Museum) . Built in the 6th year of Tiancong (1632 A.D.) , it is one of the early buildings of Shengjing imperial palace built by Huang Taiji. It is a hard mountain type of building with five-room front covered with glazed tiles and the roof was decorated with green trim. The utmost top of the gable of Daqing Gate are 4 protruding porch heads at the south and north. All three sides of the porch heads are inlaid of 5-colored glaze, with protruding sea water and cloud dragon ornamentation and all kinds of animals symbolising good luck. The animals are delicately carved and look very lifelike.

Chongzheng Hall At the very centre of the front yard of the middle section, Chongzheng Hall, popularly known as the "Throne Room", is the most important building at Shenyang Palace Museum. The whole building is structured of wood, with 5 rooms at the front and 3 rooms in depth. The front and back porches are in the style of hard mountain. There are partition doors. Both the front and back porches are surrounded with stone carved railings. The roof is covered with yellow glaze tiles and decorated with green trim. The main ridge is decorated with 50 colored glaze dragon and flame beads. This was where Emperor Huang Taiji met his officials, treated foreign envoys and dealt with important affairs. In 1636, the ceremony for changing the Late Jin national name to Da Qing was held here. The emperors who took "east inspection" held celebration ceremonies such as "paying homage to imperial tombs finished".

Phoenix Building Standing on the 4-metre-tall black brick base at the north end, Phoenix Building has three storeys. The roof is covered with yellow glaze tiles and decorated with green trim. As the tallest building in Shengjing, it was one of the "8 Shengjing scenic spots" and was named "Phoenix Building under the morning sun" and "viewing tower at Phoenix Building". In Phoenix Building is hung the "Purple Air comes from the east" (a propitious omen) plaque handwritten by Emperor Qianlong himself.

Qingning Palace It is a building of hard mountain style with 5 front rooms and front and back porches. This is the "central palace" for the residence of Emperor Qing Taizong Huang Taiji and his queen. The door is at the second room in the east, the west side in the room forms the pattern of "package room". The big wide removable window is simple in style. The gate of the palace is not of partition board type, and right in front of the gate of the palace is erected "solon rod", which originated from the traditional Manchu style. The roof is covered with yellow glaze tiles and edged with trim. Square eave columns are used in the front and back of the palace. The column cap is decorated with animal faces, and the sandalwood square column is decorated with colored drawing, which is the imitation of Han and Tibetan architectural art.

Wenyuan Pavilion Built in the 47th year of Emperor Qianlong (1782 A.D.) specifically for storing *the Wenyuan Pavilion Si Ku Quan Shu* (*Complete Library in the Four Branches of Literature*) , with *Integration of Ancient and Modern Books* also being stored here. Now the main building of the west section of Shenyang Palace Museum, its architectural pattern is an imitation of Tianyi Pavilion in Ningbo, Zhejiang Province. It has six front rooms and two storeys. It is a multi-eaves building of hard mountain type, with front and back porches, and the roof is covered with black glaze tiles and edged with green trim, while the front and back eave columns are painted green. All doors, windows and columns are painted green, and the color painting on the eaves are mainly in such cool colors as blue, green and white, which are in strong contrast with the red and gold eaves of other palaces. The themes of the color paintings also differ from the running dragons and flying phoenixes usually seen in palace buildings, but are such themes as "The White Horse Offering Books" and "Calligraphy Books" that are in harmony with the function of the book-storing pavilion and that give the impression of classic elegance and pure freshness.

The canopy architetural pattern and layout is the vivid and concrete representation of the Eight Banner System that had developed from Manchu's hunting experience in palace building. It is the only one of its kind in all ancient Chinese palace buildings. The architectural style and structure of Shenyang Palace Museum does not only reflect regional characteristics, but also expresses the idea of the ethnic integration that was in accord with the ruling thought of the Qing regime. Besides, the materials used in Shenyang Imperial Palace being in between those of the imperial and those of the rich people, this was consistent with its ruling status and reflected the situation at the early pioneering period of Qing Dynasty, and has very high value for the study of ancient architecture and culture.

Significance of the Heritage

Shenyang Palace Museum has become a famous tourist scenic spot not only for its palace buildings of multi-ethnic style, but is also renowned world wide for its rich collection of cultural relics and treasures. The cultural relics of Ming and Qing Imperial Palaces are especially precious and can be rightly called national treasures. The Exhibition of Cultural Relics and Treasure of Shenyang Palace Museum displays best attire, champleve enamel ware, calligraphy and painting, sculpture, lacquerware and chinaware. The cultural relics collectively represent the high craftmanship of Chinese working people and the artistic style of the Qing imperial court and reflect the standard of production technology in Ming and Qing dynasties, and thus have important appreciative value and research value.

Among the historic relics, art treasures and handicraft articles of Ming and Qing dynasties collected and displayed in Shenyang Palace Museum are many crafts from cultural communication between China and the West, unique among which are clocks, watches and glasswares. These crafts of high skill give a full show of the creative wisdom and artistic ability of foreign craftsmen, while at the same time bear historical evidence of cultural communication and trade between China and the West in the 17th and 18th centuries.

The Great Wall

Fighting all the way over 20000 li[Li is a Chinese unit in measuring distance. One li is half a kilometer.] *in the Long March, we will not be counted as men if we failed to reach the Great Wall.*

— by Mao Zedong

The Great Wall, also named "the ten-thousand-li Great Wall", refers to the large-scale defensive structure of China built over different periods in history to prevent the intrusion of northern nomadic tribes. State Administration of Cultural Heritage of China declared in Juyong Pass Great Wall on June 5th 2012 that after five years survey it was finally concluded that the total length of the Great Wall of different dynasties in China is 21196.18 kilometers and the distribution area cover 15 provinces (including municipalities and autonomous regions)-Beijing, Tianjin, Hebei, Shanxi, Inner Mongolia, Liaoning, Jilin, Heilongjiang, Shandong, He'nan, Shaaxi, Gansu and Qinghai-and heritage sites of the Great Wall including walls, trenches, monocoque construction, forts and supporting facilities amount to over 43721 altogether. This is the first time the Chinese administration scientifically, systematically measured the total length of the Great Wall.

The Great Wall in Different Periods

During Spring and Autumn period and the subsequent Warring States period, principalities of Zhou built beacon towers and joined them with walls to prevent intrusion of other countries. Hence the earliest Great Wall appeared. According to historical records, over 20 principalities and dynasties constructed walls in Chinese history and the total length is over a million li and the walls built in Qin Dynasty, the Han Dynasty and Ming Dynasty respectively are over 10, 000 li in length. In most provinces, municipalities and autonomous regions in north China there are ruins of the Great Wall and beacon towers today.

The Wall of the Qin Dynasty The Great Wall in the north of China was first built by three states during Warring States period, namely, Qin, Zhao and Yan.Ever since the Reform of Shangyan, Qin began to push the policy of booming the country and strengthening the military power. Emperor Qin Shi Huang enlisted 300, 000 people for the construction of the Great Wall and created this miraculous work in human architectural history. Objectively speaking, the Great Wall played a positive role in preventing the intrusion and incursion of the Huns and provided a peaceful environment for the development of economy and culture in the heartland of China. Sun Yat-sen once commented, "Though Emperor Qin Shi Huang is condemnable for his cruelty, the construction of the Great Wall in his reign is beneficial to later generations and may compare with the well-known ancient ruler Dayu's feat in controlling floods."

King Wulingwang of the State of Zhao decreed in the 26th year of his reign (300 B.C.) the construction of the Great Wall. The wall built by Zhao started from Dai and Mountain Yin westward to the Yellow River to prevent the possible plundering and looting of the Huns on the north.

The State of Yan is the weakest one among the seven powers of Warring States period and the state exerted itself after King Zhaowang ascended the throne, "Yan also constructed walls from Zaoyang to Xiangping and founded new counties such as Shanggu, Yuyang, Youbeiping, Liaoxi and Liaodong to resist the Huns."

The Wall of the Han Dynasty From the reign of Emperor Wendi to Emperor Xuandi, the Han Dynasty constructed a wall of nearly 10, 000 li from the city Ershi of Dawan in the west to the north bank of River Heilong. This is the longest wall in history and the ancient Silk Road ran parallel to it over half of the total distance. The walls built by Qin, Zhao and Yan had still performed its defensive function up to the early period of the Han Dynasty, though this capability had been greatly weakened in comparison to the Warring States period. Later on Emperor Wudi successfully defeated the Huns and drove them to today's Mongolian area and had the walls built by General Mengtian of Qin Dynasty reconstructed and a new outer wall constructed. Only then were the walls of Qin, Zhao and Yan abandoned and its defensive capability ceased.

The Wall of the Tang Dynasty The wall along River Mudan, reputed as "the Great Wall of the Tang Dynasty", was formally listed on the Great Wall World Cultural Heritage of China on November 6th, 2011.

This wall was a defensive system set up to defend Heishui Mohe on the north during Bohai period; so it's the same as the Great Wall in nature.

The Great Wall of the Ming Dynasty In order to guard against the intrusion of Dada and Wala, two Mongolian branches, Ming Dynasty never ceased its efforts in constructing the Great Wall. From Emperor Hongwu's reign to that of Emperor Wanli large-scale constructions had been undertaken over twenty times and so a wall of 6350 kilometers was completed. This wall stretched from Jiayu Pass of Gansu Province to Mountain Tiger in the east of Liaoning Province. Apart from the "Outer Wall", "Inner Wall" and "Inner Three Passes" were also constructed. The Inner Wall was built on the basis of the old wall of Qi in the Northern and Southern Dynasties. It stretched from the west of Pass Pianguan on the border of Inner Mongolia and Shanxi Province and went eastward via Pass Yanmen and Pass Pingxing into Hebei Province and then went northeast via Laiyuan County, Fangshan District and Changping District to Pass Juyong, and then it went eastward to Pass Sihai of Huairou County where it joined the Outer Wall. So the wall of Ming Dynasty was centered on Pass Zijing and went from north to south approximately. The "Inner Three Pass" wall went parallel to "Inner Wall" in many areas and the distance between them was only a dozen kilometers in some places.

Current Main Sites

Badaling Great Wall Among the Great Wall spots Badaling is most solidly built and well-preserved and the most representative section of the Great Wall of Ming Dynasty. It is located in Yanqing County of Beijing and 1015 meters above sea level. It is well situated and hard to access and has been an indispensible battleground for military strategists. In Ming Dynasty it had been an important fort in its own right and was also outpost for Pass Juyong and provided a defense for Beijing, the capital of China.

Mutianyu Great Wall Mutianyu Great Wall is located in Huairou District of Beijing and counts as one among the 16 new scenic spots of Beijing. It connects Juyong Pass in the west and joins Gubeikou Pass in the east. Famous views like Jiankou, Niujiaobian and Yingfeidaoyang are located on the west end of Mutianyu and so it is also a wonderful part of the Great Wall.

Simatai Great Wall Another distinctive section of the Great Wall is Simatai: here the mountains are steep, the vegetation dense, the views novel, the design exquisite and the facilities complete. It is located in the town of Gubeikou, northeast of Miyun County and 120 kilometers from Beijing. It starts from Wangjing Tower in the east and stretches to Houchuankou in the west and coverts 5.4 kilometers in distance. This section of the Great Wall is uniquely designed and novel-structured. Professor Luo Zhewen, a specialist of the Great Wall study, made the comment that the Great Wall is the wonder of the world while Simatai is the wonder of the Great Wall. Simatai is the only ancient architectural site where the original appearance of Ming walls has been preserved.

Gubeikou Great Wall Gubeikou presents the most complete great wall structure in history. It is made up of the wall of Northern Qi Dynasty and the wall of Ming, and comprises four sections: Mount Wohu, Mount Panlong, Ranges Jinshanling and Simatai. Gubeikou is a fort between Pass Shanhai and Pass Juyong, and is the only passage from Liaodong Plain in the Northeast of China and Inner Mongolia to the heartland of China. Undoubtedly it is also a hot battlefield for strategists, especially in the Five Dynasties of Liao, Jin, Yuan, Ming and Qing when major or minor battles to seize Gubeikou had scarcely ceased.

Shanhai Pass Great Wall Shanhai Pass is located in the point where the Great Wall joins the sea. The Great Wall within Shanhai Pass is 36 kilometers in total length and comprises seven castles, namely, Guancheng, Dongluocheng, Nanyicheng, Beiyicheng, Weiyuancheng and Ninghaicheng. They are surrounded by city walls which are 4769 meters long, 11.6 meters high, over 10 meters thick. The walls are tall and solid and quite imposing. There are four gates to enter this city in the four quarters and in the southeast and northeast corners there are turrets. In the center of the city there are grandiose Bell and Drum Towers. The whole structure is massive and solid for defense.

Jiayu Pass Great Wall Jiayu Pass is the west end of the Great Wall, the first fortress in Gansu Corridor as well as an important stage along the Silk Road. It was built in the fifth year of Hongwu (1372 A.D.) and has an area of over 33500 square meters. It is the most well-preserved pass-city hitherto and has the whole set of defense work-Inner City, Outer city and trenches. On the four corners of the pass-city there are two-storey turrets shaped like a tower.

Juyong Pass Great Wall Juyong Pass, celebrated as "the No. One Pass in China", is one of the oldest and most well-known passes along the Great Wall. It is most prominent in the large scale of the construction work and the profundity of cultural connotations among the passes. It is located in Guangou Gorge 48 kilometers to the northwest of Beijing. Here the steep mountains on both sides of the gorge confronting each other with a stream flowing through.

Significance of the Heritage

The Great Wall is the greatest military defensive work in ancient history of the world. It is not simply a wall with no supporting facilities; rather, it connected all the points along the wall to form a line and then a plane, i. e., all the beacon fires, passes, forts, pass-cities and military strongholds along the route are woven into a close net and so form a systematic defensive work. The forts, the pass-cities and military strongholds with permanently stationed troops constitute a comprehensive defensive structure performing the function of fighting, commanding, observing, communicating and concealing.

In cold weapon era the Great Wall defensive work was quite effective in military affairs. In Qin Dynasty, "the wall was built in the north of the country and the barriers were under our control, and the Huns were defeated and retreated over 700 li. Henceforward they dared not go southward to graze their horses." (*New Book: Visiting Qin*) Later in Emperor Wudi's reign of the Han Dynasty, "forts were built, beacons set up, the outer wall constructed, garrisons established to defend this area. And so the frontier areas were no longer disturbed." (*The Book of Han: the History of the Huns*) Those historical records show that the construction of the Great Wall is not only a measure for positive defense, but also a strategy for building up power for further movement.This is the fundamental reason for the construction of the Great Wall.

The main work of the Great Wall is tall walls stretching over 10, 000 li and they were mostly built on the top of ranges and delineated a clear-cut outline along the zigzagging mountains. The Great Wall is shaped like a majestic dragon leaping over the north of China and so stands for the Chinese. Along the 10,000-li wall there were hundreds of passes, forts and thousands of lookouts and beacon towers breaking the monotony of the uniformed wall. They render the undulating frame of the wall much steeper and so harder to access. There is great artistic charm in this military work.

Mausoleum of the First Qin Emperor

The Mausoleum of Emperor Qin Shihuang (the First Qin Emperor) is located in the eastern suburb of Lintong, Shaaxi Province. It is 5 kilometres away from Lintong and 36 kilometres away from Xi'an. It is not only the first emperor mausoleum built in Chinese history, but is the biggest one as well. Since 1974, 1.5 kilometres to the east of the mausoleum, 3 terracotta army pits have been discovered; 8,000 terracotta figurines, over 100 war chariots and tens of thousands of real weapons have been excavated. In 1980, 2 large-sized bronze carriages were excavated in the west side of the mausoleum. The discovery of the Mausoleum of Qin Shihuang aroused world-wide amazement and attention. It is the biggest underground military museum and has been acclaimed "the Eighth Wonder of the World".

Architectural Arrangement

"Emperor Qin swept the universe, and like a tiger he surveyed the world. Seven hundred thousand convicts were recruited, to build his tomb at Lishan Mountain." These memorable lines were composed by the great poet Li Bai, singing the praises of the brilliant achievements of emperor Qin Shihuang and describing the vast scale of his mausoleum project. As a matter of fact, in terms of scale, the number of workers and the length of construction, the mausoleum of Qin Shihuang has seen no earlier precedent. It started the practice of extravagant burial for later emperors to imitate. The construction of the mausoleum accompanied Qin Shihuang's lifelong political career: he started the project when he ascended the throne at the age of 13.

The Terracotta Army Pits were meant as an exterior section of the mausoleum of Emperor Qin Shihuang. According to records, the planning and designing of the mausoleum were presided over by Shihuang's Prime Minister Li Si, and General Zhang Han was in charge of supervising the construction.The whole project took 38 years. At that time,the whole kingdom of Qin had a population of about 20 million, and as many as 720,000 forced labourers took part in the construction. The yellow earth used for constructing the tomb was taken from an area 2,000 metres to the south, between Sanliu Village and the quarry. It has a multi-level yellow cliff, 5 to 25 metres high. The huge amount of stone used for constructing the mausoleum was transported completely by human labor from Mount Zhong and Mount Jun'e on the northern bank of the Wei River. It requires little imagination to realize how arduous the construction was.

The whole mausoleum is divided into a tomb section and a burial objects section. The tomb section takes up 8 square kilometres and is composed of an inner chamber and an outer chamber.The tomb is in a rectangular cone shape. The mausoleum rides west to east. With heaped earth forming a mound at the centre, the mausoleum is divided into 4 levels, namely, the underground palace as the central part, and successively there are the inner city, the outer city and the part outside the outer city, all very well arranged. It occupies 56.25 square kilometres of land.The interior of the city is 2.13 square kilometres. The wall of the city is made up of an inner wall and an outer wall, both of which are organised on a north-south axis, mutually coordinated to create a rectangular shape of homocentric square with the long sides facing north and south and the short sides facing east and west. The total length of the city wall is 12 kilometres, similar in length to the Ming Great Wall of Xi'an.

The Process of Unearthing

In March 1974, Yang Zhifa, a villager from Xiyang Village to the east of the mausoleum, while digging a well, hoed out a clay warrior head. Then archaeologists finally excavated the Terracotta Army Pit of the Mausoleum of Emperor Qin Shihuang. The discovery became a global sensation.

From 1974-1977, Shaaxi archaeologists excavated 3 Qin terracotta army pits in the southeast of Xiyang Village in Lintong County. All the pits are paint pot tunnel buildings made from earth and wood. Pit No 1, discovered in January 1974, is the biggest. It is rectangular with a size of 14,260 square metres. Among the 40 columns in the pit that are composed of war chariots, 38 columns of all warriors and chariots face east, with the rest of the warriors on the edges, as flanks and as rear guards respectively facing south, north and west. Judging from the density of the excavated section, there are more than 6,000 terracotta warriors and horses in Pit No.1.

Pit No.2, discovered in 1976, is 20 metres away to the north of Pit No.1. It is in the shape of a set square, and covers an area of about 6,000 square metres. Judging from excavated materials, about 1,400 terracotta warriors and 89 wooden chariots are buried in this pit. Pit No.3 is 25 metres to the north of the west side of Pit No.1. It is 120 metres away from Pit No.2 in the east.This pit is in an inward curving form, covering an area of 520 square metres. Inside it are buried 1 wooden war chariot, 4 clay horses and 68 clay warrior figurines, who stand along the four walls in a ring, facing inward and looking at each other.

Judging from the form and structure and equipment of the figurines, Pit No.1 stands for the main body of the army that is composed of infantrymen and war chariots, and Pit No.2 is the combination of infantrymen, cavalrymen and chariot soldiers, while Pit No.3 represents the headquarters that command both Pit No.1 and 2.

Terracotta Figurines and Bronze Chariots

All the terracotta figurines excavated from the Terracotta Warriors and Horses Pit show a strong touch of military hue, so they are all warrior figurines. Classified according to clothing, there are war-robe figurines and armour figurines; and according to identity and status,there are officers and soldiers. The officers may be divided into senior officers (commonly referred to as generals) , intermediate officers and low-ranking officers. According to army branch, the figurines can be divided into infantrymen, chariotmen, cavalrymen and crossbowmen. Classified only according to hat and armour, the senior officers wear hats made with feathers of brown-eared pheasants and armour with fish scale patterns, the intermediate officers wear long plate-type hats and armour with decorative border, while low-ranking officers have long plate-type hats and armour without decorative border. Soldiers wear no hats. Soldiers wearing armour have a higher position, but all the armours have no decorative patterns. Judging from the afore-mentioned classification, the Qin army was an iron army that enjoyed complete branches and a stringent system of social stratum.

The bronze chariots were discovered 20 metres away at the west side of the mausoleum. In 1980 when carrying out trial excavation in the bronze chariots pit, archaeologists found in a wooden-chambered tomb two large-sized bronze chariots in tandem that were stowed on end. They were already broken then and were later repaired and restored. The main body of the bronze chariots are made of bronze, and some of the accessories are gold and silver. Metal processing technologies in Qin Dynasty secured brilliant achievements, and this was collectively reflected in the manufacture of the bronze chariots in the mausoleum of Emperor Qin Shihuang. The chariot is made up of over 3,000 components. The craftsmen used various technologies of casting, welding, inlaying, movable link connection, snap-fastener connection, and spiale connection, to put together the complete chariot, attaining a very high technological level.

Significance of the Heritage

The historical facets reflected in the Qin terracotta figurines are both rich and far-reaching, and provide unique value in understanding the various historical aspects of architecture, costume and institutions, especially the institutional history of mausoleum.

What is most stunning about the Qin Terracotta Warriors and Horses is their remarkable artistic achievement. The thousands of big and valiant clay figurines, arranged as a whole in nearly 20,000 square metres of space, embody the outstanding ability of ancient artists in mastering grand materials and in realising systematic taste and artistic creativity. Their majestic momentum arouses in the hearts of visitors of all nationalities a powerful feeling of admiration.The terracotta warriors appear different from one another and are perfectly lifelike, which prove how outstanding the artists were at expressing bodily structures and facial expressions, and at using all kinds of colors and depicting details. The realistic style of the art works has left us a superb ancient artistic model, and at the same time, the art works have kept for us a priceless historical record of that age.

The cultural relics excavated in the Terracotta Warriors and Horses Pit have also expanded greatly our knowledge about the scientific and technological levels of the Qin Dynasty. The large numbers of real objects vividly embody the development standard of the production forces at that time. As far as the history of science and technology is concerned, many materials discovered here are astonishing. Besides, the military contents as exhibited by the thousands of terracotta warriors and horses doubtless ly provide the most important and most lively data for studying military history. Many materials have helped upgrade people's knowledge about ancient military affairs.

Temple of Heaven: an Imperial Sacrificial Altar in Beijing

Sacrifice to Heaven, as a cultural act of human beings praying to spirits for bestowing good fortune and dispelling disaster, used to be an important aspect of the the life of Chinese people in ancient China. From the legendary "3 Sovereigns and 5 Emperors" right to the end of the Qing Dynasty, the sacrificial ceremony to worship heaven had been in practice for over 5000 years, which is truly a long history.

In 1420, the 18th year of the reign of Ming Emperor Yongle, the Temple of Heaven was built to worship heaven and earth, modelled on the Temple of Heaven and Earth in Nanjing. Back then, the sacrificial ceremony was carried out at the main hall. In 1530, the 9th year of the reign of Emperor Jiajing, following the suggestion of his minister, the Emperor decided to offer separate sacrifices to heaven and earth, and so the Circular Mound Altar was built to the south of the main hall for sacrifices particularly to heaven, and Fangze Altar was built to worship earth outside of Anding Gate in the north of the city. In 1534, the 13th year of the reign of Jiajing, the Hall of Prayer for Good Harvest was decommissioned, and in the 19th year the construction of Daxiang Hall began, and was completed in the 24th year.In 1751, the 16th year of the reign of Qing Emperor Qianlong, Daxiang Hall was renamed Hall of Prayer for Good Harvest, and later was repaired and expanded on several occasions.

Architectural Arrangement

In the city of Beijing, the Temple of Earth in the north was for worshiping earth, the Temple of Heaven in the south was for worshiping heaven, the Altar of the Sun in the east was for worshiping the sun, and the Altar of the Moon in the west was for worshiping the moon. Among all of the four altars, the Temple of Heaven is the most splendid.

The Temple of Heaven is the collective name for the Circular Mound Altar and the Altar of Prayer for Good Harvest, and it was the place where the emperors of the Ming and Qing dynasties held ceremonies to worship heaven and to pray for good harvests. The altar was enclosed by two walls which form the inner Outer Altar. The wall of the altar is square to the south and round in the north, symbolising that heaven is round and the earth square. The main buildings are in the Inner Altar. The Circular Round Altar is to the south, and the Altar of Prayer for Good Harvest is to the north. The two altars, separated by a wall, are on the same south-north axis. The main buildings in the Circular Mound Altar include the Circular Mound Altar and the Imperial Vault of Heaven; the Altar of Prayer for Good Harvests contains the Hall of the Prayer for Good Harvests, the hall of the Heavenly Emperor, and the Gate of Prayer for Good Harvests. The famous Hall of Prayer for Good Harvests, the most grand and splendid building in the Temple of Heaven, at the most northern corner, was imagined to be closest to heaven. In 1545, the 24th year of the reign of Ming Jiajing Emperor, it was changed into a three-tiered round hall, covered from the top with black, yellow and green glazed tile, signifying everything in heaven and on earth. In 1751, the 16th year of the reign of Qing Emperor Qianlong, the three-color tile were replaced with the same blue glazed tile and gold roof and the place was renamed the Hall of the Prayer for Good Harvests, specifically used for praying for grain in early spring.

The whole design of the Temple of Heaven, from the architectural layout to the handling of every detail, gives emphasis to the idea of Heaven. When one stands in 300-metre-long corridor and looks around, the first thing one sees is the vast sky and the Hall of Prayer for Good Harvests symbolising Heaven, and one can't help feeling close to heaven.

The main buildings in the Inner Altar are on the south-north axis. The Circular Mound Altar to the south was for worshiping heaven; the Altar of Prayer for Grain in the north was for praying for good harvests. The two altars are connected by the Danbi Bridge (also called Haiman Avenue, or Sacred Way) , 360 metres long and 30 metres wide, with the north side being higher than the south side. In the altar are such main buildings as the Hall of Prayer for Good Harvests, the Hall of the Heavenly Emperor, the Circular Mound Altar, the Imperial Vault of Heaven, the Fasting Hall, the Beamless Hall, the Long Corridor and the Bicyclic Wanshou Pavilion. The other places of historic interest and scenic beauty include The Echo Wall, the Three Sound Stones, and the Seven Star Stone.

Main Buildings

The Circular Mound Altar The Temple of Heaven is the collective name for two altars: the Altar for Prayer of Grain and the Circular Mound Altar. The double walls enclosing the temple separate it into Inner Altar and Outer Altar, both of which are square in the south and round in the north.

The Circular Mound Altar was the place where the sacrificial ceremony for heaven was held. The main buildings here include the Circular Mound, the Imperial Vault of Heaven, the Side Hall, the Kitchen, Sanku and the Slaughter Pavilion, and accessory buildings such as the dressing platform and Wangdeng, etc. During the Ming Dynasty the Circular Mound was a three-storey, blue glazed tile round altar. In 1749, the 14th year of the reign of Qing Emperor Qianlong, it was enlarged, the original blue-glazed tiles being replaced with white marble.

The Imperial Vault of Heaven At the north of the Circular Mound Altar, the Imperial Vault of Heaven was the site for making offerings to the gods worshipped at the Circular Mound Altar, the place for housing the plates that identified the deities worshipped. It was originally a building of double eaves and conical roof, but in 1752, the 17th year of the reign of Qing Emperor Qianlong, it was changed into a golden-roofed, single-eaved, conical building. The brick-wood structure, with no crossbeam, relies on 8 peripheral columns, 8 gold pillars and many bucket arches to support the roof, making clever application of the principles of mechanics. The three ceiling caisson, arrayed in multiple levels, is very remarkable and rarely seen in ancient buildings. The eave of the hall is covered with blue glazed tile, the canopy top is in gold, and the walls are built of round bricks set on seam. Seen from a distance, the building is like a huge sapphire umbrella with a golden top.

The Echo Wall If one stands on the round-heart stone at the middle of the Circular Mound platform and gives a low call, one can hear echoes from all directions as if many people were all responding at once. The emperor of old days would interpret it as a sacred edict delivered by god in heaven. Actually, it is an echo generated by an obstruction to the sound wave.

The Altar of Praying for Grain Built in 1420, the 18th year of the reign of Ming Emperor Yongle, the Altar of Praying for Grain was the ceremonial site for praying for a good grain harvest in the first month of Spring. The main buildings here include the Hall of Prayer for Good Harvests, the Hall of the Heavenly Emperor, the East and West Side Halls, and the Gate of Praying for Good Harvests. There are the accessory buildings of the Inner and Outer Wei Wall, the Dressing Platform, Danbi Bridge, the four Heaven Doors in the wall of the Inner Altar, the Gate of Praying for Grain in the wall of the west wall of the Outer Altar, and the Seven Star Stone to the east of the Inner Altar. The altar of the Altar of Praying for Grain is a round building combining altar and hall. It was built in keeping with following the ancient notion of "sacrificing to the emperor beneath a roof". It is a triple glazed tile building with round eaves, conical roof and golden top.

The Hall of Praying for Good Harvests This building is unique in that it is both magnificent and rich in ethnic flavor. It reflects the unique astronomical concepts and stringent architectural thought of ancient Chinese people, and expresses the ancient Chinese people's great respect for heaven and their great hope for abundant harvests. 33 metres high, with a 24.2 metres diameter, the magnificent hall is one of the highest buildings in old Beijing. The round triple eave conical roof contracts in size as it rises, completely covered with blue glazed tile, symbolising heaven. The top is in gold, and overhead is the dragon and phoenix Caisson, with the pattern of dragon and phoenix at the centre. The huge 3-tier roof rely on the 28 landed pillars for support. The 4 pillars in the middle are called Dragon Well Pillars, symbolising respectively Spring, Summer, Autumn and Winter. The 12 open spaces created by the 12 red paint gold pillars surrounding the Dragon Well respectively represent the 12 months in a year. The 24 open spaces further out respectively stand for the 24 solar terms in a year; at the same time, the 28 pillars also stand for the 28 constellations in heaven.

Danbi Bridge The 360-metre-long, 30-metre-wide bridge is the corridor connecting the brick gate of the Altar of Praying for Grain and the South Heaven Gate (Chengzhenmen) , and also the axis connecting the praying altar and the Circular Mound Altar. Danbi Bridge has three stone ways: the Sacred Way is in the middle, and the east way is Yudao, that is, the road used only by emperors, and the west way is Wangdao, that is, the kingly way. The bridge is high in the north and low in the south. The north end is 4 metres high, and the south end 1 metre high. In this way, when going north, one is going upward, as if approaching heaven.

The Hall of Abstinence It is at the southwest corner of the Altar of Praying for Grain. Here are the Beamless Hall, the Bedroom Hall, The Bell Hall, the Duty Room and the Patrol Step Gallery, buildings of special use for etiquette, living, services and security. Covered with green glaze tile, the buildings are enclosed in double walls and are protected by two royal ditches. With strict layout and elegant environment, the Fasting Hall is a representative example of worshiping and fasting buildings in ancient China.

Divine Music Department Located at the west outer altar of the Temple of Heaven, it was the place for practising worshiping music in Ming and Qing dynasties, and has been described as the most advanced school for music learning during the Ming and Qing dynasties. The interior of the hall is 600 square metres, with six pillars and five open spaces, and alley gates in east and west directions. It is now used as an area for Zhonghe Shaoyue, that is, traditional Chinese imperial music, for performing ancient worshiping music and dance. It is also the main exhibition hall of the bells and chimes used in Zhonghe Shaoyue.

Significance of the Heritage

Built in the first part of the 15th century, Beijing's Temple of Heaven is a perfectly preserved altar temple building group. In its overall layout and its individual buildings, it symbolizes the relationship between earth and heaven—the human world and God's world—which stood at the heart of Chinese cosmogony, and the special role played by the emperors within that relationship.

From the choice of site, planning, architectural design, to the sacrificial ceremony and music and dancing, everything here follows the Yin, Yang and Wuxing (five elements) theories of the ancient Chinese *Zhouyi,* or *the Book of Changes*, and succeeds in fully representing the ancient Chinese people's knowledge of heaven, the relationship between man and heaven, and people's hopes for heaven.

The buildings of the Temple of Heaven exhibit in every aspect the symbolic and profoundly meaningful artistic forms particular to ancient China. The scale and the number of components repetitively and collectively use the number 9, which symbolises heaven and emphasizes the connection with heaven.

Combining the application of ancient philosophy, history, mathematics, mechanics, aesthetics and ecology, the Temple of Heaven is a gem among ancient altar temple buildings. With its perfect combination of ancient Chinese architectural technology and art, the Temple of Heaven has become a symbol of Beijing.

Summer Palace, an Imperial Garden in Beijing

The Summer Palace is the biggest and most completely preserved existing imperial garden, one of the four most famous gardens (the other three are Chengde Summer Mountain Resort, Suzhou Humble Administrator's Garden and Suzhou Lingering Garden) in China. Located in Haidian District of Beijing, and 15 kilometres away from downtown Beijing, it covers an area of about 290 hectares. The Summer Palace is mainly comprised of Wanshou Mountain and Kunming Lake. The lake occupies 220 hectares, making up 3/4 of the total size of the garden. Centring around Foxiangge Pavilion, there are over 3,000 rooms in a variety of structures such as pavilions, terraces, open halls, gallery and sheds. Grand in scale, the whole scenic area is an outstanding synthesis of the architectural art of traditional Chinese gardens.

Architectural Arrangement

The Summer Palace was originally named the Garden of Clear Ripples. Its construction began in the 15th year of the Qianlong Era (1750) of the Qing Dynasty, and lasted for a full 15 years. Of the famous "three mountains and five gardens" (Jingyi Garden at the Fragrant Hills, Jingming Garden at Yuquan Mountain, the Garden of Clear Ripples at Wanshou Mountain, the Summer Palace and the Garden of Everlasting Spring) in Beijing, it was the last to be built during the Qing Dynasty. In 1750, in order to please his mother, Empress Dowager Xiaosheng, Emperor Qianlong turned this place into the Garden of Clear Ripples at the cost of 4.48 million taels of silver. This garden, as the centre, was connected to the four gardens on both sides and together they formed an imperial garden stretching for over 20 kilometres from Tsinghua Garden to the Fragrant Hills. In 1860, under the reign of Emperor Xianfeng, the Garden of Clear Ripples was burned down by the Anglo-French Allied Forces. In 1888, under the reign of Emperor Guangxu, the Empress Dowager Cixi, under the guise of raising money for the navy, used 5 to 6 million taels of silver, had Lei Tingchang head the reconstruction, and changed the name of the garden to the Summer Palace. In 1900, the Summer Palace was damaged by the Allied Forces of 8 Countries, and the many treasures here were looted. In 1903, it was renovated. In 1924, the Summer Palace was turned into an open garden to tourists. After 1949, the Summer Palace underwent repair on many occasions. On March 4, 1961, it became one of the first group of Important Historical Monuments under Special Preservation. In November 1998, it was listed in *the World Heritage List*.

The Summer Palace Scenic Area can be roughly divided into three parts: the front of Wanshou Mountain, Kunming Lake, and the rear of the mountain/rear of the lake. The front of the mountain, with Foxiangge Pavilion as the centre, is comprised of a huge group of main buildings that are gorgeous, imposing and magnificent. The rippling Kunming Lake, which takes up 3/4 of the total size of the whole park, lies at the south foot of Wanshoushan. Nanhu Island in the lake is connected with the bank by the beautiful 17-Arch Bridge. At the south of the lake is the West Dyke that has 6 beautifully shaped bridges over it. To the rear of the mountain, the rear lake with its swirling blue water and towering ancient pines creates a quiet, peaceful and elegant environment.

The architectural style of the Summer Palace absorbed the best elements of buildings all over China. The palace area and the inner court area in the east are typical of courtyards in northern China, with the enclosed compounds being connected by a porch; the lake area in the south is typical of the style of Hangzhou's West lake, with the West Dyke dividing the lake into two sections, showing full Jiangnan style; the north of Wanshoushan, with the White Pagoda and the bunkerlike buildings, is in typical Tibetan lama temple style; Suzhou Street in the north, with the many shops and the interrelated waterways, reflects the typical style of the region of rivers and lakes in southeast China.

Combining the great achievements of traditional art of garden construction, the Summer Palace, borrowing the scenery of the surrounding environment of mountains and water, is full of the grand and luxuriant momentum of Chinese imperial gardens, while at the same time, is rich in natural interest, thus it embodies fully the garden constructing principle of "made by man, yet like nature." Wanshou Mountain and Kunming Lake make up the basic structure, more than 100 buildings, 20 courtyards, and 1,600 precious old trees dot the garden. Among the buildings, Foxiangge Pavilion, the Gallery, Stone Boat, Suzhou Street, 17-arch Bridge, Xiequyuan, and the big Opera House are all well-known and representative structures.

Main Buildings

Mount Wanshou(longevity) Wanshou Mountain is a spur of the Yan Mountains, 58.59 metres high and with an altitude of 108.94metres, overlooking Kunming Lake. In 1494, Luoshi, the foster-nurse of Emperor Xiaozong of the Ming Dynasty, built Yuanjing Temple in front of the mountain. In 1750, Emperor Qianlong of the Qing Dynasty, built on the old site of Yuanjing Temple the Big Bao'en Yanshou Temple, celebrating his mother's 60th birthday. The next year the mountain was renamed Wanshou Mountain, and earth excavated when digging Kunming Lake was piled on the mountain in such a way that the east and west slopes were symmetrical in their gentle rise, creating the main focus for the garden. The buildings were built by following the shape of the mountain. From the Ornamental Archway "Yun Hui Yu Yu" at the foot of the slope, all the way to Paiyun Gate, the Second Palace Gate, Paiyun Hall, Dehui Hall, Foxiangge Pavilion, to Wisdom Sea at the top, all the buildings form a level by level rising axis. The present Wanshou Mountain buildings were rebuilt by Cixi after the destruction wrought by the Anglo-French Allied Forces.

Kunming Lake As the main lake of the Summer Palace, Kunming Lake takes up 3/4 of the total area of the park. The front section in the south is rippling blue waves, the mists and waves stretch far into the distance; stretching across the lake is West Dyke, lined by peach trees and willow trees; the Seventeen-Arch Bridge also stretches across the lake, and on the three islands in the lake are classic buildings of different style. The separation of the islands and the dyke creates levels over the lake surface, thus avoiding monotony. The West Dyke and the six bridges over it were an intentional imitation of Su Causeway and its six bridges on Hangzhou's West Lake, making Kunming Lake all the more like West Lake. The area around West Dyke is notable for its blue waves and drooping willows, and the vista is broad. Green trees along the banks and the dyke create pleasant shade, combining with glittering lake water to present a natural beauty of close lake and distant mountain redolent of Jiangnan (the lower Yangtze valley) .

Foxiangge Pavilion Foxiangge Pavilion, the centre of the garden's architectural design, is a grand religious building in a tower style. During the reign of Emperor Qianlong (1736-1795) of the Qing Dynasty, a 9-layer life-prolonging pagoda was under construction, but the work was ordered to stop at the eighth layer and the structure was turned into Foxiangge Pavilion. In 1860, the 10th year of Emperor Xianfeng's reign, it was destroyed at the hands of the Anglo-French Allied Forces. During the reign of Emperor Guangxu (1875-1908) , a building to the same design was rebuilt on the original site to enshrine Buddhist statues. As an imitation of the Six Harmony Pagoda in Hangzhou, and built on a 20-metre stone base, this pavilion is 41 metres high, 8-faced, 3 storeys, and has 4 layers of eaves. 8 lignum vitae pillars inside the pavilion support the roof. With its complex structure, it is a gem among classical buildings.

The Summer Palace Gallery Cloisters and Pavilions are frequently used architectural forms in gardens. The Summer Palace Gallery begins in the east with Yaoyue (inviting moon) Gate, and ends in the west with Shizhang Pavilion, with Paiyun Gate in between. The two sides are decorated with the four pavilions of Liujia, Jilan, Qiushui and Qingyao, standing respectively for Spring, Summer, Autumn and Winter. The total length is 728 metres, divided into 273 sections, and has 548 pillars. The gallery has long been famous for its exquisite architecture, winding and changing shape, and rich color paintings. On every one of the beams in the gallery are painted color paintings, which number 14,000 pieces in total.

The Four Big Continents In the central areas behind Wanshoushan is a group of Han-Tibetan buildings that occupies an area of 20,000 square metres. Taking advantage of the hilly site, Sumeru Lingjing (now turned into a platform) features 3-metre-tall pillars column on its two sides, while the main building of the temples, Xiangyan Zongyin Pavilion, lies behind. All around it are the Four Big Continents symbolising the Buddhist world, including: Dongsheng Continent, West Niuhuo Continent, South Shanbu Continent, North Julu continent and eight little continents built in different forms of towers. The eight little continents include south, southwest, northeast, northwest and the four lamaist pagodas representing "the four wisdoms" of red, white, black and green in the Buddhist Scriptures. At the top of the pagodas are 13 layers of circular "xianglun" that stand for "the 13 skies" in Buddhist scriptures. The shape of the pagodas are unconventional, and the modelling upright and good-looking. Between the Four Big Continents and the eight Little Continents are two uneven platforms, one representing the moon and other representing the sun, symbolising that the moon and the sun surround Buddha.

The Big Opera House Inside Dehe Garden, the Big Opera House is one of the three (the other two are Qingyin Pavilion in Chengde Summer Mountain Resort and Changyin Pavilion in the Forbidden City) big opera stages of the Qing Dynasty. The Big Opera House in Dehe Garden was built for the 60th birthday of the Empress Dowager Cixi specifically for her to watch opera. Being 21 metres tall, it is second in height only to Foxiangge Pavilion, the tallest building in the Summer Palace. The theatre consists of three storeys, two of which were backstage for dressing and face-painting. Above the top board are seven "heaven wells," and inside the floor are "earth wells". At the bottom of the stage are a well and five square pools. When presenting ghost operas, the actors could come down from "heaven" and appear from "earth". Water could also be drawn to the stage.

Significance of the Heritage

As a large-sized imperial garden, the Summer Palace reflects its own unique ideas and artistic achievements in world gardening history. It imitates the splendor of nature, and by further refinement, processing, and creativity, it combines natural beauty with man-made beauty, extending and expanding the limited space to form a special environment that is delightful and changing and satisfies the standard of "worthy of seeing, of strolling, of sightseeing, of residing." The Summer Palace was the last of China's great imperial gardens. Its outstanding gardening artistic value and important scientific, cultural and historic value make it one of the most attractive tourist sites and the common cultural asset of humanity at large.

Mountain Resort and Its Outlying Temples, Chengde

As the biggest existing classic imperial garden in China, Chengde Summer Mountain Resort, also named "Chengde Detached Palace" or "Rehe Temporary Dwelling Palace", consists of palaces for the emperor, an imperial garden and the magnificent temples. It occupies an area of 5,640,000 square metres and has an over 10,000-metre-long wall winding around it. Compared with the Forbidden City in Beijing, the Summer Mountain Resort took on the original essence of the natural environment, absorbed the scenery of both Jiangnan and the area beyond the Great Wall. It has become one of the four most famous gardens of China, the other three being the Summer Palace in Beijing, and the Humble Administrator's Garden and Lingering Garden in Suzhou.

Architectural Arrangement

On his inspection tour to the north, Emperor Kangxi discovered Chengde to have good terrain, comfortable climate, beautiful scenery, and was directly linked with the original homelands of the Qing Dynasty in the north. As the passageway of the Qing emperors, it both overlooked the area of China within the Shanhaiguan Pass and also surveyed the Mongolian tribes to the north. Thus Kangxi Emperor decided to build a temporary palace here. Construction started in the 42nd year of the reign of Emperor Kangxi (1703) , and by the 52nd year (1713) , 36 spots had been built. From the 6th year (1741) to the 57th year of the reign of Emperor Qianlong (1792) , another 36 spots and the eight temples outside of the resort had been built, and the area inside the wall was extended to 564 hectares. It was a huge imperial garden.

The resort absorbed the architectural and artistic essence of both south and north. The buildings here were not big, and black bricks, grey tiles and wood of original color were used to make the structures look simple, elegant and moderately solemn. They were in strong contrast with the Imperial Palace in Beijing, which had yellow tiles and red walls, gilded and colorfully decorated, magnificent and dazzling. The buildings here had the style, structure and engineering approaches similar to the southern gardens, while inheriting methods commonly used in the north, thus creating a perfect combination of the architectural art of both parts of China.

The Summer Mountain Resort includes four sections: the palace, the lake, the plain and the mountain.

The palace area is on the flat south bank of the lake. This was where the emperors managed their political affairs, held celebrations and had their living quarters. It takes up 100,000 square metres and consists of four groups of buildings: the emperor's palace, Songhe (Pine and Crane, standing for longevity) Studio, Hall of Wanhe Songfeng (Pine Breeze in the Myriad Gullies) , and the East Palace. The lake area to the north of the palace area includes about 43 hectares of islets and islands. Eight islands divide the lake into sections of different size and create distinct gradation. The islets and islands are scattered in picturesque disorder among the rippling green waters, evoking the atmosphere of Jiangnan . At the northeast corner is the famous Rehe Spring. The open and spacious plain area lies at the foot of the mountain to the north of the lake area. Here we find the Ten-thousand Tree Yard and Horse Pasture where green grass and luxuriant trees grow, redolent of grassland scenery. The mountain area, making up 4/5 of the whole place, is in the northwest of the resort. Here, among rolling hills and tumbling ravines are found many buildings and pavilions, as well as Buddhist and Taoist temples. The whole resort, with the southeast being rich in water and northwest being mountainous, is a miniature of the natural landform of China.

Main Buildings

As one of the three biggest ancient building clusters in China, the Summer Mountain Resort has the characteristic of "gardens in the hills, and hills in the gardens". There are over 120 groups of buildings of various size, among which are the 36 spots identified with four characters during the reign of Emperor Kangxi and the 36 spots described with three characters at the time of Emperor Qianlong that together form the famous 72 spots of the resort. The most famous spots include:

Songhe (Pine and Crane) Studio During the reign of Emperor Kangxi, the Empress Dowager came to the resort and stayed at Songhe Qingyue in Xiyu. In the 14th year of Emperor Qianlong (1749) , he had another building with 8 courtyards built to the east of the Central Palace and named it Songhe Zhai for the Empress Dowager. Back then in Songhe Zhai, "green pines are always seen outside the door, and white cranes dance at the courtyard", with even reindeers strolling leisurely. Behind Suicheng Hall was another structure known as the Hall of Joyful Longevity (later renamed "Yuexing Ju") for the Empress Dowager.

The Central Palace As the main building of the palace area, the Central Palace was built in the 50th to the 52nd years of Emperor Kangsi, and was renovated and rebuilt in the 19th year of Emperor Qianlong (1754 A.D.) . The 10,000-square-metre building consisted of 9 courtyards, including Lizheng Gate, the Meridian Gate, Yueshe (viewing archery) Gate, Danbo Jingcheng Hall, Study of Four Knowledge, 19 Zhao Rooms, Hall of Yanbo Zhishuang, Building of Yunshan Shengdi, Youyun Gate and some waiting rooms, side halls and cloisters. The palace was divided into a "front waiting area", the office part where the emperor dealt with military and political affairs, and "the back living quarters", the living area where the emperor and his women lived. The main hall, called "Danbo (Tranquil Frugality Jingcheng (Respectful Sincerity)", was built of precious cedar, and thus was also named Cedar Hall. This was where the emperor worked and grand ceremonies were held.

The East Palace Built on lower terrain than the Central Palace and Songhe Zhai, the East Palace lay to the east of Songhe Zhai. In the front wall of the East Palace was opened another gate, called Dehui (accumulation of virtues) Gate. It was similar in form to Lizheng Gate. Inside Dehui Gate, the main buildings on the central axis included in the following sequence gate rooms, 11 main halls, and Qingyin Pavilion, the Pavilion of Happiness and Longevity, Qinzheng (Diligence) Hall, etc. In 1945, the Japanese army invaded Chengde and burned down the East Palace to celebrate their "victory". Now only the foundation remains. Qingyin Pavilion, popularly known as the Grand Opera House, was similar in form to the existing opera houses in Changyin Pavilion at the imperial palace in Beijing and Deheyuan at the Summer Palace. The pavilion was 3-storeys tall, with a magnificent appearance.

Hall of Wanhe Songfeng This was the main hall where Emperor Kangxi received officials, marked memorials, read and wrote. In 1722, Emperor Kangxi discovered that the fourth son, Hongli (later Emperor Qianlong) , of his fourth son Yinzhen was smart and quick to learn. So fond of him was he that he had Hongli brought into the palace. In the summer of this same year, Hongli went with his parents and grandfather to Chengde, and the emperor gave the side hall of the resort, Wanhe Songfeng, to Hongli for his residence. While eating or marking memorials, Kangxi would ask Hongli to be with him so that he could teach this grandson day and night. After becoming the emperor himself, Hongli named this place "Ji En (recalling favor) Hall". In the 30th year of the reign of Qianlong (1765) , the emperor wrote *Record of Ji En Hall at the Mountain Summer Resort*, commemorating Emperor Kangxi's love and care.

Puning Temple Built in the period 1755-1758, this was also named Great Buddha Temple, as there was a large wooden Buddha in the temple. This structure imitated the design of the Three Maya Temple in Tibet. The layout was in accordance with the structure of the world as defined by Buddhist teachings, with the Mahayana Pavilion at the centre signifying Sumeru Mountain and the surrounding buildings signifying the Four Great Regions. Anyuan Temple was an imitation of Kuldja Temple in Yili of Xinjiang; Putuo Zongcheng Temple and Xumi Fushou Temple were constructed imitating respectively the Potala Palace and Tashilhunpo Monastery in Lhasa. The whole temple occupies an area of about 23,000 square metres, consisting of the main buildings of the Bell and Drum Tower, the Tablet Pavilion, Tianwang Hall, the Main Hall and Mahayana Hall.

Pule Temple Popularly known as Round Pavilion, Pule Temple is at the north of the resort. Built in the 31st year of the reign of Emperor Qianlong (1766 A.D.) , the 24,000-square-metre construction consists of two sections: front and rear. The front section is made up of the Mountain Gate, the Bell and Drum Tower, Tianwang Hall and Zongyin Hall; the rear section consists of a Mandala. Over a massive stone Mandala is built the round Xuguang (rising sun) Pavilion. It has a double—eave umbrella top covered with yellow glazed tiles. In the pavilion is set up a three-dimensional mandala, with a copper Happy Buddha enshrined in it. The north pavilion is similar in design to the Hall of Praying for Good Harvest at the Temple of Heaven in Beijing.

Putuo Zongcheng Temple This lies directly north of the Summer Mountain Resort. Putuo Zongcheng was the Chinese translation of the Potala Palace in Tibetan, therefore it was also named the Little Potala Palace. The construction began in the 32nd year of the reign of Emperor Qianlong (1767) and lasted four years. Taking up an area of 220,000 square metres, this is the biggest one of the eight outer temples. There were originally about 60 buildings of different size, most of which had flat roofs and white walls. Da Hong Tai, the main building, is a dark red square building, the roof of its central Hall of Unification of All Dharma is covered with gilded copper tiles. This was the place for important religious ceremonies, for the Qing emperors to meet important leaders of ethnic minority tribes, imperial princes and court ministers. The temple is surrounded by towering ancient trees, the enviroment is quiet, and the scenery is excellent.

Shuxiang Temple To the north of the Summer Mountain Resort, Shuxiang temple is adjacent to Putuo Zongcheng Temple. An imitation of the Shuxiang Temple at Mt. Wutai in Shanxi, it was built in the 39th year of the reign of Emperor Qianlong (1774) . It was mainly a Han-style temple, and the lamas here were mostly Manchu. The main god enshrined here was Wenshu Buddha. As Emperor Qianlong was popularly regarded as the reincarnation of Wenshu Buddha, it was also named "the family temple of Qianlong".

Significance of the Heritage

The summer palace was built by the Qing emperors for the political purpose of appeasing and uniting the frontier minorities and solidifying the country's unification. After the completion of the construction of the resort, the Qing emperors spent a large amount of time here every year dealing with military and political affairs and receiving foreign envoys as well as political and religious heads of the frontier minorities, thus making it the second political centre of Qing Dynasty.

The Summer Mountain Resort is the essence of the construction experience of imperial gardens and temples. The construction realised the perfect combination in form of "palace" and "garden", and a high level of unity in combining "dealing with political affairs" and "relaxation and recreation". It had a distinct political function.

The construction inherited and developed the traditional idea of building a classic garden so as to "turn man-made beauty into nature, conforming to yet transcending nature", incorporating many of the classic Chinese cultural contents of philosophy, aesthetics and literature, thus making it a microcosm of traditional Chinese culture. Through the creative use of all kinds of materials and technologies, this turned out to be an outstanding example of a natural landscape garden in which the structures themselves were presented in a garden-like fashion.

Imperial Tombs of the Ming and Qing Dynasties

The Imperial Tombs of the Ming and Qing dynasties are distributed in Beijing, Hebei, Liaoning, Jiangsu and Hubei. They comprise Huangling, Xiaoling, Zuling, the Thirteen Ming Tombs and Xianling of Ming Dynasty and Yongling, Fuling, Zhaoling, and the Eastern and Western Qing Tombs. These well-preserved tombs reflect the most elite burial ritual system of feudal society in China and the world outlook, outlook on life and death, morality and customs of the thousand-years old feudal society, while they also reflect the highest level of planning ideas and architectural art.

Mausoleum buildings make up an important part of ancient Chinese architecture. The rules and regulations governing them were influenced by many factors such as social ideas, economic strength, imperial attitudes, and aesthetic standards, so each mausoleum has its own characteristics. After more than a thousand years' development and evolution, the ancient Chinese mausoleum rules and regulations reached peak in the Ming and Qing dynasties.

Zhu Yuanzhang, the founding emperor of the Ming Dynasty greatly reformed the mausoleum system of earlier dynasties: the upside-down bucket shape of the original tomb mound was changed to a round top, sacrificial facilities were added, and the square courtyard was changed to a rectangle. Having inherited the Ming system and further improved it, the Qing mausoleum brought classical tomb construction to its final peak.

First of all, the Qing mausoleum was more concerned about the quality of environment. Such factors as hydrology, geology and climate were strictly investigated, while more emphasis was laid on topographical features of mountains and rivers. It was required that the chosen environment should fully satisfy the principle of "harmony between man and nature". Secondly, more emphasis was placed on the harmony and unity of buildings and the environment. The configuration of buildings combines with surrounding topographical features to create an ideal mausoleum atmosphere. Thirdly, architectural quality was further emphasized. Qing mausoleums are not only stable and big, but also splendid and imposing.

Xiaoling of the Ming Dynasty

Ming Xiaoling (Xiaoling of the Ming Dynasty) is located below Wanzhu Peak at the south foot of Zijin Mountain in Nanjing. Adjacent to the Sun Yat-sen Mausoleum to the east, and bordering Meihua Mountain to the south, Xiaoling is the biggest imperial tomb in Nanjing, and also one of the biggest imperial tombs in ancient China.

Xiaoling is the joint tomb of Zhu Yuanzhang, the founding emperor of the Ming Dynasty and his empress. It was named Xiaoling for the fact that his wife was posthumously titled "Xiaoci". As the first Ming tomb, Ming Xiaoling is imposing and magnificent. It represented the highest achievement of early Ming architecture and stone carving art, and directly influenced the structure of the imperial tombs of Ming and Qing dynasties during the subsequent 500 years. The imperial tombs of the Ming and Qing dynasties that with the passage of time came to be distributed in Beijing, Hubei, Liaoning and Hebei all follow the regulation and pattern of Ming Xiaoling in Nanjing.

Having seen much upheaval over the centuries, the wooden portion of many buildings no longer survives. However, the pattern of the tomb still maintains its original magnificent momentum. The underground palace remains intact and preserves the original authenticity of the old buildings and the completeness of the spatial layout.

Architectural Arrangement

Ming Xiaoling, surrounded by mountains and streams, is a harmonious combination of humanistic and natural landscape. The tomb is grand in size, and the pattern of it is rigorous.

The stone carving of the 2,400-metre-long Sacred Way here is the only one that is not straight, but circles around Meihua Mountain to form a bend that looks like the Big Dipper. Along the Sacred Way in sequence come the Dismount Archway, Restraint Monument, the big Gold Gate, Pavilion of Sacred Merit Monument, Way of Stone Animals, Stone Baluster Column, Generals, Ministers and Lingxing Gate. Inside Lingxing Gate and to the northeast of it is the main body of the tomb. Along this south-north axis that faces Dulong Fu come one after another Jinshui Bridge, Civil and Military Gate, Xiaoling Gate, Xiaoling Hall, Inner Red Door, Fangcheng Minglou and Baoding. The placement of all these structures along one axis reflects the style of Chinese traditional architecture.

In terms of architectural design, Ming Xiaoling began the pattern of building Fangcheng and Minglou in front of the heaped-earth mound and the Treasure City, making the back part of the tomb more magnificent and pre-eminent. All the big buildings such as the big Gold Gate, the Pavilion of Steles, the Main Sacrificial Hall and Fangcheng, all have stone sumeru slabs as their foundation, making the buildings look stable, solid, solemn and majestic. The top of the larger buildings, based on their importance in the tomb, are covered with glazed tile components of different size and different color, showing wealth and rank, flamboyance, loftiness and stateliness.

Significance of the Heritage

Ming Xiaoling, having more than 30 buildings and stone carved art works of different style and function, is grand and orderly in overall layout, while each single building here being massive and magnificent, and the workmanship of detailed decoration is excellent. The geographical environment of the tomb is characterized by attractive rolling hills, and the "Big Dipper" layout gives it strong cultural significance. The Sacred Way is characterised by a perfect combination of human construction and natural environment. It was laid out to match the zigzag mountain shape, thereby reflecting profound traditional cultural concepts and distinctive personality. The Sacred Way stone carvings, of various style, are plain and massive, grand as a whole and delicate in detail, representing the highest level of stone-carving art in the early Ming.

Ming Xiaoling embodied the political thought, social culture, aesthetic consciousness, architectural technology and state financial power of the early Ming. It inherited the superior elements of the Han, Tang and Song imperial mausoleum system, and also created a new imperial mausoleum system. The layout and architectural form of the mausoleum have a distinctive period style and possess significance as a model that would later be followed.

The Thirteen Ming Tombs

The Thirteen Ming Tombs, with a total size of more than 120 square kilometres, are situated below Mount Yan in Changping some 50 kilometres to the northwest of Beijing. From May 1479, the 7th year of the reign of Emperor Yongle, to the time when the last emperor of Ming Dynasty, Emperor Chongzhen, was buried in Siling, for a period of over 230 years, resplendent and magnificent tombs of 13 emperors, 7 concubines and one eunuch, 13 emperors, 23 empresses, 2 crown princes, over 30 concubines and one eunuch were buried here. It is a well-preserved tomb group where the largest number of emperors were buried. The time sequence of the construction of the 13 tombs is as follows: Changling, Xianling, Jingling, Yuling, Maoling, Tailing, kangling, Yongling, Zhaoling, Dingling, Qingling, Deling, Siling. Changling and Dingling are the most famous of the 13 tombs for their complete design, grand scale and imposing demeanor.

Architectural Arrangement

The Ming Tombs are a united whole, while at the same time each tomb is an independent unit of more or less the same size. Each tomb was separately built in front of a mountain. Except for Siling that is in the southwest corner, all the other tombs are distributed on the right side and left side of Changling in the shape of a fan. Under the direction of traditional Fengshui theory, from the choice of site to planning design, it was emphasized that the buildings be in harmonious unity with the natural mountain and river, water flow and vegetation. A perfect state of "shaped by heaven, created from land"was pursued, reflecting the rich content of traditional Chinese culture. The famous British historian Joseph Needham highly regarded this layout of tombs on the hillside, saying that the imperial tombs were a great achievement in Chinese architectural design, and the content of the whole pattern is possibly the greatest example of a marriage between architecture and landscape art.

The Stone Memorial Archway Being the first building in front of the tomb area, the Stone Memorial Archway composed 5 principal columns, 6 pillars, and 11 floors, all carved of white marble. At the architrave and the top and bottom of the pillar stones are carved relief of dragons, cloud patterns, Kylins and lions. The whole building is grand in structure and exquisite in carving, reflecting the superior level of stone craftsmanship in the Ming Dynasty.

The Stele Pavilion In the middle of the Sacred Way, the Stele Pavilion is a large and tall square pavilion with a double-eave hipped-roof, and uplifted corners. Inside the pavilion is housed a 6-metre-tall stone monument of dragon head and turtle tarsus, and on the monument is inscribed "Great Ming Changling Sacred Merit Stele". The text is over 3,500 characters in length, composed by Zhu Gaochi, Ming Emperor Renzong, and written by Cheng Nanyun, a famous calligrapher of the early Ming period. In the four corners of the Pavilion are 4 white stone ornamental columns that look solemn and vigorous. On the east side of the pavilion, there was once a temporary palace for the use of later emperors and consorts when they came to conduct sacrificial ceremony, but it no longer survives.

The Stone Carving Group along the Sacred Way From the two hexagonal stone columns to the north of the Stele Pavilion to the Dragon and Phoenix Gate, along the 1000-metre-long Sacred Way are erected 24 stone beasts and 12 stone figures that look lifelike and are dedicatedly carved. There are 6 types of beasts, 4 of each type, 2 standing and 2 kneeling. The stone figures consist of officials of special merit, ministers and generals, 4 of each type, all had been the intimate courtiers of the emperor during his lifetime, and all stand holding executive warrants, all looking powerful and pious, signifying the majesty of the emperor in his lifetime and meaning that the dead emperor had the ministers and beasts at his command and could still control everything in the underworld.

Lingxing Gate Lingxing Gate, also called Dragon and Phoenix Gate, compose 3 doorways formed by 4 stone columns that are similar to the ornamental archway, with cloud boards and exotic beasts carved on them. At each door architrave is decorated a stone carved fire bead, hence the gate was also named "Flame Archway". A temporary palace originally stood to the northwest of the Dragon and Phoenix Gate, for the emperor and empress to stay when they came for sacrificial ceremony.

Key Tombs

Ming Changling Changling, at the south foot of the main peak of Tianshou Mountain, is the joint tomb of Emperor Chengzu, Zhudi (whose reign title was Yongle) , the third emperor of the Ming Dynasty, and his empress. Among the 13 tombs, this is the biggest and earliest built, and its above-ground structures are the best preserved. The towering Minglou is the symbol of Changling. It is the ancestor tomb of the 13 tombs, while also one of the the main tourist attractions in this tomb area.The 120,000-square-metre underground palace is square in the front and round in the back. In front of the first courtyard is the tomb gate, a palace-style building of single eaves and gable and hip roof ; in front of the second courtyard is Ling'en Gate, five rooms long and 2 rooms deep, 14.57 metres tall from the bottom to the topmost point of the roof. The paving stones between the stairs of the middle way are carved shallow relief patterns, of excellent craftsmanship. Inside the gate, toward the north end of the central axis is the massive towering Ling'en Hall, 9 rooms long and 5 rooms deep, with a total area of 1956.44 square metres. It is one of the rarely seen big palaces in China. All the components of the big hall are made up of Chinese cedar, and 60 huge columns support the roof of the hall. The interior is not splendidly decorated, but quite quaint and elegant.

Ming Dingling Ming Dingling is the tomb of the 13th emperor of Ming Dynasty, Zhu Yijun (reign title Wanli) , and his two empresses. The main buildings here include Ling'en Gate, Ling'en Hall, Minglou and the underground palace. It occupies an area of 180,000 square metres. It is the only tomb among the 13 Ming tombs to have been excavated.The total layout of the buildings above the ground is square in the front and round in the back. In the front is a spacious courtyard house with three courtyards, and in the back is a big Baocheng. The three white marble bridges in front of the tomb lead to the tall big Pavilion of Monument, surrounded by the buildings of the Department of Sacrifice, the Animal-slaughter Pavilion, Dingling Office of Supervision and other structures, with over 300 rooms. Ling'en Hall in the Outer Luocheng has a double eave roof, is 7 rooms long and 5 rooms deep, standing over a sumeru stylobate. Inside the yard is a Lingxing Gate with two column ornamental archways on the axis.After the founding of the People's Republic of China, Dingling was excavated for historical scientific research. Over 3,000 precious objects of all kinds were found buried in the tomb.

Ming Zhaoling Located at the east foot of Dayu Mountain, Ming Zhaoling is the joint tomb of Zhu Zaihou (reign title Longqing) , the 12th Ming Emperor Muzong, and his three empresses. Zhaoling is the first tomb to have been repaired and restored on a big scale among the 13 Ming tombs, and it is also one of the tombs to be open formally to tourists.The 35,000-square-metre Zhaoling suffered great damage after the collapse of Ming Dynasty. What were left intact include Ling'en Gate, Ling'en Hall and its east and west Side Halls, Fangcheng, Minglou and Baoding. During the reign of emperor Qianlong of the Qing Dynasty, the Qing government, in order of mitigate the national conflicts, repaired the Ming tombs. The Minglou, Ling'en Gate, and Ling'en Hall of Zhaoling were restored. The repair improved the system of the tomb, yet the original architectural pattern was changed. The Minglou was simplified, Ling'en Gate and Ling'en Hall were decreased in size. For the purpose of restoring the original look of Zhaoling, the repair and restoration work began in April, 1987. The Minglou, Ling'en Hall, Ling'en Gate, the two side halls, the Sacred Merit Stele, the Animal-slaughter Pavilion, the kitchen and the library have all been restored.

Xianling of the Ming Dynasty

In March of the 16th year of the Ming Emperor Zhengde (1521) , Zhu Houzhao, Ming Emperor Wuzong, died without offspring. Following the teachings of Ming Emperor Taizu, Zhu Yuanzhang, that "the younger brother should succeed his elder brother after his death", Zhu Houzhao, conferred with the title of Prince Xing not long earlier, was welcomed to Beijing to take the throne and was named Ming Emperor Shizong. Once he was on the throne, Zhu Houzhao establishes his own system of succession and, against the objection of his ministers, conferred on his late father Zhu Youyuan the posthumous title of Emperor. After the late Zhu Youyuan was named emperor, the former tomb of King Xingxian was upgraded and rebuilt in accordance with the standards pertaining to an emperor's tomb. In April of the 3rd year of Jiajing (1524) , the tomb of the former king was renamed Xianling.

Xianling, located at Mount Chunde 7.5 kilometres to the east of Zhongxiang City, Hubei Province, is the joint tomb of the parents of Ming Shizong, Emperor Jiajing, built first in the 14th year of Zhengde (1519) . The 1.83 square kilometre tomb is the only tomb of an emperor of Ming Dynasty in central-south China, and the largest single tomb of all the emperor tombs of the Ming Dynasty. Its "one tomb, two mounds" structure is the only one of its kind in all imperial mausoleums of all dynasties.

Architectural Arrangement

Considered as a whole, the architectural pattern of Ming Xianling is very much like a huge "precious bottle", with inner and outer enclosed parts. The outer wall is 6 metres high, 1.8 metres wide, and over 3,500 meters long. The red-walled yellow-tiled building, undulating with the mountain, is very imposing and magnificent. At the south of the outer city are double gates, called the New Red Gate and the Old Red Gate. On each side of the gate is a dismount monument, on which is inscribed the calligraphy of the powerful Ming Dynasty minister Yan Song. Inside the gate, the stone Sacred Way leads all the way to the inner enclosure. In the middle is Lingxing Gate, with 6 square pillars and 3 doors. The pillars are supported at their bases by drum-shaped bearing stones, and at the top of each pillar is an unicorn. On both sides of the Sacred Way in front of Lingxing Gate are lined 8 pairs of stone beasts, including lions, Xie Zhi, camels, recumbent elephants, kylin (Chinese unicorn) , standing horses and recumbent horses, 2 officials and 2 officers, all carved out of whole blocks of white marble.

The Treasure City (tomb site) comprises the front wall and the back wall, connected with Yaotai in the middle. The plane design of the Grave City is in the shape of a dumbbell, with defensive structures built into the wall. In front of the Grave City is a square city platform, below which is arch-top corridor and over it Minglou house. Most buildings in the mausoleum have carved stone bases in sumeru style. The Yunlong Danbi (red stairway) , Water-dispersing Panlong and the components of the gallery railings in front of Ling En Hall exhibit consummate carving techniques and are classic works of stone carving art during the Ming Dynasty.

The layout of Xianling, making use of traditional Chinese Fengshui theory, takes the surrounding landscape as a central element of the architectural composition. In accordance with the principles of "combining Yin and yang", "facing water, with hills behind", the left peak of Mount Songlin was treated as the ancestor mountain supporting the Xuangong ("mysterious palace"—the underground palace housing the emperor's coffin) , and on the left side of Mount Songlin is Shashan protecting the two sides of the mausoleum, together with Tianzigang being the Anshan of the mausoleum, thus forming an immediate environment that is highly harmonious with nature.

As for the architectural layout, Xianling makes full use of the table land in Mount Songlin to build in sequence the dismount monuments, the gate, the pavilion, the look column, the stone animals, the memorial archway and the bridge by following the mountain shape and leading all the way to Xiangdian (the main hall of the mausoleum) , Minglou (the tall building in front of the mausoleum) and Baocheng (the building above the underground palace) . Evenly arranged and going up progressively, the buildings express the sense of order of the feudal rituals. The buildings are surrounded by mountain and water, and they complement each other as if created by nature to form a perfect work that combines architectural art and environmental aesthetics. Xianling is unique in construction methods in that there are two underground palaces in a single mausoleum, the golden-bottle-shaped outer Luocheng, the zigzag winding Yuhe River, the dragon-shaped Sacred Way and the inner and outer Mingtang pools, which are only seen in this mausoleum of the Ming Dynasty.

The Eastern Qing Tombs

The Eastern Qing Tombs, under Mount Changrui in northwest Zunhua in Hebei Province, comprises 15 tombs (5 emperor tombs, 4 empress tombs, 5 concubine tombs, 1 princess tomb) where emperors, empresses, imperial concubines, princes and princesses (161 individuals in total) are buried. The Eastern Qing Tombs is the most comprehensive and best preserved imperial tomb building group in China.

The 15 tombs here are arranged in accordance with the traditional concepts of "high status occupies the center,", "respect for seniority" and "distinctions between high and low". Xiaoling, the tomb of Shizu, Shunzhi Emperor, the first Manchu emperor to rule over China, is on the south-north axis, beginning in the south at Jinxing Mountain ending in the north at the main peak of Changrui Mountain, occupying the position of highest authority. The other tombs, in accordance with the seniority in the family level, are arranged on both sides of Xiaoling from east to west in the shape of a fan. To the left of Xiaoling is Jingling of Emperor Kangxi, next to Jingling is Huiling of Emperor Tongzhi; on the right side of Xiaoling is Yuling of Emperor Qianlong, and further right is Dingling of Emperor Xianfeng. The tombs are arranged to form the pattern of sons and grandsons attending father and grandfather, symbolising clear relationship of heir succession and expressing the wish for everlasting rule over the country.

Management of the Eastern Qing Tombs lasted for two centuries and a half, almost the length of the Qing Dynasty. Many of the people buried here were important and influential in Qing history. The tombs contain rich historical information that provides rare materials for studying the mausoleum regulations, burial system, sacrificial rituals, architectural techniques and crafts, and they also constitute typical cases in the study of the politics, economy, military affairs, culture, science and art of the Qing Dynasty.

Architectural Arrangement

The Eastern Qing Tombs, imitating Ming Dynasty practices from planning organization to architectural pattern, have a common entrance that begins with the Stone Arch and the Red Gate, then the common Sacred Way, the stone animals, the Beiting (pavilion built over a stone tablet) and ends with Huabiao (the ornamental column) . The sequence of the layout is as follows: the five-hole stone Quanqiao Bridge, the Ornamental Archway, Beiting, the three-hole Quanqiao Bridge, the big Yuetai, the Palace Gate, Long'en Hall and the right and left side halls, then Shiping Bridge, Yuetai, Liuli Gate, Wugong (the five containers in which offerings are put in when offering sacrifices to ancestors) , Fangcheng (with Minglou above) , Moon City, Baocheng, Baoding. The tombs of emperors, empresses, princes, princesses and concubines follow one after another. The arrangement of the tombs follows a strict hierarchy. A set of stylized regulations had been formed and they were strictly followed.

The basis for choosing the site for the mausoleum of the Qing emperors was traditional Chinese Fengshui theory. The ideal mountain and river situation was deliberately pursued so as to satisfy the imagery of "unity of man and nature", and the Eastern Qing Tombs perfectly reflect this concept.

The buildings of the Eastern Qing Tombs are magnificent, imposing and exquisite. In this huge complex comprising over 580 single buildings, there are many architectural wonders, such as: the Stone Memorial Gateway that has the widest surface of all memorial gateways in China: its imitation-wood structure of five spans, 6 pillars and 11 storeys was constructed with remarkable skill; the 6,000 metre main Sacred Way of Xiaoling, the best preserved of its kind in China, rising and falling with the mountain shape, has strong artistic appeal; the exquisite Buddhist stone carvings in the underground palace of Yuling of Emperor Qianlong have been acclaimed as the acme of perfection; the luxury of the decoration of three gold-covered halls of the tomb of Cixi is rarely seen in the world, and the stone carving with the phoenix above the dragon shows ingenuity of the craftsmen.

The woodwork and stonework of all the tombs here reflect exquisite skills, and can be rightly said to be the summation of palace buildings of the Qing Dynasty. Xiaoling has the most stone animals, and all 18 pairs of stone animals look simple and vigorous; Yuling of Qianlong is the biggest and most splendid; Dingdongling of Cixi is the most exquisite building. Only four of the 15 tombs are open to tourists, including Yuling, the tombs of the East Empress Dowager and the West Empress Dowager (Cixi) , and the tomb of Xiangfei (Fragrant Concubine) .

The Western Qing Tombs

Below Mount Yongning 15 kilometres to the west of Yi County of Hubei Province, and 120 kilometres to the southwest of Beijing, the Western Qing Tombs is one of the mausoleum groups of the Qing emperors. It is named the Western tombs for the fact that it lies at the west of the Eastern Tombs in Zunhua of Hubei Province. Here are 14 tombs, including 4 tombs of emperors, 3 tombs of empresses, 3 tombs of concubines, 4 tombs of lords, princesses and A Ge (young princes) and two accessory buildings, Yongfu Temple and Xinggong (temporary imperial palace) . Together they make up an important part of the mausoleum architectural art of China.

Construction of the Western Tombs first began in the 8th year of the reign of Emperor Yongzheng (1730) , and lasted until the early 19th century. The four emperor tombs are grand in size and of rational layout. The well-preserved palaces are splendid, and the stone carvings exquisite, while at the same time, they are of various style and rich in meaning. The standard of the tombs of empresses, concubines, lords, princesses and A Ge all strictly followed the feudal system of hierarchy. Although they have suffered damage over the years, the tombs are mostly well preserved.

With their large amount of material objects and written records, the Western Tombs reflect in various aspects the mausoleum artistic style and the great development and changes in the religious beliefs of the imperial family from the 1830's to the early 20th century, and they have made a great contribution to the creativity and development of ancient Chinese mausoleum architectural art. As such, they possess unique historical, artistic and aesthetic value.

Architectural Arrangement

Occupying an area of about 100 square kilometres, the Western Tombs extend to Lianggezhuang Village in the east, Zijingguan in the west, Dayan Bridge to the south and the Qifengling Mountains to the north. There are four emperor tombs, namely, Tailing of Emperor Yongzheng, Changling of Emperor Jiaqing, Muling of Emperor Daoguang and Chongling of Emperor Guangxu. There are three tombs of empresses and seven tombs of concubines, princesses and lords. With Tailing below the main peak of Mount Taining, the other tombs are on the east and west sides.

At the south entrance of the Western Tombs is a stone Memorial Archway, then come in sequence the big Red Gate, Shengde Shengong Beilou, the Seven-arch Bridge, the stone animals, the Dragon Phoenix Gate, Sacred Way Beilou, then come Long'en Hall, Fangcheng Minglou and Baoding of Tailing, the main tomb among Western Tombs. All these buildings are connected by the 2.5 kilometre long Sacred Way from the south to the north. There is only one stone Memorial Archway at the entrance of the Eastern Tombs, while at the Western Tombs, there are three. The stone animals and the Dragon and Phoenix Gate lie behind the seven-arch bridge, while at the Western Tombs, they are in front of it.

Muling is the tomb of Emperor Daoguang and his two empresses. Without Fangcheng Minglou, and being small in size, and the Long'en Hall being only engraved but not painted, Muling appears plain and elegant compared with the red-walled, glittering and imposing buildings. On the caisson ceiling in the hall are carved many flying dragons, implying that the dragons are to fly to heaven, inhaling cloud and exhaling mist but spraying no water, so as to keep the interior of the tomb dry.

The Three Shengjing Tombs

Shengjing, the present Shenyang, the Chinese translation of the original Manchu name is "prosperous city". It is the place where the Qing Dynasty, the last Chinese Dynasty, began to flourish. The tombs of the founding emperor of the Qing Dynasty and his father and grandfather, namely Qing Yongling, Qing Fuling and Qing Zhaoling. The tombs were located in Shengjing, and thus acquired the name "the Three Shengjing Tombs".

Key Tombs

Fuling Also Named Dongling, Fuling is the joint tomb of Nurhachi, the founder of the Qing Dynasty, and his wife. The construction began in 1629 and was basically completed in 1651. After further construction during the reigns of Emperor Shunzhi, Emperor Kangxi and Emperor Qianlong, there resulted a grand imperial tomb group with complete facilities.

The low-front, high-rear pattern of Fuling was prompted by the shape of the mountain. From the south of the tomb a red wall surrounds the tomb, in the centre is the Red Gate, and outside the gate facing each other are a pair of stone lions and a pair of ornamental columns, along with a stone archway and a dismount monument carved in the five languages of Manchu, Mongolian, Chinese, Hui and Tibetan. The Red Gate is a long sacred road, with four pairs of stone beasts of sitting lions, standing horses, lying camels and sitting tigers on both sides. At the end of the Sacred Road are 108-step flight of stairs built by making use of the mountain shape, signifying the 36 Tiangang (ancient name of star) and 72 Disha (ancient name of star) . Above the stairs is an ornamental archway of double eave hipped-roof, covered with yellow glazed tile. Inside the archway is "Da Qing Fuling Sacred Merit Stele" written by Emperor Kangxi in Chinese and Manchu. Further north is the castle-like Fangcheng, and at the centre to its south is Long'en Gate, with a 3-storey hipped-roof gatehouse above. At each of the four corners is a turret, and in the middle of the city is Long'en Hall, standing above massive sumeru-style stylobate, in which a wooden god board is enshrined. Behind the hall is a portal, above which is the big Minglou of double-eave hipped-roof. The stone monument inscribed with "the Tomb of Taizu Gao Emperor" is set in the middle of the Minglou. The buildings inside the Fangcheng are all covered with yellow glazed tile, and on the supporting columns of red basic layer and in the space between the columns are painted "Hexi" murals (also called palace murals) .

Zhaoling Zhaoling is the joint tomb of Huang Taiji, Emperor Taizong, and his wife. It is the biggest of the three tombs in Shengjing, and also has the most complete structure. Being located in the north of Shenyang, it is also known as the Northern Tomb. The construction of Zhaoling began in 1642, the 8th year of Chongde, and was completed in the same year with Fuling. During the reign of Emperor Kangxi and Emperor Jiaqing, Zhaoling was enlarged and expanded to occupy an area of about 480,000 square metres. 38 buildings remain there until now. Built on flat land and enclosed by a wind wall, it looks very much like a small city. All the main buildings are on a single axis, and from south to north come in sequence: the Sacred Bridge, the Ornamental Archway, the Red Front Gate, the Stele Pavilion, Long'en Gate, Long'en hall, Minglou and Baoding. Ling'en Hall in the middle of the Fangcheng stands on the delicately carved granite stone pedestal, covered with yellow glazed tile, having carved beams and painted rafters, gold plaque and red wall. With Minglou behind it and side halls on the left and right sides, and turrets in the four corners, it is just like a myriad of stars surrounding the moon, exceptionally majestic and solemn. To the north of Fangcheng is Baocheng, in the shape of a half moon. The inside of Fangcheng is called Baoding, and below Baoding is the underground coffin chamber. Looking around at the top of Baoding, all around are trees that make you feel as if in a city of mountain and forest.

Now, Zhaoling has been turned into Beiling Park.

Yongling The smallest one of the Three Shengjing Tombs and taking up an area of 10,000.1 square metres, Yongling is nonetheless the earliest prototype for the three tombs. The construction of Yongling, the ancestor tomb of the Manzhu Qing imperial family, started in 1598. In this tomb area are buried the Liushizu (the sixth generation ancestor) , the great grandfather, grandfather, father and two uncles of Nurhachi and their wives. The tomb palace comprises the dismount monument, the front palace yard, Fangcheng, Baocheng, Shengshengsuo, the Icehouse, and Fruit House. Qiyun Mountian behind it is just like a screen, and Suzi River in the front is just like a jade belt, Yancong Mountain on the other bank of the river faces Mount Qiyun in the distance. Situated in such an environment, Yongling appears very magnificent.

The gate of the front courtyard of Yongling is named the Front Red Gate or the Front Palace Gate. It is a hard mountain type of building with glazed tile roof. It is 3 rooms wide and 2 rooms deep. Each room has a pair of wood fence gates, painted red. As the ancient custom left from the "trees and fences mark a village" of Jiangzhou Jurchens, this kind of wood fence is the only one of its kind in all the emperor and empress tombs of the Qing Dynasty. In the middle of the front courtyard stand side by side four single eave hipped-roof stele pavilions of four generations of ancestors. Arranged according to the order of having the senior in the middle and the junior on the right, the older on the left and the younger on the right, the monuments of the four generations of ancestors are in the sequence of Zhao, Xing, Jing and Xian. The main hall in the Fangcheng is called Xiangdian, where the god boards cards of the four generations of ancestors are enshrined. This was the place for sacrificial ceremony.

Significance of the Heritage

As an important part of the Imperial Tombs of Ming and Qing dynasties, the Three Shengjing Tombs, from the methods of construction to the complete architectural design, its ceremonial rituals, and the official system of managing the tombs, were comparable to those of the imperial tombs of the Ming and Qing dynasties. At the same time, the Shengjing tombs were the products of a specific period in the process of the flourishing of an ethnic emperor in northeast China, therefore, they contain cultural information of the ideological concepts, aesthetic interest, architectural level, customs and habits of the Manchu ethnic group at that stage. Each one of the three tombs is an independent system, small in size, yet complete in pattern. They have all the ritual facilities, and the tomb pattern combines elements of religion, belief,with a sensitivity to the natural environment, creating a unity with the choice of site and its plan and design The tombs provide historic evidence of ancient architectural form, carving, painting and comprehensive ideas, and also constitute tangible objects for modern viewers to appreciate.

The Grand Canal

China was the first country in the world to dig canals. In 486 B.C., Fuchai, the king of the Wu Kingdom during the Spring and Autumn Period, dug in Yangzhou the first canal, Han Ditch, and constructed Han City. Generations of construction created the Grand Canal that runs 1,794 kilometres from south to north crossing the provinces and cities of Beijing, Tianjin, Hebei, Shandong, Jiangsu, Zhejiang and Anhui.

As the earliest, longest, and most lasting manmade canal with the biggest spatial span, the Grand Canal is a valuable heritage that the Chinese nation has left to the world.

Historical Origin

Dating from the time of Fuchai, the Grand Canal has a history of nearly 2,500 years. In 495 B.C., in order to conquer the Yue Kingdom, Fuchai cut the canal from Suzhou to Wuxi and Changzhou that joined the Changjiang River in Benniu. In 486 B.C., King Fuchai of the Wu Kingdom, in order to defeat Qi Kingdom so as to contend for hegemony in Central China, dug what was called Han Ditch, a watercourse from Yangzhou to Huaiyin that connected the water systems of the Changjiang River and the Huai River This was the earliest canal in China, and in the world.

In the 7th century, the Sui Dynasty ended civil disorder and achieved the unification of China. In order for the goods and materials of the Jianghan Plain and the wealthy regions in Jiangnan (south of the Changjiang River) to be steadily transported to Luoyang, in 605, Emperor Yangdi of the Sui Dynasty ordered the building of the "Tong Luo Canal" from Luoyang to Huai'an to connect the water systems of the Yellow River and the Huai River, and the "Jiangnan Canal" from Zhenjiang to Hangzhou, thus forming the south-to-north Grand Canal.

In the 13th century, in order to avoid having the watercourse make a detour via Luoyang, the Yuan Dynasty dug successively "Luozhou River" and "Huitong River" that connected the natural rivers and lakes between Tianjin and Qingjiang, and Han Ditch and Jiangnan Canal to the south of Qingjiang were repaired, thus forming a grand, convenient and speedy water transportation channel leading all the way to Hangzhou.In 1293, the famous scientist Guo Shoujing dug the canal that led to Jishuitan in the capital of the Yuan Dynasty. Thus was formed the 1794-kilometer-long Grand Jing-Hang Canal from Beijing in the north to Hangzhou in the south.

Composition of the Heritage

The Grand Canal includes the Sui-Tang Canal, the Jing-Hang Canal and the Zhedong Canal, all of which underwent large-scale construction in the Spring-Autumn and the Warring States Period, the Sui Dynasty and the Yuan Dynasty.

The Sui-Tang Grand Canal

With Luoyang being the centre, the Sui-Tang Grand Canal began in Yuhang (Hangzhou) in the south and ended in Zhuojun (Beijing) in the north. The total length that the Sui Dynasty dug was 2700 kilometres, crossing more than 10 latitudes, going from south to north across the wealthiest southeastern coastal area and the great North China Plain, and 8 provinces and cities of Zhejiang, Jiangsu, Anhui, Henan, Shandong, Hebei, Tianjing and Beijing. Having connected the 5 water systems of the Yellow River, the Huai River, the Changjiang River, Qiantangjiang River and Haihe River, it was a great transportation artery between the south and north, and played a great role in Chinese history. It was a great water conservation project created by the ancient Chinese people, and is also the earliest and longest canal. After having been straightened and repaired in the Yuan Dynasty, the Jing-Hang Grand Canal as we see it today, having a total length of 1794 kilometres, was constructed.

The Jing-Hang Grand Canal

The Jing-Hang Grand Canal is, with the Great Wall, one of the two largest construction projects of ancient China. According to geographical location, it is divided into 7 segments:

Tonghui River It is 82 kilometres in length. It goes from Shenshan Spring in Baifu Village of Changping District, Beijing through Kunming Lake to Jishuitan, Zhongnanhai and exits Chongwen Gate to flow east. It makes a southeastern turn at present-day Yangzha Village of Chaoyang District to go into Luhe River at Zhangjiawan Village of Tongzhou District.

The Northern Canal The section from Tongzhou District, Beijing, to Tianjin, with a length of 186 kilometres, is called the Northern Canal.

The Southern Canal The section from Tianjin to Linqing in Shandong, 400 kilometres long, is called the Southern Canal.

The Lu Canal This section of the canal, about 500 kilometres long, from Linqing to Tai'erzhuang, is called the Lu Canal.

The Middle Canal This section of the canal, 186 kilometres in length, from Tai'erzhuang to Huai'an of Jiangsu, is called the Middle Canal.

The Li Canal The Li Canal, about 180 kilometres in length, is from Huai'an to Guazhou.

The Jiangnan Canal The Jiangnan Canal, about 330 kilometres long, is from Zhenjiang to Hangzhou in Zhejiang.

At present, the length of the seasonal navigable waterway of the Jing-Hang Grand Canal has reached more than 1100 kilometres. Over the 660 kilometres of navigation channel south of Pi County in Jiangsu, ships of 500 tons can proceed without obstacle.

The Zhedong Canal

The Zhedong Canal got its name from the Eastern Circuit of Zhejiang in the Tang and Song dynasties. The canal in the territory of Zhejiang Province, having its centre in Shaoxing, the famous historical and cultural city, begins in Xiaoshan in the west, crosses Cao'e River and flows through Shaoxing City to the Yong River in Ningbo in the east. The total length is 239 kilometres. The part of the canal initially dug during the Spring and Autumn Period was located in the ancient Shanyin waterway in the territory of Shaoxing (the capital of the Yue Kingdom) . During the Western Jin Dynasty, He Xun, an official in Shaoxing, directed the excavation of the Xixing Canal, formed with the canal to the east of the Cao'e River a complete canal that began at Xixiao River in the west and ran to Dongxiao River in the east. When the Southern Song Dynasty initially made Shaoxing its capital, the Shaoxing section of the Zhedong Canal became the imperial river of the then ruling family, while at the same time it was an important trading channel.

Distribution of the Heritage Sites

According to historical periodization and naming custom, the Grand Canal is divided into 10 segments. The heritage selected respectively the typical segments of the canal and the important heritage spots, including 27 heritage rivers, with a total length of 1011 kilometres and 58 related sites. The types of heritage include such remains of the hydraulic project as floodgate, dyke, dam, bridge, water gate, track road, wharf and critical levee section, and such ancillary facilities and management facilities of the canal as warehouse cellar, government office, temporary imperial palace, guild hall, and levy station, and some ancient buildings and historical and cultural blocks that are related closely with the cultural meaning of the Grand Canal.

As the southernmost part of the Jing-Hang Grand Canal and the beginning of the Zhedong Canal, Hangzhou is an important place on the Chinese Grand Canal. Eleven spots in Hangzhou City were inscribed as the first heritage spots and segments, including 6 heritage locations: Yicang, the site of the Fengshan Watergate, the Qiaoxi historical zone, the wharf of Xixing Guotanghang, Gongchen Bridge; and five segments of waterway: the segment of Hangzhoutang, the Hangzhou segment of the Jiangnan Canal, the Shangtang segment, the Hangzhou Zhonghe River-Longshan River segment, and the main section of the Zhedong Canal.

In the segment of Yangzhou City, there are Shuidou Gate, ancient Dongguan Ferry and ancient Wantou Ferry that reflect the heritage of ancient harbor, hydraulic construction and city construction in Yangzhou, and there are the remains left by ancient emperors on their tours to Yangzhou, such as the ancient Guazhou ferry Jinchunyuan, and residence building clusters such as Heyuan and Geyuan of the Yangzhou salt merchants that display their enormous wealth.

In the Huai'an segment, we find the site of the house of the governor of Grain Transportation in its heyday along with ancient wharfs; the Grain Transportation Museum that displays the history of grain transportation; the grand water interchange formed by the intersection of the canal, the ancient Yellow River and the Huaihe River, and a large number of cultural relics left by famous historical figures who grew up by the banks of the Grand Canal.

The important cultural heritage spots of the Luoyang segment of the Grand Canal include: the site of Hanjiacang, the site of Huiluocang, the site of Tianjin Bridge, the segment of Luohe River inside the city and parts of the Chan River.

The Shandong segment of the Grand Canal flows through five prefectural-level cities, including 15 heritage spots along 8 sections of the canal. The heritages spots here cover the remains of all kinds of hydraulic facilities that give a sense of the creativity of the scientific inventions employed in the traditional project of the canal and the exemplary characteristics of the technological system. Nanwang hub was a large-scale comprehensive hydraulic and waterway hub constructed to solve the problem of crossing a water ridge, and it is the most scientifically significant spot along the Grand Canal.

A 71-kilometre-long river channel on the Tianjin segment was selected, including a 48-kilometer section of the Northern Canal from the junction of Jianhe River at Kuang'er Harbor in Wuqing District to the mouth of Sancha River; and a 23-kilometer section of the Southern Canal from the mouth of Sancha River to Yang Liuqing Town of Xiqing District.

2 sections of the river channel and 2 heritage spots were selected in the Beijing segment. The 2 sections of river channel are respectively the old Beijing city section of Tonghui River-Shichahai in Xicheng District and the old Yuhe river channel in Dongcheng District, and the Tongzhou section of Tonghui River. The 2 heritage spots are respectively Wanning Bridge and Eastern Buya Bridge.

Significance of the Heritage

As the longest and oldest manmade waterway in the world and the largest and most wide-ranging civil engineering project before the Industrial Revolution, the Grand Canal facilitated the unified jurisdiction of the communication of materials and territory between southern and norhern China, reflected the superb wisdom, determination and courage of the Chinese people, and represented the outstanding achievement of Eastern Civilization in hydrotechnics and management capability. Having undergone over 200 years of continuous development and evolution, the Grand Canal still plays an important role in transportation, flood discharge, irrigation and water delivery, and is an indispensable and important way of transportation in the regions along the Grand Canal. From ancient times up to the present, the Grand Canal has played an important role in safeguarding the economic prosperity and social security of China.

Yin Xu

Yin Xu, the capital site of late Shang Dynasty on both banks of the Huan River, is situated in the surroundings of present-day Xiaotun Village of Yindu District, Anyang City, in Henan Province. The sites of royal tombs, palaces and the royal ancestral shrines area in Yin Xu, together with the site of the Shang city to the north of the Huan River, form a great and magnificent Yin Xu ruin. From Pangeng to Dixin (Zhou) , the Shang Dynasty had its capital here for 273 years, making it the earliest capital in Chinese history whose location can be accurately ascertained.

Its status as capital proved by literature, archaeology and oracle bones (inscriptions on bones or tortoise shells of the Shang Dynasty) , the Yin capital Anyang was the first ancient Chinese capital. The ancient name of Yin Xu was "Bei Meng",but it was also known in oracle inscriptions as "Shang Yi" and "Da Yi Shang". From 1300 B.C. when Pangeng moved the capital to Yin, to 1046 B.C. when Dixin was overthrown, over the time period of 273 years, 12 kings of 8 generations, including Pangeng, Xiaoxin, Xiaoyi, Wuding, Zugeng, Zujia, Linxin, Kangding, Wuyi, Wending, Diyi and Dixin, were rulers here. This place had been the political, economic, cultural and military centre of late Shang Dynasty. After the fall of the Shang Dynasty, it was gradually reduced to ruins.

Architectural Arrangement

Centring around Xiaotun palaces and the royal ancestral shrines area, the general layout of Yin Xu was distributed along the banks of the Huan River in a radial ring. The ancient capital, whose history can be traced back over 3,300 years, was in an open form.

North Bank Shang City

In January, 1999, a huge new site of the Shang city was newly discovered 2 metres underground to the northeast of Anyang Yin Xu. The plane of it was square, 2200 metres long from north to south, 2150 metres wide from east to west, the total area amounting to about 4.7 square kilometres, its direction being 13 degrees east of north. It has been established that in the south section of the north-south axis were distributed palaces and royal ancestral shrines. The underground relics prove that this city was older than Yin Xu, the late Shang capital according to traditional concepts. Its distribution slightly overlaps with the old area of Yin Xu, but as a whole it was on the north bank of the Huan river, thus it was named by academic circles as "North Bank Shang City."

The site of North Bank Shang City, along with the sites of palaces and royal ancestral shrines and the sites of royal tombs together form the scope of Yin Xu ruins in their declaration as having World Heritage status, and they truly embody the originality, completeness, and value expected for a World Heritage site. They added up to the richness of contents and lended Yin Xu weight in its claim for World Heritage.

The Ruins of Palaces and Royal Ancestral Shrines

The more than 50 architectural sites are divided into three groups of palaces, ancestral shrines and sacrificial altars. A bronze site was also discovered. In the palace site a large amount of such precious relics as oracle bones, bronze vessels, jade vessels and precious stone vessels have been excavated. Yin Xu relics, which include some of the most notable creations of China and the world at large, contain the creativity, wisdom and outstanding skills of ancient Yin people.

The palaces and ancestral shrines, constructed mainly of loess and wood, had as their foundation solid and tall tamped-earth platforms. The foundations of the buildings had column bases, with frames supported by wood columns, while the walls were constructed of rammed earth, and the roofs were covered with thatchgrass. The modelling of the buildings appeared solemn and respectful, plain and elegant, showing strong characteristics of Chinese palace architecture and representing the advanced level of palace architecture at the early stage of ancient China.

The famous tomb of Fu Hao was one of the most important archaeological discoveries in the palace and ancestral shrines area of Yin Xu since 1928. It is the only tomb of a Shang royal family member that can be connected to oracle bones and for which we can establish the date, identity and status of its occupant. In the palaces and ancestral shrines area were also distributed a large number of oracle-bone storage cellars. Since the discovery of oracle bones at the end of the 19th century, about 15,000 oracle bones have been excavated.

The Ruins of Royal Tombs

The ruins of the Yin Xu royal tombs take up an area of 11.3 hectares and face the ruins of the palaces and ancestral shrines area across the river. Here was where the Shang kings were buried and where sacrifices were conducted. These are the earliest complete royal tombs known in China. 12 big royal tombs and over 2500 sacrificial pits have been found in the area. The big royal tombs, mostly in the shapes of the characters 亚, 中 and 甲 , had grand tomb chambers and were vast in shape and structure. The biggest tomb measures 1803 square metres and is 17 metres deep. The coffin chamber and coffin were extremely luxuriant, and the funerary objects were exquisite. The osseous remains of the several thousand humans who were sacrificed here reveal that most of these people, mostly young men along with some women and children, were beheaded. The number of people buried in each pit varied from 8 to 10. In the 191 sacrificial pits excavated in 1976 alone were found 1178 human skeletons, the existence of these sacrificial pits bearing historical testimony to the cruel human sacrifice system of the Shang Dynasty. The Yin Xu tombs' burial system, distribution pattern, burial mode and sacrificial rites represented the highest level of royal tomb construction in the early history of ancient China. The discovery of these tombs gave sure proof of the historical position of the Yin Xu Shang capital and laid important groundwork for exploring the origins of Chinese civilization.

The Site of Sacrifice Field

In the Shang Dynasty, on ceremonial occasions the kings would sacrifice people as well as livestock as offerings to their ancestors and gods. This is known as the "human sacrifice system". Those killed were mostly prisoners of war, and a small number were slaves. The kings and aristocratic slave owners would engage in human sacrifice when they worshipped their ancestors, when they appealed for protection from the gods, when they built palaces and when they prayed for rain, making this place a huge public sacrifice field. In the surrounding area of the big royal tombs, over 2,000 sacrificial pits were discovered, with many remains of the bodies of human sacrifices. According to incomplete statistics, 13,052 people were used as human sacrifices, and 1,350 oracle bones and 1,992 pieces of inscriptions among Yin Xin oracles had to do with human sacrifice.

Scientific and Technological Level

During the Yin Xu period, natural scientific technology as represented by bronze vessels reached an advanced standard in global terms. Archaeological excavations indicated that the handicraft industry during the Yin Xu period was unusually advanced, not only being very diverse, but also attaining a very high technological level . Some of the main handicraft production lines, such as bronze metallurgy, jade carving, earthenware, bone carving, vehicle making, spinning and weaving, had reached a sizable scale.

The Yin Xu era also made great achievements in other fields of science and technology.

According to the records of oracle inscriptions excavated here, the Yin people could accurately record solar eclipse, lunar eclipse and the stars. The Yin calendar was a combination of solar and lunar calendar, the whole year being divided into 12 months, with a leap month added to resolve the discrepancy between the two measures.

In mathematics, the Yin people had the digital concepts of 1, 10, 1000 and 10,000 and had adopted the decimal system.

In medicine, more than ten diseases had been recognized in the late Shang Dynasty, and were treated with medicine as well as acupuncture and massage.

Bronze Vessels

China's ancient bronze culture has strong national characteristics and artistic style. The more than 4,000 pieces of bronze vessels excavated in Yin Xu, including sacrificial vessels, musical instruments, weapons, tools, accoutrements, ornaments and works of art, formed a bronze civilization dominated by bronze sacrificial vessels and weapons, having attained a peak of development in the Chinese Bronze Era. The bronze carriage unearthed in Yin Xu had made extensive use of bronze parts, having a single shaft and two wheels, the structure being both delicate and complicated, which reflects superb compound mechanic technology and bronze casting technology. The existence of a large number of bronze sacrificial vessels in Yin Xu proves that the Chinese bronze culture had reached the highest stage. The exaggerated and mysterious style contains a rough and strong primitive tension and artistic charm, reflecting the religious emotions and aesthetic concepts uniquely belonging to the ancient Yin Shang people. The outstanding achievements of Yin Xu in the field of bronze casting made it one of the key bronze civilizations in the ancient world.

Stone Vessels and Jade Vessels

Besides the solemn-looking bronze vessels, Shang civilization is also famous for its large number of stone vessels and jade vessels. The jade vessels of the late Shang Dynasty have as their representatives the jade vessels excavated in the tomb of Fu Hao in Anyang Yin Xu. The 755 jade vessels can be divided into the seven categories of sacrificial vessels, honorary vessels, tools, utensils, ornaments, works of art and miscellaneous devices. Jade vessels in the shapes of animals and human beings greatly outnumber those in geometric shapes. Jade dragons, jade phoenixes and jade parrots look distinctive and lively. The jade human figurines, either standing or sitting or kneeling, are different in attitude and are all vivid.

According to experts, the source materials of the jade vessels excavated in Yin Xu are mainly Hetian jade and Liaoning jade, so it can be said that over 3,000 years ago during the Shang Dynasty, there was already the "gold and stone way" leading to Xinjiang, more than 1,200 years earlier than the "silk road" that began in the 2nd century B.C.

The discovery of the Yin Xu jade vessels does not only help us to have a fairly comprehensive understanding of the jade carving technology at the time, but it also provides important reference to the study of the history of jade carving, artistic history, and the social, economic and cultural aspects of the Shang Dynasty.

Significance of the Heritage

The excavation of Yin Xu confirmed the existence of the Chinese Shang Dynasty, reframed the early ancient history of China and enabled the Shang history recorded in traditional literature to become true history. The Shang buildings represented by palaces, ancestral shrines and big royal tombs set an example for palace buildings and imperial tombs in China's early ancient period. The 15,000 pieces of oracle bones excavated in Yin Xu gave the earliest clues to the present Chinese system of characters used by one quarter of the world's population. The Yin Xu relics as represented by bronze vessels and jade vessels and Yin Xu burial customs as represented by human and animal sacrifice and the burial of humans, horses and chariots provide unique proof of the cultural tradition of the late Shang Dynasty.

Site of Xanadu

In his *Travels*, Marco Polo described Xanadu in this way:

"The marble palace is truly beautiful. The inside of the rooms are all painted with gold and decorated with birds and beasts, which are extremely exquisite. The excellence of the artistry is a feast for the eyes."

Xanadu, the remains of the capital of the Yuan Dynasty, is 20 kilometres to the northeast of the seat of government of Zhenglan Qi, Xilin Gol League, Inner Mongolia, and on the north bank of the Shandian River. This prairie capital established by the northern horse-riding people in northern China is considered to be a marvellous product of the blending of the agricultural culture of central China and the prairie nomadic culture. Historians say that it is comparable to the ancient Italian city of Pompeii.

Historical Origin

In 1256, following the order of Mongke Khan, Kublai appointed Liu Bingzhong to build at the bank of Luanshui River in Lingbei castle and palaces. Liu Bingzhong chose the site at Jinlianchuan, and built the city in three years. It was a prairie capital combining the features of nomadic culture and traditional Chinese architectural style.

In 1259, Mongke Khan marched his army against the Song Dynasty. He died in Mt. Diaoyu in Sichuan, and after his death, Kublai made peace with the Southern the Song Dynasty decisively and withdrew north from the frontline of Yuezhou. In March of the next year, Kublai used Kaiping as his base and connected with the Mongolian imperial princes. In October, Kublai ascended the throne in Kaiping, establishing the Yuan Dynasty. Then he led his army north, took over the capital Helin and forced Ariq Boke to step down from the throne and moved west. From then on, Kaiping became the capital and the Central Secretariat was established to control the political affairs of the whole country. The development of Yuan history entered a new stage at that point.

In 1263, Kaiping, after enlargement and reconstruction, was formally titled Xanadu, and the Zongguanfu Department was established. The next year, Yanjing was renamed Zhongdu, the Central Capital. In 1267, a new city was built in the northeast of the Central Capital. In 1272, the name Central Capital was changed to Dadu, the Great Capital. From then on, the Yuan Dynasty had two capitals, with Dadu the capital and Xanadu the Summer Capital. All of the main government departments had their offices or subordinate offices in Xanadu, which was still an important national political centre.

Architectural Arrangement

Having a special geographical location, Xanadu was close to Helin, the political and military centre of the original Mongol Khanate. As an important hub connecting the east, the west, the south and the north, it played a key role in communicating with and controlling the powerful Mongolian clan aristocracy in Mobei, and had a decisive political and military position. It was not only on the front line for dealing with the Mongolian clan rebels, but was also the highest decision-making place for devising strategies. Therefore, the Quriltai (enthronement) of the early emperors of the Yuan Dynasty, such as Kublai, Tie Muer and Haishan, were held in Xanadu.

While adopting the ancient traditional Chinese layout of cities, the overall pattern of Xanadu took into consideration the Qionglu Yurts of ancient Mongolian nomadic life. The city layout was not quite regular, and each building group had their own walls, reflecting the architectural style of a temporary residence.

According to records, Xanadu once had a population of 110,000, and the perimetre of the city wall was more than 8 kilometres. There were about 60 government departments, and over 160 temples and monasteries of all kinds. The post-road extended in all directions, acting as the transportation hub between Mobei and Central China. The city comprised three walled compounds—the Palace, the Imperial City, the Outer City—as well as Guanxiang, the neighborhood outside of the city. The city walls were rammed with yellow soil, while the walls of the Palace City and the Imperial City were built of bricks and stones, The Outer City was square in shape, each side of it was 2200 metres. It had four gates and Wengcheng, that is, a small town outside the city gate. The inside of the city was divided into two sections with a cob wall, with the northern section being the Imperial Garden, and the southern section being government offices, businesses and workshops. The area surrounding the capital had many sacrificial sites and tombs.

Main Buildings

The Imperial City Square in plane, the Imperial City was at the southeast corner of the Outer City. There were 7 seven main streets, "four horizontal and 3 longitudinal", and the buildings were distributed irregularly, like a temporary palace. The exterior city wall was built of bricks and stones. The temples, the Imperial Academy and some large buildings were inside the Imperial City. At the north of the Outer City was the Imperial Yuanyou (enclosed ground for raising animals) and the golden-top Big Tent "Brown Hair Hall". In the east, south and west outside of the Outer City were Guanxiang, which occupied a large area and now has left many construction remains. Guanxiang was where ordinary people lived and where the shops, workshops and storehouses were found.

The Palace City As the centre of the whole city, the Palace City had three gates, namely, Donghua, Xihua and Yutian. The city wall was wrapped with bricks. In the four corners of the wall were watchtowers. Yutian Gate in the south, the main road for entry, was the most important gate and as such it was on the same axis as Mingde Gate, the south gate of the Imperial City. There were about 60 government office buildings, over 160 temples of all kinds, the halls of Daming, Yitian, Baoyun, Chenli, Cifu, Hongxi and Ruisi, the Pavilions of Da'an, Yanchun, Liangxiang, Zitan and Ninghui, and the important buildings of Luzhu, Yingzhou and Zhentang. As the most important building inside the Palace City, Da'an Pavilion was the symbol of Xanadu. The centre and the big palaces at the centre of the northern city wall were on the axis, and most other buildings were arranged symmetrically. The halls, Pavilions and sheds each had their own characteristics, being different in shape and size, of different color and style.

The Outer City 18-19 kilometre in perimetre, the Outer City was completely built of earth. It was at the northwest of the Imperial City. To the north was the Imperial Garden of the emperor, while the south was the site for government offices, temples and workshops. The three Guanxiang areas respectively in the east, south and west were the sites for shops, resident houses and storehouses. In the west of the city was the Imperial Villa. 5 kilometres around the Imperial Villa were mainly Temporary Imperial Palaces and tents. There was another big Imperial Garden that occupied an area of 25 square kilometres. In the northern suburbs were many temples and monasteries of all kinds. In 1358, the Red Turban Rebels took over Xanadu, burned down the buildings and ended the history of Xanadu as the provisional capital.

The Sacrificial Area and the Tomb Area In the area surrounding the Xanadu site are a series of subsidiary remains, mainly including the sacrificial site of Yangqun Temple, the Anvil Hill Tomb Area, the Woniushi Tomb Area, the Yikeshu Tomb Area and the Dongliang Pavilion Site.

The Yangqun Temple Sacrificial Site was 35 kilometres to the northwest of Xanadu. Comprised of four sacrificial sites, it was built by the upper nobles of Yuan Dynasty to worship their ancestors. All four sites were enclosed by stone walls and incorporated sacrificial altars, white marble sculptures and sacrificial buildings.

Three of the Yuan Xanadu tomb areas, including Anvil Hill, Woniushi and Yikeshu, have been discovered. The Anvil Hill Tomb Area is on the southeast and northwest slopes of Anvil Hill 8 kilometres to the southeast of the Xanadu Site. There are more than 500 tombs here, most of which are made of stone. 73 tombs have been excavated. Woniushi Tomb Area is on the slope of Mt. Xiangyang, 20 kilometres to the northwest of the Xanadu Site. 15 tombs here have been excavated. The surface part of the tombs are piled up with natural stones into convex shape. Most of the tombs are cremation tombs and are divided into the three kinds of brick coffin, wood coffin and vertical rectangular coffin pit. The pattern of Woniushi Tombs was regular; they are quite well-preserved and fairly rich in funerary objects. They were the tombs of the Han Chinese who lived in Xanadu during the Yuan Dynasty. Yikeshu Tomb Area is on the slope of Mt. Shanwan 12 kilometres to the northwest of ancient Xanadu. 26 tombs have been excavated. Tombs here are rich in funerary objects. Many gold vessels, silver vessels, porcelains, and copper and metal vessels have been discovered.

Significance of the Heritage

The location and the environment of the Xanadu Site reflect the common influence of the values and lifestyles of both the Mongolian and the Chinese. The design model of the city also reflected the mutual influence of these two cultures. It was through the blending of the Mongolian and Chinese ideas and institutions that the Yuan Dynasty could expand its rule to a great part of the then known world. The Xanadu Site represents an unique example of the city planning that combined the elements of different ethnic groups.

The Xanadu Site of the Yuan Dynasty provides extraordinary evidence of the supreme rule of the Yuan conqueror Kublai, which included the absorption and changing of the culture and political system of the conquered, and the conqueror's resolve and efforts to keep and maintain the original cultural tradition.

The location, environment and city pattern of the Yuan Xanadu Site prove the co-existence and blending of nomadic culture and agricultural culture. The city planning of the Chinese way of combining garden and landscape was necessary for the lifestyle of the Mongolians of the Yuan Dynasty, and thus was produced an outstanding example of city layout representing an important stage in human history.

The Yuan Dynasty established a powerful empire stretching across Europe and Asia. It conquered 40 countries and had a territory of 30 million square kilometres, exerting a very significant influence on human history. The capital of the Yuan Dynasty was of course a global political and cultural centre during that period.

Xanadu played an important role in the history of exchanges between China and foreign countries. In the Yuan Dynasty, foreign communication was frequent, with businessmen, merchants, traders and craftsmen coming from not only central China, but also from central Asia and Europe, who brought in metal containers, daily necessities and luxury goods, and took away livestock products. They helped promote the economic prosperity of the Mongolian area centering around Xanadu.

The position of Xanadu in the history of science and technology is even more important. As early as during the reign of Mongke Khan, Chengyingque,the astronomical observatory in Kaiping, was established. At the invitation of Mongke Khan, the Persian scientist Jamal al Din established the astronomical observatory where he invented many large astronomical instruments and formulated the Permanent Calendar.

Capital Cities and Tombs of the Ancient Koguryo Kingdom

Koguryo was an ethnic regime on the ancient Chinese frontier. In 37 A.D., the 2nd year of the reign of Emperor Yuandi of the Han Dynasty, Zhu Meng from Fuyu founded the kingdom in Koguryo County of Xuantu Prefecture (in the present Xinbin County of Liaoning Province) of the Western Han Dynasty, later, the capital was moved to Heshenggu City (present day Wunü mountain city in Huanren County, Liaoning Province) . In the 3rd year of Yuanshi of the Western Han Dynasty (3 A.D.) , the capital was moved to Guonei City, and at the same time was built Weinayan City (both are in Ji'an County of Jilin Province) , then in the 4th year of Shiguang (427 A.D.) in Northern Wei Dynasty, the capital was moved to Pyongyang. In 668 A.D., the Koguryo regime was destroyed by the united forces of the Tang Dynasty and Silla of Korean Peninsula.

The Koguryo regime was one of the influential ethnic regimes in northeastern China, and played an important role in the process of historical development in northeastern Asia. It created a splendid ancient civilization, and left in Jilin, Liaoning and some other places rich historical remains and cultural relics.

Main Bulildings

Since the 1990s, archaeologists have excavated many Koguryo capitals and tombs of nobles in Ji'an and Huanren, and have repaired some naturally damaged emperor tombs, revealing the rich cultural content of the Koguryo and making clear the outline of the Koguryo culture. The heritage site encompasses mainly Wunu mountain city, Guonei City, Wandu mountain city, 12 imperial tombs, 26 tombs of nobles, Good Taiwang monument and the No.1 accompanying grave at Jiangjun tomb. The capital cities, the imperial tombs and the tombs of nobles are especially precious for their important historical and cultural value.

The Capital Cities

As the capitals of the early and middle Koguryo Dynasty (from the 1st century to the 5th century) , Guonei City and Wandu Mountain City (originally Wei Nayan City) are characterised with the mutual interdependence of the plain and the mountain cities. Among the city sites of the Middle Ages in Northeastern Asia, both Guonei City and Wandu City are outstanding examples of capital construction. Guonei City is one of the few plain type of capital sites where stone city walls still remain and where the remaining city wall still looks stable and solemn. The layout of Wandu mountain city made smart use of the mountain shape and was reasonably planned, perfectly realising the harmonious blending of natural landscape and human creation. The remains of the palace site exposed by archaeological excavations reveal the splendid bearing of the original construction. As the capitals used for the longest time by the Koguryo regime, Guonei Vity and Wandu City both give evidence of the glorious Koguryo Civilization that had been submerged in history.

Wunü mountain city was the first capital created by the ethnic Koguryo regime in northeastern ancient China. As the earliest city of the over 100 Koguryo mountain cities along the banks of the Yalu River, it is grand in size, complete in system, and very well preserved. Inside the city are distributed the important architectural sites and life and military sites that have very rich cultural meaning. The construction of Wunü mountain city inherited the tradition of mountain city construction of northern China, yet big breakthroughs and innovations had been made in such aspects as choice of site, layout, the building of walls and the processing of stones. In the architectural history of ancient northeastern Chinese people, this city had milestone significance.

The Imperial Tombs and the Tombs of Nobles

The ancient Koguryo tombs in Ji'an City are the remains of the slave kingdom of Koguryo . On the surrounding plain of Ji'an City are distributed more than 10,000 ancient tombs of the Koguryo period, the world-famous "Donggou ancient tombs". The large tombs such as the Taiwang tomb, the General tomb and the Qianqiu tomb reflect the historical development process of the Koguryo Kingdom. The dozen or more ten large Koguryo tombs represented by the Taiwang tomb and the General tomb and big number of the Fresco tombs of the nobles are an epitome of the Koguryo architecture. What is more significant is that they fully embody the organic blending of the local cultural heritage and the surrounding cultural influences, especially those from the main part of China. As classic examples of Koguryo cultural work, they are an inspiration to prosperity.

The Monument of Good Taiwang According to historical documents, established in 414 A.D., the 10th year of Yixi during the reign of the Eastern Jin Emperor Andi, the Stele of the Good Taiwang has 1590 years of history. It was made of a huge complete stone column with slight chiselling. The monument is 6.39 metres tall, and the width of the four sides vary from 1.34 to 2 metres. The square column shaped weighs 37 tons, having no inscription at the top. Without support from any external strength, the whole monument stands on an irregular granite slab.

The Good Taiwang, named Tan De, was throned in 391 A.D. at the age of 18, and died at 39. The 22 years under his reign saw an unprecedented prosperous period in the Koguryo history, and the Good Taiwang Monument was established by King Changshou in memory of his father's achievements. The monument text recorded the fact that the Monument of the Good Taiwang was established by the 20th King Changshou of the Koguryo Kingdom for the memorial of the Good Taiwang, the 19th Koguryo King. It told about the legends of the origin of the Koguryo people and the founding of the kingdom, and the inheritance relationship of the first three kings. It recorded the great achievement of the Good Taiwang who had fought many wars to expand the Koguryo territory, the number of tomb-guarding households, their origin and related regulations about tomb guarding. There are now only three known Koguryo relics with written inscriptions, and the Monument of the Good Taiwang is the one of the three with the most detailed contents, thus it is of great importance for the study of the Koguryo politics, military, culture, institutions, tradition and its relationship with Xinluo, Baiji and the Japanese islands.

The Taiwang Tomb The construction of Taiwang tomb, the tomb of the 19th king of Koguryo Kingdom, began in 391 A.D. Of the surviving Koguryo tombs, it is the only one whose date and owner are accurately known. The Taiwang tomb has a stone chamber with square altar stairs. The tomb is square, with the edge length being 66 metres, and the remaining height being 14.8 metres. It is built up of several altar stairs. Each altar stair is composed of several layers of delicately carved rectangular strip stone. The four walls of the tomb chamber are built by flatly laying the polished stones. The chamber is covered with a huge stone as the tomb roof. The whole tomb is huge in size, and has plain structure.

By the Taiwang tomb, there used to be a Tomb monastery enshrining the tomb keeper of Guangze King. On the walls of the monastery were paintings and poems. The poem by Ke Zongqi, the Fugong of Qing Dynasty, in 1824 described the occasion of worshipping the Taiwang tomb: "Every year we come to Qingxi to worship our ancestor, bringing wine, ox and goat, jostling with other mourners. Recalling the place where the old vines incarnated, the old monastery was under the setting sun in the west."

Koguryo Fresco Tombs The Koguryo tombs are located in Ji'an City, Jilin Province. The Koguryo people were brave and bellicose, and that explains why many frescoes of the earlier period represent scenes of soldiers and battles. More contents have to do with palaces, Pavilions, stables, wells, guards, maids, ox, horse, chicken and dog, trees and flowers, the sun, the moon and the stars. The fresco also describe Fuxi, Nüwa, Huangdi, Shennong, gods, Buddhist monks and Taoist priests that are typical of central Chinese culture, reflecting rich Confucian, Buddhist and Taoist influence. There are few written materials left by the Koguryo, and the little information about it merely scattered in ancient books; the rich content of the Koguryo ancient tomb frescos provide important references for experts and scholars to study the Koguryo history, culture and customs.

The Bagua Map in the Koguryo Imperial Tomb This Bagua Map was found in the lower left corner on the north wall of the chamber of the No. 4 "Five Helmet Tomb" of the Koguryo Tombs of the Nobles in Ji'an, Jilin Province. In the fresco is painted the image of a Taoist priest: he is sitting on the lotus platform with cross legs, with the left leg bending and the right leg erect. He is bowing his head, with hair falling down. Wearing a green feather robe, he is painting a Bagua Map with one hand. This earliest Bagua Map with strong personality in the fresco on the chamber wall of the Koguryo Tombs of the Nobles has important significance for the study of *Book of Changes* and the cultural history of northeastern China.

The General Tomb At the foot of Mt. Dragon 5 kilometres northeast of downtown Ji'an, Jilin Province, there is a huge tomb similar in shape to the Egyptian pyramids. This is the General Tomb, sometimes known as the "Pyramid of the East". This square altar stair tomb belongs to the 20th King, Changshou King, of the Koguryo Kingdom.

Constructed in the early 5th century, the General Tomb was built of more than 1100 evenly cut rectangular granite stones, filled in between with pebbles and gravel. For fear of the stones being moved outward by their own weight, on each side of the grave, 3 huge stones were laid to protect it. Except for one stone at the north side, all the stones remain complete to this day. The tomb is 12.4 metres tall. The outward form of the tomb is 7 steps of stairs, and the opening of the tomb is at the middle of the fifth step.

According to documentary sources, "the Changshou King" was "tall and vigorous, bold and generous". After inheriting the kingdom of his father, "the good Taiwang," he continued expanding the territory of his kingdom, and in order to develop the southern Korean Peninsula, he moved his capital to Pyongyang. The Koguryo regime reached its peak under the reign of the Changshou King, when it was one of the most powerful countries in northeastern Asia.

Qianqiu Tomb It is located on the 200-metre-high slope on the eastern bank of Maxian River, 3.5 kilometres to the west of Ji'an City. Huge and in the shape of a mountain, it is called Qianqiu Tomb because of the Chinese characters "qianqiu wansui" (longevity) inscripted on the brick. This is a square altar stair tomb of stone chamber, almost square shaped, with the side length being 80-85 metres. The remaining incomplete height is 15 metres. The top of the tomb is flat and is about 20 square metres. Among a heap of stones are several processed huge strip stones. Large amount of fragments of semicircle-shaped tile, pan tile and bricks with characters remain on the tomb. The architectural pattern of Qianqiu Tomb is the same as that of the General Tomb, but it is several times larger than the General Tomb. It can be said to be the champion of the Koguryo tombs. It is a Koguryo imperial tomb.

Significance of the Heritage

The Koguryo created a glorious history. The large amount of historical remains are mainly found in Jilin and Liaoning provinces and represent irreplaceable physical evidence for this period of history. Having created a culture rich in ethnic characteristics, in its middle and late periods, the Koguryo had been deeply influenced by the culture of central China; as a result, Confucianism, Buddhism and Taoism became very popular. The stable Koguryo mountain city, the massive tombs, and the splendid frescos in ancient tombs have become an important component of Huaxia (Chinese) Civilization. Acclaimed as "the art treasure house of northeast Asia", the Koguryo frescos recorded the special culture of the ethnic group in ancient northeast China.

Temple and Cemetery of Confucius and the Kong Family Mansion in Qufu

In the southwest of Shandong Province there is a county-level city one fifth of whose population is surnamed Kong. This is "the sacred city in the east"—Qufu, with a history of over 5,000 years. As the famous saying goes, "the rituals and music over thousands of years may be traced back to the state of Lu in East China, the Chinese wearing different dresses and caps all revere the king with no crown." It is on account of Confucius that Qufu has become well-known all over the world. Confucius, one of the world's great thinkers, was the founder of Chinese Confucianism. During a long period of over 2,000 years Confucianism has grown to be the orthodox culture of China and influenced the countries in East and South-East Asia and come to be the cornerstone of the whole oriental culture.

Main Buildings

In order to "commemorate and offer sacrifices to Confucius annually," Duke Ai Gong of Lu consecrated the house of Confucius as "temple" the second year after the death of Confucius (478 B.C.) . At that time the whole property only consisted of "three temple rooms," in which were preserved the clothes, caps, musical instruments, carriage and books of Confucius. Later on, with the succeeding dynasties conferring more and more titles on Confucius, the Temple of Confucius underwent continuous maintenance and expansion. By the time of the Ming and Qing dynasties the monument had reached its present scale.

The Temple of Confucius

This is a massive monument full of magnificence and grandeur and also the largest venue for commemorating the Confucius. Inside the temple there are nine courtyards and three axes with the north-east axis the central one. The temple is 630 meters long and 140 meters wide. The architecture comprises over 460-bay halls, altars and pavilions with a total area of about 16,000 square meters. There are 54 stone arches and 13 Imperial Stele Pavilions within. The main buildings within the temple are the stele pavilions of the Jin and Yuan dynasties, Kuiwen Pavilion, Xing Altar, Deyang Tiandi Workshop of Ming Dynasty, and Dacheng Hall and Residential Hall rebuilt in Qing Dynasty.

Kuiwen Pavilion Also called Bibliotheca, it is a pavilion dedicated to the collection of books and pieces of calligraphy from succeeding emperors. It is a four-bracket, three-flying-eave structure with red-painted walls and yellow tiles. It has singular architectural artistic style and is a tall building second only to Dacheng Hall.

Thirteen Stele Pavilions They are located between Kuiwen Pavilion and Dacheng Stone Arch. Eight of the pavilions are in the south while five are in the north. They are generally called "imperial stele pavilions." There are over 50 massive stone monuments of the Tang, Song, Jin, Yuan, Ming and Qing dynasties. The Chinese characters in those monuments are in different styles, including xing, cao, li and zhuan.

Dacheng Hall It is the main hall and the core structure of the Temple of Confucius. In the Tang Dynasty it was called "The Hall of Prince Wenxuan." In the second year of Emperor Yongzheng's reign in the Qing Dynasty (1724) this hall was rebuilt. It is a nine-ridge double-eave structure covered by yellow tiles. It has carved beams and painted rafters with eight caissons decorated with the patterns of yellow dragons and royal seals. In the center of the double flying eaves is a board with three gilded characters " 大成殿 "carved in the shape of Emperor Yongzheng's handwriting. The hall is 24.8 meters tall, 45.69 meters long and 24.85 meters wide. It is built on a 2.1-meter-tall terrace and is the tallest building in the temple and also one of the three ancient halls in China. In the center of the hall is the statue of Confucius with the statues of Yanzi, Zengzi, Zisi and Mencius on the left and right. The four statues are called "the four subordinate statues". On the two sides are also 12 statues, namely, Minsun, Rangeng, Ranyong, Zaiyu, Duanmuci, Ranqiu, Zhongyou, Yanyan, Boshang, Zhuansunshi, Youruo and Zhu Xi, generally called "the twelve sages." Those 16 scholars are generally recognized as the orthodox successors of Confucianism. The ten stone columns in front of the hall bear openwork carvings of two dragons playing with a pearl. They are carved of a rock taking ascending shape. This lively and exquisite work is a treasure among stone carvings.

Cemetery of Confucius

The Cemetery of Confucius is located two kilometers to the north of Qufu county seat, with an area of over 3000 mu. In China it is the largest clan cemetery, used for the longest period of time and preserved most completely; it is also a man-made garden. There are many ancient trees projecting umbrella-like shades. It is said that the disciples of Confucius each planted a tree from his home town in the cemetery and so there are large varieties of trees in the graveyard. Tombs and monuments in the cemetery are numerous. Apart from the tombs of Confucius, Kong Li and Kong Ji (the latter two being the son and grandson of Confucius) there are also tombs of Kong Lingyi, Kong Yugou, Kong Wenshao and Kong Shangren. Not far from Zhushui Bridge is a ceremonial hall for holding the altar of incense in commemorating Confucius. Beside the hall the big tomb in the center is that of Confucius and in front of the tomb is a gigantic stone memorial with characters written by Huang Yangzheng in zhuan style identifying the tomb as that of Confucius. On the east is the tomb of his son Kong Li (the Marquis of Sishui and in front of which is the tomb of Kong Zisi (the Duke of Shu Sheng of Yi State) . East of the tomb of Confucius are three pavilions which housed imperial guests when Emperor Zhenzong of the Song Dynasty, and Emperors Shengzu and Gaozong of the Qing

Dynasty came to commemorate Confucius. In Chinese the pavilions are called Zhubi Pavilions meaning the stopover place of the emperor.

Among the tombs there is one of a celebrity named Kong Shangren. He was a great playwright of Qing Dynasty and well-known to the Chinese on account of his play The Peach Blossom Fan. His tomb is in the northeast corner of the outer side of the inner circle. On the stone monument are the characters identifying the host of the tomb as well as his official rank. Kong Shangren once guided Emperor Kangxi on a royal tour of the Temple of Confucius and the cemetery. His learned knowledge and lively explanations left a deep impression on the emperor.

The Kong Family Mansion

The Kong Family Mansion, close to the Temple of Confucius, is the dwelling of the direct male descendants of Confucius who inherited the title of Duke of Yan Sheng from their ancestors. Of traditional residences in China it is second in size only to the Imperial Palace of the Ming and Qing dynasties. The mansion covers an area of over 240 mu and comprises 463 rooms in the form of hall, tower or pavilion along the central, east and west axes. Along the east and west axes are respectively the home temple and the academy, while the main buildings assemble along the central axis. The buildings here may be divided into two sections: the front section is made up of official rooms while the back section is made up of inner residential quarters. The official rooms consist of three main halls and six side halls while the residential quarters consist of the front main rooms, the front hall building, the back hall building and the back five rooms. The last section of the mansion is the garden.

The main hall of the mansion is the place where Duke Yan Sheng read the decrees, gave audiences to officials, exhorted domestic discipline and clan regulations and tried major cases. It is also the venue where ceremonies are held on festivals and anniversaries. The armchair in the middle is covered by tiger skin with colorful fur and looks quite splendid.

The second main hall is also called the back hall. It is the place where Duke Yan Sheng received higher-rank officials (above the fourth grade) and the venue where the Duke gave examinations on rituals and music to junior scholars under the trust of the emperor. In the central section of the hall are two big boards with Chinese characters " 钦承圣绪 " The four characters mean receiving royal favors continuously. and" 诗书礼乐 " The four characters mean poetry, books, rituals and music, the four fields which constitute the main body of Confucianism. respectively with several stone monuments beside. Among them the Chinese character " 寿 " This letter means longevity. written by dowager mother Cixi was granted to Duke Yan Sheng when Lingyi Kong went to Beijing to celebrate the birthday of the dowager mother in the twentieth year of Emperor Guangxu's reign (1894) .

Behind the three halls are the inner chambers of the mansion. In the north is a seven-bay main hall named the front main room. It is the parlor where the masters and mistresses of the mansion received very close relatives and kinsmen and also the main venue where they held family banquets and wedding and mourning ceremonies. In the main hall antiquities of a great variety are displayed.

Preserved Artifacts

The historical, scientific and artistic value of the monumental complex is revealed by the collections they harbor. The most famous historical artifacts kept by the Kong Family Mansion are ten items from the Shang and Zhou dynasties, also called "the ten ceremonial utensils". They are time-honored and exquisite in patterning. They used to be bronzeware kept by the imperial court and were granted to the mansion in the 36th year of Emperor Qianlong's reign. Apart from this, over 300 buildings and 1,300-bay ancient architecture of the Jin, Yuan, Ming and Qing dynasties reflect the architectural regulation and features of each period. Over 1,000 pieces of Han stone reliefs, carved pictures depicting the life of Confucius, and stone dragon carvings all reflect the change and evolution of stone carving art. Over 5,000 stone steles since Western Han are not only treasures of Chinese calligraphy, but also precious materials for studying politics, thoughts, economy, culture and art of ancient China. Over 100,000 tombs provide objects for studying the burial system of China. Over 17,000 ancient trees are living samples for studying ancient phenology, climatology and ecology. Among 100, 000 artifacts collected, the most famous ones include costumes of the Yuan and Ming dynasties, the portrait of Confucius, portraits of Duke Yan Sheng and his wife and ceremonial utensils. The costumes of the Yuan and Ming dynasties are rare artifacts and valuable in studying ancient costumes and textile technology. Over 300,000 files and archives of the Ming and Qing dynasties kept in the Kong Family Mansion are the richest private archive and provide important documents for studying the history of the Ming and Qing, especially regarding the economy of the two dynasties.

Significance of the Heritage

The Temple of Confucius and the Kong Family Mansion are concentrated embodiments of Chinese architectural styles over nearly a thousand years and represent the pinnacle of architectural achievement during Ming and Qing dynasties. The architecture mostly uses wood as the frame structure and employs various brackets for support. The courtyard layout of the architecture pays much attention to symmetry. The architectural complex of the temple and the mansion has condensed the cream of architecture of previous dynasties and embodies the architectural beauty to the utmost degree. Meanwhile the plan, design, and ornament of the building also reflect the essence of Confucianism. The spatial treatment of paying attention to structure and total layout incorporates the notion of harmonious coexistence in Confucianism. The particular example is the temple of Confucius which is a prominent embodiment of the architectural inclination of Confucianism and may be called a masterpiece and model of the architectural aesthetics of "harmony." In this sense the temple is a sublime palace of culture and art in East Asia. The 17,000 ancient trees in the cemetery of Confucius are not only witnesses to the evolution of the three architectures, but also precious objects for the study of ancient phenology, climatology and ecology.

Classical Gardens of Suzhou

The city of Suzhou, located in the lower Yangtze River alongside Lake Tai, is extremely rich in natural resources and superior in geographical environment. Suzhou has been the political, economic and cultural center of the East Yangtze Delta region (also called Jiangnan Region) since 514 B.C. when the Wu Kingdom built its capital here during the Spring and Autumn Period. Suzhou enjoyed prosperity in commerce and industry and abounded in talents, especially masters gifted in gardening, architecture, arts and crafts, and painting. All these circumstances provided conditions for the emergence and development of classical gardens of Suzhou.

The history of classical Suzhou gardens may be traced back to the 6th century B.C. when the king of Wu set up his royal hunting garden, and the earliest recorded private garden is Pijiang Garden of the Eastern Jin Period (the fourth century A.D.) . Later dynasties witnessed a boom in garden-construction and a growth in the number of prestigious gardens. During the Ming and Qing dynasties Suzhou was the most prosperous area in China and private gardens were built both in and outside the city. There were over 200 gardens from sixteenth to eighteenth centuries and over several dozen of them are still in good shape even today. Therefore classical gardens of Suzhou enjoy a singular position in the history of garden-building and possess great value.

Landscape Characteristics

Suzhou gardens have been compared to freehand paintings of mountain and water, with profound cultural connotations, since the garden-creators often were inspired by traditional Chinese paintings and poems and created evocative scenes by piling rocks, digging ponds and planting trees and flowers. As a result Suzhou gardens have been described as "soundless poems, three-dimensional paintings," due to their lyrical, pictorial qualities.

Suzhou gardens highlight the beauty of nature and all the landscapes are designed in accordance with natural geographical features. Garden creators used techniques such as scenery-borrowing, scenery-corresponding, scenery-dividing and scenery-separating to make gardens appear variable and full of views. The landscapes of mountain and forest in the urban environment show mankind's harmonious existence in nature.

One important feature of Suzhou classical gardens is that they are not only products of history and culture but also vehicles of traditional Chinese ideology and culture, which are manifested in the names of the buildings, the inscriptions of horizontal boards, the couplets, the carvings, furnishing and the allegorical meanings of the trees, flowers and even rocks. Such items are not only ornaments decorating the gardens but also vehicles of history, culture, thoughts and science. And so they inlaid rich spiritual connotations in physical existence. Philosophical ideas and various schools of Confucianism, Buddhism and Taoism find expression in classical Chinese poetry, decorating and elevating the landscapes inside the garden and eliciting fine sentiments in visitors, who finds their minds enriched and their spirits uplifted. In the gardens are also preserved works of distinguished calligraphers. Visitors may have the chance to see these rare works of art of high value.

Main Scenic Attractions

In the Ming and Qing dynasties garden-creating reached its peak, creating over 280 private gardens and courtyards in Suzhou. Among these, some are still in good shape and open to the public. They are Small Wave Pavilion (Canglang Pavilion) and the Net Master's Garden from the Song Dynasty, the Lion Forest Garden of the Yuan Dynasty, the Humble Administrator's Garden and the Garden of Cultivation of the Ming Dynasty, and the Lingering Garden, the Lotus Root Garden, the Garden of Delight, the Zigzag Garden and Tingfeng Garden (Maple-Listening Garden) of the Qing Dynasty. The Humble Administrator's Garden, the Lingering Garden, Net Master's Garden and the Mountain Villa with Embracing Beauty are listed as world cultural heritage sites by UNESCO for their exquisite craft and distinctive artistic features. Apart from these four, Small Wave Pavilion, the Lion Forest Garden, the Humble Administrator's Garden and the Lingering Garden represent different styles of Song, Yuan, Ming and Qing and so are referred to as the four celebrated gardens of Suzhou.

The Humble Administrator's Garden This garden is located on No. 178 Dongbei Street in the old Suzhou district with an area of 78 mu. First built in the early 15th century A.D., it still retains its elegant and delicate features of a southern waterside town, despite hundreds of years of vicissitudes. Ming garden design is still preserved in this time-honored garden which is celebrated as "the most superior private garden in China".

The garden is divided into four sections: east, middle, west, and the living quarters. The middle is the choice part with pretty hills and ponds, elegant halls and pavilions, and rich flowers and trees; the west section is calm and tranquil with winding corridors along the water; the east is spacious with grassy slopes and clumps of bamboo by the water.

The Lingering(Liu Yuan)Garden This garden, located on Liuyuan Road, has been hailed as "No. 1 garden in Wu region" for its compact layout, elegant style and rich views.

The Lingering Garden features spacious and splendid halls and exquisite furnishing. The creator of this garden made use of various architectural complexes to separate the whole garden into several units with distinctive features and connect those units with zigzag verandas. These verandas integrate with the various topology and landscape-sometimes they climb up a hill, sometimes they zigzag along a pond-and add depth and variety to the views in the garden. The total length of the verandas exceeds 700 meters.

The Net Master's Garden This garden is a typical medium-sized residential garden with supreme artistic features and cultural value. It was first constructed in the Southern Song Dynasty and got its present name during Emperor Qianlong's reign in the Qing Dynasty. It is composed of two parts: residential quarters in the east and courtyards in the middle (the main courtyard) and west (the inner courtyard) . The residential area is made up of three sections and the halls are all tall and spacious. It is typical of an official residence during the Qing Dynasty. The halls consist of palanquin hall, main hall and drawing hall with elegantly decorated interior and finely-carved bricks on the exterior. This garden may be regarded as a representative dwelling for officials of feudal society. There are comparatively more buildings in the main courtyard and so this courtyard is separate into two parts. The garden is regular and symmetrical in layout while the inside is separated into different sections based on the landscape.

The Canglang Pavilion Situated at Sanyuanfang in the south of the city, Canglang Pavilion enjoys the longest history among the surviving Suzhou gardens. The layout of this garden is natural and harmonious and this site is deemed a masterpiece of fabulous conception and proper techniques. The scenery inside the garden is natural and primitive, excelling in naturalness rather than exquisite craftsmanship. The scenery outside this garden highlights water and produces feelings of a water town while the inside view features buildings set around rockeries and connected by a veranda. Along the pond there is a covered winding walkway connecting all the pavilions around water. It links the water outside the garden with the rockeries inside, presenting a good example of scenery-borrowing.

The Lion Forest Garden This is one of the four celebrated gardens in Suzhou, with a history of over 650 years. It harbors not only various buildings such as pavilions, halls, corridors typical of Suzhou gardens, but also landscapes of hills, rocks and caves which wins the title of "a land of rockeries" for this garden. The rockeries have 21 entrances altogether; deep and winding horizontally, they zigzag up and down vertically. Poet Wei Tan of Yuan Dynasty once wrote,"I am said to reside in the city, yet I seem to perch among rockery forests." These poetic lines provide a fine description of this garden.

The Mountain Villa with Embracing Beauty This villa, called "Yi Garden", is an ancient garden features rockeries. It excels in conception, uniting one hill, one lake, trees and architecture into one whole. The rockery and lake are singular, rendering this tiny garden quite imposing. The rockery piled by Mr. Ge, the designer, is an extraordinary piece of work: though it covers less than half a mu, it is intensively detailed with various sceneries after every step. The peak tops at the southeast, while the subordinate peak appears a little dwarfed in the northwest, with a stream flowing between them. There are risky paths, caves, ravines, precipices, ridges and cliffs on the rockeries as if they are real. The peak rises to 7.2 m while the ravine runs 12m in length. The path covering more than 60 meters takes visitors up and down and creates the sensation of climbing a mountain.

Significance of the Heritage

Classical Suzhou gardens, integrating garden and residence, can serve multiple purposes of enjoyment, tourism and accommodation. This form of construction is actually a kind of creation originating from people's attachment to nature and pursuit of harmonious coexistence with nature, and the desire to beautify and perfect their living environment in a densely populated city of scarce natural scenery. Zhuozheng Garden (the Humble Administrator's Garden) , Liu Garden (the Lingering Garden) , Wangshi Garden (the Net Master's Garden) and Huanxiu Villa (the Mountain Villa with Embracing Beauty) with comprehensive architectural types and intact shape are four representative works displaying in a systematic and all-round way the layout, structure, shape, style, color, decoration, furniture and furnishings of classical gardens of Suzhou. They are representative vernacular architecture of the Ming and Qing dynasties, reflecting the sophisticated residential culture of the East Yangtze Delta region in this period. They once influenced the tone of architecture of all the cities in southern China and promoted the design, conception, layout, aesthetic orientation and construction technology of vernacular architecture. Therefore they reflect the way of living and etiquette of people in southern China and serve as a physical record when we explore and study the folk customs in Southern China in ancient times.

West Lake Cultural Landscape of Hangzhou

"West Lake Cultural Landscape" began in the 9th century, took shape in the 13th century and came to a thriving stage in the 18th century. The spot is comprised of five types of landscape, including authentically and completely preserved natural landscape, the so-called "Ten West Lake Scenes" and the 240-hectare West Lake Longjing Tea Plantation, which are located around the West Lake and the surrounding mountains in western Hangzhou in an area of 43.3 square kilometres.

Landscape Characteristics

"West Lake Cultural Landscape" includes the following sites: Su Causeway, Bai Causeway, Lesser Yingzhou, Huxinting (Heart of the Lake Pavilion) and Sir Ruan's Mound; these together form the landscape configuration of "Two Causeways and Three Islands" that gradually took shape from the 9th century to the 19th century; the spacious relationship of "mountains on three sides and city on one" , comprised of the waters of the West Lake, surrounding mountains in the south and north, and city landscape on the east side of the lake, formed in the 12th century and still remains to this day.

The lake area is famous for the beautiful scenery of Su Causeway and Bai Causeway that cross West Lake and separate it into five sections: Outer Lake, North Inner Lake, West Inner Lake, Yue Lake and South Lake. At daybreak, lingering night fog hanging over the lake creates the pretty scene of "Liuqiao Yanliu" (six bridges and misty willows) . Gushan, the biggest natural island in the West Lake area, Su Causeway and Bai Causeway crossing the lake, the three small artificial islands, namely, Small Yingzhou, Huxin Pavilion and Sir Ruan's Mound standing in the centre of the Outer Lake, and Leifeng Pagoda on Xizhao Mountain and Baochu Pagoda facing each other across the lake, form the basic pattern of "one mountain, two pagodas, three islands, three causeways and five lakes."

Main Scenic Attractions

The titled scenes of "Hangzhou West Lake Cultural Landscape" mainly consist of "The Ten Sights of the West Lake" , namely, Dawn on the Su Causeway in Spring, Curved Yard and Lotus Pool in Summer, Moon over the Peaceful Lake in Autumn, Remnant Snow on the Duan Bridge in Winter, Fishing Viewing at the Flower Pond, Orioles Singing in the Willows, Three Ponds Mirroring the Moon, Two Peaks Piercing the Clouds, Leifeng Pagoda in the Sunset, and Evening Bell Ringing at Nanping Hill.This series of scenes involve such features as seasons, time periods, meteorological phenomena, animals and plants, combined with such landscape elements as gardens, houses with courtyards, Buddhist temples, pavilions and pagodas. Each of these has its own aesthetic subject, expressing vividness, or serenity, or solitude, or a sense of "zen".

Gushan Gushan is the biggest island in West Lake area. It is connected with the lakeshore through Bai Causeway and Xiling Bridge respectively to the east and west. There are many places of historic interest and scenic beauty on the island; most outstanding among them are Zhongshan Park, Zhejiang Provincial Museum, Wenlan Tower, Xiling Seal Club, Fanghe (Crane Releasing) Pavilion, the Tomb of Qiu Jin, Yu Mansion, Mucai Pavilion (Tomb of Su Xiaoxiao) .

Zhongshan Park had been the imperial garden for the temporary imperial palace before it was turned into a park in 1927 to commemorate Sun Yat-sen. Fanghe Pavilion is at the northeastern corner of Gushan, built for the commemoration of Lin Bu, the lofty Song scholar famous for "taking a plum tree as his wife and cranes as children". Zhejiang Provincial Museum, on the south side of Gushan, has a collection of over 100,000 cultural relics. Wenlan Tower, located at the northwestern corner of Zhejiang Provincial Museum, was built during the reign of Emperor Qianlong of the Qing Period for conserving *the Si Ku Quan Shu (Complete Library in the Four Branches of Literature)* . It is modelled after WenyuanGe (Pavilion of Literary Profundity) in the Imperial Palace in Beijing. Xiling Seal Club, established in 1904 at the southwest corner of Gushan, got its name because it was close to Xiling Bridge. It was a famous painting and calligraphy art group in modern Chinese history.

Bai Causeway and Su Causeway The Bai Causeway begins at Duan Bridge and extends for about a kilometer to the west past the Brocade Belt Bridge, joining Gushan at "Calm Lake Autumn Moon." Peach and willow trees grow on either side, creating the best vantage point for viewing the West Lake and the surrounding mountains.

The Su Causeway used to be known as Sir Su's Causeway. At its southern end it starts near Nanshan Road at the foot of Mt. Nanping, and to the north it extends to just east of the Yue Fei Memorial, crossing the West Lake to a length of 2.797 kilometres, with a width of 30-40 meters. According to the Southern Song gazetteer *Lin'an Zhi*, "During the Yuanyou period Dongpo reported that he had dredged the lakebed and built a causeway for several li from south to north across the lake, planting willows and flowers on either side of the path with a total of six bridges, providing much convenience to walkers." Later the causeway was repaired and replanted several times, and it is now one of the most famous sites on the West Lake.

Duan Bridge Duan Bridge is at the beginning of Bai Causeway in the east. In *the Legend of the White Snake*, a folktale, Duan Bridge is where the heroine Bai Suzhen met the hero Xu Xian, thus making it the most famous bridge among the West Lake bridges.

In ancient times, there were eaves above the gate, so when it snowed, the snow in the middle fell on the eaves and only on both ends of the bridge was there snow, so that when seen from a distance it seemed as if the bridge was broken, hence the bridge became known as Duan (broken) Bridge. Duan Bridge was the only way leading to Gushan . After snow, people swarmed to Duan Bridge to appreciate the snow-covered West Lake. At such time, the snow-covered Gushan and the West Lake were all the more charming and thus this sight was called "Remnant Snow on the Duan Bridge".

Hupao Spring(Running Tiger Spring) Hupao Spring, a spot with "spring" as its subject, is for watching the spring, listening to the spring, tasting the spring and trying the spring. While at the same time, this is also a historical and cultural area, with the Dinghui Temple on Daci Mountain to the south of the West Lake, in which the legendary monks Xing Kong, Ji Gong and Master Hongyi stayed during their lifetimes.

Legend has it that Master Xing Kong of the Tang period visited the mountain and found that there was no water although the scenery was attractive. He decided to go elsewhere. Suddenly a god appeared to tell him that two tigers would come to dig a spring. The next day, two tigers did indeed come and dig out a spring. Ever after since, "Longjing tea and Hupao spring" have become "the two wonders of the West Lake".

Lingyin Temple Foremost among all West Lake temples and one of the most important centres of Buddhist activities in the coastal areas of southeastern China, Lingyin Temple has demonstrated the direct influence of Buddhism (especially Zen Buddhism) on the scenery of West Lake. The 2 stone pagodas and 2 Dharani pillars are meticulously carved, the imitation wood buildings are lifelike and are valuable cultural relics.

Feilaifeng The Feilaifeng sculptures form the biggest Buddhist cliffside group of statues in southeastern China, and it is also the Buddhist grotto in the Han Chinese area that enshrines the most Tibetan Buddhist statues. Having preserved the important link in the development and change of the art of Buddhist sculpture since the late Tang period, it fills in the gaps of the history of grotto art from the Five Dynasties to the Yuan Dynasty and thus occupies an important place in the history of Chinese grotto art.

Significance of the Heritage

Created and built by Bai Juyi and Su Shi, great ancient writers in ancient China, the West Lake cultural landscape highlights the philosophy of "harmony of man and nature", and embodies the three great Chinese traditional cultures and beliefs of Confucianism, Daoism and Buddhism. It transmits such traditional Chinese cultures as Buddhist worship, seclusion, tea and Zen, loyalty and filial piety, and book collection. It also bears witness to the clash in JIangnan during the 13th and 14th centuries of two highly advanced Asian civilizations, namely, the prairie civilization of the Mongolian Yuan Dynasty, and the agricultural civilization of the culture of the Song Dynasty. It reflects the creative spirit of Chinese scholars and literati in landscape designing at the height of agricultural civilization. The landscape has survived hundreds of years and is still completely and authentically preserved and continued. The West Lake has played an important role in the history of landscape design in China and neighboring countries and in the history of cultural communication from the 9th century to the 20th century.

At the same time, "West Lake landscape" is directly related to two of the 4 famous Chinese traditional love legends, *the Legend of the White Snake* and *Liang Shanbo and Zhu Yingtai*, which have had great impact both in the field of traditional Chinese literary art and in people's lives.

Historic Centre of Macao

The Historic Centre of Macao retains the historic essence of Macao's more than 400 years of communication between China and the West. It represents the oldest, the biggest, the most complete, and the most concentrated historic city in China in which Western buildings are the main element and in which Western and Chinese buildings add to each other's splendor. It is an important witness to the spreading of Western religious culture in China as well as in the Far East. What's more, it is the fruit of over 400 years of the communication and complementing of Western and Chinese cultures and the coexistence of different cultures. The Historic Centre of Macao (which used to be known as The Historic Buildings of Macao) is a collection of 22 historical locations and sites centering around the old downtown on Macao Peninsula.

Historical Origin

In Mid-16th century, as a response to the new situation of foreign trade, the government of the Ming Dynasty marked off a section in the southwest of Macao Peninsula for foreign merchants, mainly Portuguese, to reside and do business. Before 19th century, Macao had developed into the main port for foreign trade in China and was also an important international port in Asia. The prosperous trade business attracted people from all over the world and thus turned Macao into an international city inhabited by Europeans, Asians, Africans and Americans. The Portuguese named this city enclosed within walls the City of God's Holy Name, and the present Historic Centre of Macao was its core zone.

During the last 400 years or more people from various places such as Portugal, Spain, Holland, Britain, France, Italy, America, Japan, Korea and even Africa came here, bringing with them different cultures, different occupational skills,different customs and habits, and built in the Historical Centre of Macao houses, churches, roads, forts and even graveyards. They launched a colorful life, including all kinds of cultural life. Macao, taking advantage of this opportunity, started the trend and became the earliest and most important Chinese city to establish contact with modern Western culture. It is also the Chinese city most influenced by modern Western culture. At the same time, the foreigners living in Macao, using various ways, introduced to the world all the Chinese cultural ideas and customs that they saw in Macao. Macao was also a window through which foreigners learned about China.

The foreigners living in Macao brought with them their architectural tradition, making Macao the first stop for modern Western architecture's spread into China. All the buildings of the Portuguese in Macao reflect a close relationship with native Portuguese buildings. In fact, some of the main post-Renaissance architectural styles and forms, combined with the different Asian architetural elements, became new variants in Macao and produced a unique architetural style.

Landscape Characteristics

Due to the communion of Chinese culture and Western culture at the historical centre of Macao, most of the buildings are characterised by the combination of Chinese and Western elements. Most buildings in the city proper are still very well preserved or keep their original functions, including the site of the oldest church, the oldest Christian graveyard, and the oldest Western fort building group in China.

During the late Ming and early Qing, large numbers of Catholic priests used Macao as their base for missionary efforts. They actively devoted themselves to missionary work and construction in the Far East and created many Firsts in China, such as the first Western university (St. Paul's School) , the first Western hospital (Raphael Hospital) , the first Western theatre, the first modern lighthouse, the first printing house using Western metal platemaking and printing Latin (Affiliate Printing House of St. Paul's School) , the first foreign-language newspaper (*A Abelha da China*) , to name just a few. St. Paul's School (no longer exists) and St. Joseph's Seminary, founded by the Jesuits, trained a large number of people for Catholic missionary career in Far East and China, while at the same time, also educated many Chinese priests and made great contributions to Sino-Western cultural communication.

Main Scenic Attractions

The Historic Center of Macao is a historical block centering around the old downtown of Macao, and the buildligs are connected by adjoining squares and streets, including: A-Ma Temple, Moorish Barracks, Lilau Square, Mandarin's House, St Lawrence's Church, St. Joseph's Seminary and Church, St. Augustine's Square, Dom Pedro V Theatre, Sir Robert Ho Tung Library, St. Augustine's Church, Leal Senado Building, Senado Square, Sam Kai Vui Kun (Kuan Tai Temple) , Holy House of Mercy, Cathedral of the Nativity of Our Lady, Lou Kau Mansion, St. Dominic's Church, Ruins of St. Paul's, Na Tcha Temple, Section of the Old City Walls, Mount Fortress, St. Anthony's Church, Casa Garden.

St. Dominic's Church It is also referred to as Banzhangtang Church or St. Domingo's Church. Built in 1687 by Christian priests when they first came to Macao, it is 400 years old.

The church shows a strong artistic flavor. The ceilings are beautifully decorated, and the color of the crown patterns are especially elegant and exquisite beyond compare.The gorgeous Baroque pillars represent one of the most magnificent altars.

St. Augustine's Square Formerly named Mopanshan, it is small, but it enjoys a quiet and elegant natural environment and features humanistic and religious sights. Famous buildings in this area include: St. Augustine's

Church, Dom Pedro V Theatre, St. Joseph's Seminary, Sir Robert Ho Tung Library, etc. The road, with its wave pattern of stones, together with the buildings, shows a strong European flavor and makes the visitor feel exceedingly relaxed and comfortable.

Senado Square This is the square in front of IACM, and the buildings on both side of it were built in late 19th century and early 20th century. On the right side are the classical Post Office Building and neoclassical Holy House of Mercy. On the left are a series of 3-storey neoclassical buildings with cloisters. The buildings are in different colors and reflect a strong influence of South Europe.

Ruins of St. Paul's The Ruins of St. Paul is the remains of the anterior of St. Paul's Church. The church caught fire in January, 1835 and the anterior was the only part that survived. St. Paul's Church at that time was of distinguished air and enjoyed a prominent position, as the biggest Catholic church and the first Western university in the Far East.

Significance of the Heritage

The Historic Centre of Macao is the oldest existing Western architectural heritage in China , and is the comprehensive reflection of the architectural art of both East and West. It witnessed the development of Western religious culture in China and the Far East, while at the same time it also witnessed the historical origin of China spreading its folk religion to the West. It is a unique reflection of the pluralistic co-existence of Chinese and Western cultures, creating a very distinctive combination among Chinese historical cities.

Fujian Tulou

Fujian Tulou are constructed mainly of clay, wood, stone and bamboo. A certain ratio of un-burned sandy clay mixed with glutinous sandy soil was tamped with plywood to build 2-storey or higher houses. Tulou were the special product of ancient adobe architectural art improved and perfected by Han Chinese from central China, that is, the ancestors of Hakka people, who migrated from the Yellow River basin to the Yangtze River basin, and from there to the Dingjiang River basin. Fujian Tulou are famous for being wide in distribution, great in number, rich in types and perfect in preservation. With a total number over 30,000, Tulou are especially concentrated in southwest Fujian Province. Mainly built by Hakka people, they are also known as Hakka Tulou.

Historical Origin

Fujian Tulou, as the symbol of Hakka culture, are well-known for long history, numerous types, grand size, sophisticated structure, comprehensive function and rich connotation. With high historical, artistic and scientific value, Tulou have been described as "a unique and legendary form of mountain architecture."

Fujian Tulou appeared during the Song and Yuan dynasties, and developed and came to a peak in the Ming and Qing dynasties and the Republican period. Both the oldest and the youngest circular tulou are found in Chuxi of Yongding. Jiqinglou, with a diametre of 66 metres, is 600 years old, while Shanqinglou, with a diametre of 31 metres, is only 30 years old.

The origin of Fujian Tulou can be traced back to several influential migrations by Han Chinese from central China. During the Yongjia years of the Western Jin Dynasty, that is, the 4th century, in response to frequent wars and severe natural disasters in northern China, local people swarmed southward and thus started the history of hundreds of years of Han Chinese from central China moving continuously to Fujian. Migrants from central China merged with local people in south Fujian to form the Fulao population, characterized by their Minnan dialect. Those Han Chinese from central China who eventually came via Ganzhou in Jiangxi province to the mountainous area of west Fujian formed another important population, that is, Hakka people characterized by their Hakka dialect.

Moutainous southwest Fujian, where Fujian Tulou are located and where Fulao and Hakka people interact, was a rugged, steep and sparsely populated region where once wild beasts swarmed and bandits ran rampant. Communal living was the requirement of the firmly-ingrained traditional Confucian ideas brought over from central China, and, more importantly, it reflected a practical need to gather strength in order to collectively resist external enemies. Built by smartly taking advantage of the mountainous environment, reasonably arranged, and following traditional concepts of Fengshui in architectural planning, Tulou satisfied the requirements of communal living and defense by making ingenious use of the narrow and small flat land in the mountains and local materials of adobe, timber and pebble, thus producing a self-contained style of multi-storey adobe building that were cost-efficient, stable, highly defensive, and extremely aesthetic. These unparalleled residential houses of the mountain people had taken the long-pedigree rammed earth technology to an ultimate stage.

Landscape Characteristics

Popularly called "Adobe buildings", the Tulou feature modelling, decoration and construction craft rarely seen in the world. They were built mainly with adobe mixed with fine sand, lime, bamboo chips and batten, the mixture of which was repeatedly rubbed, pounded and pressed. The main characteristics of Tulou include: the combined use of soil and wood, closed externally and widely open internally, grand in size, beautiful in form, rich in types, making good use of local materials, cleverly designed so that a clan can live communally. The unique shape, superb technologies used, rich cultural connotation and the communal living of so many families, all these characteristics help make Tulou different from any other buildings the world over and thus may rightly be described as a wonder of the world.

Fujian Tulou include three typical styles, namely Wufenglou (five-phoenix structure) , rectangular and circular. Considered as a whole, Wufenglou, centred by three main halls, reflect a clear sense of primary and secondary, and meant the continuation and development of ancient courtyard style originating from the middle and lower reaches of the Yellow River, the birthplace of Han Chinese culture. The layout of rectangular tulou is similar to that of Wufenglou, yet with a thick and solid earthen wall extending from the upper main hall to the whole exterior, which greatly increased the defensive effect. Round tulou had a more intensified defensive function; at the same time, the hierarchical difference was greatly weakened.

Another characteristic of Fujian Tulou is that the structure is very well arranged, with all rooms being the same in size. Having only one gate for entry and a high, thick wall, most tulou are moisture-proof and warm in winter, heat-insulating and cool in summer.

Known as "gateless Hakka tulou museum of China", Fujian Tulou vary greatly in form and appearance, but may be divided into two main systems, namely, rectangular Tulou and round Tulou, covering over 20 kinds of architectural forms. Among the large number of tulou, round tulou are the most representative.

Round tulou are the most typical kind among all the local tulou, usually extending out layer after layer from a centre by following different perimeters, just like waves on a lake that nestle inside each other. At the center of round tulou is the clan temple, and from inside out come in sequence the ancestral hall and gallery, with residential rooms in the outermost layer. Uniform in size, all rooms in tulou are around 10 square metres. Sharing stairs makes it practically impossible for families to keep anything secret. Known as "the prince of tulou", Zhencheng Lou, a dramatic residential buildings, may be the most beautiful round tulou.

Main Scenic Attractions

The 46 tulou considered as World Cultural Heritage are composed of six groups of four buildings. There are three groups of buildings in Yongding county, while Nanjing county and Hua'an county have three groups, including the Chuxi tulou cluster and the Hongkeng tulou cluster in Yongding county, and the Tianluo tulou cluster and Hekeng tulou clusters in Nanjing, and the Dadi tulou cluster in Hua'an county. Mainly distributed in the mountainous areas of west and south Fujian,these tulou are known across the world for unique architectural style and long historical and cultural tradition.

Chuxi Tulou Cluster Located in Chuxi Village, Xiayang Town, Yongding County, Chuxi tulou cluster consist of five round tulou and several dozen rectangular tulou that unfold naturally like a pattern. The most typical Hakka residential tulou are Jishanlou, Jishantang and Shanqinglou. The structure of Shanqinglou is special among the traditional Hakka's Weilongwu (round-dragon house) in that it is a reverse round-dragon, which is rarely seen in the Hakka region of east Guangdong.

Hongkeng Tulou Cluster Built in different time periods and of different forms and size, the Hakka tulou in Hongkeng Village, and the ancestral temple, religious temple and school are on the banks of a brook. Very well arranged and in picturesque disorder, the houses stand in perfect harmony with the mountains, streams, village paths, little bridges and fields that together make a beautiful picture. Occupied by the Lin family, the Hongkeng tulou cluster consists of dozens of tulou of all types, including round tulou, rectangular tulou, palace tulou, wufenglou (5 phoenix) , and mansion-style, built from the 16th century (Ming Dynasty) to modern times. These buildings bear special witness to traditional Chinese adobe architectural art and traditional culture.

Gaobei Tulou Cluster Located in Gaobei Village, Gaotou Town, Yongding County, the Gaobei tulou cluster is a representative example of Yongding tulou. Dozens of tulou, of different height, are situated at the foot of a hill and close to a stream. Built in the Ming period, Wuyunlou with stoneless foundation tells the long history of tulou, and the elaborate Qiaofulou reflects the sincerity of overseas Chinese people's love for their hometown and their home country. The numerous tulou, as a natural part of a natural environment, present to viewers an incomparably beautiful rural scenery.

Tianluokeng Tulou Cluster Located in a long narrow small valley and halfway up a high hill in Shangbanliao Village, Shuyang Town, Nanjing County, the Tianluokeng tulou cluster consists of five buildings. Four round buildings surround a rectangular building, which looks like a blossoming plum flower. Looking at the buildings in a car going down the zigzag road, with the change of perspectives, Tianluokeng landscape is constantly and magically changing, with the round tulou now in front and then behind and the rectangular tulou now disappearing from sight and then coming into view.

Hekeng Tulou Cluster Located in Qujianghekeng Village, Shuyang Town, Nanjing County, the Hekeng tulou cluster followed the planning layout principle of "keeping in line with climate and geography". The round and rectangular tulou were planned at the same time but built separately. Fourteen large-sized tulou are set in an area of less than 1 square kilometre, thus making Hekeng tulou the most densely configured of all Fujian tulou, which reflects the unique feature of the villages composed of tulou blending into the natural envionment. The seven rectangular tulou built in the Ming and Qing dynasties and the seven round tulou of modern times form two groups, each shaped like the Big Dipper.

Dadi Tulou Cluster Located in Dadi village, Xiandu town, in Hua'an county of Zhangzhou municipality, the Dadi tulou cluster consists of Eryilou ("The King of tulou") , Nanyanglou ("Fujian Tulou Museum") , Dongyanglou (Livable Model) and such surrounding spots as Xuantiange, Jiaying Temple, Cixian Monastery and Chaxiang Street, which make an important part of the World Cultural Heritage "Fujian tulou". Built on hills, every aspect of the three tulou, from location to shape and arrangement, embodies the principle of "harmony between man and nature", and can be regarded as a classic work of fengshui.

Significance of the Heritage

As an architectural form of which Fujian Hakka people are proud, tulou are a treasure of Fujian residential buildings and can be considered an epitome of the combination of "Heaven, Earth and Man" for the humanistic dimensions contained in them. The history of tulou is also the history of village families. Residents of tulou can talk with ease and fluency about their family origin without having to look at their genealogy. Moreover, the tall buildings made of common local materials embody the great creativity and superb wisdom of the Hakka people in overcoming natural obstacles.

The massive Fujian tulou transmit a deep cultural tradition. The thought-provoking couplets and plaques, the private schools coexisting with tulou, and the murals and colored drawings for enlightening and educating people, all reflect generations of Hakka families' ideal of "cultivating one's moral character and managing the family's affairs well" and the pursuit of "striving for perfection". The highly praised couplet hanging in Zhenchenglou of the Yongding Hongkeng tulou cluster reads:

In striving you find no leisure. You must work hard whether you are small or young or old;

Making fame is no easy thing. You should care about everything whether of the family or country or the world over.

Old Town of Lijiang

The Old Town of Lijiang, also called Dayan Town, is located in Lijiang city of Yunnan province in the southwest of China. It is one of the "Four Best Preserved Historical Towns" in China, along with Langzhong in Sichuan, Ping Yao in Shanxi and Shexian in Anhui.

Without any walls around the city, Lijiang Old Town features clean and smooth flagstone roads, handcrafted houses with traditional wood and earth construction, as well as a number of waterways and bridges. The history of the town can be traced back to antiquity, when the ancient Qiang people moved here. They worked hard in this land and built their own Naxi Kingdom. The later generations of the ancient Qiang people are therefore called Naxi people, who are still the majority ethnicity group in Lijiang.

Located in Hengduan Mountains of southwest China, Lijiang has a distinct altitudinal belt of climate. Situated in the plateau with snowy mountains, it has nevertheless abundant rainfall with distinct dry and wet seasons. Autumn is the most beautiful season in Lijiang with clear sky, crisp air, colorful trees and flowers set against the distant Yulong Snow Mountain.

Structure and Layout

Sifangjie Square is typical of ancient streets in Lijiang. It is not only the center of the old town, but also the trade and commerce center of northwest Yunnan.

Near the mountains and by the rivers, Lijiang Dayan town is simple and natural without any grand city walls or wide roads. Houses are built along the ups and downs of the terrains and rivers with wood, stone and mud. In a mixed style of Han, Bai and Tibetan houses, the folk houses feature a unique layout of "houses on three sides and wall on one side". On every house side, there are three rooms in two storeys. The middle room facing south is for the senior members of the family while the rooms in the west and east are occupied by younger ones. The courtyard in the middle of the house is delicately floored with pebbles and tiles with intricate carvings. The central room facing the entrance usually has six lattice windows carved into flowers and propitious birds and animals. The attached wide verandas are usually good space for relaxation.

Landscape Characteristics

Different from any other important cities of ancient China, the Old Town of Lijiang does not adhere to the city building rules prevalent in the center of China which require a symmetrical structure and constructive defense. In the Old Town of Lijiang there are no mathematically built roads or guarding city walls. The town is naturally protected by mountains on three sides and connected by river on the other side. The river winds through the town past each house. The streets are varied, narrow and connected like veins. The genuine architecture in picturesque disorder makes the charm of this old town.

The town and architecture are the materialization of social life. Folk houses, compared to government buildings and temples, reflect in a better way the economic development, culture, customs and religion of a certain population or region. The folk house architecture of the Old Town of Lijiang is the best embodiment of Naxi architecture style. Its layout and structure are adapted to the specific conditions and life style of Naxi people. Combining some elements from Han, Bai and Tibetan folk houses and designed to be earthquake proof, shaded from the sun, and rain proof, with ventilation and decoration, these folk houses developed their own style, contributing to the architectural and cultural heritage of China.

Main Scenic Attractions

Shuhe Ancient Town Shuhe, or "Shaowu" in Naxi language, means the village at the foot of high peaks. As one of the earliest settlements built by Naxi ancestors in Lijiang, the well-preserved Shuhe ancient town was an important town along the ancient tea and horse trail. It is regarded as the live sample of the transition of Naxi ethnicity from the agricultural civilization to the commercial civilization.

Baisha Ancient Town Situated on the north of Lijiang and right at the foot of Yulong snow mountain, Baisha ancient town is an important part of the World Cultural Heritage of Lijiang. As the place of origin of the Mu family, the town of Baisha built by the family is regarded as the most authentic representation of Naxi culture. Baisha Fresco in Liulidian (Glazed Palaces) and Dabaojigong, which is typical of Lijiang Fresco, blends multiple religions such as Tibetan Buddhism, Chinese Buddhism, Taoism and Dongba religion, reflecting the traditional painting styles of Han, Bai, Tibetan and Naxi ethnicities as a result of the openness of Naxi society during Ming Dynasty.

Ancient streets Sifangjie is a trapezoid square of about 4000 square meters. Floored with colorful pebbles, it is lined on both sides with numerous shops. The highest point in the west is Kegongfang, a unique three-storeyed archway. In the west there is the West River and in the east the Middle River. An operative gate was built on West River to utilize the drop between West River and Middle River to wash the streets. From the four angles of Sifangjie square extend four main streets of the old town: Guangyi Street, Qiyi Street, Wuyi Street and Xinhua Street, from each of which cobwebby streets diverge and converge to cover the whole town. This forms an intricate and open layout centered in Sifangjie and spread along streets.

Ancient bridges Along the Yu River in the Old Town of Lijiang, there are 354 bridges, which means 93 bridges in each square kilometer. There are varied forms such as covered bridge, stone arch bridge, stone slab bridge, wooden slab bridge, etc. Famous ones as Suocui Bridge, Dashi Bridge, Wanqian Bridge, Nanmen Bridge, Ma'an Bridge and Renshou Bridge were all built during the Ming and Qing Dynasty. Dashi Bridge (Big Stone Bridge) , located 100 meters east of Sifangjie, is regarded as the best of all. This double stone arch bridge, over 10 m long and almost 4 m wide, was built by Chieftain Mu during the Ming Dynasty. The arch is built of slate and the gradual bridge deck is floored by traditional colorful stones.

The Mu Residence The Mu Residence was the government office of the hereditary Chieftain Mu. It was established in Yuan Dynasty, flourished in Ming Dynasty and then rebuilt in the spring of 1998 after years of war. The museum of the Old Town was set up inside the residence.

The reconstructed Mu Residence occupies about 3 hectares and faces east. Along the axis are 15 constructions in the style of antique looking architecture: Zhongyi Arch, Wanjuan Pavilion, Hufa Hall, stage, courtyard, corridors and resting spots. It is appraised as the architectural representation of the ancient music of Lijiang.

Wufeng Pavilion (Five Phoenix Pavilion) Located in the north of Heilongtan Park, Wufeng Pavilion was originally called "Fayun Pavilion" and was built in 1601 during the Ming Dynasty. It was announced as a protected site of Yunnan province in 1983. The pavilion is three-storeyed, with a height of 20 meters. The roof of each storey is decorated with eight cornices. The 24 cornices in total look like five flying phoenix. It is supported by 32 pillars, the four of which in the middle are 12 m high. The ceiling is painted with Tai Ching diagram, flying Apsaras, dragons and phoenix. The smooth lines and colorful patterns reflect the painting styles of Han, Tibetan and Naxi ethnicity.

Dongba Culture

Since ancient times the Naxi people have created a unique culture which is primarily preserved within their Dongba religion. The Dongba culture includes Dongba characters, Dongba scripts, Dongba painting, Dongba music, Dongba dance, Dongba religious instruments and a series of worship ceremony.

Hieroglyphic Dongba Characters As the only hieroglyphic writing alive in the world, the Dongba characters are well cherished as a precious cultural heritage since 1970s by worldwide academia. The 1400 hieroglyphic characters are still in use today. Representative books by Chinese researchers include *Naxi Hieroglyphic Patterns, Naxi Hieroglyphic Dictionary*, etc.

Naxi Ancient Music Dating back to the 14th century, Naxi ancient music is the oldest music of Yunnan province, and one of the oldest of China and probably the world. Composed of Baisha Music, Dongjing Music and Huangjing Music (lost now) , Naxi ancient music blends Taoism ritual music, Confucius ceremonial music as well as the poems and tunes from Tang and Song Dynasty into its unique style and so has been appraised as a "living fossil of music." The most fascinating elements in Naxi ancient music are three time-honored elements: the tunes passed down from ancient times, the instruments handed down hundreds of years ago, and the old performers.

Dongba Ceremonies The Dongba religion followed by Naxi people is a transitional one from Naxi primitive religion to more fully developed religion. The essence of Dongba culture is carried by the thirty kinds of Dongba religious ceremonies which were recorded in the Dongba scripts with hieroglyphic characters. The culture is presented and inherited in the form of religious ceremonies, which, closely related with the daily life of Naxi ancestors, tried to explain the conflicts between man and nature, man and society.

Dongba Painting There are three kinds of Dongba painting: wooden painting, paper painting and roll painting, which is the most famous one. The best representative of all is Shenlu Painting, 14 m long and 30 m wide, demonstrating the paradise, man's world and the hell in three parts in rough lines and unaffected style. The Baisha Fresco, painted in temples of Ming and Qing Dynasty by a Han painter, features vivid and genuine figures in smooth lines.

Dongba Wood Carving Dongba sculptors carve round, square and stereo patterns on azalea wood in lines and relief. These detailed or abstract patterns, drawn from daily life scenes such as playing music, carrying a load, ploughing, farming, tropical flora and birds, or from epic stories, are genuine reflections of their ethnicity culture.

Significance of the Heritage

In the past eight hundred years, the Naxi population together with other minorities who have been living in the old town created splendid cultures of their own. The streets, memorial archways in the square, water-supply system, bridges, house decorations, inscribed boards, couplets and steles all reflect the aesthetics and cultivations of Naxi people in religion, literature and arts. In particular, the rich Dongba culture and Baisha Fresco are precious relics of traditional arts of human history.

Ancient City of Ping Yao

Ping Yao ancient city is located in the middle of Shanxi province. It is a famous cultural city with over 2,700 years of history.Through over five centuries of continuous evolution and development, the Ancient City of Ping Yao is now an outstanding example of a Han Chinese city of the Ming and Qing dynasties (14th-20th centuries) that has retained all its features to the most exceptional degree in China. The ancient city has long been recognized as "a treasure house of Chinese historic architecture". The number of old buildings and the quality of their preservation are of a rare standard in the country, and possess significant value for historic, artistic and scientific studies in urban change, urban construction, human dwelling forms and traditional culture development during traditional times.

Historical Origin

There has been an urban settlement on the site of Ping Yao ever since the Western Zhou Dynasty, when it was fortified during the reign of Emperor Xuan (827-782 B.C.) . With the implementation of the system of prefectures and counties in 221 B.C., Ping Yao became the seat of a county (the most grassroots unit for a local town setting in China) administration, and continues to play that role. In 1370, during the reign of the Ming Emperor Hongwu, the city was greatly extended; its original city wall is still well preserved. The area comprises six large temple complexes, administrative offices for county and municipal administrations, and other historic buildings, all remaining in their original forms. More than a hundred cross-streets within the city, maintain their original appearance and are lined with shops built in the 17th-19th centuries, effectively preserving the historic townscape.The city has 3,797 traditional houses, over four hundred of which offer high conservation value and present unique local style.

Structure and Layout

Ping Yao ancient city was built completely in accordance with traditional urban planning style and layouts of cities of the Chinese Han nationality. In the closed city, four avenues, eight side streets and seventy-two lanes interweave with one another. They have clear functions and well-ordered layouts. The residences are all Siheyuan (quadrangles) made of black bricks and grey tiles with clear axes and bilateral symmetry. The cave-dwelling-like brick houses express a particularly strong sense of local flavor. The antique architecture authentically reflects the bustling townscape style of the Ming and Qing dynasties. The city walls, streets, residences, shops and temples in the ancient city all remain largely intact, with the original form and layout mostly unchanged. They constitute an integral part of the existing historical relics in Ping Yao.

The city walls of Ping Yao have six barbican gates. The east and west sides have two gates each. If you gaze across the old city from a height, you may find that its shape is like that of a tortoise sitting ready to move. The southern gate of the city is like the head of a tortoise, with the northern gate as its tail. The four barbican entrances in the east and west of the city resemble the paws of the tortoise. Therefore people named it "Tortoise Town". In ancient times, Zhongdu River used to wind just outside the southern gate. The landscape inspired ancient literati's reverie, "Splashing around in front of the turtle, with hills and waters facing the sun, that's just the way, to build a city." The ancient Chinese people worshipped the Four Benevolent Animals (Qilin, Dragon, Turtle and Phoenix) , which included tortoises, and they regarded tortoises as animals of auspiciousness and longevity. Thus the way "Turtle Town" was constructed, as people believed, carried the profound meaning of making this ancient city as firm as a rock and able to last for ages, relying on the power of the tortoise.

Landscape Characteristics

In 1370, during the reign of the Ming Emperor Hongwu, Ping Yao was greatly extended, leaving the ancient city walls the best-preserved in China. Wanfo Shrine, the main shrine of Zhenguo Temple, dating back to 963 A.D. of the Five Dynasties, is one of China's most precious timber-structure buildings in existence.With 2,052 existing painted clay statues made in the Song, Yuan, Ming and Qing dynasties, Shuanglin Temple, first built in 571 A.D. during the reign of the Northern Qi Emperor Wuping, has been described as an "oriental art gallery of Chinese painted statues".The 12th-century Main Hall of the Confucian Temple is a classic example of a Confucian temple constructed in the Song and Jin dynasties. Rishengchang Exchange Shop has been hailed as "the World's No. 1 Shop" and "Land of Wealth". The Qingxu Daoist Temple, founded in the second year of Emperor Xianqing's reign in the Tang Dynasty, is noteworthy for the rare constructional technique used-a system of suspension beams and pendant columns. All over the city and in its vicinity, there are a thousand ancient stele inscriptions and colorful glaze objects in various forms, crafted in different historic years.

Main Scenic Attractions

Temple of the City God Cheng Huang Miao (Ping Yao Temple of the City God) is located on the Chenghuangmiao street in the southeast of Ping Yao City. The whole temple is composed of Temple of the City God, Caishen (Fortuna, god in charge of fortune in Chinese legends) Temple, and Zaojun (god in charge of food) Temple.City God is one of the major gods that ancient Han ethnic universally idolized in their religious culture. Hence there is an old saying, "Once in trouble, the Emperor visits the Temple of Heaven, but this is where the magistrate comes." In history, particularly in the Ming Dynasty, the City God was appointed to a higher official title than the magistrate. As Zhu Yuanzhang, the first emperor of

Ming Dynasty, issued in an imperial edict, each city and town had to build its own Temple of the City God, symmetrically arranged with the county government structure, in order that "yin and yang carry out their respective duties." This explicitly reflects the ancient notion of "Men and Gods co-ruling the world".

Ping Yao City Wall The Ancient City of Ping Yao has three valu able treasures, and the ancient city wall is one of them.During the initial settlement of the city, the city walls were just built of rammed earth and on a relatively small scale. In 1370, during the reign of the Ming Emperor Hong Wu, the city was greatly extended into such a scale as it is now. The circuit of the city walls measures about 6 km in length. There are 3,000 crenels in the exterior of the wall top, and 72 massive bastions on the city walls to watch out for enemies. It is said they are the symbols of Confucius' 3,000 followers and 72 virtuous people. In addition, a Kuixing Court housing the Kuixing god of literature, art and culture was built in the southeast corner of the ancient city during the late Qing Dynasty, blessing the cultural fortune of the whole city. Thus it can be seen that Confucian thought inspired by Confucius exerted a far-reaching influence.

Zhenguo Temple Zhenguo Temple is a few kilometers away northeast from the northern gate of Ping Yao, and ranked as the second of the "Three Treasures" of Ping Yao. Its Ten-Thousand-Buddha Hall was first built in the 10th century during the Five Dynasties (907-960) . It is one of the three oldest timberworks in China, with a history of over a thousand years. Inside the temple there are color-painted sculptures that date back to the Five Dynasties, which are rare and valuable in terms of statuary art.

Shuanglin Temple Reconstructed in 571 A.D., the second year of the Emperor Wuping reign of the Northern Qi Dynasty, the Shuanglin Temple, the third of the "Three Treasures" of Ping Yao, is located southwest of the city. The ten large halls in it house more than 2,000 colorful sculptures reflecting the exquisite skills of the artisans of the Song, Yuan, Ming and Qing dynasties, thus earning it the title of "ancient painted sculptures museum".

Fortuna Temple Enclosed in the ancient city, there is a well-preserved Fortuna Temple (Temple for the God of Fortune) . The temple occupies a relatively small area of 833 square meters, with rooms circulating around one single courtyard.The gate of the temple is a brick arch, with a corridor passing across in front of it. The rites and music house was built above the doorway, and behind the east and west corridors were built compartments. On a high pedestal in the center, Xian Shrine stands in the front, while the cave-like Fortuna Shrine is in the back. Three main figures, Bi Gan, Guan Yu and Zhao Gongming are in the shrine to be worshipped. The entire temple possesses a rigorous layout as well as a majestic shape.

Rishengchang Exchange Shop The rectangular compound of Rishengchang Exchange Shop faces north and is 65 meters long and 20 meters wide. In total it occupies over 1,300 square meters. The shop is within a compound with three courtyards, all in elegant layout and smart style. Enclosing high walls, grand courtyards and deep corridors, it feels majestic on the outside and graceful on the inside.

Significance of the Heritage

The numerous cultural relics of the ancient city represent perfectly the developments in architectural style, construction method and material applications over many historical periods. Moreover, they also reflect multi-ethnic art evolution and aesthetic achievement across different regions in ancient China.

The city planning and design completely follows and executes Chinese traditional etiquette dominated by Confucian thought. The internal street layout, with the south and north avenues as the axis, is strictly a bilateral symmetry: the Temple of the City God on the left, opposite the county government on the right; the Confucian Temple on the left, opposite the Guan Yu Temple on the right; the Taoist Temple on the left, opposite the Buddhist Temple on the right. The main cross-streets are lined with residence buildings, most of which are built in the form of quadrangles, with harmony, modesty, discipline and tranquility as encouraged by Confucian traditions. It is an exceptionally well-preserved example of a traditional Han city. Ping Yao ancient city was built completely in accordance with traditional urban planning style and layouts of cities of the Chinese Han nationality. As an outstanding example of a Han city from the 14th to the 19th century, retaining all the Han features in history and culture, it is of great value for studying social forms, economic structure, military defense, religious beliefs, traditional thought, traditional ethics and dwelling design.

In the second half of the 19th century the banking community of Ping Yao, where the headquarters of the most influential banks and financial institutes were located, dominated Chinese financial life. The city emerged as one of the leading commercial cities in modern China, and retained that status well into the present age.

Founded in the fourth year of Emperor Daoguang of the Qing Dynasty (1824) , Rishengchang, the first draft bank in China, was the banking center of China. Its branches could be found in over 30 cities and commercial ports in China, and even in Europe, America and Southeast Asia. It was famed for "World-wide Remittance". Its establishment and development were conducive to promoting national finance circulation and accelerating capital turnover, thus making an outstanding contribution to national industry and commerce at the time and opening a new chapter in Chinese financial history.

Ancient Villages in Southern Anhui—Xidi and Hongcun

Situated in the Huangshan Scenic Area in Yi County, Anhui province, eastern China, the two traditional villages of Xidi and Hongcun are the most representative of the ancient villages in southern Anhui and are widely known for their idyllic sights, well-preserved settlements, exquisitely-crafted Huizhou-style architectures, and rich historical and cultural heritage.

Historical Origin

Tucked away in the mountains in southern Anhui, Yi county, a small county with a population of a little over one hundred thousand, is home to Xidi and Hongcun. The county's unique allure, typical of non-urban settlements in southern Anhui, once inspired the great Tang Dynasty poet Li Bai to write, "The small idyllic county of Yi/in the sunset a hundred miles of rosy clouds above and mist between /A blessed land home to lush vegetation/and a people respectfully dressed in the style past."

Dating to the Huangyou reign period in the Northern Song Dynasty (1049-1054) , Xidi is nearly a thousand years old. Surrounded on all sides by mountains and built along two streams running through it from the north and east before converging at the Huiyuan Bridge to the south, the village is boat-shaped and features a mostly eastbound layout which then spreads towards the north and the south. A north-south street and two roads along the streams constitute the main framework of the village. The village is a picturesque tableau of balanced development of alleyways and buildings, flexible spatial arrangements and plain and elegant-colored architectures.

Dating back to the first year of the Shaoxing reign period (1131) in the southern Song Dynasty, the 19-hectare village of Hongcun was once a stronghold of the Wang clan. More than 140 buildings from the Ming and Qing dynasties have survived to date and dot the village-scape. Hongcun's historic buildings are laid out in orderly fashion, flanked by cream-colored walls and capped with grey tiles. Chengzhi Hall, the grandest and most exquisite of them all, known as "the exhibition hall of Huizhou-style woodcarving crafts," is adorned with richly-layered, elaborate and lively woodcarvings that are still magnificent after more than a hundred years.

Landscape Characteristics

The scientific value of the villages of Xidi and Hongcun is particularly reflected in their settlement planning, fire safety design, living environment, cultural ecology, cultural landscape and cultural integration. Traditional villages often experience a kind of "snowballed" development and as they expand in size, the problem of erratic roads and waterways becomes prominent. In contrast, the development of many villages in southern Anhui has obviously been well planned, with organized street layouts and efficient water systems. From the perspective of cultural ecology, the evolving relationship of the ancient villages and the natural environments in southern Anhui is one of conditioning, adaptation, reproduction and selection. From the perspective of cultural landscape, the ancient villages in southern Anhui reflect the inward-looking, stylistic harmony and ethical core of traditional Chinese culture. From the perspective of cultural integration, the villages in southern Anhui are an outward expression of the economic competence of Huizhou merchants and the ideology of Huizhou people.

The location selection, layout and architectural form of Xidi and Hongcun followed the geomantic theory of *the Book of Changes* (《易经》) and reflect the traditional Chinese philosophy of harmony of man and nature as well as respect and longing for nature. The seamless integration of these elegant Ming and Qing-era residence complexes with the natural landscapes creates a living environment both scientific and enriching. These villages embody the essence of traditional Chinese residences. The unique water systems of Xidi and Hongcun are models of hydraulic engineering that integrate functionality and aesthetics. The ox-shaped water system in Hongcun in particular reflects extraordinary human intelligence in harnessing and transforming nature.

Main Features of Huizhou-style Residences

Respect for the Natural Environment and Landscape Ancient Huizhou was meticulous in its selection of locations to build villages in which a host of factors such as the local topography, landscape, directions of water and wind flows all came into the consideration. The constructions are often set in a beautiful landscape of waters and hills, well integrated with the natural environment and rationally planned with convenient traffic.

An Aesthetically-pleasing Look and Visual Integrity The unique form of tilting horse-head gables rising and falling on top of the enclosing walls lends a playful variation yet a sense of integrity to all residences. As a characteristic element of the Huizhou-style architecture, the horse-head gable, along with whitewashed walls and dark tiles and a background of green hills and clear waters, make for an organic and elegant picture.

Flexible Layout of Aligned Courts from Front to Back In the floor plan of these ancient residences, a building unit is a central light court with its surrounding courtyard and enclosing high walls, houses and a main hall. But there is also a rhythmic spatial variation depending on the specific function, size and ground features.

Intricate Decorative Details Huizhou's three carving traditions (brick carving, stone carving and wood carving) birthed stunning crafts and arts. The carved works, such as the carved brick lintels, the stone-carved perforated windows and the carved wood columns fronting the hall, have become an integral part of the buildings and a key feature of the Huizhou style.

Main Scenic Attractions

Chengzhi Hall Located in the middle of Shangshuizhen Street, Chengzhi Hall was built in the 5th year of the Xianfeng reign in the Qing Dynasty (1855) as the private residence of Dinggui Wang, a big salt merchant in the late Qing Dynasty. This wood-structure building has a total of 9 light courts and 60 rooms of various sizes, covering an area of 2,100 square meters, with the floor area being 300 square meters. As a well-preserved large residence, the building also boasts a magnificent collection of brick, wood and stone carvings.

South Lake Academy South Lake Academy, located on the north bank of the South Lake, was historically comprised of six private schools, together called "Yihu Liuyuan," built in the late Ming Dynasty. In the 6th year of the Jiaqing reign in the Qing Dynasty, the six schools merged and went through reconstruction to become one institution called "Yiwen Family School," also known as "South Lake Academy". The academy bears the traditional look of Huizhou-style academic buildings and is comprised of Zhidang Hall, Wenchang Pavilion, Qimeng Pavilion, Huiwen Pavilion, Wanghu Tower and Qi Garden.

Ruiyu Courtyard Built in the 3th year of the Xianfeng reign in the Qing Dynasty, the Ruiyu Courtyard is more than 140 years old. The building's original owner came from an old and established Huizhou merchant family and his business mentality is reflected in the architecture: shoe-shaped ingots with the word "Fortune"(" 富贵 ") on top are carved on the brick lintels over the doors; a drainage design allows all rain waters to stream down the inner slopes of the four-side roofs into the light court, which is a metaphor for the linkage of fortunes; and carved, gold-traced patterns of "Flowers and Bird of Four Seasons" on the decorated brackets over the surrounding structures symbolize the moment of renewal and good fortunes throughout the year.

Taoli Garden Built in the Xianfeng reign of the Qing Dynasty, Taoli Garden was both a private residence and a children's private school, owned by the Xidi merchant Hu Yuanxi. The two-story house features a structure of three aligned courts from front to back, each in front of a main hall with three rooms on both sides (for the first two courts, the three rooms on each side was built with two small rooms back to back with the third room) .

A unique "upstairs light well" was constructed on the second floor of the building surrounding the second court, allowing the whole structure to get sufficient sunlight and ventilation. There are also peepholes on the upstairs wood-carved railings for young ladies of the house to peek at visiting marriage candidates.

Eastern Garden and Western Garden The architecture of the Western Garden is in a typical Chinese garden style. The three buildings of the residence were aligned and connected by a long and narrow courtyard, which was then partitioned by walls into the front, middle and back courts. Arched doors and rectangular perforated windows decorated the partitioning walls and cypresses and flowers embellished the courts, along with rockeries, elevated flower stands, bathing pools and potted plants. All of these were meticulously designed and laid out to reflect the bearing and taste of the house's owner.

Only a few steps away from the Western Garden, the Eastern Garden was built by the father of Hu Wenzhao, the owner of the Western Garden, for the latter's education. Measured by feet, the main hall of the building are only ten steps in width, embodying the traditional Chinese saying that preparation for a successful life starts with ten years of hard study. A wood mosaic titled "Ice Cracks" mounted on the door of the west chamber suggests excellence doesn't happen overnight, just as hard and thick ice require more than just one day of cold weather; and another wood mosaic titled "Five Bats" (bat is symbol of happiness in Chinese culture) suggests that a happy life only comes after hard works.

Significance of the Heritage

The ancient villages in southern Anhui, including Xidi and Hongcun, refer to a cluster of traditional villages located in the mountain regions south of the Yangtze River in Anhui province that share a common regional cultural background and strong features of the old Huizhou culture. The mountain regions in southern Anhui have a long history and deep cultural roots where a large number of traditional buildings and villages have been preserved to a remarkable degree. Similar and distinctive in appearance, these ancient settlements were cleverly integrated with the local topography and landscapes. In the Ming and Qing dynasties, these areas began to thrive in culture and education as a wealthy Huizhou merchant class gave strong support to the development of their hometowns. Returning to their native places, these merchants began to build houses with the concepts of elegance, gentility, purity and originality in mind, which lent these ancient villages a richer cultural environment and a more distinctive look.

The biggest difference between the ancient villages of Xidi and Hongcun from other ancient villages is that the construction and development of these villages in southern Anhui are independent of agriculture to a large extent. In terms of their self-awareness, lifestyle and taste, the inhabitants of these villages greatly surpassed common rural and urban dwellers and strived to be more in keeping with those of the scholars and officials. As a result, a strong cultural atmosphere was established in these villages.

The villages of Xidi and Hongcun emerged along with the thriving of Huizhou merchants in the Ming and Qing dynasties, and developed a unique architectural form that shows exquisite design and superb craftsmanship to a maximum extent within a limited construction space. Later, the merchant class gradually declined, but the Huizhou-style architecture was preserved in the villages. Therefore, these surviving villages possess significant historical and architectural value.

Kaiping Diaolou and Villages

The towers are located in Kaiping, Guangdong Province. As a special type of Chinese village building, Diaolou are multi-storeyed tower buildings taking the 3 functions of defence, living and Eastern and Western architectural art. According to existing evidence, Kaiping Diaolou came into being at least in the late Ming Period (16th century) , and as a group of buildings of unique features have already established an image in the late 19th century and early 20th century as the embodiment of the history, social pattern and cultural tradition of overseas Chinese. 1,833 diaolou survive to this day and are known as the Model of Overseas Chinese Culture and A Gallery of Thrilling Architectural Art.

Historical Origin

The rise of Kaiping Diaolou was closely related to the geographical environment of Kaiping and the social public order in old times. Kaiping was low-lying and had a dense river network often out of repair. Frequent floods caused by typhoon and storm deeply affected people's lives. Besides, Kaiping was remote at the juncture of four counties, including Xinhui, Taishan, Enping and Xinxing, and as such, it had long been neglected by all. As a result, social order was very bad and bandits were rampant, and local villagers built diaolou for self-defence.

In December 1922, some bandits plundered Kaiping Middle School. They were exposed by the searchlight of Yingcun Diaolou and were surrounded from all directions by local armed villagers who took back the principal and 17 students. This event caused a great sensation all over the county and overseas Chinese were very happy upon hearing the news and felt that diaolou had played an important role in preventing banditry. They came back to their hometown with money and supported the building of diaolou. Many diaolou were built. At its peak, the number of diaolou reached 3,000. To this day, there are still over 1,400.

Landscape Characteristics

The architectural style and decorative art of Kaiping Diaolou are varied and breathtaking. As for the comprehensive design, constructive components and ways of expression, traditional Chinese architetural art and Western architectural style were fused; and western architectural style included many different types, such as ancient Greek colonnades, ancient Roman arch and pillar, Islamic leave-shaped arch and metal carving, Gothic arch, Baroque pediment, the decorative techniques of the Art Nouveau Movement and the Industrial architectural expression form, which were all used in the building of Kaiping Diaolou. It is not simply an adoption of the architectural art of a certain place at a certain time, but a fusion and product of all kinds of Chinese and Western architectural styles.

Most of the Western-style buildings on Chinese territory were mainly forced in by Westerners' guns and thus had a strong hue of transplantation by western colonists, while Kaiping Diaolou fully reflect the confidence, openness and tolerance of overseas Chinese in voluntarily absorbing advanced foreign cultures. A peerless art and an unique culture were created in building the several thousands of diaolou.

Main Scenic Attractions

Jinjiangli Diaolou Group Jinjiangli is subordinate to the Xiangang Town. During the Guangxu years (1875-1908) of the Qing period, the Huang family built this village according to plan. In later years, one after another, Ruishilou, Shengfenglou and Jinjianglou, were built. Of the three, Jinjianglou was built with funds from villagers in 1918 in the middle area at the back of the village. Jinjianglou is typical of public buildings. A reinforced concrete structure, it is 17.36 metres high, with 5 storeys. The top storey is a cantilevered platform. On the parapet are plaster molding patterns. Simple in structure and plain-looking, it is typical of defensive diaolou. Ruishilou stands on the east side of Jinjianglou. It is located at the main axis of the village houses and is typical of residential houses. The facade of Ruishilou adopted Western window lintel architrave and colonnade molding. In the many plaster molding patterns are traditional Chinese contents such as Fu (blessing) , Lu (fortune) , Shou (longevity) and Xi (happiness) , containing under the Western surface strong traditional cultural atmosphere. The style of the building is basically that of the Italian castle in the Middle Ages. Shengfenglou was built in 1928 by Huang Xiufeng, who made his fortune by doing business in the United States. It is 12.34 metres high, in 7 storeys, structured in reinforced concrete. Having a refined and beautiful shape, it is full of the emotional appeal of Indian buildings. It is a typical residential diaolou.

Zili Village Diaolou Group Zili Village is under the jurisdiction of Tangkou Town, Kaiping City. 12 kilometres from Kaiping in the east, it consists of 3 villages inhabited by Fang Family, namely, Anheli (folk name Litouzui) , He'anli (folk name Xincun) and Yong'anli (folk name Huangniling) . Litouzui Village was the first to be established in 1837. Sporadically scattered, the residential houses in this village stay in harmony with the surrounding environment. The Diaolou in Zili Village are beautifully built and well-preserved. They are harmoniously arranged and in picturesque disorder. Thousands of hectares of cropland surround the diaolou. Small field trails, with green trees and tall bamboo on both sides, lead to the village, which makes one feel as if in arcadia. The 9 diaolou and 6 cottages are the fruits of a blending of Western and Chinese style, and yet each one has its own characteristics. They can be called the "essence of diaolou architecture."

Maxianglong Diaolou Group Located in Southeastern Baihe

village, Baihe Town, the Maxianglong Diaolou Group was built by the Huang and Guan families in the late years of Qing and early years of the Republic of China. Now there are 506 villagers of 171 households, 80% of whom are Overseas Chinese who live in America, Canada, Australia, etc.

Maxianglong Village has the magnificent Baizu Mountain behind it and overlooks the crystal-water Tanjiang river. The 5 villages scatter naturally among green mountains and blue water. There are a forest of bamboo and trees, with singing birds and fragrant flowers; the ecological environment is excellent. The 13 diaolou here, uniquely designed and well-preserved, are hidden among dense bamboo forest at the back of the village and stay in great harmony with nearby residential houses and natural environment. Looked at from the distant mountain top, the village is just like paradise.

Yinglonglou Located in Sanmen Village, Chikan Town of Kaiping City and built by the Guan Family in Jiajing years of Ming Dynasty, Yinglonglou is the earliest extant diaolou. It occupies an area of 152 square metres and has a construction size of 456 square metres. Of brick and wood structure and in 3 storeys, 11.4 metre high, it occupies the commanding height of the whole village. The building has a traditional flush gable roof. It is plain in style and simple in shape. The square shape of the building shows no trace of foreign influence, and thus it is representative of traditional Kaiping Diaolou.

Fangshi Denglou Built collectively with funds raised by the Fang Family in 1920, Fangshi Denglou is located on the north slope of Tangkou village, Tangkou town of Kaiping City. In reinforced concrete structure, the building is 18.43 metres high and in 5 storeys. The top is a pavilion with a western dome roof. It is supplied with an early western generator, a searchlight for early warning and guns. It is a typical watch tower.

Canadian Village Canadian Village, formerly named Yaohuafang, built by Canadian Chinese, is located in Lingyuan Village, Chikan Town. The village was designed by a famous Canadian planner. The 10 ancient residential houses and 1 diaolou were mostly built in the 1920s and 1930s. Different architectural styles, such as additional Chinese plaster molding, Roman column, circular arch and carved wood patterns, were adopted to make it a typical building fusing Chinese and Western styles.

Significance of the Heritage

The 1,833 Kaiping Diaolou fused the architectural elements of different countries. They have different styles and are in picturesque disorder. The materials, functions and structures show that Overseas Chinese were deeply influenced by such Western concepts as openness and freedom. The Kaiping villagers voluntarily studied the Western material culture, institutional culture and conceptual culture of the time and practiced them in building diaolou, the crystallization of Overseas Chinese culture of that time.

Meanwhile, Kaiping Diaolou also reflect the transition of Chinese rural society in modern times. The architectural style and interior furnishings show that the villagers' awareness, concept and life style were changing from traditional agricultural society to modern society. That is to say, Kaiping Diaolou and Ancient Village contain rich historical information on Overseas Chinese and record the contribution made by Overseas Chinese to their country of residence, to their hometown and even to the whole of Chinese society at a specific time in modern social transition. This part of history was completely saved in a remote Chinese village, which is rare and precious in the field of World history.

Mount Qingcheng and the Dujiangyan Irrigation System

Mount Qingcheng and Dujiangyan are located in west Sichuan where there are high mountains and deep valleys at the northern section of Hengduan mountains. As the transition zone from the Sichuan Basin to the Qinghai-Tibet Plateau, the geological structure of this area is complicated. The weather here is warm and humid. The geological history is long. With a wide variety of living creatures, this is the area in the world where subtropical mountainous biodiversity is best preserved.

Uniquely blessed, Dujiangyan Scenic Area enjoys rich resources, including Dujiangyan, the large irrigation project, and Longchi National Forest Park, the so-called "Paradise on earth" , as well as Mount Qingcheng, the famous Taoist mountain.

Dujiangyan Irrigation System

Main Scenic Attractions

The Irrigation System Scenic Spot The three big centerpiece projects of Dujiangyan are built in the area where the Minjiang River emerges from the mountains. Surrounded by mountains, with the big river flowing in the middle, this site impresses visitors with magnificent views and excellent scenery. The building clusters built in different periods to address various needs, such as Erlang Temple, Fulong Temple and the office building of the Department of Water Resources, are exquisite examples of ancient buildings. Yuleiguan, Guanlan Pavilion, the Chain Bridge and Nanqiao Bridge are other treasures of ancient architectural art. These structures, together with the Minjiang River and the Dujiangyan project, collectively form the main body of the cultural heritage.

Baopingkou (Mouth of Precious Bottle) Diversion Mouth In accordance with the water flow and the characteristics of the terrain, Li Bing cut at the place where the slope was gentle a wedge-shaped opening 17m wide at the bottom. The mouth of the gorge is 19m wide in dry season, and 23m in flood season. According to *Yongkang Military Record*, "At the time of spring plowing, it is as precious as gold, and thus was given the name 'Gold Irrigation Port' ." That explains why Baopingkou Mouth was called Gold Irrigation Port in ancient times. Baopingkou Mouth is the neck of the inner river through which water enters, and is the key irrigation facility that makes it possible for the inner river to "regulate water flow at the will of man". The natural scenery at Baopingkou Mouth is magnificent. It has been called "Lidui Blockading Gorge", and is one of "the ten famous spots of Guanyang".

Feishayan Feishayan Spillway, 200m long and 2m high, is at the tail of Jingang Dam and at the front part of Lidui. Historically, it was formed by piling cages of pebbles, which are now replaced by cement. When water volume in the inner river is small, Feishayan, like a dam, makes water go into Baopingkou ; while in flood season extra water automatically goes into the outer river. Although simple in appearance, Feishayan is the key facility protecting the Chengdu Plain from flood. Not only does it act as spillway in flood season, but it also makes use of the whirlpool effect produced when water overflows Feishayan into the outer river, thus effectively reducing sedimentation at Baopingkou.

Yuzui (Fish Mouth) Diversion Dike Yuzui is the most typical and most important project within the Dujiangyan Irrigation System. Built at the natural bend where the Minjiang River flows out of the mountains and using the principle of bend circulation, Yuzui can automatically regulate the ratio of water flow for the inner and outer rivers in flood season and dry season. As a result, it ensures that the downstream area of the inner river do not suffer damage of flood, while on the other hand, it ensures that there is enough water for spring plowing. Another important function of Yuzui is its effective solution of the problem of sediment discharge.

Fulong Temple Fulong (conquering dragon) Temple, on Lidui. Three sides of it fall sheer, and one connects to the wide dam through 42 stone steps about 10m wide, so that it looks especially imposing. The original building had two storeys; after the building of Li Bing Hall in the late Qing Dynasty the main hall have three stories. In 1959, Yuhuang Hall and Xiyulou were combined and turned into a showroom of reinforced concrete, bricks and wood. In the front hall is exhibited the stone image of Li Bing that was dug out of the riverbed in 1974 while building the floodgate of the outer river. 2.9m tall and 4.5 ton in weight, the statue was carved in the Eastern Han Dynasty and is now over 1,800 years old. As China's earliest surviving stone image in high relief, it is extremely valuable.

Erwang Temple Located at the foot of Yulei Mountain outside the west gate of the present Dujiangyan City, the ancient building cluster of Erwang (two kings) Temple was built in memory of Li Bing, the builder of Dujiangyan and the prefect of Shu County in Qin Dynasty, and his son Erlang. Erwang Temple was first built in the Northern and Southern dynasties, but the present existing building was rebuilt in the late Qing Dynasty and early Republican period. The three golden characters on the mountain gate were the work of Feng Yuxiang, the patriotic general. Inside the temple are enshrined the images of Li Bing and Erlang, and on the stone wall are embedded the dicta of Li Bing and later generations regarding water management. They have been described as the Three Character Classic of water management.

Mount Qingcheng, the famous Taoist Mountain

Complicated in geological structure, Mount Qingcheng is the eastern branch of the south section of Qionglai Mountains. This area lies within the humid climate zone of Sichuan Basin in subtropical Central Asia. Being neither too hot in summer nor too cold in winter, with ample rain and high humidity, the area is shrouded in cloud and fog, thus providing an ideal condition for the growth of all kinds of plants that stay green all year round. There are rich resources of flowers, with various kinds of fruit plants, foliage plants and herbs. For the Taoist who pursue simplicity and worship nature, the natural environment found here is undoubtedly a blessed spot.

As a world-famous mountain known for its beautiful natural landscape and numerous Taoist temples, Mount Qingcheng has long been a tourist attraction and an ideal spot for reclusive life and self-cultivation. With Tianshi Cave being the centre of all the Taoist temples at the mountain, there are some other ten temples, namely, Fujian Temple, Shangqing Palace, Zushi Hall, Yuanming Palace, Laojun Pavilion, Yuqing Palace and Chaoyang Cave, etc. All these buildings give full expression to the Taoist pursuit of being at one with nature. By adopting the traditional symmetrical layout and in accordance with the terrain and landform, all the buildings are smartly structured. The precious "Mobao" (treasured scrolls of calligraphy or painting) left behind by literary men has enhanced the rich humanistic taste of this mountain. For the in-depth study of ancient Taoist philosophical thinkings, Mount Qingcheng has great academic and artistic value.

Main Scenic Attractions

Hall of Zushi(Founding Master) Also named Hall of Zhenwu, the Hall of Zushi, built in the Tang Dynasty, is on the hillside of the mountain at the rear right of Tianshi Cave. It boasts of a quiet and beautiful environment, and inside it can be found the sculptures of Zhenwu Zushi, Lu Dongbin and Tie Guaili, the fresco of the Eight Gods and poetry steles.

Shangqing Palace Situated at the No.1 peak of Mt. Qingcheng, it is on the slope 500 metres away from the top of the peak. First constructed in Jin Dynasty, the present temple was built during the reign of Emperor Tongzhi of Qing Dynasty. There are such inscriptions on the precipice as "the fifth famous mountain under heaven" and "the No.1 Mt. Qingcheng Peak". Li Laojun, the founding ancestor of Taoism, is enshrined here. There are the sculpture of Lao Zi and the wood carved Daode Jing (the Scripture of Ethics) .

Tianshi Cave It was first constructed in the Daye period of Sui Dynasty. Tianshi Cave, embracing on three sides by hills, with one side facing the water, growing towering old trees, enjoys quiet and excellent environment. The present temple, built in Qing Dynasty, is grand in size and finely carved. Here can be seen many precious cultural relics and old trees. According to legend, Zhang Daoling preached here at the late years of the Eastern Han Dynasty, and his sculpture and that of his 30th generation descendant, Xujing Tianshi. The main hall inside the temple is San Qing Hall, behind which are the historical sites of Huang Di Temple and Tiashi Cave. At the lower right corner of Tianshi Cave is the small Temple of Three Emperors, where are enshrined the stone sculptures of the emperors Xuanyuan, Fuxi and Shennong.

Significance of the Heritage

As an ancient irrigation system characterized by the diversion of water without the use of a dam, Dujiangyan is not only a great miracle of hydraulic technology in China, but is also a pearl among world irrigation projects. Taking full advantage of the geographical condition of higher terrain in the northwest and lower terrain in the southeast, and based on the special situation of the river's egress from the mountain, water vein and water flow, the project makes the best use of conditions and succeeds in diverting water without a dam, and providing gravity irrigation. The project enables the different functions of diking, water division, flood discharge, sand discharge, and flow control to benefit from each other's contributions and form a complete system to make sure that the comprehensive benefits of flood-control, irrigation, water transportation and water for people's everyday use are fully realised. What is greatest about it is that it has been in use for over 2,250 years and is still playing an irreplaceable role. Having as the precondition of no damage to natural resources and making full use of natural resources to serve human beings, Dujiangyan turns harm into benefit, and enables the three elements of man, land and water to unify in a highly harmonious way. It thus opened a new era in the history of ancient Chinese water conservancy.

The influence of Mount Qingcheng Taoism on Chinese Taoism is beyond measure. To this day, Mount Qingcheng is still the main site for the promotion of Taoism culture in China. The ancient Taoist temples at Mount Qingcheng, still well preserved, are priceless heritages.

Cultural Landscape of Honghe Hani Rice Terraces

Honghe Prefecture in Yunnan Province is located to the south of Mt. Ailao, and is inhabited by 7 ethnic groups, including Hani, Yi, Dai, Miao, Yao, Zhuang and Han. Over hundreds of years, the hard-working people of different ethnic groups have cultivated more than 360,000 mu of terraces and together they have created a colorful gallery of borderland folk customs, one that's been called "the most magical land sculpture".

The Honghe Hani terraces are a wonder of agricultural civilization, created mainly by Hani people together with people of other ethnic groups by making use of the local geographical and climatic conditions, summarized as "four seasons coexist on the same mountain, and the weather differs markedly within a ten-li radius." According to records, the terraces have existed for over 1,300 years, stretching among such counties as Yuanyang, Lvchun, Jinping, etc, along the southern bank of the Honghe River. Yuanyang alone has 190,000 mu of terraces. Abundant water, high moisture and swirling mists help make the valleys and terraces appear reserved and mysterious.

Historical Origin

Each one of the "terrace mountains" is just like a huge non-textual history book that visually exhibits the long history of Hani ancestors' tenacious struggles and survival under natural and social pressure. According to the ancient Hani *Legend of Heaven, Earth and Man*, Dayu (big fish) created the Universe and the first human couple, Zhita the man and Tapo the woman. Tapo mothered 22 children, the 3rd one of whom, a dragon, grew up to be the Dragon King in the sea. He showed his gratitude to Tapo for having nurtured him by giving her 3 bamboo tubes, each containing things. In one of the bamboo tubes was rice seed. That is to say that Hani people think that there was rice at the very beginning of the world, which means that the Hani people were one of the first peoples to domesticate wild rice and rice planting has been an ancient production activity for the Hani. Over hundreds of years, Hani people domesticated the wild rice in the 3 rivers basin of Mt. Ailao and turned it into land rice, which were later improved into water rice. Bestowed with exceptional ecological environment, the 3 rivers basin became one of the earliest areas where people domesticated and grew rice.

Cause of Formation of Hani Rice Terraces

The first and foremost contributing formation factor of the magnificent and unique Hani Terraces has to do with the naturally special geographical structure. The huge size of high-mountain forest on Mt. Ailao and the vertical change of vegetation supply the local forest and land with strong transpiration and great water-storing function that form a natural system of forest—water source—terraces.

The 7 ethnic groups of people who inhabit this mountain in Yuanyang, roughly speaking, live according to altitude. The riverside area, with an altitude of 144-600 metres, is inhabited by Dai people. From altitude 600-1000 metres is valley, inhabited by Zhuang people. The lower mountain part, altitude 1000-1400 metres, is home to Yi people. Hani people live on the higher mountain, with an altitude of 1400-2000 metres. The high mountain part over 2000 metres of altitude is inhabited by Miao and Yao people. Han people mainly live in towns and along highways. The higher mountain inhabited by Hani people enjoys warm temperature and rich rainfall, with an average yearly temperature of about 15℃ and 1,670 hours of yearly sunlight, which is ideal for the growth of rice.

Ever since they came to this place during the Sui and Tang periods, the ancestors of Hani people began to cultivate terraces to grow rice. During more than 1,200 years, Hani people have exerted great talent and creativity and have dug hundreds of ditches. The ditches are like silver belts encircling the mountains. The collected water flows along the ditches, first into the high terraces, and when they are filled, the water then flows into the lower terraces, filling them, until finally the water flows into valleys and rivers. In this way, each ditch is a mountain spring, and each piece of terrace is equivalent to a canal; as ditches and rivers connect with each other, performing month after month and year after year an endless song of mountain life.

Landscape Characteristics

The ecological system of Yuanyang Hani terraces has the following characteristics: above each village there is bound to be a dense forest that supplies the village with water, timber and firewood, characterized by a sacrosanct cluster of trees that is revered as having special powers. Below the village are hundreds of stacked layers of terraces that supply the Hani people with their basic condition of existence and development, that is, grain. The village in the middle between the forest and terraces consist of ancient-looking mushroom-shaped houses for people to stay in for a peaceful life on earth. This structure is highly regarded by cultural ecologists to be a four-dimensional Isomorphism of river—forest—village—terraces that is highly coordinated between man and nature, a sustainable and benign ecological system. This is the beautiful home of the Hani people who have lived and thrived here for hundreds of years.

Yuanyang is full of high mountains and the fall in elevation between terraces is very substantial, with the greatest drop being over 1,500 metres and the slope being as long as several kilometres. Take one slope for an example. The highest of the terraces consists of as many as 3,000 levels, which is extremely rare both at home and abroad. With the undulating of the mountains, each plot of terrace differs from all others in color, and seen from the distance, there is an obvious distinction between one terrace and the next. Big and small villages lie scattered among the terraces. What is especially worth of visiting is the area around Laohuzui (tiger month)

, where the terraces give viewers the strongest stereoscopic sense, and the slope is most precipitous, hence the strongest color differences. The terraces of Longshuba, on the other hand, are totally different, being less grand in scale, but more delicate and gorgeous.

Main Scenic Attractions

There are 3 main scenic spots in Yuanyang Hani Terraces, namely, Bada, covering over 2,300 acres of terraces, Laohuzui (tiger mouth) , covering 998 acres, and Duoyishu, covering over 1,600 acres. All terraces are built on mountain slopes, the gradient varying from 15-75 degrees.

Bada Scenic Spot Also known as Malizhai Scenic Spot, Bada is located 43 kilometres to the south of the county seat and 15 kilometres to the east of Xinjie. With large area, elegant lines and strong stereoscopic effect, the terraces here look quite magnificent. Beginning at Malizhai River at an altitude of 1,100 metres, over thousands of levels of continuous terraces stretch to the mountain top at an altitude of 2,000 metres, carrying the Hani villages of Malizhai, Bada, Shangmadian and Quanfuzhuang, etc. high into the clouds. Looking at the terraces at Malizhai Tea Factory, the thousands of acres of terraces are just like an ocean, glittering with waves that awaken a sense that this is a lost paradise. After four in the afternoon and under the sunset, the vast expanse of whiteness of the slopes turn into pink and red, which then turn back into pink and white. Hani villages have exquisite scenery, simple plain folk customs and hospitable villagers.

Laohuzui Scenic Spot Laohuzui Terraces is 50 kilometres away from the county seat of Yuanyang. Distributed deep in the valleys and in the shape of a colossal stamen, the 500 acres of terraces differ in shape and look like thousands of snakes sleeping quietly among flowers. Laohuzui Terraces is the most representative and most magnificent of Yuanyang terraces, and when viewed from the high Laohuzui, they are just like unending sea waves, and when looked at carefully, there seem to be two running horses or an thousand-year-old turtle quietly lying in the mountains, relating the vicissitudes of the history of Hani ancestors cultivating terraces. Looking westward, under the sunset, countless levels of terraces rising from deep valleys in the south to mountain top in the north form a contrast of red, white and black, which is dazzling to the eyes. While looking eastward in some distance, you will see the hundreds of acres of terraces connecting to the seven and a half round-shaped mountains and forming a stereoscopic sea.

Really, whichever spot at Laohuzui you choose to look down at the terraces below, you would surely feel as if looking at a piece of watery Jiangnan ink painting and hearing a thrilling field song.

Duoyishu Scenic Spot 55 kilometres east of the county seat and 25 kilometres east of Xinjie, Duoyishui Scenic Spot consists of 5 Hani villages and 4 Yi villages and includes about 1,000 acres of continuous terraces in Aicun Village and Dawazhe Village. This scenic spot exhibits such scenery as clouds, terraces, villages, multicultures of Hani and Yi, and 4,000 acres of primitive forest in the Provincial Natural Protection Zone.

Terraces here, with three sides bordering mountains and one side falling back into a deep valley, are in the shape of a huge gulf. The numerous villages scattered on the three mountainsides have mushroom-shaped houses that look like sailboats gearing up to go. Looked at from the high mountain behind Huangcaoling Village, the upper half of the whole terrace is gentle-sloped and looks as if thousands of snakes were wriggling, while the lower half is precipitous and stretches deep into the valley, causing the shining white of the "huge gulf" to look like a huge waterfall plunging from the south to the north. It is a matchless sight!

Significance of the Heritage

Agricultural economy is the most basic value of the terraces. At the beginning, terraces development was closely related to population increase and convenience of tillage, irrigation and the need to conserve soil and water. For hundreds of years, confronted with the living environment of high mountains and valleys, Hani people have created and synthesized a set of successful experiences in ploughing terraces. They built embankments and ridges in accordance with different terrain and different soil,and they made use of the natural conditions of "no matter how high the mountain, the water is just as high" to get unending water into terraces through ditches and streams.

Hani people have created their own culture that in turn has brought about great internal cohesion, with Hani terraces being its cultural symbol. Hani terraces are a miraculous testament to a people's survival. Though not a natural landscape, they have a refreshing force, manifesting that we still have tradition, having witnessed the most important agricultural civilization in China's history of development.

Peking Man Site at Zhoukoudian

Zhoukoudian Peking Man site is located on Mt. Longgu, at the village of Zhoukoudian in Fangshan District, 48 kilometers southwest of Beijing. The site proper is about 50 kilometers from Beijing, at a spot where mountains and plain meet-with the North China Plain to the southeast and a mountainous area to the northeast. The mountains near Zhoukoudian are mostly made up of limestone, with many natural caves, big or small, formed through the effects of water. An east-west natural cave about 140 meters long has been nicknamed "ape-man cave". Here, in 1929, the Chinese paleontologist Wenzhong Pei unearthed teeth, bones and a complete skull of primitive men and found evidence of Peking Man's lifestyle, hunting practices, and use of fire. The remains proved that human beings began to appear in the Beijing area 500,000 years ago. This discovery established the irreplaceable position of the Zhoukoudian site in the worldwide study of prehistoric humanity.

Living Environment

The discovery of broken, burned bones in ashes indicated that Peking Man had knowledge of cooked food. Relying on their collective resources, they struggled to live in harsh natural conditions. Changes of season, natural disasters, wild animals, and diseases all posed great threats to them. Fossil test of dozens of Peking Man reveals that their mortality rate was very high, with many individuals dying before the age of 14. It is clear that living conditions were quite unfavorable.

Peking Man chose quartzite, flint, and sandstone from nearby riverbanks and slopes to make tools through simple direct percussion that served different purposes in life and work. Scientists have inferred from the excavated fossils of animals and plants that the area of Zhoukoudian was previously warmer than today's north China and so there were thick forests and abundant water here. With the global climatic changes this area also underwent changes between cold and warm, dry and wet weather over several hundred thousand years. Fortunately Peking Man had learned how to use fire and this greatly improved his adaptability to the environment.

Physical Features

Peking Man had already covered a long distance in the process of human evolution, yet they still retained some primitive features, such as a low skull, prominent brow, short face and protruding lips. The average brain volume is only a little more than 1000 ml, about two-thirds of the brain capacity of modern men. They are short and stout with a height of 156 cm for men and 144 cm for women; they have short legs and long arms and a protruding head. The bones of their four limbs are very like those of modern men and enabled them to walk steadily on the ground.

The fossil of a Peking Man skull (frontal bone) was unearthed in an excavation directed by famous paleontologist Wenzhong Pei in 1966; it is the only Peking Man skull (frontal bone) still preserved in China. This frontal bone is of the same period as the missing skull fossil.

The primitive features in Peking Man's head are similar to those of Java ape-man and so they both belong to the stage of Homo erectus. The spade-shaped incisors, broad noses and low, flat faces as well as the mandibular torus in the inner side near the front of the lower jaw bone all show that they have clear traits of the Mongoloid race. The marrow cavity of their lower limbs is small with a thick wall, while the size, shape, proportion and muscle insertion of their legs are very similar to those of modern men. This fact indicates that they were already good walkers. As for their upper limbs, the extent of similarity with modern men is even higher except for the small size of the marrow cavity and thick walls. This fact shows that their arms can perform activities very similar to those of modern men.

Archaeological Findings

Peking Man's Use of Stoneware Marks the Beginning of Human History

Even in the beginning of the Paleolithic age, Peking Man had known how to select rocks to make stone implements. This indicates that Peking Man had learned to use primitive tools to work, which is the fundamental difference between men and apes. The relics of Peking Man include stoneware, bone tools, antler spades and traces of fire. In the Zhoukoudian site thousands of stone implements have been unearthed; the rocks for making the stoneware were all picked from nearby. Among sites of the same period none can match Zhoukoudian in possessing relics of stoneware culture in such quantity and of such quality.

The Date of Man's Use of Fire has been Shifted Several Hundred Thousand Years Earlier

In caves where Peking Man once lived, colorful ashes of four to six meters in thickness were discovered. This indicates that Peking man had already known how to use, control and keep fire, a sign of progressing from the animal world into the world of human civilization. The traces of fire discovered in locality 1 of Zhoukoudian site have advanced the history of man's use of fire by hundreds of thousand years.

Providing Evidence for Studying the Historical Changes of Ecological Environment

The study of Peking Man and the surrounding natural environments show that the geological features of Beijing half a million years ago are approximately the same as today: there are dense forests in the hills and mountains, with various animal species. But large areas of prairie and desert also appeared. The traces left by ostriches and camels show that

Beijing area had experienced climatic changes from warm and moist to cold and dry over a long period.

Excavation Process

Zhoukoudian locality 6 is the site discovered earliest, by the Swedish scientist Andersson in 1918.

In 1921 Andersson together with American paleontologist Granges and Austrian paleontologist Zdansky discovered locality 1 and then locality 2. In 1927 Black formally identified the three teeth discovered in Zhoukoudian as belonging to Sinanthropus Pekinensis. In that same year excavation of the Zhoukoudian site was formally begun. Chinese geologist Jie Li took part in the excavation and discovered locality 3 and 4. In 1929 Wenzhong Pei discovered locality 5, 7 and 8 and the first Peking Man skull. In the same year the locality where Peking Man was discovered was numbered as locality 1 and the rest were subsequently numbered 2 to 9.

In 1930 fossils of the Upper Cave Man (dating from about 20,000 years ago) and their cultural remains were discovered in the Zhoukoudian site. Yet subsequent wars led to the loss of the fossil samples of Peking Man and Upper Cave Man discovered from 1927 on. Those fossils are still missing today—a worldwide puzzle in the history of modern paleontology. After the founding of People's Republic of China, excavation of the Zhoukoudian site was resumed and large quantities of precious materials were obtained. Up to now archaeologists have unearthed fossil skulls, mandibles, teeth and plenty of stoneware, bone work and antler spades and discovered traces of fire. In 1953 Zhoukoudian Site Museum was set up in the Zhoukoudian Peking Man site and opened to the public.

Important Spots

Locality 1

Locality 1 is also called "the ape-man cave". It was originally a natural limestone cave, 140 meters from west to east and 40 meters high; the widest place is 40 meters from north to south and the narrowest place in the west is only 2 meters in width. From about five million years ago Peking ape-man began to live here now and then for a period that lasted between 200, 000 and 400, 000 years. The skeletons, relics, traces and the collapsed stone and sand flowed in from outside the cave and deposited layer by layer, forming a large deposit of 13 layers in thickness.

In 1921 and 1923 Swedish geologist Andersson and Austrian Paleontologist Zdansky discovered this locality and conducted trial excavation. In 1927 a well-preserved lower molar of man was found and named by Professor Grabau "Peking Man", and this name has been adopted and used up to now. On November 2nd 1929 Wenzhong Pei discovered the first intact fossil of a human skull. In 1949 excavation was resumed after a break of 11 years. From 1951 to 1980 several excavations were conducted. This locality had been excavated for 23 years altogether and about 203 pieces of Peking man fossils have been unearthed, including six skulls which were complete or nearly complete, 3 areas with fire remains and over 100, 000 pieces of stoneware. Meanwhile fossils of 98 types of mammals were also unearthed.

Locality 2

Locality 2 was discovered by Andersson, Granger and Zdansky in 1921; it is also one of the two areas first discovered in the Zhoukoudian site. This spot is about 200 meters away from locality 1. It is about 15 meters tall, 2 meters thick and the stratum is brownish red clay. Scholar Zhongjian Yan first studied it and numbered it locality 2. Among the finds there are 22 types of mammal fossils, one reptile fossil and one bird fossil. They all belong to Medio-Pleistocene Age.

Locality 4

Locality 4 is located on the southern slope of Mt. Longgu and about 70 meters away from locality 1. This spot is 46 meters above the level of Zhoukoudian River. The opening of the cave faces southward. When it was discovered by Lin Bu and Jie Li in 1927, most of the top of the cave had collapsed and the fallen materials were piled up in the open air. Ten years later, in 1937, this locality was excavated and over 40 types of mammal fossils were discovered. In the beginning of 1973, locality 4 was excavated under the direction of Yumin Gu. The deposits being dug is 6.5 meters thick. The finds include a large number of stoneware, traces of fire and one fossil of human tooth. Appraisal revealed that this tooth was an upper left front molar fossil of early Homo Sapiens about 200, 000 to 100, 000 years ago.

Significance of the Heritage

Zhoukoudian Site is the fossil man site with the richest, most vivid, and most comprehensive collection of fossil types hitherto unearthed in the world. It is also the site where the study of fossil man is most profound. The discovery of Peking Man has provided helpful evidence for the theory of human evolution and is a great contribution by Chinese archaeologists to world paleontology. The discovery of Peking Man and research on their culture settled the dispute over the identity of homo erectus since the discovery of Java Man-whether homo erectus is ape or man. It is proven that Homo erectus provides the most important link in the transition from ape to man in the earliest history of mankind. They are descendents of Australopithecus and ancestors of later Homo sapiens. Peking Man has the typical features of Homo erectus while the use of fire further highlights their human identity. The discovery of Upper Cave Man and their remains further confirms the development and continuation of Peking Man. The discovery of Peking Man laid foundation for the study of Chinese fossil man and their culture, and Zhoukoudian is thus a virtual treasure house of ancient civilization.

Silk Roads: the Routes Network of Chang'an-Tianshan Corridor

The Silk Road was the main corridor of economic, political and cultural communication between the East and the West in ancient China. Beginning in Chang'an (present-day Xi'an) , the capital during the Western Han period, and then in Luoyang, the capital during the Eastern Han Dynasty, the Silk Road cut across Mt. Longshan, passed through the Hexi Corridor, Yumen (Jade Gate) Pass and Yangguan Pass to reach Xinjiang, and then passed oases and the Pamirs to cross Central Asia, West Asia and North Africa to reach Africa and Europe. The original function of the road was to transport the silk produced in ancient China, and therefore, when in the 1870s the German geographer Ferdinand Freiherr von Richthofen named it "the Silk Road", the name was widely accepted.

Historical Origin

The Silk Road generally refers to the commercial route in the north of Eurasia, in contrast with the ancient Tea Horse Road in the south. At the time of Emperor Wudi of the Western Han Dynasty, Zhang Qian first opened up the Silk Road, and the Romans acquired Chinese silk through the Parthian Empire, the Kushan Empire and the Aksum Empire. At the end of the Western Han Dynasty, the Silk Road became impassable due to the harassment of the Huns.In 73 A.D., Ban Chao of the Eastern Han Dynasty reopened the route to the Western Regions that had been cut off for 58 years, and for the first time extended the route to Europe. Following the cross-continental route between Asia and Europe, Chinese silk products such as silk, silk fabric, damask silk, satin and thin tough silk were steadily transported to Central Asia and Europe, thus accelerating the friendly interaction between China and other Asian and European countries and becoming a road of friendship that linked up Eastern and Western cultures.

Distribution of the Heritage Sites

Along the Silk Road are altogether 33 representative heritage sites of 5 different types, including the heritage of central towns, the heritage of commercial and trade cities, the heritage of transportation, religious heritage and related sites. There are 22 archaeological sites and sites of ancient buildings within the Chinese territory, of which 4 are in Henan, 7 in Shanxi, 5 in Gansu and 6 in Xinjiang. Kazakhstan and Kirgizstan respectively have 8 and 3 sites.

The site of Daming Palace of the Tang Dynasty in Chang'an City

Daming Palace, the political centre of the Tang Empire, was the biggest palace building cluster in ancient China and even across the world. Located at Longshouyuan to the north of Chang'an, the capital of the Tang Dynasty, Daming Palace, formerly known as Yong'an Palace, was first built in 634 A.D. Taking up an area of 350 hectares, the biggest of the 3 main palaces (Daming Palace, Taiji Palace and Xingqing Palace) in Chang'an had more than 50 palace halls and pavilions, and it has been hailed as the Holy Place of the East along the Silk Road. From Emperor Gaozong, most of the emperors of the Tang Dynasty resided here and dealt with state affairs here. For over 200 years, it was the political centre of the country. In the late years of the Tang Dynasty, Daming Palace was destroyed in the flames of war.

The Big Wild Goose Pagoda

The Big Wild Goose Pagoda is regarded as a symbol of the ancient capital Xi'an. Built in the 3rd year of Yonghui (652 A.D.) by Xuanzang to store scriptures, the pagoda includes 7 floors and is 64.5 metres tall. As the earliest and biggest Tang brick pagoda in the style of a square pavilion that survives to this day, the Big Wild Goose Pagoda is a typical material proof of the architectural form of the Indian Buddhist temple that spread to Central China with Buddhism and was integrated into Chinese culture. It is a landmark structure that concentrates the wisdom of the Chinese working people.

Built by Tang imperial order, the Big Ci'en Temple to which the Giant Wild Goose Pagoda belonged was the most famous and magnificent Buddhist temple in Chang'an in the Tang period. Presided over by Master Xuanzang himself, it was one of the three major centres for Buddhist scripture translation and had an important position in the history of Buddhism in China.

The Ruins of Luoyang City of the Han – Wei Dynasties

The ruins of ancient Luoyang, the site of the capital of the Eastern Han, Cao Wei, the Western Jin and Northern Wei dynasties, are about 15 km to the east of present-day Luoyang City of Henan Province. The city, when first built here in the early years of the Western Zhou Dynasty, was called "Chengzhou". It was at the north of Luoshui River, and thus was named Luoyang. For over 540 years, it was successively the capital of the Eastern Zhou, the Eastern Han, Cao Wei, the Western Jin and Northern Wei dynasties. Among all Chinese capital sites, this ruined city has the longest history as a capital, is the biggest in scale and is fairly well preserved. For more than 1000 years, it had influenced later capitals in such aspects as architetural structure, design and planning.

Some 10,000 metres of the wall of the inner city still survive on the east, north and west sides, the highest spot being as high as 9 metres, mainly including the site of Changhe Gate, the front gate of the palace city, and the site of Taiji Hall, the main hall of the palace; the site of Yongning Temple, the imperial temple of the Northern Wei; White Horse Temple, the first official Buddhist temple in China; the site of the Imperial College, the national college of the Han and the Wei dynasties; the sites of Mingtang and Piyong, the royal sacrificial architectures of the

Han-Wei period; the site of Lingtai, the earliest astronomical observatory in ancient China and the large tomb at Jincun, the imperial mausoleum of the Eastern Zhou Dynasty, where large amount of national treasure were excavated.

The Site of Yumen (Jade Gate) Pass

Yumen Pass, 90 km to the northwest of Dunhuang City, Gansu, was first established when Emperor Wudi of the Han Dynasty opened up the road to the West Regions and set up the four Hexi counties. It got its name for the importation of jades from the West Regions that was conducted in this area. During the time of the Western Han, it was the gateway going to various places in the West Regions. From Yuanding to Yuanfeng (from 116 B.C. to 105 B.C.) , the great wall from Jiuquan to Yumen was constructed, and Yumen Pass was then established and became an important military post of the Han Dynasty and a vital communication link of the Silk Road.

Mt. Maiji Grottoes

Mt. Maiji Grottoes got their name from their shape that resembles a farmer's wheat stack. The grottoes were cut into a vertical cliff at the height of 20-80 metres and had a width of 200 metres. 194 niches survive, with 54 on the east cliff and 140 on the west cliff. There are more than 7,800 clay sculptures, stone tier clay sculptures, and stone statues. The great Buddha on the east cliff, the biggest image, is 15.8 metres tall, and there are over 1,000 square metres of frescoes.

Among the grottoes on the east cliff, the Nirvana Grotto, the Thousand Buddha Corridor and the Seven Buddha Pavilion on the Scattering Flowers Building are the most beautiful, while on the west cliff are the Hall of Thousands of Buddhas, the Cave of Paradise, and Grottoes No. 121, No. 123, No. 127 and No. 165, which are the most notable grottoes. More than 30 clay sculptures remain to this day. Grotto No. 4 at Mt. Maiji is the biggest grotto in China that imitated traditional Chinese architectural style, and it provides important material for studying wood-structured architecture of the Northern Wei Dynasty. It truthfully reflected the outer and inner features of the already sinicised Buddhist hall of the late Southern and Northern Dynasties, and had great significance in the history of the development of grottoes.

The Grottoes of Bingling Temple

The Grottoes of Bingling Temple, cut in the early years of the Western Jin (about the 3rd century A.D.) , are on the cliff at the west side of Dasi Valley of Mt. Jishi, some 40 km to the southwest of Yongjin County, Linxia Hui Autonomous Prefecture, Gansu Province. The surviving 183 grottoes, housing 694 stone statues, 82 clay sculptures and about 900 square metres of frescoes, are distributed along the 200-metre-long and 60-metre-high cliff on the west bank of Dasi River. The grottoes have as their main body the "natural great Buddha" (Grotto No. 169) on the higher part of the cliff and numerous medium-sized and small grottoes in the middle section of the cliff.

Jiaohe Ruins

The ancient city of Jiaohe is in Ya'erzi Valley, 11 km to the west of Turpan City, Xinjiang. It was initiated and constructed from the 2nd century B.C. to the 5th century A.D. by the Cheshi people, and reached its peak at the time of the Southern-Northern Dynasties and the Tang Dynasty. It is the biggest, oldest and best preserved city of earth construction in the world, and is also the most completely preserved capital site of more than 2,000 years in China. Anxi Frontier Command, the highest military and political institution of the Tang Dynasty in the West Regions, was first established in ancient Jiaohe.

The ruins of the ancient city have been very completely preserved. The city is 1600 metres from south to north, and the widest place is about 300 metres from east to west. The city was composed mainly of a temple area, dwelling area and government office area. It took up a total area of 470,000 square metres, and 360,000 square metres of construction sites survives. Most of the buildings were built in the Tang Dynasty, and the architectural composition has unique characteristics. The city preserves the architectural characteristics of Central Chinese cities before the Song Dynasty.

Kizil Grottoes

Also named Kizil Thousand Buddha Cave or Kizil Stone Cave, Kizil Grottoes are on the cliff of Mt. Mingoytagh in the southeast of Kizil Town of Bay County, Xinjiang, and to the south of it is the Muzat River Valley.

Cut in about the 3rd century A.D., Kizil Grottoes are the earliest and westernmost large-scale grotto cluster in China. The construction gradually came to a stop in the 8th and 9th centuries. It is the only grotto in the world whose construction lasted for so long a time. There are 4 sections of grottoes, with 236 grottoes being formally numbered. Most statues were destroyed, but exquisite frescoes remain in 81 caves as the cultural heritage of the ancient Qiuci Kingdom.

Significance of the Heritage

As the channel of fusion, communication and dialogue between the East and the West, the Silk Road has made a great contribution to the common prosperity of human beings for nearly 2,000 years. The Silk Road took shape in the 2nd century B.C., came to prosperity in the 6th to the 14th centuries, and remained in use until the 16th century. It was distributed in the territories of present-day China, Kazakhstan and Kyrghyzstan. The Silk Road witnessed communication of the economic, cultural and social development of the Eurasian continent, especially the communication between nomadic civilization and settled civilization. It was an outstanding example in having facilitated the development of big towns and cities through long-distance trade . It was directly related to such major historical events as Zhang Qian's diplomatic mission to the West Regions, and reflected profoundly the spreading of such religions as Buddhism, Manicheism, Mazdaism and Zoroastrianism, and ideas of urban planning. The Silk Road was the communicating artery of the Eurasian continent, and was a bridge between the three major cultures of China, India and Greece.

Historic Ensemble of the Potala Palace, Lhasa

The Potala Palace

The world-famous Potala Palace stands at the top of the Red Mountain in Lhasa, Tibet. "Potala" is the Sanskrit transliteration of "Boat Island". It is also translated as "Putuo Luo" or "Putuo", originally refering to the island where Arya Avalokiteshvara (the Bodhisattva Guanyin) has his home.The Potala Palace in Lhasa is commonly called second Mount Putuo.

The Potala Palace has been described as "the pearl at the roof of the World". It is known across the world for the layout of the palaces, civil engineering, metal smelting, paintings and sculptures. It is an embodiment of the excellent artistry of Tibetan, Han, Mongolian and Manchurian craftsmen, and represents the great construction achievements of the Tibetan people.

Historical Origin

Construction of the Potala Palace started in the 7th century A.D. According to legend, Songtsen Gampo, after moving his capital to Lhasa, in order to marry Princess Wencheng of the Tang Dynasty, specifically built three 9-storey buildings with over 1,000 rooms and named them "the Potala Palace". On one side of the ensemble was the bedroom of the Tibetan King. At the top of the palace in the middle was a Buddhist pagoda. On the other side was the rear palace. Between the rear palace and the middle palace was a hanging copper-iron bridge 4 storeys high. In 1645 (Wood Chicken year in the Tibetan Calendar) , the 5th Dalai Lama, in order to consolidate the local theocratic power of Ganden Phodrang, with Sonam Rabtan being the director of the project, reconstructed the White Palace and the palace walls, the city gate and the turrets. He also moved the political organ from Drepung Monastery to this location. In 1690 (Iron Horse year in the Tibetan Calendar) , Sangye Gyatso expanded the Red Palace in order to build a funerary stupa for the 5th Dalai Lama. Following the collapse of the Tubo Dynasty, large parts of the ancient palace were destroyed in flames of war, and the rest were damaged by lightning and other natural calamities, which gradually reduced the size of the Potala Palace. After the reconstruction in the 17th century, the Potala Palace was the winter residence of succeeding Dalai Lamas, as well as the ruling centre of Tibetan theocracy. Later Dalai Lamas added 5 golden tops and some ancillary buildings. In 1936 (the year of the Fire Mouse in the Tibetan Calendar) , the building of the stupa of the 13th Dalai Lama formed the present scale of the Potala Palace.

Main Buildings

The 13-storey Potala Palace, whose main building is composed of the White Palace on the east side, the Red Palace in the middle and the white dormitories for monks on the west side, including such ancillary buildings as the Sutra Printing House at the mountain foot and the rear garden, Zongjiao Lukang (Dragon King Lake) . The 3 buildings, all pinkish white, towering at the peak of the Red Mountain, are both holy and magnificent and are referred to by native Tibetans as "the White Palace".

The White Palace The East Chapel on the 4th floor is the biggest palace hall in the White Palace of the Potala Palace. It is 717 square metres in area. This is where such main religious and political ceremonies as the Dalai Lama's enthronement and the celebration of new policies took place. The 5th and 6th floors were the offices and living quarters for the regents. On the 7th floor, that is,the top floor, there were two winter palaces for the Dalai Lama. As they enjoyed day-long sunshine, these palaces were respectively called East Sunshine Hall and West Sunshine Hall. The West Sunshine Hall (Solange Leo Gio, Yue) is the original hall, while the East Sunshine Hall (Gandan Langse) was built later by modelling after it and share similar arrangements, were respectively the living palaces for the 13th Dalai Lama and the 14th Dalai Lama as well as their offices. Inside the palaces,there are a praying hall, sutra hall, sutra-learning hall and bedrooms, which are all luxuriously furnished.

The Red Palace The most important buildings of the Red Palace are the stupa halls of generations of Dalai Lama. There are altogether 5 stupa halls that belong respectively to the 5th, the 7th, the 8th, the 9th and the 13th Dalai Lama. All the stupa halls share similar shape and structure, but differ in scale. The biggest among the 5 stupas, Hidebayashi Shizuki, is dedicated to the 5th Dalai Lama. It is 3 storeys high and is supported by 16 huge square columns. At the centre is laid the stupa of the 5th Dalai Lama, with the stupas of the 10th and 12th Dalai Lama on both sides. The Memorial Hall in the Stupa Hall of the 5th Dalai Lama, the Big West Hall (Cuo Qinlu, also named Scipitso) , the biggest hall in the Red Palace, is over 6 metres high and covers an area of 725.7 square metres. In the west part of the Red Palace is the Stupa Hall of the 13th Dalai Lama, Gelai Dunjue. Built in 1936, it is the newest building in the Potala Palace. Besides the stupa, there is also enshrined a silver statue of the 13th Dalai Lama and a "Manza" (a kind of religious object) woven with 200,000 pearls and corals.

The King's Hall (Qujie Zhebu) and the Saint's Hall (Paba Lakang) are said to have been built in the Tubo Dynasty. The King's Hall is in the centre of the Potala Palace, and under it is the peak of Mount Maburi. According to legend, this was where Srongtsen Gampo meditated and now the extremely precious statues of Princess Wencheng, Princess Bhrikuti and Lu Dongzan etc. are enshrined.

The Characteristics of the Architecture

The Potala Palace, built on the mountain, now covers an area of

410,000 square metres and has a construction area of 130,000 square metres. The main building of the palace has 13 storeys and is 115 metres high. It is completely stone and wood structured. The building looks majestic and gives the impression of uniqueness. The substantial granite walls, the smooth wall collar made of Chinese tamarisk twig, the glittering golden roof, the huge gilded precious bottles, all of which are bright and colorful and complement each other, embody the attractive character of ancient Tibetan buildings.

The design and construction of the palace took into account the pattern of sunlight on the high plateau, and the base of the walls are wide and solid, and under the wall bases are tunnels leading to all directions and vents. All halls and bedrooms have skylights, which let light come through and also regulate the air. The pillars are decorated with all kinds of sculptures, and on the walls there are over 2,500 square metres of colored mural.

Among the thousands of examples of the architectural types that combine Tibetan Buddhist temple with palace, the Potala Palace is the most prominent as far as architectural art is concerned, and it is the only one of its kind in China and even in the whole world.

The Potala Palace stands on a small mountain in the north-western suburbs, 2000 metres from Lhasa. In the minds of local religious believers, this small mountain is just like Mountain Potala (Putuo) where Arya Avalokiteshvara (Guanyin) has his home. It is composed of the White Palace in the east and the Red Palace in the middle. Arranged on mutiple levels, with many twists and turns, the Potala Palace is built in such a way in that the building blends into the mountain setting and the building and mountain make a perfect whole. The palace stands tall and majestic, lofty and spectacular. The walls are in white and red and the roofs are gilded, and together they create a strong artistic appeal. It is the symbol of the city of Lhasa, as well as the unique cultural heritage site on the plateau of snowland.

The Potala Palace is a stone and wood structure. The outer wall is as thick as 2 to 5 metres, and the base of the wall is buried into the rock. The wall, as high as 10 metres, is constructed entirely of granite. At set intervals molten iron was poured between the stone blocks, both to reinforce the structure and to enhance the walls' resistance to earthquakes. The roof and window frames are of wood construction, with jutting eaves and upturned corners, and gleaming copper tiles. The glistening roofs incorporate gable and hip roof style and pavilion style, which possess the Han Chinese architectural style. The walls under the eaves are decorated with gilded copper ornamentation, in the form of the eight precious Buddhist ritual objects, which conveys a rich flavor of Tibetan Buddhism.

The Potala Palace used to be the ruling centre for the Tibetan theocracy and is closely related to the key historical figures such as Songtsen Gampo, Princess Wencheng, Princess Khri b'Tsun and generations of Dalai Lama, which makes it important historically and religiously. In Sasoon Langjie Hall is enshrined Emperor Kangxi's longevity tablet (in Tibetan, Han, Manchurian and Mongolian) and Emperor Qianlong's scroll, which reflect the subordinate relations that the Dalai Lamas had with the central governent. The Potala Palace can be rightly called a museum of architectural art and Buddhist art, and it is the symbol of the unity of the Chinese people of different nationalities and national unification.

Preserved Artifacts

Over a period of more than 300 years, the Potala Palace has collected and kept many historical relics, including Sakyamuni Buddha's relics, 108 letters and 2500 scriptures (especially precious are the Pattra Leave Sutra written with gold from such places as Kangyur and Sindhu, present day India) , and all kinds of gold and jade documents from the central goverments of Ming and Qing dynasties coronating the Dalai Lamas, gold seals and the Gold Bottle given by Emperor Qianlong to select the reincarnation boy for the Dalai Lama. There are also the 8 stupas, the biggest of which was built for the 5th Dalai Lama that cost 3,721 kilograms of gold and over 10,000 precious stones. The stupa is wrapped up in gold and is decorated with large numbers of pearls and jewels. Also kept here are all kinds of gold and silver artifacts made by Tibetan artisans, religious instruments and honorary objects and art works, which are of rich variety and priceless value. Stored in the Potala Palace are a large number of books that cover all fields from Buddhist classics to medicine, astronomy and calendar. All these relics have enormous significance and value for the study of Tibetan politics, economy, history and culture.

"Thangka", Tibetan transliteration, is the kind of painting most characteristic of Tibet. It is a kind of scroll painting, framed with colorful satin, and painted on thin tough silk, cloth or paper. The contents of Thangka are mainly about religious figures, religious historical events and religious doctrines, and also touch upon such themes as the astronomical almanac of Tibet and Tibetan medicine. In the Potala Palace there are nearly 10,000 Thangkas, the biggest of which is as big as several dozens square metres.

Protection and Maintenance

Ever since the founding of the People's Republic of China, the government has always paid great attention to the protection and management of the Potala Palace. In 1988, the State Council decided to pay a huge sum of money to give Potala Palace a large scale restoration, which started in October, 1989. The project, cooperatively carried out by Tibetan and Han engineers and technicians, was finished in five years. Less than 10 years later, in 2002, the second phase of the maintenance of the Potala Palace started, intended to strengthen the underground foundations, replace the woods damaged by moths and repair the frescos. In the same year, repairs to Norbulingka and Sakya Monastery were also carried out. Up to the early summer of 2008, the workers have completed the strengthening of the ancient underground foundations of the Potala Palace, and the repairing of 17 ancient buildings, including the Red Palace and the White Palace. The building project of the Treasure Museum is completed. The fresco repair work, some of the roof of the Snow City, and the renovation of the interior environment of the Treasure Museum have also one by one been finished. The present Potala Palace, with a completely new image, stands on the top of the holy mountain in the snow-covered plateau.

Significance of the Heritage

The existing design, arrangement, materials, craftwork and decoration of the Potala Palace very well maintain the original historical state that has passed down from the first building in the 7th century and succeeding expansion and reconstruction. The many buildings, from different dynasties and different time periods, all make ingenious use of the mountainous topography. As a result, the whole building appears to be exceptionally imposing and majestic, harmonious and complete. The palace rises up in various layers, twisting and turning, melding organically with the mountain setting. This is the most direct feeling that Potala Palace gives visitors and it is also its most notable characteristic. The Potala Palace represents not only a creative breakthrough in its overall architectural artistry, but also reaches unparalleled heights in its aesthetic achievement.

Jokhang Temple

In November 2000, the UNESCO listed Jokhang Temple on *the World Heritage List* as the Extension Project of the Potala Palace, and Jokhang Temple became a world cultural heritage site. (Norbulingka was listed in 2001.)

Jokhang Temple, also named "Zula Kang" and "Jokhang" (meaning Buddhist temple hall in Tibetan) , is a Buddhist temple of Tibetan Buddhism that is located at the old city centre of Lhasa. First built in the 21st year of the Zhenguan Era in theTang Dynasty (647 A.D.) , it was built by the Tibetan King Srongtsen Gampo to commemorate Princess Bhrikuti's arrival in Tibet. The more than 1300-year-old temple enjoys a supreme status in Tibetan Buddhism.

The Characteristics of the Architecture

Jokhang Temple is the most glorious surviving Tubo building. As the earliest Tibetan civil architecture, it created the layout pattern of the Tibetan plain type temple. Jokhang Temple, having combined the architectural styles of Tibet, the Tang Dynasty, Nepal and India, has become a model of Tibetan religious buildings through the ages.

Jokhang Temple has a construction area of over 25,100 square metres and has more than 20 palace halls, notably Maitreya Hall, Guanyin Hall, the Hall of Three Generations of Kings and Tara Hall. The main hall, 4-storey high, has a typical Han-style golden roof and bucket arch and typical Tibetan-style watchtower and carved beams. Under the eaves of the second and third floors of the main hall are lined 103 wood-carved crouchingng beasts and sphinxes. The Tibetan-style murals of the Picture of Princess Wencheng Going to Tibet and the Picture of Building Jokhang Temple are close to 1,000 metres long.

It is often said that "Jokhang Temple had been there first, and then the city of Lhasa came into being." Both geographically and sociologically, Jokhang Temple is the centre of the Lhasa. The circle of the Hall of Sakyamuni Buddha at the centre of Jokhang Temple is called "Lang Kuo", the circle around the exterior wall of Jokhang Temple is called "Ba Kuo", and the street outside the temple is called "Ba Kuo street", that is, Bajiao Street. With Jokhang Temple being the centre, the big area including the Potala Palace, the Medical King Mountain and Ramoche Temple make up Lin Kuo. The three rings from the inside to the outside are the routes taken by Tibetan people in carrying out their prayer ceremony.

Preserved Artifacts

Among the thousands of cultural relics collected in Jokhang Temple, the gilt copper full-length statue of the 12 year old Sakyauni is the most exquisite and valuable. It is said that the statue is the exactmimage of the Master Buddha of 2500 years ago, and seeing the statue is just like seeing the Buddha himself. It was brought from India into China and was later taken by Princess Wencheng into Tibet and has been enshrined at Jokhang Temple ever since. Lhasa's fame as "the Sacred Land" is tied in with this statue.

Other extremely valuable relics in Jokhang Temple are a sandalwood sculpture and 8 sandalwood pillars in front of the Hall of Sakyamuni, all of which were made in the 7th century. After over 1400 years, they still remain intact and will produce a ringing metallic sound when knocked.

Significance of the Heritage

Jokhang Temple is not only a sanctuary for enshrining numerous Buddhist statues and holy things for believers to worship, it is also a fully-articulated and authentic representation of the tantra doctrine Mandala, the ideal pattern of the universe in Buddhism. In front of the temple, incense burns all day long, and the pious kowtowing of believers has made deep marks the length of a human body on the stone floor in front of the gate. The ever-burning tens of thousands of ghee lamps have recorded the never-ending footprints of pilgrims and have stored the eternity of time.

On one of the three stone pillars in front of the entrance to Jokhang Temple is carved the Document of the Alliance between the Tang Dynasty and Tubo in both Han Chinese and Tibetan, signed in 823 A.D. This was a witness to the deep friendship between the Han and Tibetan peoples. On another pillar is carved the Vaccination Paper (the pillar was erected to commemorate the event that during the reign of Emperor Qianlong of Qing Dynasty, the central government taught the Tibetan people the method of vaccination to prevent smallpox) . This proved the care of the central government for the Tibetan people. Looking down at the square of Jokhang Temple from the golden roof of the temple, you can see the Potala Palace on the distant mountain on the right. The willow trees closer by, called "princess willow" and said to have been planted by Princess Wencheng, signify the ever-lasting and deep-rooted friendship between the Han people and the Tibetan people.

Norbulingka

Norbulingka, meaning "the treasure garden" in Tibetan, is located in the western suburb of Lhasa. First built in the 1740s (during the era of the 7th Dalai Lama) , it was the place where generations of Dalai Lama stayed for the summer and handled political affairs. It is a typical Tibetan garden. Having undergone more than 200 years of expansion, the whole garden takes a area of 360,000 square metres and is home to more than 100 kinds of plants, some of which are common to the Lhasa area, some of which are exotic flowers and rare herbs taken from the south and north Himalayas, while some are precious flowers transplanted from inland China or foreign countries. This can be rightly called a High Plateau Botanical Garden.

Main Buildings

Norbulingka is made up of the Kesang Phodang (phodang means "palace" in Tibetan) , the Golden Phodang and the Takten Migyur Phodang, and each one of the palaces consists of the three main sections of the palace section, asection in front of the palace and the forest section. The building cluster centring around Kesang Phodang is at the southeast of the south courtyard inside the second enclosing wall. The building cluster with Tsokyil Phodang (the pavilion in the midst of a lake) being the main body and about 120 metres to the northwest of Kesang Phodang, is the most beautiful scenic spot at Norbulingka. The building cluster with the Golden Phodang being the main body is at the west of Norbulingka. The buildings, mainly making use of wood and stone and being neatly planned, are typical of Tibetan architectural style.

The outstanding characteristics include: terraces on the higher levels, pools at the lower levels, adapting to the natural conditions, and putting emphasis on the view. Huxin Palace, the Dragon King Pavilion and the Golden Lingka are hidden among the lush trees. The fresh air and the quiet environment impress visitors with the plain and natural sentiment that belongs specifically to Tibetan gardens. This is the biggest man-made garden in Tibet, with the best scenery and the most historical sites.

Preserved Artifacts

The cultural relics preserved in Norbulingka may be, overall, divided into two types: one type being the religious relics made in local Tibet, the other type being all kinds of treasures given by the central government of successive dynasties and emperors to the upper strata of Tibet. The gold copper statue is the most famous locally made religious relic. It is delicately made, well-proportioned and bright-colored. The gilding over the Buddhist statue is thick and heavy, and the gilded surface has a high degree of finish. Such ornaments as the Buddha's crown, earrings, armlets, bracelets and the ribbon are all inlayed with turquoise. All these spectacular features proved that after the mid-18th century, the local Tibetan Buddhist statue-making technique had reached a mature stage of independent development.

In addition to the Buddhist statues and pagodas, the collection of thangkas makes another bright spot. Large number of all kinds of paintings by the Miangtang School, Khyentse School and Gachi School are preserved in Norbulingka, the figures in these paintings being vividly and delicately portrayed, making them very precious.

Besides, the murals on the walls of the main halls and palaces are also truly outstanding. They count as exceptional art treasures of Tibetan culture.

Significance of the Heritage

As the biggest man-made Tibetan garden in Tibet, Norbulingka conbines both Tibetan and Han architectural style and is the masterpiece of Tibetan garden construction. The many artistic treasures preserved here not only have high artistic value, but also prove the friendly interaction between the Tibetan and Han peoples for more than a thousand years.

Mogao Caves

Dunhuang was an important town along the ancient Silk Road. The precious artistic objects housed in Mo Kao Grotto at Dunhuang are treasures representative of the cultural communication between China and the world.The Chinese people are proud of Mo Kao Grotto.

Mo Kao Grotto is on the cliff of the east side of Mingsha Mountain which is 25 kilometres southeast of Dunhuang City, Gansu Province. Mo Kao Grotto has five levels and is 1600 metres long from north to south. As recorded, in the year 366 A.D., the monk Lezun saw a shining golden light as if thousands of Buddhas were in front of him while passing this mountain, so he cut the first grotto on the cliff. Later, such monks as Faliang continued building caves and meditating here. They named this place Mo Gao Ku,meaning "at the height of desert," which was later shortened to Mo kao Grotto.

Historical Origin

Dunhuang, since the Han and Wei dynasties,has been populated by Han people and many minorities, which has resulted in the convergence and fusion of different cultures. At the same time, Dunhuang was also in the corridor connecting the western world and inland China. Ever since ancient times, Buddhist believers among local officials, powerful families and poor people alike, donated money for cutting grottoes, molding statues and painting pictures. Merchants, envoys and monks travelling along the Silk Road, praying for a safe crossing of deserts and gobis or hoping to gain entrance to the Kingdom of Heaven, hired large numbers of craftsmen to cut niches and mold statues on the cliff of Mingsha Mountain to enshrine the Bhuddist images they worshipped.A thousand-year (covering the dynasties of Eastern Jin, Northern Liang, Northern Wei, Western Wei, Northern Zhou, Sui, Tang, the Five Dynasties, Song, Western Xia and Yuan) of continous work left to later generations a colorful art treasury of Buddhist culture.

The Northern Dynasties

In the dynasties of Northern Wei, Western Wei and Northern Zhou, the rulers believed piously in Buddhism and the nobility gave generous support to building the grottoes, which grew rapidly. 36 grottoes were cut during the Northern Dynasties,and the earliest ones, No.268,272 and 275 were carved during Northern Liang. The shapes were mainly those of meditation grotto, central pillar grotto and sanctuary grotto. The painting of this period are mainly composed of flying apsaras, supporting Bodhisattvas and the Thousand Buddha. At the beginning, round moldings were usually a combination of one Buddha and two Bodhisattvas; later, two disciples were added.

The molded figures look strong and healthy, with demure and tranquil expression. The style is plain and substantial. Earlier frescoes usually have earthy red as background color, and there are added such colors as dark green, green, and white, whose combination creates a feeling of warmth and density. The figures are tall and straight with simple and vigorous lines, which are characteristic of the Buddhism of the Western Region. After the Western Wei Dynasty, the background color is usually white and the color tends to be delicate, while the style is free and easy, which is typical of the culture of inland China.

Sui-Tang Period

During the Sui and Tang dynasties,the prosperity of the Silk Road brought Mo Kao Grotto to its palmy days. The more than 300 grottoes of Sui and Tang dynasties that have survived to this day are mainly palace hall grottoes, altar grottoes, 4-wall-3-niche grottoes and big statue grottoes, while the meditation grottoes and central pillar grottoes disappeared.

The fresco of the Tang Dynasty are magnificent, and statue painting and sutra painting have reached perfection. The stautes, looking simple, loyal and plump, are representative of inland China style. Tall and big statues appeared for the first time. Group statues are usually made up of seven or nine figures, whose perfect modelling complement with the frescoes.

The Five Dynasties and Song

There are now over 100 grottoes built in the Five Dynasties and Song period,most of which were rebuilt and re-painted earlier gorttoes.The styles were mainly altar grotto and palace hall grotto. From late Tang to the Five Dynasties, the Guiyijun governor Zhang and Cao families that ruled Dunhuang were pious Bhuddist believers and presided over the cutting and building of the Mo Kao Grotto, which explains the large number of pictures and rich comtent of supporters. Both the statues and frescoes followed the late Tang style, but toward the end of the period, the forms became more and more formulaic, the content was somewhat more diversified, but lacked the creative vigour and passion of the Tang Dynasty.

Western Xia and Yuan

There are now 85 Western Xia and Yuan grottoes, 77 of which were from Western Xia. The form of the grottoes and the fresco sculpture basically inherited earlier styles. In mid-Western Xia grottoes can be seen the images of Huihu kings,and in the frescoes from late Western Xia, there appear contents concerning Tibetan Tantra. There are only 8 Yuan grottoes,all of which were newly cut. The round-shape altar inside square grotto first appeared and the frescoes and sculptures were basically related to Tibetan tantra. After Yuan Dynasty, Ming Dynasty blocked the pass, as a result, Mo Kao Grotto stopped building and expanding and gradually disappeared into oblivion.

Dunhuang Art

The art of Dunhuang Stone Grotto is three-dimensional art combination of construction, sculpture and painting. The ancient artists, while inheriting the Inland Han Chinese culture and the traditional ethnic art heritage of the people in the Western Region, learnt and put into practice foreign art skills and produced Chinese Buddhist art works with local Dunhuang characteristics. These art works provide precious materials for people to make researches into ancient Chinese politics, economy, culture, religion, ethnic relations and friendly mutual interaction between China and foreign countries.They have become a common cultural treasure and spiritual wealth for all humanity.

The Art of Colorful Molding

The earth of the cliff of Mo Kao Grotto is soft and loose, so it is not suitable for making stone statues, as a result, all the statues are made with wood frames and earth, except for the four big Buddhas that are made with stone and earth. All the statues are Buddhist gods and Buddhas that are composed of individual statues or group statues. In group statues, the Buddha is usually in the centre, with disciples and bodhisattvas, from as few as three to as many as eleven, standing on both sides of him. The colorful stautues are made with different styles, including round molding, floating molding, shadow molding and good works molding, etc. The statues appear to be very real and show rich imagination, excellent conception and great artistic achievements on the part of the sculptors. Besides,the statues are perfectly compatible with the frescoes and they make each other all the more powerful and beautiful.

The colorful statues represent the essence of Dunhuang Art. There are different kinds of figures, including buddhas, bodhisattvas, disciples, king of heaven, Buddha's warrior attendant, strong men and gods. As they were made in different time periods, these statues were different in style, too. The styles of "thin image with delicate bone", "Cao costume emerging from water" of Wei, Jin and Northern and Southern dynasties and the "Wu's clothes floating in wind" from the Tang Dynasty, fully represent the artists' extraordinary imagination and singular ability to control various artistic styles.

The Fresco Art

The Mo Kao frescoes are painted on the four walls and on the top of the grottoes and in the niches. They are rich in contents, including the seven kinds of genres of Buddhist figures, Buddhist stories and historical events, story of a scripture, gods and monsters, supporters, decorative designs. There are also many pieces describing the various aspects of social life such as hunting, farming, spinning and weaving, communications, battles, construction, dancing, weddings and funerals. They provide an artistic representation of folk culture and historical evolution over 1500 years, from the 16 kingdoms to the Qing Dynasty. They also make up important material objects for studying Chinese Art history.

The Dunhuang fresco figures, especially flying Apsaras, are very lifelike. The Tang people praised the flying Apsaras, describing them as "heavenly clothes flying, while you feel the movement of wind all over the wall." Flying Apsaras have become the symbol of Dunhuang Fresco, and the Flying Goddess playing the Pipa by holding it on her back is the height of Dunhuang art. Through bright colors and flying lines, the ancient artists expressed their warm and passionate dreams for the ideal heaven and they make us feel their tireless passion spreading over the endless desert.

The Art of Architecture

Among the over 500 existing grottoes, 492 still have paintings and color statues. Classified by construction and function, the grottos are of the following kinds:central pillar, palace hall (central altar) , upside-down top, big image, nirvana, meditation, monk room, shadow and burial. There are also some Buddhist pagodas.The biggest grotto is over 40 metres high and 30 metres wide, and the smallest is no taller than 0.33 metre. The central pillar form, as a foreign style and kept in early grottoes, reflects the fact that ancient artists learnt and assimilated foreign art and made it their own and created masterpieces of architecture that survive to this day. The almost completely Tang and Song wooden eaves outside many grottoes are hard-to-find real materials of traditional ancient wooden structure and have extremely high research value. In the grotto protection area, there are many Buddhist pogodas, some of which are from the Five Dynasties period, the Song Dynasty and Werstern Xia Dynasty.

Significance of the Heritage

Ever since the discovery of over 5,000 volumes of religious and secular books, Dunhuang Art had shocked the world and Dunhuang Studies has become a globally distinguished school.

Mo Gao Grottoes has 492 grottoes, more than 45,000 square metres of frescoes, 2,400 painted sculptures, 4,000 flying Apsaras, 5 Tang and Song architectures of wood structure, thousands of lotus-shaped beryls and tiles. This is an extensive, profound and comprehensive art palace composed architecture, painting and sculpture. The contents involve the different fields of art, history, economy, culture and religion of ancient society. As the biggest existing Buddhist art treasure house that is most completely preserved in the world and "the art pearl of the East", Mo Gao Grottoes has great historical, artistic and scientific value. It is the historical treasuere of the Chinese, and an excellent cultural heritage of human being.

Yungang Grottoes

Li Daoyuan, the famous geographer of the Northern Wei Dynasty, recorded the magnificent sight of the Yungang Grottoes in his *Shuijingzhu (Annotated River Classic):*

Caves are dug by cutting the rocks and opening the mountain. Rarely are seen such lifelike images of such imposing scale. With mountain hall and water palace, temples lie within each other's sight. Pools in the forest are like a brocade mirror, dazzling the eye.

Historical Origin

The Yungang Grottoes are located on the southern slopes of Mt. Wuzhou in the western outskirts of Datong in Shanxi Province. They were first developed in the Northern Wei era and are the first large grottoes whose carving was sponsored by the high nobles of a royal house. The grottoes are set against the mountain and extend from east to west for one kilometer. The cluster of grottoes is divided into east, central, and west sections. The east grottoes contain mainly Buddhist pagodas and are known as the pagoda cave. The central portion includes the earliest and most imposing sculptures. The western section was developed relatively late, consisting mainly of works dating from after the Northern Wei transferred its capital to Luoyang. There are a total of 252 niches, with more than 51,000 images. The biggest Buddhist images is 17 meters tall and the smallest is just a few centimetres. The five Tan Yao grottoes were designed with a rigorous unity and count as a classic achievement from the first peak in Chinese Buddhist art.

The Yungang Grottoes, along with the MoKao Grottoes in Dunhuang, Gansu, the Longmen Grottoes in Henan, and the Tianshui Maiji Grottoes in Gansu, are regarded as Chine's four great grottoes; the Yungang, Mokao, and Longmen Grottoes, along with the Dazu Grottoes near Chongqing, have all been designated as World Heritage sites.

The Art of Yungang Grottoes

Carving Style

Yungang Grottoes was the first large Buddhist grotto temple sponsored by the court in the central mainland (China) , as well as a representative work of early Chinese grotto art. Yungang grottoes are famous across the world for royal demeanor, variety of subject matter, delicate carving, rich content and magnificent artistic beauty. Characterised by the fusion of cultures of the west and the east and the distinctive nationalization process connecting the North and the South, Yungang grottoes are unique among Chinese grotto art. The large number of actual images and written historical materials reflect in different ways the important changes in grotto art style of the 5th and 6th centuries and in religious beliefs of the North; they have made great contribution to the innovation and development of Chinese Buddhist art. The historic, artistic, and scientific value of the Yungang Grottoes surpasses that of other early grottoes.

Key Grottoes

1-20 among the 45 main grottoes existing currently (2012) are the oldest grottoes that provide the richest and most valuable contents, while they have also been the earliest to open to the public. The Five Caves of Tan Yao are the most famous and are said to be "the best of the best".

The Five Caves of Tan Yao are the present caves 16-20. Being spacious, the caves have a U-shaped plan and arched roofs, and the main statue takes up most of the space.

Cave 16 This cave is famous for Jiyue (music and dancing girls) . The giant statue, chin up and chest out, standing on a lotus pillar in the middle of the cave, is extraordinary in bearing and is called a "male beauty". The other Buddha statues are either handsome and delicate, or solemn and dignified; they either stand wearing thousand-buddha cassocks, or sit with palms holding together devoutly. On the walls are carved thousand Buddhas and niches, all the Buddhas having vivid appearance and wonderful posture. As such they are truly breathtaking.

Cave 17 This is special in that the floor inside the cave is lower than the ground outside. The main statue, Cross-legged Buddha, is 15.5m tall, with the face, two arms and most of the parts in backlight having collapsed, and the legs remaining to be carved. The Buddha wears a crown, and his robe is decorated with necklace, armlet, and snake streamer at the chest.

Cave 18 Having a door and a window, the outer look of Cave 18 is basically similar to that of cave 19. The main statue is a standing Buddha, with standing attendant Bodhisattvas, standing statue of Buddha and statue of Bhikkhu (monk) . The main statue, 15.5m, is standing on a low and flat lotus pedestal; he has a high bun on his head, a round plump face with no makeup, big eyes, high nose, lop ears, and is smiling brightly. He is wearing a cassock with no right sleeve, and on the cassock are attached small sitting statues. Two statues, about 9m tall, stand on his right and left; their appearance is much like that of the main statue. Short and sturdy, they are wearing cassocks.

Cave 19 This is the biggest of the Five Caves of Tan Yao. With door and window, the main cave has a U-shaped plan and arched roof. The main statue is 17m tall and takes up most of the space. Having a high bun on his head, and with a round plump face wearing no makeup, it looks very like the great Buddha in Cave 20. The big Buddha sits on the floor of the cave, without a pedestal. He is dressed similarly to the big Buddha in Cave 20. All over the walls inside the cave are carved thousand-buddhas, while there are two comparatively big Buddha statues standing among the thousand-buddhas on two sides of the front wall. A child, said to be Rahula, son of Buddha, is standing in front of the standing Buddha who is touching the child's head.

Cave 20 Acclaimed the symbol of Yungang carvings, the great Buddha sits cross-legged in open air. This is a sitting staute of Sakyamuni Buddha, 13.7m tall; the part above the chest remains well preserved as a result of the hard stone used. The statue is giant in stature, has round plump face, thin lips, high nose and heavy shoulders. He has a solemn expression. He is wearing cassock with the right arm naked. The flame pattern in backlight, and the embrossed sitting Buddha and Flying Apsaras are very colorful, thus rendering the main Buddha all the more strong and magnificent. In front of the cave is a pavilion of five rooms and four wooden structures, with a glazed tile roof built in the early years of the Qing Dynasty. It is a magnificent building.

Jiyuetian(entertainers in heaven) in Yungang Grottoes

Cave 12 of Yungang Grottoes is also called Music Grotto, as inside the cave are carved many Jiyuetian. More than ten kinds of instruments are presented here, including konghou (an ancient plucked stringed instrument) , a kind of harp, wicker horn and crooked lute, which came from Central Asia in earlier times, as well as panpipes, ancient guqin (a seven-stringed plucked instrument in some ways similar to the zither) , ancient zheng (a 21-or 25-stringed plucked instrument in some ways similar to the zither) and xunan (ancient egg-shaped, holed wind instrument) , which were traditional Chinese instruments. The carvings provide precious visual materials for the study of music and dancing history both at home and abroad. They are the fruits of the combination of multiple cultures of ancient times, and the accumulation of deep and sustained folk music and dancing art of different nations. According to statistics, instrument carvings are found in 22 caves, with over 500 carved instruments of 27 kinds and over 60 music bands.

Significance of the Heritage

Magnificent in style and having rich and colorful contents, Yungang Grottoes have been acclaimed a treasury of ancient Chinese sculpture art. The Buddha, Cialis and flying apsaras are all lively and vivid, and the sculptures on the columns are delicate and exquisite.

Three main periods can be identified in the construction: the Early Period (460-465) , the Middle Period (471-494) and the Late Period (494-525) . The style of grottoes of different periods differ and each has distinctive characteristics. The Five Grottoes of Tan Yao of the Early period are magnificent, and have the emotional appeal of Western Region sculpture, being simple and unsophisticated. The grottoes of the Middle Period are well-known for their delicate carvings and sumptuous decorations, and reflect the complicated, changeable and palatial art style of Northern Wei. The grottoes of the Late Period are small in size, yet the statues, thin, handsome and moderately-proportioned, are the models of the grotto art of northern China and the origin of "shougu qingxiang" (thin images) . Yungang Grottoes inherited the realistic art style of the Qin and Han dynasties, and also began the romantic style of the Sui and Tang dynasties.

Longmen Grottoes

As one of the great grottoes of China (the other two are the Mogao grottoes in Dunhuang, Gansu and the Yungang grottoes in Datong) , Longmen grottoes are located in Yique Valley 6 kilometres south of Luoyang. Yique is the ancient name for the place where Xiang Mountain and Longmen Mountain stand facing at each other, with Yihe River flowing between them. After Emperor Yang of the Sui Dynasty moved his capital to Luoyang, he had the front gate of his palace face Yique. Chinese emperors claimed to be "true dragon and son of heaven", therefore, from that time on, Yique was customarily called Longmen, literally Dragon Gate. According to Bai Juyi, the great Tang poet, "As for the scenery of the suburbs of the capital Luoyang, Longmen has the best of all."

Historical Origin

Lasting for 400 years, the intermittent building of the Longmen grottoes continued through the dynasties of the Eastern Wei, Western Wei, Northern Qi, Northern Zhou, Sui, Tang and Northern Song. Large scale construction was carried out for over 140 years during the Northern Wei and Tang dynasties, and as a result, Northern Wei grottoes make up to 30% of all Longmen grottoes and Tang grottoes make up 60%. Only 10% were carved in the other dynasties. According to statistics, there are now 2,345 niches, more than 70 Buddhist pagodas, and more than 110,000 statues on the two mountains. The statue of Buddha Vairocana, the biggest Buddha statue, is 17.14m high. The prestigious Twenty Inscriptions of Longmen and *Yique Niche Stele* by Chu Suiliang, among the over 2,860 steles and inscriptions, respectively represent the best example of Weibei (tablet inscriptions of the Northern Dynasties) and Tangkai (regular script calligraphy of the Tang Dynasty) .

The Art of Longmen Grottoes

Carving Style

As the place where the imperial families and noble families of Northern Wei and Tang dynasties made the most statues, Longmen grottoes reflect the purpose and behavior of the inperial families and as such have the rich flavor of national religion. A great deal of material evidence concerning religion, art, architecture, music, apparel, and medicine is housed here, making it a great artistic museum of stone carving. The statues of the two different dynasties reflect the distinct styles of different time periods. The Northern Wei statues here have turned from the rough, stately and vigorous characteristics of the Yungang grottoes to having a richer atmosphere of life and being active, moderate, delicate and pretty. These statues of the Northern Wei have long and narrow faces, thin shoulders, and flat, straight chests. Carved in a level and straight way, the clothes appear strong and unadorned. This exotic and dazzling array of stone art work provides a precious record of the fusion of traditional Chinese culture and foreign civilizations.

In contrast to theNorthern Wei artistic style of admiring thin figures, Tang artists favored plumpness. As a result, the Tang statues have round faces, heavy shoulders, and uplifted chests. The clothes are carved in a round way and thus look natural and smooth. Having inherited the fine traditions of the Northern Wei and absorbed the culture of the Han Chinese, the artists of the Tang statues of Longmen grottoes have created an strong, active, purely natural and realistic style that embody the strong material and spiritual strength of the Tang Empire, and represent the highest achievement of the carving art of the Tang Dynasty.

Key Grottoes

Fengxian Temple Fengxian Temple, which got its name because it was subordinate to the then imperial temple Fengxian Temple, houses the biggest-sized and best group of cliff stone statues among all Longmen Grottoes. This grotto was carved in the early years of Emperor Gaozong of the Tang Dynasty. Reflecting the distinctive features of Buddhist statuary art of the Tang Dynasty, the Buddhist statues in this grotto are plump, calm-looking, life-like and touching. Nine great statues are housed here, with Lushena Buddha, the Sambhogakaya Buddha of Sakyamuni Buddha, in the middle. The statue is 17.14m tall. Having the look of a wise and amiable middle-aged woman, the statue stands for noble character, rich feelings, open-mindedness and elegant appearance. As such it has great artistic glamor.

Qianxi Temple Qianxi Temple, the biggest grotto at the northern side of West Mountain at Longmen, was built in the early Tang Dynasty. A t the caisson at the top of the grotto is a lightly carved lotus. The chief Buddha, Amitabha, is sitting straight at the Sumeru Desk. With plump face, uplifted chest, robe hanging down before his seat and having a well-proportioned body and wise appearance, the statue impresses viewers with a feeling of serenity and kindness. On the right side of the chief Buddha is the leading disciple Kassapa, and on the left the little disciple, Ananda. Beside the disciples are Guanyin and Manjusri Bodhisattva. Amitabha and the two Buddhas on both sides of him are collectively called "Three Saints of the West", that is, the three gods in charge of the Western Elysium who are the objects of belief of the Jodo sect of Buddhism.

Binyang Grotto "Binyang" means greeting the rising sun. The carving of the three grottos of Binyang began in the Northern Wei period, but a palace coup brought the plan to an end and only the Middle Binyang Grotto was completed. It was not until the early Tang period that the main statues of South Grotto and North Grotto were carved.

The interior of the Middle Grotto is horsehoof-shaped. At the centre of the fornix top is a lotus canopy composed of a huge lotus of multi petals, surrounded by eight entertainer Rakutens and two celestial supporters who, with swirling costume, hover around the lotus canopy. They are truly beautiful and affecting.

The grotto of Binyang South Grotto was cut in the Northern Wei period, but the main Buddha statues were completed in the early Tang Dynasty. Amitabha, the chief Buddhist image, has a plump face and body and heavy shoulders, reflecting the early Tang style of admiring plumpness.

Wanfo (Thousands of Buddhas) Grotto Wanfo Grotto got its name for the 15,000 little Buddha statues that were carved on the north and south sides of the grotto. This is the grotto that provides the most comprehsensive combination of stone statues among all the Longmen grottoes. Amitabha, the chief Buddhist image in this grotto, sitting on a two-tier lotus, has plump, round face and heavy shoulders. The simple and smooth robe Amitabha is wearing was carved in the round-graver method. Each one of the little statues is 4cm tall. At the wall bases on both sides are six slender and graceful entertainers dancing beautifully to the sound of melodious music.

Lianhua (Lotus) Grotto This was named Lianhua (lotus) grotto for the big lotus carved at the roof of the grotto. This grotto was carved in the Northern Wei period. The flying apsaras around the lotus are slender, graceful and composed, having thin waists and wearing longuettes. Sakyamuni, the chief Buddhist image in this grotto, is wearing a cassock which is in the style of ample gown and loose girdle. The gathers of his cassock are simple and sprightly. The two disciples are bas-relief. Kassapa, on the left hand of Sakyamuni, has deep eyes, high nose and protruding bones and veins on his chest and is holding a pewter staff. He looks like an ascetic from the Western Regions. Here can be found the most tiny Buddhist statues just 2cm tall that are carved on the upper part of the south wall of the grotto. These small images are vivid, delicate and lifelike.

Guyang Grotto Located at the south section of Longmen Mountain and cut in 493 A.D., Guyang Grotto is the earliest one of the Longmen Grottoes; in it are housed the richest Buddhist contents, with the highest standard of calligraphy art. On the roof there is no lotus caisson, and the floor is in horsehoof shape. The chief statue, Sakyamuni, in a cassock of double-collar-sagging style, having thin face and smiling eyes, is sitting calmly at the square table.

Yaofang (Prescription) Grotto Yaofang grotto was named as such for the many prescriptions of the Tang Dynasty carved on the gate of the grotto. Over 150 prescriptions are concerned with internal medicine, surgery, paediatrics and the five sense organs. All the medicinal materials prescribed in these prescriptions could be easily found, much to the convenience of the common people. The prescriptions not only can cure common diseases, but can also deal with difficult miscellaneous diseases. For example, "Prescription for Choking" is for the treatment of esophagus cancer. As the earliest existing carved prescriptions in China, the prescriptions kept in Yaofang Grotto has great significance for the study of Chinese medicine.

Significance of the Heritage

Longmen Grottoes and niches display the best and the largest Chinese art of the period from the late Northern Wei Dynasty to the Tang Dynasty (493-907 A.D.) . The art works that give full and accurate illustration to Buddhist subject matter represent the peak of Chinese rock carving art.

Longmen Grottoes are incomparable for its superiority of the geographical location and the beauty of the natural environment. The large amount of real images and written materials reflect in various ways the development and changes in different fields of ancient China, such as politics, economy, religion, and culture, and made agreat contribution to the innovation and development of grotto art. The historical, artistic, scientific and aesthetic value of the Longmen Grotttoes marks them as among the most representative works of grotto art. Also, Longmen grottoes provide rare and precious materials for the study of ancient Chinese politics, economy, religion, geography, clan names, folk custom, art, medicine as well as cultural communication between China and other nations.

Dazu Rock Carvings

Located in Chongqing Municipality and within Dazu county, Tongnan County, Tongliang County and Bishan County, Dazu Rock Carvings preserve a considerable number of stone sculptures from the Tang and Song dynasties. Dazu Rock Carvings is the generic name for the grotto art embodied mainly in the cliff sculptures in the territory of Dazu county. There are over 70 clusters of Dazu sculptures, numbering 100,000 works in total. As the most famous clusters and the best examples of later grotto sculpture in China, the Baodingshan cluster and Beishan cluser consist mainly of Buddhist images, while Confucian and Taoist images coexisit. Grand in scale, excellent in art, and rich in subject matter, Dazu rock carvings enjoy equal popularity with the Dunhuang Mokao Grotto, Yungang Grotto and Longmen Grotto.

Historical Origin

Established during the Tang Dynasty in 758 A.D., Dazu county was subordinate to Changzhou Prefecture. In 885 the seat of Changzhou Prefecture was moved from Jingnan County to Dazu, and until 1279 (during the Southern Song period) , Dazu was the seat of the Changzhou Prefectural government. The "Wushan (Five mountain)" rock carvings were completed during these nearly 400 years.

The earliest remaining rock carvings are the Jianzishan rock carvings cut in 650 A.D., during the early Tang Dynasty. In the two centuries that followed, the Shengshui Temple rock carvings were the only ones newly cut. The two early and middle Tang carvings are no more than twenty in number. Not until the seat of Changzhou Prefecture government moved to Dazu in 885 A.D. did rock carvings gradually thrive.

In 892 A.D. (the Tang Dynasty) , Wei Junjing, the prefectural governor and Jingnan Military Commissioner, while building Yongchangzhai village which could "store grain enough for ten years, and station many tens of thousands" , started carving images in Beishan (Northern Mountain) . From 907 to 965 A.D. (the period of the Five Dynasties and Ten Kingdoms when Sichuan was the Shu Kingdom, historically known as Early Shu and Late Shu.) , prefectural and county officials, local gentry and common folks, and monks and nuns followed his example and created the first high point in the history of rock carvings.

The Art of Dazu Rock Carvings

In accordance with the inner rule of aesthetics and the rule of form, the Dazu Rock Carvings made use of both realism and hyperbole in the three-dimensional carvings to give different figures their own distinct features of personality. The emphasis was put on the strong contrast of good and evil, beautiful and ugly, and the contents represented were close to life, which produces intense aesthetic appeal and great social educational effect. The arrangement shows a smart combination of art, religion, science and nature. Aesthetically, the carvings blend mysteriousness, naturalness and elegancy into one, thus fully reflecting the traditional Chinese culture's aesthetic emphasis on admonitory examples.

The Baoding Rock Carvings The Baoding Rock Carvings is situated 15 kilometers to the northeast of Dazu County seat. These sculptures were carved over a seventy-year period from 1179 to 1249, in an effort initiated by Zhao Zhifeng , a famous monk of Shu. Baoding Rock (Grotto) Carvings consist of 13 clusters of sculpture, and the number of images amount to over 10,000. The Big Buddha Gulf and the Small Buddha Gulf are the biggest in size. There are over 360 huge carved images, the most well-known of which include the Six Paths of Reincarnation, Guangda Baolou Pavilion, 3 Sacred Huayan (Kegon) Images and images of Avalokitesvara.

Nanshan Rock Carvings The Nanshan Rock Carvings, 86-metre long and 3.5-10.2-metre high, were produced between 1131 and1162 (the Southern Song Dynasty) . Five grottoes of carvings, including Sanqing (the 3 gods who enjoy the highest position in Taoism) Ancient Cave, Houtu Shengmu Temple, Longdong (Dragon) Cave, Emperor Zhenwu Shrine, etc., consist mainly of Taoist subject matters. Take as an example Sanqing Ancient Cave. The 421 statues, mainly those of the highest Taoist god "Sanqing", accompanied by the gods "Siyu" (the four assistants for the 3 most important gods in Taoism) , Shengmu and Wangmu, vividly reflect the historical fact that, in the 12th century, Taoism had changed from the worship of Laojun and "Sanguan" (Three gods of heaven, earth and water) in the earlier period to a belief in "Sanqing" and "Siyu" that had a distinct system of gods and a clear hierarchy of gods. This is the most elaborately carved grotto among all Taoist grottoes of the Song Dynasty. As for the contents, this cave represents the most complete and systematic material presentation of the Taoist pantheon in the Song Dynasty, and as such, has great religious, historical and artistic value.

Beishan Rock Carvings Located 2 kilometres to the north of Dazu County seat, Beishan Rock Carvings were initiated in 892 A.D. (during Zhaozong's reign in the Tang Dynasty) and continued throughl the Five Dynasties, Northern Song and Southern Song. They include close to 10,000 sculptures at the various sites of Fowan, Yangpanpo, Guanyinpo, Beita Temple and Foeryan, etc. On the 300m long 7m high cliff are 6 steles, 55 pieces of prefactory remarks and inscriptions about statue cutting, 8 pillar columns, 1 picture of "Wenshushili (the Manjusri Bodhisattva) visiting patients" and 264 grottoes of rock statues. The Buddhist statues at Fowan are elaborately carved, and look urbane in body posture and unique in style. Wei Junjing Monument, Cai Jing Monument and Ancient Book of Filial Piety Monument, only found here, are not only precious examples of calligraphy, but also fill a gap in the historical record and as such are extremely valuable. Fowan rcok carvings are divided into two sections, with the southern section being carved mainly in the Late Tang and Five Dynasties and the northern section mostly in Nothern Song and Southern Song. Late Tang statues look dignified and plump, simple and honest, in plain dress with fluent lines. Freed of the influence of foreign culture and showing the carving features of the transitional period, the statues of the Five Dynasties look exquisite, ingenous and colorful, with the dressings turning from being plain to complicated. The statues of the Northern Song and Southern Song embody notably Chinese flavor.

Shizhuanshan Rock Carvings Shizhuanshan is rare as a typical site where the statues of the three teachings of Buddhism, Taoism and Confucianism coexist. In Grotto No.6 are a statue of Kongzi and the shrines of the ten philosophers, with Confucius, the founder of Confucianism, sitting on the front wall, and the ten most famous disciples of his on the side walls. Grotto No. 7 presents three Buddhas sitting on a lotus, with a dragon under each seat. Buddha Pilu is in the middle, wearing a tall flowery hat embellished with a golden disc, and wearing a double-breasted Buddhist robe with wide sleeves, two hands folded on the chest in Mudra style. Losana Buddha is on the left, his hair bound in a spiral-shaped bun. Sakyamuni Buddha, with a similar bun and in cassock, is on the right, with his right hand at the chest, narrating Dharma. In Grotto No. 8 are Laozi, the founder of Taoism, in sitting position, and 7 gods and sages, standing on his right and left . According to the carving record, all three groups of carvings were cut by the famous sculptor Wen Weijian using donations from rich landowners.

Shimenshan Rock Carvings There are both Buddhist statues and Taoist statues in this site, with the Taoist statues having special characteristics. The statue of Qianliyan (clairvoyance) outside Grotto No.2, the shrine of the Jade Emperor, has copper-bell-like eyes that look as if they could see things at a great distance. Having a strange ugly face, Shunfenger (Clairaudience) appears to be listening to something. These two statues are exaggeratingly presented as abundant in muscles; their meridians and veins are fully visible.In Grotto No.7, Wutong Dadi (Great Single-legged Emperor Wutong) , his left foot standing on a firewheel, has a wide forehead and deep eyes, big mouth and thick lips, with his sash flying; it makes one feel as though he is coming and going at the speed of wind. In Grotto No. 10, the shrine of Sanhuang (three emperors-legendary figures, including the emperor of heaven, emperor of earth and emperor of man) are 35 statues, represented realistically, that all look debonair and delicate, more human than god. Grotto No. 12, the shrine of Great Emperor Dongyue (God of Mountain Tai) , houses 98 statues, with Emperor Dongyue and Queen Shuming in the middle, reflecting the outstanding position of the Dongyue family in Taoist god system from the 10th century to the 13th century (the Song Dynasty) . Those belonging to Buddhist subject matter include Yaoshi (Master Pharmacist) Shrine, Water Moon Guanyin (Avalokitesvara) Shrine, Sakyamuni Buddha Shrine, Shisheng (ten saints) and Guanyin Shrine, Kongquemingwang Shrine and Helidimu Shrine, etc. Grotto No.6 with its representations of Shisheng (ten saints) and Guanyin, is the most refined of all.

Significance of the Heritage

As typical Dazu Rock Carvings, the rock carvings of Mt. Beishan, Mt. Nanshan, Mt. Shizhuanshan, Mt. Shimensha (also known more simply as"Five Mountains") is an important part of China's grotto art as well as the most grandiose page of world grotto art from the late 9th century to mid-13th century. The rock carvings of "Five Mountains" are well known across the world for their great size, elaborate carving, variety of subject matter, rich content and complete preservation. Dazu Rock Carvings differ from earlier grottos as the great achievement of statues of the three teachings of Buddhism, Confucianism and Taoism. The clear ethnic characteristics and true-to-life characteristics make it an independent school in China's grotto art. The great amount of actual images and written materials exhibit the important development and changes of grotto artistic style and folk religious belief from the 9th century to the mid-13th century. It has made great contribution to the innovation and development of China's grotto art. It is a treasure house of world heritage with unique characteristics.

Mount Emei Scenic Area, including Leshan Giant Buddha Scenic Area

Over Mount Emei the half moon hangs in autumn,
Its reflection shines on Pingqian, the rushing water flows.
In the moonlight I started from Qingxi to Three Gorges,
How I missed you on my Yuzhou voyage.
—Li Bai Song of the Moon over Mount Emei

Mount Emei, located in the county-level municipality of Mount Emei in Sichuan Province, has a scenic area of 154 square kilometers. Its peak, Wanfoding, is 3,099 meters above sea level. It is a national-level mountain area featuring natural scenery in conjunction with Buddhist culture.

Even before the Eastern Han Dynasty, legends about divine beings had been spreading in China, including that of Emperor Xuanyuan (An ancient emperor in Chinese mythology.) quizzing an immortal about Taoism, Ge You retiring into the mountains in a quest for immortality, and Jieyu of Chu choosing to live as a hermit in Mount Emei after satirizing Confucius for the latter's attempt to realize his ideals in the Spring-and-Autumn Period. Since all those legends took place in Mount Emei, this mountain became a fascinating resort of immortal beings to ordinary people. Later on, Mount Emei was listed as the seventh among the 36 havens of immortal beings, and so it became a famous Taoist resort. Taoism at Mount Emei developed in the Wei and Jin dynasties and reached its peak in the Tang Dynasty.

There is a Taoist book titled *Xianjian* (meaning identifying immortal beings) which lists ten famous men as "Ten Friends of Immortal Beings". Two distinguished poets of the Tang Dynasty Chen Zi'ang and Li Bai both visited Mount Emei in a quest for divine truth. Li climbed Mount Emei and lived in the mountain for quite some time when he was young. He composed a poem titled *Climbing Mount Emei*, in which there are famous lines like "In the land of Shu there are many mountains where immortals dwell/Mount Emei is one far beyond compare/Looking about, I try to climb to a vantage point/It is such a wonder, one cannot fully apprehend." The renowned poet not only praised Mount Emei as the supreme mountain, but also noted how Taoism flourished there. Even today, some temples and places in Mount Emei still retain Taoist names, such as the Hall of Chunyang, Yuxian Temple, and Xianfeng Temple. Yet among the Taoist figures only Zhao Gongming, god of wealth, is still worshipped by monks and laymen.

In the Song Dynasty Emperor Taizu and his successors spared no efforts in supporting Buddhism and Mount Emei was finally established as the bodhimanda of Bodhisattva Samantabhadra and so became a sacred mountain of Buddhism. In the Ming and Qing dynasties large numbers of Buddhist temples were erected due to governmental support and consequently Buddhism became the dominant religion in this mountain.

Main Scenic Attractions

Main Scenic Spots in Emei Scenic Area

Jiulao Cave (meaning the cave of nine immortal beings) Jiulao Cave is the largest cave of Mount Emei, with a total length of about 1,500 meters. The name of the cave comes from the legend that there used to be nine immortal beings practicing Taoism in the cave. The modern poet Lin Sanzhi has a poem entitled *Jiulao Cave*, in which he writes, "From the green pine trees comes the wind, and towers rise in a half sky. Inside there is a tame monkey, whistling sadly with grief now and then. The old monk summons the monkey, feeding it with green plums. They gently stroke each other, as affectionate as two little toddlers."

Jinding (Gold Peak) Jinding is the peak of Mount Emei with quite a number of beautiful views. It is 3,077 meters above sea level and the last stop of an Emei tour. Huazang Temple of the Tang Dynasty is situated on the top of the peak, its roof covered by tin-tiles. In this spot you may see the four wonders of Mount Emei-the sunrise, the sea of clouds, the Buddhist halo, and sanctuary lamps.

Baoguo Temple Baoguo Temple is the gateway to Mount Emei and the center for holding various Buddhist activities. It was built in the Wanli reign period of the Ming Dynasty and used to be named "Huizong Tang" (meaning the hall converging different sects". Inside, the enshrined sculptures include that of Budhisattva Samantabhadra (the number one disciple of Sakyamuni) , Guangchengzi (the incarnation of the founder of Taoism) and Lu Tong (a celebrated Confucius scholar) and so representatives of the three sects are all worshiped jointly here. The temple has an area of nearly 40,000 square meters. The main buildings include the gate of the temple, Maitreya Hall, Main Hall, the Seven-Buddha Hall, Samantabhadra Hall and Sutra Depository. They are arranged along the central axis and rise gradually with the mountain.

Qingyinge Qingyinge, also called Woyun Temple, is located in the place where the Black River and the White River converge, 710 meters above the sea level. Enshrined and worshipped in the temple are Buddha of Sakyamuni, Manjusri and Samantabhadra. Below the attic there is Shuangfei Pavilion (meaning the pavilion of double flying) with two bridges on either side like the wings of a bird. Under the pavilion where the two rivers join there is a giant rock as tall as 3.3 meters. Since it is shaped like the heart of an ox, it is named "Ox Heart Stone". Liu Guangdi, one of the six martyrs put to death at the end of the Wuxu Reformation (The reformation led by Emperor Guangxu of the Qing Dynasty in the year 1898.), once wrote a couplet for this stone, "Shadows of two rainbows flying double, heart of an ox for thousands of years."

Four Great Wonders of Mount Emei

The sea of clouds The sea of clouds in Mount Emei consists of low clouds; the peaks appear in the clouds as if they are many isles in the sea. The encircling clouds render the mountain a fairy land. The isles may also be compared to floating boats on the breakers and so this scene conveys the Buddhist notion of "the barge of mercy ferries all the miserable people to the world of bliss". The modern poet Zhao Puchu has lines describing this scenery, "The sky clothes itself with rosy clouds to welcome the sunrise, the peaks rise above the sea of clouds to float as barges."

The Sunrise Mount Emei towers on the west brim of Sichuan Basin, overlooking the vast land of the Tianfu Plain. Tourists climbing the peak may have fine extensive views, their minds cleansed. As the sun rises the sky turns rosy with thousand rays of sunlight shooting to the land. Mount Emei presents her graceful figure as if newly clothed in a golden cloak. Fan Chengda of the Southern Song Dynasty wrote the lines, "Clouds clothe the world for mortal beings, the sun accompanies me to make a journey through the world."

The Buddhist Halo The Buddhist Halo, also called the glory of Mount Emei, is said to be the brilliant rays from the brows of Samantabhadra. Actually the halo is a natural phenomenon resulting from the diffraction and diffusing reflection of the sunlight when the rays penetrate the clouds. Tan Zhongyue describes the scenery in the following lines, "What appears in the air? Not the cloud, not the fog, unique in color and splendor. Toward higher places take a look, everybody is a Buddha with a halo behind."

Sanctuary Lamps In the moonless nights sometimes you may see a dot of light appearing suddenly below Sheshen Rock. It is just the size of the light from a firefly. Then several dots of light appear and then many more. They float in the dark valley here and there and are referred to as sanctuary lamps by Buddhists. The famous Chinese meteorologist Zhu Kezhen listed it as one of the three mysteries of Mount Lu. Over thousands of years people made varied inferences and offered various explanations for the sanctuary lamps. Yet it remains a mystery even today. The monk Xincheng has a poem entitled *Sanctuary Lamps*, "From east of the steep cliff float dots of red. Some far, some near, flying in the misty sky. The flames are cold for thousands of years, their light wavering on the walls in the wind. When everybody has fallen asleep in the silent night, the lamps hang everywhere in the temple."

Leshan Giant Buddha

Leshan Giant Buddha, also called Buddha Maitreya, or Jiading Buddha, is located in Qiluan Peak at the east foot of Mount Emei. The carving of this Buddha began in the early years of the Kaiyuan reign period in the Tang Dynasty (713 A.D.) and lasted 90 years. The Buddha faces the river, backed by the mountain; it is the largest surviving cliff stone sculpture in the world. There is a saying that "the mountain is a Buddha and the Buddha is a mountain". The Buddha Maitreya sits sedately facing west with a total height of 71 meters. The meticulous carving, smooth lines, well-proportioned body and grand and imposing gesture all capture the grandeur of the high Tang style. The Buddha has high artistic value and rich cultural connotations. It is a treasure of Chinese culture and precious heritage in world history and culture.

Over hundreds of years from the Ming and Qing dynasties Leshan Buddha has been subject to weathering and heavily damaged. After the founding of People's Republic of China the government invested 0.5 billion RMB to do reconstruction work of the Buddha and improve the surrounding environment. Now the Buddha has taken on a new look and appears more authentic and complete.

Significance of the Heritage

According to archaeological evidence, the earliest settlers appeared in this region as early as ten thousand years ago. The human history of this region with documentary records and historical traces stretches back over 2,000 years. During such a long period of time the early settlers created splendid culture and left a rich historical heritage. The introduction of Buddhism, the construction of temples and the prosperity of Buddhism added a flavor of mystery to this "Fairy Mountain of Shu" well-known for its magnificence and beauty. Buddhist culture, especially Buddhism, constitutes the main body of its history and culture. All the architecture, sculptures, musical instruments, rituals, music and art manifest the strong flavor of religious culture and distinctive features. There are over 30 temples all together on this mountain, among which Feilai Hall and the Beamless Brick Hall of Wannian Temple are first-rate and second-rate national protection spots. All the architecture embraces local tradition and the style of local dwelling with elegant and modest furnishing. The temples are all exceptional in location, design and construction and possess both the majesty of temples and the beauty of landscape. They have become models of architectural artistry in scenic areas of China.

Historic Monuments of Dengfeng in "The Centre of Heaven and Earth"

In the cosmological perspective of early Chinese people, China was at the centre of heaven and earth, while the centre of heaven and earth was Songshan of Dengfeng. The early Chinese dynasties established their capitals in Dengfeng to symbolise that their power was conferred by god. Prompted by the concept of "centre of heaven and earth", the various cultural schools, such as ancient social institutions, astronomy, Confucianism, Buddhism and Taoism, were keen to set up their core base at Songshan, and thus it gradually became the centre of Chinese civilization. Representative structures of various dynasties associated with social institutions, religion, science and technology, and education were gathered here and have been well-preserved, which give this place great historical, artistic and scientific value.

Main Scenic Attractions

Taishi Que Located below Huanggai Peak of Taishi Mountain, to the east of Dengfeng city, this is on the axis 600 meters in front of Zhongtian Pavilion in Zhongyue Temple. First built in the 5th year of the Yuanchu reign period (118 A.D.) of Emperor Hanan, Taishi Que was built with black-grey stones. It consisted of East Que and West Que, with 6.75m between them; facing each other like doors, the two Que were the symbolic gates of Taishi Temple. The Que had a rectangular plan, topped with an eaved roof, built of stone, but imitating the design of a wooden structure. Each of the Que was composed of a mother Que and a child Que. As an important witness to the practice of offering sacrifice to the god of Taishi Mountain, Taishi Temple was a model of ancient buildings designed for ceremonial purpose, and as such has great value for the study of architectural history, artistic history, and the social conditions of the Eastern Han Dynasty.

Shaoshi Que As the sacred way Que of Shaoshishan Temple in the Han Dynasty, Shaoshi Que is to the west of Shilipu Village, which lies on the southern slopes of Songshan, 6 kilometers west of Dengfeng City. Shaoshi Temple and Taishi Temple were built in the Qin Dynasty, and during the reign of Emperor Andi of the Han Dynasty, the Que was built in front of the temple. Behind the Que is a platform, 60m long from east to west and 40m wide from north to south, on the site of the original Shaoshi Temple. According to *Stele Record for Tang Shaoyi Temple* written by Yang Jiong, the name of Shaoshi Temple was changed to Shaoyi Temple in the Tang Dynasty, and its god was in the form of a woman, said to be the younger sister of Tushanshi. In the Yuan period, "Shaoyi" was said to be Lei Zu, the Chinese silkworm goddess. Yang Huan, a poet of the Yuan Dynasty, wrote a poem about Shaoyi Temple when he visited Zhongyue (i.e. Songshan), "On the roadside, the twin Que have become old, with wild weeds growing in the deserted temple; now and then mountain girls come burning incense for better silk."

Qimu Que Qimu Que, below Wansui Peak in south Songshan, 2km to the northwest of Dengfeng City, was the symbolic gate in front of Qimu Temple in the Han Dynasty. 190m to the north of Qimu Que was a huge cracked rock, called "Qimu Rock". According to *Huai Nan Zi*, the writings of Prince Huainan, occupied with combating flood, Dayu passed his home three times but did not enter. His wife, Tushanshi, turned into a big rock, which cracked and gave birth to Qi, hence there circulated in later generations the story of "hearing the drum and taking food to her husband".

The Observatory It is located in Zhougong Temple 13 kilometres at the southeast of Dengfeng City. The buildings still existing here, from the south to the north, include the Screen Wall, the Gate, the Instrument Door, the Sundial Platform of Zhougong, the Round Ridge Roof of Zhougong Temple, the Main Hall, the Observatory and the Temple of Emperor Yao, etc. The Observatory, built from 1271-1294 A.D., is the earliest existing observatory in China that is still very well preserved. It is also one of the earliest astronomy buildings in the world.

The Sundial Platform of Zhougong Popularly known Shadowless Table, the stone table for memorial purpose was the legacy of the Shadow Measuring Template of ancient times. According to legend, Zhougong (that is, Ji Dan) , the second son of King Wen of Zhou Dynasty, came here and measured the shadow for the construction of Luoyang. In the 11th year of Kaiyuan of the Tang Dynasty (723 A.D.) , Nangong Shuo, the astromomical officer, erected the 2.16-metre-tall Stone Table by modeling after the Shadow Measuring Template of Zhougong. The stone Sundial Platform consisted of pedestal and stone pillar. The stone pillar was the dial, and the pedestal was the template. At the top of the template was the roof, and on the south side of the template was carved the characters "the Sundial Platform of Zhougong". The main function of the Dengfeng Observatory was to measure the length of the shadow of the sun so as to master the solar term changes of the four seasons concerned with agriculture.

Zhongyue Temple First built in the 2th century B.C., Zhongyue Temple is the biggest surviving ancient Taoist building cluster; it is built to the highest specifications and is the best preserved of any in China. Richly ornamented, with carved beams and painted rafters, the whole temple has a similar layout pattern to the Forbidden City. The ancient cypress trees planted in Qin and Han dynasties, tablet inscriptions of the Northern Wei Dynasty and the iron man of the Song Dynasty authentically reflect the long process of the development and rich meaning of Taoist culture and have witnessed the history of Taoist culture, in which the belief in "the centre of heaven and earth" is deeply embedded.

Songyang Academy of Classical Learning It was first established in the 8th year of Taihe in the Northern Wei (484 A.D.) , and it became the best of the four famous academies in the country. It was the earliest academy in China, and was the originating place and spreading centre of Cheng-zhu Neo-Confucianism. Distinguished Confucian scholars, such as Sima Guang, Fan Zhongyan, Cheng Yi, Cheng Hao, etc. gave lectures one after another, and the academy acquired great fame. Many restoration and expansion projects during the Jin, Yuan, Ming and Qing dynasties, resulted in the present size and rigorous arrangement. The academy maintains the construction layout of the Qing Dynasty—an axis construction of 5 courtyards, from south to north successively the front gate, Hall of the Sage (Confucius) , Lecture Hall, Daotong (Confucian orthodoxy) Temple and Collection House. On both sides of the axis are side buildings and Jingyizhai of the West Courtyard. There are 25 buildings and108 rooms. The plan layout and material objects have unique features and illustrative value in the study of ancient Chinese academic buildings, the educational system, and Confucian culture.

Building Cluster of Shaolin Temple

The Building cluster of Shaolin Temple consists mainly of three parts: Changzhuyuan (what is usually called Shaolin Temple) , Talin (the Forest of Pagodas) and Chuzu (initial ancestor) Temple. The main body of Shaolin Temple is Changzhuyuan, having a series of seven buildings along a single axis, which from south to north are successively the Mountain Gate, Hall of Heavenly King, the Main Hall, Dharma Hall, Abbot Yard, Lixue Pavilion and Thousand-buddha Hall.

Changzhuyuan This was first built in the 19th year of the Taihe period (495 A.D.) of the Northern Wei Dynasty. Over 30 buildings built in Ming and Qing dynasties are still preserved within the monastery, and each one of them has a heart-touching story to tell. The relics of 500 Arhats Facing Pilu, Shaolin Quan Manual and the fresco of 13 Monks Holding Sticks Saving Prince Qinwang (the later Emperor Tang Taizong) reflect the cultural communication between China and other countries, the fusion of Chinese culture with other cultures and innovation and development made by Chinese artists.

Chuzu Temple Chuzu Temple, one of the historical building clusters of the Centre of Heaven and Earth, is located at Mt. Fuqiu under Wuru Peak 2 kilometres northwest of Shaolin Temple. The small building cluster was built by the later monks in memory of Bodhidharma facing the wall and meditating for nine years in the Dharma Cave of Shaolin Temple.

Talin (Forest of Pagodas) The Talin of Shaolin Temple, housing the tombs of the prestigious monks of all generations, is situated at the west side of the temple. The pagodas are in all kinds of shapes, such as square or hexagonal, columns and cones, straight and parabolic, round and bottle-shaped, carved from a single rock, etc. Most famous and most representative among the pagodas are: Fawan Pagoda, erected in the 7th year of the Zhenyuan Era of the Tang Dynasty; Putong Pagoda, erected in the 3rd year of the year Xuanhe Era of the Song Dynasty; Xitang Pagoda, the 2nd year of the Zhenglong Era of the Jin Dynasty; Zhonglin Pagoda, of the 27th year of the Zhiyuan Era of the Yuan, Tanran Pagoda of the 8th year of the Wanli Era of the Ming Dynasty; and Bi'an Pagoda of the 5th year of Kangxi of the Qing Dynasty.

Biggest in size, Talin of Shaolin Temple has the most pagodas of any Buddhist monastery in China. There are 241 brick-stone pagodas of the dynasties of Tang, Song, Yuan, Ming and Qing and 2 modern pagodas. The whole Talin takes up an area of 14,000 square metres. Shaolin Talin is a precious treasury for studying ancient brick-stone buildings and the carving art of China.

Significance of the Heritage

Most representative of the Dengfeng "Centre of Heaven and Earth" complex, and as the most scientifically, technologically, artistically and historically valuable ancient buildings, 8 sites and 11 historical and cultural heritages passed through the dynasties of Han, Wei, Tang, Song, Yuan, Ming, Qing, constituting a visual architectural history of over 2000 years of Central China.

Shaoshi Que and Qimu Que are the oldest models of national-level ceremonial buildings of China; Zhongyue Temple and Taishi Que are the most comprehensive examples of China's ancient ceremonial building pattern; the Songyang Academy of Classical Learning, the earliest academy spreading Lixue, a Confucian school of idealist philosophy of the Song and Ming dynasties, worshipping Confucian sages and holding tests, is the carrier of the now defunct academy culture; Songyue Temple Pagoda, Shaolin Temple building clusters, and Huishan Temple are the momuments of the development of Buddhism in different time periods in China, and have influenced, in the course of over a thousand years, the religious architectural pattern in a wide range. This building cluster is very rare, when one takes into consideration such factors as architectural type, standard of achievement, length of time, richness of meaning, and depth and breadth of influence. They are outstanding examples of ancient buildings associated with social institutions, religion, science and technology, and education in China.

Ancient Building Complex in the Wudang Mountains

Situated in sounthwest Danjiangkou City in northwest Hubei Province, the Wudang Mountains, also named Taihe mountains and Xuanyue mountains, is a famous Taoist holy place. In an area of 400 square kilometres, there are 72 peaks, 24 caves, 3 pools, 9 springs, 10 ponds, 9 wells, 10 rocks, 9 platforms, and many Taoist temples. Xu Xiake, the famous Ming traveller, considered that "Xuanyue is above Wuyue (the five ancient Taoist mountains, including Mt. Tai, Mt. Hua, Mt. Heng, Mt. Song and Mt. Heng)."

The long history of Mt. Wudang is closely related to Taoism. According to *Tujing* (the Map Classic) , "Wudang is the home of gods. Many gods and people came and stayed here ever since the establishment of the religion." From the Zhou Dynasty to the end of the Eastern Han Dynasty, Wudang had already been a place attractive to hermits and those who practiced immortal cultivation and alchemy. With the birth of Taoism in the later years of the Eastern Han Dynasty, Mt. Wudang gradually turned into the main place of Taoist activities in China. In the periods of the Three Kingdoms, Wei, Jin and the Southern and Northern dynasties, there was a notable increase in the number of people who came here for immortal cultivation, and Mt. Wudang was already named "Taihe" and "Xianshi", names rich in Taoist hue. The rulers of the Tang Dynasty claimed to be the descendants of Laozi (Li Er) and as such, respected and supported Taoism to give it leading position among the three main religions. During the Zhenguan period (627-649) of the Tang Dynasty, many grand Taoist temples were built; they were enlarged in the Song and Yuan dynasties and came to a peak in the Ming Dynasty.

Landscape Characteristics

By making full use of the high and magnificent mountain settings and the steep and secluded cliff caves, every temple was built in a suitable position so as to form a harmonious whole with the surrounding forest, rocks and streams. Some temples are huge and grand, some are small and exquisite, some are hidden in deep valleys, some are built on cliffs, and the buildings create with the beautiful mountain an unique humanistic scenery that gives visitors a marvellous aesthetic feeling and intriguing sensation of being in a fairyland. The buildings achieve great harmony with the natural environment.

From Jingle Palace to Tianzhu (Heavenly Pillar) Peak, there are thirty-three clusters of buildings constructed by the imperial house, all of which are arranged by strictly following the regulations instituted according to status. Large-size Taoist temples adopt architectural norms restricted to the royal family, in that the main axis is given emphasis, clearly reflecting the guiding principle of "the imperial authority as the axis".

Various in types, using a wide range of materials and all kinds of design, structure, decoration and furnishing, all the Wudang buildings, be they wood temples, bronze palaces, stone rock temples, or statues in bronze, wood, stone, or clay, have reached an extremely high technological and artistic level. Meanwhile, this is also the place of origin of Wudang Taoism, Wudang Taoist Music and Wudang Martial Arts, which have added new content to traditional Chinese culture.

Main Scenic Attractions

Jindian (Golden Shrine) Popularly known as "Golden Summit", Jindian is situated at the top of Tianzhu Peak, the main peak of Mt. Wudang. The wood building structured in the form of a palace built in Ming Dynasty is as wide as its depth and has twelve pillars all around. The altar, with the sitting statue of Zhenwu Dadi, the god of water in Taoism, is set in front of the screen of the back wall. Above the altar is hung a huge golden plaque with four chacters reading "Jin Guang Miao Xiang" (golden ray and wonderful image) written by Emperor Kangxi of Qing Dynasty. Every part of the shrine, including the tiles and wood pieces, are so precisely structured and well-knit that after five hundred years of erosion by wind and rain, they still remain just as magnificent as if new, reflecting the high level of China's foundry industry.

Zijincheng(Forbidden City) Built in the 17th year of the Yongle era (1419) , "Zi" in Zijincheng means "the purple air coming from the East", signifying a propitious omen, and "Jin" means forbidden place of the imperial family, so it is obvious that Zijincheng, besides protecting Jindian, the golden shrine, is endowed with political connotation. Also named Huangcheng (Imperial City) , Zijincheng is 10 to 30m tall and 344m in perimetre. It is at the top of Tianzhu Peak and is constructed of strip stone, each one of which is close to 500 kg. When seen from a distance, with the glow of light hanging over it, the golden palace looks magnificent and attractive. Lingguandian Gallery just inside Nantianmen (South Heavenly Gate) Gate appears dark, deep and chilly. At the top of the stone stairs is a small piece of flat land on which is the tin-made Lingguandian Palace, small and ancient looking, a rare relic.

Zixiao Palace Below Zhanqi Peak at northeast Wudang Mountain, Zixiao Palace, whose main buildings are about six hundred years old, is the best preserved Wudang palace. Making full use of the terrain, which is steep vertically but spacious laterally, the whole building follows an axis, advancing level by level to form three courtyands that are distinct in priorities and solemn in air, reflecting the dignity of this ceremonial site.

Nanyan Palace Located at the precipice of Nanyan (also known as Zixiaoyan and Duyangyan) , touching the blue sky at the top and close to a gully down below, among surrounding steep peaks and green woods, Nanyan Palace is the most beautiful among the 36 scenic spots of Mt.

Wudang. The building of Nanyan Palace started in the Tang Dynasty, and it was enlarged in the Song, Yuan, Ming and Qing dynasties. It consists of 640 rooms and halls. The comprehensive planning of the Nanyan Palace building cluster, near hillside and resting on rocks, is ingenious, making clever use of the terrain. Breaking away from the traditional absolute symmetrical way of layout and pattern, the palaces, halls and temples here are built on precipice and cliff. The man-made buildings are just like the work of nature in that they stay in great harmony and integration with nature, thus realizing the high conception of "the unity of nature and man".

Fuzhen Temple Fuzhen Temple is also known as Taizipo (Crown Prince Slope) . Taking advantage of the special terrain of Shizi (Lion) Peak, this ancient building group, called the "Serpentine Yellow River Wall", was elaborately designed in accordance with the cultivation story of Zhenwu. Just inside the second gate is a spacious, quiet and comfortable courtyard where there are small yards. Wubulou (Five-step Building) is in the front, Huangjingge Pavilion and Cangjingge Pavilion are in the middle, and Taizidian Hall is high on the platform in the back. The layout, the left and right sides being asymmetrical and the height of the buildings varying, is perfectly tuned and fully exemplifies the notion of the Taoist principle "Quietism".

Mozhen Well Also known as Chunyang Palace, Mozheng Well is a courtyard-styled Taoist temple built in the period of Emperor Kangxi. It is smartly arranged and compactly structured. There remain 52 rooms composed of the Mountain Gate, the Main Hall, the Side Hall, Laomu Pavilion and East Taoist Yard. The picture of *Zhenwu Cultivating Immortality* in the Main Hall vividly illustrates the stories of Zhenwu cultivating immortality and turning into an immortal god. The style of the painting is simple and primitive. Inside the yard is an ancient well, with an iron pestle erected beside it. According to legend, enlightened by the philosophy that "When enough efforts have been made, an iron pestle can be turned into a needle" edified by Mulao, incarnation of Ziyunjun, the Crown Prince Zhenwu finally turned into a god.

Significance of the Heritage

Among the ancient buildings in Mt. Wudang, the palaces and temples collectively reflect the artisitic achievement of both secular and religious architecture in the three dynasties of Yuan, Ming and Qing, and represent the highest standard of Chinese art and architecture in nearly a thousand years. The combination of the beauty of mountain and water with that of architecture gives the ancient building complex of Mt. Wudang its unique features of serenity, emptiness and holiness. The application of all kinds of techniques and skills, such as "scene borrowing" and "reality and unreality", produced remarkable architectural scenery.

The surviving four Taoist palaces, two palace sites, two Taoist temples and numerous shrines and rock temples are kept intact as far as format, style, materials used and techniques are concerned. The main buildings, with palace and temple as the centre, are distributed in the basin or mesa, nunneries and shrines are close to palaces and temples, and rock temples are built on perilous peaks, which together result in the great scenery of "a nunnery every five li (2.5 kilometre) and a palace every ten, with exquisite red-walled, green-roofed buildings." Being nearly perfect in aspects of architectural art and aesthetics and rich in ancient Chinese cultural and scientific connotations, the temples supply physical evidence for the study of early Ming politics and examples for the research of Chinese history of religion and ancient architecture.

Mount Wutai

Buddhism was first introduced into China in the Eastern Han Dynasty. According to historical records, in December of the tenth year of the Yongping period (67 A.D.) envoys sent west to seek Buddhist wisdom by Emperor Mingdi returned to Luoyang with two eminent monks from India, Kasyapa Molten and Dharmaratna. In the following year the two monks went to Mount Wutai with permission from the emperor to build a temple. After the temple was completed it was named Vulture Temple due to the shape of the mountain. Since then Mount Wutai has become the center of Buddhism in China. Dafu Vulture Temple here and the Temple of the White Horse in Luoyang are the two earliest temples in China.

Main Scenic Attractions

Five Peaks

Dongtai (East Flat-topped Peak) This is also called Wanghai Peak (meaning the peak for viewing the peaks) with the top shaped like the spine of a turtle. It is located 10 kilometers to the northeast of Taihuai Township and is 2,795 meters above the sea level. The top is smallest in area with only 70,000 square meters. According to legend there was a Wanghai Tower on the top of this peak previously and from the tower one could see the sunrise over the East Sea. Presently, although the tower is no longer there, one can still watch the sun rise and have a good view of the scenery and the changing clouds. Pagoda Lizi, built during the Xuanhe reign period (from 1119 to 1125) , still stands on this peak. It has the appearance of an overturned bowl-shaped Lamaist pagoda.

Xitai (West Flat-topped Peak) This peak is also called Guayue Peak. 23 kilometers from Taihuai Township, it is 2,773 meters above sea level with an area of about 280, 000 square meters. It is surrounded by peaks. Previously there was Falei Temple built on the summit, with a sculpture of Manjusri Bodhisattva mounted on his lion in this temple.

Nantai (South Flat-topped Peak) This is also called Jinxiu Peak. 25 kilometers to the south of Taihuai Township, it is 2,485 meters above sea level with an area of about 140, 000 square meters. The peak is steep and looks beautiful with all the green vegetation. Puji Temple, on the summit, has a sculpture of Manjusri, Bodhisattva of wisdom.

Beitai (North Flat-topped Peak) This is also called Yedou Peak, about 25 kilometers away from Taihuai Township. It is the highest peak among the five peaks, at 3,058 meters above the sea level. The towering peak is called "the roof of North China". On top of the peak is Lingying Temple with the sculpture of Manjusri Bodhisattva Immaculate.

Zhongtai (the Central Flat-topped Peak) This is also called Cuishi Peak, 10 kilometers from Taihuai Township with an area of 150,000 square meters on the top. This peak is bigger than the other four. To the northwest of the peak is Taihua Pool, to the north is Ganlu Spring, to the southeast is Yulong Pool with three springs beside the pool. Yulong Pool is the place where the five streams to the north and south rise. On the top of the peak there is Yanjiao Temple, with a statue of Manjusri Bodhisattva. There is also Qiguang Pagoda, built in the Ming Dynasty, with four small pagodas on the four corners resembling the five flat peaks (or terraces) of Mount Wutai.

Ten Great Temples

Foguang Temple It is situated in Foguang New Village. The main hall is the East Hall, constructed in the 11th year of the Dazhong reign period of the Tang Dynasty (857 A.D.) , a bit later than the main hall of Nanchan Temple, and it ranks number two among the surviving wooden structure buildings in China. The architecture, sculpture, frescos and inscriptions of the Tang Dynasty in the temple are of high historical and artistic value and are called the "Four Wonders of the Tang Dynasty."

Xiantong Temple Xiantong Temple is situated to the north of Taihuai Township, within the area of five peaks. The seven Jiuhui halls were a Huayan bodhimanda laid by Master Miaofeng with rubbed bricks in accordance with the order of Emperor Shenzong of the Ming Dynasty (1606) . This temple was originally built in the Yongping period of the Eastern Han Dynasty (58-75 A.D.) and named Dafu Vulture Temple at that time. Later on it was rebuilt by the Xiaowen Emperor of the Northern Wei Dynasty and renamed Garden Temple. It underwent another reconstruction in the reign of Emperor Taizong of the Tang Dynasty and got the name Huayan Temple. Emperor Taizu of the Ming Dynasty (named Zhu Yuanzhang) had the temple rebuilt and presented to this temple a horizontal tablet with the name " 大显通寺 " (Great Xiantong Temple) . Later the temple underwent further expansions and repairs and finally took on its present shape. It now had an area of 80,000 square meters, with over 400 bays of structures. It has its own prominent features and is well preserved.

Tayuan Temple It is located to the south of Xiantong Temple in Taihuai Township and originally was a pagoda chamber of Xiantong Temple. In the Ming Dynasty the Stupa Pagoda was rebuilt and so this chamber became one separate temple. Since there is a tall white pagoda, this temple got the name Tayuan Temple (meaning the Pagoda Chamber Temple) . The towering white pagoda is the main emblem of this temple; it appears magnificent among the temples of this famous mount.

Pusading Temple It is located on Vulture Peak to the north of Xiantong Temple in Taihuai Township and is the largest Tibetan Buddhist Temple of Mount Wutai. It was first built during the reign of Emperor Xiaowen of the Northern Wei Dynasty and underwent many reconstructions in later dynasties. From the Yongle Period in the early Ming Mongolian and Tibetan Lamaist monks began to reside in Mount Wutai and so it has become the number one Tibetan Buddhist Temple among all the temples in Mount Wutai. The temple claims an area of 45 mu, and the halls and other buildings are laid out in accordance with the shape of the mountain. There are 108 stone staircases in front of the temple. Inside there are Hall of Heavenly Kings, the Bell-and-Drum Tower, Mahavira Hall, etc. All the halls are covered by three-colored glazed tiles.

Shuxiang Temple It is located to the west of the Cheng Temple of the Putuo Sect, at the north foot of Lion Valley. In the 26th year of Emperor Qianlong's reign (1761) , the emperor accompanied his dowager mother to make a pilgrimage to Shuxiang Temple. The emperor was impressed by the serene visage of Manjusri Bodhisattva and "memorized the Buddha's visage and returned to Beijing". After their return the dowager mother had the Buddha statue sculptured in stone according to what she saw in the temple and had the statue placed in a niche in Baoxiang Temple of Mount Fragrance. In the 39th year of the Qianlong reign period (1774) , Emperor Qianlong had a statue of Manjusri sculpted according to that of Baoxiang Temple and a temple built in Chengde to harbor this statue. This temple was manned by Lamaist monks of Manchu nationality and so this temple was called the home temple by the royal court of Qing Dynasty.

Bishan Temple It is located at the foot of Beitai, two kilometers to the northeast of Taihuai Township. It was first built during the reign of Emperor Yingzong of the Ming Dynasty and is the largest temple in Mount Wutai, providing free meals and accommodation to monks and lay Buddhists. (Such temples are called Shifang Temples) . If the pilgrims lack fare when they start, they may even get a special subsidy from the temple. For this reason many pilgrims make a point of visiting this temple during their pilgrimage.

Jinge Temple Jinge Temple is located to the north of Nantai and the south of Zhongtai. Among the temples of Mount Wutai, this temple is above 1,900 meters in height, virtually the most lofty location. This temple has aq close relationship to the spread of Vajrayana in China and the founder of this sect, Master Bukong.

Nanshan Temple It was first built in the Yuan dynasty. The whole temple comprises seven terraces divided into three sections. The lower section made up of three terraces is called Jile Temple, the middle section of one terrace is called Shande Hall and the upper section of three terraces is called Youguo Temple.

The stone and clay sculptures in the temple are most characteristic. They are about Buddhist legends, Taoist anecdotes and patterns of trees and flowers. They feature fine cutting and exquisite patterning and may be deemed a wonder of Mount Wutai.

Longquan Temple This temple is located on the slope of Jiulonggang, 5 kilometers south of Taihuai Township. Longquan Temple used to be the home temple of the Yang Clan of Generals (according to Chinese lore, male and female members of this clan successively became generals to support the Northern Song Court against foreign invasions) . There is a spring named Longquan (meaning "dragon's spring") and so the temple is named after it. It was first built in Song Dynasty and rebuilt in the early years of the Republic of China. It occupies an area of 15,950 square meters and comprises 165 bays of halls and monk rooms. Presently there are three courtyards respectively of Screen Wall, Terrace and Memorial Gateways.

Puji Temple Puji Temple is 25 kilometers to the south of Taihuai Township and 2,485 meters above sea level. The flat peak has an area of about 140,000 square meters. The peak is steep and the flowers are luxuriant, so it is also named Jinxiu Peak. On the flat top is Puji Temple with a statue of Majusri, Bodhisattva of wisdom.

Significance of the Heritage

Mount Wutai enjoys a long history. During a 15-century-long span of history, a large-scale, magnificent, classical and solemn temple complex emerged that was perfectly integrated with the natural environment. The scale and time span of the temple architecture render it number one in Asia and the world. The temples of different size, shape and layout have their own particular features and manifest the concept of "man and nature in one" and display to the utmost "the Golden Mean" of Confucianism and the philosophical idea of "everything is a unity of yin and yang" of Laozi. It is a witness to the history of Buddhism in China with unique implications and values. Mount Wutai is utterly unique.

Mount Taishan

Mt.Taishan, named Mt.Dai in ancient times, also named Mt. Daizong, is located in the middle of Shandong Province. To the south it is adjacent to Qufu, the home town of the Confucius, and to the north it comes close to Jinan, the city of springs. It is about 200 kilometers from east to west and 50 kilometers from north to south and so this mountain covers an area as large as 426 square kilometers. The highest peak of Mt. Taishan, Yuhuangding (meaning the top of Jade Emperor) , is located to the north of Tai'an and 1,545 meters above sea level. Mt. Taishan stretches between three cities, namely, Tai'an, Jinan and Laiwu and runs through the middle of Shandong with the main range, branch range, and complementary range stretching into a dozen surrounding counties. The natural landscape of Mt. Taishan is imposing and magnificent, and the mountain has also accumulated a rich body of cultural associations over several thousand years. It is deemed an epitome of Chinese spirit and culture.

Scenic and Historic Sites

The views of Mt. Taishan are well-known for grandeur. The stacking mountains with massive shapes set off by the pine trees and huge rocks together with the changes of clouds and vapor imbue this mountain with both masculine strength and feminine beauty. It is both magical and solemn, and so has come to be regarded as a mountain possessing a number of outstanding qualities associated with Chinese mountains.

The scenic spots of Mt. Taishan are centered on the highest peak, with other sites of interest scattered around. They feature a fusion of natural scenery and cultural relics. There are 156 peaks, 138 cliff ranges, 72 famous caves, 72 unusual rocks, 130 valleys and gullies, 64 waterfalls and lakes, 72 famous springs, over ten thousand ancient or famous trees, 58 temples, 128 ruins, 1,239 stone steles and 1,277 cliff inscriptions. The spots are mainly distributed on the north and south slopes of the mountain, on the summit, and at Lingyan.

Main Scenic Spots

The 18 Hairpin Bends There are three sets of hairpin bends in Mt. Taishan. From Kaishan to Longmen is "the loose 18 bends"; from Longmen to Shengxianfang is "the neither tight not loose 18 bends" while the set of stairs from Shengxianfang to Nantianmen is called "the compact 18 bends". The three sets of 18 bends make up over 1,630 stairs altogether. On either side of "the compact 18 bends" there is a huge rock in the air looking like Buddha's head reclining on a pillow in profile and so nicknamed "guest-greeting Buddha". The 18 bends are the steepest section of the ascending flight, with a grade of 70 to 80 degrees. This section is one notable spot on Mt. Taishan. Here the opposing cliffs on either side are clear-cut, with the steep stairs between. Viewed from a distance, this flight looks like an aerial ladder to the Gate of Heaven.

South Gate of Heaven At the end of the 18 Hairpin Bends is the Gate of Heaven or Gate of Heaven Pass, 1,460 meters above sea level. It is in the lower section between the confronting Flying Dragon Rock and Flying Phoenix Range and so the Gate of Heaven appears to be an entrance way supplied by nature. The gate is of tower design with a stone vaulted doorway above which is inscribed "South Gate of Heaven" on the horizontal tablet. The gate structure looks quite imposing with red walls and yellow-tiled roof.

Dai Temple This has been described as the pre-eminent temple on one of China's famous mountains. It was first built in the Qin and Han dynasties and later expanded in the Song. It used to be the imperial residence when emperors came to Mt. Taishan. Before holding the Fengshan ceremony on Mt. Taishan, they would first hold a ceremony here before climbing the mountain. Tiankuang Hall to the north of Ren'an Gate is the main structure, built in the second year of the Dazhong Xiangfu period (1009). This hall is built on a rectangular stone platform and surrounded by carved railings on three sides. It is 48.7 meters long, 19.73 meters wide and 22.3 meters tall. This is a double-eave structure with hip and gable roof covered by painted tiles. There are painted brackets in this building and eight bright-red columns under the eaves. This gigantic hall of splendor and grandeur matches the Taihe Hall in the Forbidden City in Beijing and the Dacheng Hall in Qufu. Together these buildings are known as "the three grand halls in ancient China".

Four Wonders of Mt. Taishan

Sunrise on Mt. Taishan This is the most splendid view at Mt. Taishan and also an important emblem of this mountain. Viewing sunrise on the peak has always been a fascinating event to tourists and also inspires men of letters to compose famous lines. At daybreak, tourists standing on the top of the peak look eastward and see a thread of dark gray sunlight turning light yellow, and then turning orange. The rosy clouds on the whole sky merge with the boundless clouds on the horizon and it seems a gigantic oil painting has fallen from heaven. On the glittering sea the sun removes the curtain of clouds and rises slowly from the horizon as if a floating palace lantern. In an instant, the sun shines and bathes all the surrounding mountains in splendor.

The Jade Dish among the Clouds The clouds and fogs of Mt. Taishan have various shapes. Sometimes billowing clouds are like foam on the sea while at other times dark clouds roll across the sky as if rivers and seas have been overturned. Looking downward from the mountaintop one may see silver clouds merging with dark clouds and converge into a running torrent. Such sceneries are so exciting that they never fail to stir your feelings.

The Evening Clouds at Sunset If you take a walk and look westward as the sun goes down, you will see colorful clouds, bright as rose or white as snow. The rosy sunshine in the sea of clouds appears grand and intoxicating.

The Gold Belt of the Yellow River This scene, like the previous one, largely depends on the season and the weather of Mt. Taishan. In autumn when the sky is high and the weather fine, take a look around, the graceful scenery of the nature can be taken in one glance.

The Four Buddhist Temples

Lingyan Temple This temple is located in the northwest foothills of Mt. Taishan in Wande Township, Changqing district, Jinan. It was first built in the Eastern Jin Dynasty and has a history of over 1,600 years. This time-honored temple has rich Buddhist legacy and is called the first temple among "the four most well-known temples" since the Tang Dynasty. The other three are Guoqing Temple of Zhejiang Province, Qixia Temple of Nanjing and Yuquan Temple of Hubei Province.

Puzhao Temple It is located below Linghan Peak at the foot of Mt. Taishan. Embraced by peaks outside, with the pavilions, towers and halls in the shade of pine and cypress trees, this temple has a lofty atmosphere. It is said to be built during the Northern and Southern Dynasties and has undertaken repairs and expansions in succeeding dynasties. With the main hall and Mosong Building as the main architecture, this temple has three courtyards. On the two sides of the temple there are hall verandas, meditation rooms and gardens. There is Shaiyue Pavilion in the temple, under whose roof is a stone table which will give off chimes of bells and Qing (Qing, a kind of ancient Chinese musical instrument.) on being beaten. When General Feng Yuxiang (Feng was a high-rank Kuomingdang general.) lived a secluded life in Mt. Taishan he composed the couplet, "the winding paths in the clouds are suitable for growing bamboo, and empty pavilion under the bright moon is opposite to Mosong Building." The courtyard in the back of the temple is called Julin Chamber. Inside there is a pine tree with canopy-like crown. A personage of literary reputation visited this chamber during Emperor Guangxu's reign and titled this pine tree "First-Rank Courtier". Now this chamber has been converted into a memorial. There are couplets on two sides of the door, "here the pine tree is dark green, the bamboo fresh green; there the sky is just a brick for me, the earth a tile."

Zhulin Temple This is in the valley on the west of Mt. Taishan, a temple of graceful scenery with bamboos surrounding the temple and pine and cypress trees inside. Of this temple it has been written, "Clear streams flow by the little path in the mountains. Wending one's way along the meandering track, every step will bring a new view." The origin of this temple is now in obscurity. Since the Tang Dynasty this temple has been rebuilt several times. According to historical record, a distinguished monk Fahai had this temple rebuilt in the Yuanzhen Period of the Yuan Dynasty. The reputation of this temple reached far and pilgrims came from far away: from east Shandong to the east, north Hebei province to the north, Shanxi province in the west, and the Yellow River in the south. Later this temple was burned down and presently a new temple of Tang style is being reconstructed.

Yuquan Temple It is located to the north of the summit and can be reached from Tai'an by highway. In the vicinity are Lotus Peak, Incense-Burner Peak, the Site of Zhouming Hall and Tianjing Gulf on the southeast; Motian Ranges to the west; Rice Shed on the south; Mt. Fandao and Mt. Changcheng to the north. So this temple may be described as surrounded by mountains and dense woods with tall cliffs and secluded valleys. It was initially built by monk Yisuo of the Northern Wei during Northern and Southern Dynasties and rebuilt by monk Shanning of the Jin Dynasty. In the Yuan Dynasty monk Pujin added a Seven-Buddha Tower in this temple. In later years this temple went through various cycles of prosperity and decline.

Significance of the Heritage

Mt. Taishan, together with Mt. Heng (衡) in the south, Mt. Hua in the west, Mt. Heng (恒) in the north and Mt. Song in the middle makes up the five famous Mt.s in China. It has been hailed as "foremost among the five famous Mt.s" and "the No. 1 Mt. in China". Since the sun rises in the east, the east is regarded as the cradle of life, the symbol of hope and good luck. For this reason, ancient Chinese often regarded Mt. Taishan as a god and prayed to the mountain god for good weather for the crops. So Mt. Taishan has become "the mountain of good auspices" and "the abode of the gods," nurturing life. Ever since ancient times Mt. Taishan has been the object of occult beliefs for Chinese. As the saying goes, "if Mt. Taishan is safe and sound, the whole world is safe and sound." Legend has it that in ancient times no fewer than 72 kings toured Mt. Taishan and offered sacrifices to this holy Mt. Emperor Qin Shi Huang was caught in the rain when climbing the Mt. and left the legend of the five minister-pines. Emperor Wudi of the Han Dynasty visited Mt. Taishan eight times and greatly admired it, saying, "So tall! So supreme! So large! So singular! So imposing! So astonishing! So confounding!" In all dynasties emperors would ascend this mountain to perform Fengshan ceremony and offer sacrifices to heaven. They also built temples and made statures of gods and inscriptions in Mt. Taishan. Men of letters in ancient times worshipped this mountain even more and composed poems and essays in their tours. Today there are over 20 ancient architectural complexes and over 2,200 stone steles and stone inscriptions.

Mount Huangshan

Mt. Huangshan was formerly named "Yishan" because of its dark color of peaks. Legend has it that Xuanyuan, the ancient Yellow Emperor in Chinese mythology, did alchemy on this mountain and so Emperor Xuanzong of the Tang Dynasty, who strongly believed in Taoism, renamed this mountain Mt. Huangshan. Xu Xiake, a geographer of the Ming Dynasty, who climbed Mount Huangshan twice, wrote, "I have seen many mountains in the world, but none of them can match Mt. Huangshan. Standing on its peak, I had the feeling that there were no other mountains in the world worth visiting." In December 1990, Mt. Huangshan was listed in *the world cultural and natural heritage* by UNESCO, and in February 2004 it became a global geographic park.

Mt. Huangshan, in the beautiful southern part of Anhui, is a renowned national scenic mountain. It is about 40 kilometers long from north to south and 30 kilometers wide from east to west, covering an area of about 1,200 square kilometers with the core scenic area of 160.6 square kilometers. It stretches over the counties of Yi and Xiuning, Huangshan District, and Huizhou District, with a total area of 1,078 square kilometers.

Mt. Huangshan's imposing peaks are the result of crustal movements, subsequent uplift as well as the impacts of glaciers and natural weathering. Mt. Huangshan is well-known for "36 large-scale and 36 small-scale peaks" and its highest peak, the Lotus Flower Peak (Lianhua Peak) , reaches up to an altitude of 1, 864 meters. The Lotus Flower Peak, together with the spacious and flat Bright Summit Peak (Guangming Peak) and the precipitous Celestial Capital Peak (Tiandu Peak) tower in the center of Mt. Huangshan scenic area surrounded by 77 peaks over 1,000 meters in altitude. These overlapped green pinnacles form a three-dimensional rhythmic, magnificent and imposing picture.

The body of Mt. Huangshan is mainly composed of granite from the period of Yanshan Movement; it grew into a vertical structure with many crisscross cracks. Magnificent and beautiful granite caves and channels formed due to long-term erosion from water. Actually there are 30 ranges, 22 cliffs, 7 caves and 2 passes altogether in this mountain. The rock mass on the front mountain has fewer joints and most of its rocks are weathered into egg-shaped ones, and the body of the mountain looks very spectacular, while that of the back mountain has more joints and has been weathered into vertical rocks and the mountain body is very precipitous. Hence Mt. Huangshan forms unique geological features of "majestic mountain front and beautiful mountain back".

Flora and Fauna Resources

Mt. Huangshan is a natural park of animals and plants with great diversity in rare species. Mt. Huangshan enjoys a complexity in natural environment and the ecosystem maintains stability and balance, while the plants are zoned vertically with complete flora. There are also an alpine swamp and alpine meadow abounding in green plants. The forest coverage is 56% and vegetation coverage is as high as 83% in Mt. Huangshan. This mountain is the habitat of 1,452 species of wild plants, of which the metasequoia is under state first-class protection, four species including "gingko" under state second-class protection, eight species under state third-class protection. And the list also covers ten endangered species such as "caulis dendrobii". There are 28 plant species which are initially found in Mt. Huangshan or bear "Mt. Huangshan" in their names. Among them the tea "Huangshan Maofeng" and medicine "Huangshan ganoderma lucidum" are the most famous both home and abroad. There are also over 300 animal species endemic to Mount Huangshan among which 14 species such as sika deer, black muntjacs, barking deer, serows and long-tail pheasants are under state wild animal protection.

Scenic and Historic Sites

Main Scenic Areas

The Jade Screen This area is centered on "Jade Screen Tower" with Lotus Flower Peak and Celestial Capital Peak as main part, and including other beautiful sites such as "Three Islets of Fairyland", "Hundred Step Ladder", "Yixiantian (A Gleam of Sky)", "New Yixiantian" and "Dragon-headed Fish Cave". Celestial Capital Peak, located to the south of Jade Screen Tower and one kilometer away from the Tower, is the steepest of the three main peaks of Mt. Huangshan with an altitude of 1,830 meters. An old poem remarks that visitors returning from other famous mountains will still be stunned by the sight of this peak. On the top of Celestial Capital Peak, there is the inscription " 登峰造极 " meaning "reaching the summit of perfection", reminding viewers that "at the far side of the ocean the sky becomes the shore, and on the top of the peak I am the summit."

The Northern Sea This area is a large open zone in the heartland of Mt. Huangshan between Bright Light Peak, Shixin Peak, Lion Peak and White Goose Peak with an altitude of 1,600 meters and covering 1,316 hectares. This scenic area is a typical scenery spot of Mt. Huangshan, assembling peaks, rocks, coves, terraces as well as pines and clouds, unfolding a magnificent, fantastic and spectacular landscape.

The Hot Spring It was originally named Taoyuan Fairyland. This area centers around Lansheng Bridge (Beauty-Embracing Bridge) with Taohua Stream (Peach Blossom Stream) and Xiaoyao Stream (the Stream of Serene Existence) winding past. Ciguang Pavilion, once known variously as Ciguang Temple and Zhusha Nunnery, is 25 minutes' walk from Lansheng Bridge. The pavilion was first built in the Jiajing reign period of the Ming Dynasty and was named by the emperor as "Ciguang

Pavilion for State Protection" in the 38th year of his reign.

White Clouds Situated in the west of Mt. Huangshan, this area covers 1,655 hectares. With Diaoqiao Nunnery at the center, the area is a unique secluded spot assembling characteristic elements of Mt. Huangshan (peaks, pines, stones and springs) .

The Pine Valley This area is at the rear, northern part of Mt. Huangshan, starting from North Gate, famous for its beauty in contrast to the precipitous front of Mt. Huangshan. The valley is surrounded by Lion Peak, Camel Peak, Bookcase Peak and Tower Peak. This scenic spot has fascinating rocks such as "Transcendent Viewing the Sea" and "Guan Yu Blocking Cao Cao", water scenery including Feicui Pond and Five Dragon Pool, and ancient buildings like Songgu Buddhist Temple.

The Cloud Valley It is a low and open valley with an altitude of 890 meters in the eastern part of Mt. Huangshan. Fu Yan, a man of letters in the Ming Dynasty, wandered here and crafted the words "Cloud Valley" at the request of a monk. The temple has been called Cloud Valley Temple ever since. The main scenic spots are Cloud Valley Cottage, ancient trees, grotesque rocks, Nine Dragon Waterfall and Thousand Foot Spring.

Four Wonders of Mt. Huangshan

The Four Wonders of Mt. Huangshan refer to the spectacular pines, bizarre rocks, sea of cloud, and hot springs which are unique to Mt. Huangshan.

Huangshan pines are a variant of Chinese pines formed by unique landform and climate in Mt. Huangshan. The wonder is that Huangshan pines root in hard rock with no soil and absorb nutrients and water from the crevices of the rocks. The verdant and vigorous pines have become symbols of tenacious vitality. Grotesquely-shaped rocks, which are well-known for their unique shape and large quantity, are another wonder of Mt. Huangshan. Still another wonder, the sea of clouds, can be viewed in any season though winter is the best, when Mt. Huangshan has peaks as its body and clouds as its garment. And the last wonder is the hot springs, whose fountainhead starts from the foot of Peak Ziyun with an altitude of 850 meters. The water can be used for drinking or bathing because it's full of bicarbonate. According to legend, the Yellow Emperor took a bath here and got his rejuvenation so that the spring is called "Divine Spring". Mt. Huangshan hot springs have certain effects on treating diseases in digestive, nervous and cardiovascular systems, and some skin diseases in particular.

Significance of the Heritage

Mt. Huangshan has a unique culture and was a cradle for the landscape painting school, since it has merged various cultural identities and codes of different social strata in different times.

Due to its richness in historical and cultural associations Mt.Huangshan has over 200 relics such as temples, pavilions, bridges and cliff inscriptions, which are dotted among the mountains and produce an ancient and elegant atmosphere.

Lushan National Park

"Viewing horizontally you see ranges, yet peaks appear if you take a side view; landscape changes as you move from far to near, high to low. The true face of Mt. Lushan is lost to my sight, for it is right in this mountain that I reside."

This poem, entitled *On the Wall of Xilin Temple*, by Su Dongpo (Su Shi) of the Song Dynasty, gives full expression to the changing views of Mt. Lushan seen from far and near. Here is a fine example showing the function of culture to nature-if culture merges with nature in a singular way, it will enrich and intensify the beauty of nature and give nature the finishing touch. As a result, nature will be more lively and glamorous. Mt. Lushan is just such a famous mountain of culture.

Residing in Mt. Lushan, you feel its range of temperature, view the fogs and clouds encircling the mountain, and perceive the unpredictable changes of this mountain and its various facets. You will be touched by the beauty of this scenic area.

Mt. Lushan is a cultural mountain with a long history; you will see famous historical and cultural sites everywhere. For thousands of years numerous men of letters or celebrities left us large numbers of paintings, calligraphy and poems depicting the mountain. Legend has it that Yu, a ruler of ancient China, once passed Mt. Lushan when he was engaged in dredging Jiujiang, a section of the Yangtze River. Emperor Qin Shi Huang also visited this mountain when he toured South China. Literary giants like Tao Yuanming of the Eastern Jin Dynasty, Li Bai, Du Fu, Bai Juyi of the Tang Dynasty, Fan Zhongyan, Su Shi, Lu You of the Song Dynasty and Wang Yuanming of the Ming Dynasty all visited Mt. Lushan and composed poems here; the patriotic general Yue Fei of the Northern Song Dynasty, the anti-Yuan martyr Wen Tianxiang of the Southern Song Dynasty, the famous doctor of traditional Chinese medicine Li Shizhen and the famous traveler-geographer Xu Xiake of the Ming Dynasty all toured Mt. Lushan.

Flora and Fauna Resources

Mt. Lushan abounds in biological life and its ecosystem is multilayered. In summer Mt. Lushan is cool and frequented by clouds and fogs. The plants here show features of the Tertiary period and grow exuberantly, so vegetation is rich. With the increase of altitude and the vertical distribution of water and heat on the mountain surface, there is a progression of evergreen broadleaved forests and mixed forests of broadleaved evergreen and deciduous trees from the mountain foot to the top. The plants here include 210 families, 735 genus, and 1,720 species. The botanic types can be categorized as belonging to temperate zone, tropical zone, sub-tropical zone, East Asia and North America, and so Mt. Lushan is a natural botanical garden. There are 171 types of birds resident here and the number of migratory birds is as large as over one million. Among them is the world's largest flock of cranes, making up 95 percent of the total number of white cranes in the world.

Scenic and Historic Sites

Mt. Lushan is about 25 kilometers in length and 20 kilometers in width. Its highest peak is Hanyang Summit, 1,474 meters above sea level. Streets in Guling Township are 1,167 meters above sea level. The towering Mt. Lushan presents different postures. Viewed from afar, Mt. Lushan is a mountain flying along the Yangtze River; viewed from nearby, a thousand peaks join each other, hand in hand; viewed horizontally, Mt. Lushan is like an iron bastion standing by Poyang Lake; viewed from the side, Mt. Lushan is like a stone pillar lost in the clouds.

Main Scenic Spots

The main scenic spots of Mt. Lushan include Wulao Peak, Three Tier Waterfalls, Donglin Temple and White Deer Cavern Academy. The scenic spot covers an area of 302 square kilometers, with a peripheral protection zone of 500 square kilometers. Mt. Lushan abounds in traces left by the Fourth Glacier Stage-rivers, lakes, slopes, peaks, and so on. There are so many landforms that this mountain may be called a geological park. The singular culture of Mt. Lushan endows it with important scientific and aesthetic value.

Guling Township This is an unusual mountain town on Mt. Lushan with the title of "a garden city in the clouds". The westbound road from this town leads to West Lake. It is also named Flowery Path Lake. Since this lake is shaped like a cello and the spring water produces the tinkling of a cello, it has also been dubbed Cello Lake. This is the second largest man-made lake of Mt. Lushan with an area of 100,000 square meters. By the waterside, Lake Heart Pavilion presents fine scenery.

The Immortal Cavern Take a walk along the westbound path in Jinxiu Valley for about 500 meters and you will reach the Immortal Cavern. This cave is the result of natural weathering. It is 14 meters long, 12 meters wide and 6 meters tall. The top of the cave is covered by fingerlike rocks shaped like Buddha's hand, so it is also called Buddha Hand Rock. In the cave there is a spring flowing out from a crack between the stones that is called Yitang Spring. The couplet "Water dripping from tall mountains for thousands of years ceaselessly, clean spring water flowing over countless rocks with no rest" gives a vivid description of the scene. It was not until the Qing Dynasty that Buddha Hand Rock had become a blissful cave for Taoists and was renamed the Immortal Cavern. Inside the cave is a statue of the Taoist immortal Lü Dongbin in a niche reestablished in the 1970s. He has a special status, revered as both a teacher and an ancestor, a Confucian as well as a Taoist.

Wulao Peak The name of this peak comes from the scenery viewed from Haihui Temple at the foot of the mountain-five seated old men sitting together. If you view Wulao peak from different perspectives, you will see those peaks are quite different, one resembling a poet whistling in the wind, one resembling an enterprising warrior in old age, one resembling a passionate scholar, one resembling a monk witnessing the ups and downs of mortal beings, one resembling a white-haired fisherman angling in Poyang Lake. Great poet Li Bai once commented on this scene, "Wulao Peak in the southeast of Mt. Lushan, a jade lotus carved against the sky."

Sandie Waterfalls

Sandie Waterfalls is also called Three Tier Waterfalls and Water Curtain Spring. Ancient men say, "Among the waterfalls of Mt. Lushan, the most wonderful one is Three Tier Waterfalls." It has won acclaim as the first wonder of Mt. Lushan. Water from Dayue Hill and Wulao Peak converge and flow out from Dayue Hill, passing through the rear of Wulao Peak and pouring onto a big rock (first tier) from the hanging mouth on the north cliff, and then the water spills on another rock (second tier) and sprays on still another rock (third tier) . The water-spraying Sandie Waterfalls seems to contain a thousand egretss flying up and down; or thousands of pearls going in different directions. The scene is enchanting.

Donglin Temple Donglin Temple is located in the west foothills of Mt. Lushan; it is the cradle of the Buddhist Pure Land Sect of China. During the 11th year of the Taiyuan reign period of the Eastern Jin Dynasty (386 A.D.) , a celebrated monk named Huiyuan set up a temple on Mt. Lushan and lectured on the doctrines of Buddhism. He promoted the Amitabha Pure Land School and founded the Lotus Society. This temple reached its prime in the Tang Dynasty and had 310-bay halls, wings, pagodas and rooms all together. Before going to Japan, the distinguished monk Jianzhen of Yangzhou visited Donglin Temple and crossed seas to Japan with Monk Zhi'en from Donglin Temple, introducing the doctrines of Monk Huiyuan and the Pure Land School to Japan. Even today the Donglin School of Japan regards Monk Huiyuan of Donglin Temple as its ancestor.

Significance of the Heritage

Mt. Lushan used to be an education base and center of religions in ancient times. White Deer Cavern Academy was established in 940 A.D., and this academy was the paramount one among the four famous academies in China. The educational ideas put forward here by Zhu Xi, a master of the Song Dynasty Neo-Confucianism, became the principles of education in ancient China and his doctrines also had a significant impact on the educational history of the world.

White Deer Cavern Chamber was originally the hermitage where Li Bo, a young man from Luoyang in the Tang Dynasty, studied. During the Shengyuan period of the Southern the Tang Dynasty, "a school was established and some farmland was purchased", and the White Deer Cavern was formally recognized as the home for "Mt. Lushan Classical Studies", thus indicating that the White Deer Cavern had been converted into a school. In the early years of the Northern Song Dynasty many academies were established in the whole country and "Mt. Lushan Classical Studies" was then renamed White Deer Cavern Academy and gradually expanded in scale and became one of the four most renowned academies in China.

In 391 A.D. Buddhist leader Huiyuan set up Donglin Temple, the earliest temple garden in China. This distinguished monk resided here for 36 years, founding Pure Land Buddhism, and so Mt. Lushan became the center of Buddhism in South China. In the fifth century a monk of the Southern Dynasty, Lu Xiujing, established the Nan Tianshi Sect in Mt. Lushan. Ma Zudaoyi of the Tang Dynasty founded the Liji and Weiyang Sects in Mt. Lushan and exerted great influence. In the Song Dynasty the temples in Mt. Lushan reached a total of 361. In the Ming and Qing dynasties, Islam and Christianity also began to set up religious buildings here to spread their teachings. Over the space of 1,600 years Mt. Lushan became a mountain harboring five religions.

Xinjiang Tianshan

Xinjiang Tianshan, referring to the east part of Tianshan within the boundary of China, stretches 1,760 kilometres, making up over 2/3 of the total length of the mountain range. Lying across the whole territory of Xinjiang, it is the natural geographical boundary between the Junggar Basin and the Tarim Basin, and is the unique sign of Xinjiang geography. Xinjiang Tianshan is one of the seven biggest mountain ranges in the world, the biggest mountain chain of the world in an arid area of the temperate zone, and is also the biggest independent mountain in the world that goes from east to west. Xinjiang Tianshan Natural Heritage Site, 5,759 square kilometres in size, is comprised of four areas, including Bogda of Changji Hui Autonomous Prefecture, Bayinbuluke of Bayinguoleng Mongolia Autonomous Prefecture, Tomur of Aksu Prefecture, Kalajun-Kuerdening of Ili Kazak Autonomous Prefecture.

Flora and Fauna Resources

Many mountain peaks of the Tianshan Mountains are snow-covered all year round. Below the 3000-metre snowline, however, are rich animal and plant resources. In the foot hills and river valleys of Tuomur Peak and Bogda Peak, spruce trees and pine trees grow everywhere and stay green in all seasons. On the south and north slopes of Tomur Peak are dense forests, and this is one of the main timber-producing areas of Xinjiang. In the spruce forest, wild rose, codonopsis pilosula and over 80 medical herbs grow very well; in the subalpine meadows, blooming trollflowers dance in the wind; in the riprap close to the snowline, snow saussurea blossoming in severe cold send out fragrance and bring vitality to the ice world. Tianshan area is also the gene pool of excellent forage grass. Most of the 55 gramineous plants discovered so far are excellent forage grass and play an important role in developing animal husbandry.

Many rare birds and beasts are found here in Tianshan. Ridges and peaks under 3,000 metres altitude, and the dense forests of the hilly areas and in the prairie make natural habitat and reproduction places for all kinds of fowls and beasts. Marmots, otters, argali, snow leopard, lynx, Tianshan antelope, and Tianshan deer are protected rare species.

Scenic and Historic Sites

Well-known Snow Peaks

Among the Tianshan mountain ranges, more than ten peaks are over 5,000m altitude. Besides Tomur, the highest peak, the other main peaks include Khan Tengri Peak, Bogda Peak, Vaski Kavli Mountain, and Delasike Bashan Mountain at the bordering between China and Kazakhstan. These high mountains, snow-covered all year round, looked at in the distance, standing between heaven and earth, appear magnificent and indomitable, full of profound mystery.

Bogda Peak Bogda Peak, at an altitude of 5,445 metres, is the highest peak of Mt. Bogda in the eastern part of Tianshan. The part of the mountain over 3,800 metres is covered by snow all year round, thus is called Snow Sea. On the whole of Mt. Bogda, there are altogether over 300 glaciers, 1/4 of which are in the Bogda Peak area. The biggest glacier, on the north slope of Bogda Peak, occupies an area of 11 square kilometres and melts intensely in the summer to form many glacier rivers, rushing down the mountain and making a deafening roar.

Half way up Bogda Peak, within in the territory of Fukang City, is a natural high mountain lake in the shape of a half moon that is called Tian Chi, Heaven's Pool. The water in the lake is transparent and crystal as jade. On the east and west sides of the main lake are two pools, and the one 500 metres at the east side of is called the Little East Tian Chi, whose ancient name was Heilong (Black Dragon) Pool. Legend has it that this was where Xiwangmu, the West Queen, bathed, so it is also called Cleaning Stream and Washing Basin.

Tomur Peak "The bright moon arising among Tianshan Mountain, looking as if it is among a sea of clouds." Tomur Peak, taller and more magnificent than Bogda peak, with its peak in the sky, is the highest peak among the Tianshan mountains. Tomur, meaning "iron" in Uighur (so, Iron Peak) , is situated in Wensu County, Akesu Prefecture, close to the border between China and Kirgizstan, 20 kilometres to the southwest of the border mountain, Khan Tengri Peak. There are more than ten high mountains over 6,000 metres in altitude. The glacier in the Tomur area is over 2,800 square kilometres, and is the biggest modern glacier in China. The main peak and the surrounding area of ten hectares was listed as the Prefectural Natural Protection Area in 1980, mainly protecting the high mountain glacier and the forest below the glacier, the biological communities and ecological environment.

To the north of the peak area is the old site of Wusun Kingdom at the time of the Han Dynasty, the original birthplace of Pegasus Horse and Ferghana Horse.

Main Scenic Spots

The Stone Gate of Tian Chi The Stone Gate is the natural pass to enter Tian Chi Scenic Area. It is roughly a hundred metres wide, and the width at the narrowest spot is only 10 metres. In between two peaks, Stone Gate is the valley forced open by a river, which explains why it is also called Stone Valley. The stone walls, tens of metres high, about 100 metres long, are just like two open door planks. The dark reddish brown stones look as if made of iron, hence was named Iron Gate. Inside the gate, Sangong River rushes along. It can be rightly said that "Cut so skillfully as if by spirits, the thoroughfare leads to the blue sky."

The Footbath of Wangmu, West Queen The Little Dragon Pool, also named the Footbath of Wangmu, is down below the right side of the 3rd of the Fifty Skies. It has an altitude of 1,660 metres. The water of Tian Chi infiltrating from underground into the pool is just like top-quality wine, and also like the fine muscles and delicate skin of Wangmu, and legend has it that it was the footbath of Wangmu. The water of the pool mirrors the pine trees around the pool, which impresses viewers as quiet and deep.

The Little West Tian Chi Waterfall Not too far away from the Little West Tian Chi, on the right side of the road is the Little West Tian Chi Waterfall. Having tens of metres of drop, the waterfall is just like a drawn silver curtain, behind which you feel as if you saw the pretty image of Wangmu washing and dressing herself.

Wentao (listening to waves) Pavilion has been newly rebuilt at the old site. It is an octagonal pavilion, having two storeys, red pillars, and yellow glazed tile roof. Tall and spacious, the pavilion is magnificent.

Crocodile Spitting Pearls Climbing over the mountain at the south of the Little East Tian Chi is the northern bank of the big Tian Chi. The northern bank of Tianshi is a huge natural dyke-dam that was formed by a pile of ancient glacial moraine and the remains of hillsides. 289 metres high, the whole dyke-dam is very much like the tail of a crocodile, thus was named Crocodile Dam. At the east side of the dam has been built an artificial sluice gate named Crocodile Sluice Gate. Tian Chi water falls down to form a waterfall over 10 metres high, called Crocodile Spitting Pearls. The waterfall rushes into the valley of Black Dragon Canyon and forms with the mountain streams a pool, which is the Little East Tian Chi. Crocodile Spitting Pearls, Ice Pool Silver Curtain and Hanging Spring Flying Waterfall are collectively called the Three Waterfalls of Tian Chi.

Xi Wangmu, West Queen Ancestor Temple Located at the east bank of Tian Chi in the northwest of Bogda Peak, Xi Wangmu Ancestor Temple, at an altitude of 2000 metres, is one of the oldest Taoist temples at the highest altitude. According to legend, Xi Wangmu here cultivated the way and became an immortal, hence it was called Xi Wangmu Ancestor Temple.

Significance of the Heritage

As a typical natural mountain landscape in the dry area in northwest China, Xinjiang Tianshan includes the permanent snow and ice belt, the grass-covered prairie and platform belt-middle mountain canyon forest belt-Low mountain steppe zone-gobi and desert, which show an obvious vertical band of natural landscape. The landscape resources of Tianshan reflect very important sightseeing and scientific value. The nature of the landscape is characterised mainly by a complete vertical plant landscape belt, snow mountains and glaciers, and high mountain lakes, while it has as its cultural contents the Jade Pool Myth of ancient times, religions and ethnic customs.Therefore, Tianshan is important for the following scientific and protection values: Mountain biodiversity in arid areas, the genetic resources of specifically local plant seeds, the habitat of endangered wild animals and plants.

Mount Wuyi

Mount Wuyi, in the southwest of Wuyishan City in northern Fujian Province, occupies a total area of 60 square kilometres. As a typical Danxia landscape, it has been hailed as "blue water and red mountain" and "the most beautiful mountain in southeast China". Possessing striking views like Huangshan, steepness like Huashan, waterfalls like Lushan, and charming harmony of landscape like Guilin, Mt. Wuyi has multiple charms, delicate and exquisite.

The evergreen broad-leaved forest at Mount Wuyi is the most typical of its kind in China, while it also has the most kinds of species and the most completely preserved forest ecosystem. Mount Wuyi represents the combination of the scenery of mountain and river, at the same time, the harmonious combination of human culture and nature reaches a perfect level. The Nine-bend river winds its way around the mountains; the typical Danxia mountain stands close to the river; the vestiges of a culture over 3000 years old cliff lies scattered among the hills and caves. Natural landscape is infused with culture's rich flavor.

In terms of their position in Chinese cultural history, Mount Wuyi and Mount Taishan each has its own merits. Taishan nurtured Confucius who gathered together the culmination of the academic thought of early ancient times and created Confucianism, the main body of traditional Chinese culture. Mount Wuyi brought up Zhu Xi, who bundled the academic thought after Confucius and formed the complete Confucian thinking system, Neo-Confucianism, which became the orthodox thought of the last 700-years of China's feudal society. It is generally held among both domestic and foreign scholars that Confucius is the most influential person in the history of early Chinese culture, tradition, thought, education, and ethics, and Zhu Xi is the most influential person in later history.

Scenic and Historic Sites

Main Scenic Areas

Tianyoufeng Scenic Spot Tianyou peak, a rocky ridge stretching from north to south, connects with Xianyou crag in the east and Xianzhangfeng in the west. Here the towering precipice and cliff stand over the high mountains. When it turns fine after rain, or at early dawn, the white clouds in the sky are just like sea waves, which, seen from the viewing platform, make viewers feel as if they were in Penglai Wonderland—hence the name Tianyou. Famous trees and ancient trees are found here in great number, and the evergreen broad-leaved trees are lushly green. The well-known Ming geographer Xu Xiake paid high tribute to Tianyoufeng, "It is not by the Nine-bend river, yet has all the beauty of it. This peak fully deserves the title of the number one peak."

On the stone wall by the Humajian stream at the top of the peak are dozens of cliff inscriptions of different dynasties. The biggest of the inscriptions, "First Mountain", was written by Xu Qingchao, a general of the mid-nineteenth century.

Nine-bend River Scenic Spot Ever since ancient times mountains gain in beauty from water, and the essence of the landscape of Wuyi is Nine-bend river, with a total length of 15 kilometres, which has clear water and zigzags past the mountains like a jade belt. Like a jade belt strung with pearls, the river links the 36 peaks and 99 precipices to form the unique natural beauty of the Nine-bend river scenery.

Some of the most famous peaks and the mysterious hanging coffins over the cliffs are found by the riverside of the Nine-bend river. The area is also noted for culturally significant sites such as the porcelain kiln site of the Song Dynasty at Yulin Pavilion and Wuyi Palace.

Dahongpao Dahongpao Scenic Spot is at the central part of Mount Wuyi Scenic Area, inside the famous canyon Jiulong Nest. This is a deep and long valley stretching from east to west that was shaped by a fault structure. The valley is deeply cut, the two long and deep stone walls of the valley face the nine rugged stone mountains that stand respectively to south and north, facing each other. The unique joint development has created undulating peak ridges that look like nine huge dragons, some sprawled and some ready to fly. At the mouth of the valley is a round-shaped rock, like a huge pearl for which the dragons are vying. In the valley and on the cliffs there grow strong pines and bamboos of iridescent green. The celebrated dahongpao Tea is cultivated on the valley floor. The leaves of six old tea shrubs, dating back more than 340 years, spread their leaves wide. The color, aroma, and flavor of the tea produced are preeminent among Oolong teas, and so this variety is called "the King of Teas".

Main Scenic Spots

Wuyi Great Canyon Wuyi Great Canyon includes two tourist attractions Qinglong Great Waterfall and Great Canyon Rafting. Qinglong Great Waterfall is on the west side of Wuyi Great Canyon Park. It is surrounded by dense forest and has rich water resources. A section of Tongmu Stream, which deserves the title of "The number one rafting in east China", is one of the sources of Nine-bend River and originates here. It is the purest and clearest water source of Mount Wuyi.

Mount Longjing Eight kilometres in the southeast of Mount Wuyi Natural Landscape Area, Longjingshan (dragon well mountain) is 12 kilometres away from the city of Wuyishan. In the valley, flowers bloom and trees stay green for all seasons, many kinds of birds find their homes here, and the natural ecology is balanced. As a result, some researchers describe this area as a "green lung".

According to historical record, since the Song Dynasty, Longjingshan Rain Praying Hall was the place where people prayed for rain and fortune, and it became the most lively and influential rain-praying place. Up to this day, the well from which to get water for praying for rain is still there. The main scenic sites include: Longjing waterfall, Longjing cliff, Shenshan Dahu (the big lake in the deep mountain) , viewing platform and Rain Praying Hall, etc.

Mount Huanggang Having an altitude of 2160.8 metres, Huanggangshan, titled "the continental ridge of east China", is the highest mountain in southeast China. The mountain is high and steep, and there are many peaks; as a result, the area is misty the whole year round, and owing to abundant rainfall and a warm climate, this constitutes the biggest and most complete Central Asian tropical forest ecological system in southeast China. The top of Huanggangshan is the core part of Mount Wuyi Natural Protection Zone. It is not fully open to tourists because of the special nature of the protection zone.

Shuilian (water curtain) Cave Shuilian Cave is one of the famous 72 caves of Mount Wuyi. It is in the north of Zhangtang Stream. Here, on the Danxia rock, are cut the famous words of Zhu Xi, "Ask the stream why it is so clear, it's because there is fresh water coming from the source." This place is also named Tang Yao Cave, and the Taoist temples were built here from ancient times. The inside of the cave is spacious and bright, and there are stone tables and stone benches for visitors to have a rest. By the stone fence one can stand by to view the water curtain outside the cave.

Wuyi Palace Wuyi Palace, also named Huixian Temple, Chongyou Temple, Wannian Temple, is at the south foot of Dawang peak, facing the mouth of the Nine-bend River. It was the place for emperors of all dynasties to worship Wuyi Jun, and was also one of the six most influential Taoist temples in the Song Dynasty. It suffered fire damage during several wars, and although often repaired has not recovered its past splendor. In 2008, the main hall of Wuyi Palace was rebuilt, and now the plan to completely restore Wuyi Palace is being implemented step by step.

Wuyi Boat Coffins Wuyi Boat Coffins and Hongqiao Wood Boards are the vestiges of burials by the ancient Yue people, and are over 3000 years old. The so-called boat coffin is actually a coffin in the shape of a small boat. The outer shape of the boat coffins may be divided into two types: one type of boat coffin is in the shape of a boat, with the two ends perking up; the other type is in the shape of a square box, popularly called "Han". The coffins were laid on the cliff tens of metres above the ground and remained intact for thousands of years, therefore, they are regarded as precious matter and are titled "changting" (open boat) , "xianzhou" (god's boat) , "xianren room" (god's room) , "golden coffin" and "Chengxiang boat". Hongqiao Wood Board, the appendages of boat coffins, were used to support the coffins or build a plank road. The funerary objects in the coffins are simple and unsophisticated, but rich in variety. The cotton cloth fragments in the coffins are the earliest real cotton textiles discovered in China up to now, and constitute very valuable materials for the study of pre-Qin Chinese history and the now disappeared ancient Min people.

Significance of the Heritage

Mount Wuyi is a historically and culturally famous mountain. As early as the Neolithic Age, the ancient Yue people were already living and multiplying here; and the Jiahechuan (that is, boat coffins) , and Hongqiaoban (a kind of precious wood board) that still remain on the steep precipices and cliffs are relics left behind by ancient Yue people. Emperor Wudi of the Western Han Dynasty sent envoys to Wuyishan to offer sacrifice by using dried fish to Wuyi Jun, the mountain god of Wuyi. Emperor Xuanzong of the Tang Dynasty granted titles to famous mountains and big rivers, and Mt. Wuyi received one such honor, the event inscribed on a stone monument. The emperor also ordered that the forests be protected and not be felled. At the end of the Tang Dynasty and the beginning of the Five Dynasties period, Du Guangting in his book *A Record of Blessed Spots* listed Wuyishan as one of the 36 blessed spots under the sun. In 1095 A.D., during the Song Dynasty, when a prayer for rain was answered, the Lord of Wuyi was given the title Wuyi Xiandao (revealing the truth) Zhenren (Immortal being) .

Mount Sanqingshan National Park

Mt. Sanqingshan is located on the border between Yushan County and Dexing County in Shangrao, Jiangxi Province. It is the main peak of the Huaiyu Mt.ain range. Mt. Sanqingshan is made up of three main summits: Yujing, Yuxu, and Yuhua, representing the Taoist trinity. A Chinese phrase "Three steep peaks, as though the Three Pure Ones are seated on their summits" explains why it came to have this name. Of the three peaks, Yujing (1,819.9 meters above sea level) is the highest. It is also the fifth highest Mt.ain in Jiangxi Province, and the source of Xin River. Mt. Sanqingshan is a renowned Taoist sacred Mt.ain with outstanding scenery, sometimes described as the most beautiful landscape in China.

The magic and magnificent landscape of Mt. Sanqingshan have resulted from particular geological and meteorological conditions, and are a product of crustal movement over time. In geological history, Mt. Sanqingshan has undergone many great changes over 1.4 billion years. About twenty or thirty million years ago, Himalaya orogeny—also known as neotectonic movement—sequentially took place, and Mt.ains were dramatically uplifted as heavy water flows created downward erosion effects, resulting in huge topographical differences. Owing to the fact that Mt. Sanqingshan was situated in a geological environment where there was frequent and vigorous movement, a system of faults and joints developed and spread almost everywhere in the Mt.ain, especially in the vertical dimension. The Mt.ain continued to uplift under long-term weathering erosion, forming a grotesque landscape of peaks touching the sky, along with yawning abysses and deep valleys. The creation of the Mt. Sanqingshan scenic area can be regarded as a heavenly creation and masterpiece of nature.

Flora and Fauna Resources

Mt. Sanqingshan has four very distinct seasons, with correspondingly beautiful scenery: in spring, flowers flourish, rich in color; in summer, green shades are everywhere, refreshing; in autumn, leaves seem to be dyed in colorful shades of red, and in winter, it is snow-covered, a crystal world. This is what Mt. Sanqingshan is all about—a place full of vigor and soul.

The evolution of the biological world over 200 million years has created on Mt. Sanqingshan a unique ecosystem of middle and sub-tropical east-humid evergreen broadleaved forest, a home to 2,373 species of high plants and 1,728 species of wild animals. In the Quaternary Ice Age, the vegetation of Mt. Sanqingshan was not severely affected by the ice-sheet, thus providing a biotic shelter for many ancient plant species and enabling an ancient plant community and a diversity of species to be preserved. Mt. Sanqingshan has become a rare conservatory of natural life. Among the botanical varieties distributed in East Asia and North America, China in total has 117 genera and Mt. Sanqingshan possesses 68 genera, accounting for 58% of the Chinese total. Therefore, in addition to its important scientific values for geology and geomorphology, Mt. Sanqingshan also possesses notable importance for biology and ecology studies.

Taoist Culture

The Taoist culture in Mt. Sanqingshan was initiated by Ge Hong in the Jin Dynasty, so he holds a special place of honor in the Mt.ain. During the Shengping reign of the Eastern Jin Dynasty, he and Minister Li took up residence on Mt. Sanqingshan, making pills of immortality and writing books and practicing Taoist doctrine. Ge Hong thus became a leading thinker of Taoism and the first exponent of Taoism on Mt. Sanqingshan.

Thanks to Taoist practices, Mt. Sanqingshan became widely known in the following dynasties. In the Tang Dynasty, Taoism in Mt. Sanqingshan gradually became popular as Taoism was respected as the national religion by the imperial court. The Lao Tzu Taoist Temple, the first Taoist shrine ever built in Mt. Sanqingshan and referred to as "the blessed spot of Sanqing", was erected where Ge Hong made pills of immortality, since when the status of Taoism in Mt. Sanqingshan was further consolidated.

Since the Song Dynasty, and especially since the Ming Dynasty, Sanqing Taoist Temple and other Taoist edifices were built in accordance with the landscape orientation as well as the notion of the Eight Trigrams, blending natural landscape and Taoist philosophy. Within miles of the Mt.ain, there became concentrated a strong Taoist ethos and Taoism was widely practiced. Modern scholarship has suggested that Sanqing Taoist Temple was a hideout for the missing Emperor of the Ming Dynasty, Emperor Jianwen. Located at the junction of the provinces of Zhejiang and Jiangxi, Mt. Sanqingshan offers access to Shanghai and Hangzhou in the east, to Fujian and Guangdong in the south, to Hubei and Hunan in the west, and to Jiangsu and Anhui in the north. While bordering Mt. Huangshan, it connects with Dragon and Tiger Mountain; and close to Mt. Wuyi, it enjoys its beauty.

Scenic and Historic Sites

Landscape Characteristics

Mt. Sanqingshan is 12.2km long from north to south and 6.3km wide from east to west. It takes the shape of a water-lily leaf, slanting from southeast to northwest. Situated in a zone of frequent and violent geological motion, the Mt.ain is characterized by numerous faults, joint development, and rocky protrusions. Due to long-term natural erosion and breakage, grotesque skyscraper-like peaks were carved out as if by a magic hand, constituting rare sceneries of serene valleys and cliffs.

The layout of the landscape is steep in the east, strange in the west, unique in the south, and beautiful in the north. It is beautiful with its simplicity and naturalness, and rare in its unity of form and spirit. Imbued with a mystical aura, it evokes a Taoist paradise. Taoist edifices from different periods blend in with the natural landscape, showing divergent splendor, elegance, and grace. That's how it earned its reputation as a Mt.ain of special charm and attraction.

Main Scenic Spots

Oriental Spring Goddess Goddess Sichun (Oriental Spring Goddess) , a granite peak located in the northeast of the Nanqing Garden, is the landmark sight of Mt. Sanqingshan. The peak looks like the silhouette of a maiden with shoulder-length hair. The natural creation is so extraordinarily lifelike as if created by gods. Legend has it that the Goddess is the 23rd daughter of Queen Mother of the West, named Yaoji. She is regarded as the incarnation of spring, hence the name "Goddess Sichun" (literally, managing spring) .

Sanqingshan Rare Pines Sanqing rare pines are one of the major features of the scenery. The rare species of pines mainly are Taiwan red pine (Pinus taiwanensis) and East China yellow pine (Pseudotsuga gaussenii) , most of which grow on the surface of cliffs, thousands of meters above sea level. The charming appearance and graceful figure of these pine trees is highly distinctive. The rare pines and grotesque peaks and pillars constitute beautiful scenery, naturally praised by tourists.

Grotesque Peaks and Pillars Mt. Sanqingshan features many grotesque peaks and pillars, of which ten are particularly memorable. The most iconic sights are the Goddess Peak and the Snake Rock. These colossal granite pillars, formed under the effect of weathering and disintegration, seem to have been specially carved and molded by nature.

Among thousands of grotesque peaks and pillars in this natural stone sculpture museum are such sights as: Yunü Kaihuai (Pure Beauty Shows Elegance) , Laodao Baiyue (Old Taoist Worshipping the Moon) , Houwang Xianbao (Monkey King Presenting Treasure) , Guanyin Shangqu (Guanyin Listening to Music) , Sanlong Chuhai (Three Dragons Rising from the Sea) and Shenlong Xisong (Holy Dragon Playing with The Pine) .

Fairyland in Clouds The sea of clouds is the most marvellous among all superb exotic sights in Mt. Sanqingshan. Elegant peaks stand erect one after another, with high-rising cliffs and deep valleys. The flow of air travels through the Mt.ains, up and down, looping around in high speed. Clouds and mist are carried up and down, whirling or stretching, forming a remarkable, ever-changing grand view of a sea of clouds. Within the Mt. Sanqingshan Scenic Area, groups of peaks tower vertically into the sky, and crisscrossing canyons and valleys divide the terrain into several seas of clouds, making it feel like a fairyland.

Sanqingshan Azalea Between April and May is the prime time for azalea blossoms, when alpine azalea flowers group like colorful clouds all over the hills and fields. Along miles of walks, the enchanting aroma turns Mt. Sanqingshan into a wonderland of flowers. There are 19 azalea varieties, including rhododendron fortunei, rhododendron simiarum, rhododendron farrerae, rhododendron latoucheae, rhododendron ovatum, and rhododendron simsii. In the azalea forest between the Goddess Peak and the Yutai Pavilion, some big trees up to several meters tall and over forty centimeters in diameter have lived for more than 1,700 years, an exceptional age. Accompanying the azalea trees, the magnolia denudata, with hand-size flowers, either fresh yellow or light pink, also grows, either along the flowing springs or reclining on the rock wall between the peaks. They are elegant and pure and quite endearing.

Significance of the Heritage

Mt. Sanqingshan is located in the southeast of the Eurasian Plate. Within the area, a history of geological evolution over one billion years has been recorded, and much stratigraphic evidence of the earth's major geological events is available. The Mt.ain accommodates a variety of ecosystems native to East Asia, with unique granite landscapes. It is an ideal place for research into the history of the earth and the formation of plate tectonics. Mt. Sanqingshan assumes various forms of terrain, as it suffered little from the Quaternary glacial impact, and possesses a large quantity of ancient relic plants. Being a biological refuge during the Quaternary glacial era, it is internationally significant for researches on the cross-continental disjunction of plant species and relic plants.

Mt. Sanqingshan is characterized by a juxtaposition of abundance and diversity of granite landforms, forest biodiversity, and particular meteorological conditions which make for landscapes of sheer peaks and grotesque rocks, old trees and famous flower species, flowing springs and cascading waterfalls, and cloud seas and fog waves. From a multi-disciplinary and multi-dimensional perspective, it shows fantastically shaped granite pillars and peaks. The unique blend of abundant granite rocks, a diversified vegetation, an ever-changing and arresting landscape, and spectacular splendor of ever-shifting weather patterns, provides the area with exceptional natural beauty, making it a unique scenic experience.

Wulingyuan Scenic and Historic Interest Area

Wulingyuan Scenic Area is located in the northwest of Hunan Province in central China. It consists of Zhangjiajie Forest Park, Suoxiyu Reserve in Cili County and Tianzishan Reserve in Sangzhi County, with an area of about 500 square kilometers. Recently a new scenic spot, Yangjiajie, was discovered. Billions of years ago this area was covered by a vast body of oceans, and by a long process of movement and carving Nature finally formed today's landscape of sandstone peaks and forests in present-day Wulingyuan.

Wulingyuan is located in the New China Third Uplift-Belt in the regional tectonic system. In its long geological history it underwent the Wuling-Xuefeng, Indosinian, Yan Mountain, Himalaya Mountain and neotectonics movements. The Wuling-Xuefeng movement laid down the basal structure of this area; the Indosinian movement fashioned the basic tectonic framework of this section, while the Himalaya Mountain movement and neotectonics movement were fundamental factors behind the formation of the unique quartz sandstone peak forest landforms and landscapes of Wulingyuan.

Flora and Fauna Resources

Wulingyuan is a wonderland of nature without artificial polishing, and also a bank of abundant botanic resources and a paradise for wild animals. There are two primeval forests in this area and forest coverage rate of this area has reached 74.75 percent. It is an important habitat of time-honored living fossils. There are over 3,000 kinds of higher plants, including 35 species of rare and endangered seed-plants in the first list of stressed national protection such as Chinese dove tree. Among the plants, Wuling pine trees are most widely distributed and have the largest number and most exotic shapes. The line "on the three thousand peaks grow 108 thousand pines trees" illustrates the growth of pine trees in this area.

Wulingyuan is also the habitat of rare wild animals. The number of macaques is fairly large, and also common is a salamander with the folk name "baby-fish".

Scenic and Historic Sites

Landscape Characteristics

Wulingyuan has five special features: unique peaks, exotic stones, deep valleys, clean water and caves.

The singular peaks of quartz sandstone are rare in and out of China and have become the matchless wonder of this resort. In an area of over 360 square kilometers there are over 3,000 peaks, of which over a thousand have a vertical height of over 400 meters. The peaks here differ from those of other places: these towering cliffs and rocks are straight and dense, like silks, bamboo shoots, line after line, pillar after pillar. They stretch on and on and look majestic and magnificent.

The caves here not only excel in quantity and scale, but also in special features. The well-known ones include the Cave of the Yellow Dragon, Guanyin Cave, Xiangshui Cave, Guiqi Cave (meaning the cave inhabited by a tortoise) , Flying Clouds Cave and Gold Snail Cave.

What sets a fine contrast to natural scenery is the simple rural lifestyle. Patches of terraces and bays of cottages are dotted among green mountains and clean streams. They merge with the mountains and forests of Wulingyuan and form a primitive and boundless painting scroll.

Main Scenic Areas

Zhangjiajie Scenic Area The landscape of Zhangjiajie is very special: there are over 2,000 stone peaks of different shapes. This area is in the bosom of mountainous lands with exuberant trees and the forest coverage rate reaches 88 percent. The slopes here are steep and the gullies deep. There are many minor scenic spots in the area, with Yellow Stone Village, Sandstone Knife Valley, Gold Whip Rock, and Gold Whip stream being the most famous.

Xiangzhi Stream is just like a fairyland with its high peaks and higher sky, clean water in deep valleys, old tracks of road in the setting sun, twittering birds and singing cicadas; Longquan Gorge looks like an ancient city wall, its cliffs forming a natural screen; Hundred Monkey Valley is the home of macaques and egrets-here crowds of macaques frequent the cliffs and the gullies while flocks of egrets perch on old branches and green leaves.

Yellow Stone Village, 1,200 meters above sea level, occupies an area of 250 mu, and is a typical spot reflecting the corrosion and peak forest terrain in Zhangjiajie; it is the largest and most concentrated landscape viewing spot.

The First Bridge in the World is a choice scenic spot of Zhangjiajie-a five-meter-thick natural flag stone bridges two peaks, as if installed there by spirits. The bridge is 350 meters tall, 20 meters long and 1.5 to 3 meters wide. The bridge is quite level, allowing a person to cross to the other peak.

Thousand-li Reunion. This spot is located in Zhangjiajie National Forest Park where two stone peaks are closely joined to each other like are a couple in embrace. Legend has it that the princess of the Dragon Palace of the East Sea fell in deep love with a young man of Emei. This greatly offended the Dragon King of the East Sea, who turned the young couple into stone peaks.

Mihuntai (The Enchanting Platform) is located in the Sandstone Knife Region of this park. Many stone peaks and columns look like tables, stools, towers, or pavilions. After each rainfall light clouds circling the mountain peaks are occasionally visible and change their shapes from time to time. Travelers get puzzled by the changing scene and wonder whether they are in heaven or on earth. That is why this spot is called Mihuntai.

Suoxiyu Scenic Area Suoxiyu is celebrated for its "two thousand mountains and eight hundred streams". In this scenic spot there are over 2,000 peaks, 19 gullies, and 6 streams. Here mountains and rivers enhance each other in beauty and form a wonderful painting scroll.

Baipu Stream (meaning Hundred Waterfall Stream) is the most spectacular view in Suoxiyu. Here you see waterfalls everywhere with water spraying in the air and torrents flowing in the valley. This stream has virtually become a "Hundred Waterfall Stream".

In Suoxiyu Valley there are over a hundred large lime caves, of which ten are open to travelers. The most distinctive cave is called Yellow Dragon Cave, nicknamed "the Underground Pearl". It opens into a cavern the size of a palace, with streams running through, together forming a massive structure with varied views.

The most spectacular view in "Ten-li Corridor" is "Fairy Ladies Worshipping Guanyin". After crossing Dongfeng Bridge and walking another 400 meters, you look eastward and seem to see a crowd of fairy ladies worshipping the serenely seated Guanyin in great piety. Three royal incense-burners giving off smoke provide a fine background for the scene of worship.

The total area of Yellow Dragon Cave is over 300 mu, with a vertical depth of over 140 meters. The total length of big and small caves is 14 kilometers. Inside the caves there are stalactites, peristeles, sheets, lime flowers and lime cataracts in various shapes. Among the stalactites there is a most wonderful one called "the magic needle calming the sea"-a transparent 27-meter-tall stone column thick at its two ends and tapering in the middle, which reaches the ceiling of the cave palace. The whole cave is just like an ancient tree spreading branches in every direction. In Yellow Dragon Cave there are caves within caves and a succession of new vistas; an amazing sight may appear at any moment to the admiration of visitors.

Tianzishan Scenic Area Tianzishan Scenic Spot is to the north of Wulingyuan and adjoins Zhangjiajie and Suoxiyu. It is one of the three major scenic spots of Wulingyuan with an area of 67 square kilometers. Here the views are singular and awe-inspiring and well-known for the height, size and quantity of the peaks.

Standing on the top of Tianzishan and looking into the distance, you may see stone peaks in strange shapes such as the "Imperial Brush" peak, the "Fairy Bridge" peak, the "Fairy Lady Presenting Flowers" peak, the "Qu Yuan Chanting Verse" peak, all showing us the craftsmanship of nature.

Tianzishan is a virgin land of natural scenery, until recently little-known given its remote location. There is a natural bridge, two natural pools, three ancient temples, four heaven gates, five flowing springs, six caves, seven scenic spots and 84 natural landscape spots. It unifies elements like singularity, steepness, grace, quietude and wildness and may be compared to a lyric or a landscape painting. Shielded by a mysterious veil, it tells enchanting stories.

The General Rock is one of the singular views of Tianzishan. The man-shaped natural rock over 90 meters tall stands on the top of a high peak, looking awesome and dignified. A lurking fog covers his visage. Yet he stands with both hands crossed behind his back in his golden armor as if he were a general directing thousands of soldiers.

Significance of the Heritage

Wulingyuan Scenic Area maintains a fairly pristine eco-system. Over 3,000 peaks of singular shapes, over 800 valleys together with the fantastic sea of clouds, mysterious caves and gushing cataracts render Wulingyuan a mountain of magnificence, singularity, steepness, grace and wildness. The singular quartz sandstone peaks are rarely seen elsewhere either in China or abroad and form matchless landscapes. The water landscapes in this park are also quite varied with streams, springs, lakes, pools and waterfalls, so that the park is celebrated for its "800 graceful waters". Wulingyuan also has luxuriant forest and a large number of Wuling pines, said to number one hundred and eight thousand.

Jiuzhaigou Valley Scenic and Historic Interest Area

Situated among the jagged alpine mountains of Jiuzhaigou County in the northern part of Sichuan Province, this Scenic and Historic Interest Area was named after the nine Tibetan villages in its vicinity. This area, about 620 square kilometers, 52% of which is covered by lush ancient forests, is rich in pools, waterfalls, snow mountains and forests. Hidden far away from crowded population centers, the pristine Jiuzhaigou valley is now comprised of six scenic regions: Changhai (long lakes) , Jianyan (spiky rocks) , Nuorilang, Shuzheng, Zharu, Heihai (black lakes) . The whole valley is well known for its "five spectaculars": emerald lakes, layers of waterfalls, colorful forests, snowy peaks and Tibetan folkways.

Flora and Fauna Resources

With a forest cover rate of over 50 percent, Jiuzhaigou valley preserves almost 30,000 hectares of natural forest and over 2,000 species of plants. It is an important habitat for many wild animals, including 170 species of vertebrates and 141 species of birds, 17 of which are nationally protected. The thick moss in the forest and the scattered feathers and fur give this valley an abundance of rustic and primitive charm.

The wild altitudinal range contributes to the diversity of flora in Jiuzhaigou valley. With its significant vertical vegetation belts, the valley is rich in zonal vegetation types of various climatic zones. The floral elements include some from almost all the major zones in the world. Many well-preserved primitive and relic plants are helpful to research about the evolution of botanical systems and floral elements.

Scenic and Historic Sites

Landscape Characteristics

Unique Water Landscape Jiuzhaigou valley is renowned for its water scenery, which stands out for its marvelous beauty amid the mountains and forests. The long, narrow valley is dotted with over a hundred crystal-clear, strange-colored blue, green and purplish pools, waterfalls, lakes and shoals. The most unique feature of this water landscape is its highland calcareous tufa pools, waterfalls and shoals. Its diversity and scale surpasses any other scenic area in China.

Beautiful Environment With plateau scenery as its keynote, blending together the emerald lakes, layered waterfalls, colorful forests, and snowy peaks, Jiuzhaigou valley has historically been regarded by the local Tibetans as a place of sacred mountains and holy lakes. The mountains, waters, forests and rocks are worshipped and protected. Since the establishment and opening of the scenic area, it has been appreciated worldwide as a fairyland.

Well-preserved Glacial Remnants Formed in the quaternary glacial period, Jiuzhaigou valley preserves a large amount of quaternary glacial remnants such as the rugged horn peaks, towering aretes, typical cirques and U-shaped valleys, charming hanging valleys and trough valleys which extend as far as 2,800 meters high. Lateral moraines and terminal moraines of the ancient glaciers in the valley were well-developed. Jiuzhaigou valley is one of the places in China that has well-preserved quaternary glaciers.

Main Scenic Areas

Shuzheng Gully The entrance to the area lies in the Shuzheng Gully, which is 13.8 km long and includes over 40 lakes—about 40 percent of the total number of lakes in the whole area. Those lakes run five or six kilometers along the valley, shining in different colors.

Zechawa Gully Zechawa Gully is in the left branch of the Y-shaped Jiuzhaigou valley. As the longest and highest one of the four touring routes of the valley, it is adorned with a number of scenic spots.

Rize Gully The essence of the valley lies in the 18-km-long Rize Gully, where one is mesmerized by the spectacular waterfalls, colorful travertine shoals and natural forest.

Main Scenic Spots

Emerald Lakes Water is the spirit of Jiuzhaigou valley, and the lakes are the most characteristic expression of that spirit. Clear and emerald throughout the year, they change with variations of color and charm according to the light and season. Over a hundred lakes, each surrounded by natural trees and flowers, connected by gushing waterfalls, are like a necklace of emeralds.

Layers of Waterfalls Jiuzhaigou valley is the kingdom of waterfalls. Rushing from deep forests, they weave different kinds of white silks, like tireless weaving machines. The widest is the Nuorilang waterfall, pouring in torrents from high steeps, like a spectacular hanging curtain. The most unique one is the Zhenzhutan waterfall in Rizegou gully, lying above a slope which has been eroded by the everlasting flows into numerous round holes. Rapid flows running into these holes are splashed into millions of drops of water, which upon the reflection of sunshine look like colorful pearls.

Colorful Forests Over half of Jiuzhaigou valley is covered by natural forests, which extend for more than 30,000 hectares. It is a habitat for more than 2,000 species of flora. In autumn, the forest is decorated by deep orange Cotinus szechuanensis, golden birches, crimson maples and dark red wild fruits. It creates a palette for Nature, the greatest artist, who paints the most incredible pictures of the forests.

Snowy Peaks The three gullies of Jiuzhaigou valley are jagged, towering and capped by snowy peaks. From the top of Gaerna mountain, one can get a bird's view of the whole valley.

Significance of the Heritage

Jiuzhaigou valley is a masterpiece of Nature. To have such a quantity of scenic spots, scenery of such beauty, and such richness of sightseeing, all within such an area of dozens of square kilometers, is truly rare.

It's hard to find anything comparable in so fully satisfying the highest standards of natural beauty. The spectacular mountains and waters of Jiuzhaigou valley display multiple facets, harnessing colors, sounds and shapes into a surprisingly multi-dimensional natural scroll.

Huanglong Scenic and Historic Interest Area

Legend has it that a long long time ago, a "Huanglong Zhenren (Taoist title, Immortal being)" retired to Yucui Peak in Huanglong Valley. The three temples he built, respectively named Front Temple, Middle Temple and Back Temple, for hundreds of years have attracted large crowds of worshipers. The Back Temple survives to the present day, and still remains a Taoist temple where the image of Huanglong Zhenren is enshrined. During every traditional temple fair held at Huanglong Temple in June on the Lunar Calendar, worshippers of such nationalities as Tibetan, Qiang, Hui and Han from hundreds of kilometres around gather together, to burn incense and worship the mountain, to make prayers, or to play and enjoy scenery, singing and dancing.

Situated in Songpan County, Aba Tibetan and Qiang Autonomous Prefecture, Sichuan Province, Huanglong Scenic and Historical Interest Area, at an altitude of over 3000 metres, is one of the highest scenic areas in China. It consists of Huanglong subdivision and Muni subdivision. The calcification of the surface of the earth, with an area of 700 square kilometres, is most characteristic of Huanglong. The main sights can be found in the 3.6-km-long Huanglong Valley, including carbonate tufa deposit in terrane structure like a giant golden dragon, snow-covered mountains, waterfalls, primitive forests and canyons.

Flora and Fauna Resources

From the foot (at an altitude of 2000 metres) to the top (with an altitude of 3800 metres) can be seen in turn mixed forest of subtropical evergreen trees and deciduous broad-leaved trees, mixed forest of coniferous trees and broad-leaved trees, subalpine coniferous forest, and alpine meadow dominated by shrubs and grass. Over ten precious animals such as giant panda and snub-nosed monkey happily live here. Special karst landform and precious rare animals and plants coexist naturally in Huanglong valley, which is described to be imposing, high, strange and wild, and enjoys the titles of "World wonder" and "Paradise on Earth".

Scenic and Historic Sites

Main Scenic Areas

Red Star Rock Located on the eastern side of Zhangla Basin and on the western slope of Minshan Mountain, it is at a high altitude and is characterized by a large number of odd peaks and rocks and glacier quake lakes resulting from the Quaternary glacial effects. Untraversed, it appears to be a mysterious place. Red Star Sea, at an altitude of 4300 metres, is in the shape of an asymmetrical star. It is quiet and beautiful, surrounded by blooming flowers. Midway up the cliff is a red rock cave, which remains a mystery how it came to acquire its blood-red hue. When winds rise and clouds accumulate, the cave is hidden in mist and feels all the more mysterious and treacherous.

Xuebaoding(Snow Mountain Peak) As the main peak of Minshan Mountain, Xuebaoding is at an altitude of 5588 metres. It is located in the east of Songpan County and is 50 kilometres away from the city. A poem recorded in *SongPan County History* descibes Xuebaoding like this: The Cliff nearly touches the sky, glittering and translucent in the universe. Among the fellow mountains, it is incomparably high and feels extremely lonesome and cold. The Five Mountains is referred to as the father of thousands of mountains. Yet, compared to the high, cliffy and sparkling Xuebaoding, it is much less impressive.

Xuebaoding is covered by snow all the year round. On the hillside are strange-shaped rocks, streams and lakes. There are 108 major lakes, and the most famous of them include Dongnan Round Lake, Xibei Square Lake, Xibei Semi-round Lake and Dongbei Triangle Lake. At the foot of the mountain, there are blooming flowers and grass, dense bushes and towering pine trees and cypress trees. The precious black goats, deer, and river deer flourish here.

Sigou (Fourth Gully) This is a big and open ancient glacier valley 12 kilometres away from Huanglong Valley. At the mouth of the gully are open and flat diluvial terraces and the small, characterful town of Huanglong is located here. The topography here is complicated and varied, from towering peaks to flat river rapids. After eons of evolution, the primitive forests, glaciers, traces of earthquake activity stay unchanged, and in coexistence with the beautiful rural scenery, they create quite a fantastic sight.

Above the watershed is a vast alpine meadow pasture. From here, one can take an aerial view of the glacier damming lakes at the headstream of Jiuzhaigou and the boundless primitive forest. The famous ancient "Longan Horse Way" in northwestern Sichuan passed by here and the wide horse road survives to this day.

Danyun Gorge (Red Cloud Gorge) The beautiful scenery of Danyun Gorge makes it one of the five most stunning spectacles of Huanglong. It is a paradise for many varieties of trees, shrubs and flowers. In winter time, it is a snow-covered world of complete white; while in summer it is totally verdant. Then during Autumn, the red maple trees turn the whole gorge into red and it is as if the crimson clouds at sunset have descended from heaven, hence this place is called Red Cloud Gorge. Mountains create clouds and trees produce wind, which explains why in Danyun Gorge it is misty and foggy everyday and visitors feel as if they have ventured into a mythical world.

Muni Valley In the primitive forest of Muni Valley there is the biggest tufa waterfall in China—Zhaga Waterfall. A huge stream of water roars down on the 140-metre-high stepped tufa rock mass and creates quite a magnificent sight. Zhaga Waterfall is at an altitude of 3270 metres, with a height of 93.2 metres and a width of 35 metres. Upstream is a lake, and downstream are a string of stepped riverbeds. Over a hundred circular waterfalls rush down over three tiers of tufa steps. The lashing of water produces spray of waves and thunderous roar, which is thrilling.

Main Scenic Spots

Huanglong Valley The valley, 7.5 kilometres long and 1.5 metre wide, is at Xuebaoding (Snow Mountain) , the main peak of Minshan Mountain and close to the origin of Fujiang, Fuyuanqiao Bridge. Everywhere in the valley are milk yellow rocks, which, seen from a distance, looks like a yellow dragon winding among the dense forest, and hence this place was named Huanglong (Yellow Dragon) Valley. In Ming Dynasty, Huanglong Temple was built to worship Huanglong, the yellow dragon. Huanglong Valley is renowned for its excellent natural scenery. It is so much similar to the "dragon" for the Chinese people that it has always been known as "Abode of Immortals on Earth" and "the symbol of China". In the valley, there spreads tufa as long as 3600 metres and there are more than 3000 colorful ponds.

Yingbin(Greeting Guest) Pond The first thing that comes into sight in Huanglong Valley is a group of small pools with beautiful clear water. This is Yingbin Pool. The pools vary in size and are colorful and of peculiar shapes. Mountains surround the pools. In sight are dense and green trees, blooming flowers, and dancing colorful butterflies. A stone road zigzags along the valley and there are now and then sightseeing pavilions that add to tourists' interest.

Huanglong Temple It is 3.5km from the entrance of Huanglong Valley. According to *Songpan County History*, "Huanglong Temple, also named Xueshan (Snow Mountain) Temple, was built by Ma Chaojin, Envoy of Army and Horses of Ming Dynasty. Legend has it that Huanglong Zhenren (Immortal Being) cultivated himself here according to Taoist doctrines, which gave this place its name. The three temples, namely Front Temple, Middle Temple and Back Temple, are within each other's sight, 2.5 kilometres away from each other."

The Front Temple is merely a ruined site. The Middle Temple used to consist of 5 halls and occupied an area of 5100 square metres, but only the Avalokitesvara Hall and the 10 Arhat statues enshrined in it survive. The Avalokitesvara Hall is at an altitude of 3558 metres and takes up an area of 2100 square metres. It is basically well-preserved. According to legend, Huanglong helped with Yu in regulating rivers and watercourses. Later generations built this temple and set up a tombstone to worship him. In the main hall of the temple, there is a sitting statue of a calm-looking Huanglong Zhenren wearing black Taoist frock.

Wucai (Multi-Colored) Pond On a 2.5-km-long slope, a stream of water flows speedily under bright sunshine, which creates for the whole valley a glittering effect that looks as if a huge yellow dragon is flying downward. With the changing of water flow speed, and because of the rising and falling of the land and the obstructing of dead tree branches and irregular stones and rocks, the calcium carbonate richly contained in the water gradually agglomerates and turns into solid tufa banks that retain the flowing water to produce a large group of interrelated colorful pools, creating the No.1 natural picture of the wonder of Huanglong. In the process of deposition, the calcium carbonate, by combining all kinds of organic matters and non-organic matters, forms calc sinters of different qualities. Theses different qualities of calc sinters, together with all kinds of changes of sunlight, cause the water from the same source to appear different in color, and people refer to this scene as Multi-colored Pond.

Significance of the Heritage

Huanglong Scenic and Historic Interest Area is located at the joint part of three units of geological formation and is especially complicated geographically. The total size of it is 1340 square metres. With the many snow mountains, waterfalls and rich resources, it is of important scientific and aesthetic value.

Huanglong is most renowned for its huge size of tufa that is various in kinds, peculiar in structure and beautiful in color. It is unique and has been a wonder of China. The keynote of Huanglong is the combination of fascinating plateau scenery and exceptional ethnic cultures. Such natural resources as sky-touching mountains, dense forest, flowing blue water,and the tufa pools, lakes, rapids, waterfalls, springs and caves, in combination with the mysterious stockades, temples and all kinds of local ethnic customs such as ploughing, grazing, singing and dancing, present a limitlessly mystical natural picturesque scene. The geographical structure in a transition state creates a complicated natural environment that holds many unsolved mysteries for scientists to answer and provide them with a great opportunity to explore nature. At the same time, at places over an altitude of 3000 metres, Quaternary glacial remains are clear and widespread, which is of great scientific value for studying modern glacier and ancient glacial remains and their relationship to tufa.

Three Parallel Rivers of Yunnan Protected Areas

The Three Parallel Rivers are Jinsha (Yangtze) , Lancang (Mekong) and Nujiang (Salween) which originate from the Tibetan Plateau and run roughly parallel from north to south in Yunnan province for over 170 km through mountains such as Dandanglika, Gaoligong, Nu Mountain and Yunling. The parallel but uncrossed rivers create a unique landscape in the world, with the straight-line distance between the Lancang and Jinsha Rivers being 66 km and less than 19 km between the Lancang and the Nujiang.

The Three Parallel Rivers protected area is the richest geological landform museum in the world. The collision between the Indian plate and the Eurasian plate 40 million years ago caused a rapid compression, upheaval, uplift and shearing of the Hengduan Mountains, which resulted in the alternation of mountains and rivers in the Three Parallel Rivers area. This landscape, with high mountains and deep valleys, snow-clad peaks and glaciers, plateau and wetlands, forests and grasslands, freshwater lakes, and rare and endangered animals and plants, is of outstanding universal value.

Flora and Fauna Resources

Consisting of the equivalents of seven climatic zones: southern, central and northern subtropical, warm, cool and cold temperate, and cold zones, the area is one of the richest regions with biodiversity and a very intuitive indicator for the environment of the earth. It is a refuge for China's rare and endangered animals and plants, harboring over 210 species of higher plants, 173 mammals, 417 birds, 59 reptiles, 36 amphibians, 76 freshwater fish, and 31 papilionidae insects, whose numbers altogether amount to the 25% of the total of the species in China. Most of the endangered animals live in the west of this area, such as Yunnan snub-nosed monkeys, antelope, snow leopards, Bengal tigers and black-necked cranes; endangered plants such as flousiana, cyathea and Chinese yew.

Main Scenic Attractions

Three Rivers

Jinsha River (Yangtze) The upper reach of the Yangtze, from Batang estuary in Yushu of Qinghai province to Yibin of Sichuan province, is called the Jinsha River, which is 2308 km long and borders to the east Zhongdian county of Yunnan province, where forests flourish in snow-capped mountains. It takes a sharp turn to the north at Shigu Naxi autonomous county of Lijiang, cutting deep into the plateau, which results in the famous Tiger Leaping Gorge. As deep as 3,000 meters at places, the gorge even surpasses the renowned Grand Canyon of Colorado by over 600 meters. In May 1935, the Chinese Red Army fought to cross Jiaoping Ferry on the gorge in order to continue their Long March.

Lancang River The upper sources of the Lancang, Zhaqu and Jiqu, originate from Tanggula Mountains in Qinghai province. They converge in Changdu of Tibet, and run southeast through the west of Yunnan to the southern border in Xishuangbanna Dai autonomous prefecture. Beyond that the river is called the Mekong. The topography along the Lancang is very complicated with crisscrossing rivers and towering mountains which create varied climatic zones. Half of the minorities in Yunnan have been living here for generations, adding their colorful cultures to the rich natural landscapes.

Nujiang River Also called Lujiang, the Nujiang originates from the southern slope of Tanggula Mountains, running horizontally through the east of Tibet to Yunnan province. It then turns south and flows through Nujiang Lisu autonomous prefecture, Baoshan and Dehong Dai and Jingpo autonomous prefecture to Myanmar, where it is called the Salween. The Nujiang rushes between Gaoligong Mountains and Biluo Snow Mountains, both at an altitude of over 3,000 m with the highest at 5060 m. Dangerous rocks and towering peaks command the heights, while the valleys are spread with luxurious plants and flowers.

The Eight Geographical Clusters

Gaoligong Mountains Gaoligong Mountains is the best demonstration area for the flora diversity in the Three Parallel Rivers region. The evergreen broad-leaf forest spreading from west to east is so far the best preserved one of its kind in China as well as East Asia, sheltering a rich variety of special flora. The outstanding scenic landforms of Gaoligong Mountains form the "Great Bend of Nujiang", the deep shearing geological landscape around and the alpine karst typically represented by the Stone Moon scenic area.

Meili Snow Mountains The Meili snow mountains are the best geological relics demonstration area of the Three Parallel Rivers, with many well-preserved ancient oceanic geological and biological relics, glacial and orogenic remains, and widespread glacial and frozen soil geomorphic development. The most representative species here is Yunnan snub-nosed monkeys, which live primarily in the Baimang Snow Mountain protected area. Around Mt Kawagebo mixed broadleaf-conifer forests and wet evergreen broad leaf forests are well preserved in their pristine state, representing the natural geographical diversity of the dry hot valleys of Lancang.

Haba Snow Mountains Haba Snow Mountains along Jinsha River encompass modern oceanic glaciers at the southernmost latitude in China, and present a typical natural landscape of integral alpine perpendicular band. In a very limited space, this area collects all the vegetation types from subtropical dry hot valleys to alpine cold zones. The coniferous forest of the cold temperate zone is the most important type of ecosystem in Haba Snow Mountains protected area, as well as the most typical alpine coniferous forest protected area in the Three Parallel Rivers region.

Qianhu Mountains Located in Xiaozhongdian village of Shangri-La County in Diqing Prefecture, Qianhu Mountains is one of the best demonstration areas for primitive vegetation and plateau lakes along Jinsha River. Roughly estimated, there are over 100 plateau lakes of different sizes, among which Bigu Tianchi and Sanbihai are the most representative ones.

Hongshan Mountains Hongshan Mountains along Jinsha River are characterized by plateau planation surfaces, ancient glacial remains with alpine karst landforms, rich flora ecosystem and plateau lakes. Nirunanbao grassland and Little Snow Moutain Yakou plateau landscape possess high value for their primitive landscape resources.

Yunling Cluster Situated between Lancang and its tributary Tongdian River in Lanping county of Nujiang, 76% of the Yunling protected area is covered by primitive forests, rich in biodiversity and widespread wild animals. According to tentative research, 28 species of mammals of 7 orders and 13 families have been identified.

Laojunshan Mountains Laojunshan Mountains are situated in the lower reach of Jinsha River. Here there are plateau glacial erosion lakes, alpine reddish sandstone landforms (Danxia) and a demonstration area for normalized protection and scenery display. The azalea forest ecosystem here includes the richest varieties of azalea along the Jinsha River. The Danxia landforms in Laojunshan Mountains are the biggest and most developed in China. The reddish sandstones dotted in the green forests are quite eye-catching.

Laowoshan Mountains Situated in the lower reach of Lancang in Weixi Lisu autonomous county of Diqing Tibetan autonomous prefecture, Laowoshan Mountains are complement the landscape resources along Lancang. Alpine lakes, plateau grasslands and wild flowers are carefully protected here. The main and undeveloped scenic spots include Xinhua Lake, Laowoshan alpine glacial lakes, a secondary tributary of Lancang: Laluo river, Hongyandong karst cave and the wild flowers in Lidiping.

Significance of the Heritage

The Three Parallel Rivers protected area possesses great geodiversity. The ophiolite and pillow lava of earth evolution, geological strata record from the Paleobiogeographic to Quaternary period, the glaciers, snowy mountains, karst caves and rivers formed from the orogeny in the continent are inexhaustible resources for scientific research and adventure. It is also one of the areas with the richest biodiversity, consisting of the equivalents of seven climatic zones: southern, central and northern subtropical, warm, cool and cold temperate, and cold zones. This is unique not only in China but also in the northern hemisphere and probably the whole world. Along the rivers are born the riverside cultures which can be dated back to thousands of years ago. Shigu Town in the upper reach of Jinsha and Yezhi Town in the upper reach of Lancang are two representative historical and cultural towns that stand out in the Three Parallel Rivers area and the Ancient Tea and Horse Route. These lively minority cultures together with the unique natural landscapes are the most precious historic and cultural heritage of this area.

South China Karst

The South China Karst region extends over a surface of half a million square kilometers lying mainly in Yunnan, Guizhou and Guangxi provinces; the region includes diversified karst landscapes.The heritage site includes three types of karst: Libo Karst, Shilin Karst and Wulong Karst. South China Karst represents some of the world's most spectacular examples of humid tropical to subtropical karst landscapes. The stone forests of Shilin are considered superlative natural phenomena and a world reference with a wider range of pinnacle shapes than other karst landscapes with pinnacles, and a higher diversity of shapes and changing colours.

South China Karst, undergoing a long geological time, represents an important and typical natural geographical feature and karst landscape. It retains ancient karst remains from the geological historical period, while also represent the important and ongoing karst process. Largely unaffected by the Ice Age, the geological history of both the mature modern karst landscape and ancient karst landscapes is very complete. Influenced by the upthrust of the Qinghai-Tibet Plateau, the evolving South China Karst has formed a structural system and evolving sequence of a tropical and subtropical karst rising and developing zone that provides precious landscape evidence for studying regional hydrological networks and the formation of the Three Gorges of the Yangtze River. Shilin Karst (Yunnan) has been chosen as a model example of all karst landscapes discovered in South China Karst. The stone forest of Shilin County reflects the event features of the evolution of karst landscapes over 270 million years.

Study of karst landscape started in China as early as in the 16th century, in the Ming Dynasty, about 200 years earlier than research was conducted by foreigners. Xu Xiake, the famous Chinese geographer, took a two-year tour to Guangxi, Guizhou and Yunnan from 1637 to 1639, making careful exploration and research into the karst area in Southwest China. Acclaimed the first scientific book of the study of karst landscape, his book *Travel Notes of Xu Xiake* provides detailed and vivid description of the landscape forms of the karst area.

Karst landscapes mainly consist of two types: ground karst and underground karst.

Ground karst includes solution groove, stone bud, tiankeng (sinkhole) and vertical shaft, karst depressions, karst valley, dry valley, needle karst, peak-cluster, isolated peak, natural bridge, and surface travertine accumulation, etc. Shilin in Yunnan represents the well-developed, tall and big stone bud cluster, the forming conditions of which include thick layer, pure quality, gentle occurrence, sparse vertical joints and hot and humid climate; peak cluster landscape is acclaimed the museum of karst landscape, Travertine deposition is a magnificent picture bestowed to humanity by nature.

Underground karst include karst cave, karst landform—stone pot, notch and accumulation landform,etc. Accumulation landform is the essence of karst cave; in karst caves of South China can be found magical cavern worlds. The deposits of gravitational water are the forming pattern of karst cave deposition landscape. Stalactite, stalagmite, stalagnate, stone curtains, and side stone embankment formed by water drops strike different poses and look dazzlingly beautiful. In addition, there are many unique and remarkable sights, some look like a blooming lotus, some are like stretching tree branches. Stone grapes and stone coral are lifelike and vivid.

Distribution of the Heritage Sites

Almost every province and autonomous region in China has karst landscape, but it exists most widely in Guangxi, Yunnan and Guizhou. In Southwest China, karst landscape covers a vast area of 550,000 square kilometers. Guangxi has the largest outcrop area, with 120,000 square kilometres, that makes up 60% of the total size of the region. In Guizhou and southeast Yunnan, karst landscape makes up 50% of the total size of each of the provinces. Karst landscape is widely distributed also in Guangdong, Zhejiang, Jiangsu, Sichuan Basin and the mountainous area of west Hubei.

In 2006, South China Karst, composed the solid Karst represented by the sword-shaped, column-shaped and pagoda-shaped karst of Yunnan Shilin, the forest karst of Guizhou Libo, and the natural bridge, land crevice and Tiankeng (sinkholes) of Chongqing Wulong, was the only asset that the Chinese government submitted to the World Heritage Committee for nomination as World Heritage. The South China Karst submitted for nomination took shape during a period of 500,000 to 300 million years, with a total size of 1460 square kilometres, 480 square kilometres belonging to the nominated area, and the remaining 980 square kilometres lying in a buffer area.

Yunnan Shilin

Shilin, located in the hinterland of the west plateau of Yunnan, is in the territory of Shilin Yi Autonomous County and 70 km from Kunming, capital city of Yunnan. Enjoying springlike conditions all year round, here it is neither too cold in winter nor too hot in summer. Shilin is a large and comprehensive tourist spot that combines natural landscape, ethnic customs, leisure and vacation, and scientific exploration in one. With karst landscape being the main content and famous for being "imposing, bizarre, dangerous, pretty, serene, mysterious, vast", Shilin has the most unique karst landscape in the world and enjoys great reputation among geologists.

Shilin took shape 270 million years ago, and only after long geological evolution and complicated changes of ancient geography was the present precious geological heritage formed. Having most of the karst landscape types on earth, it seems as if this is the gathering of all stone forests of the world. Shilin represents the three-dimensional panorama of a typical plateau karst ecosystem.

Shilin Scenic Spot covers an area of 1,100 square kilometres, and has a protection area of 350 square kilometres. Entering it is like stepping into the tunnel of time, where one can gain a full appreciation of the uncanny craftsmanship of nature. Walking in the underground labyrinth, one can see the high cliffs and rugged stone peaks that look like a powerful army of countless men and horses, or one may feel being within a mysterious ancient castle. Some stones are in the shape of birds and beasts, while others look like human beings. The stones are in all kinds of different shapes, lifelike and vivid.

What is fascinating about Shilin is not only the natural landscape, but are also the unique indigenous Sani customs. The most influential creations of the Sani culture include "a poem", "a film", "a song" and "a festival". The ancient narrative poem *Ashima*, recorded in Yi language, has been translated into over 20 languages and released both at home and abroad; *Ashima*, the first color stereo film in China adapted from the narrative poem *Ashima*, got worldwide fame. Torch Festival of Yi people, on June 14 on the lunar calendar, is the traditional festival of Sani people (Sani is a branch of Yi) , and on this day, such activities as wrestling, bullfighting and torch carnival are held; it is so spectacular that it is called "the carnival of the East".

Libo, Guizhou

Libo county of Guizhou, subordinate to Qiannan Buyi and Miao Autonomous Prefecture, borders Guangxi. Maolan National Karst Forest Natural Protection Zone, at the southeast of Libo, consists of the karst forest area in the southeast, Jialiang Town Dongting Wuzhensong Suppliance Centre, and Xiaoqikong Karst Scientific Sightseeing Area, covering a total area of 21,285 hectares—5827 hectares of which is core zone, 8910 hectares buffer zone, and 4588 hectares experimental zone.

Libo Primitive Karst Forest, Water Forest and Funnel Forest, collectively called The Three Wonders of Libo, grow on the stones.

Funnel Forest is a densely forested karst peak-cluster funnel, with dense trees and surrounded by mountains, there are funnel-shaped sinkholes that look like huge green caves. The height difference between the bottom of the sinkholes to the cone peaks varies from 150 to 300 metres. Everything here stays in its original shape. Depression forest consists of densely forested karst cone peak depressions with fields and village houses in between to form a picturesque landscape of countryside forest. Basin forest refers to densely forested karst basin (valley) . The densely forested isolated peaks and peak-clusters surround the open flat basin with fertile farmlands to constitute a magnificent basin forest landscape.

Wulong,Chongqing

Located at the southeast borderline of Chongqing, Wulong County, in the lower reaches of Wujiang River, borders Pengshui County in the east, and Daozhen County of Guizhou in the south, thus gaining the title "the door between Yu (Chongqing) and Qian (Guizhou)". The scenic spot in Wulong includes Furong Cave, the No.1 cave under the sky, the largest natural bridge clusters in Asia, and the rare and unusual Houping Sinkholes formed by karst system.

Furong Cave It is a large limestone cave, 2,400m in length and 30-50m in width and height. The size of the bottom of Huihuang Hall is over 11,000 square metres. Here there can be seen all kinds of secondary chemical deposition forms, that is, stalactites. There are over 30 main scenic spots, about ten of which may be said to be best spots in China and across the world.

The Natural Bridges Typical of karst landscape, the natural bridges in Wulong are a rare geological wonder.The scenic spot is famous across the world for the three arched stone bridges of Tianlong, Qinglong and Heilong, the largest natural bridge cluster in Asia.

The Sinkholes In Houping Village in the hinterland of the Three Gorges of Changjiang River, the Sinkholes fall within Wuling Mountain. The 5 sinkholes, with a total area of 150,000 square metres, are hidden in primitive forest and bamboos. This is a mysterious place with high and steep precipices.

Significance of the Heritage

As one of the most superlative landscapes under the sun, karst is formed on the material basis of a carbonate mainly composed of limestone and dolomite. In China, the country with the highest proportion of karst in the world, the outcrop area of carbonate rocks reaches $1.25\times106km^2$, with karst development being extremely typical. Judged from the aspects of its developmental condition and degree, and from the beauty of the landscape, South China Karst is the finest, in that it has notable universal value and significance when such factors as the unique geological landform and its developing process, ecosystem and biodiversity, and the aesthetics and ethnic culture formed around it, are taken into consideration. This has long been acknowledged and is widely recognized .

China Danxia

The bright moon is among the rosy clouds,
the beautiful stars are coming out of the clouds.
Splendor shining down from the sky above,
How bright is the rainbow of five colors.
—A Poem Written at Furong Pool by Cao Pi

In 1928, the deposit scientist Feng Jinglan, who got his Master's degree in Geology from Columbia University, noticed the wide distribution of red conglomerate layer of Tertiary (6500 million years to 165 million years ago) rock in Renhua County of Guangdong Province. In the area of Mt. Danxia, rocks 300-500m thick, weathered and eroded by water and wind, form fort-shaped peaks and peak clusters, stones of all shapes, stone bridges and caves. Aware that this was an unique landform, he named the red conglomerate layer Danxia Layer. The term Danxia was taken from Cao Pi's poem, *A Poem Written at Furong Pool*, "The bright moon is among the rosy clouds, and the beautiful stars coming out of the clouds." Danxia in the poem referred to rosy clouds in the sky.

In 1938, deposit geologist Chen Guoda named the landscape developing over the red rocks Danxia Landform, and used this landform as the mark of the Danxia Stratum. From the 1940s to the end of the 1970s, Prof. Wu Shangshi and Prof. Zen Zhaoxuan, two geologists from the Department of Geography of Zhongshan University, treated red stratum landform as a type of independent rock landform and made systematic research into it, with the result that the term Danxia Landform was widely circulated. In the 1980s, scientists made fieldtrips to about 400 Danxia landforms in 21 provinces and prefectures, and spread the study of Danxia landform to the whole country.

The most outstanding feature of Danxia landform is the wide development of red cliffs, forming the striking and steep landforms of square mountains with flat peaks, sheer sides, and gentle foothills, stone cliffs, stone peaks and stone columns. The stones of different shapes make a landscape of great visual interest, fully living up to the name of "Redstone Park".

From the the perspectives of geology and geomorphology, this geomorphological landscape, formed on the extremely thick deposits of the faulted basin at the edge of the active continent of west Pacific, is composed of red sandstone and conglomerate and reflects the Oxidation continental sedimentary basin environment under the condition of a dry and hot climate. Up to the present, 790 Danxia areas have been discovered in China, widely distributed in tropical and subtropical zones, temperate humid and semi-humid zones, arid and semi-arid zones, and Qinghai-Tibet Plateau alpine zone. According to international researches, red stratum is distributed widely in all the continents except Antarctica. The type of red landform in other parts of the world is the same as, or similar to, the type of Danxia in China. Therefore, Danxia is a special natural geographical phenomenon and red type of landform with global significance.

China Danxia is mainly found in 26 provinces and prefectures. Mt. Danxia, in northeast Shaoguan, Guangdong, characterized by crimson Danxia, is composed of red gravel continental sedimentary rocks. As the name place of Danxia Landform, Mt. Danxia got the most detailed and thorough study among all Danxia landforms in the world in such aspects as the stratum, structure, landform, development and environmental evolution. The Mt. Danxia World Geological Park established here has a total size of 319 square kilometres, and UNESCO designated it as one of the first geological parks in China in 2004.

The typical Danxia areas in China include: Taining, Mt. Wuyi, Liancheng and Yongan in Fujian; Zhangye in Gansu; Mt. Maling in Xinyi of Jiangsu; Huaihua, Mt. Wanfu in Tongdao and Mt. Liang in Shaoyang, Hunan; Mt. Longhu, Yingtan, Yiyang, Shangrao, Ruijin and Ningdu in Jiangxi; Kanbula in Qinghai; Mt. Danxia, Jinjiling, Cangshi village, Nantaishi and Mt. Wuzhi in Guangdong; Yongkang and Xinchang in Zhejiang; Mt. Baishi and Mt. Duqiao in Guangxi; Mt. Doutuan and Mt. Qingcheng in Sichuan; Mt. Cilong in Shanxi; and Chengde in Hebei.

Distribution of the Heritage Sites

Chishui in Guizhou

Chishui is located in the biggest Danxia distribution area at the point where the Sichuan basin and the Yunnan-Guizhou plateau meet. The dramatic uplifting of the plateau and the strong cutting-through of water flow caused the huge contrast in terrain. Here developed the very typical step-like valley and the very spectacular group of Danxia waterfalls, and thus was created a representative example of young Danxia—the plateau valley type of Danxia.

Chishui Danxia combines some other beautiful landscapes of nature, such as waterfall, wetland and forest. The forest coverage is over 90%. The large size of ancient vegetation, 2,359 kinds of animals and plants and precious and endangered animals and plants, reflect the most unique feature of Chishui Danxia. Chishui Danxia has very high sightseeing value for all the good things it can offer: the bright red Danxia cliffs, the springing up of single peaks and narrow ridges, the unusual mountains and strange stones, the huge caves and pretty Danxia valleys, the green forest, waterfalls and streams.

Taining in Fujian

Taining Basin records the evolutionary history of the active area at the margin of eastern continent of South China plate. The unique cliff caves, intensive deep-cut valley streams and rivers, and primitive ecosystem of the valleys and rivers constitute a rare natural feature and is representative of the type of adolescent low altitude mountain canyon; the close connection of canyon rapids and dense peak clusters does not only maintain the pristine nature of the ecological environment, biological diversity and ecological diversity, but has also created the extraordinarily beautiful landscape.

Lang Mountain in Hunan

This is characterised by a peak forest—a dense cluster of Danxia peaks, a mass of round mountain tops that look like innumerable towering bamboos or galloping horses. Lane Valley, Line Valley and Natural Bridge are grand in scale and have unique Danxia karst. The special phenomena of plants growing in an "ecologically isolated island effect" and a narrow habitat are noteworthy. This area has the most complete Danxia Plant community successional series, and is a representative place of coevolution of animals and plants. For its rarely seen natural beauty and primitive attributes, Mt. Lang is a natural Danxia landform museum, and has been called"the soul of Danxia" and "a national treasure".

Mt. Danxia in Guangdong

Having developed in the structural basin at the centre of Nanling Fold Belt, Mt. Danxia has the diversity of the Monomer type and the rarity of terrain landscape. It is the place that gave Danxia its Chinese name and is the model for the main types and basic features of Danxia. It is also the representative of group peak clusters and peak forest Danxia at a more advanced stage. It has the most tropical species composition, and is the most notable in terms of ravine rain forest. It is a model area for the study of the biological lineage, Danxia "isolated island effect" and "hot island effect".

Mt. Longhu in Jiangxi

Xinjiang basin, where Mt. Longhu is located, the outstanding feature of the combination of eroded remnant peak clusters, peak forest, single peaks and residual hills reveals that this is a representative of early old age sparse peak forest and wide valley Danxia. Here grows an uncommon low altitude subtropical evergreen broad-leaved forest, an important habitat for the important precious and endangered species. The many ancient hanging coffins in the cliff caves are smartly combined with the cultural landscape of the birthplace of Taoism to make a colorful picture of mountains and rivers.

Mt. Jianglang in Zhejiang

This mountain is located in Jianglang Township, 25 kilometres to the south of Jiangshan City, Zhejiang Province. The basin at the mouth of the valley where it is situated is a structural basin above a deep fault zone. The red stratum formed of hard volcano clastic rock group is the material guarantee for the Mt. Jianglang single peak. The rock, differing in erosion resistance, underwent erosion to different degrees and thus formed a single protruding peak. On the cliff are carved the words "The wall stands immeasurably high" composed by Zhan Ruoshui, a Ming Confucianist. Mt. Jianglang combines cliff, cave, cloud and waterfall in one mountain, and is magnificent in its steep and unusual appearance. Xu Xiake visited this mountain for three times and compared it to Mt. Yandang, Mt. Huangshan and Dinghu Peak, praising its attractive landscape.

Significance of the Heritage

China Danxia combines geological diversity, landscape diversity, biodiversity and rarity of landscape all in one. It is a special red layer landform, having as its characteristics red cliff, clusters of peaks, deep-cut valleys and beautiful scenery.

China Danxia is the only World Heritage nominee identified as a Danxia series. The total scientific, aesthetic and ecological value of the series surpasses all the World Natural Heritage sites and Mixed Heritage sites that have Danxia (red layer) as a nomination factor, and possesses features unique to a present heritage site. The wide distribution of the red layer on earth, and the differences in period of formation and space distribution show that China Danxia is an important and irreplaceable link in red layer landform and in the development of Danxia. Compared with the present World Heritage sites, China Danxia is the Danxia area with the best combination of mountain, water, and forest, and thus has outstanding Danxia landform scientific value and aesthetic value, and great ecological value. Danxia culture based upon Danxia puts particular emphasis on the harmony of man and nature, reflecting the outstanding universal value of a landscape culture with world significance.

Chengjiang Fossil Site

In the summer of 1984, Hou Xianguang, a researcher from the China Academy of Sciences Nanjing Institute of Geology and Paleontology, came to Chengjiang looking for fossils of Bradoriids that had lived in the Cambrian period. In Hongjiachong, close to Mt. Maotian, Hou Guangxian uncovered, with the blow of his hammer, a great secret that has been in hiding for 530 million years.

Mt. Maotian fossil belt in Chengjiang is 20 kilometres long and 4.5 kilometre wide. It is more than 50 metres under the ground. Occupying an area of 512 hectares, it is the most completely preserved group of marine fossils of the early Cambrian period, and demonstrates the anatomical structure of the hard tissue and soft tissue of invertebrate and vertebrate organisms. It is one of the earliest records of a complex marine ecosystem and has opened a bright window for the academic study of palaeontology.

Over the course of long geological history, animal carcasses, especially the soft parts of invertebrate animals, decay easily, and it is only under very special natural conditions that they could be preserved and turned into fossils. Geologists and paleontologists, after studying the stratum samples of Yunnan and Chengjiang, came to the conclusion that, in the early Cambrian period, the areas of east and central Yunnan, western Guizhou, Guangdong and Guangxi were seas, and Chengjiang in central Yunnan was where the sea uphove and formed a shallow part of the Yangtze Basin. As Chengjiang was close to the seacoast, it was easy for it to gather argillaceous sediments. Back then, the climate was warm, and the sea water was rich in minerals. Such benthic animals as sponges, worms, arthropods, brachiopods, zooplanktons and other such jellyfish-like animals, and many types of swimming animals and algae came into being in large numbers. Later, these aquatic animals and plants were buried suddenly by a flood or some other argillaceous sediments that happened to accumulate. Being separated from air,after a considerable period of time they turned into fossils.

Flora and Fauna Resources

Chengjiang Biota appeared during the Cambrian explosion, and except for lower plant forms like algae, many animals that represent the various forms of animals living today appeared at the same time. Altogether there are 169 genera and 191 species, 159 genera and 180 species of which were animals, 3 genera and 3 species were plant algaes.

The Chengjiang biogroup is characterised by the rare preservation of soft-bodied fossils. The biogroup fossils that have been discovered belong to many animal phyla, including sponges, cnidarians, priapulids, lobopods, brachiopods, mollusks, arthropods, and some exotic groups whose classification is not clear. In addition, there are many types of symbiotic algae. Among the animal fossil groups, jellyfish fossils fill the gaps in paleontologcial research in China. These are also the first jellyfish fossils of the early Cambrain period to have been discovered in the world.

Besides jellyfish fossils, there are also sponges, worms, brachiopods, gastropods, hyoliths, layered and other types of arthropods whose software structure and bones are perfectly preserved. As far as types and preservation are concerned, Chengjiang fauna are comparable to the famous late Precambrian Ediacaran fauna of Australia and the middle Cambrian Burgess Shale fauna of Canada. Furthermore, this discovery makes up an important link between the evolution of the two faunas of Burgess and Ediacara, and has an important bearing on answers to some basic questions about the evolution of life.

Main Fossil Scenery

Given their many types, distinct gradation, wide distribution and complete preservation, Chengjiang Mt. Maotian Animal Fossils have been acclaimed the jewels of world Paleontology, and together with the Ediacaran fauna of Australia and the Burgess Shale fauna of Canada, are treated by paleontologists as the three miracles that provide material examples of early life origin and evolution on earth.

Yunnan Worm As the distant ancestor of human being, it belongs to animal phylum, which is the ancestor of Vertebrate creatures.

The first Yunnan fossil was discovered by Hou Xianguang in 1991. He found it hard to explain certain natures and kept it in the unclassified animal group. In 1995, Prof. Chen Junyuan and some other experts and professors published a paper in the British magazine *Nature*, proposing that Yuanan worm was chordate. This meant that the origin of chordate was 15 million years earlier than the Pikaya worm of Burgess Shale.

Fuxianhu Worm It is the distant ancestor of insects. In 1993 when the Swedish paleontologist Berg Jones discovered it, he thought it was cysticercus or platyhelminth. In 1996, Chen Junyuan and some other experts, after repeated study, thought it was the ancestor of straight shrimp.

Naraoia Fossil This was a crawling mud-feeding animal on the seabed. The first Naraoia fossil was discovered on July 1, 1984 by Hou Xianguang at Mt. Maotian, removing the mysterious veil that had once concealed this site. In 1985, Hou Xianguang and his teacher Zhang Wentang published their thesis *The New Discovery of Naraoia on the Asian Continent* in *Journal of Paleontology*, and named formally the fossils discovered in Chengjiang "Chengjiang Faunas".

Hallucigenia Hallucigenia, with a big head, is the most famous Cambrian animal.

Luolishan Worm It was collected and named by Hou Xianguang and his team members in 1989.

Yunnan Torch Worm According to experts, this is a carnivorous or saprophagous animal.

Anomalocaris It was the hegemon of Cambrian ocean, and the bandit among paleontological organism.

Kunming Fish The most ancient vertebrate of the Chengjiang fossils, the Kunming fish has been called "the first fish on the globe".

Significance of the Heritage

The Chengjiang biogroup, with a panoramic portrayal, vividly represent what really happened in the "Cambrian Explosion" 530 million years ago, and fully reflect the biodiversity of the early Cambrian period. Almost all the present animal categories and many extinct creatures, under the precondition of a complete lack of ancestral vestige, magically appeared in the primitive sea of the Cambrian era, and help trace the evolution history of most present animal types to the beginning stage of Cambrian Chengjiang.

The Chengjiang biogroup provides us a complete and most ancient marine ecological community, of which we were ignorant in the past. The discovery of the fossil groups did not only let us know what animals appeared during the Cambrian Explosion, but also made it possible for us to get some preliminary knowledge of the life style and the feeding habits of different animals. The Chengjiang biogroup can also possibly help us understand the causes of the biological evolution during the Cambrian explosion and the reasons that triggered the great explosion.

Sichuan Giant Panda Sanctuaries — Wolong, Mt Siguniang and Jiajin Mountains

Sichuan Giant Panda Sanctuaries are located in Sichuan Province and include Wolong, Mt Siguniang and Jiajin Mountain. This habitat covers 12 counties or county-level municipalities of Chengdu Municipality, Ya'an Municipality, Aba Autonomous Region of Tibetan and Qiang Nationalities, and Ganzi Autonomous Region of Tibetan Nationality with a total area of 9,245 square kilometers. Presently over 30 percent of wild giant pandas live in this habitat, the largest and most complete Giant Panda habitat.

This habitat is situated mainly in the Qionglai Mountains between Dadu River and Mt. Min, between the Chengdu Plain and the Qinghai-Tibet Plateau. It stretches 180 kilometers from north to south and 40 to 70 kilometers from east to west and covers areas of 12 counties under the jurisdiction of Chengdu, Ya'an, Aba and Ganzi. It is composed of 9 scenic areas and 8 natural reserves with an area of 9,510 square kilometers. The core area of this habitat is 5,370 square kilometers and the buffer zone is 4,140 square kilometers. The area of the habitat on *the world heritage list* is 9,245 square kilometers.

Since Sichuan Province first began to implement natural forest protection projects in 1998, the area of Sichuan Giant Panda Habitat has been expanding annually. The area reached 1,770,000 hectares prior to the Wenchuan Earthquake and became home to 1,206 wild giant pandas. Through post-earthquake reconstruction Sichuan Giant Panda Sanctuaries has not only been restored but also expanded with an additional 40,000 hectares. The Giant Panda Natural Preserves have been expanded to cover 37 sites and a corridor for gene exchange of giant pandas in the wild has been established in Tudiling and Nibashan. As a result giant pandas have been under benign protection both in sanctuaries and natural preserves.

Natural Reserves and Scenic Sites

Sichuan Giant Panda Sanctuaries is made up of 7 natural reserves and 9 scenic areas in Sichuan Province.

Natural Reserves

Wolong National Preserve It is located in Wenchuan County and was set up in 1963 to protect chiefly the Giant Panda and the forest ecosystem.

Fengtongzhai National Preserve It is located in Baoxing County and was set up in 1975 to protect the Giant Panda and the forest ecosystem.

Mt Siguniang National Preserve in Xiaojin County It is located in Xiaojin County and was set up in 1996 to protect wild animals and mountain ecosystem.

Labahe Provincial Natural Reserve It is located in Tianquan County and was set up in 1963 to protect the Giant Panda, gnu, and other rare animals.

Heshuihe Provincial Natural Reserve It is located in Lushan County and Dayi County and was set up in 1993 to protect the Giant Panda and the forest ecosystem.

Jintang-Kongyu Provincial Natural Reserve It is located in Kangding County and was set up in 1995 to protect rare animals and the ecological environment.

Caopo Provincial Natural Reserve It is located in Wenchuan County and was set up in 2000 to protect the Giant Panda and the ecological environment.

Scenic Sites

Qingchengshan-Dujiangyan National Scenic Area It is located in Dujiangyan Municipality and was set up in 1982.

Tiantaishan National Scenic Area It is located in Qionglai County and was set up in 1989.

Mt. Siguniang National Scenic Area It is located in Xiaojin County and was set up in 1994.

Xiling Xueshan National Scenic Area It is located in Dayi County and was set up in 1994.

Jiguanshan-Jiulonggou Provincial Scenic Area It is located in Choungzhou County and was set up in 1986.

Jiajin Mountain Provincial Scenic Area It is located in Baoxing County and was set up in 1995.

Miyaluo Provincial Scenic Area It is located in Li County and was set up in 1995.

Lingjiushan-Daxuefeng Provincial Scenic Area It is located in Lushan County and was set up in 1999.

Erlangshan Provincial Scenic Area It is located in Tainquan County and was set up in 2000.

Sites Designated for the World Heritage

There are three sites designated for the world heritage as Sichuan Giant Panda Sanctuaries in China: Wolong, Mt Siguniang, and Jiajin Mountain.

Wolong

According to legend, one day a dragon king passed this place and was deeply attracted by the beautiful scenery here. He reclined and turned into a mountain. As a result, this area has a vivid name Wolong (meaning "reclining dragon") .

Wolong Natural Preserve is located in Wenchuan County of Aba Autonomous Region, 120 kilometers from the city of Chengdu and over 50 kilometers from Dujiangyan. It is situated at the east foot of Qionglai Mountain, an Alpine valley region descending from the Qinghai-Tibet Plateau to Sichuan Basin. There are 101 mountains over 5,000 meters above the sea level, and the Mt. Siguniang (the highest one) is over 6,250 meters above sea level. In this region are peaks at different levels circled by clouds and fogs. Vegetation is luxuriant, including primeval forest, secondary scrub forest and arrow bamboos. This preserve is very high and moist and suitable for the growth of arrow bamboos and orange bamboos and so this is an ideal area for giant pandas to live and reproduce. The Giant Panda Feeding and Breeding Pen at Hetaoping is the only Giant Panda research center in the world and a good place for viewing and accessing giant pandas.

Presently one-tenth of the wild giant panda and over half the giant pandas in captivity are living in this habitat and so it is virtually "the home of the giant panda".

Mt Siguniang

Mt Siguniang is located in the border area of Xiaojin County and Wenchuan County. It is composed of four adjoining mountains of Hengduan Mountains and hence is said to be the incarnation of four beautiful maidens according to local Tibetan legend.

Mt Siguniang is 6,250 meters above sea level and snow-capped the whole year round. The peaks magnificently penetrate into the sky.

The valleys go from south to north in the gorges and range from ten to several dozen kilometers in length. One of the valleys called Shuangqiao is over 30 kilometers long. The gorges are sometimes wide and sometimes narrow and the width may reach several kilometers. On the slopes are large areas of grassland, while streams wriggle in the gorges.

Mt Siguniang is a mysterious and beautiful land of special climate with great differences in height, abounding in animal and plant resources. At the foot of the mountain are luxurious forests and grasses as well as clean, bubbling streams. It resembles the beautiful scenery of South Europe and so has been called "the Alps of China".

Mt. Jiajin

Mt. Jiajin is located in the south of Xiaojin County, 250 kilometers from Chengdu. It is composed of two primeval ecological zones called Muchenggou and Muerzhaizhou. In December 2000 Mt. Jiajin National Forest Park with an area of 92.175 square kilometers was founded after the ratification of the State Forestry Bureau. Presently there are about 240 giant pandas living in the wild in this mountain. The number of giant pandas is about one-fourth of the total number of giant pandas in Sichuan and the same proportion of the total number in China. From 1955 on, this area has provided living pandas to the central government and the number of pandas presented by this area amounts to 46 percent of the total number of wild giant pandas enlisted by the state and 78 percent of the total number of giant pandas presented to other countries as special gifts. Actually Jiajin Mountain has become the largest supplier area of wild giant pandas. Furthermore, this habitat is also the supplier of type specimens of 82 types of vertebrate animals (including the giant panda and golden monkey) and 105 types of senior plants (including China Dove Trees) .

Significance of the Heritage

The Giant Panda fauna has experienced climatic evolution from Tertiary Period tropical climate to subtropical environment and modern Alpine subtropical and sub-Alpine cold temperate zone environment in the Quaternary Period, and is a prominent example showing the process of geological and biological development in the Quaternary Period (the latest stage in the development of the earth) . As a result, this habitat has significant scientific value in study of the classification and evolution of mammals and changes to the ancient environment.

后　记

中国世界遗产深邃的历史内涵、博大的文化精髓、巧夺天工的艺术造诣和浑然天成的自然奇迹，令人仰止。在我们萌生出版一本《中国世界遗产影像志》想法的时候，中国已拥有 45 处世界遗产，位居世界第二。而在编辑的过程中，丝绸之路和中国大运河又申遗成功，因此，本书就有了 47 处世界遗产的新出版纪录，令人欣喜。

《中国世界遗产影像志》作者阵容强大，影像丰富，颇具文化气质。本书从 100 多位摄影家的数万幅作品中，遴选了近千幅展示中国世界遗产的优秀影像，涵括历史影像、绘画、书法、地图、图表，多角度纵深地展示中国世界遗产的独特魅力；聘请了历史学、建筑学、人类学、美术史学及汉学等不同领域的十位专家担任顾问并撰稿。为了让读者充分理解中国世界遗产中所展示的不同文化和艺术形态，本书首次将中国的世界遗产分为皇家文化遗产、民间文化遗产、宗教文化遗产和自然遗产进行叙述，这也是诸多已经出版的中国世界遗产图书所不曾表达过的。

《中国世界遗产影像志》编辑过程历时一年多，它的出版得到了各方的帮助。我们在这里一并致谢。

感谢刘嘉麒、葛剑雄、楼庆西、王贵祥、黄文昆、李玉寿、周梅生、茹遂初等专家，他们为这本书奠定了坚实的史料及文字基础。感谢陈勃、孙之常、谭明、李少白、卞志武、胡锤、姚天新、何世尧、翁乃强等众多著名摄影师提供了大量照片，其中许多是珍贵的原图底片。感谢彭小华和王淑芳两位译者。感谢著名汉学家白亚仁（Allan H. Barr）担任英文终审。感谢郭旃、孙华、祁庆国、马宏杰等给了我们很多启发和帮助。

最后，感谢本书总顾问中国文学艺术界联合会副主席、书记处书记李前光先生的指导。感谢中国摄影家协会主席王瑶作为编委会主任的支持。感谢编委会副主任、中国摄影家协会秘书长高琴女士的关心。

惟愿此书终不负众望。

主编　赵迎新

2014 年 8 月

Afterword

China's world heritage sites command our attention with their rich historical associations, profound cultural essence, exquisite artistic attainments and natural wonders. At the time when we got the idea of publishing *World Heritage in China*, China already had 45 world heritage sites, the second largest total for any country. While in the process of editing, the Silk Road and China's Grand Canal were successfully listed as world heritage sites, thus, this book makes the new publication record of 47 world heritage sites. This is truly delightful.

World Heritage in China has a strong team of authors and abundant photographs. It abounds with cultural flavor. We have chosen among thousands of pictures by more than a hundred photographers some one thousand pictures to display outstanding images of China's world heritage sites, including historical images, paitainings, calligraphies, maps and illustrations that give in-depth revelation of the unique glamor of China's world heritage sites. Ten experts from different field of study , including history, architecture, anthropology, artistic history and sinology were invited as our advisors and authors.So as to enable readers to have a full understanding of the different cultures and artistic forms represented by the cultural heritage sites, this book, for the first time, classifies China's cultural heritage sites into imperial heritage sites, folk heritage sites and religious heritage sites, which no earlier books about world heritage sites in China have ever expressed.

Editing *World Heritage in China* took more than a year, and its publication was facilitated by assistance from many quarters. Here we give our thanks to all.

We express our appreciation to the experts Liu Jiaqi, Ge Jianxiong, Lou Qingxi, Wang Guixiang, Huang Wenkun, Li Yushou, Zhou Meisheng and Ru Suichu who laid a firm basis of historical data and text. We thank the famous photographers Chen Bo, Sun Zhichang, Tan Ming, Li Shaobai, Bian Zhiwu, Hu Chui, Yao Tianxin, He Shiyao and Weng Naiqiang who provided numerous pictures, including many valuable negatives from original film. We thank the translators Peng Xiaohua and Wang Shufang, and the famous sinologist Allan H. Barr, who gave the English version a final proofreading. We thank Guo Zhan, Sun Hua, Qi Qingguo and Ma Hongjie for their inspiration and help.

Finally, we thank Mr. Li Qianguang, the general advisor of this book, the vice chairman and secretary of the secretariat of the China Federation of Literary and Art Circles, for his guidance. Many thanks also to Wang Yao, director of the editorial committee, chairman of the China Photographers Association, for her support, and to Gao Qin, vice director of the editorial committee, secretary-general of the China Photographers Association, for her concern.

We sincerely hope that this book lives up to the expectations of all those involved and concerned.

Editor-in-Chief　Zhao Yingxin

August 2014

专家顾问团

葛剑雄　　历史地理学家，复旦大学教授

刘嘉麒　　中国科学院院士，地质学家，中国科普作家协会理事长

楼庆西　　中国古建筑专家，清华大学建筑学院教授

王贵祥　　清华大学古建筑研究所所长，博士生导师

黄文昆　　美术史学者，古代佛教艺术专家

邓启耀　　中山大学人类学教授，博士生导师，中国民族学会影视人类学会副会长

白亚仁　　英文名 Allan H.Barr，汉学家，牛津大学博士，美国波摩纳大东亚语文学系教授

周梅生　　世界遗产影像研究专家，著名摄影家，摄影评论家

茹遂初　　《人民画报》高级记者，著名摄影家

李玉寿　　知名历史作家

Experts and Advisers

Ge Jianxiong　　historical geographer, professor of Fudan University

Liu Jiaqi　　academician of Chinese Academy of Sciences, geologist, managing director of China Science Writers Association

Lou Qingxi　　expert on Ancient Chinese Architecture, professor of School of Architecture, Tsinghua University

Wang Guixiang　　director of the Ancient Architecture Research Institute of Tsinghua University, doctoral tutor

Huang Wenkun　　art historian, expert on Ancient Buddhist Art

Deng Qiyao　　professor of Anthropology of Zhongshan University, doctoral tutor, vice chairman of Association of Film and Television of China Ethnic Society

Allan H. Barr　　sinologist, Oxford University Ph.D, professor of the Department of Eastern Asian Languages and Literature, Pomona College, U.S.A.

Zhou Meisheng　　expert on world heritage images, famous photographer, photography critic

Ru Suichu　　senior journalist of *People's Pictorial*, famous photographer.

Li Yushou　　well-known writer of history

图书在版编目（CIP）数据

中国世界遗产影像志 / 赵迎新主编 . -- 北京：中国摄影出版社，2014.8
ISBN 978-7-5179-0070-2

Ⅰ . ①中… Ⅱ . ①中… Ⅲ . ①文化遗产 – 中国 – 图集
Ⅳ . ① K203–64

中国版本图书馆 CIP 数据核字 (2014) 第 011544 号

中国世界遗产影像志
主　　编：赵迎新
执行主编：李　健
责任编辑：张　璞　李　健
中文撰稿：李玉寿　葛剑雄　刘嘉麒　周梅生　王贵祥　楼庆西　黄文昆
英文翻译：彭小华　王淑芳
英文终审：白亚仁（Allan H. Barr）
编辑助理：赵柏钧　邢　月
设　　计：衣　钊
设计助理：胡佳南
监　　印：姚利军
出　　版：中国摄影出版社
　　　　　地址：北京东城区东四十二条 48 号 邮编：100007
　　　　　发行部：010-65136125 65280977
　　　　　网址：www.cpph.com
　　　　　邮箱：distribution@cpph.com
印　　刷：北京科信印刷有限公司
开　　本：12 开
印　　张：72（插页 32 页）
字　　数：1250 千字
版　　次：2014 年 8 月第 1 版
印　　次：2015 年 5 月第 2 次印刷
I S B N　978-7-5179-0070-2
定　　价：680.00 元

CHINA LITERATURE AND ART FOUNDATION
中国文学艺术基金会
中国文学艺术发展专项基金
资助项目

P28

P70

P100

P128

P284

P328

P376

P472

P558

P594

扫描二维码，
欣赏景观特效。

First published in the People's Republic of China 2014 by China Photographic Publishing House
No. 48, Dongsi Shi'er Tiao, Dongcheng District, Beijing 100007, China

This book was conceived, designed, and produced by China Photographic Publishing House
Printed in the People's Republic of China

World Heritage in China

General Consultant: Li Qianguang
Committee Chair: Wang Yao
Deputy Chair: Gao Qin
Committee Members: Wang Yao, Gao Qin, Zhao Yingxin, Gao Yang, Jin Yongquan, Li Yushou, Bao Su

Editor-in-Chief: Zhao Yingxin
Executive Editor: Li Jian
Editor in Charge: Zhang Pu, Li Jian
Chinese text contributors: Li Yushou, Ge Jianxiong, Liu Jiaqi, Zhou Meisheng, Wang Guixiang, Lou Qingxi, Huang Wenkun
Translators: Peng Xiaohua, Wang Shufang
English copy editor: Allan H. Barr
Editorial Assistants: Zhao Bojun, Xing Yue
Design: Yi Zhao
Design Assistant: Hu Jianan
Print Supervisor: Yao Lijun

ISBN 978-7-5179-0070-2

故宫博

北京故宫太和门。（图 / 李少白）

The Gate of Supreme Harmony of the Imperial Palace in Beijing. (Photo by Li Shaobai)